# Applied E-Learning and E-Teaching in Higher Education

Roisin Donnelly
*Dublin Institute of Technology, Ireland*

Fiona McSweeney
*Dublin Institute of Technology, Ireland*

 **INFORMATION SCIENCE REFERENCE**

Hershey · New York

| | |
|---|---|
| Director of Editorial Content: | Kristin Klinger |
| Managing Development Editor: | Kristin M. Roth |
| Senior Managing Editor: | Jennifer Neidig |
| Managing Editor: | Jamie Snavely |
| Assistant Managing Editor: | Carole Coulson |
| Copy Editor: | Shanelle Ramelb |
| Typesetter: | Cindy Consonery |
| Cover Design: | Lisa Tosheff |
| Printed at: | Yurchak Printing Inc. |

Published in the United States of America by
Information Science Reference (an imprint of IGI Global)
701 E. Chocolate Avenue, Suite 200
Hershey PA 17033
Tel: 717-533-8845
Fax: 717-533-8661
E-mail: cust@igi-global.com
Web site: http://www.igi-global.com

and in the United Kingdom by
Information Science Reference (an imprint of IGI Global)
3 Henrietta Street
Covent Garden
London WC2E 8LU
Tel: 44 20 7240 0856
Fax: 44 20 7379 0609
Web site: http://www.eurospanbookstore.com

Library of Congress Cataloging-in-Publication Data

Donnelly, Roisin.

 Applied e-learning and e-teaching in higher education / [Roisin Donnelly, Fiona McSweeney].

    p. cm.

 Summary: "This book presents international practices in the development and use of applied e-Learning and e-Teaching in the classroom in order to enhance student experience, add value to teaching practices, and illuminate best practices in the area of e-Assessment. This book provides insight into e-Learning and e-Teaching practices while exploring the roles of academic staff in adoption and application"--Provided by publisher.

 ISBN 978-1-59904-814-7 (hardcover) -- ISBN 978-1-59904-817-8 (e-book)

 1. Universities and colleges--Computer networks. 2. Internet in higher education. 3. Education, Higher--Computer-assisted instruction. 4. Education, Higher--Effect of technological innovations on. 5. Information technology. 6. Educational technology. I. McSweeney, Fiona. II. Title.

 LB2395.7.D66 2008

 378.1'7344678--dc22

                          2007051822


British Cataloguing in Publication Data
A Cataloguing in Publication record for this book is available from the British Library.

All work contributed to this book set is original material. The views expressed in this book are those of the authors, but not necessarily of the publisher.

*This book is dedicated to the life and memory of Frank Donnelly (1933-2007).*

# Table of Contents

**Foreword** .................................................................................................................................... xiv

**Preface** ....................................................................................................................................... xvi

**Acknowledgment** ....................................................................................................................... xxii

**Section I**
**Partners in the E-Learning and E-Teaching Process and Academic Development**

*The chapters in this section examine e-learning and e-teaching from the viewpoints of the educational developer, the learners and the tutor, as well as discussing the value of online academic development programmes for e-tutoring.*

**Chapter I**
"Oily Rag" or "Winged Messenger": The Role of the Developer in Multiprofessional Teams ............. 1
    *Sabine Little, CILASS, Centre for Inquiry-Based Learning in the Arts and Social Sciences,*
        *University of Sheffield, UK*

**Chapter II**
The Role of the Tutor in Blended E-Learning: Experiences from Interprofessional Education .......... 18
    *Rhona Sharpe, OCSLD, Oxford Brooks University, UK*
    *Jillian Pawlyn, School of Health & Social Care, Oxford Brookes University, UK*

**Chapter III**
Modeling Best Practices in Web-Based Academic Development ......................................................... 35
    *Diana K. Kelly, San Diego Miramar College, USA*

**Chapter IV**

A Reflection on Teachers' Experience as E-Learners ........................................................ 56

    *Tony Cunningham, School of Real Estate and Construction Economics,*
        *Dublin Institute of Technology, Ireland*
    *Claire McDonnell, School of Chemical and Pharmaceutical Sciences,*
        *Dublin Institute of Technology, Ireland*
    *Barry McIntyre, School of Business and Humanities, Dun Laoghaire Institute of Art,*
        *Design and Technology, Ireland*
    *Theresa McKenna, National College of Art and Design, Ireland*

**Chapter V**

Opening Online Academic Development Programmes to International
Perspectives and Dialogue ................................................................................................ 84

    *Catherine Manathunga, TEDI, University of Queensland, Australia*
    *Roisin Donnelly, The Learning and Teaching Centre, Dublin Institute of Technology, Ireland*

**Chapter VI**

Embedding E-Learning in Further Education ................................................................... 108

    *Louise Jakobsen, Park Lane College, Leeds, UK*

### Section II
### Accessibility in E-Learning

*Without access there can be no learning and without accessibility there is exclusion. These are the issues of two chapters in this section. The potential of eLearning to improve accessibility as well as the problems are discussed.*

**Chapter VII**

Access and Accessibility in E-Learning ........................................................................... 130

    *Catherine Matheson, East Midlands Healthcare Workforce Deanery,*
        *University of Nottingham, UK*
    *David Matheson, Medical Education Unit, University of Nottingham, UK*

**Chapter VIII**

E-Learning for All? Maximizing the Impact of Multimedia Resources for Learners
with Disabilities ............................................................................................................... 152

    *Morag Munro, Learning Innovation Unit, Dublin City University, Ireland*
    *Barry McMullin, Electronic Engineering, Dublin City University, Ireland*

## Section III
## Designing E-Learning and E-Teaching Experiences

*The chapters of Section III cover the design of online courses and eLearning tools as well as appropriate pedagogical strategies and learning theories in relation to various topics and subject disciplines in higher education.*

**Chapter IX**

Enhancing Students' Transition to University through Online Preinduction Courses........................ 178
  *Ursula Wingate, King's College London, UK*

**Chapter X**

A Methodology for Integrating Information Technology in Software Engineering Education .......... 201
  *Pankaj Kamthan, Concordia University, Canada*

**Chapter XI**

Using Technology in Research Methods Teaching ............................................................................. 220
  *Gordon Joyes, School of Education, University of Nottingham, UK*
  *Sheena Banks, School of Education, University of Sheffield, UK*

**Chapter XII**

Instructional Design for Class-Based and Computer-Mediated Learning: Creating the Right
Blend for Student-Centered Learning ............................................................................................... 241
  *Richard Walker, E-Learning Development Team, University of York, UK*
  *Walter Baets, Euromed Marseille École de Management, France*

**Chapter XIII**

Online Communities of Inquiry in Higher Education........................................................................ 262
  *Ann Donohoe, School of Nursing, Midwifery and Health Systems,*
    *University College Dublin, Ireland*
  *Tim McMahon, Centre for Teaching and Learning, University College Dublin, Ireland*
  *Geraldine O'Neill, Centre for Teaching and Learning, University College Dublin, Ireland*

**Chapter XIV**

Using Multipoint Audio-Conferencing with Teaching Students: Balancing Technological
Potential with Practical Challenges .................................................................................................. 289
  *Nick Pratt, University of Plymouth, UK*

**Chapter XV**

The Alliance of Problem-Based Learning, Technology, and Leadership............................................ 309
  *Timo Portimojärvi, University of Tampere, Finland*
  *Pirjo Vuoskoski, Mikkeli University of Applied Sciences, Finland*

**Section IV**
**Online Assessment**

*As assessment is an integral part of learning in higher education a discussion of e-learning and e-teaching would not be complete without examination of this topic. The two chapters in this section discuss formative and summative online assessment.*

**Chapter XVI**
The Use of Online Role Play in Preparing for Assessment ................................................. 328
    *Stephen Millard, School of Business and Management, Buckinghamshire New University, UK*

**Chapter XVII**
Mastering the Online Summative Assessment Life Cycle ................................................... 347
    *Simon Wilkinson, Medical Education Unit, University of Nottingham, UK*
    *Heather Rai, Medical Education Unit, University of Nottingham, UK*


**Compilation of References** ................................................................................ 369

**About the Contributors** .................................................................................. 406

**Index** ................................................................................................. 413

# Detailed Table of Contents

**Foreword** ........................................................................................................................... xiv

**Preface** ............................................................................................................................... xvi

**Acknowledgment** ............................................................................................................... xxii

## Section I
## Partners in the E-Learning and E-Teaching Process and Academic Development

*The chapters in this section examine e-learning and e-teaching from the viewpoints of the educational developer, the learners and the tutor, as well as discussing the value of online academic development programmes for e-tutoring.*

### Chapter I
"Oily Rag" or "Winged Messenger": The Role of the Developer in Multiprofessional Teams ............. 1
*Sabine Little, CILASS, Centre for Inquiry-Based Learning in the Arts and Social Sciences, University of Sheffield, UK*

This chapter provides a discussion of the changing role of the learning or educational technologist from a background support figure to one central to innovative change in the development and presentation of an online environment. The multifaceted and overlapping roles of the educational technologist are considered in the context of the development of a new module for undergraduate students in higher education. The unique position of the educational technologist as a "winged messenger" able to bring knowledge and expertise across faculties in a higher education institution is emphasised.

### Chapter II
The Role of the Tutor in Blended E-Learning: Experiences from Interprofessional Education .......... 18
*Rhona Sharpe, OCSLD, Oxford Brooks University, UK*
*Jillian Pawlyn, School of Health & Social Care, Oxford Brookes University, UK*

This chapter presents the viewpoint of tutors teaching through a blended-learning format. It aims to draw attention to the impact of technology on tutors' roles in higher education. Issues such as the choice to incorporate e-learning, and confidence and competence in the use of technology are raised. The authors present findings from a case study of tutors' experiences in changing from a traditional face-to-face to a blended-learning format in teaching interprofessional education to health care students.

**Chapter III**

Modeling Best Practices in Web-Based Academic Development..........................................................35
*Diana K. Kelly, San Diego Miramar College, USA*

In this chapter, the author explores the benefits of preparation for e-teaching by participating in a fully online programme as a learner, thus connecting the e-tutor experiences of Chapter II with the e-learner experience of Chapter IV. Concerns about the efficacy of e-teaching are considered in relation to quality, student persistence, and criticisms. The author then presents a discussion of best practice in preparation for e-teaching illustrated by description and reflection of the author's experiences as an e-learner.

**Chapter IV**

A Reflection on Teachers' Experience as E-Learners .............................................................56
*Tony Cunningham, School of Real Estate and Construction Economics,*
*    Dublin Institute of Technology, Ireland*
*Claire McDonnell, School of Chemical and Pharmaceutical Sciences,*
*    Dublin Institute of Technology, Ireland*
*Barry McIntyre, School of Business and Humanities, Dun Laoghaire Institute of Art,*
*    Design and Technology, Ireland*
*Theresa McKenna, National College of Art and Design, Ireland*

This chapter is written from the perspective of e-learners and, through the personal reflection and discussion of four e-learners, provides advice and suggestions pertinent to course designers and e-tutors. Some of the issues raised are the role of individual factors in e-learning, technological competence and confidence, peer support, the benefits of a blended format of delivery, technical difficulties, the impact of assessment on learning, and the role of the tutors, complementing those mentioned in the two previous chapters.

**Chapter V**

Opening Online Academic Development Programmes to International
Perspectives and Dialogue .............................................................84
*Catherine Manathunga, TEDI, University of Queensland, Australia*
*Roisin Donnelly, The Learning and Teaching Centre, Dublin Institute of Technology, Ireland*

Taking up the topic of online academic development of Chapter III, this chapter discusses the value of incorporating international guests into online academic programmes. Through reviewing literature and two case studies, distinct advantages are offered for students and teachers alike, such as becoming part of an international community of practice and understanding international higher education contexts. The introduction of new perspectives on teaching and learning are discussed. The limitations of online international collaboration are also considered and ways of addressing them are suggested.

**Chapter VI**

Embedding E-Learning in Further Education..................................................................................... 108
    *Louise Jakobsen, Park Lane College, Leeds, UK*

The author presents e-learning as a culture change within an educational organisation and examines the potentials and difficulties that the use of e-learning has from the viewpoint of students and staff. Although the discussion is located within the further education sector in the United Kingdom, the use of examples and suggestions from Jakobsen's experience makes the content relevant beyond this sector.

## Section II
## Accessibility in E-Learning

*Without access there can be no learning and without accessibility there is exclusion. These are the issues of two chapters in this section. The potential of eLearning to improve accessibility as well as the problems are discussed.*

**Chapter VII**

Access and Accessibility in E-Learning .......................................................................................... 130
    *Catherine Matheson, East Midlands Healthcare Workforce Deanery,*
        *University of Nottingham, UK*
    *David Matheson, Medical Education Unit, University of Nottingham, UK*

The opening chapter of this section looks at the issues of access and accessibility in e-learning, setting these issues in the context of access and accessibility within higher education, particularly focusing on debates in the United Kingdom. The authors examine the positive and negative aspects of e-learning with regard to access and accessibility, taking into consideration economic, technological, and geographical factors, as well as disabilities.

**Chapter VIII**

E-Learning for All? Maximizing the Impact of Multimedia Resources for Learners
with Disabilities .............................................................................................................................. 152
    *Morag Munro, Learning Innovation Unit, Dublin City University, Ireland*
    *Barry McMullin, Electronic Engineering, Dublin City University, Ireland*

This chapter continues on the theme of accessibility and provides the practitioner with practical solutions and recommendations for the development of accessible educational e-learning material. The authors provide the reader with a useful examination of educational multimedia in relation to its accessibility to potential higher education students, taking into account differences in learning styles and preferences, and sensory and mobility impairments. A case study illustrates the problems that can make e-learning material inaccessible. The legal implications of the provision of accessible material are considered and accessibility guidelines are discussed.

## Section III
## Designing E-Learning and E-Teaching Experiences

*The chapters of Section III cover the design of online courses and eLearning tools as well as appropriate pedagogical strategies and learning theories in relation to various topics and subject disciplines in higher education.*

### Chapter IX

Enhancing Students' Transition to University through Online Preinduction Courses........................ 178
*Ursula Wingate, King's College London, UK*

In this chapter, the design and evaluation of an online induction resource for students prior to entering and during their first year in higher education is discussed. It is set in the context of widening participation and issues affecting student retention in higher education in the United Kingdom. The design of the resource is described using the theoretical frameworks of situated, experiential, and constructivist learning. Its purpose is explained and details of its evaluation through qualitative research are discussed.

### Chapter X

A Methodology for Integrating Information Technology in Software Engineering Education.......... 201
*Pankaj Kamthan, Concordia University, Canada*

In this chapter, Kamthan uses an example of software engineering to discuss the integration of information technology into education, both inside and outside the classroom. He points out that the integration of technology requires taking account curriculum content, goals and outcomes, teaching and learning strategies, the participants involved, as well as the selection of the most suitable available resources. Advantages and limitations of the integration of information technology are outlined and guidelines for educators are provided.

### Chapter XI

Using Technology in Research Methods Teaching............................................................................ 220
*Gordon Joyes, School of Education, University of Nottingham, UK*
*Sheena Banks, School of Education, University of Sheffield, UK*

Addressing the questions of reported problems in teaching research methods to postgraduate students in the United Kingdom, this chapter describes an ongoing action research project on developing a Web-based resource for the teaching and learning of research methods that aims to enable new researchers to develop skills and knowledge. The authors discuss partnership between higher education institutions and the relationship between teaching and research within higher education, and draw out the importance of flexibility and reusability with regard to online resources.

**Chapter XII**

Instructional Design for Class-Based and Computer-Mediated Learning: Creating the Right
Blend for Student-Centered Learning ............................................................................................ 241

*Richard Walker, E-Learning Development Team, University of York, UK*

*Walter Baets, Euromed Marseille École de Management, France*

This chapter discusses the implementation and evaluation of three models of instructional design that
position blended learning with a learner-centred pedagogic framework. In particular, it focuses on the use
of e-learning tools to support knowledge building and discourse among communities of learners. Although
located in the context of management courses, the experiences and insights of the authors offer designers
and instructors a selection of models for course delivery that may be applied to any discipline.

**Chapter XIII**

Online Communities of Inquiry in Higher Education ...................................................................... 262

*Ann Donohoe, School of Nursing, Midwifery and Health Systems,*
*    University College Dublin, Ireland*

*Tim McMahon, Centre for Teaching and Learning, University College Dublin, Ireland*

*Geraldine O'Neill, Centre for Teaching and Learning, University College Dublin, Ireland*

This chapter discusses the development, delivery, and evaluation of an online reflective practice resource
developed to facilitate registered nurses to critically reflect on practice. The author explains the theoretical framework of the community of inquiry and presents findings of an action research study using this
framework. The chapter provides practical insights into the development and use of online communities
of inquiry, particularly with regard to facilitating reflection on practice.

**Chapter XIV**

Using Multipoint Audio-Conferencing with Teaching Students: Balancing Technological
Potential with Practical Challenges ............................................................................................... 289

*Nick Pratt, University of Plymouth, UK*

Continuing on the topic of designing online resources for professional practice, this chapter discusses
the use of multipoint audio-conferencing to enable students to discuss and reflect on their professional
practice while undertaking work-based learning during initial teacher training. The author advocates
the consideration of technology from a sociocultural perspective and argues that the use of technology
needs to be embedded in changes in teaching practice as well as knowledge of how learning occurs. As
with the previous chapter, practical insights into the use of conferencing as a resource are provided for
the reader.

**Chapter XV**

The Alliance of Problem-Based Learning, Technology, and Leadership ........................................ 309

*Timo Portimojärvi, University of Tampere, Finland*

*Pirjo Vuoskoski, Mikkeli University of Applied Sciences, Finland*

This chapter reports on a study that aimed to explore whether problem-based learning as a pedagogical strategy and information technology as a medium affects the group learning process on the topic of

leadership. The transformative and reflective potential of problem-based learning as a way of developing leadership skills (such as self-management, team leadership, and patient empowerment) within the health care profession is evaluated in combination with the facilitative potential of online resources.

**Section IV**
**Online Assessment**

*As assessment is an integral part of learning in higher education a discussion of e-learning and e-teaching would not be complete without examination of this topic. The two chapters in this section discuss formative and summative online assessment.*

**Chapter XVI**
The Use of Online Role Play in Preparing for Assessment ............................................. 328
    *Stephen Millard, School of Business and Management, Buckinghamshire New University, UK*

This chapter examines the use of the discussion board in a virtual learning environment for role play as a way of effectively preparing for assessment. Acknowledging the use of technology for the provision of certain types of online summative assessment, Millard provides an argument for the use of a virtual learning environment for effectively preparing for more discursive assessment types. The value of role play for the acquisition of information, reflection, and perspective taking as well as increasing student participation is noted, and the advantages of conducting role play asynchronously online are discussed.

**Chapter XVII**
Mastering the Online Summative Assessment Life Cycle ............................................. 347
    *Simon Wilkinson, Medical Education Unit, University of Nottingham, UK*
    *Heather Rai, Medical Education Unit, University of Nottingham, UK*

This chapter provides practical advice and indicates possible pitfalls in developing, delivering, and grading online summative assessments. The authors thoroughly cover the process of online summative assessment, providing the reader with accessible details of the process of developing and administering summative assessment online. Factors such as item development, quality assurance, item selection, examination delivery and analysis of results are considered. Although the topic is discussed in the context of the large-scale assessment of medical students in the United Kingdom. Practical tips are given applicable to the design of all online assessments.

**Compilation of References** .................................................................................. 369

**About the Contributors** ..................................................................................... 406

**Index** .................................................................................................................. 413

# Foreword

Teaching in a traditional face-to-face setting is a very complex activity. The complexity is even further extended when teaching is delivered online or electronically due to the lack of standard cues such as tone of voice, eye contact, body language, and so forth, which are key tools for human communication.

Technology-enhanced learning is at the core of using innovative and emerging technologies to facilitate and support learning in both online and blended settings. The success and promotion of effective learning is dependent on a range of factors: the learner's ability, sound pedagogy, the nature and alignment of the curriculum, assessment, sociocultural and accessibility issues, and so on. Indeed, the success of technology-enhanced learning is underscored by sound pedagogy and promotion of the effective use of technology in teaching and learning by scholars and practitioners like Betty Collis, Hirumi, and Palloff and Pratt.

Drawing on current knowledge, experience, and evidence-based practice from a range of perspectives, this book focuses on

- developing, teaching, and assessing online programmes,
- academic development,
- the use of technology for collaborative learning, and
- the potential of learning technology for developing skills transferable to students' future professions.

This edited collection of chapters by Roisin Donnelly and Fiona McSweeney entitled *Applied E-Learning and E-Teaching in Higher Education* brings together respected practitioners from across the globe, representing diverse disciplines and perspectives, to share experience, knowledge, current thinking about good practice, and enhancement of the learner experience. In addition, from a discipline perspective, the book places the spotlight on the effective integration of pedagogy and technology, the use of technology in teaching research methods at higher degree levels, collaborative learning within multiprofessional teams, and online communities of inquiry.

The book makes a valuable contribution to the pool of resources that inform knowledge and practice of e-teaching and e-learning in higher and tertiary education. The editors have made a start in opening up the debate and discourse on contemporary practice, as well as posing the challenge of how contemporary applied e-learning and e-teaching practice might change to better prepare facilitators of e-learning to meet the needs of the future generation of learners. The book is a source of valuable advice, hints and tips, and case studies of how to successfully integrate e-learning into higher education, accounting for all participants in the process, and to make e-learning more accessible using technology, encourage collaborative learning and reflection, and create online formative and summative assessment.

I recommend the book to you.

*Dr. Charles Juwah*
*Aberdeen, Scotland, UK*
*May 2008*

*Charles Juwah is senior educational development officer and teaching fellow in the Department for the Enhancement of Learning, Teaching and Assessment at Robert Gordon University, Aberdeen, United Kingdom. His responsibilities include providing leadership for pedagogy in MA Higher Education Learning and Teaching, the university's flagship course for initial teacher training and continuing professional development of academic staff. He is also the director of research for the doctoral degree in educational development. His research interests include curriculum development, online education, assessment, personal development planning, e-portfolios, and research supervision. Charles is an independent expert for EU Tempus Projects in the Russian Federation, and recipient of the 1996 Scottish/UK National Training Awards for Individual Achievement.*

# Preface

During the last 800 years, higher education has shown its sustainability, adaptability and transformable capability. Today there is increasingly a need to negotiate the complexities of the Information Age, which become more and more demanding as we are influenced by technology and the greater interconnectedness of nations and their peoples. Our new knowledge societies require more flexibility in their educational structures to adapt more readily to new styles of learning and teaching, new intellectual and social needs, and new levels of skills development. Such transformation is often referred as "The Learning Revolution" (Oblinger and Rush, 1997) and is taking place in a new era of global digital competition in higher education.

Critical research to date on the application of theory to e-learning practice has been epistemic in focus at times, but widespread and plentiful in addressing such issues as what is e-learning and e-teaching and how does online learning occur. Practical case studies abound in the literatures of learning technologies and e-learning in higher education. In the broad field of e-learning, research has demonstrated that problems have emerged in higher education practice because in many instances it is based on anecdotal evidence and minimal theory, there is a questionable validity of tests, a lack of control groups and objective learning measures, and difficulty in comparison of results across domains. Some of the identified research gaps at the beginning of the new millennium have been variations in tutor moderation, online debating, student perceptions of the e-learning environment, development of online learning communities, critical thinking and problem-solving applications in synchronous and asynchronous environments, peer tutoring and online mentoring, student retention, conceptual referencing and online collaboration (Bonk and Wisher, 2000).

However there remains a growing fissure: trying to determine whether or not good e-teaching, of any kind, supports or encourages good e-learning is a thorny issue. There is not a generic definition of good e-teaching that suits all contexts and student cohorts, primarily because the terms good 'e-teaching' and 'effective student e-learning' are subjective and context dependent. Applied e-learning and e-teaching in higher education cover multiple possibilities, including the interactions between the learner, teacher and a growing range of technologies available today. This book is a contribution towards a collective inquiry which pools experience, pinpointing gaps and indications of perceived needs in this large and sometimes blurred field. The themes in the book have emerged from the authors themselves, as they chose to write about issues that are pertinent to them as practitioners and researchers in higher education. Ultimately this book aims to provide directional choices for academics in higher education through the provision of guidelines shared by a variety of academics across disciplines. It is argued that the questions raised and the issues analysed in this book have become more urgent and pertinent in recent years for academic staff and those charged with providing flexible opportunities for their development. This book therefore makes a case for an analysis of key on-the-ground themes for academic staff and academic developers alike.

Each of the chapters in this book presents a number of strategies to assist the academic in coming to grips with one of the tensions facing them today in balancing the discourse and practice of student-centredness with an era of massification. Tied to this are the skills and experiences required by both staff and learners to make the successful transition to alternative learning environments. It has also been important to identify critical activities and actions which are required to facilitate this transition at higher education institutions. Undoubtedly, there have been high demands placed on both staff and learners to deal with these changes in education, influenced by the rapid development and implementation of information technologies. This is because not only does the Internet represent a revolution for the learner, it also represents a sea change in the way that learning is delivered and supported and the consequent skills and techniques needed by the lecturer (Duggleby, 2000). The professional debate, and emerging practice today, surrounding the use of the Internet as a teaching, and by association a learning and assessment tool seems to be putting academics under increasing pressure. In an age where the use of Information and Communication Technologies is almost regarded as essential to everyday activity, teachers are dealing with demands to adapt their teaching to accommodate the new technologies. Discussing the development and delivery of online summative assessment, the chapter by Heather Rai and Simon Wilkinson also converses on the roles and responsibilities of key stakeholders involved.

Much has been written about the use of such technologies impacting not only on the ways in which staff teach but also on the ways in which learners learn. There remain significant numbers of staff and learners who are not adequately prepared or equipped to operate effectively in emerging alternative learning environments, particularly those environments which are technologically mediated. The chapter by Louise Jakobsen presents e-learning as an organisational culture change and suggests a way of implementing it. The adoption of learning technologies as everyday teaching tools has been placing pressure on academic staff; for some, using e-learning to deliver instruction is forcing them to rethink the ways in which they teach and learners learn, a theme mentioned by many of the authors. They are beginning to acknowledge that transferring the teaching techniques they have used in the past to an e-learning environment does not necessarily provide satisfactory results.

Indeed the authors in this book point out the advantages of e-learning environments for facilitating new student-centred ways of learning. This is the central issue of the chapter by Richard Walker and Walter Baets. The chapter by Ann Donohoe, Tim McMahon and Geraldine O'Neill and separately that by Nick Pratt focus on reflection in work-based learning. Steve Millard, in his chapter, looks at online role-play, not only as preparation for assessment but also as a way of encouraging the development of transferable skills such as information seeking, reflection and perspective taking. In Ursula Wingate's chapter, the potential of e-learning for reflection on epistemological issues and new ways of learning are discussed. Morag Munro and Barry McMullin examine how the use of technology in higher education can improve accessibility for all students. They also illustrate how design can make material inaccessible. This is echoed in the chapter by Catherine and David Matheson.

This book has also provided an ideal opportunity to explore key issues in professional academic development provided by the current movement towards increased use of e-teaching and learning technologies and the emerging field of online pedagogies, where future possibilities are largely unknown, and traditional notions of development may no longer be appropriate. Whilst this may offer particular threats to established beliefs and values within many disciplines, it can also help meet the demands from academics and institutions for increased flexibility in modes of teaching and learning. This research is an opportunity to problematise the very notion of "academic development". Many of the chapters include this issue. For example, Diana Kelly's chapter looks at academic development in preparation for eTutoring; Tony Cunningham et al. discuss the experiences of being e-learners and how this can transfer to an e-tutoring role; Catherine Manathunga and Roisin Donnelly write about the potential of an international dimension to academic development programmes. Academic development suggests that the main focus is the development of skills and knowledge in individuals, and that the change is about changing academics; this research proposes that what needs to be explored is the engagement of academics in negotiating the process of change happening in their teaching environment, and as part of their everyday practice of adapting to change.

This book will outline ways in which the discussion around e-learning academic development for academic staff can be broadened to include a more critical, more effective approach to design and implementation. A further issue worthy of exploration concerns the nature of effective academic e-learning development. It is suggested here that understanding the nature of academic work in e-learning and e-teaching is critical if we are to understand today's higher education environment. As higher education has expanded, and more attention has been given externally to its quality, higher education institutions have naturally begun to devote more attention to the academic development function. This growth in academic development has been reflected in the establishment, in many institutions of higher education globally of centres for academic practice, staff development, learning and teaching, and a myriad of other titles. The challenge for those charged with developing teaching in higher education is to engage academics in a discourse of teaching and learning. Rowland (2005, p8) suggests that there is a lack of correlation between effective teaching and effective research, and believes this is likely to be the result of the weakness of a culture of enquiry (in both teaching and research) in higher education. Such a culture requires learning, teaching and research to be mutually enhancing.

Does effective academic development result in improved e-teaching or blended learning which in time leads to enhanced student learning outcomes? Chapters in this book illuminate these questions, and the studies outlined may contribute towards a better understanding of the emerging conceptions and practical approaches used by academic staff and e-learning developers. It important to foster a lecturer's increasing knowledge of effective pedagogical practices for successful e-learning, and this is most effective when the lecturers who are starting out as online educators can experiment and develop their skills in a safe and reliable environment.

The intention throughout the book has been to provide an overview of relevant components of e-learning theories rather than give a complete exploration of such theories. However the research reported by various authors does provide discussion of a variety of theories and pedagogical strategies, for example the chapter by Timo Portimojärv and Pirjo Vuoskoski explores the use of problem based learning in learning about and developing leadership skills. Pankaj Kamthan argues for the combination of teacher-led (objectivist) and student-led (constructivist) learning to fuse student learning in and outside the classroom. It is hoped that future research will utilise the analysis and arguments presented here to contribute to further research in the field.

There appears to be a mutually sustaining cycle of reaction to the benefits of e-learning in higher education. Although online instruction is seen by many as a major breakthrough in learning and teaching, it has had its share of critics who do not believe it can actually solve difficult learning and teaching problems and who consider that many barriers hinder effective e-learning. Critics of e-learning have regularly noted that there is little evidence of its ability to improve learning outcomes, despite substantial worldwide investment in its development, and its wide uptake. Even when research about e-learning has been published showing that it is effective, or at least no less effective than other approaches, misgivings are held about the validity of that research.

A persistent challenge for higher education is to promote the development of highly complex knowledge structures, generic skills as well as transferability of knowledge and skills to future professional work. Emphasis is given today to problem-solving, team work, oral communication, the search for information from multiple sources and self- and group-directed initiatives. As e-learning is introduced into academic teaching, expectations arise as to how new learning technologies will contribute to this end. Issues that are educational in nature – such as sustainable content management (particularly discussed by Pankaj Kamthan as well as Gordon Joyes and Sheena Banks), sound pedagogical strategy, and learner support – can all too often be left at the periphery. An interesting component of research into the application of e-learning and e-teaching is the exploration of the role of the tutoring process as a central instructional strategy, integrated fully in everyday learning and teaching in institutions, in contrast to current practice that regards online tutoring as a tangential activity. In their examination of the changing role of the tutor to an eTutor, Rhona Sharpe and Jill Pawlyn provide valuable information about the key differences.

In fact, technology often puts teachers in the role of learner alongside their students. This represents a big change from the traditional role of the teacher as the one with all the knowledge and right answers. Instead, students are given the chance to see their teachers perhaps acquire a new set of skills. Teachers who are not threatened by this change in roles report that the experience sensitizes them to the learning process in unexpected ways, giving them new insights into their students as learners. Engaging in the process of exploring technology with their students further provides teachers with an opportunity to demonstrate aspects of problem solving and learning that are rarely made visible in more product-oriented classrooms. Technology-supported constructivist approaches are particularly energy-intensive for teachers who themselves have not been taught in this way and who need to acquire both the pedagogical and the technological skills required. Even when they have mastered the needed skills, many teachers find it difficult to sustain constructivist teaching approaches over time.

In addition to the role of the eTutor is the part played by the educational technologists in creating viable online learning resources. The first chapter, by Sabine Little, considers the role of the e-learning developer, in particular as part of a multi-disciplinary team. Today, there is an ever-increasing wide range of e-learning technologies available for the more traditional teaching and learning strategies; amongst others there are games, simulations, social networking tools, learning portals, learning object repositories, knowledge management tools, learning content management systems, Blogs, Moblogs, Vlogs, PodCasting, Wikis, ePortfolios. As highlighted earlier, the technologies that have revolutionized information exchange and enabled distributed learning continue to change at a rapid pace and influence advances in e-learning. Many studies have noted a relative emphasis on training in the use of technology at the expense of academic development that focuses on pedagogy and embedding technology into learning and teaching practices (McNaught, 2000), a point that is taken up by some of the authors in this volume.

However, as discussed in the chapters by Nick Pratt and Ann Donohoe et al. the key to understanding how telecommunication technologies can enhance learning is to realise that the use of interactive telecommunication technologies alone does not ensure that meaningful interaction will occur. Two-way communications, whether synchronous or asynchronous, do not necessitate meaningful interaction. Adding a discussion forum, scheduling a few chat sessions, and using email will not lead to meaningful interactions. Nor do streaming media and animated graphics guarantee interaction. In order for interaction to be meaningful it must enhance student performance and/or the learning experience. The technology itself enables various types and levels of interaction, whereas learning theory provides insight as to how and when these tools should be used to enhance learning. This is why an understanding of underpinning learning theory and pedagogical principles is vital.

The growth of e-learning requires the development of new instructional strategies that promotes an interactive collaborative learning environment. Unfortunately many novice teachers find it difficult to plan and manage meaningful e-learning interactions. When a teacher's repertoire of instructional strategies is limited to teacher-directed methods, they can end up relying heavily on self-instructional text or lecture-based materials, failing to promote meaningful interactions among students, the instructor and content (Hirumi, 2002). Of course the real problem is that insufficient time, training and resources forces educators to revert back to what they know: teacher-directed instructional methods.

The challenge for education, then, is to design technologies for learning that draw both from knowledge about human cognition and from practical applications of how technology can facilitate complex tasks in the workplace. These designs use technologies to scaffold thinking and activity. Computer scaffolding enables learners to do more advanced activities and to engage in more advanced thinking and problem-solving than they could without such help.

When students use technology as a tool or as support for communicating with others, they are in an active role, rather than the passive role of recipient of information transmitted by a teacher, textbook, or broadcast. The student actively makes choices about how to generate, obtain, manipulate, or display information. Technology prompts students to actively think about information, making choices, and executing skills in a manner that is not typical in teacher-led lessons. Each student can be involved in independent or small-group work with the technology. Moreover, when technology is used as a tool to support students in performing authentic tasks, the students are in the position of defining their goals, making design decisions, and evaluating their progress.

McConnell (2006) argues that, surprisingly, there has been little research looking at what actually happens in online learning communities: to date, we know very little about how they are formed, how members negotiate shared meanings about the nature of the community, how they work in the community and how the dynamics of learning in communities are controlled and what the effects of this are for those involved. We also know very little about the eventual outcomes of learning communities, and how members work together to produce meaningful learning outcomes. The chapter by Cunningham et al. sheds light on this from a practitioner perspective.

All told, exploring applied e-learning and e-teaching is a challenging area. It is essential that all academics willing to engage in this process acknowledge that they too are learners and will need to engage in ongoing reflection on their teaching and learning practices. Taking a reflective pause regularly is important, and taking time out from busy practice to write a chapter, each author in this book has been offered just that. We believe that the result has been worthwhile.

## STRUCTURE OF THE BOOK

The book is divided into four sections, each focusing on a theme relating to applied e-learning and e-teaching. The first section, *The Partners in the e-learning and e-teaching Process And The Role of Academic Development*, contains chapters which examine e-learning and e-teaching from the viewpoints of the developer, the tutor and the students as well as examining academic development.

The emphasis in Section II is on accessibility, examining it in a broad context as well as with regard to the use of multi-media in higher education as a way of improving accessibility.

The chapters of Section III all focus on designing for e-learning and e-teaching, looking at various issues and subject disciplines. The potential of e-learning for student induction, the use of e-learning for class-based and independent student learning in software engineering and the development of an online resource for learning about research are the subject matter of the first three chapters. The use of e-learning tools to support knowledge building, discourse, reflection and collaboration among learners in management, nursing and teaching education is dealt with in Chapters XII, XIII and XIV. Chapter XV looks at the partnership between problem based learning and technology in developing leadership skills in the field of health care.

Section IV concentrates on the area of online assessment. The first chapter here looks at role play as a way of preparing for discursive forms of assessment while the second chapter describes the process of developing and administering summative assessment online.

## REFERENCES

Bonk, C. J., and Wisher, R. A. (2000, August 2-4) Adapting e-learning Tools from Educational to Training Environments. Paper presented at the 16th Annual Conference on Distance Teaching and Learning, Madison, WI.

Duggleby, J. (2000) *How to be an Online Tutor*. Aldershot, Hampshire; Brookfield, VT: Gower.

Hirumi, A. (2002) A Framework for Analyzing, Designing, and Sequencing Planned e-learning Interactions, *Quarterly Review of Distance Education 3*(2), 141-160.

McConnell, D. (2006) *E-learning Groups and Communities*. Maidenhead: The Society for Research into Higher Education & Open University Press.

McNaught, C. (2000) Technology: The Challenge of Change. In R. King, D. Hill and B. Hemmings (Eds). *University and Diversity*, (pp.88-102). Wagga Wagga, NSW: Keon Publications.

Oblinger, D.G. and Rush, S.C. (1997) *The Learning Revolution. The Challenge of Information Technology in the Academy*. Bolton, MA: Anker Publishing Co, Inc.

Rowland, S. (2005) Intellectual Love and the Link between Teaching and Research, in R. Barnett (ed). *Reshaping Universities*. (pp.92-10). Milton Keynes: Open University Press/Society for Research in Higher Education.

# Acknowledgment

The editors would like to acknowledge the help of all involved in the collation and review process of the book, without whose support the project could not have been satisfactorily completed. Deep appreciation and gratitude is due to Dr. Kevin O'Rourke for his suggestions on enhancing aspects of the book, and we would also like to acknowledge Heather Probst for her editorial support services.

Most of the authors of chapters included in this book also served as referees for chapters written by other authors. Sincere thanks go to all those who provided constructive and comprehensive reviews.

Special thanks also go to the publishing team at IGI Global, whose contributions throughout the whole process from inception of the initial idea to final publication have been invaluable.

Closer to home, we would like to thank the Donnelly and McSweeney/Ryan families for their un-wavering support and encouragement throughout—in particular, Rhiannon, Adam, and Leon for putting up with their absentminded mothers.

*Editors,*
*Dublin*
*May 2008*

# Section I
# Partners in the E–Learning and E–Teaching Process and Academic Development

*The chapters in this section examine e-learning and e-teaching from the viewpoints of the educational developer, the learners and the tutor, as well as discussing the value of online academic development programmes for e-tutoring.*

# Chapter I
# "Oily Rag" or "Winged Messenger":
## The Role of the Developer in Multiprofessional Teams

**Sabine Little**
*CILASS, Centre for Inquiry-based Learning in the Arts and Social Sciences,
University of Sheffield, UK*

## ABSTRACT

*This chapter has been composed as a piece of reflective practice, and as such traces and researches the development of a new technology-rich first-year module from the point of view of one particular developer, myself. The main emphasis in my role was on advising and assisting with the development of a student learning experience that provided, above all, an inquiry-based learning environment for students to acquire the skills necessary to succeed in their ongoing degree. Technology and e-learning offered a number of interesting options for development and implementation, necessitating the further brokering of technological expertise. The chapter highlights the collaborative issues that occur in a multiprofessional team working in such a developmental environment, and explores the role of the developer and how this role might be interpreted by other staff and institutions. The chapter concludes by offering ideas for future research into what remains an emerging field of scholarship.*

## INTRODUCTION

The constant development of new technologies over recent years has made it less and less possible for individual lecturers to remain abreast of developments and make informed choices regarding the use of technologies for new courses and modules without consulting others. At the same time, the creation of specialist technology or pedagogical support units at many institutions has meant that, frequently, more support than ever before is available: The issue is its discovery and utilisation. As a result, the development of new technologically rich modules is becoming an increasingly collaborative process, requiring not only group work skills, but also advanced project management practices from all involved.

## BACKGROUND

The context for this chapter results from a government-funded initiative to establish Centres for Excellence in Teaching and Learning (CETLs) at higher education institutions in England and Northern Ireland. In 2005, 74 such CETLs were established, all building on existing excellence within institutions, and all with a strong remit to support new learning and teaching initiatives. At the University of Sheffield, the Centre for Inquiry-Based Learning in the Arts and Social Sciences (CILASS) currently supports 19 departments within three core faculties, namely, the Faculties of Arts, Social Sciences, and Law. Two learning development and research associates (LDRAs), one specialising in information literacy and the other in networked learning, support inquiry-based learning projects within these departments, and also broker support from professional learning services within the institution, such as the library and the Learning Development and Media Unit (LDMU). In searching the literature, it appears that the terminology describing the role of an individual involved in planning, advising on, and developing academic content and pedagogy, which includes the component of technology, is by no means clear (Fraser, 2001; Oliver, 2002; Wright & Miller, 2000). For me, the role of an LDRA for networked learning originally seemed a very specific description, especially within the main remit of inquiry-based learning. There are, however, distinct overlaps with the more traditional roles of learning technologist, educational developer, educational technologist, academic developer, and further variations on the same themes. For this reason, this chapter draws on literature from all

these fields to explore the issues surrounding the collaboration that leads to the implementation of innovative projects in the field of e-learning.

Oliver (2002) identifies the role of educational technologist as being both marginal (in terms of contract and security) and powerful (in terms of remit linked to "strategic priorities," p. 245). His study, based on six interviews with learning technologists, identifies issues that are mirrored in this study. This included the time commitment a collaborative development requires, tensions between responsibility and marginality, and the way in which the developer or technologist is regarded by senior management and/or collaborating academics. Further issues involved the specific skills required of the role, such as constant repositioning of context from project to project, fast acquisition of knowledge related to such context both at the subject and pedagogical level, and the requirement to stay abreast with technological developments in the field. Hicks (1997) outlines the future of the educational developer with the need to be entrepreneurial about the role and position, to lead the institution in the area of educational technology, and to play an active role in determining strategic directions. Wright and Miller (2000) seek to outline future professional development and accomplishment for the educational developer, a future that includes the "integration of scholarship and practice" (p. 21), a focus that does not feature in Oliver's paper. However, both Oliver and Wright and Miller describe a role that, potentially more so than others, is fast paced, instrumental for institutional change, and highly demanding, yet not necessarily recognised for its importance. Gosling (2001), in reviewing the work of educational development units in the United Kingdom, draws on work by several authors (e.g., Candy, 1996; Hounsell, 1994; Moses, 1987). He remarks that the work traditionally classified as carried out by educational development units—curriculum design, learning support, staff development, organisational and policy development, and student learning development—overlooks the scholarly component of the role. To remedy this, he adds to the list two points relating to the informed debate about learning, teaching, assessment, and curriculum design, and to the promotion of the scholarship of teaching, learning, and research into higher education goals and practices.

There is further evidence of a blurring of roles between the academic developer and more traditional academia. Blass (as cited in Blass & Davis, 2003) illustrates the emergent model of the future academic as including the following:

- identification of new forms of conversations with students,
- increased ICT usage,
- monitoring of student performance,
- increased visibility through technology,
- creativity and innovation,
- the ability to deliver key skills, plus cognitive skills and the development of reason,
- rapid information processing,
- appreciation of global contexts,
- the role as a change agent, and
- the delivery of workplace education.

Although this model no doubt falls short on several levels (there is, for example, no mention of research activity), the parallels with Wright and Miller's (2000) analysis of job announcements for educational developers are clear: Educational developers are expected (amongst other things) to promote teaching excellence, develop teaching and learning materials, consult faculty to develop programme direction, advise faculty on pedagogical issues, facilitate peer coaching and mentorship, teach in an appropriate discipline, coordinate programmes, research teaching and learning issues and publish on these, and serve on committees and interact in regional and national networks. This blurring of roles has the potential to be both helpful and a hindrance to educational developers seeking to establish their own field. Bath and Smith (2004) address this point when they seek to situate the academic developer be-

tween teaching, research, and service, identifying an emerging "academic tribe." Brew (2006) asks the question: "Does the research that academic developers do give their work legitimacy [or does it] detract from the day to day practical work of helping others in higher education to develop their teaching and student learning?" (p. 74), highlighting the balancing act developers engage in on a daily basis.

D'Andrea and Gosling (2001) promote development as a holistic approach across the institution, bearing in mind strategic concerns as much as the individual student's experience. The developer, as a crosscutting change agent, thus becomes a "winged messenger" in facilitating this approach, a role that I identify with and that will be further discussed below. For the purpose of this chapter, therefore, literature from both the area of educational development and educational technology will be drawn upon to highlight the emerging understanding of a professional role that is ever changing and depending on context, and whose holder must be equally adaptable to circumstances.

In order to explore this role further, this chapter draws on existing literature as well as research and evaluation data from one particular collaborative project involving a multiprofessional team. Furthermore, data will be drawn from the LDRA blog, a private research blog kept by the two learning development and research associates (including myself), which traces the role on a day-to-day basis.

## The Module and the Collaborative Team

The module that was developed as part of the collaboration in question took place in the School of Law, involving approximately 250 first-year undergraduate students in Semester 2. Entitled Understanding Law II, the module introduces students to the various professional aspects the discipline entails and forms a follow-up module to Understanding Law I in the first semester. The module had received funding to integrate inquiry-based learning components into the learning experience, giving students more responsibility regarding the pace of learning, choice of topics, and collaborative research experience. Several of these goals ran in parallel with perceived advantages of e-learning, as Blass and Davis (2003, p. 229) state, "the control of pace, place, time and style of presentation and interaction shifts more towards the learner." The development of an e-learning approach (or networked learning, incorporating the notion that technology is used to promote connections between individuals as well as between the individual and the computer; Jones, 2004) therefore seemed an appropriate option to address the individual learning needs of the 250-strong student body.

The module contained some traditional face-to-face lectures and seminars, as well as a variety of networked leaning components. These included a major presence in the institutional virtual learning environment (VLE) WebCT™ Vista. This WebCT component included a weekly workbook with tasks for students that built on lectures and were discussed at seminars. An online learning diary provided an inquiry-based learning element and was kept by students to aid reflection and revision, logging personal responses to readings and allowing learners to put their learning in context. An initial application for funding was made in July 2006, focusing on buyout time for academic staff to develop content on WebCT and support requests to develop a CD-ROM with readings and tasks for students to keep after the module finished. The project received funding and thus began the collaborative process, involving three members of academic staff within the School of Law, the departmental technical support officer, a producer/educational designer and a graphic designer from the institution's Learning Development and Media Unit (LDMU), and me, the LDRA for networked learning from CILASS. An initial meeting explored the background behind

the bid, and it transpired that, as part of an ongoing agreement with a local law firm, external funding was available for the CD-ROM, which was the reason for its inclusion in the bid. At this meeting, several plans and suggestions were made as to how the module might build successfully on the preceding one, both in terms of content and the learning process. Both the producer and the LDRA suggested a more collaborative, inquiry-based learning approach for students, which was supported by the academic staff. This meant that this component now involved asking students to work in groups and to choose one aspect of their degree so far they thought worthy of further research to be presented at a celebration of learning held at the end of the module. The format of presentation was entirely left to the students, although suggestions were made that students might choose an enhanced PowerPoint presentation, a video, or a podcast (for the purpose of this chapter, this term describes an audio file rather than subscribed downloadable content). This meeting provided a pivotal role in the working relationship, as will become apparent later. Training was available for students to achieve the technological skills to produce their contribution in the medium they desired, and ongoing collaborative support ensured that groups had a point of contact for any disagreements and difficulties. In parallel to this collaborative element, the electronic workbook and learning diary were completed independently and formed the basis for reflection on lectures, seminars, and readings, thus feeding into revision. Overall, the module sought to adopt a community-of-inquiry (Garrison, Anderson, & Archer, 2000) approach, at the centre of which stood the collaborative element, supported and facilitated through technology. Ling (2007), in researching the extent to which a successful community of inquiry might be established online, states that the three kinds of presence (cognitive, teaching, and social presence) associated with the model can all be achieved through online contact only. Our situation was considered to be an artificial context for a module that took place on campus, leading to the combination of approaches outlined here. Furthermore, it was felt that a blend of virtual and campus-based interaction would go some way in scaffolding more dependent learners toward increased independence (O'Neill, Singh, & O'Donoghue, 2004). The module was assessed by examination, a component that could not be altered at the stage of planning. This was originally seen as a flaw in the development process. In the end, the module incorporated one seen examination question that asked students to illustrate the group project, identify learning from both the subject content and the collaborative process, and reflect on the group experience. This transpired to be a very happy medium for the module and helped students deal with the more complex issues around group work and technology as they could be certain they would be assessed on their ability to engage with the process reflectively.

## ISSUES AND SOLUTIONS

The complexity of the project demanded certain planning processes simply to allow the project to take place from a logistical point of view. Issues, however, were frequently resolved within very short periods of time, allowing planning to move forward. Rather than separating issues from the way in which they were resolved, this section therefore tackles the various complications and considerations as they arose, providing data from the research around the project as necessary.

### The Multiprofessional Team

As the term *e-learning* is more problematised and less and less synonymous with resources online, and as technology allows for development in ever-different directions, so the multiprofessional team around e-learning development grows. As outlined above, the core development team around Understanding Law II involved seven individuals,

including three academic members of the Department of Law, one subject technician, two members of staff from the Learning Development and Media Unit (one producer/educational designer and one graphic designer), and one LDRA for networked learning within the context of inquiry-based learning. Discussions quickly developed an understanding that the producer/educational designer's role was very similar to my own, and continuous communication was necessary to allow for a reshaping and resharing of responsibilities, which is further discussed below. In line with the fluidity of the environment, however, development did not stop there, and other members of staff were involved insofar as their professional role touched upon the needs of the projects. Staff who taught on the module had to believe that the e-learning component, despite its complexity, was worth the extra effort and support it in their teaching. Those staff who had worked on the module's predecessor, Understanding Law I, were a valuable source of information and advice, and helped shape the way in which the module was taught. The department's subject librarian and the institution's digitisation officer had considerable input in making content accessible online through the digitisation of readings and the creation of online reading lists. Whilst the librarian was not involved directly in the development of content, the various ways of allowing the students to access resources were discussed and brought forward (Littlejohn, 2005). At the University of Sheffield, the library already has substantial input into e-learning development through the creation of an information skills resource, which is transferable to any module on WebCT. Through the resource, students learn how to access and evaluate resources, and how to reference correctly. As this resource is often adapted to the needs of various departments, subject librarians are involved at a more active level of development.

Other members of staff involved included a technician on hand to loan out equipment to students wishing to create a film; due to student numbers, any loan was to last no longer than a day at a time, and coordination of equipment coming or going was a complex issue. Similarly, the university's central WebCT support aided the development of the virtual learning environment.

With the module involving a development team as large as this, it would be easy to assume that such behind-the-scenes development goes unnoticed by the students; however, this was not the case. Asked as part of a focus group to identify the members of staff involved in the development of the module, students named nearly all members of the wider team, with the exception of the graphic designer, the central WebCT support, and the institution's digitisation officer, effectively linking a total of 12 members of staff to their module. Asked what they thought of such a development process, students in the focus group were seen to engage not only with the content, but with the teaching approach as well: "I think it's helped having different approaches from different people putting into how it's [the module] run. You can see—I thought you could see...why the different lecturers were involved, as well" (Student A, student focus group).

The academic members of staff were originally linked by students to their subject specialty, without being connected to a specific learning and teaching approach, or a specific e-learning component. As part of the project, however, students came in contact with further members of the team through specialist filming and podcasting training sessions, when hiring out equipment, during the final showcase, and as part of the module evaluation. Therefore, having developers and support staff involved meant students allocated the various approaches to these individuals, who in their eyes stood not for any particular aspect of the law, but for filmmaking, WebCT, and group work. The smooth collaboration between the various staff members also allowed students to maintain their trust in the system. Although fully aware that the way this module was taught was new to the department, a student remarked,

*I thought about it being new, and I don't think it affected me. I didn't think, Oh, they don't know what they're doing, or anything, or feeling like a guinea pig. It could have been quite scary, but I think they made quite a bit of effort to tie it all together, and tying it into the exam. You can't talk to second-years about the way they've done this, but I think they did that really well. (Student B, student focus group)*

## Getting the Multiprofessional Team to Work

So how do 15 members of staff end up creating one module that provides a coherent, positive student learning experience, incorporating several learning technologies and the institutional VLE?

For the module under consideration here, it appears that certain assumptions and presuppositions regarding role distribution and expertise were laid aside and restructured to fit into the new structure of a multiapproach development team. Several of the more innovative components of the module illustrated clearly the need for expertise in three distinct areas, namely, subject content, technology, and the inquiry-based learning approach, involving collaboration, reflective learning, and self-study skills. The success of the project built on the understanding that everyone would be willing to engage with all components to a point of minimum understanding to allow communication to take place, but also to recognise and trust in the expertise of those whose main responsibility the component is. None of the components had only one expert, and the overlap was on occasion considerable. Lack of subject knowledge was in part overcome by the fact that all members of staff not from the Department of Law had worked on the previous module, allowing for familiarisation with the subject matter at a basic level. The freedom of inquiry given to the students as part of the collaborative component helped here as well as it meant the outputs of groups made sense to the subject layman and allowed for communication and research with student participation to take place. This mutual awareness facilitated the development of support systems as part of the development process, a particularly challenging task bearing in mind the complexity of the learning environment (both virtual and face to face) that had been created as part of the module. In evaluating support-system concerns in relation to a three-year collaborative project (extended learning environment network, ELEN), funded by the Teaching and Learning Technology Programme in Britain, Diercks-O'Brien (2002) found that the technology dependency e-learning brings adds a number of support issues to any list of concerns staff and students might have about a new venture. In the case of the ELEN project, these concerns were as follows:

- Uncertainties about responsibility for student IT training and support,
- Problems with student access due to inadequate technical and support infrastructures,
- A shift in priority to see online learning as technology rather than task driven,
- Project leaders who were unaware of the amount of technical and pedagogical support needed in order to develop online learning projects,
- Project leaders who were unaware of administrative support needs, and
- The impact of institutional IT and teaching and learning strategies on project development and support needs.

What made the Understanding Law II project successful was that the core team's collaboration went beyond the necessary expertise-related engagement and branched out into a feeling of ownership and stake in the success of the project. In part, this ownership was related to the visibility of the project: A celebration-of-learning showcase involving 250 students can by default be no low-key event, and the stakes were no doubt raised through the high visibility of the module.

A further considerable component, however, was the level at which each member of the core team was able to work to their strengths and interests, thus facilitating the sense of ownership. As part of the research, the producer who supplied the training in filming for students, and the learning development and research associate who advised and supported technological and collaborative development, met for a reflective discussion to identify why the project had been successful.

## Oily Rag or Winged Messenger?

In a successful collaborative team, the support issues mentioned above will most likely be divided among the staff involved depending on their expertise, but overall responsibility for the success of the project remains an interesting question. Oliver's (2002) study highlights that the role of the learning technologist is "shaped by a distinct combination of autonomy, a lack of authority and responsibility for initiatives" (p. 249). In order to explore these perceptions in context, a reflective discussion took place between myself and the producer/educational designer working on the project (attributed as Danielle below). This discussion took place in May 2007. Despite the different job titles, there was a distinct overlap of experience and day-to-day work; however, there were also substantial differences in our understanding of our role and the project, which are further outlined in this section. Regarding Oliver's concerns, these were echoed only partially during the reflective discussion, although it certainly seemed that any validation of our role in general depended on the academic staff members: "And it depends on the academics, I guess—if they're big *I-am*s, then you won't get much acknowledgement, but if they're not like that, they'll be more vociferous in their appreciation, and they'll see it as a team job" (Danielle).

Despite the fact that both of us saw ourselves as facilitators during the project, the way this role is expressed is very different. One such impression was put forward by the producer/educational designer:

*I'm happy to be, you know, an oily rag. I've always seen myself, actually, as an oily rag. I'm very happy with not being in the limelight; I don't want to be standing at the front. I'm just not into it. I hate being the centre of attention, and I'm just very happy to facilitate things in the background. (Danielle)*

However, another way to express the role can be found on the LDRA blog, where I wrote, in the context of a different project,

*What I wanted to write about though is what I call my winged messenger role—we discussed ways forward regarding group work, and during the two hour meeting, I told them about...ten concrete examples, narrated and points of interest drawn out for a specific audience. ...I feel competent that I can forward that information and am aware of exciting new projects around the university, I feel happy to see an immediate positive reaction, and I guess in a way...not powerful, but....maybe "important"???? "useful"???? because I can make these links when very few other people (apart from [those in similar roles]) can. On those days, I love my job.*

Whatever the perception of the role, it is very much the enthusiasm of all involved that makes the work worthwhile. As the producer/educational designer puts it,

*I guess it's personal chemistry, and there are some people...that you just click with, you know. They can understand what you're bringing, they're happy for you to offer things, they're receptive, but they also know what they want. ....It's always about a dialogue....And sometimes, you find somebody who's really up for it, and then...you have fun. (Danielle)*

If there are considerations about a power relationship to be had, it appears that, although the developer may bring knowledge from other projects, it is

*Because there was a strong relationship of trust between...the academics, because, you know, you never know whether they're going to deliver, and these, they did deliver, and they worked really hard, and the thing that was produced I thought was really very good. ....And if you know [everybody], and you know what their strengths are, then you can play to their strengths. And it frees things up, it means you can go beyond a base level, and you can be free, and it gives you space to try things out. (Danielle)*

The above quote underlines the suggestion made by Healy and Jenkins (2003) that academic developers and discipline academics can raise the status of teaching in higher education through collaboration and valuing each other's contribution. Something that might be worth considering at this point is that, frequently, developers work within the academic's context and not vice versa. Innovation has different meanings in different contexts, and what might be a far cry from the comfort zone for one department might be the next department's bread and butter. The ideas of fun and freedom expressed during the discussion become reality when developers are invited to become active stakeholders in the project: when the multiprofessional team stands as a team of experts into which the developer feeds from both a technological and a pedagogical point of view. The following section of the chapter explores whether the e-learning context, specifically, holds potential for this kind of relationship.

## The Developer in the E-Learning Context

The chapter so far has highlighted the role of developers as catalysts—crosscutting change agents whose access to innovative development across the institution leads to insights and strategic awareness not as easily accessible to staff bound to a particular academic department. As Oliver (2002) highlights, the role of the educational technologist is one that emerged over recent decades in response to developing technologies. It is frequently the development of these technologies, or indeed of e-learning, that is cited as a catalyst for change (Conole, White, & Oliver, 2007), and the change this brings for the academic (Salmon, 2000). Shephard (2004) identifies the differences between "helping staff to help themselves" and "doing it for them" (p. 71), a fundamental difference between academic development in using technology and providing a technological support service. The role of the developer remains frequently overlooked despite what seems to be an often inseparable connection between the two. Looking in the other direction, however, much of the literature dealing with educational development highlights the impact technology has had on the role (Land, 2004). In talking to developers in various contexts, both formally and informally, it appears that, by and large, they thrive on flexibility and spontaneity, juggling several projects at the same time and having to adjust to new contexts quickly and competently, living in a constant state of problem solving.

*If projects work well, we hear little about them; there is then some kind of interim phase where things start going wrong, and we still don't hear, then they reach crisis point, and immediate reaction is required, often with nearly impossible deadlines to keep up with. This makes any kind of advance planning difficult….In this role, there's a process of understanding the crisis…then it involves acquiring the information it takes to solve the problem, and potentially contacting somebody else to actually do the work.…Overall, I deal well with crisis, as long as I'm in control—it's the constant flux of dependency on other people's competence and willingness, whilst still feeling*

*responsible for a project's success that makes my stress levels soar. (educational developers' blog)*

When everything goes more or less to plan, however, the state of crisis is more of a state of excitement: a constant adrenaline rush of exploring different avenues and brokering connections—the winged-messenger component of the role. Technology and the way in which it advances can make this component even more pronounced, as was highlighted in the following discussion:

*There is this ethos of technology which is constantly developing, interest in learning and teaching, and…a sense that it's new territory, so you're developing it. And I think if you work in this field and you care about it, then you're always going to be wanting to try new things, and because the rate of technological change is so…fast, then you get to try new things all the time. It is just irony that you spend [time] on something, developing something, and you finish and you think "yeah, this is it, this is the thing, this is…" and then something else happens, technologically, and you're off in another direction. And that's, you know, that's very exciting! (Danielle)*

In the example cited above, it is interesting that having to start from scratch is not described as a frustrating experience; instead, there is an almost playful engagement with having new challenges all the time: a work that is never finished. One reason for this may be that, despite new work needing to be carried out technologically, from a pedagogical point of view, the developer's work is never lost; it gets reused across projects, and expertise gained in one context gets the opportunity to be applied much quicker elsewhere than other roles might allow for.

The advantages of having more than one developer with a technology-area specialism working on the project become apparent in the following comment:

*The role that both you and I played was as a kind of catalyst. And we did that—I'm convinced that the reason we did it, particularly with a group of 250 students, was because we both egged each other on. And we both egged each other on because it was a dialogue. And you could say we were just getting carried away, or you could say that we felt empowered to take risks…and that's when the job starts to get exciting and interesting for me. (Danielle)*

In planning the collaborative component of the module, the two developers and the module leader met originally to discuss the WebCT content and how the module would build on the preceding one. In the previous module, student face-to-face colloquia had been facilitated by more mature students, and the plan was that this semester, the groups would be self-facilitating. This very quickly led to the suggestion that, in order for this approach to be effective, the groups would need a tangible inquiry task or outcome to work toward. A creative, student-led outlet was discussed, with the potential of creating a resource that could be showcased to others. It was further suggested that the size of seminar groups (15 students) would be too large for any meaningful collaboration. Whilst the considerable number of students was an issue everybody was aware of, it was never treated as a barrier—only as a reason for trying things slightly differently from the way other departments or projects might address the same issues. E-learning and multimedia here provided the perfect opportunity to support the work on several levels:

- WebCT as an existing and already utilised tool to remind students of deadlines and provide updates,
- online booking for face-to-face training in the use of technologies,
- e-mail support for students facing technical problems or wishing to book equipment,
- high-end-spec collaborative learning spaces that allowed students to come together to create their final product,
- WebCT as an online discussion tool for students to raise both technical and conceptual issues,
- laptop technology to allow 45 groups to present their work simultaneously in one big learning space,
- a CD-ROM with all multimedia student projects allowing students to take their own and other's work away and present and use them in different contexts, and allowing staff to use the best student work in their future teaching (in consultation with the students).

In reminiscing about this pivotal meeting, both developers have, on several occasions, discussed why this project ended up being so much more innovative than its original plan, and the usual end point of discussion is the fact that suggestions from developers were continuously met with open ears and appreciation. In comparing notes, it transpires that, in many projects, the developer might suggest an idea that goes deliberately beyond the comfort zone of the academic or department in an attempt to reach a compromise that allows for calculated risk taking and innovation. Hearing the positive response to all ideas voiced at the meeting resulted in what the quote above describes as either getting carried away or feeling empowered to take risks, a position that, according to Oliver (2002), staff in the developer and learning technologist role do not necessarily find themselves in very often, but which, coupled with an increase in developer-driven research, could bring about considerable change in the future of e-learning development.

## CONCLUSION

In working on the module, it became quickly obvious that all team members were willing to engage with each other at a professional level, recognising the diversity of expertise available and seeing this as a strength. Inglis, Ling, and Joosten (1999) highlight this—the recognition of each other's expertise as part of the collaboration—as one of the crucial factors of successful learning and teaching development. Although the personal reasons behind engaging with the project might have been different, the fact that the students' learning experience remained central to the development process helped maintain focus and certainly steered the development in the direction of networked learning components at both the collaborative and the individual level. The focus on inquiry-based learning also helped unite the various threads of thought into a coherent learning experience.

The background section to this chapter outlines the role of the educational developer or learning technologist as an agent of change; however, the project illustrated the role of academics in the process. The educational developers and learning technologists might be the winged messengers, carrying news of good practice between departments, or the oily rags, who do background work, develop materials, set up resources, and then blend into the background. The members of lecturing staff, however, are ultimately the ones who will implement the new developments with the learners: They need to believe in the process as much as the developers that came before them, or the evaluators who come after them. With this in mind, the roles are remarkably similar. As outlined in the background to this chapter, a blurring of roles is occurring (Blass, as cited in Blass & Davis, 2003; Wright & Miller, 2000), where educational developers and academics share many aspects of their respective multifaceted job descriptions, calling for close collaboration and mutual support.

The multiprofessional team that was the focus of this research project was remarkable insofar as it had an even balance between lecturing staff and development staff. On the development side, three individuals collaborated with the lecturing

staff to achieve the best possible module development. With their specific expertise in multimedia production, WebCT design and development, and inquiry-based learning and networked learning development, the three roles were differentiated enough to necessitate three experts. At the same time, however, all development staff had at least a working knowledge of each other's professional area, enhancing the collaboration, facilitating communication about the project, and highlighting once more the need for a portfolio of skills necessary to the educational developer or learning technologist. All three developers were prime examples of the particular species of developer involved in e-learning that was described above: keen to try new things, thriving on exploring unknown issues and problems, and collaborating to find solutions for these issues. The fact that the academics involved took a real interest in the pedagogical value of the relevant technologies rather than seeing developers as technical support staff unrelated to the pedagogy meant that the entire team engaged in a continuous discourse both throughout the planning and the running of the module. For the developers involved, this meant input at a higher strategic level, including forward planning, sustainability, reusability of resources, and student involvement in taking the project forward through dissemination of student work across other modules. As a result, the module ended up as a patchwork of good practice that had evolved in other departments across the institution when adapted for context. It also allowed the advancement of some more adventurous ideas, including those that were previously considered very difficult to solve, if not unsolvable, such as group work with large student numbers. The input from three developers and/or support staff allowed a far more encompassing overview of the possibilities e-learning held to support the module, in turn providing for a more coherent experience for the student, who, despite the multifaceted use of various technologies, saw the module as one fluent structure rather than considering technology to be "bolted" onto lectures.

## FUTURE RESEARCH DIRECTIONS

There is no doubt that the educational developer or learning technologist can and may adopt the role of either oily rag or winged messenger in a multiprofessional team, or indeed any other role or function described in this chapter. The increasing use of a variety of technology and the resulting increase in team size, however, do not only spell changes for academic staff. Developers, too, will have to rethink their role and specialist area at a time when the profession is still considered to be emerging. It is likely that the future will see both a blurring of roles (between developer and technologist) and a specialisation that allows for true expertise in one particular field, involving not only experience, but also research and scholarship (Brew, 2002; Harland & Staniforth, 2003). Whilst this chapter sets the ball rolling in exploring some of the various roles in the multiprofessional team from the developer's perspective, much more remains to be done to identify just how e-learning has affected and might affect the development of new learning activities, modules, or courses over the coming years. There is scope for a long-term study researching the changing role of the developer over time, but also for in-depth research into the ways in which the various developer and technologist roles within any one particular institution can and might feed into the strategic e-learning development of that institution. In the United Kingdom, the role of CETLs has involved the creation of new posts in addition to already existing units offering educational development and learning technology support. In some CETLs, these roles have a specific pedagogical approach or specific context in mind, such as inquiry-based learning, active learning, work-based learning, creative learning, learner autonomy, and so forth. This means the emergence of developers and technologists who have the opportunity to engage with development (including e-learning development) from a specific pedagogical angle. In many other countries, a thriving distance learning market holds great potential to explore how development takes place, whether from a departmental or an institutional vantage point, and how these developments are supported. There is scope for a comparative study of institutions seeking to provide developmental support for e-learning at the departmental level and those who have centralised support systems in place.

With all this in mind, however, it should not be forgotten that the very complex role of the developer or learning technologist is still under-researched. Recognised as an emerging profession and, in the United Kingdom, a topic of study seeking to provide accreditation, it is a role that draws people from a variety of backgrounds few other professions in the higher education system can rival. The personality traits, skills, expertise, and knowledge inherent in such a diverse group of individuals have much to offer to the field of e-learning and as such warrant further investigation.

## ACKNOWLEDGMENT

Thank you to Dr. Philippa Levy, CILASS, University of Sheffield, and the reviewers for their helpful comments on an earlier version of this chapter.

## REFERENCES

Bath, D., & Smith, C. (2004). Academic developers: An academic tribe claiming their territory in higher education. *International Journal for Academic Development, 9*(1), 9-27.

Blass, E., & Davis, A. (2003). Building on solid foundations: Establishing criteria for e-learning development. *Journal of Further and Higher Education, 27*(3), 227-245.

Brew, A. (2002). Research and the academic developer: A new agenda. *International Journal for Academic Development, 7*(2), 112-122.

Brew, A. (2003). Making sense of academic development: Editorial. *International Journal for Academic Development, 11*(2), 73-77.

Candy, P. (1996). Promoting lifelong learning: Academic developers and the university as a learning organisation. *International Journal for Academic Development, 1*(1), 7-19.

Conole, G., White, S., & Oliver, M. (2007). The impact of e-learning on organisational roles and structures. In G. Conole & M. Oliver (Eds.), *Contemporary perspectives in e-learning research: Themes, methods and impact on practice* (pp. 69-81). Abingdon: Routledge.

D'Andrea, V., & Gosling, D. (2001). Joining the dots: Reconceptualizing academic development. *Active Learning in Higher Education, 2*(1), 64-80.

Diercks-O'Brien, G. (2002). Implementing a virtual learning environment: A holistic framework for institutionalizing online learning. In R. Macdonald & J. Wisdom (Eds.), *Academic and educational development: Research, evaluation and changing practice in higher education (staff and educational development series)* (pp. 140-151). London: Kogan Page.

Fraser, K. (2001). Australasian academic developers' conceptions of the profession. *International Journal for Academic Development, 6*(1), 54-64.

Garrison, D., Anderson, T., & Archer, W. (2000). Critical inquiry in a text-based environment: Computer conferencing in higher education. *Internet and Higher Education, 11*(2), 1-14.

Gosling, D. (2001). Educational development units in the UK: What are they doing five years on? *International Journal for Academic Development, 6*(1), 74-90.

Harland, T., & Staniforth, D. (2003). Academic development as academic work. *International Journal for Academic Development, 8*(1/2), 25-35.

Healy, M., & Jenkins, A. (2003). Discipline-based educational development. In H. Higgins & R. Macdonald (Eds.), *The scholarship of academic development* (pp. 47-57). Buckingham, United Kingdom: Society for Research into Higher Education & Open University Press.

Hicks, O. (1997). Career paths of directors of academic staff development units in Australian universities: The emergence of a species? *The International Journal for Academic Development, 2*(2), 56-63.

Hounsell, D. (1994). Educational development. In J. Bocok & D. Watson (Eds.), *Managing the university curriculum: Making common cause* (pp. 89-102). Buckingham, United Kingdom: Society for Research into Higher Education & Open University Press.

Inglis, A., Ling, P., & Joosten, V. (1999). *Delivered digitally: Managing the transition to the knowledge media.* London: Kogan Page.

Jones, C. (2004). Networks and learning: Communities, practices and the metaphor of networks. *ALT-J, Research in Learning Technology, 12*(1), 81-93.

Land, R. (2004). *Educational development: Discourse, identity and practice.* Maidenhead, United Kingdom: Society for Research into Higher Education & Open University Press.

Ling, L. H. (2007). Community of inquiry in an online undergraduate information technology course. *Journal of Information Technology Education, 6*, 153-168.

Littlejohn, A. (2005). Key issues in the design and delivery of technology-enhanced learning. In P. Levy & S. Roberts (Eds.), *Developing the new learning environment: The changing role of the academic librarian* (pp. 70-90). London: Facet Publishing.

Moses, I. (1987). Educational development units: A cross-cultural perspective. *Higher Education, 16*, 449-479.

Oliver, M. (2002). What do learning technologists do? *Innovations in Education and Teaching International, 39*(4), 245-252.

O'Neill, K., Singh, G., & O'Donoghue, J. (2004). Implementing elearning programmes for higher education: A review of the literature. *Journal of Information Technology Education, 3*, 313-323.

Salmon, G. (2000). *E-moderating: The key to teaching and learning online.* London: Kogan Page.

Shephard, K. (2004). The role of educational developers in the expansion of educational technology. *International Journal for Academic Development, 9*(1), 67-83.

Wright, W. A., & Miller, J. E. (2000). The educational developer's portfolio. *The International Journal for Academic Development, 5*(1), 20-29.

## ADDITIONAL READING

Beetham, H. (2001). *Career development of learning technology staff: Scoping study executive summary.* JISC Committee for Awareness, Liaison and Training Programme. Retrieved June 2, 2007, from http://www.elt.ac.uk/ELT%20documents/institutional/execsum.pdf

This scoping study provides an interesting overview over roles, responsibilities, and activities of learning technologists in the United Kingdom, and formed the basis for several future research projects.

Beetham, H., & Bailey, P. (2002). Professional development for organisational change. In R. Macdonald & J. Wisdom (Eds.), *Academic and educational development: Research, evaluation and changing practice in higher education* (pp. 164-176). London: Kogan Page.

This chapter outlines the EFFECTS project, which aimed to support staff in a wide range of institutions in embedding learning technologies into curricula.

Brew, A. (2002). Towards research-led educational development. *Exchange: Ideas, Practices, News and Support for Decision Makers Active in Learning and Teaching, 3*, 25-26.

This brief article outlines the need for academic developers to participate in research activity and issues surrounding this endeavour, bearing in mind the multifaceted role.

Brew, A. (2003). The future of research for academic development. In H. Eggins & R. Macdonald (Eds.), *The scholarship of academic development* (pp. 165-181). Buckingham, United Kingdom: Society for Research into Higher Education & Open University Press.

This is a longer article arguing the case for academic developers engaging in research on their own practice. Brew makes a clear point for the dual role of the developer as support to others and a researcher in his or her own right.

Collett, P., & Davidson, M. (1997). Re-negotiating autonomy and accountability: The professional growth of developers in a South African institution. *International Journal for Academic Development, 2*(2), 28-34.

This article provides a more international perspective, giving an interesting overview of academic development in one particular institution.

Although 10 years old now, this is an interesting contribution to the field.

Conole, G. (2006). What impact are technologies having and how are they changing practice? In I. McNay (Ed.), *From mass to universal HE: Building on experience* (pp. 81-95). Buckingham, United Kingdom: Society for Research into Higher Education & Open University Press.

Approximately a decade after the Internet first came into use as a teaching tool, this chapter provides a useful reflection on how technologies have changed teaching and learning at universities.

Dempster, J., & Deepwell, F. (2003). Experiences of national projects in embedding learning technology into institutional practices. In J. K. Seale (Ed.). *Learning technology in transition: From individual enthusiasm to institutional implementation* (pp. 45-62). Lisse, The Netherlands: Swets & Zeitlinger.

Situated within the context of the United Kingdom, this chapter summarises and evaluates several projects that were aimed at embedding learning technologies at an institutional level, outlining successes and lessons learned.

Ellaway, R., Begg, M., Dewhurst, D., & Macleod, H. (2006). In a glass darkly: Identity, agency and the role of the learning technologist in shaping the learning environment. *E-Learning, 3*(1), 75-87.

This article proposes a typology of learning-technology support provision based on the context within with educational technologists operate. It gives a critical overview of several of the identities a learning technologist might have to maintain.

Errington, E. (2004). The impact on teacher beliefs on flexible learning innovation: Some practices and possibilities for academic developers. *Innovations in Education and Teaching International, 41*(1), 39-47.

This article from New Zealand provides valuable insight in how teachers' beliefs shape their willingness in engaging in learning and teaching innovation, and how this knowledge can be helpful to the developer.

Hanson, J. (2003). Encouraging lecturers to engage with technologies in learning and teaching in a vocational university: The role of recognition and reward. *Higher Education Policy and Management, 15*(3), 135-149.

This article provides an insight into how one particular institution in the United Kingdom has sought to implement reward and recognition for staff, and also addresses some of the difficulties that arise when engaging in action research at your own institution.

Kowch, E. G. (2005). Do we plan the journey or read the compass? An argument for preparing educational technologists to lead organisational change. *British Journal of Educational Technology, 36*(6), 1067-1070.

This brief article argues for further research that is needed in order to explore fully the role educational technologists play in leadership positions, and the impact this may result in. There is very little to be found in this field, so Kowch's argument certainly warrants future research.

Lytras, M., & Naeve, A. (2006). Semantic e-learning: Synthesising fantasies. *British Journal of Educational Technology, 37*(3), 479-491.

This article provides a useful introduction to the idea of semantic e-learning, as well as an argument for its use as a way to bring together learners, teaching staff, and educational technologists.

Mintz, J. (1997). Professionalization of academic developers: Looking through a North American lens. *International Journal for Academic Development, 2*(2), 22-27.

This article looks at issues faced by academic developers in North American institutions, giving an interesting juxtaposition to other international contributions outlined here.

Murphy, J. (1994). Improving the effectiveness of educational development: Concerns, constraints and recommendations. *Higher Education Research and Development, 13*(2), 213-230.

Although dated now, this article provides an interesting snapshot of how educational development has evolved over time. Several more recent publications have built on this one: a valuable resource for those interested in the history of educational development.

Naeve, A. (2001). *The knowledge manifold: An educational architecture that supports inquiry-based customizable forms of e-learning.* Department of Numerical Analysis and Computer Science: Kungl Tekniska Högskolan. Retrieved June 2, 2007, from http://citeseer.ist.psu.edu/cache/papers/cs/27067/http:zSzzSzcid.nada.kth.sezSzpublikationerzSz..zSzpdfzSzCID-162.pdf/the-knowledge-manifold-an.pdf

This article reports on the concept of the "knowledge manifold," which operates on the basis of several educational design patterns and requires a number of individuals to collaborate together to achieve it successfully.

Oliver, M. (2003, September 8-10). Community, identity and professionalisation: Are learning technologists a community of practice? In J. Cook & D. McConnell (Eds.), *Research proceedings of the 10th Association for Learning Technology Conference (ALT-C 2003)* (pp. 259-272). University of Sheffield & Sheffield Hallam University.

Oliver here explores the concept of community of practice as it may or may not relate to the professional field of educational technologists, asking some pertinent questions about the evolution of the field.

Oliver, M., Sharpe, R., Duggleby, J., Jennings, D., & Kay, D. (2004). *Accrediting learning technologists: A review of the literature, schemes and programmes* (ALT Accreditation Project Rep. No. 1). Retrieved June 2, 2007, from http://www.ucl.ac.uk/calt/alt-accreditation/Initial_review.doc

This report provides an interesting overview and summary of issues relating to the accreditation of learning technologists; it forms an excellent starting point for further research.

Stiles, M., & Yorke, J. (2003, April 8). *Designing and implementing learning technology projects: A planned approach.* Paper presented at the EFFECTS Embedding Learning Technologies Seminar, London. Retrieved June 2, 2007, from http://www.jiscinfonet.ac.uk/Resources/external-resources/eltfinal.doc

This paper recognises the need for additional planning resulting from e-learning vs. traditional teaching, and proposes a planned approach to help the various professionals involved to keep an overview of the development in question.

Surry, D., & Robinson, M. (2001). A taxonomy of instructional technology service positions in higher education. *Innovations in Education and Teaching International, 38*(3), 231-238.

The authors of this article analysed 449 job adverts in the field of educational technology, developing eight categories of defined jobs with specific roles and responsibilities. It is a highly interesting exploration of the many aspects that make up the role of the educational developer or learning technologist.

Trowler, P. (1998). *Academics responding to change: New higher education frameworks and academic cultures.* Buckingham, United Kingdom: Society for Research into Higher Education & Open University Press.

Focusing on one institution in the United Kingdom, this book gives a detailed overview on how change influences attitudes and beliefs of professionals working in the institution, and how these responses can be explained.

Wills, S., & Alexander, S. (2000). Managing the introduction of technology in teaching and learning. In T. Evans & D. Nation (Eds.), *Changing university teaching: Reflections on creating educational technologies* (pp. 56-72). London: Kogan Page.

This chapter looks at two Australian institutions, as well as a study conducted in 20 Australian universities, highlighting the factors that are necessary for the successful introduction of information and communication technology.

# Chapter II
# The Role of the Tutor in Blended E-Learning:
## Experiences from Interprofessional Education

**Rhona Sharpe**
*OCSLD, Oxford Brookes University, UK*

**Jillian Pawlyn**
*School of Health & Social Care, Oxford Brookes University, UK*

## ABSTRACT

*This chapter reports on an implementation of blended e-learning within three modules in the School of Health and Social Care at Oxford Brookes University. All preregistration students within the school are required to take an interprofessional education module in each year of their study. These three modules have undergone a radical redesign, prompted by the school and university strategies for e-learning and the European and UK National Health Service IT skills agenda. The redesign resulted in a blended-learning strategy that combined face-to-face teaching with online work of increasing sophistication during each of the three modules. In each module, there was an emphasis on collaborative, interprofessional learning. Interviews were conducted with seven members of the course teams to ask them about their perceptions of their roles as tutors in this blended environment. Analysis of the interview transcripts revealed five elements of the tutors' roles: relationships with students, supporting group work, supporting professional learning, managing the blend, and developing new tutoring skills. The implications are discussed for improving staff development for tutors in this case study and for our understanding of blended learning more generally.*

## BACKGROUND

### Online Tutoring in Blended Environments

The role of the online tutor has been discussed for more than 20 years now, producing wide-ranging descriptions of the roles undertaken by tutors that cover pedagogical, social, managerial, and technical functions (see Berge, 1995), and advice and guidance for tutors (Mason, 1991; Salmon, 2004). Despite the attention that has been paid to documenting the online tutor's role, there is still a need for us to more fully understand the impact of increased use of technology on teachers' roles in higher education today. In part this is due to the changing context: the shift from tutors operating fully online to a blended-learning environment. The research on the tutor's role has largely been conducted on courses where students are working online at a distance, and students and tutors never meet. For example, Moule (2007), in a critique of Salmon's e-moderating framework and working from a health care background, argues that "the five stage model has not reflected the potential available to use e-learning as part of an integrated approach that includes face to face delivery" (p. 39). The use of blended learning is increasing rapidly in the United Kingdom (HEFCE, 2005), North America (Bonk, Kim, & Zeng, 2006), and Australia (Eklund, Kay, & Lynch, 2003), and we are only just starting to unpick what this means for the tutor.

In part our need to understand online tutoring in the blended context is also due to the mounting evidence that there are variations in how tutors take on their expected roles and the difference this makes to students who have high expectations of online tutors (e.g., Connolly, Jones, & Jones, 2007; Miers, Clarke, Lapthorn, Pollard, Thomas, & Turtle, 2005). We are starting to see more publications reporting not the early successes of computer-mediated communication, but more realistic struggles to get students to engage at all (e.g., Ham & Davey, 2005) or at the standard expected (e.g., Clouder & Deepwell, 2004). This point is important. We should not assume that all staff will have the same responses to teaching online as the early adopters. We note that many early adopters were educationalists themselves and teaching other educators or postgraduate students. Historically, online courses have been designed with a clear pedagogy based on notions of collaboration and constructivism that are understood and adopted by designers and tutors alike (Bennett & Lockyer, 2004; McConnell, 2000). Other qualitative studies of the teacher's role have examined the beliefs and behaviors of those tutors who were also the course designers and early adopters of technology (McShane, 2004). It is important that such staff are not the only ones whose voices are heard as we develop guidance for online tutors.

As blended learning becomes embedded into the practices of higher education, many more staff are involved, some of whom have not made an active choice to adopt technology, have not been involved in the pedagogical redesign decisions, and are not all sharing the same responsibilities. In the case study described here, the course redesign led to a compulsory change in the lecturers' roles to blended teaching for approximately 30 staff. Capturing the perceptions and experiences of these staff represents a valuable addition to our current knowledge of the demands, challenges, and rewards of tutoring online within a blended context.

### Blended Learning within the School of Health and Social Care

In 2004 the university had produced a strategy for e-learning that required each school to debate and explore how they could best use technology (see Sharpe, Benfield, & Francis, 2006). Each school was expected to develop, publish, and maintain their own e-learning strategy, part of which included the identification of high-impact e-learning implementations in their own context. The School of Health and Social Care was committed to providing opportunities for both staff and students to develop the necessary skills for continuing professional development in an increasing technologically enhanced workplace. The following needs were identified (Garrett, 2003):

- A requirement to maximize the use of available resources and promote efficient use of resources (both human and physical) within the school,
- A need to develop alternative methods of delivery to release some of the existing burden upon limited school resources,
- A need for staff development to build up skills in the use of ICT and educational technology for e-learning,
- Relocation to a single site where room size posed limitations to the size of teaching groups, and
- Delivering modules containing large numbers of students.

The interprofessional modules were identified by the school as a high-impact project in the school e-learning strategy. The interprofessional learning component is delivered through three PiP modules, one in each year of study across a 3-year undergraduate programme. Interprofessional education (IPE) and interprofessional intervention are of paramount importance for the success of current and future professional practice. In past decades in the United Kingdom and overseas, there has been a growing interface between health and social care sector services. Considerable attention has been given to IPE with students in the health and social care professions, particularly nursing, midwifery, health visiting, occupational therapy, physiotherapy, social work, and others in the health sciences, as well as medicine. The school adopted the definitions of interprofessional education and interprofessional intervention from Zwarenstein, Reeves, Barr, Hammick, Koppel, and Atkins

(2000) and applied these to their course design under the heading of interprofessional learning (Colyer, Helme, & Jones, 2005).

Students working toward 10 professional degrees take these modules, including four nursing pathways, midwifery, social work, physiotherapy, occupational therapy operating department practitioners, and paramedics. It was envisaged that redesigning these modules to be delivered via a blended approach would provide opportunities for the following.

- Flexibility: Student and staff study time, 24/7 access to resources, and learning on demand.
- Inclusivity and differentiation: accommodating different learner preferences and adaptable resources suitable for diverse learners.
- Extension beyond core learning activities and materials.
- Extension of opportunities for students to learn with and from each other (cooperative, collaborative, and interprofessional learning).
- Development of student and staff skills in line with the European and UK National Health Service (NHS) IT skills agenda.

In addition to making use of online resources, it is important for today's health professionals to be able to make use of online professional development opportunities. For example, Blair (2002) identified the often isolated working environments of learning-disability nurses, indicating that they may have limited access to learning opportunities due to geographical and financial boundaries, with many being employed by small organizations without the capital to fund higher education in the traditional sense. He emphasized the importance of e-learning opportunities for this small professional group as a means of communicating via networking and access to resources for continuing professional development.

## The Design of the Partnerships in Practice Modules

Interprofessional education has been criticized for being "shared listening rather than shared learning," for example, when students from different programmes all attend the same lecture (Ashford & Thomas, 2005, p. 125). In the redesign of the PiP modules, we were aiming for interprofessional learning, described by Colyer et al. (2005, p. 14) as the "process through which two or more professions learn with, from and about each other to improve collaboration and the quality of service." It was hoped that the interactive, participatory nature of online activities would promote not just learning alongside other professions, but learning about and from them.

The PiP modules focus on three themes. The first module, Academic Level 1, focuses on responding to others. This module is the foundation of the Partnerships in Practice series; it introduces key concepts, values, and skills pertinent to working in partnership with individuals and was being delivered to large groups of students (400+) in a lecture format. The focus of the second module, Academic Level 2, is on responding to the individual. It is an integrated and interdisciplinary study of diversity and inclusion policies and their impact on practice. This is considered within the context of health and social care and from the perspective of working in partnership with individuals, groups, or communities. This module was being delivered through lectures, seminars, and face-to-face group work. The third module, Academic Level 3, focuses on valuing diversity. This module is an integrated and interdisciplinary study of the evidence base of working in partnership within diverse teams and agencies and across professional and organizational boundaries. This module was being delivered through lectures and seminars.

The identification of the PiP modules in the school e-learning strategy led to targeted staff development for course teams. Staff were invited to an intensive 2-day course-redesign experience facilitated by central educational developers and learning technologists. This brought together the school learning technologist and e-learning champion with the module and programme leaders and some tutors. The course team was guided through a curriculum planning process supported by such tools as blue-sky thinking, storyboarding, and risk assessment, culminating in presentations to critical friends.

The first PiP module was redesigned from a predominantly lecture-based format to teaching entirely through seminar groups working on collaborative tasks. The students were time-tabled to attend a facilitated seminar each week on campus and had time allocated for study. There was a blend of face-to-face and online student activities based on interactive learning methods and an interdisciplinary approach to knowledge and key concepts. There was a strong emphasis on learning from and about others (team members, users, agencies, etc.) in order to improve collaboration and the quality of care. Students had access to a range of discussion-based activities in the discussion areas within the virtual learning environment (VLE) where they worked through planned activities. Members of each group could negotiate whether to undertake their study activities face to face or online.

The second PiP module was also redesigned from a predominantly lecture-based format to one taught entirely through seminar groups working on collaborative assessed tasks. Once again, the cohort was divided into seminar groups that met each week, face to face, and had access to a range of facilitated discussion topics within the VLE. The substantial difference here was the level of expectation in engagement. Students in this model were required to develop a set of ground rules for their subset and communicate this with other seminar set members. They were required to work through a series of planned activities including working collaboratively on a case-study vignette and were encouraged to share resources with each other as they worked together. This module was assessed on the production of a joint paper focusing on the case study. Students were supported in developing team working roles through face-to-face activities, with additional tools and resources available in the VLE (e.g., Belbin team roles; Belbin, 1993).

The third PiP module was originally delivered by lectures and supported by seminar groups. To prepare them for professional registration, students worked with peers in developing their own professional portfolio of interdisciplinary skills, working in partnership within diverse teams and agencies and across professional and organizational boundaries. Similar to the previous modules, the student cohort was structured into seminar sets; however, subsets were not allocated within the VLE. In this module, students formed their subsets in face-to-face discussion groups.

A range of technologies were utilized in the redesign of the modules to enhance the presentation of course materials delivered within the VLE and augment the student learning experience, including the following.

- WebCT (Web Course Tools, now called Blackboard Learning Environment v 4.0) was the VLE then utilized by Oxford Brookes University. We primarily focused on the presentation of core teaching materials and resources in the content pages and utilized the discussion facility for discussion, reflection activities, and file sharing when working on group activities.
- Macromedia Flash and embedded media clips were integrated to enhance the presentation of the e-learning environment.
- Respondus™ was used to develop formative assessment quizzes and surveys (http://www.respondus.com).
- Students were provided with key texts as e-books where available and links to electronic journals via the university library catalogue,

the emphasis being on ensuring materials were accessible both on and off campus.

The direct face-to-face teaching contact was reduced for these modules to allow for the additional time that students would work either independently or in subgroups. We specifically encouraged students to plan regular opportunities for accessing the VLE and check the discussion topics for any messages from people in their subgroups or the module team. This was different from the previous approach, which only required the students to engage with the module content once a week during the lectures or seminars.

## Implications of the Redesign for Tutors

As a result of this redesign, from 2004 to 2005, approximately 30 school staff and over 40% of all health and social care undergraduates were involved in blended learning through the PiP modules. The first cohort going through the redesigned modules (some 400+ students) was divided into seminar sets of approximately 20 to 25 students; these sets were further divided into four professionally mixed subsets for the purpose of group tasks and project work. The set leaders were required to facilitate discussion both face to face and online. In both environments, discussions needed to be suitably professional in both their focus and in the academic terminology used. Netiquette (Alexander, 2000), respect, and valuing of diversity needed to be upheld at all times. We recognized the challenges in teaching in a blended environment and identified that breaches of confidentiality and discriminatory practices might occur, and that these needed to be treated in the same light as in a face-to-face classroom discussion.

Teaching syndicates each comprised three seminar sets and their set leaders. Within each syndicate, a tutor was identified as a lead tutor who took the role as e-moderator for the syndicate.

E-moderators had previous experience in facilitating learning within a VLE and were technically confident and competent in using the tools and resources within it. The e-moderator's role was primarily one of collegiate support and guidance for their teaching colleagues in the syndicates and the overseeing of the discussion areas, supporting set leaders to facilitate student learning.

We developed role outlines for e-moderators and set leaders informed by the work of Rowntree (1995), Salmon (2004), and Shank (2001). In these we emphasized the importance of effective time management and communication of online availability to students when developing ground rules at the beginning of the module. We encouraged teaching staff to plan their online teaching in the same manner as they plan their time in the classroom with one specific modification, namely, duration of contact. It is more productive to organize tutor time so he or she "dips in and out" of the VLE on a daily basis, that is, visits quickly and often, rather than spend intense and long periods of time. This way, the tutor can keep up with discussions as they unfold, keep the conversations alive, and stimulate student learning.

## METHODOLOGY

The rationale for conducting interviews with teaching staff was to hear first-hand accounts of the experience of the tutor delivering blended learning in interprofessional education. This approach is endorsed by Guion (n.d.), who states that the purpose of conducting in-depth qualitative interviews is "to deeply explore the respondent's point of view, feelings and perspectives" (p. 1).

Interviews were conducted with seven members of staff who had taught on at least one of the blended PiP modules in the year prior to the interview. Six of the seven interviewees had taught on the Level 1 module and the other on Level 3 only. Of the Level 1 tutors, one had additionally taught on Level 3 and one on all three

PiP modules. Even within the modules, there was a wide range of experiences of online teaching during the previous year. Some tutors had both facilitated face-to-face seminars and watched over the online areas of those students in their seminar groups, and other tutors had volunteered to be e-moderators, which involved supporting a number of seminar groups and their seminar leaders. Taken together, the tutors had observed and/or facilitated a range of assessed and nonassessed online activities. All the interviewees had attended some training on the university VLE prior to tutoring, and some had attended specific course briefing. As a group, they expressed variable levels of confidence and competence in using IT to support student learning.

The interviews were semistructured with three sets of questions concerning:

- Experiences of being an online tutor in a blended environment, including their intentions, understanding of their roles and responsibilities, and the impact of the online working on what they did in class,
- Observations of their student's behavior and learning, including interactions and relationships with staff and other students and impact on their learning to be health professionals, and
- Suggestions for any improvements to the course and preparation of tutors.

Throughout the interviews, tutors were asked to provide examples to support their responses where ever possible.

The interviewees gave written permission for the interviews to be recorded on audiotape, and the tapes were transcribed. The transcripts were coded using open coding and axial coding processes by the principal investigator to identify emerging themes and their associated properties, dimensions, and subcategories (after Strauss & Corbin, 1998). The first reading of the transcripts produced five major themes. Subsequent reading and coding produced several subthemes. This interpretative methodology drew on the investigator's knowledge of the programme and the expected use of the blended approach in the modules.

## EMERGENT THEMES

Five major themes emerged from the qualitative analysis.

1. Relationships between staff and students
2. Support for student group work
3. Support for professional learning
4. Teacher management of the blend
5. Development of new tutoring skills

These themes and their subthemes are shown in Table 1 and are explored below.

## Relationships Between Staff and Students

Five of the tutors thought that the nature of their relationships with students had changed in the blended course, with some making comparisons with their experiences of teaching in previous versions of the PiP modules before they were redesigned in blended mode. Three of these tutors were uncomfortable with the changes, which they felt meant that they did not get a sense of their students as individuals. They noted that it took longer than usual to put names to faces: "There is a real difference in my relationship with the students [in the blended course] in that I didn't get to know them as people very well" (Tutor 1).

One of the tutors, who had been working on the Level 1 module where all lectures had been replaced by seminars, felt that they needed to start from scratch developing relationships in the seminars:

*If at some point you give them a lecture...they know who you are.... Then you go into a seminar, you have something to start working with.... If you just go in cold to the seminar, I find it much harder because then you have to start 30-plus one-to-one relationships with no beginning. (Tutor 2)*

However, it is likely to be a more complex situation than just not getting to know individual students. Tutor 4 talked about the separation of students' personas on the Web from their perso-

*Table 1. Themes and subthemes emerging from interviews with tutors*

| Themes | Subthemes |
|---|---|
| Relationships between staff and students | Difficulty in getting to know students<br>Students with increased access to tutors<br>Time spent on introductory activities |
| Support for student group work | Formation of supportive student-led community<br>Support for the process of group work<br>Less dependence on the tutor<br>Accelerated group work |
| Support for professional learning | IT skills<br>Teamwork skills<br>Language and communication skills |
| Integration of face-to-face and online teaching | Routines and time management<br>Clarification of expectations of tutors and students |
| Development new tutoring skills | Need for role descriptors<br>Technical support provision for students<br>Further skills development |

nas in the class and their difficulty in reconciling these, even toward the end of the module: "The student knows who you are and they come in and they've had what you think has been a very intimate discussion with them online...but you're not sure which face it is" (Tutor 4).

Tutor 1 felt that the impact of this perception of increasing distance between tutors and students was that they were not as able to draw on the experiences and backgrounds of the group members in face-to-face classes. This tutor also reflected that there was no evidence that this made any difference to students:

*I don't think that the students actually felt that I hadn't been there for them or that they didn't know me. [Indeed for them] I was available...in a more flexible way to them and it did mean that I could give very specific and thought-out responses. (Tutor 1)*

This point about the blend allowing tutors to be more accessible to students was a common theme: "I think they had more access to me and I had more access to them so...rather than feeling like a Monday-morning seminar, it felt as though the module spread over the week much more" (Tutor 6).

Finally, tutors noted that although in general they felt increased separation from their students, this was not the case for all students; indeed for some, it was the opposite: The blend "did allow for some relationship development which would not have occurred with some of the quieter members" (Tutor 4).

As this was the first run of the PiP modules in blended format, tutors were keen to suggest strategies to enable them to build relationships with their students, including making photographs of students available and spending more time on introductory activities. Tutor 3, who felt somewhat lacking in confidence in her online tutoring skills at the start of the course, spoke of spending a lot

of time on the introductions, and using these to build up relationships with students:

*I picked up a fair bit about people as individuals at that stage in a way that they phrased their little notes to me and stuff; I got the impression... of who was keen, who was hacked off, who was interested, and who was treating it as a bit of a laugh. (Tutor 3)*

## Support for Group Work

The second emergent theme was the tutors' perceptions of how the students worked together in groups and the impact of this on their tutoring roles. The tutors gave many examples of how they had seen the students supporting each other online and a feeling of a developing community of learners.

Tutors provided many examples of students taking active roles within their groups, which helped to build a sense of community. For example, there were students providing support to individual group members who, for instance, did not participate for the first couple of weeks: Being online "gave the student an opportunity to sort of say officially online—to post up an apology almost—and I think my group really responded to that and all wrote nice responses" (Tutor 1).

There was also a student whose attendance was affected by chronic illness who chose to explain that to the group in their online discussion:

*Every single one of the group put a response up that was very thoughtful...saying we really value your presence in the group, we think you are contributing, and now that we understand that we will support you even more.... I think [they] then went and talked to her face to face. (Tutor 1)*

Other tutors gave examples of students contacting each other via e-mail or the VLE if they had missed sessions and to organize the group work process:

*They did a lot of saying where they were, "I can't come this week," or "I can't do this this week but I'll see you here," or "I'll phone you there," so there was sort of, like, team tactics with the WebCT, informing each other what was going on. (Tutor 3)*

Another tutor reflected on how the VLE allowed all members of the group to contribute: "There would be someone in the group who had done the readings and would share that online rather than sitting in the corner" (Tutor 4).

Finally, another tutor exemplified how the VLE facilitated the students in answering each other's questions: "I think it gave the opportunities to discuss further, and one of the things that seemed to be happening was the students were answering students' questions, especially in the wider forum, which was very encouraging" (Tutor 7).

These actions all helped to promote a sense of a student-led community. Tutors noted that such interactions were often supported by a small number of students giving very mature, informed responses and getting thanks for that from other students.

It is worth noting that tutors were aware that students have always worked together, and some thought that the student-led community observed here "might just be perception because the traffic was more transparent" (Tutor 6).

Some tutors made direct comparisons between face-to-face and online work in terms of community building. Tutor 5 commented that the feeling of belonging to a community was created by having online areas where everyone participated together, as well as the working areas for smaller groups. This tutor noted how different this was from a large lecture, where although all the students might be physically together, they tend to be sitting with, and interacting with, a small group of friends. A second example was provided by one of the module leaders who ran an online assignment-query discussion, which was well used by students. The tutor felt this was

more egalitarian than the assessment queries, which were didactic face-to-face sessions that had been run in previous years toward the end of the module.

As well as offering social support to one another, the tutors noted that some groups completed the group-work tasks more efficiently and progressed through the work at a faster pace than in previous years. Tutors ascribed this to the fact that online, students did not chitchat about what television programmes they had watched, for instance, and just got down to work; another reason given was the reduced demand for finding time to meet in already busy schedules. For example, for some mature students who attended class on site for only 2 days, which were booked solid for teaching sessions, it would have been difficult to complete the group work without the online communications.

The tutors found that these student-led communities, working efficiently together, were less dependent on them as tutors. A number of tutors mentioned that the students had been surprised when they had joined in their online conversations and they themselves had felt like they were "eavesdropping" (Tutor 4) or "barging in" (Tutor 5). In the face-to-face classes, it was noticeable that the groups were working more independently and required less facilitation:

*There was a couple of days I came in and I felt totally superfluous; they were working away, some of them had laptops actually with them, and I said, "Hi I'm here, does anyone need any help?" and it was like "No, no, no; we'll let you know." (Tutor 3)*

Tutor 4 thought the online work accelerated the group process and reduced the amount of teacher time needed to facilitate that: "It seemed that those groups needed more work from an external facilitator to get them functioning together where these groups seemed to be more ready to engage once they got into the classroom because they had already done some of the discussion" (Tutor 4).

## Support for Professional Learning

The three PiP modules aimed to promote interprofessional learning both through their content and their mode. The tutors were supportive of the prominence given to online work as part of the skills set needed by health professionals, even if the students did not always see why it was necessary:

*We had some students saying how they didn't think they'd come here to do so much IT…. I think they had but they're rather misinformed on the way practice is going if they think it's not going to be part of their professional lives. (Tutor 5)*

Another tutor commented, "[Learners] who aren't getting involved in Web-based learning activities are going to be disadvantaged in the future" (Tutor 7).

One clear example of why learning to work online was valuable concerned the need for health professionals to adopt appropriate language, and to learn

*that communication has consequences and that anything that you e-mail or WebCT could be used in evidence against you…. I think that they've got used to being accountable for their communication and if that means that a few shocks have put them off, I'm not sure that's such a bad thing that they have to think quite carefully. (Interview 5)*

In terms of how much interprofessional learning was achieved, the tutors were supportive of the blended design to facilitate group work. They recognized that the goals of interprofessional learning would be different at each level. For example, at Level 1, working alongside students from other professions was sufficient: "In the first year the goal should be for them to learn how to

work with others, period, and not be preoccupied with the professions" (Tutor 4).

There was agreement that the students had learnt about working in a team, and this was an important first step in interprofessional education: "It just got in so early in their professional experience so that all that learning about others and learning with others was happening…. I'm really keen to see what happens to that group as they go through" (Tutor 7).

## Integration of Face-to-Face and Online Teaching

One of the interesting features of this study was that it was based on the experiences of teachers in blended contexts rather than fully online courses. The tutors gave examples of their perceived benefits of the blend, including giving continuity between the face-to-face sessions, making tutors more accessible, and offering flexibility in scheduling.

One tutor said, "It felt that there was continuity between the classes because you didn't feel necessarily that you had sent them off—they'd gone off and gotten lost through the week" (Tutor 4).

Another tutor stated, "I think they had more access to me and I had more access to them so…rather than feeling like a Monday-morning seminar, it felt as though the module spread over the week much more" (Tutor 6).

Regarding flexibility, one tutor said, "I think for me the great advantage of WebCT is that people can work together without having to be face to face, and coming from a satellite campus, I think that's a massive advantage" (Tutor 7).

The tutors were helping students to integrate what was happening online and face to face. Most tutors used the online discussions as a way to see what issues were arising for students and to tackle those in class. One tutor stated, "I looked to see what queries were coming up and if it was a query that I thought was actually worth sharing with the whole group, I'd then take that back the following Monday and say this has come up" (Tutor 6). Another said, "I used the face-to-face time to make sure I'd understood what they were asking of me and to share any difficulties that had been going on within the groups" (Tutor 3).

Six of the tutors had established a routine of logging in either before or after class to see what was happening and answer any queries. The remaining tutor was aware of the need to be "far more systematic" in logging in next time. In addition, some tutors developed a routine of proactively writing to their students on a weekly basis: "I got into a routine of writing to them all after the session on Friday as a way of putting together what we'd done in the session" (Tutor 3).

This tutor noted that the important aspect of this was not necessarily what she said, but that she was showing that she had listened to what the students had said and was responding to it. She used this weekly message to give specific feedback on what she thought they were doing well in their group work and what was being expected of them. It is noticeable that this tutor used the face-to-face sessions to clarify what tutors were expecting of her, and weekly online messages to help students understand what were being expected of them.

Tutors were also making choices about what to use each medium for. This might in part be due to the tutor's experience and preference. For example, Tutor 2 was concerned when he found the students were drawing heavily on their personal experiences in their work rather than their academic background, and found it "much easier to handle that kind of thing in a seminar group."

## Development of Tutoring Skills

There was general agreement that tutors should be trying to provoke discussion online. One tutor said, "I thought it would be good to…get them talking online and giving them the space and time online because there is that flexibility to think about their answer" (Tutor 1). Another stated,

*I tried to provoke wider discussion because it seemed that students were being invited to come out with some fairly immediate responses, and so I tried to push them into thinking about those…. I played devil's advocate and waited to see what results I got. (Tutor 2)*

However, the same tutors also expressed some confusion about the precise nature of their roles and felt "quite threatened by it and a little overwhelmed to start with" (Tutor 3): "It wasn't clear to me to what extent I was supposed to be engaging in dialogue with them…so I chose to define the role myself" (Tutor 2).

Specific examples of roles and activities tutors took on were

- Being available online to promptly respond to student comments,
- Supporting students who were making very good comments,
- Modeling behaviors expected online,
- Encouraging students to use the online discussions, and
- Giving technical support.

For a minority, these roles were seen to be similar to their previous tutoring roles in face-to-face courses: "They've felt like the same behaviors that I would be performing in the classroom in terms of group process" (Tutor 4).

However, most were aware that different tutor behaviors were important online; for example, Tutor 5 aimed "just to get there as quickly as possible and to acknowledge that they'd make an effort," and saw it as quite a responsibility to get there quickly and do more than "pat the students" on the head for posting, saying something useful to them in response.

The technical support was a little contentious. Some tutors spent time in the face-to-face sessions going through how to use the system, not just at early stages, but throughout the course, for example, helping students in managing navigation when there are many messages. Other tutors did not think this was their job and/or did not feel confident themselves about taking on the technical-support role.

In general, tutors became aware of the need to prepare tutors and were keen to develop their own skills further: "I'm very committed to developing my online tutoring skills because I know it's going to happen, it's inevitable, and so I need to know how to do it as best as possible" (Tutor 1).

## DISCUSSION

As a small-scale evaluation, this study aimed to help us understand the impact of increased use of technology on the roles of the tutors with the School of Health and Social Care. We found that tutors did think that the blending of their courses was changing their relationships with students. On the one hand, they were concerned with the difficulty in getting to know their students as individuals, and they were developing ways of doing this in the blended context. On the other hand, they felt that they were more accessible to students even if they were not quite sure who they were or who they had been talking to. This finding contrasts sharply with the established literature based on fully online situations, which have frequently reported that teachers get to know their students better online than they do face to face (McShane, 2004). We found that staff were supportive of the use of technology to facilitate interprofessional learning for health professions and were keen to develop their own teaching strategies and skills to implement this.

Of most interest was the finding that students were using the technology to develop and sustain a student-led learning community. Although this has been noted in other evaluations of online interprofessional learning courses (Miers et al., 2005), our emphasis here was on its impact on the tutor's role. We found that the students made use of the availability of access to each other to support the group-work process they had been asked to undertake. Some students behaved in ways that helped both small task groups and the wider learning community to function effectively and efficiently. The tutors recognized that some students have always worked together, for example, in setting up their own study groups. However, they noted that the visibility of this process online and its ability to involve students who might previously have been excluded through time-tabling demands, personal circumstances, illness, or preferences for interacting in groups changed the nature of the relationships between students and between staff and students.

The tutors interviewed found that the blended course redesign led to changes in the ways that students worked together, and this had an impact on the tutoring role. In both face-to-face and online contexts, tutors found students needing less facilitation. In the online mode particularly, tutors were sometimes unsure of the role they should take and when to intervene. Again, this is in contrast to the existing literature. The well-established models of online learning assume the dominant position of the e-moderator in scaffolding student learning in a constructivist environment (e.g., Berge, 1995; Denis, Watland, Pirotte, & Verday, 2004; Goodyear, 2001; Salmon, 2004). Berge, for instance, sees the pedagogic role of the tutor as questioning and probing students in order to encourage discussion around key concepts, principles, and skills. Goodyear specified that the tutor's role would be expected to change in networked learning environments from lecturer to guide, and from provider of content to designer of learning. Timmis et al. (2004) found some support for this in their Study of the Online Learning Experience (SOLE) project. They also found evidence as we did here of tutors encouraging increased student self-direction. Case studies from health care follow a similar theme, suggesting, for instance, that online tutors adapt the cognitive element of their role to prompt more reflective postings from their students (Wilson, Varnhagen, Krupa, Kasprzak, Hunting, & Taylor, 2003).

We proposed at the beginning of the chapter that findings in our study might differ from the existing literature because much of the literature is based on tutor and student experiences in fully online, even fully distance, courses. Looking at our interviews, it might also be that learners are using technology to support their informal learning because they are entering higher education with different expectations, attitudes, and prior experiences of how technology is used to support learning. Looking at bit more closely at the issues tutors raised about when or whether to intervene, we find that this has been noted before in the literature (e.g., Monteith & Smith, 2001), although, as we might expect, it has been related to the tutor's job to scaffold constructivist learning environments. In our study, the wording used by tutors is important. They were concerned about not wanting to "eavesdrop" or "barge in": not phrases used by facilitators of learning guiding a structured learning activity but by those witnessing student led-learning groups. The emergence of such patterns of interaction amongst students is consistent with recent findings from studies of learners' experiences that say students are using technology extensively to support informal learning and social networking, and that this is often out of sight of their tutors (Conole, de Laat, Dillon, & Darby, 2006; Creanor, Trinder, Gowan, & Howells, 2006).

The tutor in a blended-learning context cannot ignore the informal support groups that are operating in many places out of sight. He or she is not formally taking on the role of the e-moderator as a teacher might do in a fully online course. It is becoming clear that to tutor in a blended context, tutors likely need to demonstrate their other skills, such as facilitating the process of setting up student-led groups and helping them to sustain themselves. We have some idea of the strategies that might help in such situations, but much more needs to be done.

In our situation here at Brookes, we have recommended that PiP module tutors

- Are provided with clear descriptors of their roles, informed by the intentions of the design of the course in which they are teaching,
- Are given time in their workload plans to include an allocation of hours for online teaching,
- Are encouraged to spend time in the introductions to find out about their students and to generate their own ways of getting to know their students,
- Are encouraged to adopt regular and consistent strategies for managing the blend like writing after a face-to-face session to link this session and online sessions,
- Need more flexible scheduling in blended courses to allow time in face-to-face sessions to discuss things that have been arising online, and
- Support the development of student skills needed for group work as an important precursor to interprofessional learning.

These recommendations are equally valid for colleagues elsewhere who are planning to deliver teaching in a blended learning environment.

## FUTURE TRENDS

It was not the purpose of this chapter to produce a comprehensive guide to the tutor's role. Others have already done this and found that it is important to select roles that suit the context (Denis et al., 2004). Within the blended-learning context in one academic school in one university, this work has led to the development of a role descriptor for our e-moderators in the interprofessional learning modules. It has also led to lobbying for staff to receive time to work online and for the school to invest in developing their e-moderators. Looking to future work, it will be interesting to see how the role of the tutor in blended-learning environments comes to be specified.

In a recent review of evaluations of blended learning, we identified engaging in course redesigns as crucial to the embedding of e-learning (Sharpe, Benfield, Roberts, & Francis, 2006). This was particularly notable where studies described a blended course that had been developed in response to a real and relevant problem at the course level or with very clear design principles set in advance. The PiP redesign is a good example of this. In the redesign of the PiP modules, we made use of the VLE and digital resources to facilitate interaction and communication between the students and tutors and reduced face-to-face modes of teaching and learning. As e-learning moves from a period of being led by individual innovators to large-scale implementations resulting from transformative course-level redesigns, it is crucial that we understand the impact of the introduction of technology for all those involved.

## CONCLUSION

Like other qualitative evaluations, this study set out to capture the experience of tutors through an interview method. Their experiences need to be seen within the context in which they undertook their role: interprofessional learning modules that had recently undergone radical redesign prompted by the national and local strategies to engage health care staff and students in using information and communication technologies. This study was unusual in that the seven staff interviewed were teaching in a blended, rather than fully online, context and had been required to do so through the course redesign. A number of themes emerged from the analysis: tutors' perceptions of a changing relationship between themselves and their students, their role in supporting student group work and professional learning, how teachers manage the blend, and the need for developing new tutoring skills.

## FUTURE RESEARCH DIRECTIONS

This small case study has hinted that the established models of online learning and tutoring, based on socioconstructivist principles, may not be well suited to the more recent use of technology to support large groups of undergraduate learners in blended settings. Future research needs to approach this issue from both the perspectives of tutors and learners. From the tutor's perspective, future research should be directed at uncovering the roles that tutors take on when supporting learners and the skills and strategies they find useful to, for example, reduce the perceived distance between themselves and their students. From the learner perspective, we need to know how learners are using communicative tools to support required group-work tasks, or indeed to support their study through informal networks. In this context, what are their expectations of the tutor's role and what do they find useful?

## REFERENCES

Alexander, G. (2000). *Netiquette*. Retrieved August 21, 2007, from http://sustainability.open.ac.uk/gary/papers/netique.htm

Ashford, M., & Thomas, J. (2005). Interprofessional education. In H. Burgess & I. Taylor (Eds.), *Effective learning and teaching in social policy and social work* (pp. 124-137). Oxford, United Kingdom: Routledge Falmer.

Belbin, M. (1993). *Team roles at work*. Oxford, United Kingdom: Butterworth Heinemann.

Bennett, S., & Lockyer, L. (2004). Becoming an online teacher: Adapting to a changed environment for teaching and learning in higher education. *Educational Media International, 41*(3), 231-244.

Berge, Z. L. (1995). Facilitating computer conferencing: Recommendations from the field. *Educational Technology, 35*(1), 22-30.

Blair, J. (2002). E-learning: A virtual challenge for educators. *Nursing Times, 98*(31), 34-35.

Bonk, C., Kim, K.-J., & Zeng, T. (2006). Future directions of blended learning in higher education and workplace settings. In C. Bonk & C. R. Graham (Eds.), *Handbook of blended learning: Global perspectives, local designs* (pp. 550-568). San Francisco: Pfeiffer Publishing.

Clouder, L., & Deepwell, F. (2004). Reflections on unexpected outcomes: Learning from student collaboration in an online discussion forum. *Networked Learning Conference.* Retrieved October 25, 2007, from http://www.networkedlearning-conference.org.uk/past/nlc2004/proceedings/individual_papers/clouderanddeepwell.htm

Colyer, H., Helme, M., & Jones, I. (Eds.). (2005). *The theory-practice relationship in interprofessional education.* Retrieved June 25, 2007, from http://www.health.heacademy.ac.uk/publications/occasionalpaper/occ7.pdf

Connolly, M., Jones, C., & Jones, N. (2007). New approaches, new vision: Capturing teacher experiences in a brave new online world. *Open Learning, 22*(1), 43-56.

Conole, G., de Laat, M., Dillon, T., & Darby, J. (2006). *Student experiences of technologies (LXP): Final report and appendices.* Retrieved June 25, 2007, from http://www.jisc.ac.uk/elp_learneroutcomes

Creanor, L., Trinder, K., Gowan, D., & Howells, C. (2006). *The learner experience of e-learning (LEX): Final report.* Retrieved June 25, 2007, from http://www.jisc.ac.uk/uploaded_documents/LEX%20Final%20Report_August06.pdf

Denis, B., Watland, P., Pirotte, S., & Verday, N. (2004). Roles and competencies of the e-tutor. *Proceedings of Networked Learning Conference 2004.* Retrieved June 25, 2007, from http://www2.uca.es/orgobierno/ordenacion/formacion/docs/jif-pev5-doc4.pdf

Eklund, J., Kay, M., & Lynch, H. (2003). *E-learning: Emerging issues and key trends.* Australia: Australian National Training Authority.

Garrett, B. (2003). *School of Health and Social Care e-learning strategy.* Retrieved November 9, 2004, from http://www.brookes.ac.uk/virtual/documents/files/Health_and_SocialCare-DraftSchoolRBLStrategy2003.doc

Goodyear, P. (2001). *Effective networked learning in higher education: Notes and guidelines.* Retrieved June 25, 2007, from http://csalt.lancs.ac.uk/jisc/Guidelines_final.doc

Guion, L. (n.d.). *Conducting an in-depth interview.* Retrieved August 21, 2007, from http://edis.ifas.ufl.edu/pdffiles/FY/FY39300.pdf

Ham, V., & Davey, R. (2005). Our first time: Two higher education tutors reflect on becoming a "virtual teacher." *Innovations in Education & Teaching International, 42*, 257-264.

HEFCE. (2005). *HEFCE strategy for e-learning.* Retrieved October 25, 2007, from http://www.hefce.ac.uk/pubs/hefce/2005/05_12/

Mason, R. (1991). Moderating educational computer conferencing. *DEOSNEWS, 1*(19). Retrieved October 25, 2007, from http://www.emoderators.com/papers/mason.html

McConnell, D. (2000). *Implementing computer supported co-operative learning* (2nd ed.). London: Kogan Page.

McShane, K. (2004). Integrating face to face and online teaching: Academics' role concept and teaching choices. *Teaching in Higher Education, 9*(1), 3-16.

Miers, M., Clarke, B., Lapthorn, C., Pollard, K., Thomas, J., & Turtle, A. (2005). *Learning together on-line: Student and staff experience of interprofessional on-line groups.* Centre for Learning and Workforce Research in Health and Social Care, University of West of England. Retrieved June 25, 2007, from http://hsc.uwe.ac.uk/hsc/pdf/research/learning_together_online.pdf

Monteith, M., & Smith, J. (2001). Learning in a virtual campus: The pedagogic implications of students' experiences. *Innovations in Education and Teaching International, 38*(2), 302-311.

Moule, P. (2007). Challenging the five-stage model for e-learning: A new approach. *ALT-J, Research in Learning Technology, 15*(1), 37-50.

Oxford Brookes University Centre for E-Learning (OBU C4eL). (2005). *E-learning strategy 2005-2008: Embedding e-learning.* Retrieved August 21, 2007, from http://mw.brookes.ac.uk/download/attachments/1900739/Appendix+2-5+e-L+Strategy+2005-08+post+consultation+vers51.pdf?version=1

Rowntree, D. (1995). *The tutor's role in teaching via computer conferencing.* Retrieved August 21, 2007, from http://www.iet.open.ac.uk/pp/D.G.F.Rowntree/Supporting%20online.htm

Salmon, G. (2004). *E-moderating: The key to teaching and learning online* (2nd ed.). London: Routledge Farmer.

Shank, P. (2001). *Asynchronous online learning instructor competencies.* Retrieved August 21, 2007, from http://www.learningpeaks.com/instrcomp.pdf

Sharpe, R., Benfield, B., & Francis, R. (2006). Implementing a university e-learning strategy: Levers for change within academic schools. *ALT-J, Research in Learning Technology, 14*(2), 135-151.

Sharpe, R., Benfield, G., Roberts, G., & Francis, R. (2006). *The undergraduate experience of blended e-learning: A review of UK literature and practice.* Retrieved December 12, 2006, from http://www.heacademy.ac.uk/4884.htm

Strauss, A., & Corbin, J. (1998). *Basics of qualitative research: Techniques and procedures for developing grounded theory.* Thousand Oaks, CA: Sage.

Timmis, S., O'Leary, R., Cai, C., Harrison, C., Weedon, E., Trapp, A., et al. (2004). *Student and tutor roles and relationships (SOLE thematic reports series).* Retrieved June 25, 2007, from http://sole.ilrt.bris.ac.uk/roles.pdf

Wilson, D., Varnhagen, S., Krupa, E., Kasprzak, S., Hunting, V., & Taylor, A. (2003). Instructors' adaptation to online graduate education in health promotion: A qualitative study. *Journal of Distance Education, 18*(2), 1-15.

Zwarenstein, M., Reeves, S., Barr, H., Hammick, M., Koppel, I., & Atkins, J. (2000). Interprofessional education: Effects on professional practice and health care outcomes. *The Cochrane Database of Systematic Reviews* (Issue 3, Art. No. CD002213.DOI:10.1002/14651858.CD002213). Retrieved August 21, 2007, from http://www.mrw.interscience.wiley.com/cochrane/clsysrev/articles/CD002213/frame.html

## ADDITIONAL READING

These three books offer practical guidelines on how to conduct qualitative research and analysis, with a particular focus on research interviews and suggestions on conceptual frames of reference for thinking about them.

Bazeley, P. (2007). *Qualitative data analysis with NVIVO* (2nd ed.). Thousand Oaks, CA: Sage.

Kvale, S. (1996). *InterViews: An introduction to qualitative research interviewing.* CA: Sage Publications.

Richards, L. (2005). *Handling qualitative data.* Thousand Oaks, CA: Sage.

These three resources are an amalgamation of recent and current thinking and practice on interprofessional education in both universities and the workplace across health and social care.

Centre for the Advancement of Interprofessional Education (CAIPE). (n.d.). Retrieved from http://www.caipe.org.uk

Hughes, M., Ventura, S., & Dando, M. (2004). On-line interprofessional learning: Introducing constructivism through enquiry-based learning and peer review. *Journal of Interprofessional Care, 18*(3), 263-268.

Freeth, D., Reeves, S., Koppel, I., Hammick, M., & Barr, H. (2005). *Evaluating interprofessional education: A self-help guide.* Higher Education Academy Health Sciences and Practice Network.

These are two popular and practical generic Web sites on the role of the online tutor, and an interesting insight on the improvisational role of the online tutor in the context of legal education.

Emoderators. (n.d.). Retrieved from http://www.emoderators.com/moderators.shtml

Online Tutoring Skills Project (OTIS). (n.d.). Retrieved from http://otis.scotcit.ac.uk

Maharg, P. (2005). Portrait of the online tutor as Thelonius Monk directions. *UK Centre for Legal Education, 11.* Retrieved October 25, 2007, from http://www.ukcle.ac.uk/directions/previous/issue11/maharg.html

The first journal article critiques a well-known model for e-moderating in higher education whilst the second presents qualitative research on interactions in five online courses involving staff that currently lecture or support learners in further and higher education at the University of Glamorgan and its partner colleges throughout Wales.

Lisewski, B., & Joyce, P. (2003). Examining the five-stage e-moderating model: Designed and emergent practice in the learning technology profession. *Alt-J, Association for Learning Technology Journal, 11*(1), 55-66.

Jones, N., & Peachey, P. (2005). The development of socialization in an on-line learning environment. *Journal of Interactive Online Learning, 3*(3), 1-20. Retrieved August 21, 2007, from http://www.ncolr.org/jiol/issues/showissue.cfm?volID=3&IssueID=12

These final three readings are included to capture the importance of e-learning and blended-learning course design, with a particular focus on the pedagogical challenge of designing for fruitful interaction in online and blended courses. All include personal practices and an outline of the tools and policies used to enhance interactivity with students, among students, and between students and course content.

Mabrito, M. (2004). Guidelines for establishing interactivity in online courses. *Innovate, 1*(2). Retrieved October 25, 2007, from http://www.innovateonline.info

Macdonald, J. (2006). *Blended learning and online tutoring.* Aldershot, United Kingdom: Gower.

Sharpe, R., & Oliver, M. (2007). Designing courses for e-learning. In H. Beetham & R. Sharpe (Eds.), *Rethinking pedagogy for the digital age: Designing and delivering e-learning* (pp. 41-51). Oxford, United Kingdom: Routledge Falmer.

# Chapter III
# Modeling Best Practices in Web–Based Academic Development

**Diana K. Kelly**
*San Diego Miramar College, USA*

## ABSTRACT

*This chapter makes a case for the importance of preparing e-teachers by requiring them to have an experience as an e-learner. The chapter begins with a review of the challenges and criticisms of e-learning. Some of the literature indicates that e-learners have been dissatisfied with their learning experiences. Some academics have concerns about the rigour of courses offered through e-learning. The literature of academic development and e-learning is used to link theory with practice. The chapter provides examples of best practice in the preparation of academic staff for e-teaching. Two case studies of lived examples of e-teaching preparation are provided from a North American perspective. Future research directions are outlined, with research questions to be explored regarding the link between the preparation of e-teachers through e-learning and the quality of the e-learning experience for students.*

## INTRODUCTION

Academic staff in higher education are enthusiastic about getting involved in e-teaching, yet most are getting started with no experience as an e-learner. Experiencing e-learning from the learner's perspective is immensely helpful, if not essential, for effective e-teaching. Ideally, it would be best to experience a very positive and involving model of e-learning, which may be used as a model for one's own e-teaching. This chapter is a presentation of a lived example of academic development through e-learning.

The aim of this chapter is to make a strong case for the preparation of e-teachers through successful completion of a fully online programme to prepare for e-teaching. International examples of e-teaching programmes will be included, including lessons learned from participation in two North American Web-based e-teaching programmes: one generic programme (for anyone from any institution), and one programme offered by a university for new e-teachers.

## BACKGROUND

Whenever new or innovative teaching methods are used, it is normal for sceptics and critics to express concerns about the quality of teaching and learning, and e-learning has attracted some criticism. While some studies have shown "no significant difference" between learning outcomes in face-to-face classrooms and in the e-learning environment (Joy & Garcia, 2000), other studies have shown high attrition rates in e-learning, student frustrations with inexperienced e-teachers, and frustrations of e-teachers with poor student participation and learning outcomes.

While all of these criticisms cannot be directly linked to the quality of the preparation of the e-teachers, some of the frustrations of novice e-teachers show that preparation for e-teaching is a significant issue that does contribute to the quality of the overall teaching and learning experience for students and teacher.

Academic staff who plan to begin e-teaching usually need some professional development to provide an introduction to the new learning and teaching environment. According to a recent study in the United States, two thirds of 320 colleges and universities surveyed require academic staff to complete some training prior to teaching online (Lokken & Womer, 2007). Professional development for e-learning often takes the form of face-to-face workshops, one-on-one assistance and mentoring, and sometimes hybrid or blended e-learning experiences. The focus of some profes-

sional development is on the use of the technology, or on the development of materials to put up on a Web site for students. Some academic development programmes are also focused on the use of e-learning technology to enhance student learning.

The main point of this chapter is to consider the potential benefits of a professional development programme that is provided fully online. Some universities currently provide professional development preparation for teaching online through classroom instruction in computer labs or through blended learning formats. The premise of this chapter is that, while these approaches are useful, it may be even more effective for academic staff to have the opportunity to experience e-learning fully at a distance as their students will. This chapter will focus on the role of effective professional development fully through e-learning to prepare teachers for high-quality e-teaching that is focused on student involvement and learning. First the criticisms of e-learning will be explored to determine what needs to be done to improve the quality of e-learning. Second, best practices in professional development will be examined, including possible ways of translating these to the preparation for e-teaching. Third, research on the current practices in academic development for e-teaching will be explored. Finally, recommendations will be made for the improvement of the preparation of e-teachers in the future.

This chapter is not a research-based chapter, but rather a detailed review of the existing literature on the challenges of preparing academic staff for teaching in the online environment, and some of the best practices that are emerging in the field.

In this chapter, the terms *e-teaching, e-learning, Web-based learning,* and *online learning* refer to any instructional course component delivered using the Internet, whether provided fully at a distance or in a hybrid or blended format. E-teaching refers to the processes used by teachers, and e-learning refers to students learning online.

## ISSUES, CONTROVERSIES, PROBLEMS

Several concerns are addressed frequently in the literature of e-learning: the quality and rigour of instruction, including learning outcomes; student persistence; and student satisfaction.

### Concerns about the Quality and Rigour of E-Learning

There is a perception, particularly among those who have not experienced e-learning, that it is much less rigourous for learners and teachers than face-to-face classroom-based learning. A recent report from the Sloan Consortium (Allen & Seaman, 2006) notes that although perceptions of quality in e-learning have improved somewhat since 2003, only 62% of chief academic officers surveyed believe that learning outcomes are the same as face-to-face learning, and only 16% believe outcomes are superior in e-learning.

The highly quoted report *The No Significant Difference Phenomenon* (Russell, 1999) was a meta-analysis of research studies that showed evidence that the learning outcomes from e-learning were no different than learning outcomes in traditional courses. However, since then, others, including Phipps (2000) and Joy and Garcia (2000), claim that the original analysis was flawed and that cause and effect cannot be determined because the research did not control for extraneous variables. Joy and Garcia recommend that rather than looking at the use of technology as an issue to be debated, it is more important to focus on learning by considering this question: "What combination of instructional strategies and delivery media will best produce the desired learning outcome for the intended audience?" (p. 38).

In a meta-analysis of many studies of learning effectiveness in e-learning courses offered at a distance, Zhao, Lei, Yan, Lai, and Tan (2005) found that interaction is the key element that contributes to student learning outcomes. More interaction among students and teacher, including both asynchronous and synchronous interactions, was the most important element in many studies of e-learning.

### Problems with Student Persistence in E-Learning

Student persistence in online distance learning courses is another concern. Although it is difficult to obtain accurate statistics on dropout rates, higher education officials in the United States estimate that student persistence is generally 10 to 20 percentage points lower in e-learning courses (Barefoot, 2004; Carr, 2000). A more recent study of over 300 colleges in the United States shows a much smaller difference in student retention in semester-length modules: 72% for distance learning and 78% for face-to-face modules (Lokken & Womer, 2007).

While theories on persistence in face-to-face learning emphasise engagement and social cohesion, Gibbs (2004) points out that an attempt to adapt these theories to the online environment have not been successful. However, according to one study, feelings of isolation, anxiety, or confusion can contribute to decisions to drop out of online courses (King, 2002). Several studies have found that students underestimate the workload of e-learning and will drop out when they feel they have fallen too far behind (Aqui, 2005). Jo Tait (2004) of the Open University (United Kingdom) explains that student persistence is difficult to address because there are many factors that may contribute to students' decisions to drop out. However, she also points out the important role of tutors in distance learning, and the need for academic development to teach in ways that enhance student persistence. One example of this comes from an introductory computer module at a community college in Tyler, Texas. The e-teacher, Emilio Ramos, reported that when he started holding regular chats and provided more interactive discussions for his students, his course completion rates jumped from 62% to 90%. Ramos says, "The key to having low attrition and successful completion in the online medium is the ability of instructors to keep the students engaged, and that requires quite a bit of effort from the instructor's point of view" (as cited in Carr, 2000).

## Student Criticisms about the Quality of E-Learning

Some of the criticism of e-learning has come from students. In a large-scale study of students who have participated in Web-based distance learning in the United States (Noel-Levitz, Inc., 2006), students responded that the following areas needed improvement in e-learning: the quality of instruction, the responsiveness of e-teachers to students' needs, and timely feedback from e-teachers. Experienced e-learners would agree. After dropping out of an online astronomy module mid-semester, a student said, "It wasn't worth the headache. The instructor wasn't a bad teacher. He just did not have the experience with online courses" (as cited in Carr, 2000). The instructor was teaching online for the first time and had not set up the course materials and labs properly.

Other studies reinforce these findings, including a study of Canadian university students (Stodel, Thompson, & McDonald, 2006). When asked to compare their experiences in face-to-face classes with online classes, students expressed concerns about the quality of the online asynchronous discussions. Some felt that they were too drawn out, going over the same issues too many times. Others were unhappy with the flow of the discussion and felt that students were really just "checking in" rather than paying close attention to what others had already written on the discussion board.

Despite the criticisms about the quality of e-learning and the concerns about the consistency and rigour of e-learning, it is possible to address these concerns by preparing e-teachers more effectively.

## SOLUTIONS AND RECOMMENDATIONS

To examine the solutions, it is important to first look at best practices for the preparation of e-teachers. Two case studies of e-teaching preparation will be described in detail as concrete examples of the best practices outlined.

## Best Practice to Prepare for E-Teaching

In determining best practices for preparing for e-teaching, it is important to examine four dimensions of the preparation. First, how do novice e-teachers learn to teach online? Second, how can best practices in academic development for face-to-face teaching be translated into the preparation of e-teachers? Third, which methods of professional development are currently used in preparing academic staff for e-teaching? Fourth, what is the focus of the professional development programmes to prepare new e-teachers?

## First, How do Novice Teachers Learn to Teach?

Those with no background in teaching and learning often try to reproduce what they have experienced as students. If they have seen excellent lectures, they will try to emulate them. If they have experienced small group work and lively discussions, they will try to create a similar learning environment for their own students. They often tend to use the teaching methods that best suit their own learning style.

How do novice e-teachers learn to teach online? If novice teachers tend to reproduce what they have experienced as students, what happens if they have never experienced e-learning? If they do not have a frame of reference or a prior e-learning experience to draw upon, it is very challenging to begin to teach online. This is confirmed in an article written from the perspective of a first-time online teacher. Using a reflective approach through teaching journals, student feedback, and analysis of online discussions, Yu and Brandenburg (2006) analysed several dimensions of a first-time e-teacher's experience. The issues and frustrations that were raised indicated a lack of experience in e-learning as a learner, and a significant lack of preparation to teach online. In particular, the importance of facilitating student interactions and collaboration was a lesson learned through hard experience. In a case study of another very frustrated novice e-teacher, Choi and Park (2006) outlined very similar issues and concluded,

*If the new online instructor had had training regarding the pedagogical issues of online teaching and vicarious experiences through experienced online instructors, she could have been better prepared and had a different impression about online teaching. This implies that training for online instructors should be designed with more focus on the pedagogical issues of online teaching and on vicarious experiences with the actual online teaching rather than on technical issues. (p. 322)*

The University of Hull developed a tutor training programme for e-teaching based on a model that started with face-to-face workshops, progressed to 4 weeks of online teaching observation, and ended with 12 weeks of online teaching practice. In their extensive evaluation of this programme, it became clear that one of the major issues was the lack of experience in e-learning as learners. The participants could only imagine what it might be like as an e-learner, and they only had a few weeks of experience as an observer (not learner participant). The programme evaluation also noted the importance of modeling practice in the tutor training programme that matched the group work and interactive discussions that would be expected of tutors when they were teaching (Bennett & Marsh, 2002).

## Second, Which best Practices in Academic Development may be used Effectively in Preparing E-Teachers?

The following characteristics of academic development programmes are important to consider for long-term impact and positive changes to teaching practice: a long duration, social construction, a focus on content, an experiential model of learning, and reflection on learning.

Longer duration programmes are more effective than short-term workshops. Several studies have shown that activities for academic development that are longer in duration tend to have a more substantial impact on making changes to teaching practice over the long term (Hinson & LaPrairie, 2005).

The social construction of learning through cohorts is important for long-term impact on teaching practices. Tom Angelo (2001, p. 100) explains, "Faculty [academic] developers intent on change must engage their colleagues in constructing or adapting new, shared, contextually relevant concepts, rather than presenting faculty [academic staff] with imported prefabricated models for adoption."

Academic development programmes linked clearly to the content of teaching are more meaningful for teaching practice. When lecturers have opportunities to apply their learning to teaching in their own discipline, they are more likely to make changes to enhance their teaching. In a successful programme of professional development for online course development at Louisiana State University, participants moved from learning and practicing new skills in using the e-learning platform to applying the skills into their own courses (Hinson & LaPrairie, 2005). Another study of over 1,000 science and mathematics teachers found that professional development activities with a focus on content knowledge and active learning had the greatest positive impact on increases of knowledge and skills in teaching, which changed the teachers' teaching practices. In addition, those activities that were longer in hours of participation and spanned a longer period of time had the greatest positive impact (Garet, Porter, Desimone, Birman, & Yoon, 2001). Most lecturers consider teaching methods to be linked strongly with the discipline, so they are more likely to be accepting of ideas and advice on teaching from those within their own discipline. Those in a department who have a solid background in learning theory and teaching and learning methods can be very effective consultants to their colleagues. According to Maxwell and Kazlauskas (1992, pp. 356-357), "expert consultation by colleagues on specific teaching matters were among the most effective modes of development."

Experiential or situated learning is the notion of experiencing a model of teaching and learning to be used in a real-life situation. If learning is embedded in the context in which it will be used, it will be more meaningful to the participants (Brown, Collins, & Dugiud, 1989). Ideally, the learning experience should provide authentic situations and activities, process models, collaborative constructions of knowledge, and opportunities for reflection (Herrington & Oliver, 1995). Staff developers at Southern Cross University in Australia call their module a "staff immersion" programme that immerses participants in the role of online students, who learn about the potential for online interaction (O'Reilly & Brown, 2001).

Stephen Brookfield (1993, p. 21) explains the importance of becoming learners to learn about teaching: "I argue that regularly experiencing what it feels like to learn something unfamiliar and difficult is the best way to help teachers empathise with the emotions and feelings of their own learners as they begin to traverse new intellectual terrains."

By experiencing a well-designed and well-facilitated e-learning course about teaching online at a distance, new e-teachers understand from their own experience what a good e-learning experience feels like. The University of Southern Queensland drew upon the ideas of situated and experiential learning to develop a situated staff development model for e-teaching (Taylor, 2003). This successful model included awareness building for novice e-teachers experiencing the actual e-learning environment with authentic activities, a small amount of face-to-face training, online reflection, and peer mentoring.

Reflection on the learning experience and possible application to teaching must go hand in hand with experiential learning. Cowan (2003) points out that we learn from experience only if we also reflect upon that experience: "What have I learnt from that which will be useful to me in the future?" (p. 207) is a useful question for stimulating reflection on a learning experience. Cowan calls this "reflection for action," expanding upon Schön's (1988) model of reflective practice.

## Third, Which Methods of Professional Development are used to Prepare for E-Teaching?

Whether teaching and learning occurs fully at a distance or in a blended format with some face-to-face meetings, academic staff must be well prepared to teach effectively in this new learning environment. This preparation often includes an orientation to the course management software, such as WebCT™ or Blackboard™, and usually takes the form of a face-to-face course or a series of workshops that include some underpinning learning theories, the use of features of the e-learning platform, and the development of materials to load to the course Web site. There are several examples of this type of workshop designed to prepare those who are new to e-teaching, including the Jump Start programme at Indiana University Purdue ("IUPUI Jump Start Program Prepares Faculty to Teach Online," 2006), the CampusNet online workshop provided by the University of Houston, Texas (Kidney, 2004), and the Xanadu project at the University of Turin, Italy (Trentin, 2006).

While these face-to-face workshops are helpful, they might not provide the same experience as an online e-teaching course. How will the new e-teacher learn what a good discussion looks like? How will teachers understand the experience of a new e-learning student if they have never participated in an e-learning module?

Blended or hybrid e-learning is the format of choice for some university professional development programmes, including the e-moderating course offered by the University of Glamorgan (Fitzgibbon & Jones, 2004). However, blended learning comes with the challenge of finding an appropriate time for the face-to-face sessions.

Some programmes are fully online self-paced tutorials. Prospective e-teachers are expected to work through the materials to learn to teach online. While this provides experience in using the course management software, and often gives prospective e-teachers a look at innovative possibilities for course materials and assessments, the self-paced workshops lack one of the most important aspects of e-teaching: the facilitation of online discussions.

Fully online e-teaching programmes offered at a distance include the e-moderating programme at the Open University, United Kingdom (Salmon, 2006), and the two case studies described later in this chapter. This model provides a comprehensive experience in e-learning for the prospective e-teachers and, if well modeled and well facilitated, provides a positive experience for future e-teachers to draw upon when they begin teaching online.

## Fourth, What is the Focus of E-Teaching Programmes?

The focus of e-teaching programmes has been evolving. Some programmes still focus on the use of the technology for e-learning, including how to use various features of the specific e-learning course management software, such as WebCT™, Blackboard™, Moodle™, and so forth. As a part of this focus, novice e-teachers are most interested in learning how to develop materials for a module

Web site with a content-driven focus when preparing to teach online. As Dianne Conrad (2004) noted in her study of novice e-teachers, teachers' overall concerns stemmed from their perception of their role as "deliverers of content." They appreciated the e-learning platform as a place to put more content to be accessed by their students. However, they did not seem to be concerned about issues of social interactions among learners, and facilitation and mentoring of learners. The participants in Conrad's study took part in face-to-face workshops and one-on-one mentoring sessions that focused only on the use of the technology for e-learning. While this is a necessary part of professional development for e-teaching, the professional development focus must go beyond a focus on technology and content.

A study of over 500 members of the Multimedia Educational Resource for Learning and Online Teaching (MERLOT) indicated that the focus of interest for e-teachers has shifted from technology skills training to enhancing skills in e-moderating for high-quality online learning (Kim & Bonk, 2006). Gilly Salmon's (2006) well-respected work in this field indicates that this is a crucial component in successful e-teaching. Using Vygotsky's "zone of proximal development" as a model, those who provide e-teaching workshops online can help the academic staff to develop their skills in facilitation by modeling behaviours in asynchronous discussions that will be more productive for their learning development, including questioning techniques that probe for deeper learning (Welk, 2006). Through this modeling, participants will experience the type of facilitation that will help them to be more effective facilitators of online asynchronous discussions.

To summarise, high-quality e-teaching programmes focus on the learning theories and principles that have been proven to be effective in face-to-face teaching, adapting them to the e-learning environment. The "Seven Principles of Effective Teaching," originally developed by Chickering and Gamson, were used by Graham,

Cagiltay, Lim, Craner, and Duffy (2001) to provide a useful way of looking at the qualities of teaching that help students learn in the online environment. These seven principles include contact between students and teacher, cooperation among students, active learning, prompt feedback to students, time on task, high expectations, and diverse talents and ways of learning. By applying these same principles to e-learning, e-teachers can fine-tune their teaching practices.

## TWO CASE STUDIES: MODELS OF THE FULLY ONLINE E-TEACHING PROGRAMMES

To provide concrete examples of model programmes to prepare e-teachers, two programmes are described (Kelly, 2000, 2002). Both programmes were provided fully online at a distance with no face-to-face meetings. This was an intentional part of the design to give participants the same experience that learners will have when they participate in a fully online programme rather than blended or hybrid learning.

The first case study describes a postgraduate-level certificate programme open to anyone in the world who has teaching experience in education, higher education, or in professional development in the business world. The second case study describes a programme that was designed specifically for Walden University to prepare tutors to work online at a distance with postgraduate students in the PhD in education programme.

The most important similarities between the programmes are the strong grounding in learning theory, a focus on facilitating active learning through asynchronous discussions and collaborative activities, and, most importantly, providing a relevant learning experience in context and allowing reflection on this experience.

## University of California at Los Angeles: Online Teaching Programme

In 1999 I decided to update my skills as an academic and learn about online classes. Because my time was limited and my day-to-day schedule was somewhat unpredictable, I was happy to find a fully online certificate programme on teaching online offered by UCLA (University of California at Los Angeles, http://www.uclaextension.edu). The certificate programme consisted of five core modules and one elective module. The school recommends taking two modules at a time, so I started with the first two core modules: Introduction to Online Technologies and Developing Curriculum for Online Programs. Other core modules were Teaching and Learning Models for Online Courses, Internet and Online Teaching Tools, and Practicum in Online Teaching (a capstone course). I chose the module Multimedia Production as my elective module. Modules were offered in 4-week or 6-week periods in four terms each year. Taking two modules each term, it was possible to complete the certificate programme in three terms over 9 months.

### Flexibility in Learning

Although there were clear starting and ending dates for each module, the time students put into the actual course work was entirely flexible. Almost all of the collaborative work and online discussions were asynchronous. Each module usually had 10 to 15 participants, and only those who were experienced teachers were accepted into this programme. Some were from very remote areas, and they were happy to participate in this online programme because they had no university within traveling distance.

People have often asked how much time this online programme required of me as an e-learner. My experience was that, as with any course, it depends on the student's level of interest and motivation. Students could spend as much time online and completing assignments as they wanted to, but on average, I probably spent about 10 hours per week on each module, and more when major assignments were due. Those 10 hours per course (20 hours per week for two courses) were spread out over lunchtimes, evenings, weekends, and generally whenever I had a chance to work on assignments.

## International Participation

As a fully online programme offered at a distance, we had a very international group of participants from many parts of the world including Hong Kong, Saudi Arabia, Australia, Switzerland, and North America. This resulted in rich discussions with an international perspective. We learned quite a bit about educational issues in other countries and gained some new ideas. Having such broad international participation would not have been feasible if face-to-face sessions had been required.

## Mandatory Student Orientation

After enrolling I received a welcoming e-mail from OnlineLearning.net, UCLA's online learning provider. It recommended ordering textbooks soon, and provided links to several places where textbooks could be ordered online. The e-mail also included information about how to download the necessary software from Embanet, the online course management system, which was a simple process.

Prior to the start of the first module, it was required that all participants complete a four-part online self-paced orientation to the Embanet software. There were dire warnings that those who did not complete the entire orientation would be removed from the module. Although this sounded a bit harsh, it soon because obvious that the online orientation to the software was absolutely essential to the experience. Students learned how to use the asynchronous discussion groups, submit assignments, participate in synchronous chat, go to the course resources, get help from Embanet, and so forth. Without this orientation and the easy availability of Embanet's technical-support team (by phone and e-mail), this fully online programme would have been very frustrating, if not impossible.

## The Importance of Technical-Support Systems for E-Learners

High-quality e-learning is impossible without good technical support in place, ideally 24 hours per day, 7 days a week. If this is not possible, then it should be available at specified times when usage is highest, particularly on weekends and evenings. It can be incredibly frustrating if the course Web site crashes, especially when an assignment is due. Embanet had a habit of doing this periodically. Fortunately, Embanet had excellent technical support for major problems like a Web site crash or individual student problems such as software incompatibility. Students could e-mail or call the technical-support desk for immediate assistance with any problem.

## Providing a Welcoming Learning Environment

As with any face-to-face class, introductions at the beginning of each module help students to become involved more quickly. Online learning is no different. Participants have a desire to make connections with other students, but the e-teacher must facilitate this. This initial interaction on the discussion board also helps e-learners get into the habit of checking in to the course Web site regularly to see if anyone new has added their introduction.

About a week before the module started, we received a welcoming e-mail from the e-teacher. She asked all of us to go to the course Web site and introduce ourselves, including our background, our interest in online learning, and what we were hoping to achieve, as well as any personal details we wanted to share. As a good student, I was happy to follow her directions and thought I would be the first one there, but I was not. Everyone was enthusiastic about getting started. It was interesting to learn that they were not only from higher education, but also from secondary education and from training and development.

## Facilitation of Asynchronous Discussions

At the beginning of each module, the e-teacher provided general discussion guidelines, or netiquette rules, which emphasised the importance of participating, contributing, and encouraging. With these guidelines, our discussions were very positive and encouraging. Even when someone in the class was struggling with an issue, many would respond positively to offer advice and encouragement.

The online asynchronous discussions were lively and stimulating, and the teacher was an active participant, sometimes providing answers to questions that were raised, and sometimes raising new stimulating questions. Because the discussions were written and asynchronous (occurring whenever someone felt like submitting a discussion item), they were much more thoughtful than the typical face-to-face discussion. People had time to read another student's thoughts, digest them, and respond thoughtfully. Students also became great resources for the rest of the group. If one person raised a question, often two or three others would respond with answers or online resources. The teacher did not feel obliged to be the only one providing answers. In fact, the teacher was truly a "guide on the side," actively participating and guiding the discussion but encouraging the students to provide the majority of input.

All of the online modules seemed to follow the same pattern in terms of organization, discussions, and assignments, but the quality of the learning experience was really influenced by the tone set by the teacher. Those modules in which the teacher was less involved seemed to be less interesting and less involving for the students. The modules with the greatest interaction and that stimulated more learning were those in which the e-teacher was actively engaged on a daily basis, and showed his or her enthusiasm for the e-learners, the topic, and the discussions through comments that were worded in the most positive way. These modules were so involving that I found myself checking into the course Web site several times a day to see the new postings: at lunchtime in front of my computer and most evenings.

## Practical and Relevant Assignments

The assignments for each module were very practical, relating the theoretical readings to the creation of online materials. However, one big difference was that we submitted our assignments to the module Web site so all e-learners in that module could look at the assignments and offer formative comments and suggestions before final submission. The comments were very positive and affirming, and when suggestions were offered it was in the spirit of helpfulness: e-learners helping other e-learners. This was all a part of the process of learning how to provide formative feedback to e-learners, as well as modeling an excellent collaborative process to be used with our own students.

## Group Projects

Some of the course projects and assignments were done in groups. It is possible to do group work online if it is well organized and facilitated. One assignment was to create a fictional module Web site around a particular topic. In my small group (members were assigned by the teacher), there was one member in Switzerland, one in New York, one in Texas, and two in California. We decided who would do which piece of the project, and most of our work was done asynchronously through our own group discussion site that the teacher had set up on the course Web site. We also decided to try a synchronous chat just to check in with the group members. Considering the 9-hour time difference between California and Switzerland (and the others in between), we determined a time that would work for all of us. It worked pretty well, but at times it was somewhat confusing because just as I thought of a response to someone's comment, there were three other responses about something else. So, the asynchronous mode generally worked best to pull our project together. We were happy with the course Web site we created as a team, and it was also interesting to see how the other groups developed their course Web sites.

## Lessons Learned as an E-Student

From this experience, I learned that e-teaching is completely different from a scheduled lecture or tutorial meeting 3 hours per week. It is much more flexible. As prospective e-teachers, we wanted to know how much time an online module requires of e-teachers. Our e-teachers answered truthfully that the busiest time in online courses is on the weekends because that is when most students have the time to do some concentrated work. So e-teachers plan to be online several times on weekends to respond to questions and problems. In addition, they check in everyday to read student comments and assignments, facilitate discussions, and address questions. If our e-teachers were traveling to a conference, they would often let us know that they would be out of touch for a particular period of time until they had their laptop set up in the hotel room. Because e-learners may also contact the teacher privately through e-mail on the module Web site, the best teachers also felt that it was important to be quick in responding to these individual queries. However, e-teachers usually said that questions that were not of a personal nature should be addressed to the discussion board so that other students may

respond, and/or see the teacher's response. There is no question that e-teaching online takes a lot of time and dedication, and a learner-centred approach to e-teacher availability.

As with any learning and teaching method, online learning is not the preferred learning mode for everyone. Some of the people in the online course said that they really missed the face-to-face contact or hearing the voices of the teacher or the other students. Perhaps it is a learning style issue. On the UCLA Web site (and other university Web sites), there is a self-assessment tool for prospective online students to determine how well suited they may be for the e-learning experience. It is important for prospective e-learners to recognize that e-learning also takes much more self-discipline and self-motivation than a face-to-face class. Those who think it will be easier are in for a big surprise. Anyone looking for an easy ride really does not belong in an online programme.

The final module of the UCLA programme was a supervised e-teaching experience with Alfred Rovai, who has written widely on e-teaching practices and was an excellent mentor to us one on one. After receiving the UCLA Certificate in Online Teaching, I was able to immediately apply my learning to create some online self-paced workshops for lecturers interested in learning new teaching strategies. These e-workshops were also designed to provide a test experience as an e-learner, allowing one to see how e-learning works, how it feels, the pitfalls, and the advantages.

## WALDEN UNIVERSITY: ORIENTATION FOR NEW FACULTY MENTORS

### Background on Walden University

Walden University (http://www.waldenu.edu) is an accredited postgraduate university that started in 1970 based on the learner-centred principles outlined by Harold Hodgkinson, professor at

University of California at Berkeley, in his 1969 article in the journal *Soundings*. The founders of Walden, inspired by Henry David Thoreau, envisioned an institution that would provide the opportunity for adults to earn doctorate degrees as scholar-practitioners so that they might develop into leaders committed to the betterment of society.

Walden University is fully accredited by the Higher Education Commission in the United States, offering master's and doctoral programmes in education, management, nursing, health sciences, psychology, social service, public policy, and engineering. Walden University is based in the United States and has 20,000 online students from 95 countries, including a partnership with the University of Liverpool for three online programmes: the MBA, MS in IT, and MA in information systems management. Walden is part of the large Laureate International Universities network that includes a total of over 240,000 students in 25 universities in 16 countries.

## Mentoring Research Students Online

In December 2005, I was invited by Terry O'Banion to join Walden University as a faculty mentor in the College of Education, working part-time at a distance, supervising and mentoring doctoral-level students in the Community College Leadership and Adult Education Leadership programmes. Terry O'Banion is the director of the Community College Leadership programme and was very enthusiastic about Walden University's focus on learning, as outlined in his 1997 book *A Learning College for the 21st Century*. He explained that the doctoral students at Walden must complete three "knowledge area modules" (KAMs) prior to beginning work on their dissertations. In other doctoral programmes in the United States, these might be considered equivalent to the required qualifying exams that are normally completed prior to the dissertation. These KAMs are very lengthy, analysing the breadth, depth, and

application of a particular topic relevant to the area of the student's academic work. Each KAM focuses on a different theme: KAM I is Principles of Social Change, KAM II is Principles of Human Development, and KAM III is Principles of Social Systems. Within each KAM, the *breadth* portion is a study of major theorists, the *depth* portion is a study of the current literature that applies the theory to a specific topic, and the *application* portion provides students with the opportunity to apply what has been learned in the *breadth* and *depth* sections through a mini research study or a real-world project aimed at creating a positive social change.

## Mandatory Orientation for New Mentors

As a new faculty mentor, I was required to complete a 12-week orientation programme provided by Walden University starting in January 2006. This programme was similar in some ways to the UCLA programme described earlier, with a strong focus on learning theory, facilitation of discussions, and provision of good support to students. However, the major difference in the programme is that we also needed to learn the "Walden way" of KAMs, learning agreements, personal development plans, and the methods for submitting and assessing work. Our online orientation was facilitated by an experienced Walden faculty mentor from the education programme, who had a wealth of experience she was willing to share with us. The group was small with only four of us, but we had well-facilitated discussions around issues of e-teaching and mentoring at Walden University. In order to pass the orientation, we were required to participate in all discussions, complete all assignments and projects (usually one each week), and successfully pass an exam at the end of the orientation course. Those who were unable to complete all of the work were invited to participate in another upcoming orientation, but were not allowed to teach for Walden until successful completion of the full orientation. This fully online orientation was an excellent model for new faculty mentors to experience learning at Walden before starting to teach there.

## Lessons Learned from the Walden Orientation Programme

Walden University has a unique structure with its KAMs, and new doctoral students can become very frustrated in the early stages. Without the extensive orientation programme, as a faculty mentor, I would have been equally frustrated. However, by providing a safe environment for new e-teachers to learn about Walden's structures and methods, I was able to provide my early students with the support and advice they needed. Because the programme is fully online for students, it was important for the prospective mentors to gain experience as learners in the same e-learning environment. Of course, some things will be learned only through the experience of working with mentees, but the preparation through the orientation programme provided a firm foundation for us as new mentors.

After examining the best practices in the preparation of e-teachers and two case-study examples of e-teachers prepared through e-learning, it is important to look at the future trends in e-teaching and e-learning.

## FUTURE TRENDS

With the rapid growth of e-learning and exponentially growing demand for fully online courses, universities are starting to pay more attention to the need for professional development to prepare e-teachers more effectively. Some universities offer their own professional development programmes in e-teaching, although most are short in duration and few are fully online. It will be important in the future for universities to consider how to best prepare novice e-teachers for

effective online teaching and include facilitation and e-moderating to promote deep learning and student success. Will all institutions provide their own fully online e-teaching programmes, or will many academic staff participate in programmes offered by a few institutions that already have excellent programmes in e-teaching? In either case, the need for providing a fully online experience will be met.

## CONCLUSION

The purpose of this chapter has been to highlight one important way of supporting academic staff in higher education who are thinking of introducing e-learning as a way of enhancing student learning. This is a critically important part of applied e-learning and e-teaching in higher education. Without good preparation for e-teaching, the quality of e-learning experiences for students will vary widely.

After my two experiences as an e-learner to prepare for e-teaching, I strongly believe in the importance of having a high-quality experience as an e-learner fully at a distance before attempting to be an e-teacher. Universities and colleges that are serious about the quality of their e-learning programmes require their prospective e-teachers to complete a programme or module in online teaching as an e-learner prior to teaching online. If it is not feasible to offer this programme within the institution, it would be worthwhile to support academic staff in participating in high-quality programmes offered by other institutions.

Prospective e-teachers who want to provide a high-quality learning experience for their e-learners should plan to participate in a well-organized, well-facilitated fully online course to see how it feels from the student perspective, whether or not it is required by their own universities. Through this type of immersion in e-learning as professional development, it is likely that the quality of online instruction will continue to improve, resulting in better student e-learning outcomes in the future.

## FUTURE RESEARCH DIRECTIONS

Further research must be done in the future to demonstrate the links between e-teacher preparation and student learning and success. Although all research on student success is challenging due to the number of variables that contribute to learning outcomes, it will be necessary to demonstrate the effectiveness of the professional development programmes to prepare e-teachers. Without this evidence, it is difficult to justify a lengthy professional development programme that models best practices in e-learning because these programmes are expensive. This research may also reveal some new ideas for professional development that will enhance e-learning outcomes in the future.

Research in the area of preparation for e-teaching should ideally analyse student learning outcomes, including completion and success rates in e-learning modules and courses. In programmes or courses with high success rates, how are the e-teachers prepared? How many of the e-teachers have participated as e-learners? Literature on e-teaching has often shown, through interviews or surveys of e-teachers, that quite a few felt unprepared when they started e-teaching. It would be interesting to find universities with e-teachers who felt well prepared to determine how many of these e-teachers had an e-learning experience first.

The student perspective is another important area to include in researching this issue. What do students look for in an effective e-teacher? Are the characteristics of e-teachers different in universities that provide preparation for e-teaching through e-learning? How much interaction and involvement in learning do students experience with e-teachers who were e-learners first in comparison to e-teachers who did not have their own e-learning experiences?

Future research in the area of Web-based academic development as preparation for e-teaching must be linked to the literature of academic development, experiential learning, and e-learning. The objective of this research will be to bring together relevant learning theories with e-teaching in order to provide the best possible e-learning experience for our students.

## REFERENCES

Allen, I., & Seaman, J. (2006). *Making the grade: Online education in the United States.* Needham, MA: The Sloan Consortium (Sloan-C). Retrieved July 7, 2007, from http://www.sloan-c.org/publications/survey/pdf/making_the_grade.pdf

Angelo, T. (2001). Doing faculty development as if we value learning most. In D. Lieberman & C. Wehlburg (Eds.), *To improve the academy* (Vol. 19, pp. 97-112). Boston: Anker Publishing Company, Inc.

Aqui, Y. (2005, June 27-30). *Characteristics of the online learner: Experiences, participation level, and achievement.* Paper presented at the Meeting of the National Educational Computing Conference (NECC) of the International Society for Technology in Education, Philadelphia. Retrieved January 9, 2007 from http://center.uoregon.edu/ISTE/uploads/NECC2005/KEY_7030859/Aqui_Aqui_OnlineLearnerCharacteristics-NECC2005_RP.txt

Barefoot, B. (2004, February). Higher education's revolving door: Confronting the problem of student drop out in U.S. colleges and universities. *Open Learning, 19*(1), 9-18.

Bennett, S., & Marsh, D. (2002, January). Are we expecting online tutors to run before they can walk? *Innovations in Education and Teaching International, 39*(1), 14-20.

Brookfield, S. (1993). Through the lens of learning: How the visceral experience of learning reframes teaching. In D. Boud, R. Cohen, & D. Walker (Eds.), *Using experience for learning* (pp. 21-32). Milton Keynes, United Kingdom: The Open University Press.

Brown, J., Collins, A., & Dugiud, P. (1989). Situated cognition and the culture of learning. *Educational Research, 18*(1), 32-42.

Carr, S. (2000, February 11). As distance education comes of age, the challenge is keeping the students. *The Chronicle of Higher Education.*

Choi, H., & Park, J. (2006). Difficulties that an online novice instructor faced. *The Quarterly Review of Distance Education, 7*(3), 317-322.

Conrad, D. (2004, April). University instructors' reflections on their first online teaching experiences. *Journal of Asynchronous Learning Networks, 8*(2), 31-44.

Cowan, J. (2003). Learning from experience. In P. Kahn & D. Baume (Eds.), *A guide to staff and educational development* (pp. 192-211). London: Routledge.

Fitzgibbon, K., & Jones, N. (2004, March). Jumping the hurdles: Challenges of staff development delivered in a blended learning environment. *Journal of Educational Media, 29*(1), 25-35.

Garet, M., Porter, A., Desimone, L., Birman, B., & Yoon, K. (2001). What makes professional development effective: Results from a national sample of teachers. *American Educational Research Association Journal, 38*(4), 915-945.

Gibbs, G. (2004, February). Editorial. *Open Learning, 19*(1), 3-7.

Graham, C., Cagiltay, K., Lim, B., Craner, J., & Duffy, T. (2001, March/April). Seven principles of effective teaching: A practical lens for evaluating online courses. *The Technology Source.* Retrieved July 4, 2007, from http://www.technologysource.org/article/seven_principles_of_effective_teaching

Herrington, J., & Oliver, R. (1995, December 4-6). *Critical characteristics of situated learning: Implications for instructional design of multimedia.* Paper presented at the Annual Conference of the Australasian Society for Computers in Learning in Tertiary Education (ASCLITE), Melbourne, Australia. Retrieved July 4, 2007, from http://www.ascilite.org.au/conferences/melbourne95/smtu/papers/herrington.pdf

Hinson, J., & LaPrairie, K. (2005). Learning to teach online: Promoting success through professional development. *Community College Journal of Research and Practice, 29*, 483-493.

IUPUI Jump Start program prepares faculty to teach online. (2006, September 15). *Academic Leader.*

Joy, E., & Garcia, F. (2000, June). Measuring learning effectiveness: A new look at no-significant-difference findings. *Journal of Asynchronous Learning Networks, 4*(1). Retrieved July 5, 2007, from http://www.sloan-c.org/publications/jaln/v4n1/pdf/v4n1_joygarcia.pdf

Kelly, D. (2000, August 18). Adventures on the cyber shop floor. *Times Higher Education Supplement.* Retrieved January 9, 2007, from http://www.thes.co.uk/search/story.aspx?story_id=63580

Kelly, D. (2002, July 1-4). *Being an online learner before becoming an online teacher: Ten lessons from experience.* Paper presented at the Improving University Learning and Teaching (IUT) Conference, Vilnius, Lithuania.

Kidney, G. (2004, June). When the cows come home: A proven path of professional development for faculty pursuing e-learning. *T.H.E. Journal, 31*(11). Retrieved July 3, 2007, from http://the-journal.com/articles/16803

Kim, K., & Bonk, C. (2006). The future of online teaching and learning in higher education: The survey says. *Educause Quarterly, 4*, 22-30. Retrieved January 10, 2007, from http://www.educause.edu/ir/library/pdf/EQM0644.pdf

King, F. (2002). A virtual student: Not an ordinary Joe. *The Internet and Higher Education, 5*(2), 157-166.

Lokken, F., & Womer, L. (2007). *Trends in e-learning: Tracking the impact of e-learning in higher education.* Washington, DC: Instructional Technology Council. Retrieved July 7, 2007, from http://www.itcnetwork.org/Trends_in_Elearning_2006.pdf

Maxwell, W. E., & Kazlauskas, E. J. (1992). Which faculty development methods really work in community colleges? A review of research. *Community/Junior College Quarterly, 16*, 351-360.

Noel-Levitz, Inc. (2006). *National online learners' priorities report.* Iowa City, IA: Author.

O'Banion, T. (1997). *A learning college for the 21st century.* Washington, DC: American Association of Community Colleges.

O'Reilly, M., & Brown, J. (2001). *Staff development by immersion in interactive learning online.* Lismore, Australia: Southern Cross University. Retrieved July 7, 2007, from http://ausweb.scu.edu.au/aw01/papers/refereed/o_reilly/paper.html

Phipps, R. (2000). *What's the difference?* Washington, DC: The Institute for Higher Education Policy.

Russell, T. (1999). *The no significant difference phenomenon.* Chapel Hill, NC: Office of Instructional Telecommunications, North Carolina State University.

Salmon, G. (2006). *Scaffolding for e-moderator's development: The early years.* Beyond Distance Research Alliance, University of Leicester. Retrieved January 9, 2007, from http://www.atimod.com/docs/atim12dec12doc%20(2).pdf

Schön, D. (1988). *Educating the reflective practitioner.* San Francisco: Jossey-Bass Publishers.

Stodel, E., Thompson, T., & McDonald, C. (2006, December). Learners' perspectives of what is missing from online learning: Interpretations through the community of inquiry framework. *International Review of Research in Open and Distance Learning, 7*(3), 1-24.

Tait, J. (2004, February). The tutor/facilitator role in student retention. *Open Learning, 19*(1), 97-109.

Taylor, J. (2003, May). Managing staff development for online education: A situated learning model. *Journal of Higher Education Policy and Management, 25*(1), 75-87.

Trentin, G. (2006). The Xanadu project: Training faculty in the use of information and communication technology for university teaching. *Journal of Computer Assisted Learning, 22*(3), 182-196.

Welk, D. (2006). The trainer's application of Vygotsky's "zone of proximal development" to asynchronous online training of faculty facilitators. *Online Journal of Distance Learning, 9*(4). Carrollton, GA: University of West Georgia Distance Education Center.

Yu, C., & Brandenburg, T. (2006). I would have had more success if...Trials and tribulations of a first-time online instructor. *The Journal of Technology Studies, 32*(1), 43-52. Retrieved July 5, 2007, from http://scholar.lib.vt.edu/ejournals/JOTS/v32/v32n1/pdf/yu.pdf

Zhao, Y., Lei, J., Yan, B., Lai, C., & Tan, H. (2005, August). What makes the difference? A practical analysis of research on the effectiveness of distance learning. *Teachers College Record, 107*(8), 1836-1884.

## ADDITIONAL READING

The following sources were selected because they focus on the practical aspects of providing professional development for those who are preparing to be e-teachers. They all emphasise the importance of supporting academic staff prior to teaching online. These sources provide details of the ways in which e-teaching is much more than simply putting materials up on a Web site for students. The idea of building learning communities at a distance is a theme that runs through many of these references for further reading.

Bennett, S., Priest, A., & Macpherson, C. (1999). Learning about online learning: An approach to staff development for university teachers. *Australian Journal of Educational Technology, 15*(3), 207-221. Retrieved October 20, 2007, from http://www.ascilite.org.au/ajet/ajet15/bennett.html

This article is a case study of one Australian university's effort to provide a Web-based programme to prepare e-teachers. Central Queensland University was concerned that their academic staff had not experienced e-learning, so it designed a Web-based module to provide this experience. However, this Web-based module was not about e-teaching, but rather about the Irish potato famine. At the conclusion of the course, the participants completed a survey about what they had learned about the famine. They concluded that those who are new to the e-learning environment should "begin at the beginning—with a hands-on experience of an online course."

Developing online instructors requires more than workshops. (2004, November). *Distance Education Report.*

This brief article describes the Online Faculty Mentoring Programme that has been implemented at Central Michigan University as a requirement for those who plan to teach online in the future. Participants must observe an existing online class and participate in asynchronous discussions with peers about best practices in e-learning. The mentoring process continues as new e-teachers develop online courses and teach online.

Faculty training, on demand. (2004, December 15). *Distance Education Report.*

This brief article describes a programme at the University of Central Florida to provide a comprehensive, semester-length (70-hour) course to become certified to teach online. The course includes all aspects of online course development as well as facilitation of online discussions. Because the demand was so high for this course, the university developed a second shorter version of the course (35 hours). Those who complete this course may teach online, but may not develop or modify online courses. The University of Central Florida's online courses had increased to 1,200 at the time of this article.

Donovan, M., & Macklin, S. (1999). The Catalyst project: Supporting faculty uses of the Web with the Web. *Cause/Effect Journal, 22*(3). Retrieved October 20, 2007, from http://www.educause.edu/ir/library/html/cem/cem99/cem9934.html

This article describes the Catalyst project, which was implemented at the University of Washington to support those who wanted to become involved in e-teaching. This project took a strategic approach with a plan to provide a wide range of support services and activities for those involved in e-teaching, including a research and development centre, more department-specific workshops, and people-centred service to help e-teachers implement the technology at the desired level.

Driscoll, M. (1998). *Web-based training.* San Francisco: Jossey Bass.

This is a classic book that is a comprehensive resource on e-teaching because it describes all aspects of teaching online. It is particularly important because Margaret Driscoll focuses on the adult learner and links adult learning theory with the practice of teaching online. The chapter on Web-based interactions provides a complete analysis of all of the different types of asynchronous interactions between teacher and student, student and student, and student and course material.

Gibbons, H., & Wentworth, G. (2001). Andrological and pedagogical differences for online instructors. *Online Journal of Distance Learning Administration, 4*(3).

This article describes efforts to design online courses to meet the needs of adult learners while still achieving the same quality of learning outcomes as courses taught in the traditional classroom. It makes good links between adult learning theory and the practice of e-teaching. The paper concludes by saying, "During training, online faculty evolve from an instructor and content expert to a facilitator and resource person."

Hagel, J., & Armstrong, A. (1997). *Net gain: Expanding markets through virtual communities.* Boston: Harvard Business School Press.

This book is not specifically about teaching online, but rather it addresses how virtual communities can be formed to help businesses gain more customers. However, the principles outlined in this book for the creation of virtual communities may be applied to e-learning to provide a more involving learning experience. For instance, in the chapter about laying the foundation for virtual communities, the authors note that members will create their own reasons to participate and not leave the community. In e-learning virtual communities, the ideas presented in this book would help to develop methods to capture and hold the interest of students.

Jones, G. (1997). *Cyber schools: An educational renaissance.* Englewood, CO: Jones Digital Century, Inc.

The author of this book is Glen Jones, CEO of Jones International, Ltd., a company that provides cable television networks in the United States and owns Jones International University and other Web-based educational systems. This book outlines what is wrong with schools and universities, including the fact that most are based on a 19th-century model. Then it presents Web-based "cyberschools" as the solution, with greater focus on learning and more involvement for students. Although the author clearly has a business interest in promoting cyberschools, the book presents some compelling data and arguments in favor of e-learning, and some useful models for e-learners and e-teachers.

Kahn, B. (Ed.). (1997). *Web-based instruction.* Englewood Cliffs, NJ: Educational Technology Publications.

This is an edited book with contributing authors from universities in many parts of the world. The section "Designing Web-Based Instruction" is particularly good because the chapters in it provide very practical advice on all aspects of design for e-learning, including active learning, higher order thinking, teamwork, collaborative learning, and so forth. Although this book is now 10 years old, only a few chapters are dated.

Kandlbinder, P. (2001, July 2-5). Peeking under the covers: Understanding the foundations of online academic staff development. In L. Richardson & J. Lidstone (Eds.), *Flexible learning for a flexible society* (pp. 372-378). Proceedings of ASET-HERDSA 2000 Conference, Toowoomba, Australia. Retrieved October 20, 2007, from http://www.ascilite.org.au/aset-archives/confs/aset-herdsa2000/procs/kandlbinder2.html

This paper from the University of Sydney reports on a study of how different universities in Australia and the United Kingdom prepare academic staff for e-teaching. One section of this paper provides insights into the use of online academic development, breaking it down into categories: information centred, activity centred, and inquiry centred. It concludes that there are some challenges in implementing collaborative online academic development in universities that reinforce individual achievement among academics.

Kosak, L., Manning, D., Dobson, E., Rogerson, L., Cotnam, S., Colaric, S., et al. (2005, June 27-30). *Prepared to teach online? Perspectives of faculty in the North Carolina University system.* Paper presented at the Meeting of the National Educational Computing Conference (NECC) of the International Society for Technology in Education, Philadelphia. Retrieved October 20, 2007, from http://center.uoregon.edu/ISTE/uploads/ NECC2005/KEY_7248775/Dobson_necc_paper_RP.pdf

This paper outlines a study of the academic staff in the University of North Carolina to determine how well prepared they were to teach online. The study concluded that academic staff were satisfied with the amount of training available, the quality and relevance of the training, and the accessibility of programmes to prepare to teach online. However, the study also notes that most of the training was focused on the technical aspects of using the software, and the issues related to pedagogy and best practice were often addressed after the staff had been teaching online.

Laurillard, D. (2002). Rethinking teaching for the knowledge society. *Educause Review, 37*(1), 16-25. Retrieved October 20, 2007, from http://www.educause.edu/ir/library/pdf/FFPIU017.pdf

This paper was originally presented at a symposium on the future of higher education held in Aspen, Colorado, in 2001. Diana Laurillard's paper addresses the importance of reconsidering how we teach in higher education. The "knowledge society" presents many new challenges, and our students need a different type of preparation. Laurillard proposes a new way of teaching that uses "generic learning activity models" (GLAMs) to support students in learning the skills of scholarship. These GLAMs include Web-based and other technologies.

Organisation for Economic Co-operation and Development (OECD). (2005). *E-Learning in tertiary education.* Paris: Author. Retrieved October 20, 2007, from http://www.oecd.org/dataoecd/55/25/35961132.pdf

This policy brief provides a very broad view of e-learning through the review of a survey of e-learning in 19 tertiary education institutions in 13 countries. It provides a useful snapshot of the growth of e-learning, how institutions are encouraging academic staff to develop more e-learning, costs of e-learning, and future progress in e-learning. The article concludes with recommendations for governments to support e-learning in the future.

Paloff, R., & Pratt, K. (1999). *Building learning communities in cyberspace.* San Francisco: Jossey Bass.

This book is a very comprehensive resource on the ways in which e-learning may be used to build learning communities to enhance the involvement and learning of students. The book addresses ways to transfer collaborative learning methods from traditional classrooms to the e-learning environment. Links are made between Mezirow's theories of transformative learning and the learning communities in e-learning. This is a very useful resource on the importance of building learning communities and the ways in which this may be achieved.

Porter, L. (1997). *Creating the virtual classroom.* New York: John Wiley & Sons.

Although this book is now slightly dated, it provides a good overview of some of the issues related to distance learning that are not typically addressed in other books. These include international education, advertising the distance learning programme, and preparing grant proposals to fund distance learning projects. There is also a useful chapter on desktop teleconferencing as a method of e-learning.

Rovai, A. (2007). Facilitating online discussions effectively. *Internet and Higher Education, 10,* 77-88.

This article provides a synthesis of theoretical literature about learning and makes connections with the methods for facilitating online discussions to promote student learning. Rovai reviews the different purposes of asynchronous discussions and encourages e-teachers to use authentic topics for discussions. The article covers the design of a discussion and then the facilitation process. Rovai points out the importance of being a facilitator rather than being the centre of attention in a discussion. This may be done by emphasising student-to-student interactions. This is a very useful article for those who have some experience with e-teaching, but it does not address how to attain the level of skill that Rovai describes.

Russell, D. (2006, July 5-7). *Online professional development for innovative educators.* Paper presented at the Meeting of the National Educational Computing Conference (NECC) of the International Society for Technology in Education, San Diego, CA. Retrieved October 20, 2007, from http://www.iste.org/Content/NavigationMenu/ Research/NECC_Research_Paper_Archives/ NECC_2006/Russell_Donna_NECC06.pdf

This paper reviews a study of Web-based academic development provided for the purpose of developing problem-based e-learning for those who teach in primary and secondary (first- and second-level) education. The principles presented here may also be applied to higher education. The study found that those who are innovative in their approaches to teaching need online forums for their development where they can interact with others who are at the same level or at a higher level of innovation in their teaching.

Salter, G., & Hansen, S. (2000, July 2-5). Facilitating Web-based staff development in higher education. In L. Richardson & J. Lidstone (Eds.), *Flexible Learning for a Flexible Society: Proceedings of ASET-HERDSA 2000 Conference,* Toowoomba, Australia (pp. 612-617). ASET & HERDSA. Retrieved October 20, 2007, from http://www.ascilite.org.au/aset-archives/confs/ aset-herdsa2000/procs/salter1.html

This paper is not about preparation for e-teaching, but rather it is about the potential for using e-learning as a means for staff development in teaching and learning. A Web-based staff development module was developed at the University of Sydney based on constructivist learning principles. This module was studied at an early stage, so the outcomes of this module were inconclusive. However, the authors concluded that if a module is well designed using constructivist principles, it has the potential to be effective for staff development.

Sherer, P., Shea, T., & Kristensen, E. (2003). Online communities of practice: A catalyst for faculty development. *Innovative Higher Education, 27*(3), 183-194.

This paper explores the importance of interaction in the online teaching environment and the important role of staff development in developing teacher presence online.

Wilson, G., & Stacey, E. (2004). Online interaction impacts on learning: Teaching the teachers to teach online. *Australasian Journal of Educational Technology, 20*(1), 33-48. Retrieved October 20, 2007, from http://www.ascilite.org.au/ajet/ajet20/ wilson.html

This paper describes many approaches that can be used successfully to shape staff development activities to help staff integrate technologies into their teaching. The authors address the importance of considering the reluctance of academic staff to adopt new technologies, and they feel that by providing opportunities for them to interact online, they may overcome this reluctance.

Zilberman, D. (2002) Training online for teaching online. *Educause Resources: Effective Practices.* Retrieved January 10, 2007, from http://www. educause.edu/Browse/705?ITEM_ID=90

This article provides a case study from Baltimore County Community Colleges in their implementation of an online training course to prepare academic staff for e-teaching. One purpose of the course was to "expose participants to online learning from a student's perspective." The course has been successful because it has stimulated the development of more online courses, and participants have enjoyed the collaborative aspects of the course, which encouraged peer support in the development of online courses.

# Chapter IV
# A Reflection on Teachers' Experience as E-Learners

**Tony Cunningham**
*School of Real Estate and Construction Economics, Dublin Institute of Technology, Ireland*

**Claire McDonnell**
*School of Chemical and Pharmaceutical Sciences, Dublin Institute of Technology, Ireland*

**Barry McIntyre**
*School of Business and Humanities, Dun Laoghaire Institute of Art, Design and Technology, Ireland*

**Theresa McKenna**
*National College of Art and Design, Ireland*

## ABSTRACT

*This chapter explores the insights gained by a group of teachers from their lived experience as e-learners participating in a blended module on designing e-learning. An understanding of the student perspective on online learning was obtained, but we were also able to reflect on our participation in the module on the basis of our other roles: as teachers and potential e-tutors, and as course designers. As a result, important considerations were identified for the design and facilitation of online courses. These include the support provided to online learners, particularly over the first few weeks; appropriate assessment methods; the facilitation of online collaboration; access to the Internet; time management; and contextualising and scaffolding learning activities. Some issues relating to the implementation of effective e-learning in higher education institutions were also considered. Our lived experience as e-learners was invaluable to our development as e-tutors and module designers, and this approach is strongly recommended to achieve effective learning on how to be an effective online tutor and facilitator and how to design and develop online programmes and activities that make full use of the strengths of online learning.*

# INTRODUCTION

The authors participated in a 10-week blended learning module entitled Designing E-Learning as part of the postgraduate programme in third-level learning and teaching in the Dublin Institute of Technology (DIT), Ireland. This module allowed us to experience e-learning from the student perspective in order to help us to develop as e-tutors and course designers. In total, seven academic staff from a range of disciplines and a number of Irish third-level colleges took part. Most had only experienced learning online before to a very limited extent (accessing course material in a virtual learning environment, VLE), and two were implementing the blended delivery of modules within their programmes. The diverse background, experience, knowledge, and confidence among our group of e-learners meant that a wide range of issues and problems that online learners and tutors encounter in practice were brought to our attention.

In this chapter, we examine the insights we gained into blended learning from a student's perspective and review the current literature in this area. We also discuss our experience from the perspective of our other roles: as teachers and potential e-tutors, and as course designers. We consider the support provided to online learners, the appropriateness of assessment methods used, the range of e-learning methods experienced, and the problems encountered, as well as our reflections on the strengths and shortcomings of the e-learning environment. Finally, future trends and research directions are discussed.

# BACKGROUND

## What is Blended Learning?

Throughout this chapter, the term *blended learning* is used to describe course delivery in which a combination of face-to-face and online teaching and learning take place. Holmes and Gardner (2006) state that the rationale behind this approach is to improve traditional learning environments by incorporating e-learning where appropriate. Thus, e-learning is employed to complement other methods, not replace them, and should only be used if it enriches and enhances what is already being done (Charlesworth & Vician, 2003). Singh and Reed (2001) maintain that variation in the blend selected allows a programme of study to be tailored to the particular needs of the learner: "Blended learning focuses on optimizing achievement of learning objectives by applying the 'right' learning technologies to match the 'right' personal learning style to transfer the 'right' skills to the 'right' person at the 'right' time" (p. 2).

There are several other interpretations of what blended learning involves, including one that views it as a blend of different types of Web-based tools and media only (Whitelock & Jelfs, 2003); another proposed by Driscoll (2002) describes mixing several pedagogical approaches that may or may not include instructional technology.

In a recent review, Sharpe, Benfield, Roberts, and Francis (2006) recognise that blended learning is not easy to define. However, they recommend that the use of the term is continued because this lack of clarity allows teaching staff to develop their own particular meaning appropriate to their context. They also contend that academic staff are reassured by the implication that face-to-face contact with students is preserved in a blended learning approach. Oliver and Trigwell (2005) are of the opposite opinion, however, they argue that use of the term should be discontinued because of the problem of clarity and also because none of the interpretations include the perspective of the learner. They suggest that a move toward a student perspective would be facilitated by employing a variation theory research framework. We believe that the expression *blended learning* has now entered into relatively widespread use and that it is not practical at this stage to abandon it. However, the issue raised by M. Oliver and

Trigwell of the need to incorporate the student perspective is a very important one and will be addressed further in this chapter.

## Students' Experience of Blended Learning

As we are reporting on our own lived experience as e-learners, it is pertinent to examine the existing literature on blended learning from a student perspective. Sharpe and Benfield (2005) and Beetham (2005) have identified a lack of research exploring e-learning from the learner's perspective and emphasise that knowledge in this area is essential to underpin the development of teaching methods that incorporate learning technology. Sharpe and Benfield comment that research has concentrated on the teacher perspective and on demonstrating the pedagogic worth of online learning, but that this is understandable due to the relatively recent introduction of e-learning and a preoccupation with justifying the financial investment involved.

Sharpe et al. (2006) carried out a wide-ranging review of UK literature and practice on the undergraduate experience of blended e-learning in which they classified two main approaches adopted in higher education institutions. The first is the provision of additional support material online, which they report has been termed e-teaching (Jones & Fitzgibbon, as cited in Sharpe et al.). The second less common one involves course redesign to promote learner communication and interaction using ICT. Sharpe et al. found that learners gave a positive response in almost all cases when asked about their opinion of supplementary material being made available online to support traditional teaching. The students rated course notes as the most useful resource and are appreciative of the flexibility afforded by online access.

However, the research by Sharpe et al. (2006) showed that, in the case of redesigned courses that incorporated activities supported by technology, significant differences between individual student

experiences were reported, and the authors contend that a variation in how students view their involvement in the learning process may be an important factor. A study by Concannon, Flynn, and Campbell (2005) supports this argument. They found that individual factors such as motivation, clear career plans, peer influence, and study strategy had a significant effect on students' use of and attitude to online learning, and they point out that these are generic issues not directly related to the use of technology. They also establish that, as well as a broad variation in the willingness to use ICT for learning existing between students, even within individual learners, there was inconsistency as their attitudes varied from context to context. As a consequence, Sharpe et al. contend that course designers should aim to be "developing environments in which all learners are encouraged to learn actively and deeply" (p. 72).

Quite a number of examples of inconsistency in learner responses to blended learning have been reported in the literature. In one study on online collaborative groups, it was found that some students saw the benefit of being able to provide more reflective contributions online while others were concerned by the amount of time required to be effective participants in discussions. Also, some students were appreciative of the opportunity to learn from collaborative peer discussions moderated by a tutor, but there were others who expected that the tutor would provide a model answer and were perturbed when this did not happen (Sweeney, O'Donoghue, & Whitehead, 2004). In relation to online support, Matheos, Daniel, and McCalla (2005) report that half of the cohort of students in their study expressed a preference for learning support to be provided face-to-face by a person while the other half said that they would choose other kinds of support.

Often, issues that arise can be a result of the redesign of courses and the use of less traditional types of teaching and learning methods that accompany the introduction of blended learning rather than the learning technology itself.

Sharpe et al. (2006) refer to the example reported by Clouder and Deepwell (2004) of a group of physiotherapy students on placement who posted accounts of critical incidents in a discussion forum, but showed great reticence in commenting on other students' work. Clouder and Deepwell observed that this problem was likely to be a result of this group of learners not having experienced peer assessment before. Morris (2007) reports that allowing undergraduates the facility to post questions anonymously helps greatly to develop their confidence in an online environment. In a similar way, providing the opportunity to give online feedback to peers anonymously initially might prove to be a useful method of introducing them to peer assessment.

An area that requires careful consideration is online communication and collaboration as the dynamics of group interaction online are not yet fully understood (McConnell, 2005). Quinney (2005) describes how learners experienced a Website set up to facilitate communication and to support integration of theory and practice for social work students on placement. It was found that the discussion board was used extensively as a means of continuing collaborative learning relationships that students had established before they began their placement as well as organising and planning academic assignments. Quinney reports that very little in-depth discussion occurred online, however, and that the students said that this took place when they spoke to each other instead. A requirement to show evidence of reflection and critical analysis in their online interaction as part of their course assessment might result in an improvement in the depth of the postings in the future. Quinney also identifies a valuable topic for future research as she makes the point that a detailed examination of the views of the students who did not use the discussion forum would have provided valuable insights. Stracke (2007) has examined this area and focused her research on the students who dropped out of a blended language learning programme. It was

found that the students' perception of a lack of support and linkage between the face-to-face and computer-mediated parts of the programme, as well as a rejection of the use of computers as tools for language learning, were the main factors that influenced students' decision to leave.

Prior experience of using ICT and attitudes toward computers are identified by Sharpe et al. (2006) as two major factors that influence the student experience of blended learning. Arbaugh (2004) carried out a study that showed that learners became more positive about online work as they experienced more courses that used it. He observed that a significant increase in the learning quality and effectiveness perceived by students occurred between the first and second online courses. This emphasises the importance of tutors ensuring that they build the confidence of those with little ICT experience and provide effective support. In their research, Conole, de Laat, Dillon, and Darby (2006) found that most students now use a range of technology, including laptops, MP3 players, memory sticks, and mobile phones, in a variety of ways to support different aspects of their learning, and that they are comfortable with these tools. This is reflected in their comment that a number of students in the research they undertook rejected the term *e-learning* and preferred to just use *learning* on the basis that ICT has always been an integral part of all aspects of their lives. However, Conole et al. point out that learners with good ICT skills often lack e-literacy and need to be shown how to develop the skills required to critically evaluate online sources and information.

It has been shown that there is a need for more research on students' perceptions of blended learning. The work that has been carried out to date demonstrates that students are generally positive about the provision of extra resources and increased flexibility, but that when online collaboration and communication is introduced, significant variations in the individual learner experiences have been observed. A number of factors that contribute have been identified and they include prior experience of and attitudes to computers and variations in how students view their involvement in the learning process.

## Experiencing Blended Learning as Students to Develop Online Tutoring Skills

Munro and Walsh (2005) observe that, because online tutoring is a recent development, many academic staff did not experience it themselves as students and thus they tend to feel uncomfortable about tutoring in a Web-based environment. This was also the case for our group, and one participant identified that they wanted to gain experience in the use of discussion boards in the premodule questionnaire they completed: "I chose the Designing eLearning module because I want to spend some time developing online materials, find out more about what can be done and try out different ways of using eLearning e.g. discussion boards" (Participant D, response to premodule questionnaire on prior experience of e-learning, January 2006).

Salmon (2000) recommends that the experience of being a student in an online environment is the most effective way to acquire the skills required to manage and facilitate online synchronous and asynchronous communication. T. Smith (2005) also states that the challenges online students face can best be understood using this approach. B. Smith (2001) examined the skills and competences required to be an e-tutor and compared them with those necessary for tutoring face-to-face. She contends that although some of the skills are different, an experienced face-to-face tutor has many of the basic competences and should not find the transition to a Web-based environment too difficult provided suitable training and guidance are available.

Munro and Walsh (2005) report that the participants in their course to train online tutors using a Web-based environment commented that personal reflections were one of the most useful aspects of the course. To date, apart from the findings summarised here, very little else has been reported in the literature on the experience of students in online tutoring courses.

## CASE STUDY: THE DESIGNING E-LEARNING MODULE

The DIT postgraduate diploma module in designing e-learning that our group undertook provided an introduction to the theory and practice of online teaching and the development of online learning materials. Assessment was by means of a collaborative learning project and an individual reflective paper.

### Prior Experience of Participants

Before our designing e-learning module began, we were asked to fill out a questionnaire sent by e-mail on our previous experience of using ICT and e-learning as students and teachers. This premodule survey was designed to allow our tutor to prepare for our range of ICT skill levels. Due to a technical problem resulting in the nondelivery of the tutor's e-mail, one of the students, who was a novice e-learner, did not receive the questionnaire. As it happened, this particular participant commented later when she saw the survey that, if she had tried to answer the questions, she would have become too anxious about her lack of experience and would have backed out of her decision to take the module. The rest of the participants who had some degree of ICT skills did not report this type of response to the questionnaire. From the perspective of an online tutor, it is worth noting therefore that participants who have very little computer experience will need additional reassurance and support, particularly just before and during their induction session (Salmon, 2000; Sharpe et al., 2006). Responses from five of the course participants to an enquiry on their prior experience of e-learning as learners and tutors before they began the course are provided in Appendix 1. It is evident that the level of familiarity with ICT and the previous experience of e-learning of the participants varied greatly. One of the participants commented on their limited experience in their first discussion-board posting: "My experience with online technology is receiving and answering e-mails and even at that I could be better!" (Participant A, January 2006).

However, at the other end of the spectrum, two students on the module were developing blended delivery of some of the modules that they were teaching.

## Collaborative Learning Online

The designing e-learning module was based primarily on collaborative project-based learning (CPBL). Our group was presented with a 10-week open-ended task and we were required to design an online activity-centred module that responded to a genuine learning need. The outputs specified were a group report and a developed Web site including exemplars of online content. We produced a blended information-literacy-skills module that can now be modified for use by any of the group members and tailored to suit their particular disciplines.

CPBL is described by R. Oliver (2001) as an approach that challenges students to construct their own knowledge and understanding within a team environment and in the context of a genuine problem. He defines CPBL as engaging students in "the process of designing and creating products that meet authentic needs" (p. 7). The teacher's role is altered from that adopted in more traditional approaches as it becomes that of a facilitator or moderator (Ljoså, 1998). A number of commentators point out that interactive, collaborative learners can be well supported in a Web-based environment and remark that asynchronous online communication encourages significant peer interaction to take place (Gagné, Wager, Golas,

& Keller, 2005; R. Oliver, 2001; Roberts, 1995). Thus, when an e-learning approach is being used, it can readily facilitate the application of CPBL as a teaching and learning strategy. The benefits of using online group projects as an assessment method are emphasised by Chickering and Ehrmann (1996) who point out that they incorporate several of their seven principles of good practice in undergraduate education including active learning, student-to-student interaction, and time on task. They also report that it is often observed that learners perform at higher levels when they are aware that other students will be able to view their assignments and correspondence on the Web. Our group found this to be the case and, at times, because we were very absorbed with the collaborative group assignment, it led to some problems with finding time to work on our individual papers. As with any approach that involves online communication, it is very important to ensure the provision of clear guidelines on acceptable social interaction online, often referred to as netiquette (Beetham, 2002).

CPBL is based on a social constructivist approach and McMahon (1997) remarks that effective Web-based interactive and authentic learning can be designed based on social constructivist principles. In addition, Palloff and Pratt (2005) regard collaboration as a "hallmark of constructivist learning theory" (p. 6). The social constructivist theory of learning, which originated with Vygotsky, recognises that learning occurs in specific social contexts (Beetham, 2002). The theory claims that active learning occurs and that it centres on social interaction and shared tasks in which individuals build their learning by interacting with the environment, particularly with teachers and fellow students. Collaboration on meaningful and challenging activity-based programmes promotes exploratory learning and is regarded as a highly effective means of encouraging learning (Bigge & Shermis, 2004). The benefit of this approach is that learners can capitalise on their strengths and overcome their weaknesses while working on a collaborative task. Students also encounter alternative methods adopted by other learners. Portimojarvi (personal communication, February 13, 2006) sums up this approach as viewing "students as subjects of learning, not objects of teaching." McMahon discusses the criticisms of social constructivism, particularly that the strategies developed to deal with a problem are often not efficient and that there can be a lack of recognition that there is a certain "body of undisputed knowledge" in any subject (p. 6).

Palloff and Pratt (2005) examine how problems associated with collaborative approaches may be accentuated in online groups. The major difficulties they identify are the following.

- Participation can be a problem, ranging from dropout to underparticipation to domination in groups, and includes issues such as lack of communication, reluctance to share findings, and overexpectation. The outcome of these issues may lead to mistrust, resentment, and conflict.
- Leadership and decision making raise issues such as ineffective and aimless leadership, the formation of powerful cliques, the exclusion of less assertive members from decision making, and underrepresentation of particular viewpoints (gender issues, for example).
- Course and activity design may present difficulties, particularly in relation to time issues, technical support, and academic staff issues.
- Although online learning tends to be more inclusive, cultural issues may still be identified.

McConnell (2005) conducted an ethnographic study on the work of three online groups and provides detailed analysis of their online discussions. He describes issues that arose in relation to reactions by group members to delayed responses to messages, the detrimental impact of levels of anxiety among individuals on group performance, the influence of strong personalities, and the negative and positive effects of tutor intervention.

## Reflection

The other assessed component of the module involved writing an individual paper based on the completion of an online reflective journal. Moon (1999) comments that reflection "is applied in many fields and as a concept it helps those in learning and professional situations to make sense of an area of human functioning" (p. 91).

Beetham (2002) advises that online learners be given the opportunity to carry out self-assessment through the use of online logs or diaries.

To support and facilitate reflections by the module participants, our module tutor provided prompts each week in which she highlighted the relevance of assignments to e-learning issues and our development as e-learners (for example, considering the differences between online and face-to-face communication and how best to deal with learners who are not contributing online). These prompts were very helpful for structuring our reflections and ensuring that we were thinking about online learning at a deep level. Cowan (1998) also recommends this strategy and says that, instead of just being asked to reflect, learners should be presented with carefully considered questions that they will find useful to answer.

## Online Interactive Activities (E-Tivities)

In addition to the CPBL and reflective paper assignments, our tutor designed a series of e-tivities for formative assessment on a weekly basis. The initial online tasks set were designed to acquaint us with the online supports and resources available and to ensure that we could post and reply to discussion-board messages and create our own Web pages. The e-tivities were scaffolded and became more involved as the weeks passed, and most of them involved online collaboration. In some cases, the reflective prompts for the individual paper were linked to the task assigned that week. These activities ensured that we were engaged in active learning throughout the module. The approach that we experienced as e-learners is described by Salmon (2002) in her five-stage model.

## OUR E-LEARNING EXPERIENCE

In this section of the chapter, we discuss the main issues that arose during our e-learning experience from a student perspective and include the relevant implications from the perspective of teachers and course designers.

### Support and Resources

Salmon (2000) emphasises that learner support from an experienced tutor is essential to ensure that positive and productive e-learning occurs. At our induction session, it was clear to us that we were coming to the module from very different starting points and the novice e-learners found the learning curve very steep. We had many teething problems and the experience was a valuable insight into the emotions and frustrations that students feel when a lack of familiarity with technology prevents them from participating or keeping up. Our tutor anticipated the potential difficulties ahead of time and recommended a peer mentoring system within the group. This was taken up by two novice participants and was found to be very helpful. This combination of tutor and peer support, together with paired activities that were assigned, helped the less experienced members to cope with the demands of working online.

The importance of a vigilant and good-humoured tutor as a positive role model was a particularly valuable lesson. She demonstrated best practice in challenging and supporting each student according to his or her level and experience. Our own e-learning experience, therefore,

upholds the contention that blended learning can cater for individual learning needs. This brought it home to us that e-learning was not just about the technology, and it became apparent that technology complements rather than replaces the human dimension of learning. Our experience also supports the assertion by Gagné et al. (2005) that the effort, skill, and pedagogy of the teacher are the most important factors influencing the success of an online course. Page and Donovan (2005) concur with this stating that "the contribution of the teaching practitioner is vital" (p. 28).

The equipment required to participate in a range of activities (asynchronous discussion, online chat, videoconferences, etc.) was available as was technological support to provide assistance. Our e-tutor was ever present in a combination of face-to-face and online interaction throughout the 10-week module. We were encouraged to access the Frequently Asked Questions section of the VLE developed for the module or to ask our peers before contacting the tutor directly with a problem. This developed our independence and strengthened the group dynamic, and meant that the tutor's time was not being absorbed by minor issues.

### The Group Process

Our group tackled the various tasks at a series of CPBL tutorials held every week. At each tutorial, a different group member acted as the chairperson. As a blended approach was being used, two of these tutorials were held online and the remainders were face-to-face. Once the group had experienced the first online chat in Week 4, extra chats were often scheduled midway through the week to allow progress on the project to be communicated. Thus, we recognised the value of being able to meet online as a group in between our face-to-face contact. The tutor structured our module so that we were required to give a work-in-progress presentation on our CPBL project in Week 5 and this ensured that we focused on the task at hand.

In blended learning, personal contact between teachers and learners and among learners themselves is reduced. Significant efforts are needed to develop social relationships through discussions, chat rooms, and virtual meetings (Gagné et al., 2005). Our group did not suffer from this problem as we already knew each other and also met face-to-face weekly or fortnightly; we organised "extraordinary" meetings to progress through our group project. Face-to-face meetings were identified as critical to the success of our project and certain members suggested they would have dropped out without this face-to-face contact and peer support.

As our group members already knew each other and we had participated in some collaborative projects with other students as part of previous modules in our third-level learning and teaching programme, many of the difficulties that can arise in collaborative work were not serious issues for us. Our tutor maintained an involvement in our initial face-to-face and online group tutorials in case any significant problems arose and to provide clarification on the assessment requirements. Her suggestion to agree on ground rules for the group, which included a system of having a rotating chairperson as well as a recorder (to record ideas and act on items) each week, helped to ensure that we usually worked effectively.

The usual issues of some participants initially "lurking" online and frustration over delayed responses to postings (Salmon, 2002) were discussed among the group and reflected on with the encouragement of some tutor prompts quite early on in the module. One of the main problems we encountered during the designing e-learning module was time management. All group members reported that they found participating in the module very intense and that a lot of other aspects of their lives had been put on hold. While it was felt that the assessments and each e-tivity were worthwhile and contributed to our learning, they demanded a significant time commitment. Meeting deadlines and appointments for synchronous

discussions made us acutely aware of the many pressures of group learning and, on occasion, led to anxieties within the group. It is worth highlighting that all participants in our module were part-time students and thus time management will always be expected to be an issue. Interestingly, though, Concannon et al. (2005) identify the issue of "full-time part-time students" as a recent phenomenon in higher education institutions. These learners are enrolled in full-time courses but also spend significant amounts of their time working in part-time jobs.

Hiltz and Goldman (2005) suggest that students spend more time on collaborative online courses than traditional courses. Students find it more demanding because they must actively participate in the group work rather than passively take notes. Some learners have expressed concern over the time required to post thoughtful responses to a discussion board (Sweeney et al., 2004). Course designers may also fail to allow students adequate time to complete online course activities, causing considerable anxiety. Competing demands of individual modules may create significant pressure and disrupt students' personal lives, which can be demotivating.

The group also found it difficult to decide whether participants should work on CPBL project tasks that involved skills and knowledge they already had or that they lacked: the former being more likely to lead to a better group outcome and the latter allowing more learning to occur.

## Accessibility

Salmon (2000) has noted that students using online learning for the first time often have serious difficulties gaining initial access. Our group had some previous experience of using a VLE as students in the third-level learning and teaching programme, where we used it to access notes and announcements and, in some cases, for e-mail and some discussions. Despite our previous experience of WebCT™ and the technical support provided, some of us experienced significant difficulties. Some participants were on a dial-up connection at home, and this caused problems such as tying up family phone lines and being disconnected during the synchronous chats, leaving the participant with gaps in the thread of the discussion. One group member did not have an Internet connection at home and had to travel to a relative's house to have access outside working hours. Another participant could usually only access the Internet late at night and was often cut off without warning when using the discussion board in the early morning while the system was being backed up. Also, a member of the group was an Apple Mac user and experienced navigation problems that did not make any sense to the rest of the participants. In the first synchronous chat session, a group member inadvertently selected an option that prevented the others from seeing the contributions that she was typing.

Online approaches are not likely to be suitable for those with Internet access problems. As many families only have a single connection, competition for line time can be intense, and the cost of access may also be an issue. Gagné et al. (2005) remark that slow connection and long download times are frustrating and make participants impatient, angry, or even give up. Palloff and Pratt (2005) regard the inability to access the course or contact peers as the worst thing that can happen to an online student. Our experience supports this finding as a significant amount of the online communication over the first half of the module included accounts of problems that had occurred and requests for information and hints on how to perform tasks using the technology.

The fact that this module was blended and used a combination of online and face-to-face contact was very beneficial to participants struggling with the technology. For some people, it was such a roller coaster of new experiences and terminology that the face-to-face sessions were reassuring and provided an opportunity to discuss their problems. At all times, we were aware of the support from the institution, the extensive range of frequently asked questions in the VLE, our ever-vigilant tutor, and the bank of knowledge and goodwill coming from the group itself.

## Online Communication

Hiltz and Goldman (2005) describe the potential of asynchronous discussion as the greatest benefit offered by online learning. Classes may be spread out in space and time in what they refer to as "a rolling present" (p. 6). Students contribute at their own pace at the times and places that are most convenient for them. The group quickly identified the flexibility of using online synchronous and asynchronous communication as a particular strength of the blended approach. Participants were occasionally away from work or abroad but were able to keep in touch and play a part in the group activities. Contributions were made from Denmark, Italy, Spain, and the United Kingdom, as well as locations throughout Ireland. Discussions with online guest tutors from the University of Tampere in Finland and the University of Queensland, Australia, took place during the module. These tutors added an international dimension and provided fresh perspectives, and their contributions would only have been possible in an online situation.

We also discovered that online communication is very different from face-to-face communication. B. Smith (2001) observes that face-to-face discussion is essentially linear; one conversation is dealt with at a time. Online discussions, however, may involve a number of simultaneous discussions, and Swan and Shea (2005) describe them as growing "like crystals from multiple conceptual seeds in many dimensions at once" (p. 247). We also quickly realised that discussion online can be unstructured. We set up too many discussion threads, and this led to messages being posted to the wrong place and getting lost. This was confusing and resulted in a needlessly packed and disorganised discussion board. One participant remarked that the amount of messages being posted was overwhelming and that it was difficult to cope with. Another group member frequently did not open attachments because of a connection with a slow downloading speed.

As discussion boards provide a record of all online communication within a group, contributors can review, link to, and build on various strands. A learning environment and discussions that were rich and reflective developed as a result of this facility to review and build on previous postings. Salmon (2000) notes that many postings are actually composed off line, which shows that learners are taking the time to construct their ideas and thoughts. We found that the discussion boards, chat rooms, and e-mail facilities helped the group to "gel" and work in a committed and collaborative manner (Gagné et al., 2005; R. Oliver, 2001; Roberts, 1995). This collaboration was essential in achieving the module aims efficiently and completing our group assignment. Although some of us had used discussion boards before, the level of interaction and the e-moderating skills demonstrated by our tutor (e.g., summarising and weaving contributions, posing relevant questions) were new aspects and allowed us to observe and experience good practice firsthand.

The group was also introduced to a wider range of e-learning methods, particularly the use of the chat facility. This was new to most of us as very few had any experience with synchronous online communication within a VLE or indeed any of the proprietary chat rooms. Our tutor introduced us to our first chat and facilitated the session; after that, our chats were organised and facilitated by an appointed chairperson. The chair position rotated among all group members from week to week. The chats were summarised by the chair and posted on the discussion board for the benefit of any participant who missed the session and also to provide a record of the issues discussed.

In addition, two guest tutors used the MP3 format to record their responses to our discussion-board postings as audio files. This was a

completely new experience for all, and several of the group felt that they could relate to the tutors online more easily having heard their voices.

We also had a videoconference session with a guest tutor in Finland. This was a fascinating experience as we could see and hear the guest tutor. As it happened, technical difficulties arose as the sound broke down from our end, so initially we could hear the tutor but he could not hear us. This illustrates the need to anticipate likely technical problems and to plan out how they will be dealt with. As a result, the group suggested to the technical-support team that a central log listing technical difficulties that have been encountered and the steps that were taken to solve or get around them be established.

The depth of discussion that is possible using asynchronous online discussion is very impressive, but, with students who have not encountered this approach before, it can be challenging for an e-tutor to ensure that they participate effectively (Clouder & Deepwell, 2004). Most students have been shown to be sophisticated technology users (Conole et al., 2006) and thus would be expected to appreciate the opportunity to communicate using asynchronous and synchronous online communication, audio files, and videoconferencing to further their learning.

## Assessing Learning

One of the most immediate priorities for any learner, of course, is to determine what he or she has to do to pass a particular module. Ramsden (1992) maintains that "the assessment IS the curriculum as far as the students are concerned" (p. 187), and Biggs (2003) recommends that assessments and learning activities are aligned with learning outcomes to ensure that effective learning and teaching occurs. Ross (1997) points out the danger of undermining the intended learning outcomes if inappropriate assessment strategies are applied, and the difficulties associated with assessing groups. Therefore, it is important to examine how the module was assessed and how we experienced that assessment process. As already described, the module was assessed by a combination of a CPBL group assignment and an individual paper based on the completion of an online reflective journal. The group was of the opinion that the pass-fail assessment method applied was fundamental to the success of our learning. We found it liberating to be assessed on a criterion-referenced basis rather than a norm-referenced one. We liked the clarity of the criteria and the associated pass-fail classification, and those participants who were less confident when they began the module found this assessment approach particularly reassuring. In addition, this approach meant that competition among participants did not occur and it fostered a collaborative spirit.

We found that completing the CPBL assessment ensured that we met the module learning outcomes, and we agreed that we were motivated to reach a higher standard than we would have if we had been working individually. Some felt, though, that at times more patience and reflection from other members within the group was required, especially from those who were more familiar with a Web-based learning environment and had ambitious ideas for the project assigned. One aspect of the assessment that several group members felt strongly about was that there was no group CPBL project presentation scheduled at the end of the module. A work-in-progress videoconference presentation took place halfway through the module and the feedback received was very useful. At the end of the module, the group report was submitted, and many of the participants said that they would have liked the opportunity to make another presentation at this stage.

The reflective paper prompted us to engage in the module. It ensured that each of us was thinking about what we were experiencing throughout. At the end of Week 5 of our module, we were required to submit extracts from our reflective journal for formative feedback. Thus, we received guidance and direction at an interim stage, and

this submission of work in progress ensured that we were engaged throughout the module. Concannon et al. (2005) have commented on the benefits of designing assessment strategies so that learners must work on a continuous basis rather than allowing them the opportunity to put it off until the end of the module. In the case they describe, the introduction of computer-aided assessment made this redesign possible. We found that the online reflective journal provided us with a record of the problems, concerns, and rewards that we experienced as e-learners. It was also interesting that many of the effective e-learning practices we were researching and discussing as e-learning designers for the CPBL project were implemented in the module design, and thus, we were experiencing them as learners. In particular, we gained insights into how to effectively support online learners and to provide a framework allowing for a progressive increase in the complexity of assigned activities. Salmon (2002) emphasises the importance of both of these issues in providing effective online tutoring: "For online learning to be successful and happy, participants need to be supported through a structured development process" (p. 10).

Thus, the individual reflective piece was an important component of the module assessment as it ensured that we considered and discussed how it felt to experience blended e-learning, and that we recorded our thoughts and feelings at all stages of the module.

Both summative assessment strategies, the CPBL project and individual reflective paper, were found to be effective in ensuring that the module learning outcomes were achieved and would be recommended for inclusion in any blended course design. We would also recommend that a pass-fail criterion-referenced system be implemented as much as possible with undergraduate students, although it is recognised it is often a requirement that final-year modules are assigned grades so that degree classification is possible.

## THE DUAL DESIGNER AND E-TUTOR PERSPECTIVE: DESIGNING AND DEVELOPING OUR OWN PRACTICE

One of our central learning aims was to develop an awareness of the important issues to consider when designing blended learning. We now examine the design and development of the module produced for our group CPBL project from the perspective of e-designers and e-tutors in addition to the student perspective already discussed.

We chose to design and produce a 6-week blended activity-based information-literacy-skills module for first-year undergraduates called the Information Treasure Chest. Development of these skills is very important as the ability to find relevant information quickly and efficiently using the resources available is one of the key factors that allow lifelong and self-directed learning to occur (Sormunen, 2006). Initially, a series of interviews was carried out with staff in seven different libraries as part of a needs analysis to establish how best to make the proposed programme effective. One of the most important findings from this research was that the librarians all believed that their libraries were rarely used to their full potential, that the development of information-literacy skills should be integrated into programme curricula, and that credits should be available for any related assignments. Ambrose and Gillespie (2003) are among several authors who have made the case for the integration of information-literacy skills into curricula. Further research amongst academic and administrative staff and students was carried out as the module design was in progress.

The module aim and learning outcomes were derived from the needs analysis. The principal aim was to introduce students to library resources and to encourage the development of library research skills to enable them to make fuller use of library resources, both paper and electronic. The module also set out to build student awareness of the value of libraries in expanding, adapting, and updating their personal knowledge base throughout the lifelong learning process.

The design philosophy was developed in tandem with the aims and objectives. Some of the key issues that shaped our module design were the following.

- We wanted the learners to develop as reflective, critical-thinking problem solvers.
- We viewed the lecturer as a facilitator and tutor. Ramsden (1992) summed up this approach when he remarked that "the aim of teaching is simple: it is to make learning possible" (p. 5).
- The module would be activity driven instead of content driven. Laurillard (1993) contends that the acquisition of concepts is of no use if learners cannot apply them, and she states that it is important to provide multiple contexts for a conception instead of an abstraction alone.
- The module activities would be integrated into each subject discipline to ensure learner motivation and to differentiate our module from some generic information-literacy-skills modules already available.

The philosophy underpinning our module design was informed by four learning theories: cognitive, constructivist, social constructivist, and learner differences. Figure 1 in Appendix 2 illustrates how technology is related to these theories in the module we developed.

### VLE and E-Tivities

A template for the exemplar virtual learning environment and several examples of online content and activities using the chosen software were developed. We designed the 6-week module for the first half of a semester with 1 hour of face-to-face teaching for some of the weeks. The module begins with a face-to-face induction session during which students are given the handbook developed for the module. A workshop also takes place to teach students how to log on, navigate the VLE, and use the discussion board. The first activity is contained in the library induction pack to ensure that they have to attend a library induction session to get this task done.

From the e-tutor perspective, the e-tivities developed were carefully structured to ensure that they were scaffolded. Thus, the tasks are progressive, increasing in complexity over the course of the module, and they are designed to incorporate the five-stage framework devised by Salmon (2002). Table 1 in Appendix 3 summarises these e-tivity tasks.

Our group had identified the ability to make course materials readily available as one of the reasons why we would adopt online learning approaches. However, there can be a temptation to adopt a "shovelware" or "electronic filing cabinet" approach. To avoid this, we ensured that consideration was given as to the effectiveness and educational validity of the materials incorporated into the VLE developed. Easy and flexible navigation of the resources was also a priority.

Bonk, Kim, and Zeng (in press) make the point that it is the pedagogy used and the learning outcomes achieved that are important in a programme of study, not the type of technology involved. This was the approach taken in designing the Information Treasure Chest module, and e-learning technology was employed where appropriate in such a way that its benefits were exploited.

## SOLUTIONS AND RECOMMENDATIONS: WHAT WE LEARNED FROM OUR EXPERIENCE AS E-LEARNERS

The main issues that arose in relation to blended learning from the student, teacher, and designer perspectives are now summarised, and relevant solutions and recommendations are included where appropriate.

## Pivotal Role of the Tutor

It became very apparent to us that the tutor had an essential role in providing learner support, particularly at the beginning of a blended module. This requirement is well documented in the literature, but our interaction with the tutor during the first few weeks of our module was so effective that we want to draw attention to this issue. As we gained confidence in our online interaction and developed our background knowledge, our tutor continued to facilitate our learning and challenged us by providing progressively more difficult activities.

## Module Design

We found the formative and summative assessment methods used to assess us to be appropriate, and they had been designed carefully to ensure that the learning outcomes were achieved and that we were engaged with our learning throughout the module. One general conclusion from all participants was that 10 weeks was a very short time frame in which to complete the module, and each of us reported problems with time management and related anxiety. As all of the learning activities and assessments were of value, the participants felt that 15 weeks would have been more appropriate. The duration of the module is, however, subject to timetable constraints, and it is recognised that this change may not be feasible. If this is the case, perhaps some of the weekly online tasks could be reviewed and shortened. The participants felt that the criterion-referenced pass-fail classification used for the summative assessments was clear and fair to all and hope to incorporate it to a greater extent in their own teaching.

Another issue reported by the group was that most of the participants said they would have liked the opportunity to give a presentation at the end of the module. An evaluation questionnaire was circulated when the module was complete allowing the students a means to communicate this suggestion to the module tutor. However, as McKeachie (1996) observes, "students are not the evaluators; they simply provide data to the evaluators" (p. 7). Thus, there may well be logistical issues that would make this change difficult to implement or it could be that there were sound pedagogical reasons for having a presentation at the halfway stage of the module and not one at the end.

## Group Work Division

Regarding the issue of whether participants should choose tasks relating to the CPBL project that involved skills and knowledge that they already had or that they lacked, the recommendation in the literature is that the major component of a CPBL project must not involve students applying skills that they already had (Thomas, 2000). The issue only arose in relation to one part of the project that involved experience in using the software to produce the exemplar VLE. As it involved greater learning, the group agreed that participants who did not have previous experience would work on the exemplar VLE with the support of those who had.

## Tackling the Disadvantages and Barriers to E-Learning

It is important to have an awareness of the most common issues and problems that can arise when e-learning methods are introduced. In this way, many of the likely difficulties can be anticipated and systems can be put in place to deal with them if they occur. Several authors have produced useful recommendations and guidance in this regard (Holmes & Gardner, 2006; Salmon, 2000; Sharpe et al., 2006). As has already been discussed, the initial induction and access stage is particularly critical in online learning and requires careful

planning and support. Other problem areas that have been highlighted in this chapter include the challenge of keeping students motivated and engaged, the lack of online access, technical problems, anxiety over time management, and the need to develop social interaction online. In addition, the difficulties encountered with collaborative group work will often apply but are not exclusive to e-learning.

Issues relating to the successful implementation of online learning in higher education institutions are examined in more detail toward the end of the following section on future trends. The barriers that are often encountered relate to the provision of the necessary support structures and development of a clear e-learning strategy at an institutional level. Holmes and Gardner (2006) emphasise that structures and resources need to be put in place to facilitate Web-based learning innovations without excessive preparation and time commitments, and Mason (2001) observes that methods of reducing the time demands on e-tutors need to be found as "interaction fatigue" can set in.

## FUTURE TRENDS

Some of the relevant emerging and future trends in online learning in higher education will now be examined briefly. The potential impact on the learner experience will also be considered where appropriate.

An emerging trend of particular interest and relevance is online problem-based learning (PBL). There have been a number of recent developments in this area. Savin-Baden (2006) emphasises that the aim of online PBL is to develop and supplement what has already been achieved rather than replace it. She uses the term *blended PBL* to describe the type of approach used in the CPBL project that our group undertook.

Another development that our group feels is very significant for designing e-learning on the basis of our experience as e-learners is podcasting. Campbell (2005) explains that the term *podcast* is derived from the words *iPod* and *broadcasting*, and that this approach essentially involves making audio files available to download. Although we had limited experience with podcasting, we are all enthusiastic about its use in e-learning. Our guest tutors from Australia used this technology when they were interacting with our group. Our experience was that we felt we knew them much better as a result of hearing their voices and because of the descriptions they gave of where they were recording from. This humanisation of our interaction broke the ice and drew us in as we listened to our first podcast for educational purposes. Admittedly, there here may have been a novelty factor at play to some extent, but we found that the content of the guest tutor's audio-file contributions were much more memorable than the written discussion threads that they posted. This impact is emphasised by Campbell in the following quote: "Done well, podcasting can reveal to students, faculty, staff, communities—even the world—the essential humanity at the heart of higher education" (p. 44).

Holmes and Gardner (2006) have remarked on the potential of recording feedback when assessing work and posting the audio file for the student immediately afterward. However, they identify that there are problems associated with this rapid feedback approach if comments that have not been thought through fully are made.

Another significant emerging trend is e-portfolios. Each member of our group had already completed a teaching portfolio and thus we were interested in the possibility of completing an e-portfolio. This can include podcasts, e-mails, discussion threads, blogs, and journals. Jafari (2004) has examined the advantages and difficulties of implementing e-portfolios in higher education.

We are also conscious that there is a wider community of practitioners and academics who are willing to share online resources. In Ireland, the National Digital Learning Repository (NDLR) has recently been launched. Many other countries have developed similar repositories.

Mobile learning or m-learning is another emerging trend. While participating in the designing e-learning module, group members occasionally used mobile-phone communication. At present, most institutions have a texting software package to keep students up to date with announcements such as exam deadlines and cancelled lectures. Conole et al. (2006) have found that students use mobile phones extensively to communicate with peers and tutors. In a recent presentation, Sharples (2007) described an example of recent good practice, the MyArtSpace project, in which multimedia mobile phones were supplied to second-level students when they arrived at a museum. They were given several tasks to perform that required them to interact with the exhibits. These included taking photographs and video clips, and collecting other relevant material that they then edited back at their schools to produce an online gallery. It was found that the students spent significantly more time interacting with the exhibits and gathering information when this approach was used compared to the traditional visit format.

There are several features usually available within a VLE that our group did not have time to explore such as quizzes and animations, and having grades available for students. Thus, in addition to investigating future and emerging trends, it is also a priority to us to consolidate our knowledge and experience of the current VLE systems available and to become confident in practicing the e-learning and teaching that we have experienced firsthand before we extend into new areas.

## Institutional Support

It is important to mention issues relating to the implementation of effective online learning and teaching at the third level and the context of the strategy and culture within an individual institution. One participant in our group commented,

Before I began the module, I was very hesitant about getting involved in e-learning because of a lack of relevant knowledge and skills. Having completed the module, I am still holding back, but now it's because I'm aware of the significant amount of preparation and learner support that must be provided to implement meaningful e-learning in a way that makes use of the added value it can provide. (Participant B, March 2007)

Mason (2001) describes the approach taken by the Open University to incorporate online learning into their distance education courses. A clear policy decision was formulated to not hold all courses online as it was felt it was a waste of resources to place a great deal of text on the Internet when students were going to print them out to read more easily anyway. Instead, the institution focused on developing features such as online tutoring and conferencing as well as collaborative small-group activities. A clear and informed institution-wide strategy was obviously important in supporting staff as they developed online learning in this particular case. In other third-level institutions, the adoption and implementation of e-learning has not always been considered to the same extent. Donnelly and O'Rourke (2007) warn of the danger that adoption of online learning may be performed superficially by third-level institutions if the yardstick used is the quantity instead of the quality of the learning. They also emphasise the need for the professional development of academic staff in the area of e-learning coupled with ongoing support from experts and peers. Butler and Sellbom (2002) report that they identified three main barriers to adoption of Internet and Web technology. They are a lack of financial support, lack of institutional support, and a lack of time to learn new technologies.

## CONCLUSION

Our group of online learners found that our lived experience as e-learners participating in a carefully constructed, blended activity-based course was invaluable to our academic development as e-tutors and module designers. We gained insights into the common problems and challenges that students encounter as well as the benefits and potential difficulties associated with e-learning. We would strongly recommend this approach for learning how to be an effective online tutor and facilitator and how to design and develop online programmes and activities that make full use of the strengths of online learning. As one of the participants in our group commented, "it makes it much easier to teach using these methods having experienced them as a student" (Participant D, April 2006).

Several difficulties associated with online learning were encountered, and these are important issues for teachers and designers to consider when implementing blended learning. It is vital that the necessary support is available during the induction phase, which Salmon (2000) refers to as the access and motivation stage. The tutor has a very important role at this point in welcoming and encouraging students and making the benefits of Web-based learning apparent, as well as demonstrating good practice in their online communication. Sufficient technical support is essential to ensure that participants can access the ICT systems quickly and easily, and that any initial problems are dealt with efficiently. The fact that our group consisted of people with varying levels of prior experience meant that we became aware of the range and extent of initial learner support and motivation required and the role that peer mentoring can play. Other issues identified that can be problematic for e-learners include access to the Internet, time management, and a lack of social contact. As e-learning often involves collaborative group work, the difficulties associated with group work such as underparticipation and ineffective communication and decision making may also arise. It is important that facilitators are aware of these problems so that they can identify them quickly and take steps to remedy them.

Issues relating to the type of formative and summative assessments used were examined. Our group found that the CPBL project, the individual reflective piece, and e-tivities employed had been aligned effectively with the learning outcomes and were valuable to our learning. Thus, from both a learner and course-designer perspective, these types of assessments were appropriate and suitable for blended learning. The issue of careful planning to allow adequate time for learners to complete assignments is important and, in our case, we would have preferred a longer time frame for the module if that were possible. We also found that the criterion-based pass-fail classification used was clear to all and fostered a collaborative spirit. It is important when designing online assessments to ensure that students are active and motivated throughout the duration of the module by incorporating regular activities and milestones, as was the case in the module we experienced.

The design and development of the online information-literacy module for our CPBL assessment allowed us to develop and apply important skills and knowledge and to experience the role of e-designer. Important considerations that shaped our course design included the provision of effective learner support at the beginning of the module, scaffolding of the designed e-tivities, and the application of activities to the relevant subject discipline to provide a relevant context. Also, e-learning technology was only incorporated where appropriate and where it was felt it would genuinely be of benefit to the learners. There is a genuine need for the information-literacy-skills module we produced; it has been implemented by one participant already and will be adapted and used by several others in the group in the coming year.

We are aware of the relevant emerging trends in Web-based learning, which include online PBL, podcasting, and m-learning. These are exciting developments, but our group feels it is important to consolidate what we have already learnt and apply it in our teaching before we try to incorporate emerging trends to any significant extent.

Some issues relating to the implementation of effective e-learning in higher education institutions were also considered. Important requirements are institutional and financial support, sufficient time allocation, appropriate professional development courses for academic staff to learn new technologies, and ongoing support from experts and peers.

## FUTURE RESEARCH DIRECTIONS

At present, we are concentrating on applying the skills, knowledge, and insights developed in the designing e-learning module. For some of us, this involves adapting and using the information-literacy-skills module that we developed, while others are incorporating greater interactivity and collaborative work into existing Web-based aspects of our courses.

We hope that these developments will provide the basis for a future publication as we intend to assess the extent to which each participant in the module applied the knowledge and skills developed. We will also review the enablers and barriers we encountered to implementing Web-based learning. As discussed earlier, several factors critical to the successful introduction of e-learning have been identified in the literature (Butler & Sellbom, 2002; Donnelly & O'Rourke, 2007). We plan to compare their findings with ours. We also intend to evaluate the attitudes and opinions of our students and academic colleagues regarding the changes implemented to gain insights into their perspectives on blended learning. We would also like to examine the quality of the learning achieved when the new Web-based strategies are implemented.

In addition, we would like to examine what is meant by e-learning at an institutional level. If it is perceived that information-repository and course-management aspects are all that are involved, then there is little incentive to develop interactive activities (individual and/or collaborative) or promote meaningful online discussion. Another potential future research topic is the professional development of academic staff in the area of pedagogy and technology. We would be particularly interested in comparing the experience we had in the designing e-learning module with other approaches described in the literature. Further aspects we would like to study are the contribution that peer tutoring can make (Reilly, 2005) and the most effective strategies for ongoing support for academic staff who are actively involved in online learning.

## REFERENCES

Ambrose, A., & Gillespie, B. (2003). Information-literacy programmes and programme curricula: The case for integration. *Level, 3*, 1. Retrieved February 18, 2006, from http://level3.dit.ie/html/issue1_ambrose1.html

Arbaugh, J. B. (2004). Learning to learn online: A study of perceptual changes between multiple online course experiences. *Internet and Higher Education, 7*, 169-182.

Beetham, H. (2002). *Understanding e-learning, e-tutoring for effective e-learning resources.* Higher Education Academy. Retrieved April 3, 2007, from http://www.ics.heacademy.ac.uk/events/displayevent.php?id=22

Beetham, H. (2005). E-learning research: Emerging issues? *ALT-J, Research in Learning Technology, 13*(1), 81-89.

Bigge, M. L., & Shermis, S. S. (2004). *Learning theories for teachers* (6th ed.). Boston: Pearson.

Biggs, J. (2003). *Teaching for quality learning at university* (2nd ed.). Buckingham, United Kingdom: Open University Press.

Bonk, C. J., Kim, K., & Zeng, T. (in press). Future directions of blended learning in higher education and workplace learning setting. In *Handbook of blended learning: Global perspectives.* San Francisco: Pfeiffer Publishing. Retrieved March 24, 2006, from http://www.publicationshare.com/c083_bonk_future.pdf

Butler, D., & Sellbom, M. (2002). Barriers for adopting technology for teaching and learning. *Educause Quarterly, 25*(2), 22-28. Retrieved May 25, 2007, from http://www.educause.edu/ir/library/pdf/eqm0223.pdf

Campbell, G. (2005). There's something in the air: Podcasting in education. *Educause Review, 40*(6), 32-47. Retrieved May 16, 2007, from http://www.educause.edu/apps/er/erm05/erm056.asp

Charlesworth, P., & Vician, C. (2003). Leveraging technology for chemical sciences education: An early assessment of WebCT usage in first-year chemistry courses. *Journal of Chemical Education, 80*(11), 1333-1337.

Chickering, A., & Ehrmann, S. (1996, October). Implementing the seven principles: Technology as lever. *American Association for Higher Education Bulletin*, pp. 3-6. Retrieved February 24, 2006, from http://www.tltgroup.org/programs/seven.html

Clouder, L., & Deepwell, F. (2004). *Reflections on unexpected outcomes: Learning from student collaboration in an online discussion forum.* Paper presented at the Networked Learning Conference, Lancaster, United Kingdom. Retrieved August 20, 2007, from http://www.networkedlearningconference.org.uk/past/nlc2004/proceedings/individual_papers/clouderanddeepwell.htm

Concannon, F., Flynn, A., & Campbell, M. (2005). What campus-based students think about the quality and benefits of e-learning. *British Journal of Educational Technology, 36*(3), 501-512.

Conole, G., de Laat, M., Dillon, T., & Darby, J. (2006, December). *An in-depth case study of students' experiences of e-learning: How is learning changing?* Paper presented at the Australian Society for Computers in Learning and in Tertiary Education Conference, Sydney, Australia. Retrieved August 8, 2007, from http://www.ascilite.org.au/conferences/sydney06/proceeding/pdf_papers/p127.pdf

Cowan, J. (1998). *On becoming an innovative university teacher.* Buckingham, United Kingdom: Open University Press.

Donnelly, R., & O'Rourke, K. (2007). What now? Evaluating e-learning CPD practice in Irish third-level education. *Journal of Further and Higher Education, 31*(1), 31-40.

Driscoll, M. (2002). Blended learning: Let's get beyond the hype. *Learning and Training Innovations Newsline.* Retrieved August 7, 2007, from http://elearningmag.com/ltimagazine/article/articleDetail.jsp?id=11755

Gagné, R. M., Wager, W. W., Golas, K. C., & Keller, J. M. (2005). *Principles of instructional design* (5th ed.). Belmont, CA: Thomson Wadsworth.

Hiltz, S. R., & Goldman, R. (2005). *Learning together online: Research on asynchronous learning networks.* London: Lawrence Erlbaum.

Holmes, B., & Gardner, J. (2006). *E-learning concepts and practice.* London: Sage Publications.

*Intute Virtual Training Suite.* (2006). Retrieved February 14, 2006, from http://www.vts.rdn.ac.uk

Jafari, A. (2004). The "sticky" eportfolio system: Tackling challenges and identifying attributes. *Educause Review, 39*(4), 38-48. Retrieved May 16, 2007, from http://www.educause.edu/apps/er/erm05/erm056.asp

Laurillard, D. (1993). *Rethinking university education.* London: Routledge.

Ljoså, E. (1998). The role of university teachers in a digital era. *European Journal of Open, Distance and ELearning.* Retrieved May 5, 2007, from http://www.eurodl.org/materials/contrib/1998/eden98/Ljosa.html

Mason, R. (2001). The Open University experience. In J. Stephenson (Ed.), *Teaching and learning online: Pedagogies for new technologies* (pp. 67-75). London: Kogan Page.

Matheos, K., Daniel, K., & McCalla, G. I. (2005). Dimensions for blended learning technology: Learners' perspectives. *Journal of Learning Design, 1*(1), 56-76. Retrieved August 10, 2007, from https://olt.qut.edu.au/udf/jld/index.cfm?fa=displayPage&rNum=1780740

McConnell, D. (2005). Examining the dynamics of networked e-learning groups and communities. *Studies in Higher Education, 30*(1), 25-42.

McKeachie, W. (1996). *The professional evaluation of teaching* (Paper No. 33). American Council of Learned Societies. Retrieved May 14, 2007, from http://www.acls.org/op33.htm#McKeachie

McMahon, M. (1997, December). *Social constructivism and the World Wide Web: A paradigm for learning.* Paper presented at the Australian Society for Computers in Learning and in Tertiary Education Conference, Perth, Australia. Retrieved May 2, 2007, from http://www.ascilite.org.au/conferences/perth97/papers/Mcmahon/Mcmahon.html

Moon, J. (1999). *Reflection in learning and professional development.* London: Kogan Page.

Morris, L. (2007, August 30-31). *Pick and mix: Getting the blend right.* Paper presented at the Annual Variety in Chemistry Education Conference, Leicester, United Kingdom.

Munro, M., & Walsh, E. (2005, May 26-27). *Online tutors as online students: Preparing tutors to teach online*. Paper presented at the Sixth Annual Irish Educational Technology Users' Conference, Dublin, Ireland. Retrieved March 2, 2006, from http://ilta.learnonline.ie/course/view.php?id=18

Oliver, M., & Trigwell, K. (2005). Can "blended learning" be redeemed? *E-Learning, 2*(1), 17-26.

Oliver, R. (2001). Developing online learning environments that support knowledge construction. In S. Stoney & J. Burns (Eds.), *Working for excellence in the e-conomy* (pp. 407-416). Churchlands, Australia: We-B Centre. Retrieved April 10, 2007, from http://elrond.scam.ecu.edu.au/oliver/2001/webepaper.pdf

Page, A., & Donovan, K. (2005). *Elearning: A workbook for adult community learning*. Leicester, United Kingdom: National Institute of Adult Continuing Education.

Palloff, R. M., & Pratt, K. (2005). *Collaborating online: Learning together in community*. San Francisco: Jossey-Bass.

Quinney, A. (2005). "Placements online": Student experiences of a Website to support learning in practice settings. *Social Work Education, 24*(4), 439-450.

Ramsden, P. (1992). *Learning to teach in higher education*. London: Routledge.

Reilly, C. (2005). Teaching by example: A case for peer workshops about pedagogy and technology. *Innovate, 1*(3). Retrieved May 22, 2007, from http://www.innovateonline.info/index.php?view=article&id=15

Roberts, L. (1995). *A template for converting classrooms to distributed, asynchronous courses*. Retrieved February 4, 2006, from http://ww.unc.edu/cit/iat-archive/publications/roberts/template.html

Ross, B. (1997). Towards a framework for problem-based curricula. In D. Boud & G. Feletti (Eds.), *The challenge of problem based learning* (pp. 28-35). London: Kogan Page.

Salmon, G. (2000). *E-moderating: The key to teaching and learning online*. London: Routledge Falmer.

Salmon, G. (2002). *E-tivities: The key to active online learning*. London: Routledge Falmer.

Savin-Baden, M. (2006). The challenge of using problem-based learning online. In M. Savin-Baden & K. Wilkie (Eds.), *Problem-based learning online* (pp. 3-13). Berkshire, United Kingdom: Open University Press.

Sharpe, R., & Benfield, G. (2005). The student experience of e-learning in higher education: A review of the literature. *Brookes EJournal of Learning and Teaching, 1*(3). Retrieved August 15, 2007, from http://www.brookes.ac.uk/publications/bejlt/volume1issue3/academic/sharpe_benfield.html

Sharpe, R., Benfield, G., Roberts, G., & Francis, R. (2006). *The undergraduate experience of blended e-learning: A review of UK literature and practice*. York, United Kingdom: The Higher Education Academy. Retrieved August 20, 2007, from http://www.heacademy.ac.uk/assets/York/documents/ourwork/research/literature_reviews/blended_elearning_full_review.pdf

Sharples, M. (2007, May 23-25). *Big issues in mobile learning*. Paper presented at the Eighth Annual Irish Educational Technology Users' Conference, Dublin, Ireland.

Smith, B. (2001). *Teaching online: New or transferable skills?* Higher Education Academy. Retrieved March 21, 2006, from http://www.heacademy.ac.uk/resources.asp?process=full_record&section=generic&id=455

Smith, T. (2005). Fifty one competencies for online instruction. *The Journal of Educators Online, 2*(2). Retrieved December 21, 2006, from http://its.fvtc.edu/langan/BB6/Online%20Instructor%20Competencies.pdf

Sormunen, E. (2006). *Web searching, information literacy and learning: Web-SeaL.* Retrieved February 15, 2006, from http://www.info.uta.fi/tutkimus/WebSeal/Research_plan.pdf

Stracke, E. (2007). A road to understanding: A qualitative study into why learners drop out of a blended language learning environment. *ReCALL, 19*, 57-78.

Swan, K., & Shea, P. (2005). The development of virtual learning communities. In S. R. Hiltz & R. Goldman (Eds.), *Learning together online: Research on asynchronous learning networks* (pp. 239-260). London: Lawrence Erlbaum.

Sweeney, J., O'Donoghue, T., & Whitehead, C. (2004). Traditional face-to-face and Web-based tutorials: A study of university students' perspectives on the roles of tutorial participants. *Teaching in Higher Education, 9*(3), 311-323.

Thomas, J. (2000). *A review of research on project based learning.* Retrieved May 21, 2007, from http://www.bie.org/files/researchreviewPBL.pdf

Whitelock, D., & Jelfs, A. (2003). Editorial: *Educational Media* special issue on blended learning. *Journal of Educational Media, 28*(2-3), 99-100.

## ADDITIONAL READING

Alexander, S., & Golja, T. (2007). Using students' experiences to derive quality in an e-learning system: An institution's perspective. *Educational Technology and Society, 10*(2), 17-33.

This paper examines the application of a systems approach to investigate how online learning is experienced by learners and teaching staff at an Australian college. The authors conclude that the students' perspectives provide valuable data that will help to inform future developments in their institution. A useful review of existing guidelines on quality in e-learning is included, and a comprehensive analysis of the students' views on online learning is provided.

Baker, J. D., Redfield, K. L., & Tonkin, S. (2006). Collaborative coaching and networking for online instructors. *Online Journal of Distance Learning Administration, 9*(4). Retrieved April 12, 2007, from http://www.westga.edu/~distance/ojdla/winter94/baker94.htm

This paper discusses an approach to academic staff development that applies collaborative coaching to train staff in becoming effective online tutors and instructors. A model has been developed that entails three phases (planning conference, instructional observation, and reflecting conference). A collaborative coaching checklist is provided based on the experiences of the authors over the past 10 years.

Beetham, H., & Sharpe, R. (Eds.). (2007). *Rethinking pedagogy for a digital age: Designing and delivering elearning.* London: Routledge.

This book examines perspectives on the effective design and delivery of e-learning activities informed by pedagogy. Case studies are used very effectively to provide guidance, advice, and practical examples. The discussion of relevant design issues and considerations on the use of e-learning activities are also very helpful.

Boud, D., & Felletti, G. E. (Eds.). (1997). *The challenge of problem-based learning* (2nd ed.). London: Kogan Page.

This book highlights the significance, uses, strengths, and limitations of the problem-based learning approach. The contributions are drawn from a wide range of disciplines based in many different countries. The analysis of issues relating to collaboration and assessment of group work is particularly useful.

Collison, G., Elbaum, B., Haavind, S., & Tinker, R. (Eds.). (2000). *Facilitating online learning: Effective strategies for moderators.* Madison, WI: Atwood Publishing.

This book is aimed at novice online learning facilitators. The focus is on practice supported by a balanced theoretical framework. Effective guidance and practical advice on how moderators can effectively facilitate online dialogue among learners is provided.

Conole, G., & Oliver, M. (2007). (Eds.). *Contemporary perspectives in elearning research: Themes, methods and impact on practice.* New York: Routledge.

In this text, the important debates related to e-learning and the emerging research findings are critically discussed by a number of experienced researchers. Among the areas addressed are sociocultural aspects and the impact of policy and funding, as well as more practical issues such as using tools and resources and e-assessment. A thorough understanding of the important themes that have developed in research on e-learning can thus be gained.

Cottrell, S. (2001). *Teaching study skills and supporting learning.* Basingstoke, United Kingdom: Palgrave.

This text is based on the author's extensive experience of supporting learners in higher education. Examples and case studies on topics such as learner types, time management, and the development of critical analysis and group interaction skills are provided. The second part of the book contains a series of worksheets developed by the author. Although not designed for use in an online environment, many of these could be modified to become e-tivities without too much difficulty.

Cunningham, I., Dawes, G., & Bennett, B. (2004). *The handbook of work based learning.* Aldershot, United Kingdom: Gower.

This book provides an overview of strategies, tactics, and methods adopted to support work-based learning. The sections on networks and communities, e-learning, and computer-based training will be of interest to online facilitators. Each section contains a description of the process, provides examples, explains the benefits and limitations of the approach, and gives guidelines and hints for those about to apply it.

Field, J. (2003). Social capital in a post (modern) world. In *Social capital* (pp. 91-114). London: Routledge.

In this chapter, research on the effect of online interaction on social capital is examined and discussed. The author concludes that social capital does not seem to be impinged on and that the Internet actually seems to be complementing it as it allows people to extend existing networks and build upon face-to-face connections.

Fox, S., & McKeogh, K. (2003). Can elearning promote higher order learning without tutor overload? *Open Learning, 18*(2), 121-134.

The authors address the very significant issue of whether an online environment requires greater time input from facilitators. Selected teaching methods (peer-tutoring and resources/debates) were examined as these were expected to improve higher order cognitive skills of the learners with minimal demands on tutor time. The authors conclude that these techniques appeared not to require excessive levels of tutor input but further studies are planned.

Guldberg, K., & Pilkington, R. (2007). Tutor roles in facilitating reflection on practice through online discussion. *Educational Technology and Society, 10*(1), 61-72.

The authors examine the effectiveness of online discussions from the perspective of the impact of the topic selected and the intervention by the facilitator during the discussion. They conclude that if more emphasis is placed on the preparatory work online tutors undertake in advance of discussions, less involvement from them is required during the discussions. The guidance on a general structure for discussion topics that were found to promote effective dialogue is helpful.

Hemphill, L., & Hemphill, H. (2007). Evaluating the impact of guest speaker postings in online discussions. *British Journal of Educational Technology, 38*(2), 287-293.

The contribution of guest tutors to asynchronous online discussions is examined in this paper. Interestingly, it was found that the critical thinking skills and interest levels of the students were improved by the guest tutors, but, even when these tutors were not involved, the students still interacted a great deal and at a higher order thinking level. The conclusion the authors arrive at is that only occasional, good-quality interaction from a guest tutor is needed to see an improvement in student interest and thinking.

Hughes, G. (2007). Using blended learning to increase learner support and improve retention. *Teaching in Higher Education, 12*(3), 349-363.

As a result of widening participation, retention is an important issue in higher education. The author discusses an action research project in which effective online tutor support was incorporated into a module and, as a result, module retention was improved. The necessity for a very experienced online facilitator to be involved to ensure success is commented on.

Hughes, M., Ventura, S., & Dando, M. (2007). Assessing social presence in online discussion groups: A replication study. *Innovations in Education and Teaching International, 44*(1), 17-29.

This paper is of interest because it explores emotions such as fear, anger, and isolation experienced by e-learners. The authors describe how they have tested, adjusted, and validated a method for assessing social presence, including emotional states, among e-learners. The contribution this

approach can have to effective facilitation skills is discussed.

Laurillard, D. (2002). Rethinking teaching for the knowledge society. *Educause Review, 37*(1), 16-25. Retrieved May 25, 2007, from http://www.educause.edu/ir/library/pdf/erm0201.pdf.

The author examines the challenges being faced by higher education institutions as a result of the development of the knowledge society, one of which is that teaching methods have not evolved sufficiently. A careful analysis of how learning technology can be used to adapt teaching methods to meet the needs of the digital age is provided, but the author emphasises that academics must be prepared to become reflective practitioners and must be supported in this regard by their institutions.

Littlejohn, A., & Pegler, C. (2007). *Preparing for blended elearning.* London: Routledge.

The authors aim to help facilitators to design and implement effective blended e-learning, and their approach is to examine four aspects: space, time, activities, and tools. Issues of interest discussed include design quality, effective online learning, the devising of activities, and the management of online and off-line interactions. A number of case studies are also provided. A critical analysis of the strengths of e-learning is provided, but the authors are realistic about its limitations.

Lohnes, S., & Kinzer, C. (2007). Questioning assumptions about students' expectations for technology in college classrooms. *Innovate, 3*(5). Retrieved May 28, 2007, from http://www.innovateonline.info/index.php?view=article&id=431

An interesting ethnographic study of how a small group of college students use technology to make meaning of their experience in academic and nonacademic spaces is provided. It was found that the physical environment and the students' attitudes to learning and teaching were important factors. The importance of not making general assumptions about the extent to which students would like to see learning technology incorporated into their programmes of study is one of the main conclusions.

Maier, P., & Warren, A. (2000). *Integrating technology in learning and teaching.* London: Kogan Page.

This book provides a sound introduction into the use of information technology in educational settings. It presents a wide range of activities, checklists, and activities, and has a practice-based focus. Topics of interest examined are e-moderation, pedagogical frameworks, the production of digital learning materials, and the development of learning outcome goals.

Mason, R., & Rennie, F. (2006). *E-learning: The key concepts.* New York: Routledge.

This is a useful general reference book and guide as it explains and provides relevant Web links for all terms and topics relevant to e-learning. The introduction examines the development of e-learning and the current challenges faced, and includes suggestions for further reading.

O'Regan, K. (2003). Emotion and elearning. *Journal of Asynchronous Learning Networks, 7*(3), 78-92. Retrieved May 21, 2007, from http://www.sloan-c.org/publications/jaln/v7n3/v7n3_oregan.asp

The author interviewed 11 online learners and identified a number of common emotions that they experienced regularly: some positive (pride, excitement) and some negative (frustration, anxiety, embarrassment). The excerpts from the interviews conducted are very informative, and practical guidelines on how best to avoid negative emotions developed among e-learners are provided. A theoretical consideration of how emotion affects how people learn is also incorporated.

Price, L., Richardson, J., & Jelfs, A. (2007). Face-to-face versus online tutoring support in distance education. *Studies in Higher Education, 32*(1) 1-20.

A comparison between the experiences that students in the same distance learning course reported as a result of being provided with either online or face-to-face tutorials is discussed. The students who received face-to-face tutorials reported a better experience. As a result, the need for training in communicating online for both tutors and students is emphasised.

Roberts, T. (Ed.). (2006). *Self, peer and group assessment in elearning.* London: Information Science Publishers.

The contributors examine the principal characteristics of assessment approaches that encourage learners to take greater responsibility for their own learning in an online environment. The benefits and problems associated with the assessment strategies proposed are examined, case studies are discussed, and useful guidelines for effective implementation are provided.

Savin-Baden, M. (2000). *Problem-based learning in higher education: Untold stories.* Buckingham, United Kingdom: Open University Press.

The author explores the theory and practice of problem-based learning and considers the implications of implementing this approach. Of interest is her discussion of the student experience of dislocation, in which students experience frustration and discomfort in coping with novel and unfamiliar learning situations.

Shephard, K., Haslam, P., Hutchings, M., & Furneaux, C. (2004, April). *Synchronous online tutorials for staff development?* Paper presented at the Networked Learning Conference, Lancaster, United Kingdom. Retrieved April 4, 2006, from http://www.shef.ac.uk/nlc2004/Proceedings/Individual_Papers/Shephard_et_al.htm

The authors discuss the formation of collaborative online groups of academics engaged in synchronous online discussions about the use of e-learning tools. The detailed discussion on the benefits and shortfalls of online synchronous communication and the comparison to face-to-face communication is very useful.

Toohey, S. (1999). *Designing courses for higher education*. Buckingham, United Kingdom: The Society for Research into Higher Education & Open University Press.

The author focuses on the strategic decisions required when designing courses and offers practical advice. The challenges facing course designers and developers are examined, and of particular interest is the chapter on making learning opportunities more flexible, in which matters such as flexible delivery, resource-based learning, and online approaches are discussed.

**APPENDIX 1**

**Responses from Five of the Course Participants to an Enquiry on Their Prior Experience of E-Learning as Learners and Tutors Before They Began the Designing E-Learning Module**

*My previous experience of online learning was the use of the VLE to access course material during the previous year of this Learning and Teaching course. I do not use e-Learning in my work as a lecturer and really only use computers as a tool for writing, filing information and sending and receiving e-mails. This module was my first stab at looking at a new framework for communicating with my tutors, peers and eventually my students.*

(Participant A, April 2007)

*I had been used to sending and receiving e-mails as part of my work and I had obtained a Microsoft Office Applications Driving Licence in 2004 but I was still rarely using the internet and only going to specific sites to get particular bits of information. Our first year on the Learning and Teaching course had provided a toe in the water however, and gave me some experience of using WebCT software and by the end of the year I had managed with help to set up a VLE for one of the modules that I teach and upload some notes onto it.*

(Participant B, April 2007)

*My experience of e-learning prior to taking up the module was as follows:*
*Live video conference session where the lecturer based in Denmark provided a lecture usually lasting 45 minutes. When the session was complete, we were issued with a set of notes and expected to complete assessments online before logging on to the next lecture which was scheduled for two weeks later. The above did not come close to the experience as an eLearner on the Designing eLearning module.*

(Participant C, April 2007)

*My prior experience of providing eLearning involved the development of online quizzes with feedback in a VLE and using a VLE to deliver course information and material and to provide links to other web sites. I chose the Designing eLearning module because I want to spend some time developing online materials, find out more about what can be done and try out different ways of using eLearning e.g. discussion boards. At the moment, I only work on a need to know basis and don't have a more general overview of what can be done. My experience as an eLearner to date has involved accessing a VLE to obtain course material and information.*

(Participant D, original response to premodule questionnaire on prior experience of e-learning, January 2006)

*Having used virtual learning environments in varying formats since 1994 (Blackboard, WebCT, Moodle, WebEX), I am pleased to say that the basic premise on which all VLEs are founded remains no matter which one is used—that is the opportunity for increased interaction between lecturers and students, but, more importantly, between students and students, in a blended learning environment.*

(Participant E, April 2007)

## APPENDIX 2

*Figure 1. Relationship between technology and learning theories in the blended learning module designed for the CPBL project assignment*

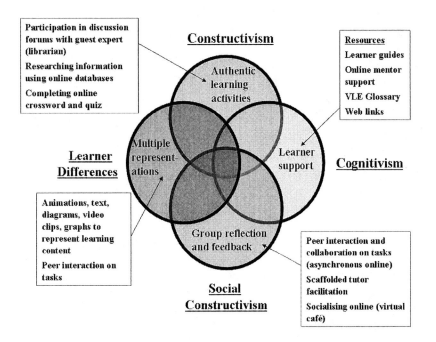

## APPENDIX 3

*Table 1. Outline of e-tivity tasks developed for the Information Treasure Chest module designed for the CPBL project assignment*

| |
|---|
| Task 1, Introductions (to be completed by Week 2): Learners post an introduction about themselves, and post a relevant URL or picture to share with other group members. |
| Task 2, Treasure Hunt (to be completed by Week 3): Learners complete an online quiz and crossword (developed using free software available at http://www.greeneclipsesoftware.com/eclipsecrossword) and have to submit several items on a treasure-hunt list to their tutor. |
| Task 3, Online Information-Skills Tutorial (to be completed by Week 4): Learners carry out a virtual information-skills tutorial for their own subject (see *Intute Virtual Training Suite*, 2006) and complete the quizzes in the tutorial. They post a short review of one key site visited when carrying out the tutorial and, in assigned pairs, look at the site that the other student they are paired with has reviewed. |
| Task 4, Poster (to be completed by Week 6): Learners work in pairs and apply their information-literacy skills to produce a poster on a topic relevant to their programme of study (e.g., The Chemistry of Hair Dyes, Sustainable Energy Buildings), interact with an expert online (a librarian), and reflect on what they have learned. |

# Chapter V
# Opening Online Academic Development Programmes to International Perspectives and Dialogue

**Catherine Manathunga**
*TEDI, University of Queensland, Australia*

**Roisin Donnelly**
*The Learning and Teaching Centre, Dublin Institute of Technology, Ireland*

## ABSTRACT

*Professional development for academic staff in higher education is receiving increasing attention. The focus has been on providing an opportunity for academic staff to enhance their effectiveness in meeting changing needs and roles in higher education. Inherent in this changing role has been meeting the challenges of technology-infused learning environments available for use today. This chapter explores the potential of online academic development programmes to increase collaboration and dialogue amongst participants through integrating opportunities for online interaction. By spotlighting two particular postgraduate programmes in Ireland and Australia, the chapter reports on present experiences of integrating international guests and considers the future of connecting people and technology for academic development in higher education.*

## INTRODUCTION

Around the world, there are increasing university and government pressures on academic staff to engage in professional development to improve their teaching and learning practices (Gibbs, 2004; Kezar, 2001; Knapper, 2004; Knight, 2002; McAlpine & Emrick, 2003). Demands are also being placed on academic development units to enable staff to realise the potential of flexible modes of learning for their students. Many higher education institutions have adopted an e-learning strategy whereby academic development is at the forefront of promoting adoption of new technologies to support learning and teaching. The Dublin Institute of Technology's (DIT) strategic plan illustrates this:

*The common objective, in all elements of the Strategic Plan, is the achievement of excellence, through processes of continuous improvement of staff and programmes...to develop modularized eLearning programmes...to foster career development for staff...to train staff to deliver web-based and other learning programmes to students internally and externally in Ireland. (DIT Institutional Strategic Plan, 2001-2015, pp. 15, 17, 19, 21)*

So, too, in the Australian context, the University of Queensland's (UQ) Teaching and Learning Enhancement Plan identifies "exploring new forms of educational interaction supported by information and communications technology" as part of its key goal of developing "flexible and engaging teaching practice," and commits the university to developing "a university approach to the support of Web-based teaching and learning materials and interactions" (UQ Teaching and Learning Enhancement Plan, 2003-2007, p. 8). Delivering on these kinds of imperatives requires those in academic development units to be increasingly creative and open to new perspectives and collaborative opportunities.

This chapter first explores the impetus for the creation and implementation of online academic development programmes, paying specific attention to the small amount of scholarly discussion on incorporating international guests into these fora. The challenges of running international online development are linked theoretically to models of professional development specifically for blended learning (the combination of face-to-face workshops and online learning activities and interaction). In particular, this chapter adapts Sharpe's (2004) professional development model for designing e-learning to these case studies. In order to set the scene for our experiences of involving international guests in our academic development programmes, the details of the contexts, curriculum design, and delivery of two diverse case studies are then presented. These case studies are in the fields of e-learning design and remote postgraduate supervision. In particular, we present evaluative data about these approaches based on a range of semistructured participant interviews from each programme over a period of 2 years. Finally, we discuss the implications of these teaching and learning strategies for academic development and for enhancing the international collaboration of academic developers. We also make some recommendations for future research directions.

## THE IMPACT OF E-LEARNING IN HIGHER EDUCATION

The pressure to embrace e-learning technologies in higher education has arisen from a number of factors beyond the mere availability of increasingly sophisticated technologies. Of particular importance have been the learning preferences and styles of the so-called Internet generation, also known as Net Gen or digital learners (Donnelly & O'Brien, 2003; Oblinger, 2006). The aptitudes, attitudes, expectations, and learning styles of these Net Gen students reflect the environment in which they were raised: one that is decidedly different from that which existed when academic staff were growing up (Oblinger & Oblinger, 2005). As Oblinger continues to argue, today's younger student learners are digital, connected, experiential, immediate, and social with preferences for learning that include peer-to-peer interaction and engagement and for learning resources that are visual and relevant. So, too, in higher degree teaching and learning, a range of online technologies are increasingly available for postgraduate supervision purposes. Supervision in this case refers to the guidance of research students in Ireland, Australia, the United Kingdom, and other countries by academic mentors that are referred to as dissertation supervisors in Canadian and American contexts. An increasing number of research students are now enrolled in higher degree studies, including masters' in research and PhD programmes, that are at a distance from their supervisors and universities. In addition, many research students travel for extended periods of fieldwork and require ways of maintaining communication with their supervisors. Online supervision raises a whole range of diverse teaching and learning challenges that require very different supervision approaches from those used in face-to-face settings and for which ICTs offer great potential (Rodger & Brown, 2000; Wisker, 2000).

It has been recognised that this increased uptake of e-learning technologies in both undergraduate and postgraduate coursework and for remote postgraduate supervision has not necessarily translated into excellent outcomes for all students (Ferrier, 1992). Indeed, there is still considerable apathy and confusion about the effectiveness of e-learning course delivery amongst students and academics alike (Shivkumar, 2006). Abrami, Bernard, Wade, and Schmid (2006) report that there has been scepticism about the use of technology to improve learning, including suggestions that it represents a threat to formal education. A number of studies report that students are dissatisfied with lecturers' use of technology for learning (Mering & Robbie, 2005; Weaver, Chenicheri, & Spratt, 2005).

In many cases, academic staff may seek to simply transfer the teaching techniques they are currently using to the new technologies, often with unsatisfactory results (Kearsley, 2000). Successful online teaching cannot be achieved by doing what lecturers always did in the classroom. In many respects, teaching online is not the same as teaching face to face. Supporting learning online through synchronous and asynchronous conferencing (bulletin boards, forums) requires teachers to have a wider range of expertise compared to working with face-to-face learning groups (Salmon, 2000). In the United States, Surry and Land (2000) suggest that enabling lecturers to use technology in their teaching means providing training that is motivating, attention gaining, and relevant, and results in confidence building. In particular, it has been demonstrated that online environments are far less conducive to didactic approaches to teaching and learning (Bowles, 2004).

In addition, Donnelly and O'Rourke (2007) argue that many academic staff lack the online experience of the Internet generation, and so do not feel as confident in an online environment as they do in a traditional classroom or postgraduate supervision setting. In this context, the problem is a social as well as a pedagogic one because it revolves around developing different kinds of communication skills and becoming adept at using the considerable array of available online communication tools. In many instances, lecturers may need to experience being an online student themselves in order to gain the necessary confidence to operate effectively in an online environment.

## INTERNATIONAL COLLABORATION IN BLENDED ACADEMIC DEVELOPMENT PROGRAMMES

There is, therefore, a clear rationale for providing academic staff with professional development that allows them to enhance their teaching and learning practice and gain confidence in using e-learning technologies simultaneously (Donnelly & O'Farrell, 2006; Panda & Juwah, 2006). There are a range of approaches to online academic development programmes already reported in the literature (Brew & Peseta, 2004; Kandlbinder, 2000; Mainka, 2007). They include fully online programmes, such as that offered by the University of Sydney for postgraduate supervisors (Brew & Peseta), and blended learning approaches incorporating both face-to-face and online components, such as the two programmes described in this chapter. So, too, they encompass fully accredited programmes, such as graduate certificates or diplomas in education, as well as voluntary academic development workshops.

All advertise similar benefits of increased flexibility and high-quality academic development support. Brew and Peseta (2004) indicate that evaluations of their online programme provided evidence of improved supervisory skills and greater knowledge of university postgraduate policies and processes. Kandlbinder (2000) argues that if online academic development programmes are designed to take an inquiry-focused approach, they are likely to "evolve into entirely new practices, in forms conducive to critical inquiry" (p. 376). More recently, an online professional development course at Napier University (Mainka, 2007) claims to provide opportunities for sharing prior knowledge, practicing new skills, supporting peers, and collaborating, and these can become the driving forces for empowering participants to identify the potential of technology in learning, teaching, and postgraduate research.

There is also a sense from the literature that some learning models driving academic development programmes in general are not making use of the shift in focus from "the sage on the stage" mentality of spoon-feeding knowledge to those who remain passive in the learning environment to the "guide on the side" concept of facilitating active and student-centred knowledge construction. Kandlbinder (2000) in particular refers to the tendency of some academic development units to adopt an information-centred transmission approach to online technologies. In order to

achieve this shift toward student-centred learning, collaboration among students needs to be encouraged and modeled as an essential ingredient in effective teaching. As Harasim (1989) argued, students need to be "involved in constructing knowledge through a process of discussion and interaction with learning peers and experts" (p. 51). Better use needs to be made of online academic development programmes to model these effective approaches to student learning for academic staff and to encourage them to discuss, argue, negotiate, and reflect upon their existing beliefs and knowledge about pedagogy.

The assortment of communication technologies made available in online programmes can enable this greater collaboration and interaction between academic developers and participants, and among participants. In particular, communication technologies, such as asynchronous discussion fora, synchronous chat sessions, and video and Web-cam interactions, broaden the pool of experts academic developers can include in their online programmes. Few scholars have investigated the impact of involving international guest lecturers in online programmes generally and in academic development programmes specifically. Referring to online student learning, ChanLin and Chan (2007) reported on the introduction of interdisciplinary experts into an online problem-based learning (PBL) course. Students in this study reported that online interactions with their peers, the teacher, the facilitator, and these experts greatly enhanced their knowledge.

Janes (2000) wrote specifically about online academic development programmes, emphasising some of the benefits of linking with international guest lecturers in an online environment. These positive features included allowing participants in many countries, with varying experiences and levels of expertise in technology-based distributed learning, to share and learn from each other. Since the beginning of the certificate programme described by Janes, participants have visited each other on special occasions across cities or continents, collaborated on projects outside the course and after its completion, and coauthored papers based on their collaborative work in the courses, which have been published in peer-reviewed journals and conference proceedings. As a result, these opportunities often generate long-term teaching and research collaborations.

This chapter argues that the participation of international guest lecturers in online course discussions can allow academic developers to model for their academic participants active and student-centred approaches to teaching and learning. In particular, through evaluative data collected from two diverse case studies in Ireland and Australia, we suggest that the involvement of international guest lecturers in academic development programmes provides additional opportunities for academic staff and their international guests to recognise, investigate, and critique their assumptions about teaching and learning; understand diverse international higher education contexts and perspectives; and enhance their capacity for clear communication and respectful, attentive listening. Developing such collaboration between courses in different institutions also allows academics to establish ongoing international research collaborations on e-learning and other areas of learning and teaching, and to embed academic developers themselves in a supportive, enriched community of academic development practice. The fact that these approaches are able to enhance academic staff learning in two very different forms of higher education pedagogy (e-learning and remote postgraduate supervision) further substantiates these claims. Before we can outline these two case studies and because there has been so little written about incorporating international guest experts into academic development programmes, this chapter will now outline the professional development models for blended learning that we have adapted for use in designing our approaches to the two case studies.

## APPLYING PROFESSIONAL DEVELOPMENT MODELS FOR BLENDED LEARNING

There are a number of models of professional development for blended learning and e-learning that we found useful in designing our approaches to interinstitutional collaboration. These models can be classified into the following categories.

1.  Practice models, where examples would be Salmon's (2000) five-step model of online learning, Laurillard's (2001) conversational model, and the CSALT (Centre for Studies in Advanced Learning Technology, 2001) networked learning model.
2.  Theoretical accounts developed in a research context and designed to provide coherent explanations of learning phenomena. Examples would be accounts written from the perspective of activity theory (Issroff & Scanlon, 2005), cognitive and constructivist theories (Thompson, 2001), or theories of individual learning differences or styles (Sense, 2007).
3.  Taxonomies and ontologies and other practical accounts exist that do not seem to fit any modeling framework such as case studies, action research reports (Zuber-Skerritt, 1992), project findings, or staff development materials. They are published through a variety of learning and teaching groups such as JISC (Joint Information Systems Committee) and the Higher Education Academy in the United Kingdom.

It is the third type of model listed above that has been selected for this book chapter because it seeks to explore the possibilities and problems inherent in interinstitutional academic development collaboration through a case-study methodology.

In supporting e-learning practice, Sharpe (2004) has proposed a typology consisting of consideration of the following characteristics to provide effective support for practitioners wishing to develop and design e-learning: usability, contextualisation, professional learning promotion, community work, and good learning design promotion. The curriculum design applied in these two online case studies addresses each of these categories, especially the issues of promoting professional learning and working within national and international academic communities. More recently, a six-stage generic model was developed for e-learning professional development (ePD) within the further education sector in the United Kingdom that is intended to support the raising of e-learning capability within the teaching and learning environment (Learning and Skills Network, 2007). With particular reference to an Australian context, Anderson and Henderson (2004) suggest a model within a pragmatic approach to extend the traditional boundaries of face-to-face training and sustain professional development for teachers in the use of e-learning. The key principles embedded in these models have also been applied in the construction of these two online academic development programmes, as will be highlighted below.

# INTERNATIONAL COLLABORATION IN ACTION

Two case studies are presented: one from the Dublin Institute of Technology, Ireland, and one from the University of Queensland, Australia. The international collaboration that took place in both programmes will then be discussed in terms of designing relevant activities to maximise the effectiveness of the participation of the guest lecturers. The intention is not to directly compare the cases per se as the subject and contexts are different. Table 1 shows a number of key variables for the two cases as it is useful to see at a glance the scope of each module.

## Case Study 1: Designing E-Learning

A postgraduate diploma module in third-level learning and teaching entitled Designing E-Learning is offered via blended delivery for academic staff in higher education in Ireland. Higgins and O'Keeffe (2004) speak of effective e-learning and good content, and express a belief that most if not all learners learn best through blended learning.

*Table 1. The scope of the two case studies*

| Module Title | Designing E-Learning | Remotely Interested: Supervising Off-Campus Research Students |
|---|---|---|
| Number of Participants | 17 academic teachers | 27 postgraduate supervisors |
| Context | Irish higher education Academic development Postgraduate diploma programme on e-learning | Australian higher education Academic development programme on remote supervision |
| Virtual Learning Environment | WebCT™ | Blackboard™ |
| Other Technologies in Use | Audio tools Blogging Discussion forum & chat Interactive whiteboard Videoconferencing | Discussion forum Online quizzes |
| Online Activities | Individual Paired Small-group problem-based learning | Individual, self-paced learning Asynchronous participant interaction and discussion |

Blended learning, as the name suggests, consists of a blend of at least two pedagogical approaches. Within the context of this Irish case study, blended learning is the integration of the face-to-face PBL in a classroom with e-learning technologies. For example, the classroom is used by the PBL group to discuss critical concepts, and the discussion boards, e-mail, and synchronous chat room in the online environment WebCT are used to encourage the international dimension to participant dialogue around the concept. In addition, where relevant, guest lecturers have recommended resources for the e-library and provided important contextual and background information for their profile area. See Figure 1 for an illustration of the module design, with specific components that have been utilised for international collaboration highlighted in blue. There are four main components to the online site: resources, module information, the PBL collaborative area (where the participants and the guest lecturers dialogue), and the prob-lem work space (where the participants work iteratively together to produce the end product of the module).

This module is part of an accredited professional development programme for academic staff. A specific approach was taken to the design and delivery of this module by using PBL as the dominant pedagogical model. An international dimension was integrated into the design of the problem by introducing online collaboration with peers in Australia over the 10 weeks of the module's duration.

Activity features at the heart of the design of the module. Communication and collaboration activities in the module included peer, lecturer, and international guest-expert communications, which all supported the participants in their questioning, challenging, and constructing of knowledge about the design of e-learning. Strands of recent thought about effective learning and professional development stress the primacy of peer

*Figure 1. Schema of the international dimension to the designing e-learning module*

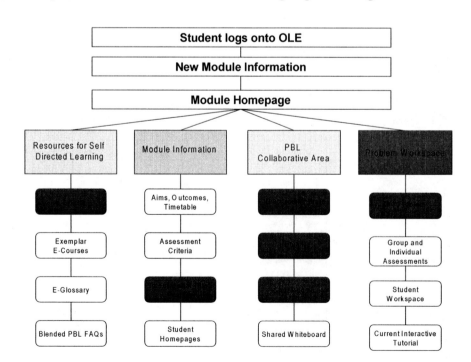

interaction, continuing reflection, the importance of experience, and the grounding of theory in practice (Kolb, 1984; Schön, 1990; Wenger, 1998). Figure 2 shows the different levels at which activity takes place. Participants begin the module with a number of activities designed to allow them to become well acquainted with each other and build trust and collegiality in their PBL groups. This evolves into a widening of perspectives by interacting with international guest lecturers. Central to this is the sharing of experience and perceptions as academics working in different disciplines, but all with the same intention of wishing to design e-learning and PBL courses. Tasks have been designed to enable the participants to engage with conceptual frameworks in the field of e-learning and PBL, and through the PBL experience, they begin the journey of applying theory to practice. The tools used to support this learning process are asynchronous discussion boards, synchronous chat rooms, reflection through blogging software, and the face-to-face PBL tutorial itself.

Liberman (2000) believes that the building of teacher networks or communities is increasingly seen as a way of fostering the conditions in which this type of development can take place. An experiential view of learning informs the way we, as academic developers, design and modify our courses as we believe that there is no substitute for our own experience delivering these courses. However, inherent in this is our belief in providing ourselves with opportunity for reflection and research and to allow both to feed into subsequent stages of course design.

## Case Study 2: Supervising Off-Campus Research Students

An online module on remote supervision, entitled Remotely Interested: Supervising Off-Campus Research Students, is offered as part of a non-accredited academic development programme on postgraduate supervision at an Australian university. This full-year programme, Becoming

*Figure 2. Activity in the module*

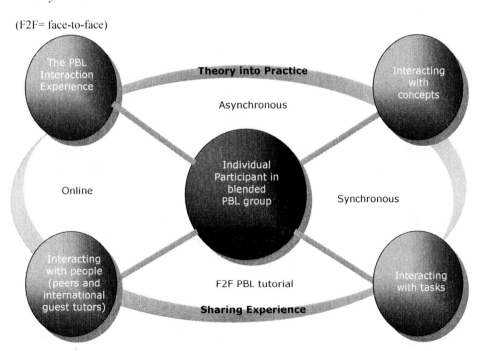

an Effective Supervisor, also adopts a blended approach to learning, containing three face-to-face interactive sessions on aspects of postgraduate supervision, one online e-learning module, and one mentoring module based within the participants' school or disciplinary area. The content and style of delivery are deliberately matched, particularly in the online module, which is about the pedagogical issues and strategies involved in supervising students from a distance using the growing array of available online technologies (Manathunga, 2002). In Australia, off-campus research students are officially classified as *remote*. They may be off-shore or international students who are located at some distance from the campus; they are enrolled in or based externally due to work and/or family commitments.

The rationale for this module is derived from a number of factors. First of all, remote or online supervision is likely to become an increasing feature of postgraduate supervision work for many supervisors as more international students elect to remain in their own countries while undertaking higher degrees in research and as mature-age students with a range of work and/or family commitments increasingly enroll in research studies. Even for on-campus students, the availability of a myriad of e-technologies that can support postgraduate supervision has led to a rapid increase in supervision via e-mail, online chat sessions and discussion fora, and a number of Web-cam technologies. Second, many supervisors lack experience in online teaching and technologies, and this module presents them with the opportunity to engage in online learning. The module participants are also from a range of disciplinary and professional backgrounds, including the health sciences, sciences, engineering, social sciences, and humanities. While the programme is largely designed for new or intending supervisors, many participants have supervised research students for considerable periods of time, ensuring that there is a full spectrum of supervision experience levels in the group. In this particular module, some su-

pervisors are already supervising remote research students while others are interested in future remote supervision; others supervise students who engage in lengthy periods of fieldwork and require extended periods of remote guidance.

In a similar way to the design of the Designing E-Learning module described in Case Study 1, the 2-week module on remote supervision requires the participants to engage in a range of activities, including reading course materials and readings, listening to example audio files, and engaging in online activities in the discussion forum (see Figure 3). In the first week of the module, which explores the issues students and supervisors face in remote supervision, former remote student and supervisor Dr. Ted Brown along with Associate Professor Sylvia Rodger joins the discussion forum. Rodger and Brown (2000) jointly wrote "Enhancing Graduate Supervision in Occupational Therapy Education through Alternative Delivery," which is used as a key reading in this part of the programme. They are able to provide the participants with additional insights into these issues from personal experience and from the research they conducted for this article. Figure 3 outlines the three main components of the online Web site. These include resources for self-directed learning, which are described above; tasks and modules, which explain the programme's stimulus material and online activities; and communications, where lecturers, participants, and national and international guest lecturers carry out the online activities and discussion. Figure 3 has also highlighted the location of the specific national and international components within the programme.

Strategies for effective remote supervision are explored in the second week of the module and are supported by the involvement in the discussion forum of Professor Roly Sussex, who provided an example audio file as an indication of the ways technology can be used to provide remote research students with feedback on their writing. It is also at this point in the programme

*Figure 3. Schema of the international dimension to a module on remote supervision*

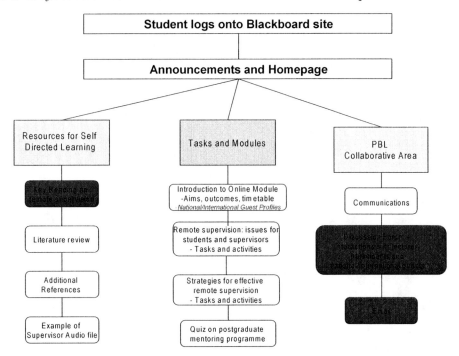

that one of the authors, an Irish practitioner on e-learning and my coauthor in this book chapter, joins the discussion forum and provides advice on the use of innovative technologies for effective remote supervision. When the programme was conducted in 2005 and 2006, she was also a remote doctorate student herself, ensuring that she could provide additional insights into the issues faced by remote research students (see Figure 3).

## Evaluation of the International Collaborative Approach

Networking with other academics and academic developers internationally is a strong feature of these modules, and practice in designing e-learning and e-supervision is enhanced by the multiple perspectives this collaboration brings. In recent years, through the Designing E-Learning module,

communities of practice have been developed with colleagues in Scotland, Finland, and most recently, Australia. In the Remote Supervision module, international online collaboration has occurred at several locations within Australia and with Ireland. The essence of these modules involves participants being brought together by joining in common activities.

In the first case study, the group meets online with the asynchronous feature of the online learning environment WebCT, which is designed to scaffold participants as they organise their PBL group task then synthesise, post, and critique the results of their deliberations. Real-time online events occur throughout this model through the WebCT Synchronous Chatroom tool, which is used for problem-solving areas of the curriculum so that the lecturer can help students on a one-to-one or one-to-small-group basis. In the second case study, participants are joined by national and international guest lecturers from Melbourne and Ireland in the asynchronous discussion forum provided by Blackboard. In both cases, participants interact with each other through posting e-mail and discussion-board questions. The strengths of this approach are the online collaborative discussions, presentations by participants, and interaction between online lecturers, participants, and international guest lecturers from Australia and Ireland.

The purpose of an asynchronous link via a discussion board was to rejuvenate the groups' work and discussions by introducing, in the first case, two guest lecturers from TEDI in the University of Queensland, Australia, and, in the second case, guest lecturers from Monash University in Melbourne, Australia, and the Learning and Teaching Centre in the Dublin Institute of Technology, Ireland. Through such expansion of physical classroom boundaries, an MP3 audio file adds live interaction to asynchronous distance learning. Such guest lecturers can be invited in to join the conference so students can interact directly with experts in their fields (Cotlar & Shimabukuro, 1995).

In the first case study, some of the varied interactions between participants and international guest lecturers included discussions about how to assess online participation, how guest lecturers can keep up with the volume of online postings, how to maintain participant motivation for e-learning and collaborative learning, how to make the most of e-learning in visual disciplines, the use of online role play, and how a guest lecturer can pick up on early signs of problems for first-year students.

The inclusion of one short vignette of guest-lecturer intervention in online discussions clearly shows the development of a key issue in the Designing E-Learning module. The topic that arose for discussion centred on the cause and impact of online bullying between students.

*Participant: These questions have being troubling me since I started reflecting on my experience as an online student. How does or can a lecturer recognise online bullying, is it peer pressure or intimidation? ...could silence or non/minimum participation in online chats and discussions be perceived as peer intimidation if for no other reason than a lack of confidence by the timid individual? [In a group learning scenario] can people who seemingly reply to each other on an individual basis throughout all online discussions be seen as not listening to the other individuals in the group? It would appear that seeing a friendship form F2F is more acceptable and obvious than seeing it form online.*

*Tutor: I think you've raised really important and difficult issues that are so different from face-to-face teaching. I think it is extremely difficult for us as lecturers to recognise online bullying, peer pressure and intimidation. There's also the whole issue of lurking and silence and what that means and how we interpret it. Silence can mean all sorts of things like busy workloads (like you say), wanting to reflect and respond to a full debate at the end, lacking confidence, lurking and getting lots from the conversation and using it in other ways etc.*

*For some quieter people, the online environment is great because they can carefully construct their responses and re-read them to make sure they make sense before sending them and it means they don't have to try and jump into fast free-flowing discussions like you do in face-to-face settings. I've heard that students whose second language is English often feel more comfortable with email and other online types of communication for those reasons.*

*Participant: Thanks! You have given me a new insight into how online responses or lack of does not always mean that the individual is being negative or over controlling. The tutor's [lecturer's] responses has now prompted me to think about my own personality and how I might be perceived online by others in my learning group.*

In addition, by sharing a number of professional and personal experiences with this participant, one of the authors was able to convey her meaning about the important issue of online bullying in a coherent and meaningful way.

The use of audio messages in this module was well received by the participants:

*Thank you for your very generous contributions and the wonderful sites and knowledge you have given us. I have just finished listening to the recorded messages. The use of the MP3 gives another dimension to eLearning, as it brings the other person to life. (online posting from DIT module participant, 2006)*

*One guest lecturer introduced us to the use of an MP3 Player to record her responses and provided the group with audio feedback to individual questions. At first I did not see the value of this and assumed it as a gimmick rather than a teaching technology to aid learning. I now believe that the wizardry of delivery tools can be used to complement instructional design. It was only after the event that I discovered how extremely important the voice recordings were and saw this as an alternative to live chat and video conferencing.*

*Replacing the typed word with voice recorded messages could make participation easier for some of my students, who can feel embarrassed by the type of difficulties they struggle to cope with such as literacy skills, slower mental processing, attention and organisational difficulties which can lead to internalized negative labels which can result in a lack of confidence. The students can verbally express their perspectives using the audio recordings and can instantly record their thoughts and feelings. (online reflective posting from DIT module Participant, 2006)*

In the second case study, a range of remote postgraduate supervision issues were debated by the lecturer, participants, and the national and international guest lecturers. Table 2 describes this list of topics when the module was delivered in 2005 and 2006.

As a result of the debate, participants were able to gain many useful insights into the issues and dilemmas associated with this breadth of topics and learn about a variety of effective online supervision strategies and technologies from national and international experts. As one participant in this module indicated, national and international guest lecturers helped students "consider some

*Table 2. Online interactions with national and international participants*

| 2005 | 2006 |
|---|---|
| • Missing subtle nonverbal cues about students having difficulties<br>• Recommended frequency of contact with remote students<br>• Positive aspects of remote supervision (written, recorded interaction, international collaboration, etc.)<br>• Research methodologies in online courses<br>• Modes of interacting with remote students including audio and video | • Costs for students of remote vs. face-to-face study<br>• Keeping student motivated and procrastination issues<br>• Required continuity of contact<br>• Negotiating with remote principal and local associate supervisors<br>• Possible lack of commitment by remote students given their other responsibilities<br>• Similarities between remote and on-campus student issues<br>• Breaking the ice with remote students<br>• Using audio for supervision interactions<br>• Useful online activities for supervision interaction |

of the complexities remote students have to face when conducting their research away from a traditional campus setting" (Remote Supervision module participant, 2006).

## Benefits of the International Collaborative Approach

Open-ended qualitative questionnaires were used in both modules to collect evaluative data and selected quotes from participants are included to illustrate the range of perceived impacts felt by the participants as each module came to a close. Participants emphasised some key benefits in using the international collaborative approach adopted in the two cases: including the provision and broadening of multiple perspectives, opening up the potential for networking, expanding the sense of being part of an international community of practice, and very importantly tackling the issue of isolation that many academics feel in their practice, revealing that colleagues from other countries and disciplines were also facing similar problems and coming up with strategies to cope with them. Each is now discussed in more detail with supporting evidence from the qualitative questionnaires.

Interacting with peers from higher education institutions internationally was regarded as important for providing multiple perspectives to learning collaboratively: "Being in a blended community of like-minded individuals was a positive and exciting experience—especially having international guest professionals. Experiencing live video conferencing, online discussions, and podcasting have left me with a great sense of achievement as a learner" (DIT module participant, 2006).

Bringing internationality into the groups to discuss the variety of ways of using different media in education proved highly influential to broadening perspectives for the participants in the module: "It was wonderful to be able to communicate with such knowledgeable academ-

ics from halfway round the world" (DIT module participant, 2005). Another participant said,

*What I really enjoyed was having other people coming in to speak with us. For example, the international guest tutors [lecturers] who joined our online discussions, which was a huge input and gave us great variety in our debates on topics. They introduced new perspectives and a touch of the exotic to our learning. (DIT module participant, 2005)*

Similar feedback was received from 2005 and 2006 participants in the Remote Supervision module. In particular, participants emphasised the effectiveness of guest lecturers: "Hearing the perspective from people from other institutions and also from people from different countries provides new perspectives and insights...and dimensions" (Remote Supervision module participant, 2005).

They also suggested that national and international guest lecturers provided an

*opportunity to see how other institutions (and individuals) manage remote student supervision. They gave me suggestions for managing remote students that I had never previously considered, e.g. using online chat [and]...helped me to appreciate other ways in which students and supervisors can interact. (Remote Supervision module participant, 2006)*

An external evaluator of the module on remote supervision also emphasised the value of incorporating multiple international perspectives. In particular, she commented on the pedagogical benefits of including "remote students and experienced supervisors...(including a supervisor of students whose second language is English, who also has suggestions for new and innovative technological tools) and an online learning expert, who are all able to contribute different perspectives on remote supervision" (external evaluator,

UQ module, 2006). She also highlighted the vast potential for networking and broadening the sense of being part of an international community of practice. She commented, "The effect of having an expert based in Ireland and on leave in Spain is to extend the 'research community' and suggest the benefits of online access." Similarly, the external examiner for the Designing E-Learning module drew attention to the importance of the international collaboration between module participants and the international guest lecturers: "From the participants' perspective, this is an innovative and exciting use of the technology to place their learning in an authentic academic context and enhance their experience of eLearning; they are truly seeing the value that technology can bring to a learning event."

Another benefit identified by participants in the Remote Supervision module was the reassurance that remote students and supervisors all around the world were dealing with similar problems and challenges. As one participant indicated,

*If the same problems are encountered by people across the board (including external and international participants) then it adds to the evidence that some issues might be universal and not just due to problems/oversights/procedures at your own university. So essentially [this]...allows you to evaluate better the "uniqueness" of the issues encountered (i.e. common, institute-specific, field-specific etc)....[It] might not help you to solve the issue but makes you feel better if you know everyone has the same problem;-). (Remote Supervision module participant, 2006)*

The technology also facilitated a burgeoning network within the module and beyond with the international guest lecturers, and this is potentially a positive force for change in practice. The participants themselves believe that digital technologies will progressively extend opportunities to engage in collaborative reflective PBL practice across disciplines:

For me the video conferencing sessions on the module with the international guest tutors [lecturers] were activating events for my learning. We had things in common with them as fellow educators and they got us to consider key learning issues as their postings were very deep and really got you to think through an issue. We continued to liaise with them for weeks after the module closed and one of the Australian tutors [lecturers] invited us to participate in their own online courses with fellow teachers from there. (DIT module participant, 2006)

## Limitations of the International Collaborative Approach

It is also important to highlight some of the limitations involved in inviting external national and international guest lecturers into online academic development programmes. First, a sense of pressure can pervade both sides of the online communication. In interacting with experts from a discipline, participants in a module can feel they are under scrutiny. There can also be pressure for international guest lecturers inherent in dealing with what can be a large number of often vague queries from participants. This can make it difficult to craft suitable responses for each participant query when, quite often, the guest lecturers are brought into the module after it has begun and are lacking knowledge about participants' contexts and backgrounds. Also, technical problems can arise at any time, and timetable issues can be a problem, especially if the international guest lecturers are from different hemispheres. Each of these limitations is now discussed in more detail with supporting evidence from the qualitative questionnaires.

While participants in the Remote Supervision module did not identify any problems with the involvement of national and international guest lecturers, it is possible to reflect upon the nature of some of the online interactions between participants and guests and to draw upon our own experience of being international guests. Some of the initial interactions between participants and guests in the Remote Supervision module appear to suggest that participants can feel under pressure, at least at first, to think of something to ask the international guest just to make them feel welcome and included in the online dialogue. This can result in very open-ended requests for information or perspectives. For example, one participant asked the guest lecturer, "From your experience, do you have a list of suggested online activities that work well for interactions between students and advisors? Are there some activities that do not work well?" (Remote Supervision module online discussion forum, August 15, 2006). The guest lecturer, in her response, clearly recognised the underlying purpose of the question and acknowledged the invitation to join the discussion by the participant: "many thanks for the question, and for bringing me into your discussion this week" (Remote Supervision module online discussion forum, August 16, 2006). It was important to recognise that such a broad question needed to be broken down in order to give a focused and meaningful response. However, this question was able to generate considerable further discussion and debate and, in many senses, even face-to-face discussions often begin broadly and then delve down into specific issues and perspectives.

Looking at this same issue from another perspective, it can also be difficult to avoid the discussions that may simply be a one-way channeling of resources and advice from experts by participants instead of a two-way exploration of key issues. In the Designing E-Learning module, a number of participants opened their dialogue with such requests.

*What are your views and advice re the evaluation of eLearning courses and can you suggest some useful websites?*

*I've two questions I'd like to ask you. It would appear from the volume of literature from Australia in the field of online learning that you guys are pretty much world leaders in this. Is that so? The other thing I'd like is any resources you can give on learner assessment. (online postings from DIT module participants, 2005)*

It is important to convey to participants that the opportunity for collaboration need not turn into an inquisition. One participant in particular set a series of long and sometimes very discipline-specific questions for the guest lecturer.

*I have been wondering how difficult is it to start an online module or programme if there has been no experience of it in one's institute. What do you feel are the initial essential requirements? Are there real benefits for the Management?*

*What type of assessment works best in a learning support site such as ours?*

*I find the on-screen comments can be a little condescending after a while. Is there another method of feedback that is low on labour, yet effective?*

*Is online learning very popular "down under"? Has it been successful in construction education?*

*Do you have any research on what students think before, during and after information skills online modules? (online postings from DIT module participants, 2005-2006)*

From a participant perspective also, there may exist what can be termed a novice-expert gap. In the Designing E-Learning module, some of the participants who had previously identified themselves as novices as regards their knowledge or experience of e-learning were initially wary of electronic discussion exchange with the guest lecturers and expressed fears of appearing inadequate in the public discussions in front of the international experts: "The guest lecturers posted encouraging introductory messages and these removed my fear of interacting with expert practitioners in the eLearning field. I learnt that the human touch is possible in this environment despite the cool nature of electronic delivery" (online posting from DIT module participant, 2006).

However, as suggested here, this can be tempered by a thorough introduction made by the experts to the participants highlighting their own journey on this pathway. Once this unease is overcome, the participants settle into a mutual development of ideas with the guest lecturers: "We look forward to your comments; it's really great to have an international dimension to our learning" (online posting from DIT module participant, 2006).

As an international guest, you can feel like you lack a lot of information about the participants' contexts and backgrounds. This can create concerns that you may be overly general or simplistic in your response or that you may have given a response that is completely irrelevant to the participants' contexts. As an international guest, one of the authors has felt that she has had to rely on the patience and good will of the participants to respond generously to her lack of understanding about their context and issues. In particular, this highlights the need in online academic programmes for cultural sensitivity and an understanding of educational practices in other countries (MacKinnon & Manathunga, 2003). These intercultural communication skills are, however, a vital part of teaching and researching in globalised higher education and, as a result, provide participants with an excellent opportunity to enhance their own skill levels.

In some ways, these limitations can be partly addressed by incorporating in the module content as much information as possible about the background and expertise of both the international guests and the participants. It also helps to provide the international guest with an indication of the projects or assessment topics being explored by

participants. As outlined in Figures 1 and 3, the authors have factored these considerations into the design of their online modules. The other way these issues can be addressed is to emphasise the importance of generosity, patience, respectfulness, and good will in online discussions. While these characteristics assist in the effective flowing of discussion in any face-to-face session (especially in intercultural learning settings), they are even more vital in online programmes, where misunderstandings may more easily occur because of a lack of nonverbal and other contextual information.

On a more pragmatic note, there may be a number of technical difficulties and limitations involved in incorporating national and international guest lecturers into online academic development programmes. One of the significant things we have learnt about online technology is to try and keep it simple. Technical problems tend to grow when crossing country borders. However, these difficulties are gradually being resolved as the technology develops. For example, until quite recently, videoconferencing was an expensive, labour-intensive, and unreliable technology. Over the past 5 years, this has dramatically changed so that now video over IP (Internet protocol) has become cheap, simple, and effective.

Time-tabling can also prove to be another obstacle. Many different course-calendar arrangements exist in our international academic world, making joint time-tabling quite a hassle. In addition, different time zones, even in asynchronous online communication, can sometimes create confusion and may increase expectations of how long international guests need to be involved in online discussions.

## DISCUSSION

Embedding an international dimension in the learning and teaching process, with special reference to the potential role of ICT in that process, is more complex than it first appears. Whilst theoretical models of professional development (e.g., Sharpe, 2004) emphasise a number of different levels such as usability, contextualisation, professional learning promotion, community work, and good learning–design promotion, we have found in practice that integrating international collaboration needs to be infused throughout all aspects of curriculum design. Through international collaboration between participants on academic development programmes, there certainly is potential to contribute to the creation and translation of knowledge about learning, teaching, and supervision. This contributes toward a flexibility of bridging across structures in such social and academic networks. We believe that the model of exchange between participants and guest lecturers in both case studies has been fruitful in unpacking the relationship between theory and practice in the pursuit of knowledge about learning, teaching, and remote supervision.

The value of international collaboration as experienced in the cases detailed in this chapter is illuminated through a consideration of how the educator can design relevant discussion activities to enhance the engagement of the guest lecturer(s) with the module participants. Brookfield and Preskill (1999) have claimed for many years to be unwaveringly committed to teaching through discussion and point to the benefits consistently enjoyed through practice. Of the 15 advantages the learner experiences from participating in discussion, a number have appeared in these case studies, particularly as evidenced by the participant quotes previously: an increase in the breadth of discussions, participants becom-

*Table 3. International online critical discourse*

| Value of International Online Discussions | Relevant Activities |
|---|---|
| Helps participants recognise and investigate their assumptions | • With the group's knowledge and permission, assign different roles to participants with some being asked to be a respectful "devil's advocate"<br>• Encourage international guest lecturers to respectfully unpack participant's implicit assumptions about e-learning or remote supervision |
| Encourages attentive, respectful listening | • Set ground rules for respectful communication in the course<br>• Model inclusive practice and respectful listening in the lecturer's own postings |
| Helps participants explore a diversity of perspectives | • Deliberately choose international guest lecturers who you know have very different perspectives from your own |
| Increases breadth and makes participants more empathetic to the experience of online students | • Ask students or former students to join in discussions of online learning<br>• Provide case studies and readings that highlight students' experiences of online learning |
| Shows respect for participants' voices and experiences | • Set ground rules for respectful acknowledgement of participants' perspectives |
| Helps participants develop skills of synthesis and integration | • Model how to effectively summarise and weave together participants' postings in the lecturer's contributions to online discussions |
| Increases participants' awareness of and tolerance for ambiguity or complexity in a topic | • Deliberately choose international guest lecturers who you know have very different perspectives from your own<br>• Present arguments for and against the use of particular online technologies to prompt debate and higher order understanding |

ing aware of the need to be more empathetic to the experience of online students, participants becoming connected to a topic, and raised awareness by participants of tolerance for ambiguity or complexity in a topic. Table 3 shows all the rewards experienced by participants in the online discussions. Recognising the importance of critical discourse within professional development, it is argued that experiencing these benefits can lead toward improvement in academics' approaches to e-learning and e-teaching.

As a result, participants are given the opportunity to engage in the final two stages of Salmon's (2000) model of computer-mediated conferencing: knowledge construction and development. This is not only valuable for students' own learning about e-design or remote supervision, or whatever topic the academic development programme is emphasising. It also models for them how effective e-moderators can encourage students to reach these higher order levels of engagement in online learning. Therefore, their comfort levels with online technologies are greatly improved (Donnelly & O'Rourke, 2007) and their own approaches to online teaching and learning are enhanced through experiential learning (Biggs, 1999; Brookfield, 1990). In particular, this experiential form of academic development enhances academics' ability to respond to the learning needs of the Internet generation and to make the most of the pedagogical and technical possibilities afforded by e-learning technologies (Oblinger, 2006; Oblinger & Oblinger, 2005; Seely Brown, 2000).

Specifically, the academic participants experience firsthand the benefits of incorporating external national and international guest lecturers in online programmes and are, therefore, more likely to adopt this approach in their own online teaching. This chapter confirms the work of Janes (2000) on the value of linking with international guest lecturers in an online environment. It has provided evidence from the voice of the participants themselves as to the coherence and depth reached in their online discussions. It also extends

Salmon's (2000) ideas about how to broaden online conference experiences, in particular by the provision of examples of online discussion activities to attain critical discourse amongst a group of interdisciplinary participants.

Academic participants involved in online academic development programmes that incorporate national and international guest lecturers also have the potential to develop ongoing teaching and research partnerships with academics around the world, as Janes (2000) also found. This chapter reveals a number of case studies of such long-term international collaboration. This is beneficial to encourage long-term partnerships among academic staff working in disciplines. It also enables the building and strengthening of academic developers' knowledge and enhances the effectiveness of the academic development international community of practice.

Teaching in higher education has often been characterized as an isolated activity, yet opportunities for lecturers to work and learn together are slowly increasing. Underlying this shift is the view that as academic staff work on new practices and teaching challenges together, they will reveal different teaching styles and experiences, express varied perspectives, and stimulate reflection and professional growth. The two case studies discussed in this chapter raise questions about how lecturers participate and learn in their professional development programmes and how to structure such collaboration to maximise lecturer learning.

## FUTURE RESEARCH DIRECTION

There is still a great deal to be thought about, debated, and researched in the area of international involvement in online academic development programmes. In particular, more case studies of the flow-on effects of online academic development and the inclusion of external participants to online student learning programmes need to be written. As part of the former, it may be important to explore large-scale rollouts in the undergraduate curriculum to move toward a more sustainable training and development culture in an institution. So, too, it would be useful to have more case studies of long-term teaching and research collaborations between academics that have occurred as a result of interacting with external participants in online academic development programmes. There also need to be more intensive evaluations of the efficacy of this approach and more longitudinal studies to confirm its effectiveness.

## CONCLUSION

This chapter has argued that the impact of international collaboration in online academic development programmes was important in these case studies. We have argued that the quality of online academic development programmes was enhanced by involving national and international guests in online discussions. A review of the literature in the theoretical and practical field of academic development and intra-institution international collaboration suggested that the presence and participation of guest speakers was important because it would allow diverse perspectives to be explored and debated. This chapter indicates how this strategy can be effectively applied to the online teaching environment, which links with the aims of this book to support academic staff in experimenting with e-learning and to value e-teaching. In particular, these case studies demonstrated that international collaboration in online academic development programmes enhances participants' abilities as teachers to help their own students recognise and investigate their assumptions, develop respectful listening and other communication skills, increase their cognitive agility, develop their capacities for critical thinking and synthesizing information and viewpoints, and increase their tolerance for ambiguity or complexity in various topics. As a

result, it emphasises the importance of teachers or lecturers experiencing e-learning from a learner's perspective before engaging in e-teaching, which is a key theme of this book.

While there is still a great deal of research needed into this issue, this chapter has confirmed a number of implications of incorporating national and international guest lecturers into academic development programmes that enhance online learning and teaching and strengthen an international academic development community of practice.

## REFERENCES

Abrami, P., Bernard, R., Wade, A., & Schmid, R. (2006). A review of e-learning in Canada: A rough sketch of the evidence, gaps and promising directions. *Canadian Journal of Learning and Technology, 32*(3), 119-139. Retrieved April 18, 2006, from http://www.cjlt.ca/content/vol32.3/abrami.html

Agostinho, S., Lefoe, G., & Hedberg, J. (1997, July 5-9). *Online collaboration for learning.* Paper presented at the Third Australian World Wide Web Conference (AusWeb97), Australia.

Anderson, N., & Henderson, M. (2004). E-PD: Blended models of sustaining teacher professional development in digital literacies. *E-Learning, 1*(3), 383-394.

Bowles, M. S. (2004). *Relearning to e-learn.* Melbourne, Australia: Melbourne University Press.

Brookfield, S. D., & Preskill, S. (1999). *Discussion as a way of teaching: Tools and techniques for university teachers.* Buckingham, United Kingdom: The Society for Research into Higher Education & Open University Press.

ChanLin, L. J., & Chan, K. C. (2007). Integrating inter-disciplinary experts for supporting problem-based learning. *Innovations in Education and Teaching International, 44*(2), 211-224.

Cotlar, M., & Shimabukuro, J. N. (1995). Stimulating learning with electronic guest lecturing. In Z. L. Berge & M. Collins (Eds.), *Computer mediated communication and the online classroom: Vol. 3. Distance learning* (pp. 105-128). Cresskill, NJ: Hampton Press.

Donnelly, R., & O'Brien, F. (2003). Towards the promotion of effective e-learning practice for academic staff development in DIT. *Level 3.* Retrieved May 20, 2007, from http://level3.dit.ie/pdf/issue1_donnelly_obrien.pdf

Donnelly, R., & O'Farrell, C. (2006). Constructivist e-learning for staff engaged in continuous professional development. In J. O'Donoghue (Ed.), *Technology supported learning and teaching: A staff perspective* (pp. 146-159). Hershey, PA: Information Science Publishing.

Donnelly, R., & O'Rourke, K. (2007). What now? Evaluating elearning CPD practice in Irish third-level education. *Journal of Further and Higher Education, 31*(1), 31-41.

Ferrier, F. (1992, July 12-15). *Not more of the same stuff: Student dissatisfaction with postgraduate courses.* Paper presented at the 15th Annual Higher Education Research & Development Society of Australasia Conference, Sydney, Australia.

Gibbs, G. (2004, June 21-23). *The nature of educational development in a changing context.* Keynote Presentation at the International Consortium for Educational Development Conference, Ottawa, Canada.

Harasim, L. (1989). On-line education: A new domain. In R. Mason & A. Kaye (Eds.), *Mindweave: Communication, computers and distance education* (pp. 50-62). Oxford, United Kingdom: Pergamon Press.

Higgins, K., & O'Keeffe, D. (2004). *An online digital engineering module companion using biomedical applications.* Paper presented at the Fourth Annual Irish Educational Technology Users Conference, Waterford, Ireland.

Issroff, K., & Scanlon, E. (2005). Activity theory and higher education: Evaluating learning technologies. *Journal of Computer Assisted Learning, 21,* 430-439.

Janes, D. P. (2000). *Teaching online in a postgraduate certificate in technology-based distributed learning.* Paper presented to the International Online Tutoring Skills (OTiS) E-Workshop. Retrieved May 12, 2000, from http://otis.scotcit.ac.uk/casestudy/janes.doc

Kandlbinder, P. (2000, July 2-5). *Peeking under the covers: Understanding the foundations of online academic staff development.* Paper presented at the Australian Society of Educational Technology & Higher Education Research & Development Society of Australasia Conference, Toowoomba, Australia.

Kearsley, G. (2000). *Online education: Learning and teaching in cyberspace.* Belmont, CA: Wadsworth/Thomson Learning.

Kezar, A. (2001). *Understanding and facilitating organisational change in the 21st century: Recent research and conceptualisations* (ASHE-ERIC Higher Education Report, Vol. 28, No. 4). San Francisco: Jossey Bass.

Knapper, C. (2004, June 21-23). *University teaching and educational development: What have we achieved?* Keynote Presentation at the International Consortium for Educational Development Conference, Ottawa, Canada.

Knight, P. T. (2002). A systemic approach to professional development: Learning as practice. *Teaching and Teacher Education, 18*(3), 229-241.

Kolb, D. (1984). *Experiential learning: Experience as the source of learning and development.* Englewood Cliffs, NJ.

Laurillard, D. (2001). *Rethinking university teaching: A framework for the effective use of educational technology.* London: Routledge.

Learning and Skills Network. (2007). *A professional development framework for e-learning.* Gillingham, United Kingdom: Impress.

MacKinnon, D., & Manathunga, C. (2003). Going global with assessment: What to do when the dominant culture's literacy drives assessment. *Higher Education Research & Development, 22*(2), 131-144.

Mainka, C. (2007). Putting staff first in staff development for the effective use of technology in teaching. *British Journal of Educational Technology, 38*(1), 158-160.

Manathunga, C. (2002). Designing online modules: An Australian example in teacher education. *International Journal of Instructional Media, 29*(2), 185-195.

McAlpine, L., & Emrick, A. (2003, August 26-30). *Discipline-based curriculum development: An opportunity for sustainable collegial faculty development.* Paper Presented at the 10th Biennial Conference of European Association for Research on Learning and Instruction, Padova, Italy.

McNaught, C. (2000). Technology: The challenge of change. In R. King, D. Hill, & B. Hemmings (Eds.), *University and diversity* (pp. 88-102). Wagga Wagga, Australia: Keon Publications.

McPherson, M., & Nunes, M. B. (2004). *Developing innovation in online learning: An action research framework.* London: Routledge Falmer.

Mering, J., & Robbie, D. (2005, July 4-7). *Education and electronic learning: Does online learning assist learners and how can it be continuously improved?* Paper presented at the HERDSA Conference, Miri, Malaysia.

Oblinger, D. (2006, September 5-7). *Listening to what we're seeing.* Keynote Presentation at ALT-C, Edinburgh, United Kingdom.

Oblinger, D., & Oblinger, J. (Eds.). (2005). *Educating the Net generation.* Educause.

Panda, S., & Juwah, C. (2006). Professional development of online facilitators in enhancing interactions and engagement: A framework. In C. Juwah (Ed.), *Interactions in online education: Implications for theory and practice* (pp. 207-227). London: Routledge.

Rodger, S., & Brown, T. (2000). Enhancing graduate supervision in occupational therapy education through alternative delivery. *Occupational Therapy International, 7*(3), 163-172.

Salmon, G. (2000). *E-moderating: The key to teaching and learning online.* London: Kogan Page.

Schön, D. (1990). *Educating the reflective practitioner.* San Francisco: Jossey Bass.

Seely Brown, J. (2000). Growing up digital. *Change, 32*(2), 10-11.

Sense, A. (2007). Learning within project practice: Cognitive styles exposed. *International Journal of Project Management, 25*(1), 33-40.

Sharpe, R. (2004). *A typology of effective interventions that support e-learning practice.* JISC.

Shivkumar, S. (2006, September 15-17). *Strategies for improving elearning effectiveness.* Paper presented at the International Workshop on E-Learning for Adult Continuing Education.

Surry, D., & Land, S. (2000). Strategies for motivating higher education faculty to use technology. *Innovation in Education and Training International, 37*(2), 145-153.

Thompson, K. (2001). Constructivist curriculum design for professional development. *Australian Journal of Adult Learning, 41*(1), 94-109.

Weaver, D., Chenicheri, S. N., & Spratt, C. (2005, November 30-December 1). *Evaluation: WebCT and the student experience.* Paper presented at Making a Difference: Evaluations and Assessment Conference, Sydney, Australia.

Wenger, E. (1998). *Communities of practice: Learning, meaning and identity.* Cambridge, United Kingdom: Cambridge University Press.

Wisker, G. (2000, April 23-24). Cross-cultural research supervision and research at a distance: Issues for postgraduate students and supervisors. In M. Kiley & G. Mullins (Eds.), *Quality in Postgraduate Research: Making Ends Meet. Proceedings of the 2000 Quality in Postgraduate Research Conference,* Adelaide, Australia (pp.43-49). Adelaide, Australia: University of Adelaide, Centre for Learning and Professional Development (CLPD).

Zuber-Skerritt, O. (1992). *Professional development in higher education: A theoretical framework for action research.* London: Kogan Page.

## ADDITIONAL READING

The following is a listing of useful references on the key issues identified in this chapter categorized under the following headings: Postgraduate Research Supervision, Blended Learning Environments, Online Academic Development, and Designing Online Collaboration.

## Postgraduate Research Supervision

Pearson, M. (2000, April 13-14). Flexible postgraduate research supervision in an open system. In M. Kiley & G. Mullins (Eds.), *Quality in Postgraduate Research: Making Ends Meet. Proceedings of the 2000 Quality in Postgraduate Research Conference,* Adelaide, Australia (pp. 103-118). Adelaide, Australia: University of Adelaide, Centre for Learning and Professional Development (CLPD).

Pearson discusses the difficulties supervisors face in adapting to use new technology to communicate with students in online modes of learning, and

argues that successful supervision of remote students should still involve some traditional methods such as occasional face-to-face meetings.

Rodger, S., & Brown, G. T. (2000). Enhancing graduate supervision in occupational therapy education through alternative delivery. *Occupational Therapy International, 7*(3), 163-172.

Rodger and Brown's study provides a comprehensive exploration of the issues and challenges both students and supervisors experience in remote supervision. They recommend a number of helpful strategies for effective remote supervision.

Stacey, E. (1997). A virtual campus: The experience of postgraduate students studying through electronic communication and resource access. *UltiBASE.*

Stacey's article explores the usefulness of establishing online discussion forums where students can discuss their research with each other. Stacey found that both students and staff regarded the online programme as an invaluable tool in helping remote students to feel motivated to continue with their studies.

Wisker, G. (2000, April 23-24). Cross-cultural research supervision and research at a distance: Issues for postgraduate students and supervisors. In M. Kiley & G. Mullins (Eds.), *Quality in Postgraduate Research: Making Ends Meet. Proceedings of the 2000 Quality in Postgraduate Research Conference,* Adelaide, Australia (pp. 43-49). Adelaide, Australia: University of Adelaide, Centre for Learning and Professional Development (CLPD).

Wisker examines a group of international students studying in Britain and then returning home to various countries to complete their higher degree studies by distance. She explores the challenges experienced by both remote students and supervisors and recommends several ways to counteract these issues.

Wright, T. (2003). Postgraduate research students: People in context? *British Journal of Guidance and Counseling, 31*(2), 209-227.

Wright identifies a number of problems students experience in studying for higher degrees in research in remote or flexible learning modes. Wright argues that to ensure a smooth supervisor-student relationship, supervisors and students should write out a contract explaining what each person expects from the other, regular progress reviews should occur, and appropriate levels of training and support should be put in place by universities for supervisors.

## Blended Learning Environments

Littlejohn, A., & Pegler, C. (2007). *Preparing for blended e-learning.* London: Routledge.

Of particular relevance to this current work is Chapter VI on environments to integrate activity blends. It recognises that blended problem-based learning is a complex construct and concept and involves detailed planning and implementation by the educator.

Savin-Baden, M. (2006). The challenge of using problem-based learning online. In M. Savin-Baden & K. Wilkie (Eds.), *Problem-based learning online* (pp. 3-13). Maidenhead, United Kingdom: Open University Press.

This text is useful for providing the educator's perspective on a range of key issues for designing and implementing problem-based learning in a blended or fully online environment. It is aimed at the development of an online pedagogy for PBL.

Reinmann, G., Macdonald, J., Donnelly, R., Fransen, J., & Poldner, E. (2007, August 28-September 1). *Blended learning in higher education: Theory and praxis.* Paper presented at the Symposium for EARLI 2007, Budapest, Hungary.

This paper provides evidence from qualitative studies of blended learning in practical situations drawing on tutors' and students' perspectives contrasted with theoretical ideas.

Uden, L., & Beaumont, C. (2006). *Technology and problem-based learning.* Hershey, PA: Information Science Publishing.

This is a practical text that provides a comprehensive overview of what is involved in integrating different learning technologies with a form of inquiry-based learning such as PBL.

Ziegler, M., Paulus, T., & Woodside, M. (2006). Creating a climate of engagement in a blended learning environment. *Journal of Interactive Learning Research, 17*(3), 295-318.

This paper describes the conversational interactions of one online learning group. A climate of engagement emerged from the data analysis as the overarching theme, capturing the essence of the participants' online interactions. Four aspects were found to constitute this climate of engagement: engaging in the online environment, engaging in dialogue, engaging as a group, and engaging in the content. A model of engagement is also proposed that captures the dynamic nature of these participants' interactions.

## Online Academic Development

Donnelly, R. (in press). Virtual problem-based learning communities of practice for teachers and teacher educators: An Irish higher education perspective. In C. Kimble & P. Hildreth (Eds.), *Communities of practice: Creating learning environments for educators* (Vol. 2, pp.). Charlotte, NC: Information Age Publishing.

This chapter explores problem-based learning in a virtual environment, concentrating specifically on how it is used to form and maintain a community of practice for educators in higher education.

Donnelly, R., & O'Farrell, C. (2006). Blended e-learning for continuous professional development of academic staff. In J. O'Donoghue (Ed.), *Technology supported learning and teaching: A staff perspective* (pp. 146-159). Hershey, PA: Information Science Publishing.

This chapter discusses a 4-week blended professional development course for higher education lecturers on e-learning, and highlights the need for streamlined learning experiences that deliver essential topics and learning materials in readily accessible formats. It is believed a central challenge here is to create and sustain quality learning environments of enduring value for teachers.

Panda, S., & Juwah, C. (2006). Professional development of online facilitators in enhancing interactions and engagement: A framework. In C. Juwah (Ed.), *Interactions in online education: Implications for theory and practice* (pp. 207-227). London: Routledge.

This chapter highlights the increased use of the Web for learning and teaching and argues that it has necessitated a reexamination of some of the issues with e-learning and the professional development of academic staff engaged in an online facilitation role.

## Designing Online Collaboration

Price, L., Richardson, J., & Jelfs, A. (2007). Face-to-face versus online tutoring support in distance education. *Studies in Higher Education, 32*(1), 1-20.

This paper explores effective online interaction and conceptions of online tutoring in distance learning environments.

Koschmann, T. D. (2002). Introduction to special issue on studying collaboration in distributed PBL environments. *Distance Education, 23*(1), 28-39.

This is an article that was very helpful in looking at how collaboration can be designed for and supported in an online PBL context.

Jones, C., Cook, J., Jones, A., & De Laat, M. (2007). Collaboration. In G. Conole & M. Oliver (Eds.), *Contemporary perspectives in e-learning research: Themes, methods and impact on practice* (pp. 74-189). London: Routledge.

This chapter focuses on the concept, practice, and research of collaboration. The complete text provides a strong theoretical foundation for the teacher in higher education wishing to explore e-learning; it is research based and considers implications for practice.

McConnell, D. (2006). *E-learning groups and communities.* Maidenhead, United Kingdom: The Society for Research into Higher Education & Open University Press.

This book discusses approaches to online course design from a specific communities and group learning perspective.

McDonald, J., & Mayes, T. (2005, June 24-26). Pedagogically challenged: A framework for the support of course designers in an Australian distance learning university. In *CRLL Conference Proceedings* (Vol. 2, pp. 397-404). Stirling, Scotland: The University of Stirling.

This is a very popular framework proposing a pedagogy for designing interaction in online courses.

# Chapter VI
# Embedding E–Learning in Further Education

**Louise Adele Jakobsen**
*Park Lane College, Leeds, UK*

## ABSTRACT

*This chapter, written from experience in implementing e-learning in further education through various roles, identifies key issues relating to embedding technologies into educational practices. From the concept that the increased expectation for technology to be used is a natural evolution, it identifies key advantages for learners and the learning process in terms of personalisation, differentiation, and interactivity. The importance of taking time to design effective resources, which include higher and deeper levels of feedback, is identified as a motivating factor, especially for independent study. The theme running throughout is the issue of developing staff skills and confidence. Ensuring training opportunities are flexible and manageable is identified as important to successful implementation. The advantages and disadvantages of face-to-face, online, cascaded, structured–play, and observational training and support techniques are highlighted alongside the introduction of a new five-step model to support gradual implementation of virtual learning environments into teaching and learning.*

## INTRODUCTION

This chapter is written from the perspective and experience of implementing and using technology in further education (FE) through various e-learning coordination and management roles, incorporating strategising and staff development responsibilities. It explores and provides examples relating to the concept of e-learning as a blend of traditional and newer techniques and tools, encompassing the use of various technologies with flexible, accessible, and inclusive characteristics to support teaching and enhance learning. It explores how the increased expectation of the use of information learning technologies (ILTs), a term still commonly used in FE linking e-learning and e-leadership (Lifelong Learning Sector Skills Council, 2005), can be dealt with as a change in culture, capitalising on existing pedagogical practices of individualised learning. Links and transferable elements suitable for higher education (HE) are discussed throughout.

Developing from the view that increased use of technology in teaching and learning is a natural evolution, three key ideas are explored.

- The section entitled "Personalisation and Differentiation" explores ways technology, including virtual learning environments (VLEs), can reach learners with different abilities, motivation, learning styles, or pace, and support various additional learning needs. The use of and potential barriers relating to e-portfolios are discussed briefly.
- "Designing Resources" discusses the advantages and disadvantages of using readily available equipment and software to create interesting, motivating, and interactive resources. Key issues relating to developing purely online resources including composing instant feedback for self-assessment are highlighted.
- "Professional Development and Implementation" details strategies that have worked to encourage and increase the use of technology, including examples of training, a descriptive model for utilising online learning environments, the provision of in-class support for first and early use of technology, the championing of roles, and the use of competitions to motivate individuals.

The chapter concludes by establishing where FE is in terms of embedding e-learning and summarises identified links to HE, suggesting where different educational environments can learn from and help each other. Further research is explored and additional reading is recommended.

## A NATURAL EVOLUTION

Arguments for the idea that the increased expectation of the use of e-learning can be dealt with as a culture change are explored initially. It is suggested that this change capitalises on existing practices of individualised learning. McKenna (2004) provides the following perspective: "Our world is transforming everyday. The technological transformations and breakthroughs…are increasing at exponential rates. We…are connecting over great distances, exploring and re-shaping our world…. Mobile telephones [and] computers…unthinkable even fifty years ago, are now considered a normal part of…twenty-first-century life" (p. 16). This links with the American Productivity and Quality Centre's (2002) vision that

*e-learning can change the paradigm of learning and transform the lecture model to an interactive model. Benjamin Franklin called for this in 1770 but he couldn't find a way. John Dewey called for this in 1916 but he didn't know how to do it. Now we have a way. (p. 6)*

Combined, the two views highlight a global change that is occurring and, in relation to the technological perspective of this publication, is a good place to start. The introduction of the knowledge economy and use of ILT in society and education is potentially the most fundamental change since the industrial revolution at the beginning of the 19th century. The resulting demand for skills, linked to the country's new economy (Byers, 2000), could result in individuals viewing the change as a revolution (Blair, 2000). However, the technological advances are simply a natural evolution rather than a revolution (Williams & Goldberg, 2005). Nevertheless the power of effective inclusion to enhance individuals' experiences is potentially more radical, as Clarke (2003) highlights, "E-learning has the potential to revolutionise the way we teach and how we learn…. This is about embedding and exploiting technologies in everything we do....It is also about...skills we increasingly need for everyday life and work."

A successful journey through change is feasible if differences between old and new processes and expectations are accepted because "the history of civilisation is one of...human adaptation to [technological] development" (H. Johnson, 2003, p. 4). Nevertheless, Bollentin (1995) and D. Johnson (2004) identify the fear of technologies as a negative to the current trend, which if not tackled sensitively can result in deepened fear of the unknown, reduced acceptance, and slow progress. Individuals can then become stressed and have a negative impact on a whole organisation (Wilson, 2001). The experience of change can affect individual effectiveness, both positively and negatively (Martin, Jones, & Callan, 2005). Overcoming the fear that changes equate to increased work is a perpetual concern (Welker & Berardino, 2005) that must be handled tactfully with honesty. Being economical with the truth where additional work, especially training, is involved is counterproductive, fosters feelings of resentment, and leads individuals to resist change more strongly. Nevertheless, the scale and pace of change can lead to the need for individuals in senior management posts to take control and firmly relay the fundamental outcomes to teaching staff of not keeping up with changes. Explaining that there is "no choice other than to embrace the new technology [because if not], they wouldn't have a job in five years time...[because students] would refuse to be taught in any other way" (Dowe, as cited in British Educational Communications and Technology Agency, 2007a, p. 22) is a powerful but realistic message.

Confusion of technological terms is not surprising as there appears to be a lack of true understanding resulting in many lecturers believing that e-learning simply means the addition of computers or a VLE. In the same way that lifelong learning has become an "elastic concept" (Dehmel, 2006, p. 49), so it is suggested by the author of the term

e-learning, which is used interchangeably with blended learning, computer-based learning, ILT, and online learning, confusing individuals further and risking complete devaluation of the concept. It is challenging as an enthusiast and leader to instill in others a realistic and diverse meaning of the term, which has now evolved from the traditional understanding of "learning online, especially via the Internet and email" (Learning and Skills Network, 2007, p. 64). Encompassing "learning facilitated and supported through the use of information and communications technology" (Joint Information Systems Committee, 2004), e-learning could simply be described as any technological intervention that supports teaching and enhances learning. Starting with a wide definition encourages some lecturers to acknowledge that they are already utilising various technologies to prepare and create resources for their lessons, and often that change in attitude can inspire an interest in doing more as it is then seen as a smaller step. A solution that has worked in all the FE organisations the author has worked in is to provide small bite-sized nuggets of information regularly. Drip-feeding snippets through many sources including booklets, bulletins, computer pop-ups, meetings, posters, and training helps individuals digest and assimilate changes more effectively. Developing new teaching methodologies and techniques is an area where HE could learn from FE because government legislation has led to a requirement for lecturers to be qualified to teach and complete a minimum of 30 hours of annual continuous professional development (CPD) from September 2007 (Institute for Learning, 2007).

Culture changes must be dealt with at every level within organisations as support and teaching staff often become disheartened if they feel managers are not committed to development. When individuals feel work surrounding changes is valued, they are motivated (Sheard & Kakabadse, 2004). However, driving change from the top is only effective if genuine support and guidance is provided at the same time. The cascade model can work effectively within large organisations, especially those widely dispersed geographically as FE colleges are, some with many community venues, particularly when there are pockets of enthusiasm and good practice. Cascading is also economical in terms of time and cost, which is vitally important because funding for training and development, particularly staff time, is usually very limited in FE. Encouraging outcomes from a technologically focused cascade scheme include higher commitment and positivism toward change from individuals whose managers are enthusiastic and keep communication lines open (National Institute for Adult Continuing Education, 2004). However, the limitations of cascading information, which include changes in perspective through individual interpretation, must be acknowledged when selecting this type of training, especially if it is the main or only strategy.

## PERSONALISATION AND DIFFERENTIATION

Educational commitments to meeting the needs of individuals, quality provision, and widening participation are key strengths associated with FE organisations in the United Kingdom (Department for Education and Skills, 2002). How technological interventions can support individuals with different learning needs is explored in this section, alongside issues related to e-portfolios.

Technology plays an important part in changing society; McBride (2005) highlights the advantages in America of new communications in reducing isolation and improving access. Nevertheless, expecting every learner to have access to technology could actually disadvantage some (Department for Education and Skills, 2002). Educational organisations are beginning to assume that everyone has access to a computer and high-speed Internet connection; however, despite the number of UK households with Internet access doubling in 4 years to about 60%

(National Statistics Online, 2006), many lecturers and learners have much less connectivity. Importantly, Greek (2006) highlights a negative trend that a significant number of individuals (4 in 10) still have no intention of installing Internet access in their homes. Therefore, for ILT to be successfully integrated into the digital society, it is essential for the technological infrastructure to be implemented or improved so that the chance of reaching the revolutionary potential that e-learning has increases (Southern, 2002).

Recognising the importance of and utilising e-learning to improve access opportunities, remove barriers, and widen participation is a vision shared by the UK Department for Education and Skills (2002) and the European Commission (2002). Introducing ILT into teaching and learning is championed by Green and Lucas (1999) as being more motivating and inspiring for learners who have become disillusioned with or face barriers in relation to traditional teaching methods. Technological advances have made realistic simulations, which enable individuals to learn by doing, a reality. Therefore, using technology can improve achievement and retention by increasing learner motivation through interactive, stimulating resources and teaching methods (Roy & Elfner, 2002). However, further research and evidence that integrating e-learning can improve retention and achievement could increase the commitment organisations make to developing and increasing the use of various technologies across all curriculum areas.

On the surface it may appear that distance learning would have less interaction, questioning, and immediate feedback due to less face-to-face contact with a tutor. Nonetheless, the author argues, from observations of teaching and learning in FE and adult and community learning (ACL) environments, that in the pressure of today's classrooms, these elements are actually not as evident and are frequently specified as areas for improvement. Newer techniques and the realisation that more thought has to go into the design of e-learning resources and delivery could lead to a much needed change, resulting in some online learning experiences being more effective than classroom-based experiences. More research needs to be done to investigate this view further as the personal experience of learning in some postcompulsory settings is in opposition to those in primary education where national strategies positively promote interaction and feedback (Department for Children, Schools and Families, 2007). The author believes that HE organisations should take this comment on board to ensure learners are kept motivated, especially as more individuals from different backgrounds, with different learning preferences, have the opportunity to study at the HE level at both university and FE campuses. Additionally, as HE programmes become more diverse and courses linked to work increase, learners need support for different modes of delivery including traditional lectures, and blended and distance learning.

Flexibility is important to improving education; utilising technology enables increased access to resources, especially when they are available in a VLE (Lewin, Mavers, & Somekh, 2003). Encouraging lecturers and students to use online learning environments can be a challenge. A descriptive five-step model developed by the author to encourage and support staff in gradually embedding the use of an online learning environment in their courses is introduced and explored in the professional development section of this chapter. Many learners access information and communicate with friends through various Web pages, social networking sites, and mobile technologies regularly. However, to encourage collaboration throughout a course, online elements must be compulsory rather than optional (Alexander, 2001) as many individuals are likely to feel they have many more noneducational activities to fill their time with. Using VLEs effectively by providing as much detail as possible, making courses transparent with no surprises, can really enhance learners' experience. Enabling the personalisa-

tion of learning journeys increases the chance of individuals taking ownership of their own learning by being able to plan efficiently because all information required is available when they want or need it. It is essential to be aware of how to work effectively with new information sources because "if our students don't know how to find [valid and reliable information], if we ourselves don't know how to do that...we are illiterate" (Richardson, 2006, p. 37). A suggestion to gently increase familiarisation with technology is to use blended delivery techniques. For example, by collecting initial thoughts or feedback in digital audio form, the author believes learners will be more comfortable verbalising thoughts than they could be if completing a paper-based form.

Providing course materials in various formats meets the needs of individuals with different learning styles. However, especially with younger learners in FE, it takes a considered effort for them to find a computer, log in, navigate to where the resources are stored in a VLE, find the version of a resource suitable for them, and then download it before they have even read it. Making use of technologies with which learners are already familiar can streamline this process. A simple technique the author has found effective is to allow learners to capture outcomes from classroom activities on their mobile phones, many of which have high-quality cameras and audio recorders built in. Text-based images can be captured from whiteboards and flip charts, and audio and video clips can be taken during activities, discussions, or debates. The advantage of this method is that learners, often without realising it, have a set of revision files on their phones that they are more likely to scroll through, especially if humour is evident during sessions as they can relive moments that include their friends and recap information without specific effort. Limitations to utilising a learner's mobile phone include confusing messages, that is, if they are not usually allowed to have phones switched on in class. Ground rules must be set and stuck to, with privileges removed if rules are disregarded to ensure this technique works smoothly.

Support available to learners during courses has improved recently with the introduction and use of electronic journals to enable reflection on progress. Some HE organisations are already utilising this support mechanism, as H. Johnson (2003) highlights, "The Open University module 'MOSAIC'...uses...a reflective portfolio assignment" (p. 17) to assess information literacy through personal experiential reflection. Positive benefits of using journals include increased linking of theory and practice because learners are encouraged to think critically about the subject they are studying and make connections with preexisting knowledge and experience, therefore internalising new information more quickly. Recent research endorses the use of electronic journals because they encompass all the advantages of paper-based logs but also help to keep motivation high because lecturers can pick up problems earlier if they are commented on in the journal and the lecturer has access to it (Adcock, as cited in Learning and Skills Network, 2007). Electronic entries also tend to be more accurate because there is encouragement to add reflections little by little and often rather than, what is more common with paper versions, to complete the journal just before submission, relying heavily on memory (Jennings, 2006).

Finally, in this section, it is important to highlight where FE is in relation to selecting, using, and embedding e-portfolios into courses. The author has used simple descriptive documents, with hyperlinks to information contained in separate files, for several years to organise evidence for assessment. With the documents being electronic, it is possible to collate many different types of files including audio and video clips as well as text-based documents, which make them accessible for learners with different needs. Despite being portable, there are limitations, especially in relation to the endorsement of accuracy as it is a very simple scheme that does not have the ability to record official examination results; it has limited transferability or role beyond simply collecting evidence. Commercially available e-portfolio systems usually have the advantage of being Web based so they are stored centrally, are accessible via any Internet-connected computer, and have areas for individual reflection and sections to record qualifications and results. However, they are often connected to a single organisation and have limited value when an individual moves to a different organisation or progresses to a higher level lifelong learning or community course in a different educational sector. To improve the usefulness of e-portfolio systems, it is important to ensure more standardisation and interoperability (Tolley, 2007), including gaining approval from awarding bodies for various assessment processes to encourage organisations to select a system for all their staff and students to use rather than having individual departments trying different tools. However, UK government legislation proposing a situation where every learner in compulsory education has a personal online space to build a record of achievement (Department for Education and Skills, 2005) is not always taken into account. Despite research identifying the importance of interoperability (British Educational Communications and Technology Agency, 2007b), further investigations are needed as some local authorities and educational organisations are still developing their own individualised e-portfolio systems rather than focusing on the potential of a system that would enable individuals to have a single e-portfolio for the entirety of their life.

## DESIGNING RESOURCES

Developing high-quality, interactive, innovative, and motivating resources is essential to the success of teaching and learning no matter what mode of delivery is being used. The availability of technology, equipment, and software has made creating interesting resources with audiovisual elements and effective feedback easier. However, learner expectations are also increasing constantly (Lewis, 2002), so tutors may need more time to keep resources relevant and high quality. Nevertheless, new concerns relating to developing resources suitable for remote delivery are becoming more evident and important as organisations in FE are moving toward delivering portions of courses at a distance to save time and survive changes in government funding, prioritising lower level skills for employment and 14-19 education (Owen & Besley, 2006).

Limited access to high-quality content is a barrier the UK Department for Education and Skills (2002) highlights as reducing the chance of reaching the full potential of e-learning. However, within educational organisations, developing resources is often the responsibility of individual lecturers or, in a few cases, departments (British Educational Communications and Technology Agency, 2005). Individuals often cite lack of time as the reason new resources are not created. However, once created electronically, resources can be updated much quicker, keeping them fresher and up to date (Rosenberg, 2001). The author believes the advantages of including audio files, hyperlinks, images, and videos quickly outweigh development time, and sharing resources with colleagues can reduce the time individuals need to gather a full set of teaching materials. Creating interactive resources that promote active learning is important as uploading original text-based resources to online learning environments is no more than retrofitting to technology, resulting in factually dry (Hoare, 2001) "electronic page-turning" (Forsyth, 1996, p. 13). Well-designed technologically enhanced activities encourage and support different levels of thinking and analysis, including many elements within the different facets of Bloom's taxonomy (Curzon, 2003), which can help learners critically analyse and understand concepts more deeply (Welker & Berardino, 2005).

Creating, developing, and updating resources are often quicker and easier when technologies are utilised; however, preparing learning objects for delivery online is more complex than traditional session planning (Agagnostopoulo, 2002). Lower achievement in online courses, often due to less effective pedagogical strategies (Jung, 2005), can be improved by enabling personalisation and differentiation through nonlinear structure and including a variety of activities, modules in different configurations, time for reflection, and audiovisual stimulation. Time needs to be allowed to compose the layout of online resources effectively to enable information to be understood at a distance without overload from solid blocks of text; sufficient description is also needed to remove the need for lecturer explanations. Software is readily available to develop interactive, motivating resources. Some like eXe (2007), Reload (2006), and Wink (2005) are shared freely through the Internet, while others are licensed and cost money. In FE, the author has found it effective to develop lecturers' skills in small increments, encouraging individuals to identify their own comfort levels, and then to provide suggestions to take resources to the next step, which could be anything from adding images to developing fully interactive Web pages.

Effective stand-alone resources contain elements that enable learners to check their progress in a meaningful way. The process of verbal or written feedback in a traditional setting needs to be translated into a form that supports learners in isolation. Many lecturers spend time creating elaborate resources, and then spend no time composing feedback for quiz and assessment elements. Many resources do not contain more than "congratulations" or "try again" for correct or incorrect responses, respectively, which can de-motivate achievers and frustrate individuals who are struggling. Comprehensive comments in quizzes provide opportunities for learners to reflect and think critically regardless of whether they respond correctly or not. Extrinsic feedback (which, for the purpose of this chapter, relates to shallow, simplistic verification comments) offers individuals a pleasantry at best, usually failing "to assess deep learning" (Littlejohn & Sclater, as cited in Salter, 2003, p. 138). Intrinsic feedback (which, for the purpose of this chapter, relates to deeper, elaborate comments that are responsive to learners' reasoning and initiate a further thought process) includes clarification details, directions to further information to encourage further learning and improve the chances of correct answers or links to higher level questions, extension tasks, and encouragement to reflect, deepen understanding, and keep enthusiasm high.

## PROFESSIONAL DEVELOPMENT AND IMPLEMENTATION

Lecturer support and acceptance is possibly the most complicated issue relating to wholly embedding e-learning into educational organisations. User approval is important to any culture change because "implementation is not just [putting in place]… [a] system…but the institutionalisation of its use" (Keen, as cited in Riley & Smith, 1997, p. 310); a system is only as effective as the users who accept it. Therefore, strategies need to be established to increase the chance of reception and adoption of new ways of working. The success of various motivational solutions including training, descriptive models, in-class support for first and early use of technology, championing of roles, and competitions are discussed in this section.

"Well planned workplace learning is…one of the most effective means of improving staff performance" (TOPSS, as cited in Cooper & Rixon, 2001); however, many organisations do not place enough emphasis on the structure and see it "as secondary in implementing major changes of practice" (M. Johnson, Benbow, & Baldwin, 1999, p. 260) to realise the benefits. Conversely, developing lecturers is essential to improve quality of service (McFarlane & McLean, 2003) because "attention

must be directed to the training of teachers to adapt to the new learning environment" (*Towards an Information Society in Western Asia*, 2003, p. 5). It is also important to remember that the majority of the current body of teaching staff who require development are "digital immigrants" (Prensky, 2001a) who are anxious about the changes, feel challenged by having to learn a whole new technological language, and would probably feel more comfortable with traditional, trainer-centred teaching. In contrast, traditional teaching is generally less flexible (DeWolfe Waddill, 2006) for newer learners termed *digital natives* (Prensky) or *millennials* (Gray, 2007) who have grown up using copious technologies and both desire and need audiovisual interactive learning materials. However, despite the UK government promising new qualifications "focusing on both e-learning support and delivery" (Department for Education and Skills, 2002, p. 38), most training is not accredited and is developed and delivered within individual organisations, which can sometimes result in poorly structured sessions.

Flexibility in training is, from experience, just as important for staff development as for general educational provision. To develop an "any time, any place, anywhere" (Jenkins, 2007) style of training suite to meet needs and requirements, a common solid structure for each session must be established. In the current role of the e-learning curriculum manager in a large FE college, the author developed a comprehensive suite of over 80 bite-sized sessions exploring many e-learning subjects, covering hardware, software, and theory, with module titles ranging from Effective Internet Searching and Digital Photography to Blogs and Wikis and Interactive Whiteboard. Progression routes were included through first-look and further look categories alongside suggested combinations, though sessions could be chosen in any combination depending on interest and time available. Hard copies of the programme, including specific aims and objectives, were distributed to managers to encourage whole team training, while all staff have access to the details on the college's online learning environment. The e-learning sessions receive positive comments in relation to their breadth and the fact that, despite being classroom based, the delivery utilises technologies and action learning to create constructive experiences for all staff. However, there is a genuine issue of staff not having time to attend training, so an alternative solution needs to be established. Research conducted for an MSc in multimedia and e-learning (Jakobsen, 2007) started the process by evaluating one possible option, online delivery, because its flexibility (Jung, 2005) "effectively facilitate[s]...critical thinking and...[improves] problem solving skills" (Chen & Yao, 2005, p. 27), which can help "turn workers into enterprising individuals" (McWilliam, 2002, p. 291) and ensure that training is closely linked to current educational thinking. Nonetheless, it is important to note that Armitage and O'Leary (2003) identify that engagement with online courses can also be negatively affected by time restraints.

Changing the use of the organisation's in-house-developed online managed learning environment (MLE) from principally a repository of static information and how-to sheets to a genuine learning setting from which courses can be delivered, monitored, and managed was the main focus of the project. It was hoped that by using technology to deliver training, familiarisation with newer methods and techniques would increase, and tutor acceptance "that they have become immigrants into a new digital world" (Prensky, 2001b, p. 7) would ensue, encouraging individuals to learn new communication methods. The theory of delivering a completely online course changed quickly when launching the module to participants when a request for a traditional face-to-face practical first session was requested. Positively, this fits with both Creanor's (2002) and DeLacey and Leonard's (2002) view that a key element to increased success of online courses is the inclusion of an element of face-to-face contact. Evidence that having a computer

qualification leads to increased confidence in using a variety of technological functions (Jakobsen, 2006) was not evident in this study. No direct correlation between participants with low experience and/or confidence with the level of support required or with the number of activities completed was evident. Participants, as expected, commented on their fear of technology breaking down, including negative views of the MLE, but positively identified areas of their teaching in which they could realistically use technology to enhance. Participants also acknowledged that there is definitely a future and strong case for online delivery to increase the flexibility of provision. Nonetheless, there remains much to organise and evaluate in terms of structure, use of tools, and online learning environments. It is important to remember that no system of delivery will suit everyone. However, by offering more choices, individuals will be able to personalise their learning journey, and, by including a technological option, some individuals will increase their skills and knowledge simply by working through a training module. HE organisations could implement the suggestions with a twist by placing the focus for the lecturer on research so that training is linked to actual intervention that is formally evaluated.

There are still only a small number of models and theories related directly to e-learning, so further research is needed. Moule (2007) highlights potential limitations of the use of Salmon's (2003) five-stage model relating to engagement in and experiences of online learning in blended learning situations. Equally, Moule's concept of an "e-learning ladder" (p. 41) to structure online learning is useful to ensure different elements are thought about and incorporated to make learning more inclusive, but could be confusing if it is assumed that it is a hierarchical model to climb rather than a conceptual representation of pedagogies along a continuum that could be used in any order. The important factor is that any model should only be a guide or starting point that should be mixed with existing or new knowledge and understanding of educational environments to create a suitable combination of theories to structure courses by. With this in mind, the author developed a five-step descriptive model, shown in Figure 1, that provides manageable steps staff should be able to follow to ultimately embed online elements into their courses through blending the use of online learning environments with traditional classroom delivery. The first and second steps of use of an online environment, the only steps evident in many FE organisations, involve a repository (British Educational Communications and Technology Agency, 1999) storing basic course documentation and resources that learners can access at any time. Differentiation is possible through the third step, when additional materials, links, interactive resources, and quizzes are uploaded to stretch more able learners, and audiovisual, revision, and explanatory materials are provided for individuals who require additional support. Providing options for learning the same subject enables individuals to personalise their own journeys. The fourth step requires lecturers to become "communal architects" (Woods, 2003) as online communities are developed through the use of Web 2.0 social networking tools including blogs, discussion boards, and wikis to stimulate alternative communication, collaborative working, and reflective thinking. Assessment completes the steps and includes a broad range of processes including gathering information in e-portfolios, providing opportunities for learners to check their own progress, accepting electronic submission of assignments, and testing online. The five-step model works effectively in FE colleges where it has been in-

*Figure 1. Five steps to embedding online elements in courses*

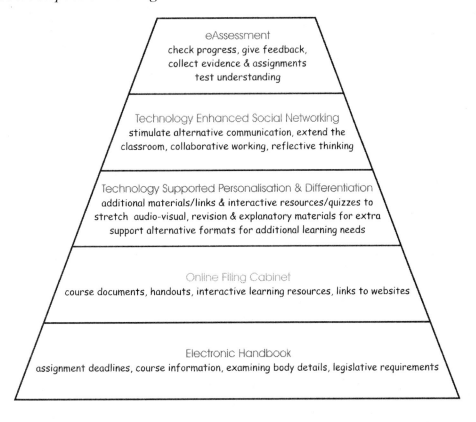

troduced to encourage and support tutors through gradual implementation of online technologies in courses. However, it would be interesting to find out if it would be received as positively, with the stages in the same or different configuration, in other FE and HE organisations.

Providing alternative support is a natural next step the author uses to supplement training sessions. Supported play sessions enable lecturers to practice skills, possibly learnt in a formal training session, in a safe environment without learners, either individually or as part of a team. An expert facilitates, ensuring all participants have equal time, but only becomes involved in the process when invited or problems are identified. Peer support flourishes where a team is working together and often leads to ongoing learning networks. The addition of learners makes some lecturers more nervous of failure, so individuals can ask for help to support the real use of technology with students. An expert, again only interfering if problems arise, takes up an unobtrusive position so as to not distract learners. In-class support works best for first and early use of new technologies, methods, or techniques and can be combined with peer observation aimed at highlighting areas where technology can enhance learning. An expert can be either the original trainer or an individual in a champion role. FE organisations have used ILT champions (British Educational Communications and Technology Agency, 2003), while e-guides (National Institute for Adult Continuing Education, 2004) were introduced into ACL environments to initiate the acceptance of change toward the increased use of technologies. However, champions need close management to ensure they effectively support changes. Those with higher standing in organisations need to lead by example because it is important to remember that "managers who actively and vigorously promote their personal vision for using IT, pushing...over or around approval or implementation hurdles...[and often

risking] their reputations...ensure...success" (Beath, 1991, p. 355).

Developing and sharing quality, transferable interactive resources can be difficult in FE due in part to lack of time, though fully utilising online learning environments with search functions can help, at least within individual organisations. A suggestion that results in a bank of good-practice examples and motivates lecturers to create inspirational materials is competition. Individual departments or whole organisations can benefit from challenging and motivating staff through an award ceremony and prizes. However, it must be acknowledged that added pressure to win can be perceived as a controlling influence, which can undermine individuals' confidence in their competence (Tauer & Harackiewicz, 1999). An EMILY (play on the term MLE) was launched within an FE college by the author, initially to establish where pockets of good practice were within the organisation and to collect transferable examples to inspire other lecturers and departments who have not embraced e-learning in any meaningful way. The focus of the promotion was to ensure that the creative talents within the body of staff are nurtured and excellence is rewarded. Entrants completed a document detailing their e-learning inspiration, methods, use, transferability, and benefits to learners to complement their resources. Judges from within the college provided the short list, and a representative from an external e-learning educational support agency (Joint Information Systems Committee's Regional Support Centre, JISC RSC) selected the three winners using the following criteria: innovation, learner impact, appropriate use of tools, quality, transferability, and the "$x$ factor." Winners received a digital camera, MP3 recorder, and memory stick for first, second, and third place, respectively, at a presentation event during a whole-college-staff development day. Participants commented that the competition was motivating while at the same time they valued the creative work that was being done to create innovative resources. Motivating and rewarding tutors in FE through competitions and acknowledgement could be complimented by partnerships with HE lecturers, who could develop the research and evaluation element of entries. Again, increased sharing of resources, methods, and techniques would help all postcompulsory education sectors learn from each other, especially within already established partnerships and consortia.

## CONCLUSION AND FUTURE RESEARCH DIRECTIONS

It is important to note that this chapter provides an initial overview of the use of e-learning within FE and only touches the tip of the iceberg in terms of implementation and use. The changes in the educational landscape to include technology are a natural evolution that enhances learning. It is evident that teaching environments, because of their commitment to learning, accessibility, and widening participation, have generally embraced the technological age through positive association, and despite some staff being resistant to change, many more individuals are excited by it. Working in small steps and being honest and realistic throughout any culture change will ultimately lead to the focus, in this case, technology becoming embedded in teaching and learning. It is suggested by the author that the strength HE institutions have in time for and encouragement in research could help FE organisations move to the next stage of implementation; nonteaching time in FE is reducing and becoming more valuable, resulting in the occurrence of smaller moves forward. Working together and sharing good practice, resources, methods, and techniques at the curriculum and organisation level could help FE organisations utilise time more efficiently by testing new resources or techniques that have already been piloted. At the same time, the sharing and collaborative work would lead to

learners having enhanced experiences through every aspect of their lifelong learning journey. However, the technological infrastructure needs to be developed to increase the opportunity for individuals from many backgrounds to access new modes of learning.

Technological developments must also involve combined working to ensure that any system, including virtual learning environments and e-portfolios, that learners use in one educational sector can transfer to another, potentially to international educational organisations, too. Lecturers and leaders must continue to strive for the best, identifying strategies and models that work to personalise and differentiate learning and helping others achieve the same results under similar and different conditions. Utilising online learning environments and Web 2.0 social networking tools widens the reach of education and extends the concept of the classroom. Enabling the use of virtual technologies challenges some individuals; however, the use of a model like the five-step method developed by the author can make the task more manageable. One of the greatest advantages of effectively using online learning environments is enabling learners to take ownership of their own learning. Ensuring all course dates, literature, resources, and session notes are uploaded and available for learners makes the whole process accessible and transparent from the beginning to end of any course. Blending traditional and newer methods can also increase individual familiarisation and confidence with technology, which has a positive effect in relation to skills needed for life and work in the digital age.

Training is essential to the successful implementation of e-learning in any organisation, and, again, by pooling resources, partnerships can collectively provide more constructive, efficient development opportunities for their staff, which in turn benefits learners. Lecturers are best supported through the availability of flexible training options, delivered when, where, and how individuals require. Providing sessions online widens accessibility, and similar to the way learners have experience in blended delivery, some lecturers will increase technological skills and confidence and be able to identify possibilities for their own teaching simply by working through a training module themselves. Developing lecturers in a real environment with learners increases confidence and is an effective follow-up to more formal skills training sessions. The cascade model complements all other forms of training and is an effective method for reaching more individuals than central training sessions delivered by an individual or team. Working closely with individuals from other educational sectors, ACL, FE, and HE practitioners could pick up hints, tips, and new ways of working that could be cascaded to colleagues in their own organisation.

Taking time to develop motivating and interactive resources is essential to their success and effectiveness as learning tools, especially for online delivery. Electronic resources are easier to keep up to date and relevant, and by including audio files, hyperlinks, images, and video clips, materials are more accessible and enable personalisation. Utilising modules of information in different configurations enables differentiation to stretch achievers and support individuals at lower levels. Effectively composed intrinsic feedback is vital to the creation of engaging resources and quizzes. Simple extrinsic yes-no responses do not inspire further exploration or reflection in learners as well as deeper, specifically detailed comments or directions, which is what is needed to promote lifelong learning. Finally, while it is generally accepted that many FE organisations are well on the way to fully embedding digital concepts, it is important to remember that financial limitations often affect the ability for organisations to consistently support developments. Nonetheless, e-learning is a constantly changing landscape and therefore all practitioners working in education need to be willing to contribute to its continued integration, development, and success.

In terms of additional research this chapter inspires, four potential options follow.

- A study to research the effectiveness of developing and using a generic introductory session to introduce the concept and use of online learning. This could, as in this chapter, be related to providing a bridging step between traditional and online delivery for staff development. It could equally be related to the introduction of online elements within courses, which are going to become more evident over the next few years, and be used to ensure learners have the skills they need. It is likely that some research in this area is already in existence from the Open University or Learn Direct in the United Kingdom.

- A study to identify and evaluate potential opportunities or methods for sharing resources, methods, and techniques. This could be focused within individual organisations but could equally, for a bigger project, involve several organisations either in the same sector or across sectors. It is likely that some research related to this issue is available from the Joint Information Systems Committee.

- A study to evaluate the wider effectiveness of the five-step model to embedding the use of a VLE into the teaching model developed by the author. Additional FE organisations at different stages of e-maturity could test the model as a way of engaging less motivated lecturers. It would also be interesting to find out if the model could work in ACL environments, where the ethos is similar to FE or HE organisations and the structure and historical way of working are very different. Because this is a new model, apart from personal information collected from practical use, there would be no preexisting research on it available.

- A study to evaluate the interoperability of e-portfolios to investigate if it would be possible for an individual to use a single linked system for the whole of his or her life. The potential of a system to be used not only locally but nationally and internationally would provide compelling reading for examination and awarding bodies. Research into the effectiveness and use of e-portfolios in different sectors of postcompulsory education would form a good foundation for this project.

# REFERENCES

Agagnostopoulo, K. (2002). *Designing to learn and learning to design: An overview of instructional design models.* LTSN Generic Centre. Retrieved March 2007 from http://www.ltsn.ac.uk/genericcentre/index.asp?id=17113

Alexander, S. (2001). E-learning developments and experiences. *Education and Training, 43*(4/5), 240-248.

American Productivity and Quality Centre. (2002). *International benchmarking cleaning house: Planning, implementing and evaluating e-learning initiatives. Consortium learning forum: Best practice report.* TX: Author.

Armitage, S., & O'Leary, R. (2003). *A good guide for learning technologists* (eLearning Series No. 4). York: Learning and Teaching Support Network Generic Centre.

Beath, C. (1991). Supporting the information technology champions. *MIS Quarterly, 15*(3), 355-372.

Blair, T. (2000). *The knowledge economy: Access for all.* Retrieved January 2007 from http://www.dti.gov.uk/knowledge2000/blair.htm

Bollentin, R. (1995). Byting back: Is technophobia keeping you off the Internet? *On the Internet Magazine.* Retrieved April 2007 from http://www.csudh.edu/psych/OTI.htm

British Educational Communications and Technology Agency. (1999). *Learning on-line: Electronic learning resources in further education.* Coventry, United Kingdom: Author.

British Educational Communications and Technology Agency. (2003). *Ferl practitioners' programme: Transforming teaching and learning with ILT.* Coventry, United Kingdom: Author.

British Educational Communications and Technology Agency. (2005). *ICT and e-learning in further education: The challenge of change.* Coventry, United Kingdom: Author.

British Educational Communications and Technology Agency. (2007a). *2007 annual review.* Coventry, United Kingdom: Author.

British Educational Communications and Technology Agency. (2007b). *E-portfolios: Technical processes, assumptions and implications.* Retrieved August 2007 from http://partners.becta.org.uk/index.php?section=pv&catcode=_pv_ep_02&rid=13637&pagenum=3&NextStart=1

Byers, S. (2000). *The importance of the knowledge economy.* Retrieved January 2007 from http://www.dti.gov.uk/knowledge2000/byers.htm

Chen, Q., & Yao, J. (2005). A cognitive model of Web design for e-learning. *International Journal of Innovation and Learning, 2*(1), 26-35.

Clarke, C. (2003). *Towards a unified e-learning strategy: Consultation document.* London: The Stationary Office.

Cooper, B., & Rixon, A. (2001). Integrating post-qualification study into the workplace: The candidates experience. *Social Work Education, 20*(6), 701-716.

Creanor, L. (2002). A tale of two courses: A comparative study of tutoring online. *Open Learning, 17*(1), 57-68.

Curzon, L. B. (2003). *Teaching in further education: An outline of principals and practice* (6th ed.). London: Continuum.

Dehmel, A. (2006). Making a European area of lifelong learning a reality? Some critical reflections on the European Union's lifelong learning policies. *Comparative Education, 42*(1), 49-62.

DeLacey, B. J., & Leonard, D. A. (2002). Case study on technology and distance in education at the Harvard Business School. *Educational Technology and Society, 5*(2).

Department for Children, Schools and Families. (2007). *Five year strategy for children and learners.* Retrieved August 2007 from http://www.dfes.gov.uk/publications/5yearstrategy/chap3.shtml

Department for Education and Skills. (2002). *Success for all: Reforming further education and training. Our vision for the future.* London: Author.

Department for Education and Skills. (2005). *Harnessing technology: Transforming learning and children's services.* London: Author.

DeWolfe Waddill, D. (2006). Action e-learning: An exploratory case study of action learning applied online. *Human Resource Development International, 9*(2), 157-171.

European Commission. (2002). *Making lifelong learning a reality for all.* Luxembourg: Office for Official Publications of the European Communities.

eXe. (2007). *eLearning XHTML editor.* Retrieved July 2007 from http://exelearning.org

Forsyth, I. (1996). *Teaching and learning materials and the Internet.* London: Kogan Page.

Gray, R. (2007). Bite-sized generation. *Human Resources*, pp. 37-38. Retrieved May 2007 from www.hrmagazine.co.uk

Greek, D. (2006). UK households snub Internet access. *Computeract!ve.* Retrieved May 2007 from http://www.itweek.co.uk/computeractive/news/2167328/growing-number-people-uk

Green, A., & Lucas, N. (Eds.). (1999). *FE and lifelong learning: Realigning the sector for the 21st century.* London: Institute of Education.

Hoare, S. (2001, March 6). Whip-hand. *Guardian Education*, p. 50.

Institute for Learning. (2007). *CPD portal.* Retrieved April 2007 from http://www.ifl.ac.uk/cpd_portal/cpd_index.html

Jakobsen, L. (2006). *What is the level of IT social services workers and what impact could this have on the implementation of the new electronically focused government social care initiatives?* Unpublished manuscript.

Jakobsen, L. (2007). *Evaluating the effectiveness of online training as a staff development tool.* Unpublished manuscript.

Jenkins, S. (2007). *UK television commercials 1955-1985. Martini: 1971.* Retrieved April 2007 from http://www.headington.org.uk/adverts/drinks_alcoholic.htm

Jennings, M. (2006, March). *SD9 teacher training transformation projects at National Institute of Adult Continuing Education.* Paper presented at the E-Guides Lead by Example national event, Birmingham, United Kingdom.

Johnson, D. (2004). *Wadda I need that I ain't got? Courage is a technology skill.* Retrieved February 2007 from http://www.doug-johnson.com/handouts/courage.pdf

Johnson, H. (2003). Product, process or pre-requisite? Information literacy as infrastructure for information networking. In *The new review of information networking* (pp. 2-20).

Johnson, M., Benbow, S. M., & Baldwin, R. C. (1999). An electronic patient record system and geriatric psychiatry: Considerations and implications. *Aging and Mental Health, 3*(3), 257-263.

Joint Information Systems Committee. (2004). *Starting point: Definition of elearning.* Retrieved

July 2007 from http://www.elearning.ac.uk/ef-fprac/html/start_defin.htm

Jung, I. (2005). Cost effectiveness of online teacher training. *Open Learning, 20*(2), 131-146.

Learning and Skills Network. (2007). *Effective teaching transforming teacher training through elearning.* London: Author.

Lewin, C., Mavers, D., & Somekh, B. (2003). Broadening access to the curriculum through using technology to link home and school: A critical analysis of reforms intended to improve students' educational attainment. *The Curriculum Journal, 14*(1), 23-53.

Lewis, C. (2002). Driving factors for e-learning: An organisational perspective. *Perspectives: Policy and Practice in Higher Education, 6*(2), 50-54.

Lifelong Learning Sector Skills Council. (2005). *E-learning standards.* Retrieved July 2007 from http://www.lifelonglearninguk.org/documents/standards/e_learning.pdf

Martin, A. J., Jones, E. S., & Callan, V. J. (2005). The role of the psychological climate in facilitating employee adjustment during organizational change. *European Journal of Work and Organizational Psychology, 14*(3), 263-289.

McBride, A. B. (2005). Nursing and the informatics revolution. *Nursing Outlook, 53*, 183-191.

McFarlane, L., & McLean, J. (2003). Education and training for direct care workers. *Social Work Education, 22*(4), 385-399.

McKenna, P. (2004). *Change your life in 7 days.* London: Bantam Press.

McWilliam, E. (2002). Against professional development. *Educational Philosophy and Theory, 34*(3), 289-299.

Moule, P. (2007). Challenging the five-stage model for e-learning: A new approach. *ALT-J Research in Learning Technology, 15*(1), 37-50.

National Institute for Adult Continuing Education. (2004). *E-guides: Lead by example.* Leicester, United Kingdom: Author.

National Statistics Online. (2006). *Internet access.* Retrieved May 2007 from http://www.ststistics.gov.uk/CCI/nugget.asp?ID=8&Pos=&ColRank=1&Rank=374

Owen, S., & Besley, S. (2006). *Funding policy watch: FE funding. 2007/08.* Retrieved August 2007 from http://www.edexcel.org.uk/VirtualContent/93790/Funding_Policy_Watch_2006_2_FE_Funding___2007_081.pdf

Prensky, M. (2001a). Digital natives, digital immigrants. *On the Horizon, 9*(5).

Prensky, M. (2001b). Digital natives, digital immigrants: Part II. Do they really think differently? *On the Horizon, 9*(6).

Reload. (2006). *Reload project.* Retrieved June 2007 from http://www.reload.ac.uk

Richardson, W. (2006). The new face of learning: What happens to time-worn concepts of classrooms and teaching when we can now go online and learn anything, anywhere, anytime? *Edutopia*, pp. 34-37. Retrieved February 2007 from http://www.edutopia.org/1648

Riley, L., & Smith, G. (1997). Developing and implementing IS: A case study analysis in social services. *Journal of Information Technology, 12*, 305-321.

Rosenberg, M. J. (2001). *E-learning strategies for delivering knowledge in the digital age.* New York: McGraw-Hill.

Roy, M. H., & Elfner, E. (2002). Analyzing student satisfaction with instructional technology techniques. *Industrial and Commercial Training, 34*(7), 272-277.

Salmon, G. (2003). *E-moderating: The key to teaching and learning online* (2nd ed.). London: Routledge Falmer, Taylor & Francis Books Ltd.

Salter, G. (2003). Comparing online and traditional teaching: A different approach. *Campus-Wide Information Systems, 20*(4), 137-145.

Sheard, A. G., & Kakabadse, A. P. (2004). A process perspective on leadership and team development. *Journal of Management Development, 23*(1), 7-106.

Southern, A. (2002). Can information and communication technologies support regeneration? *Regional Studies, 36*(6), 697-702.

Tauer, J. M., & Harackiewicz, J. M. (1999). Winning isn't everything: Competition, achievement orientation, and intrinsic motivation. *Journal of Experimental Social Psychology, 35*, 209-238.

Tolley, R. J. (2007). *I wonder when we will get some advice on the interoperability of eportfolios: BECTa Communities.* Retrieved August 2007 from http://communities.becta.org.uk/WebX?14@586. bT1FaghlZER.0@.3c40f8c7/0

*Towards an information society in Western Asia: A declaration of principles.* (2003). Beirut, Lebanon: Western Asia Preparatory Conference for the World Summit on the Information Society.

Welker, J., & Berardino, L. (2005). Blended learning: Understanding the middle ground between traditional classroom and fully online instruction. *Journal of Educational Technology Systems, 34*(1), 33-55.

Williams, J. B., & Goldberg, M. (2005). *The evolution of elearning.* Retrieved July 2007 from http://www.ascilite.org.au/conferences/brisbane05/blogs/proceedings/84_Williams.pdf

Wilson, T. (2001, May). *Information overload: Myth, reality and implications for health care.* Retrieved January 2007 from http://informationr.net/tdw/publ/ppt/overload/tsld001.htm

Wink. (2005). *DebugMode Wink.* Retrieved April 2007 from http://www.debugmode.com/wink/

Woods, R. (2003). "Communal architect" in online classroom: Integrating cognitive and affective learning for maximum effort in Web-based learning. *Online Journal of Distance Learning Administration, 6*(1). Retrieved May 2007 from http://www.westga.edu/%7Edistance/ojdla/spring61/woods61.htm

## ADDITIONAL READING

Clarke, A., & Hesse, C. (2004). *E-guidelines 1: Online resources in the classroom.* Leicester, United Kingdom: National Institute of Adult Continuing Education.

This is a practical book that explores the use of the Internet to support face-to-face learning. It identifies examples of good practice to highlight how to combine traditional learning with Web technologies and resources. It recommends Web sites for many subject areas and explores different uses for the Web in teaching and learning.

Cole, G. (2006). *101 essential lists for using ICT in the classroom.* London: Continuum.

This is a book that explores different elements of implementing technology into educational environments. Split into manageable, easy-to-digest chunks, this book is a valuable resource for all teachers regardless of their individual e-confidence and experience.

Dawson, D. (2007). *E-guidelines 12: Handheld technologies for mobile learning.* Leicester, United Kingdom: National Institute of Adult Continuing Education.

The work explores the use of various mobile technologies in community-based learning. It highlights the potential of mobile phones, MP3 players, and personal digital assistants (PDAs) to enhance learning experiences. Many of the functions are looked at through sections including "Why Use Handheld Devices in Teaching and Learning?", "Out and About and Getting Connected," "Are These Devices Accessible for Everyone?", and "How do I Get Connected?"

Edwards, K. (2001). Virtual versus classical universities: Liberal arts and humanities. *Higher Education in Europe, 26*(4), 603-607.

This article explores the inconsistencies in the development of virtual learning in higher education institutions. The identification that the humanities appear to be the least responsive department is explored and potential reasons identified. Key points covered include the need for a reevaluation of pedagogy, the need to accept a less teacher-orientated structure, and issues around helping learners educate themselves.

Essom, J. (2006). *E-guidelines 7: Attracting and motivating new learners with ICT.* Leicester, United Kingdom: National Institute of Adult Continuing Education.

Essom explores the potential of information communication technologies to engage, motivate, and interest learners. It is designed to help practitioners use technology to reach adults who traditionally may be less likely to be involved in formal learning. Examples are included about how to capture individuals' imagination through various strategies to help widen participation.

Franklin, T., & van Harmelen, M. (2007). *Web 2.0 for content creation for learning and teaching in higher education.* Retrieved May 2007 from http://www.franklin-consulting.co.uk/LinkedDocuments/web2.0_for_comment.pdf

The report focuses on the use of Web 2.0 technologies for content creation, learning, and teaching funded by the Joint Information Systems Committee and carried out between March and May 2007. It draws on existing studies, interviews with staff at universities who have implemented Web 2.0 technologies for learning and teaching, and a week-long Web-based seminar (Webinar) with expert contributions, both from speakers and the

audience. The report builds on the briefing documents that were written especially for the Webinar, together with the results of the discussions, many of which can be found on the Moodle™ site (http://moodle.cs.man.ac.uk/web2/) that was used to support the conference.

Green, H., Facer, K., & Rudd, T. (with Dillon, P., & Humphreys, P.). (2005). *Personalisation and digital technologies.* Futurelab. Retrieved March 2007 from http://www.futurelab.org.uk/resources/documents/opening_education/Personalisation_report.pdf

This report links the potential of digital technologies with the personalisation debate, with the focus on changing education to a more learner-centred approach to increase the chance of individuals reaching their full potential. The paper does not attempt to predict the future but outlines challenges and opportunities and suggests ways technologies can help and support the personalisation agenda.

Horton, W., & Horton, K. (2003). *E-learning tools and technologies.* Indianapolis, IN: Wiley.

This is a book that provides individuals with a comprehensive guide to selecting e-learning tools for specific needs. It is useful for practitioners with little or no technical knowledge and/or technologists without experience in educating. It will help individuals gain knowledge to enable them to pick suitable technological tools to support the learning process and plan how to use them. Supporting information is available online at http://www.horton.com/html/elttbook.aspx.

Hussain, S. (2005). *E-guidelines 3: Developing e-learning materials. Applying user-centred design.* Leicester, United Kingdom: National Institute of Adult Continuing Education.

This book guides lecturers through a user-centred model of designing e-resources. Written in clear language, it is ideal for those with less technical knowledge. It is suitable for all subject areas and provides examples, guidelines, and case studies to support practitioners.

Jaques, D., & Salmon, G. (2007). *Learning in groups: A handbook for face to face and online environments* (4th ed.). Oxon, United Kingdom: Routledge.

Jaques and Salmon place group learning in online environments in context alongside principals of traditional face-to-face teaching. The book includes elements on group characteristics, leadership, collaboration, communication, reflection, emotional intelligence, action research, and assessment and evaluation techniques.

Learning Technology Dissemination Initiative. (1998). *Evaluation cookbook.* Edinburgh, United Kingdom: Author.

This book provides practical suggestions and methods suitable for evaluating technological interventions. It includes recipes for different methods, information for drawing on expertise, a planning framework, guidelines, and exemplars. It is also available online at http://www.icbl.hw.ac.uk/ltdi/cookbook/contents.html

Lewis, R., & Whitlock, Q. (2003). *How to plan and manage an e-learning programme.* Aldershot, United Kingdom: Gower Publishing Limited.

The work guides individuals through best-practice examples to manage technologically based projects. It includes sections covering content to include and people to involve. This book is written with authority with clear examples in manageable chunks.

Lichtenberg, M., & Travis, J. (2002). *Creating dynamic presentations with streaming media.* Redmond, WA: Microsoft Press.

This book teaches individuals how to develop presentations into compelling training resources using Microsoft® Producer for PowerPoint® 2002. Please note this book is specific to the 2002 version

of the software: Books for other versions should be available if required.

Lim, H., Lee, S.-G., & Nam, K. (2007). Validating e-learning factors affecting training effectiveness. *International Journal of Information Management, 27,* 22-35.

The article identifies that the development of technologies has led to the expansion of online training and explores what makes online training and learning effective. It is based on empirical research that aims to establish the characteristics of effective online training and how they affect learning and training effectiveness in the workplace.

Machado, C. (2007). Developing an e-readiness model for higher education institutions: Results of a focus group study. *British Journal of Educational Technology, 38*(1), 72-82.

Machado's article explores the creation of a model to help higher education institutions assess their use of e-learning and their overall e-readiness. Based on the authors' involvement in a Tempus project (Tourism and Hospitality Studies in Central Asia, TOHOSTCA) aimed at modernising curriculum through the introduction of technologies, the ultimate aim developed into one attempting to build a common online curriculum.

Mason, R., & Rennie, F. (2006). *E-learning: The key concepts.* Oxon, United Kingdom: Routledge.

This is a fully cross-referenced book taking the reader from *A* to *Z* through key topics relating to using technology in teaching and learning.

Nance, B. (Ed.). (2007). *Platforms for success.* Leicester, United Kingdom: National Institute of Adult Continuing Education.

The book helps organisations plan and implement a learning platform strategy. It draws information from face-to-face and online debates and discussions in 2006. Based in the context that

UK government legislation requires all learners to have access to an online space, it aims to help organisations identify their own vision and requirements and implement a sustainable resource. It includes a CD-ROM with a presentation by Martin Dougiamas (Lead at Moodle™), case studies, and activity templates.

Page, A., & Donovan, K. (2006). *E-learning: An introductory workbook for staff in post-16 education.* Leicester, United Kingdom: National Institute of Adult Continuing Education.

This book introduces teachers in post-16 education in the United Kingdom to e-learning, which is now recognised in many government papers and strategies. This version of the book helps individuals with and without experience through practical hints, tips, and case studies. There is a strong theme of issues relating to the development staff will require.

Prensky, M. (2003). E-nough! E-learning is a misnomer: It's mostly just "e-teaching." For any teaching to reliably and consistently produce the results we want, we still have a lot to learn about learning. *On the Horizon, 11*(1).

Prensky's article places the focus back on the question "What is learning?" so that e-learning can be more effective.

Prensky, M. (2004). *The emerging online life of the digital native: What they do differently because of technology, and how they do it. A work in progress.* Retrieved February 2007 from http://www.marcprensky.com/writing/Prensky-The_Emerging_Online_Life_of_the_Digital_Native-03.pdf

This article explores how and why digital natives (individuals who have grown up surrounded by and using numerous technologies) analyse, communicate, coordinate, create, evaluate, exchange, share, and ultimately learn differently, and how lecturers can support these differences.

Prensky, M. (2005). Engage me or enrage me: What today's learners demand. *Educause Review,* pp. 60-64.

The article explores the intricacies of today's learners, including their needs and desires for learning.

Rossett, A., & Sheldon, K. (2001). *Beyond the podium: Delivering training and performance to a digital world.* San Francisco: Jossey-Bass/Pfeiffer.

Rossett and Sheldon explore changes in training and development, revisit fundamental theories, and evaluate opportunities technology can provide educational organisations.

Salmon, G. (2002). *E-tivities: The key to active online learning.* London: Routledge Falmer, Taylor & Francis Books Ltd.

This is a book that explores the intricacies of teaching and supporting learners online. It is full of practical suggestions for delivering successful, worthwhile, and motivating learning online. Its recommendations are based around action research to provide answers to key questions that aim to increase the use of technologies and keep teachers and learners happy throughout the whole process.

Schank, R. C. (2005). *Lessons in learning, e-learning, and training: Perspectives and guidance for the enlightened trainer.* San Francisco: American Society for Training and Development & Pfeiffer.

This book of essays explores many issues faced by instructional designers and trainers, including three key points: what can and cannot be taught, how people think and learn, and genuine technological possibilities.

Tidd, J., Bessant, J., & Pavitt, K. (2001). *Managing innovation: Integrating technological, market and organizational change* (2nd ed.). Chichester, United Kingdom: Wiley.

This book explores the wider issues of implementing change into organisations, including elements focusing on management, innovation, and strategic thinking. New models of thinking and case studies are used to evaluate techniques and establish links between innovation and the environment.

# Section II
# Accessibility in E-Learning

*Without access there can be no learning and without accessibility there is exclusion. These are the issues of two chapters in this section. The potential of eLearning to improve accessibility as well as the problems are discussed.*

# Chapter VII
# Access and Accessibility in E-Learning

**Catherine Matheson**
*East Midlands Healthcare Workforce Deanery, University of Nottingham, UK*

**David Matheson**
*Medical Education Unit, University of Nottingham, UK*

## ABSTRACT

*This chapter considers some of the major questions around access and accessibility, beginning with the most basic: just what is meant by access and how this relates to the notion of accessibility since the assumption is so frequently made that we all know so much what access and accessibility are that few writers ever bother to define them or even to set under which terms of reference they understand the words. In this respect, as we shall show, there are parallels between the e-learning access debates and issues and those surrounding access to other forms of education, in particular, higher education.*

## INTRODUCTION

This chapter examines some of the major issues and debates surrounding access and accessibility in e-learning in a primarily British context with references to other countries such as Ireland and Australia, among others. However, it is worth noting that the key issues and debates under examination to a great extent transcend national divides since without direct access there is no e-learning. This brings us to an important point in relation to the three key factors that impede access in terms of disability: failure to adjust to the needs of all learners (an impediment that the idea of universal design aims to remedy, which we discuss in this chapter), stereotypical assumptions and preconceptions of peers and teachers, and above all, the fact that with e-learning all learners can become temporarily disabled in terms of hardware and software.

It is beyond dispute that the creation of information technology has been a revolution in all our lives and its impact is inescapable: "Without question, the creation of the personal computer has been the single most important technological advance for blind people's communication"[1] (White, 2006).

With the passing of laws concerning physical access and disability discrimination across much of the industrialised world, issues of access and accessibility in all their senses are very much to the fore these days. We are well used to Web sites offering text-only alternatives and to seeing logos such as *Bobby* that indicate the attainment by the site of certain standards of accessibility in terms of user friendliness for those with visual impairments and, sometimes, dyslexia. Ironically, visual impairment only represents the most visible aspect of the debates over access and accessibility to the Web in general and to e-learning in particular. It also represents an aspect whose problems and issues are readily ignored or, perhaps worse, are seen as already solved.

## BACKGROUND

Before considering the concepts of access and accessibility in e-learning, we examine these issues in relation to higher education because issues derived from these concepts have a great deal of similarities.

### The Concepts of Access and Accessibility in Higher Education

Broadly speaking, *access, accessibility*, and *widening participation* belong to a relatively recent educational policy discourse that has now become a major policy issue in postschool education in the British context (Dearing, 1997; Department for Education and Skills [DfES], 2004; Higher Education Funding Council for England [HEFCE], 2005; Metcalf, 1997; Robbins, 1963; Scottish Executive, 2004) and worldwide (Davies, 1995; Halsey, 1992; Lynch & O'Riordan, 1998; Skilbeck & Connell,

2000). The expansion of higher education has led to a greater openness on the part of many institutions of higher education to mature, part-time, and other non-traditional students. The expansion has also led to a significant improvement in relative participation rates for women, mostly minority ethnic groups and mature students (Committee of Vice-Chancellors and Principals [CVCP], 1998). The exact position of social class is more difficult to pin down because of shortcomings in data availability and a lack of a systematic approach in how the data are analysed (Davies, 1994, 1995). However, over the past 40 years, the ratios of relative participation from lower social groups have remained fairly constant, and higher education still counts a disproportionate number of students from professional and managerial backgrounds who remain greatly over-represented while students from skilled manual, semi-skilled, and unskilled backgrounds remain underrepresented (CVCP; Dearing; DfES; HEFCE; Robbins; Scottish Executive; Scottish Higher Education Funding Council [SHEFC], 2004). Young and mature people from skilled manual, semi-skilled, and unskilled backgrounds are not only less likely to be qualified to enter higher education, but also less likely to apply if qualified and less likely to be accepted if they apply, as well as being less likely to enter higher education if they are offered a place (Metcalf; Osborne, 1999). Skilled manual, semiskilled, or unskilled people form about half the economically active population of the United Kingdom and only about a quarter of young entrants to higher education are from these groups (Office of Population and Census Survey [OPCS], 1993). The rise in the number of 16- to 19-year-olds not involved in any form of education and training is matched by a growth in their economic activity both in low-skill full-time and part-time work (Hodgson & Spours, 2000; Metcalf, 2003), especially among lower socio-economic groups, and this has prompted the British government to aim for 50% of young people entering higher education by 2010[2] (DfES).

Access can be defined as "the freedom and ability to participate in an activity" (Aldrich, 1996, p. 6). There are many factors that determine access and accessibility. However, two broad categories can be defined. The first is the nature and extent of the provision available at a particular time. The second comprises such factors as wealth, social class, sex, age, ethnicity, and physical and mental ability (Aldrich). Widening access means increasing the representation of particular subgroups that are under-represented in higher education. Participation concerns the extent to which subgroups are represented across the very mixed offerings of university and subject. Widening participation therefore means "seeking a more representative cross-section of potential entrants across universities and subjects" (Tonks & Farr, 2003, p. 26). Access to higher education might be said to exist when the drivers are stronger than the barriers, and especially when unnecessary barriers are removed, whether these be social, economic, geographical, or disability related, and where potential participants feel that the learning opportunity is for people like themselves.

Drivers can be divided into external and internal factors. Examples of the former are gaining better qualifications and better employment prospects (Ball, Davies, David, & Reay, 2002; Reay, 1998). Examples of the latter are self-improvement, the normal thing to do, and the next step (Ball et al.; Du Bois-Reymond, 1998; Reay). Barriers, too, can be divided into external and internal factors. Examples of the former are situational barriers such as financial cost, time and family commitments, and lack of qualifications, as well as institutional barriers (Ball et al.; Reay; West, 1996; Zirkle, 2004). Institutional barriers can be constructed through unwelcoming institutions and especially through lack of support and services for students, and a lack of feedback and teacher contact leading to or reinforcing a sense of alienation and isolation (Mann, 2001; Zirkle). Examples of internal barriers are academic bar-

riers such as negative attitudes toward higher education because of a lack of interest in learning (Taylor & Spencer 1994), a lack of confidence in the ability to learn (Reay; Tett, 1999; West), a lack of relevance of learning opportunities (Reay; Tett), and a negative experience of school and teachers (Lynch & O'Riordan, 1998; West). Other examples of internal barriers are sociocultural barriers such as a lack of a sense of entitlement, where higher education is seen as something for the middle class and hence a luxury to be purchased at the expense of family (Lynch & O'Riordan; Tett; West); a sense of powerlessness; a perceived lack of ability to control life and anticipate the future (Tett); and finally negative constructions of higher education and the university. They are seen as dominant cultural metaphors still imbued with mystique that maintain sociocultural and psychological barriers among underrepresented socioeconomic groups who position themselves as outside of higher education because of emotional and cultural lack of fittingness (West; Reay; Lynch & O'Riordan; Tett; Archer & Hutchings, 2000). We can add to this list the extent to which a student feels he or she fits into a particular situation (Mann, 2001; Rovai & Jordan, 2004).

How do we best explain the fact that internalised barriers are seemingly more powerful than external and internal drivers and external barriers? Are qualified potential entrants from underrepresented socioeconomic groups less likely to enter higher education because they have low aspirations and low self-confidence? Are higher education institutions not inclusive enough? Why are new policies that aim to encourage access and widen participation seemingly not effective? Do policies tend to give an unfair advantage to some groups and unfair disadvantage to other groups? Despite attempts from schools to raise aspirations and self-confidence, more inclusive higher education institutions and new policies that aim to encourage access and widen participation, including transgenerational ways of thinking, nevertheless persist, advantaging some and disadvantaging others (Du Bois-Reymond, 1998; Gorard, Rees, & Fevre,1999).

Issues of access and accessibility are also related to the changing shape and scope of higher education (Davies 1995; Scott, 1995; Williams, 1997), including changes in external structures and in the nature and scope of higher education; changes in entry requirements, qualifications, entry routes, and exit points; changes in the nature of acceptable knowledge and acceptable modes of study; and changes in the nature of society and the labour market, as well as the impact of public discourses (Hodgson & Spours, 2000) and the impact of funding policies (Woodrow, 2000). The effectiveness of access, accessibility, and widening participation is measured by monitoring institutional performance indicators and the patterns of participation using the key variables of social class, educational qualifications, disability, ethnicity, sex, age, and even geographical region and post code (DfES, 2004; HEFCE, 2005).

To summarise, entering higher education remains the consequence of the interplay of barriers and drivers that start by being outside oneself, but since barriers are culturally constructed, all barriers are ultimately internalised. Barriers and drivers are also directly related to constructions of higher education and constructions of students; in other words, they are related to views about what higher education is for, whom it is for, and how worthwhile or difficult they might be. Barriers and drivers are furthermore influenced by the impact of public discourses as well as by the impact of life history factors such as initial education and familial influences that directly affect internalised barriers. Hence, access and accessibility in higher education have not only sociocultural but also political implications linked to what interests groups such as the state, various subgroups within society, schools and teachers, higher education institutions, and lecturers, and more importantly what potential entrants think about what higher education is for and who it is for.

## Access and Accessibility in E-Learning

Cooper's (2006) stance on accessibility is that by definition its aim is to maximise itself: "Accessibility...refers to design qualities that endeavour to make online learning available to all by ensuring that the way it is implemented does not create unnecessary barriers however the student may interact with the computer" (p. 105).

We could of course nuance this stance somewhat and refer to the degree of accessibility. Nonetheless, Ron Mace's term *universal design* might usefully be employed here (Burgstahler, 2002) and kept in the back of the designer's mind as an impetus toward being aware of unnecessary barriers and hence eliminating them: "Ron Mace coined the term 'universal design' to describe the concept of designing all products and the built environment to be aesthetic and usable to the greatest extent possible by everyone, regardless of their age, ability, or status in life" (North Carolina State University, n.d.).

From this perspective, where universal design applies, then technical accessibility is maximised. However, Cooper (2006) goes further and suggests that accessibility must include all aspects of the interaction between the student and the institution:

*Disability is...an artefact of the relationship between the learner and the learning environment or education delivery. Accessibility, given this redefinition, is the ability of the learning environment to adjust to the needs of all learners. Accessibility is determined by the flexibility of the e-Learning system (with respect to presentation, control methods, access modality and learner support) and the availability of adequate alternative-but equivalent content and activities. (p. 104)*

This relationship is well illustrated by Richard Altenbaugh's (2004) comment that "we are all temporarily able-bodied and we never know when disability is just around the corner." In e-learning we see this all too clearly from the way in which any user can become disabled by the often fickle performance of software and servers. This, if nothing else, should give us an insight into the increased problems of those dependent on less-than-optimal hardware, slow Internet connections, and old software, and who have, in addition, sensory or other impairments.

If an otherwise able-bodied person suffers a temporary motor impairment, such as being obliged to type with one hand due to an injury to the other, then he or she will quickly encounter the limitations of the QWERTY keyboard, according to the English-language layout, whose only *raison d'être* was to reduce the chances of the keys on a typewriter jamming together, a long since defunct reason but one that persists to this day. Arguably, QWERTY disables everyone who does not know how to touch-type by employing an arrangement of letters whose logic is difficult to fathom, even when one knows the reason behind it.

The relationship between the learner and the learning environment extends also to the relationship between the learner and his or her peers and teachers, and to the manner in which they interact and the stereotypes and preconceptions they bring to bear. It is said that online one can be whomsoever one wants to be (as witnessed by such online worlds as Second Life, where participants create avatars that are whatever they want them to be, whether in terms of sex, age, physical attributes, etc.; Guest, 2007). Online, one only has such disabilities of whatever sort as one admits to. Thus, as Knightley (2006) tells us when discussing e-learning in the context of disabled students, "as the students were unseen, they felt accepted and welcomed by others on the basis of their contributions rather than being judged by their disability" (p. 30). This of course extends to teachers and facilitators in an online environment who can reveal as little or as much of their disabilities as they choose to (Edmonds, 2004).

Perhaps this is the essence of access: not only being able to enter but being accepted for what one does rather than judged for what one is. Equally, "learning online transcended geographical, physical, visual and temporal barriers to accessing education and reduced socio-physical discrimination" (Knightley, 2006, p. 33). E-learning therefore has the potential to take access to a new level and bring into studying groups individuals hitherto left aside. This of course demands technological and economic investment of which more anon. Meanwhile, we turn to consider some of the issues, controversies, and problems concerning access to e-learning.

## ISSUES, CONTROVERSIES, AND PROBLEMS

Access can be absolute or relative. If access is absolute, the potential participant has no prerequisites whatsoever to fulfill, whether in terms of prior accomplishments, technology, or so forth. Clearly, all but the most utopian e-learning designer would shy away from absolute access as this would mean that even the oldest PC, Mac, or BBC-Master computer would be able to make full use of the materials on offer. This would mean eschewing many of the attributes that enhance accessibility for the majority of users whose machines are probably less than 10 years old. So, if real access is relative, what are the criteria and what are the bounds?

### Criteria and Bounds for Access

Perhaps the very first criterion for access is economic. E-learning is not free to create, and it bears costs of production, delivery, assessment, and so on. In addition to this, there is the cost of support materials such as online journals and databases that are prohibitive for most private individuals and therefore only realistically accessible through an institution. Access, therefore, is first influenced by the question of who should be paying for the course. If this is to be the state, then under what conditions? If it is to be the participant, then one must consider which persons are capable of meeting the cost. Of course, this is in addition to the costs involved in getting online.

The second criterion is qualification based and concerns the question of whether higher education should be open to everyone as was the case with Sweden following its U68 reforms (Anderson, 1974). This ties in with the moral argument that is to be had over whether the potential participant should be his or her own judge as to the suitability of a course, a debate to be had elsewhere. Suffice to say that while open academic access can sound quite laudable in an egalitarian kind of way, admitting a student to a course he or she is up to but for which the student is in reality unprepared can simply serve to de-motivate and dishearten. As such, qualifications can act very successfully as a means of entrenching existing social stratification while pretending to foster social mobility.

De-motivation was frequently the case when the UK Open University offered the status of associate student to those who, regardless of prior qualification, wished to do single modules that started above the usual introductory Level 1. Resources were insufficient to support these students and offer adequate remediation (and indeed they were warned of this prior to starting), and the result was massive student desertion (Matheson, 1992). Ironically, insisting on reasonable and appropriate academic qualifications can act in a manner to increase meaningful access insofar as those crossing the threshold have the reassurance of being judged by an authority external to themselves and being adequately prepared for the course to follow, hence demonstrating potential sufficient to successfully finish the course. On the other hand, this assumes that possibilities exist for such qualification to be achieved, and this is where e-learning and other forms of distance learning can, in appropriate circumstances and

for appropriate subject areas, come to the fore for those denied such possibilities for reasons of geography, disability, or lack of help to take over some part of their responsibilities while they attend a course.

An often repeated assertion is that access is for everyone, disabled or not: "Good design for disabled people is good design for all" (Cooper, 2006, p. 104). From an egalitarian or even meritocratic perspective, this may sound good, and yet there appears to be a dearth of empirical evidence to support it. Indeed, it does not require much imagination to reason that by adopting notions of accessibility as outlined by Cooper, the end-product risks becoming encumbered while at the same time creativity is sacrificed by the efforts needed to take proper cognizance of colour schemes to accommodate dyslexics, alternate text for screen readers and text-only browsers, resizable and changeable fonts, and so on. Without much effort, one could very readily start to argue one's way into a rationalisation as to why one need take little or even no notice of issues of access and accessibility in e-learning.

Yet one need only look at a Web site that has ignored such advice to appreciate effort in accessibility, even for those of us with high-speed Internet connections, up-to-date equipment, and modern software. We suggest that you find a Web site where the pages do not scroll properly, where the font size is too small and cannot be resized, or where the contrast between text and background makes it difficult to read. It takes little effort to find such sites (see Flanders, 2007, for some suggestions). Equally, in creating a site, it takes little effort to avoid creating such barriers. In addition, "planning for access as courses are being developed is easier—and therefore less expensive—than developing accommodation strategies once a student with a disability enrolls in or a person with a disability applies to teach a course" (Burgstahler, 2002, p. 12).

Except where the very nature of a subject area excludes some part of the population (such as totally blind persons wishing to become air-traffic controllers), is there not a strong argument in favour of access being for everyone who is academically qualified? Besides this, legislation such as the Special Educational Needs and Disability Act (2001) in the United Kingdom or the Americans with Disabilities Act (1990) demand that access not be denied on the grounds of sensory, physical, emotional, or mental disability unless there are robust grounds for so doing.

Burgstahler (2002, p. 10) asserts that "if qualified individuals with disabilities enroll in distance learning courses, these courses must be made accessible to them." We would suggest rephrasing this slightly to become "if qualified individuals enroll in distance learning, these courses must be made accessible to them." If, as Altenbaugh (2004) tells us, we are all temporarily able bodied and, as is clear from the extent to which we all suffer from less-than-optimal software, variable Internet connections, and hardware failure, we all skirt the edge of disablement in one form or another. Access should therefore be inclusive of all who are qualified. If it is taken as read that access is inclusive, then there is some hope that e-learning avoids being seen as a solution to the problem of disability. Otherwise, we risk a situation where, as an anonymous reviewer (2007) of Seale in the *British Journal of Education Technology* put it, "there's too much concentration on using modern technologies to improve the learning of those with such barriers and not enough on inclusivity and integration" (p. 383). If access by the disabled remains to be seen as a problem, then one day it may be deemed to be solved. If access by all who are qualified is seen as a right, then there is no solution. Rather, there is ongoing cognizance of the need to be aware that not everyone interacts with the e-world in the same way and to take account these differences when designing programmes, software, and hardware.

Debates over for whom access is intended extends of course well beyond the disabled and include the geographically isolated, the economi-cally deprived, and so on. None of these groups are mutually exclusive.

## Access to the Internet

It is self-evident that the first step on the road to accessing e-learning is to have access to the Internet. As we see from Figure 1, this varies widely across the countries of the European Union (EU) and the European economic area (EEA).

The data used in Figure 1 compound Internet use in all possible domains, be it at home, at work, on a mobile phone, in an Internet café, or in a public library. Not all of these fora are well adapted to e-learning. For example, while mobile phones can increasingly access the Internet, it is often very difficult to read what is on the screen unless the Web site concerned has a mobile version in the manner of the UK Open University. Such sites are few and far between, and usually the user has to simply cope as best as he or she can with content designed for a screen of 40 cm or so in diagonal width. Public libraries in some places offer Internet access for free; others do so for a charge. These are, however, public places and as such are not always conducive to attempting to follow a course of study. Likewise for Internet cafés, though here the major uses are general surfing, e-mailing, and gaming. Even if the cost is acceptable to the would-be e-learner, the ambience with its noise level is unlikely to be so.

This leaves home and work as possible loci of e-learning activity. Work by its very definition is the place for work, not usually for study. Educational establishments concern only a small part of the population so in reality, for most of the population, this leaves home as the only really viable place in which to engage in e-learning. Indeed, participants in Knightley's (2006, p. 33) study "highlighted the convenience, flexibility and *necessity* of *home* access to the Internet for pursuing their courses. This raises other issues, such as the cost of computers and related software

*Figure 1. Percentage of individuals regularly using the Internet in the EU and the EEA (in 2006)*

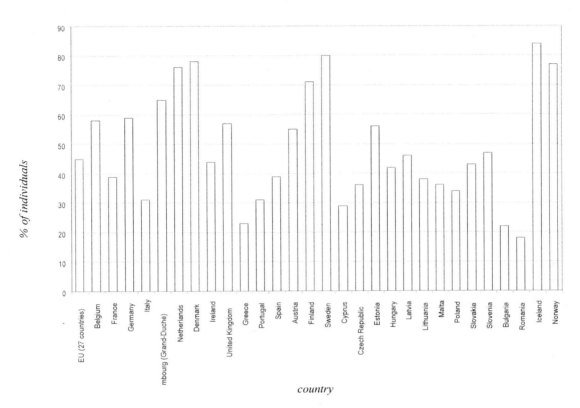

Source: Eurostat, available at http://epp.eurostat.ec.europa.eu/portal/page?_pageid=1073,46870091&_dad= portal&_ schema=PORTAL&p_product_code=ECB12560 (retrieved May 18, 2007)

and sundries, and of charges made by internet service providers."

We see from Figure 2 that at present e-learning at home is open to just over 40% of the EU population, although across the EU, home Internet use ranges from 77% in the cases of Denmark, The Netherlands, and Sweden down to 11% in the case of Romania. In the countries of the EU/EEA, geography seems to play no role in the percentage of individuals using the Internet at home, and neither does national wealth as we see relatively rich France with 35% while relatively poor Slovenia with 41%.

This of course gives no indication of how many persons actually engage in e-learning; however, that is to be construed, whether as for-

mal, nonformal, or informal learning. It is rather a measure of those who have access at all to the Internet at home, and without such access scope for e-learning is clearly limited.

## Access to Broadband and Download Speed

The kind of material that is available and accessible is contingent on download speed and, given the ever-increasing size of files and of Web pages, on household broadband access; even at its slowest, broadband is orders of magnitude faster than dial-up connections.

Unfortunately, it is clear from the file size of Web pages that authors are tending more and

*Figure 2. Percentage of individuals in the EU and EEA using the Internet at home (in 2006)*

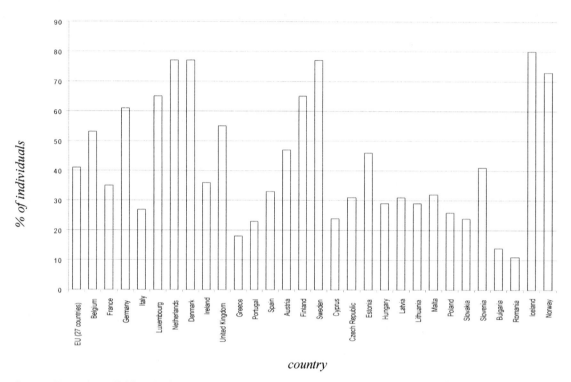

Source: Eurostat, available at http://epp.eurostat.ec.europa.eu/portal/page?_pageid=1073,46870091&_dad= portal&_ schema=PORTAL&p_product_code=ECB17685 (retrieved May 18, 2007)

more to assume that users either have broadband or that they are very patient. Hence, we see the increasing use of Flash and Shockwave animations on the welcome page. These are not always effectively streamed and sometimes demand large buffer sizes. Hence, the user even on a fast connection can sit frustrated while waiting for the animation or clip to start, never mind finish. Images are not always optimised for Web use (i.e., made as small as possible) despite this being a very readily achieved outcome in image editing software such as Photoshop or GIMP. Rather, they may be posted as is, and while this does result in far higher quality of prints and less tendency for images to pixelate when enlarged, it does mean waiting, sometimes for quite a while, for them to download to one's browser, and this even on a high-speed connection.

Then there are updates. Every Internet user with any sense will endeavour to keep software up to date, at least as far as antivirus software is concerned. The time this can take may be considerable. Warnings such as those issued by McAfee stating that downloading their antivirus updates "may take up to 30 minutes on a 56kb/s modem" certainly acknowledge the problem but do nothing to solve it. Problems of course get worse when a new version of familiar software is not reverse compatible as is the case of Microsoft Office 2007, which requires the downloading of a free compatibility pack in order for users of earlier versions of MS Office to access files created in the new software. On a 10Mb/s broadband link, this download took less than 1 minute. Notice in Figure 4 the estimated time to download on a 56kb/s modem, a speed typical of those used in

*Figure 3. Household broadband access in the EU and EEA*

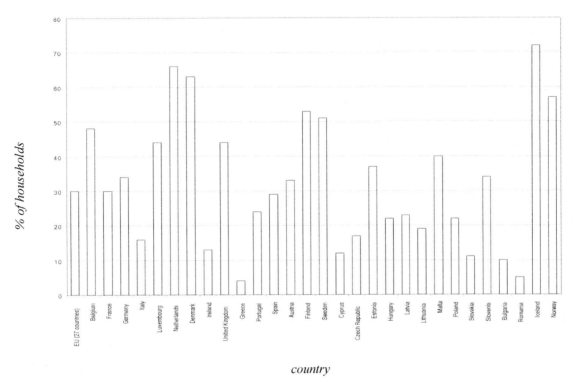

country

Source: Eurostat, available at http://epp.eurostat.ec.europa.eu/portal/page?_pageid=1073,46870091&_dad= portal&_ schema=PORTAL&p_product_code=ECB17682 (retrieved May 29, 2007)

dial-up connections. This assumes that the modem is running at full speed and that the download proceeds without a hitch. The reality is that the link might fail and the download might have to be restarted from scratch, or, most likely, the modem is running at a low fraction of its maximum speed. While this is going on, the phone cannot be used for any other purpose.

Another way to access the Internet and hence e-learning involves so-called satellite broadband, originally conceived as a system whereby one downloaded via the satellite but uploaded via the phone. Satellite broadband now employs both uploading and downloading via satellite. It is, however, considerably more expensive, even with the EU grants available in some places to help with installation, and the monthly costs in the United Kingdom are more than double the costs

of using ADSL (asymmetric digital subscriber line) or cable broadband. This simply means that high-speed links in areas without cable or ADSL are even more dependent on socioeconomic situations.

## Geographical Considerations and Infrastructure

One might expect that the greater the degree of urbanisation, then the greater the availability of high-speed Internet connections. This is true as far as the United Kingdom is concerned, where

*access was highest in London where 78 per cent of households with Internet access had a broadband connection (49 per cent of all households in the London region). Northern Ireland had the low-*

*Figure 4. Time to download an update from Microsoft*

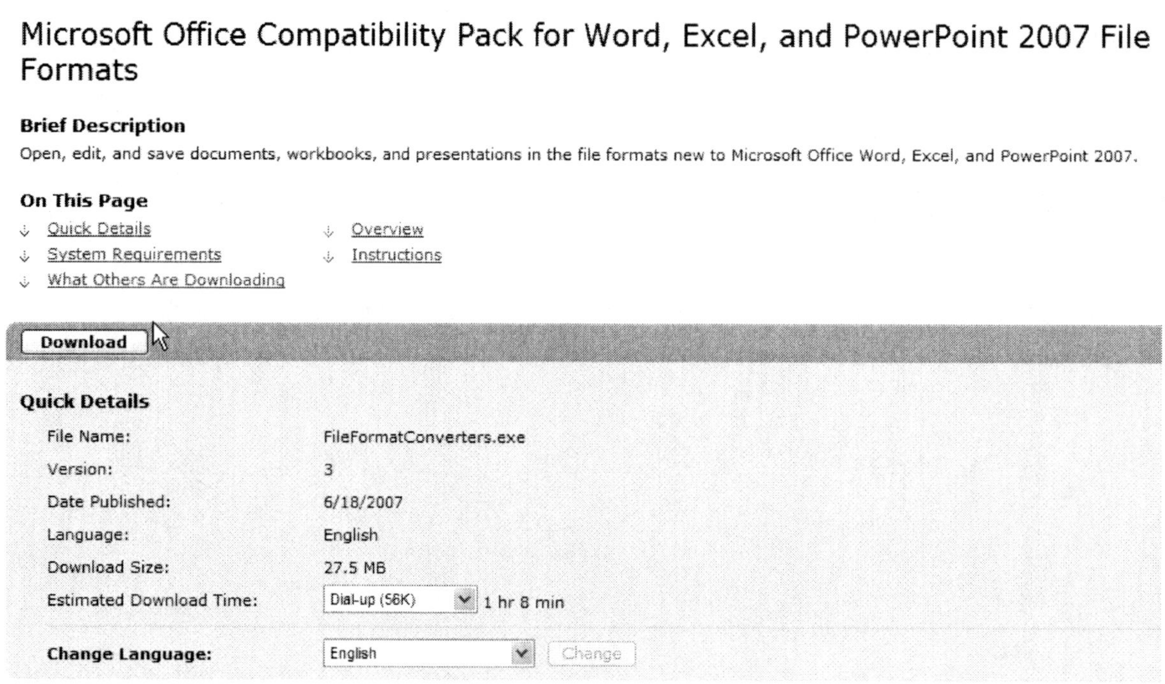

## Microsoft Office Compatibility Pack for Word, Excel, and PowerPoint 2007 File Formats

**Brief Description**

Open, edit, and save documents, workbooks, and presentations in the file formats new to Microsoft Office Word, Excel, and PowerPoint 2007.

**On This Page**
↓ Quick Details          ↓ Overview
↓ System Requirements     ↓ Instructions
↓ What Others Are Downloading

Download ⌐

**Quick Details**

| | |
|---|---|
| File Name: | FileFormatConverters.exe |
| Version: | 3 |
| Date Published: | 6/18/2007 |
| Language: | English |
| Download Size: | 27.5 MB |
| Estimated Download Time: | Dial-up (56K) ▼ 1 hr 8 min |
| **Change Language:** | English ▼ Change |

Note: Screenshot taken on October 17, 2007

est proportion of households with a broadband connection at 56 per cent (28 per cent of all Northern Ireland households)....[However] the area with the lowest access level was Scotland with 48 per cent. (Office for National Statistics [ONS], 2006)

Yet Norway, with a much more dispersed population and rather difficult geography, manages to have 57% of its households on broadband and 73% of its population aged 16 to 74 accessing the Internet from home. The essential difference lies in the telephone infrastructure. While broadband in the United Kingdom developed with cable television, with telephone companies following later with ADSL exchanges, allowing the use of multiplexing (i.e., sending more than one signal down the same line) and high rates of data compression and decompression (necessary

to increase upload and download speeds), these were entirely commercial ventures; as such, cable reaches few rural areas, and ADSL exchanges are rare outside of the urban areas. In Norway, it was the national government that decided to make broadband available to all the homes in the country. It did so using the telephone structure and by updating exchanges as well as providing additional funding for those areas in which it was economically unviable for private investment (Ananova, 2000).

## Household Income

Data on correlations between Internet access and household income are few and far between, and even the Organisation for Economic Co-operation and Development (OECD) has not updated its data since 2002.

The disparities between income groups are stark and speak for themselves.

Clearly problems abound, but there are solutions to at least some of the issues, and it is to these and recommendations that we now turn.

## SOLUTIONS AND RECOMMENDATIONS

In order to improve the accessibility and design of e-learning, the first issue to consider is how accessible a site is at all. In other words, how easily can a user find the information he or she is after? Can users readily find their way from one part to another? Can they do this without having to think?

## Improving Accessibility and Design of E-Learning

Krug's (2006) *Don't Make Me Think!* provides a lucid, and indeed often amusing but always stimulating, set of exemplified and explained precepts to follow in order for users of one's Web site to be able to do exactly what the title suggests, that is, not think but rather concentrate on getting from the site whatever they want together with whatever the designer would like them to get. Krug does not specifically discuss educational sites but all that he says is of relevance. However, educational sites and e-learning programmes depend less on passing traffic than do general sites, and hence it is easy for e-learning designers to assume that their user is sufficiently motivated as to put up with just

*Figure 5. Household Internet access by income level[1] (in 2001 or latest available year)*

| Households with Internet access as a percentage of all households | | | |
|---|---|---|---|
| | Household Internet access | First income quartile | Fourth income quartile |
| United Kingdom 2001-2002 | 40.0 | 11.0 | 80.0 |
| United States 2000 | 41.5 | 14.0 | 77.0 |
| Canada | 48.7 | 22.6 | 75.8 |
| Finland | 39.5 | 20.0 | 69.4 |
| Australia 2000 | 33.0 | 9.0 | 58.0 |
| Germany | 27.0 | 14.0 | 55.0 |
| New Zealand | 37.0 | 33.3 | 71.7 |
| Netherlands 1999 | 26.5 | 20.0 | 57.0 |
| Switzerland 2000 | 36.5 | 11.2 | 46.8 |
| France | 17.8 | 7.0 | 34.0 |
| Turkey 2000[2] | 6.9 | 0.1 | 21.4 |
| Denmark | 52.0 | 37.0 | 53.0 |
| | | | |

[1] For the United Kingdom, the first and last deciles instead of quartiles, and for Germany and New Zealand, the first and last income brackets

[2] Households in urban areas only

Source: OECD ICT database, August 2002, available from http://www.oecd.org/dataoecd/44/4/2766829.xls (retrieved June 1, 2007)

about anything. Nothing could be further from the truth. E-learners may have had the motivation (assuming they had a choice in the matter) to sign up for whatever is on offer, but this is a far cry from being able to claim they have the persistence to see it through to the end.

A second issue to consider is asking whether the e-learning user is a Web user first or a learner first, or indeed whether these different aspects of their nature simply come to the fore at different moments. One can take a step further and demand whether such a creature exists at all and propose that, rather than risking creating a mythical stereotype, one is dealing with a vast range of e-learners and that one ignores this diversity at one's peril. It is with this in mind that perhaps the first question any designer of e-learning should ask themselves concerns who the intended audience is and what equipment they can reasonably be expected to have access to. Cook and Dupras (2004) put this as their second step (their first being to perform a needs analysis, something which presumes a level of access to the learners that one may not necessarily have) but recognise that there are occasions when it has to come first. We would suggest that any start without ascertaining who the audience is and the equipment they can be reasonably expected to use (in terms of minimum specifications, including PC specifications, such as random-access memory [RAM], clock speed, etc.; browser type and version; download speed; other software; etc.) is a risky venture that relies more on hunch than on careful calculation.

It is notable that Cook and Dupras (2004) at no point make any specific mention of maximising access and accessibility within their audience. Writing as they do with regard to medical education, access and accessibility appear subsumed into part of their fifth principle and fall under the rather vague umbrella of "adhere to principles of good webpage design" (p. 698).

The Web abounds with guides to successful Web design as does the computing section of most bookshops. However, giving advice as to what to do ignores the effect of not following such advice and the horrors that may result. We could at this point enumerate the manifold ways in which Web sites can affront even the most basic common sense, but often the only way to really appreciate something is to experience it directly. With this thought in mind, and with thanks to Heather Rai and Simon Wilkinson for first bringing this to our attention, we suggest that you visit Vincent Flanders' (2007) *Web Pages that Suck 2.0* that shows examples of some of the worst design faults imaginable in Web design and explains why they are so bad. Unlike many guides to Web design that demonstrate what to do, Flanders sets out quite explicitly to show what will result if one does not follow the basic precepts of good Web design. The result is the stuff of nightmares and a salutary lesson to all who venture into Web design under whatever guise.

## Avoiding Cognitive Overload

One area of contention concerns the notions of cognitive load and cognitive overload (Clark & Mayer, 2003; Mayer & Moreno, 2003). Cognitive load theory assumes that humans can take on a limited amount of information at a time (Paas, Renkl, & Sweller, 2003), consisting of seven plus or minus two items (Clark, Nguyen, & Sweller, 2006), and that they process this information through two discrete channels, auditory and visual, as shown in Figure 6.

Mayer and Moreno (2003) give a series of examples of how a learning experience might overload the available cognitive processing, but for the sake of brevity, let us discuss just one: This concerns the situation where a student is required to view an animation while an explanation of what is happening is displayed at the bottom of the screen. The student's attention is in effect split by having to deal with two visual tasks at once: "The on-screen text is presented at the bottom on the screen, so while the student is reading she cannot view the animation, and while she is viewing

*Figure 6. Mayer and Moreno's cognitive theory of multimedia learning*

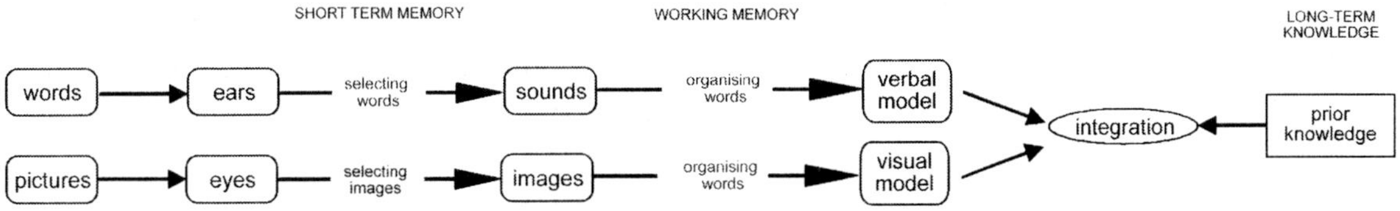

Source: Mayer and Moreno (2003, p. 44)

the animation she cannot read the text" (Mayer & Moreno, p. 45). Mayer and Moreno's solution is to present the words as a spoken narration so that they are processed by the auditory route and not the visual. This assumes that the student can actually hear the narration and is neither deaf nor in a situation where she or he cannot use speakers or headphones. It also assumes that the student cannot go back over the material, and equally assumes a high degree of linearity to viewing an animation and to reading a text rather than giving credence to the possibility of hopping between the two. Linked to this is the redundancy principle (Clark & Mayer, 2003), whereby one should use spoken narrative or written narrative but not the two simultaneously. Clark and Moreno do give some exceptions to this principle and include those occasions where there are no competing visuals (i.e., the text is effectively alone on the screen), and "where the learners are not native speakers or when the verbal material is long and complex or contains unfamiliar key words" (p. 105).

## Making Web Spaces More Inclusive

An area overlooked in the literature on redundancy is the sociocultural impact of the spoken word. The written word is not devoid of cultural connotations. Notwithstanding the actual language employed, it will employ grammatical nuances and spellings indicative of the writer's cultural heritage. These may be as subtle as using a past participle where others might use a gerund (as in the Scots

phrase "my hair needs washed" as compared to the English "my hair needs washing"). However, speech carries accent. Accent, especially in the various forms of English, carries stereotypes and expectations are built thereupon. It is indeed curious that writers such as Clark, Moreno, and Sweller (two Americans and an Australian) give no space to the cultural impact of the spoken word, which adds one more thing to the processing of the information conveyed.

In addition to paying attention to sociocultural impact, the main contention regarding redundancy comes over whether a site should cater for additional needs (and this includes those brought about by circumstances such as not having any speakers or headphones) without further ado or whether the user has to opt into such additional support. In some respects, this is a moral debate and concerns those things a person can expect as a right and those which have to be specifically chosen. It also highlights that debates over how accessible a site is at all blend with debates over accessibility for those with additional needs of whatever sort.

Legislative initiatives, enshrined in various national and supranational laws, have lent impetus to the development of more inclusive Web spaces. At the same time, there is a dawning realization that to argue that

*making sites more accessible for [the disabled] makes them more accessible for everyone...obscures the fact that the reverse actually is true.*

*Making sites more usable for the "rest of us" is one of the most effective ways to make them more effective for people with disabilities. (Krug, 2006, p. 174)*

Krug's (2006) argument is quite simply that if an able-bodied person is confused by a site, then a disabled person will likely be also and indeed may suffer all the more from, perhaps, not being able to read error messages and the like. In fact, he is inclining toward the notion of universal design as mentioned above, whereby access is built into the resource from the planning stage. This means giving the user as much control as possible over the environment so that he or she can change background colours, font sizes, pages sizes, fonts, and so on. Fortunately, Web-authoring programs, such as Adobe Dreamweaver, permit this easily through the use of cascading style sheets (CSS). Demonstrations of the utility of CSS can be found in the CSS Zen Garden (http://www.csszengarden.com). CSS is not a panacea but is a major step in the direction of allowing users to customise sites as needs be and hence make them more accessible to themselves.

Debates over access, accessibility, and design continue to burn brightly and will doubtless do so for some time to come. However, technology moves on as the creation of CSS in 1998 (Krug, 2006) shows, and for that reason we refer you to the list of Web sites presented in the additional–reading section at the end of this chapter. Attitudes and theories are of course provisional, and it is to possible developments in these in relation to e-learning that we now turn.

## FUTURE TRENDS

As previously mentioned, an area overlooked in the literature on redundancy is the sociocultural aspect to the spoken word, and to a lesser extent the written word and the cultural aspect of teaching and learning in general. Access and accessibility,

whether in relation to higher education or education in general, or whether more specifically access and accessibility in e-learning, have not only sociocultural implications but also political ones that are linked to what interest groups such as the state, various subgroups within society, providers of education, and more importantly potential service users think about what e-learning is for and who it is for.

Various mechanisms or conceptual models might be worth exploring in order to explain the lesser likelihood of participation in e-learning by underrepresented groups. Some existing conceptual explanatory models already exist, and a future trend might be to apply these models specifically to e-learning. Examples of these conceptual explanatory models are Jackson's hidden curriculum (1968, 1971) and Bourdieu's habitus and cultural capital (1990, 1997).

Jackson (1968, 1971) came up with the concept of the hidden curriculum to underline that schools do not only transmit an approved body of knowledge, but also transmit implicit messages arising from the structure of schooling. Differential achievement can be explained because education is a process of socialising practices that pass on norms and values, and maintain cultural reproduction by favouring those with more cultural resources.

Bourdieu (1990, 1997) and Bourdieu and Passeron (1977) came up with the concepts of habitus, a system of deeply ingrained structured and structuring attitudinal dispositions and assumptions subconsciously acquired from early sociocultural experiences and social conditionings, and forms of capital, but more importantly cultural capital to highlight how these exert a regulative influence upon middle-class potential entrants that makes them more likely to enter higher education. This is so because of better cultural resources and because of the fear of the threat of downward social mobility or loss of status if they do not.

The hidden curriculum, and habitus and cultural capital are attempts to explain why transgenerational ways of thinking or intergenerational family scripts persist, advantaging some and disadvantaging others. These and other various explanatory mechanisms such as Weber's social closure (1978) and Foucault's (1988) disciplinary power and finely graded hierarchies, which are variations on hidden curriculum, habitus, and cultural capital, might be worth exploring in order to explain the lesser likelihood of participation in e-learning by underrepresented groups. Another trend might be to attempt to devise a new conceptual explanatory model based on empirical research.

## CONCLUSION

With every new communications technology, readers, listeners, and viewers have been regaled with visions of an impending revolution in teaching and learning. The end of face-to-face teaching for all but the most basic learning has been heralded since the invention of the postage stamp in 1840, and repeated with the invention of radio and then television (Matheson, 1992). The degree of interactivity possible in e-learning marks it out from its predecessors as does the extent to which the learner can customise the material (in principle, at least, and increasingly in practice) so as to overcome to a maximum disabilities in terms of hearing, seeing, or reading. E-learning is accompanied by adaptive technologies that allow those physically precluded from participation in traditional teaching and learning to take a full and active part and to present to their peers whatever image they choose. They can therefore be defined in their colleagues' minds by their participation rather than categorised through stereotypes attached to some disability or another. However, "online courses do not offer a panacea for non-traditional students" (Schwartzman, 2007, p. 115). They lessen some barriers and eliminate some others, but major barriers still remain, and not the least of these concern the cost of getting

online and then the cost of accessing courses. Those in most need of adaptive technologies and of efforts being made to remove unnecessary barriers are frequently those least able to pay for them. This throws up a moral question regarding whether, in a learning society or learning age, people have the right to e-learning or indeed to any learning beyond the most basic. If they have such a right, then it is meaningless unless it is financially supported, and access to e-learning in higher education means actually being able to join university-level courses and not simply having the theoretical possibility of doing so if only one has the means.

This has only been a brief foray into the issues, controversies, problems, and solutions in regard to access and accessibility to e-learning in higher education. It has served, however, to highlight that while there are many outstanding issues, access is increasingly seen less as a problem to be solved as a set of principles that determine good practice. It also brings together practice, experiences, and research in the development and use of e-learning and e-teaching, and extends into neighbouring debates. In the end, it all comes around to the concepts basic to all e-learning and e-teaching that we all skate around the edge of disablement. We are readily prey to circumstances, whether in terms of our own physicality, our technical infrastructure, or the software we use, which all easily disable us and can be reduced to one fundamental idea: E-learning depends on access, for without access, there is no e-learning.

Access and accessibility in relation to e-learning in higher education have a brief history that has seen amazing strides forward. However, much remains to be done, and we end with a word on what some of this might consist of.

## FUTURE RESEARCH DIRECTIONS

A major area for future research on access and accessibility in e-learning in higher education concerns how issues on access and accessibility in face-to-face higher education translate (or not) into e-learning. Thus, one might examine how the drivers and barriers apparent in potential students' participation in higher education occur (or not) in e-learning in higher education. Given the fact that one can create one's own identity in e-learning and this according to whatever image one chooses, it would be enlightening to discover the role of habitus in this creation as well as knowing whether a relation, if any, exists between habitus in face-to-face higher education and in e-learning in higher education.

Habitus, cultural capital, and the hidden curriculum and its impact on e-learners in higher education await investigation. To what extent and in what ways is the hidden curriculum in higher education modified through e-learning? Does technology create a new hidden curriculum whereby there are values and norms transmitted by such simple things as download speed? How do different groups react to this?

Identity creation itself is a rich area for research. To what extent is what might be termed *identity modification* a frequent occurrence in e-learning in higher education? Are participants honest in their descriptions of themselves? If so, to what degree? If not, what aspects do they modify? Indeed, do participants reveal anything of themselves at all other than their names or perhaps some user names?

Coupled with this is the image that e-learning students create of each other. What role does, for example, a student's name play? Should students only have user names in order to avoid inadvertent (or indeed intentional) stereotyping? What issues would be raised in, for example, a class in gender studies where no one knew the gender of anyone else as everyone was identified by a unisex user name?

And related to all of these topics is the notion of participation in online activities. E-learning is well known for the lack of participation in online conferences, be they synchronous (all participants online at the same time as happens in a chat room) or asynchronous (where messages and discussions remain visible and can be contributed to by participants in their own time). Worthy of investigation are the factors that influence student participation in online activities and whether these link to any issues of access and accessibility.

## REFERENCES

Aldrich, R. (1996). *Education for the nation.* London: Cassell.

Altenbaugh, R. (2004, September 21-23). Education, disability and the march of dimes. Paper presented at the European Conference on Educational Research, Rethymno, Crete.

Ananova, N. (2000, October 15). *Norway wants Internet access for all.* Retrieved June 1, 2007, from http://www.hi-europe.co.uk/files/2000/9980.htm

Anderson, C. A. (1974). Sweden re-examines higher education: A critique of the U68 report. *Comparative Education, 10*(3), 167-180.

Anonymous. (2007). E-learning and disability in higher education. *British Journal of Educational Technology, 38*(2), 382-383.

Archer, L., & Hutchings, M. (2000). "Bettering yourself"? Discourses of risk, cost and benefit in ethnically diverse, young working-class non-participants' constructions of higher education. *British Journal of Sociology of Education, 21*(4), 555-573.

Ball, S. J., Davies, J., David, M., & Reay, D. (2002). "Classification" and "judgement": Social class and the "cognitive structures" of choice of higher education. *British Journal of Sociology of Education, 23*(1), 51-72.

Bourdieu, P. (1990). *The logic of practice.* Cambridge: Polity Press.

Bourdieu, P. (1997). The forms of capital. In A. H. Halsey, H. Lauder, & A. Stuart-Wells (Eds.), *Education, culture, economy and society* (pp. 46-58). Oxford, United Kingdom: Oxford University Press.

Bourdieu, P., & Passeron, J. C. (1977). *Reproduction in education, society and culture.* London: SAGE.

Burgstahler, S. (2002). Distance learning: Universal design, universal access. *AACE Journal, 10*(1), 32-61.

Clark, R., & Mayer, R. (2003). *E-learning and the science of instruction.* San Francisco: Pfeiffer.

Clark, R., Nguyen, F., & Sweller, J. (2006). *Efficiency in learning.* San Francisco: Pfeiffer.

Committee of Vice-Chancellors and Principals. (1998). *From elitism to inclusion* (executive summary). London: Author.

Cook, D., & Dupras, D. (2004). A practical guide to developing effective Web-based learning. *Journal of General Internal Medicine, 19*, 698-707.

Cooper, M. (2006). Making online learning accessible to disabled students: An institutional case study. *ALT-J Research in Learning Technology, 14*, 103-115.

Davies, P. (1994). Fourteen years on, what do we know about access students? Some reflections on national statistical data. *Journal of Access Studies, 9*(1), 45-60.

Davies, P. (Ed.). (1995). *Adults in higher education: International experiences in access and participation.* London: Jessica Kingsley.

Dearing, R. (1997). *Higher education in the learning society: Report of the National Committee of Inquiry into Higher Education.* London: HMSO.

Department for Education and Skills. (2004). *Widening participation.* London: The Stationery Office.

Du Bois-Reymond, M. (1998). I don't want to commit myself yet: Young people's life concepts. *Journal of Youth Studies, 1*(1), 63-79.

Edmonds, C. D. (2004). Providing access to students with disabilities in online distance education: Legal and technical concerns for higher education. *The American Journal of Distance Education, 18*(1), 51-62.

Flanders, V. (2007). *Web pages that suck 2.0.* Retrieved June 11, 2007, from http://www.webpagesthatsuck.com

Foucault, M. (1988). *Politics, philosophy, culture: Interviews and other writings 1977-1984* (L. D. Kritzman, Ed.). London: Routledge.

Gorard, S., Rees, G., & Fevre, R. (1999). Patterns of participation in lifelong learning: Do families make a difference? *British Educational Research Journal, 25*(4), 517-532.

Guest, T. (2007). *Second lives.* London: Hutchison.

Halsey, A. H. (1992). An international comparison of access to higher education. *Oxford Studies in Comparative Education, 1*(1), 11-36.

Higher Education Funding Council for England. (1997). *The influence of neighbourhood type on participation in higher education* (Interim Report). Bristol, United Kingdom: Author.

Higher Education Funding Council for England. (2005). *January 2005/03 research report: Young participation in higher education.* Bristol, United Kingdom: Author. Retrieved from http://www.hefce.ac.uk/pubs/hefce/2005/05_03/05_03c.pdf

Hodgson, A., & Spours, K. (2000, February 21). *Going to college or getting a job: Factors affecting attitudes to HE.* Paper presented at the Progression to Higher Education Working Seminar Series, London.

Jackson, P. (1968). *Life in classrooms.* Eastbourne, United Kingdom: Holt, Rinehart and Winston.

Jackson, P. (1971). The student's world. In M. Silberman (Ed.), *The experience of schooling* (pp. 76-84). Eastbourne, United Kingdom: Holt, Rinehart and Winston.

Knightley, W. (2006). Tackling social exclusion through online learning: A preliminary investigation. *Journal of Access Policy and Practice, 4*(1), 20-38.

Krug, S. (2006). *Don't make me think! A common sense approach to Web usability* (2nd ed.). Berkeley, CA: New Riders.

Lynch, K. L., & O'Riordan, K. (1998). Inequality in higher education: A study of class barriers. *British Journal of Sociology, 19*(4), 445-478.

Mann, S. (2001). Alternative perspectives on the student experience: Alienation and engagement. *Studies in Higher Education, 26*(1), 7-19.

Matheson, D. (1992). *Post-compulsory education in Suisse Romande.* Unpublished doctoral dissertation, University of Glasgow, Glasgow, United Kingdom.

Mayer, R., & Moreno, R. (2003). Nine ways to reduce cognitive load in multimedia learning. *Educational Psychologist, 38*(1), 43-52.

Metcalf, H. (1997). *Class and higher education: The participation of young people from lower social classes.* London: Council for Industry and Higher Education.

Metcalf, H. (2003). Increasing inequality in higher education: The role of term-time working. *Oxford Review of Education, 29*(3), 315-329.

North Carolina State University. (n.d.). *Profile of Ron Mace.* Retrieved May 16, 2007, from http://ncsudesign.org/content/index.cfm/fuseaction/alum_profile/departmentID/1/startRow/4

Office for National Statistics. (2006). *Internet access.* London: Author. Retrieved May 18, 2007, from http://www.statistics.gov.uk/CCI/nugget.asp?ID=8

Office of Population and Census Survey. (1993). *1991 census household composition in Great Britain.* London: HMSO.

Osborne, R. (1999, February 9). *The institutional distribution of young people from low income groups.* Address to a Joint Meeting of the Quantitative Studies and Access Network and SRHE, London.

Paas, F., Renkl, A., & Sweller, J. (2003). Cognitive load theory and instructional design: Recent developments. *Educational Psychologist, 38*(1), 1-4.

Parry, G. (1997). Patterns of participation in higher education in England: A statistical summary and commentary. *Higher Education Quarterly, 51*(1), 6-28.

Reay, D. (1998). "Always knowing" and "never being sure": Familial and institutional habituses and higher education choice. *Journal of Education Policy, 13*(4), 519-529.

Robbins. (1963). *Higher education: Report of the Committee on Higher Education under the Chairmanship of Lord Robbins.* London: HMSO.

Rovai, A. P., & Jordan, H. M. (2004). Blended learning and sense of community: A comparative analysis with traditional and fully online graduate courses. *International Review of Research in Open and Distance Learning, 5*(2), 1-13.

Schwartzman, R. (2007). Refining the question: How can online instruction maximize opportunities for all students? *Communication Education, 56*(1), 113-117.

Scott, P. (1995). *The meaning of mass higher education.* Milton Keynes, United Kingdom: Open University Press, Society for Research into Higher Education.

Scottish Executive. (2004). *Students in higher education in Scotland 2002/03.* Edinburgh, United Kingdom: Author.

Scottish Higher Education Funding Council. (2004). *Higher education in Scotland: A baseline report.* Edinburgh, United Kingdom: Author.

Skilbeck, M., & Connell, H. (2000). *Access and equity in higher education: An international perspective on issues and strategies.* Dublin, Ireland: HEA.

Taylor, S., & Spencer, E. (1994). *Individual commitment to lifelong learning: Individuals' attitudes. Report on the qualitative* (Research Series No. 31). Sheffield, United Kingdom: Employment Department.

Tett, L. (1999). Widening provision in higher education: Some non-traditional participants' experiences. *Research Papers in Education, 14*(1), 107-119.

Thomas, L. (2001). *Widening participation in post-compulsory education.* London: Continuum.

Tonks, D., & Farr, M. (2003). Widening access and participation in UK higher education. *The International Journal of Educational Management, 17*(1), 26-36.

Weber, M. (1978). *Economy and society: An outline of interpretive sociology.* New York: Bedminster.

West, L. (1996). *Beyond fragments.* London: Taylor and Francis.

Williams, J. (Ed.). (1997). *Negotiating access to higher education: The discourse of selectivity and equity.* Buckingham, United Kingdom: Society for Research into Higher Education & Open University Press.

Woodrow, M. (2000). Putting a price on a priority: Funding an inclusive higher education. *Widening Participation and Lifelong Learning, 2*(3), 1-5.

Zirkle, C. (2004). *Access barriers experienced by adults in distance education courses and programs: A review of the research literature.*

Retrieved May 16, 2007, from http://hdl.handle.net/1805/273

## ADDITIONAL READING

Where a source features in the main text of this chapter, it is referenced here as it was in the text. Bibliographical details for sources that do not feature in the main text are given in full. It goes without saying that all these sources should be critically engaged with and their espoused positions and advice scrutinized.

Aldrich (1996) gives a useful outline of debates about access to education in a historical context. Thomas (2001) offers a comprehensive introduction to issues of access and accessibility in higher education.

Jackson (1968, 1971) and Bourdieu (1990, 1997) as well as Bourdieu and Passeron (1977) are useful for their theoretical reflections and the conceptual models of hidden curriculum, and habitus and cultural capital that they offer on issues of inequalities in access, and barriers to access to education and higher education.

The hidden curriculum draws attention to the fact that pupils learn things that are not actually directly taught nor are part of an approved body of knowledge. Importantly, implicit messages in are transmitted via a process of socialisation that passes on norms and values and thus maintain cultural reproduction by giving more encouragement to those with more cultural resources. Sociocultural habitus and cultural capital underline that potential entrants do not simply weigh courses of action in terms of their utility and cost effectiveness in achieving a desired goal, but that they evaluate the desired goals in relation to a framework of personal values not always understood in terms of their usefulness but in terms of embedded sociocultural habitus and material, and in relation to discursive and psychological social-class differences.

Access and accessibility in e-learning in particular and on the Web in general have spawned a large number of guidelines and suggestions for good practice, among which the Worldwide Web Consortium (http://www.w3.org) "develops interoperable technologies (specifications, guidelines, software, and tools) to lead the Web to its full potential." This includes advice and norms for CSS as well as for a range of accessibility technologies. The *Web Accessibility Initiate 2.0 Guidelines* (2007, http://www.w3.org/WAI) is essential reading for anyone interested at all in access and accessibility in e-learning, as is the IMS Global Learning Consortium in its *Guidelines for Developing Accessible Learning Applications* (2002, http://www.imsglobal.org/accessibility/accv1p0/imsacc_guidev1p0.html) and its *Access for All Meta-Data Overview Version 1.0: Final Specification* (2004, http://www.imsglobal.org/accessibility/accmdv1p0/imsaccmd_oviewv1p0.html).

The National Centre for Accessible Media (http://ncam.wgbh.org) offers free software plug-ins as well as advice on accessibility issues. Its aim is "to expand access to present and future media for people with disabilities; to explore how existing access technologies may benefit other populations; to represent its constituents in industry, policy and legislative circles; and to provide access to educational and media technologies for special needs students."

Microsoft carries out its own research on accessibility, a result of which has been the steady growth of accessible technologies being embedded in Microsoft software. An example of their research is the following.

Microsoft. (2004). *The wide range of abilities and its impact on computer technology.* Retrieved from http://download.microsoft.com/download/0/1/ f/01f506eb-2d1e-42a6-bc7b-1f33d25fd40f/ResearchReport.doc

The UK Open University's *Web Accessibility Guidelines and Techniques* (http://kn.open.ac.uk/public/workspace.cfm?wpid=2451) is an easily usable set of recommendations for Web designers in general and for designers of e-learning in particular.

For a focus on dyslexia and accessibility, http://www.accessibility101.org.uk offers a set of suggestions coupled with research background. CSS Zen Garden (http://www.csszengarden.com) shows what can be done in an accessible manner with cascading style sheets, while the Royal National Institute of the Blind's (RNIB) Web Access Centre (http://www.rnib.org.uk/xpedio/groups/public/documents/code/public_rnib008789.hcsp) offers regular updates on how accessibility technology (both software and hardware) is advancing. In addition, the RNIB's main site (http://www.rnib.org.uk) tackles all sorts of issues around visual impairment and accessibility. To see what the world looks like to a colour-blind person, Vischeck (http://www.vischeck.com/vischeck) provides a free online service that allows the user to simulate how colours are seen by those with colour blindness. Vischeck also includes a free program to allow users to optimise images (in Adobe Photoshop) for use by people with colour blindness.

Theofanos, M., & Redish, J. (2003). *Guidelines for accessible and usable Websites: Observing users who work with screen readers.* Retrieved from http://redish.net/content/papers/interactions.html

This is one of the few pieces of academic writing on how the Internet looks to a user of a screen reader.

Further academic writings can be found for free at http://klaatu-dev.pc.athabascau.ca:8080/dspace/handle/2149/354, which hosts the Centre for Distance Education of the Athabascau University in Canada.

There are also various free online journals that are relevant here, such as the *International Review of Research in Open and Distance Learning* (http://www.irrodl.org/index.php/irrodl).

Vincent Flanders' (2007) *Web Pages that Suck 2.0* (http://www.webpagesthatsuck.com) is a perfect lesson on what not to do on a Web site. Although not specifically aimed at educational Web sites, though these are not excluded, Flanders' examples and his (and his contributors') explanations of what makes these sites so bad are a lesson to us all. In addition, Flanders updates the site regularly with the principle aim of getting designers to do the right thing by showing them the consequences of not doing it.

Further books to read include Clark and Mayer (2003) and Clark, Nguyen, and Sweller (2006), who are generally considered to be major figures in the domains of multimedia and e-learning, but who are not always as sensitive as they might be to issues of access and accessibility. However, the best book on access and accessibility is Krug (2006). Krug is stimulating, lucid, and amusing, and everything he says is of relevance to the design of e-learning, especially his well-crafted remarks on access and accessibility.

Although Cook and Dupras (2004) make a number of assumptions concerning the technological attributes of their intended Web users, theirs is an interesting and engaging exposé of how to develop Web-based learning materials and some of the pitfalls to avoid. Mayer and Moreno (2003) give food for thought on how to maximise the cognitive accessibility of e-learning materials, although they do apply, except in some rare circumstances, the redundancy principle whereby one does not have a textual version of the spoken word or a spoken version of text, but rather one should have the written word or the spoken word but not both at the same time.

## ENDNOTES

[1] The E-Access Technology for All conference is the United Kingdom's leading annual event on access to all technologies, including the Internet, PCs, mobile phones, and digital TV and radio, that is run by people with disabilities. Peter White was a keynote speaker (see http://www.headstar-events.com/eaccess06/).

[2] Much of this expansion is expected to be through 2-year foundation degrees to be developed in collaboration with employers.

# Chapter VIII
# E–Learning for All?
## Maximizing the Impact of Multimedia Resources for Learners with Disabilities

**Morag Munro**
*Learning Innovation Unit, Dublin City University, Ireland*

**Barry McMullin**
*Electronic Engineering, Dublin City University, Ireland*

## ABSTRACT

*This chapter examines some of the tensions that may exist between e-learning and accessibility in higher education, and aims to redress the balance between them. The chapter necessarily involves some significant technical detail. It examines and reports on the accessibility issues associated with particular e-learning technologies that are either current or emerging in this dynamic field. The discussion attempts to provide practitioners with practical advice that will assist them in designing multimedia-based e-learning that is both innovative and inclusive. Integral to this is a framework for best practice for the development of accessible educational multimedia.*

## INTRODUCTION

E-learning has significant potential to enhance, or even transform, the learning experience for all students in higher education (HE). It creates pedagogical opportunities that were previously too impractical, or even impossible, to implement in the traditional lecture, tutorial, or laboratory setting. It also generates options for participation that are independent of time and place (Bradley, Haynes, & Boyle, 2005; Downes, 2005; Gil, Blanco, & Auli, 2000; Tuthill & Klemm, 2002).

E-learning in the specific form of educational multimedia, for example, animations, simulations, games, and video, may also generate opportunities for disabled students, in particular, to participate more fully and more independently in HE (D. Sloan, Stratford, & Gregor, 2006). It is ironic then that e-learning resources and activities often actually disadvantage students with disabilities, reinforcing old barriers, building new ones, and even contributing to a second digital divide (Seale, 2006). Given that the use of multimedia-based e-learning is likely to become increasingly prevalent in HE, students with disabilities may be further disadvantaged, stigmatised, or even discouraged from entering postcompulsory education if this is not addressed.

## BACKGROUND

The term *e-learning* pertains to a range of applications of technology in support of teaching and learning, including materials and activities delivered via the Internet, via a local intranet, or via CD-ROM. This chapter focuses specifically on the accessibility of educational multimedia, including text and hypertext, images, photographs, diagrams and charts, animation and interaction, and video and audio. We define designing for accessibility in e-learning in this context as the practice of ensuring that all teaching and learning resources and activities can be used by the widest possible range of potential students, regardless of any visual, aural, motor, cognitive, or neurological impairments.

Although some guidelines for developing accessible e-learning resources exist, these have been criticised for being difficult to interpret and implement, especially where educational multimedia is concerned. In addition, educators and designers may be confused or apprehensive about whether they should incorporate multimedia into their designs (Mirabella, Kimani, Gabrielli, & Catarci, 2004; D. Sloan & Stratford, 2004). A

further concern is that, given that much of the current literature is focused on guidelines, standards, and legislation, some HE practitioners may have begun to consider that the objective of accessible design is primarily to comply with rules rather than to help learners learn (Seale, 2006).

## ISSUES, CONTROVERSIES, PROBLEMS

### Educational Multimedia: A Double-Edged Sword?

Although e-learning has potential to enhance and support teaching and learning in HE, a significant number of students entering postcompulsory education have disabilities that may impact on their ability to engage with educational multimedia. In this section, we highlight, via a case study, some of the barriers to learning that multimedia may impose on students with disabilities.

### Opportunities Presented by Educational Multimedia for Students with Disabilities

Well-designed e-learning resources and activities may enhance the learning experience for students in HE on many levels. For example, Web-based resources and activities can provide opportunities for individualised, self-directed learning and may facilitate more flexible participation options (Cairncross & Mannion, 2001). The Web 2.0 technologies (such as social computing networks, communications tools, blogs, and wikis) may create new opportunities for collaboration, dialogue, and shared knowledge construction (Downes, 2005).

Animations, simulations, and games can generate further teaching and learning possibilities. Multimedia can appeal to different learning styles and preferences. For example, visual, auditory, and exploratory learners may have preferences for particular media combinations (Montgomery, 1995). Animations and simulations can help to clarify complex and abstract concepts or create learning opportunities that "can only exist online, not in 'real' classrooms" (Burbules & Callister, 2000, p. 277). Multimedia may also allow access to information and situations that are time or place dependent, or that are too expensive, dangerous, or impractical to access directly, for example, via virtual laboratories (Gil et al., 2000) and virtual field trips (Tuthill & Klemm, 2002). Games may promote motivation and engagement, and can help to develop problem-solving skills (Fasli & Michalakopoulos, 2005; McFarlane, Sparrowhawk, & Heald, 2002), while mobile and context-aware devices may offer opportunities for ubiquitous "'any time, any place' multimedia learning experiences" (Bradley et al., 2005, p. 97).

Educational multimedia also has specific potential to create opportunities for disabled students to participate more fully and more independently in HE.

- A mobility-impaired student can interact with his or her peers and participate in virtual field trips from home.
- Via animations and simulations, concepts and processes can be clarified for a student with cognitive difficulties.

- Via a screen reader (software that translates text displayed on screen into audio format) or Braille display (a device that dynamically converts on-screen text into Braille format), a blind student can access books and articles as soon as they are published in electronic format instead of waiting to have them converted into audio or Braille format.

## Barriers to Learning

Despite its potential for supporting and enhancing learning and teaching in HE, e-learning is often a significant barrier to students with disabilities. Table 1 summarises some of the disabilities that may impact a student's ability to interact with e-learning materials and resources.

As Tables 2 to 5 indicate, all multimedia formats are potentially problematic if they are used inappropriately, or where an equivalent alternative to formats that cannot be accessed by some individuals is not provided. For individuals with multiple disabilities, there may be multiple possible barriers to participation.

## Case Study

Consider the multimedia resource shown in Figures 1 and 2. This resource allows students

*Table 1. Disabilities that may impact a student's ability to interact with e-learning*

| Disability | Visual | Auditory | Motor/Mobility | Cognitive/Neurological |
|---|---|---|---|---|
| Examples | • Total or partial loss of vision<br>• Low vision<br>• Colour blindness<br>• Cataract<br>• Glaucoma | • Deafness<br>• Partial loss of hearing | • Arthritis<br>• Damage to or loss of limb(s)<br>• Difficulty with coordination of limbs<br>• Repetitive strain injury<br>• Cerebral palsy | • Attention deficit disorder<br>• Autism<br>• Dyslexia<br>• Dyscalculia<br>• Epilepsy |

*Table 2. Barriers presented by text, hypertext, and navigation*

| Visual Disability | Auditory Disability | Motor/Mobility Disability | Cognitive/Neurological Disability |
|---|---|---|---|
| **Are text, hypertext, and navigation barriers to learning?** | | | |
| YES<br><br>• If screen layout or navigational elements are inconsistent<br><br>• If purely visual layout and arrangement conveys significant information<br><br>• If content does not include appropriate structural and semantic information (headings, lists, etc.)<br><br>• If flickering or flashing text is used | | YES<br><br>• If navigation via alternative devices or voice-recognition software is not supported<br><br>• If precise control of a pointer is required for navigation<br><br>• If content does not include appropriate structural and semantic information (headings, lists, etc.) | YES<br><br>• If screen layout and use of terminology is not consistent<br><br>• If content cannot be interpreted by text-speech software<br><br>• If content does not include appropriate structural and semantic information (headings, lists, etc.)<br><br>• If flickering or flashing text is used<br><br>• If language used is not consistent and clear |

*Table 3. Barriers presented by images, photographs, diagrams, and charts*

| Visual Disability | Auditory Disability | Motor/Mobility Disability | Cognitive/Neurological Disability |
|---|---|---|---|
| **Are images, photographs, diagrams, and charts barriers to learning?** | | | |
| YES<br><br>• If they cannot be scaled or magnified without distortion<br><br>• If colour alone is used to convey information<br><br>• If an equivalent textual alternative is not provided<br><br>• If content does not include appropriate structural and semantic information (internal data relationships, etc.) | | | YES<br><br>• If content does not include appropriate structural and semantic information (internal data relationships, etc.) |

*Table 4. Barriers presented by interaction*

| Visual Disability | Auditory Disability | Motor/Mobility Disability | Cognitive/Neurological Disability |
|---|---|---|---|
| **Is interaction a barrier to learning?** | | | |
| YES<br><br>• If being able to see the screen is required to participate<br><br>• If interaction via control devices other than a mouse is not supported | | YES<br><br>• If very precise control of a pointer is required<br><br>• If control via alternative devices or voice-recognition software is not supported | |

*Table 5. Barriers presented by animation, video, and audio*

| Visual Disability | Auditory Disability | Motor/Mobility Disability | Cognitive/Neurological Disability |
|---|---|---|---|
| *Are animation, video, and audio barriers to learning?* | | | |
| YES<br><br>• If they cannot be scaled or magnified without distortion<br>• If colour alone is used to convey information<br>• If a synchronised alternative to visual content is not provided (e.g., audio description)<br>• If audio content cannot be controlled or turned off | YES<br><br>• If a synchronised text-based equivalent to audio is not provided (captions) | YES<br><br>• If control via alternative devices or voice-recognition software is not supported | YES<br><br>• If no prior warning about flickering, flashing, or moving content is provided<br>• If moving content, video, or audio cannot be controlled or turned off |

*Figure 1. Acid-base titration resource in drag and drop exercise*

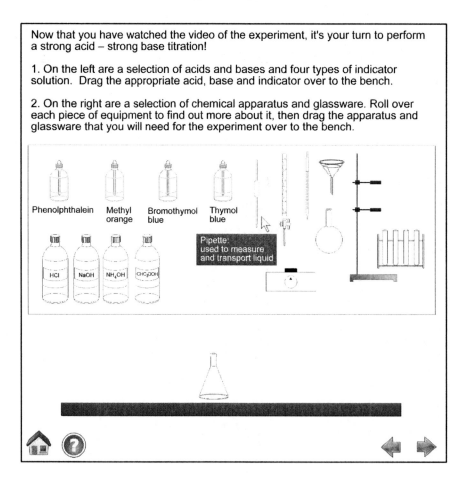

to participate in a virtual acid-base titration: an experiment commonly used to determine the concentration of an unknown acid or base solution. It employs a range of typical multimedia elements.

- Video footage of the experiment with audio commentary.
- Animation of the chemical reaction and animated titration curve (graph that shows how the pH of the acid-base solution changes over time).
- Mouse rollovers that allow hidden parts of the screen to be revealed.

- Virtual participation in the experiment via a drag and drop matching exercise.

This could be an invaluable learning resource for many students. It would allow participation in the experiment in a safe environment, from any location, and as many times as is required. It would allow visualisation of complex processes that are not visible to the naked eye. Most importantly in the current context, it may also improve accessibility for those learners who might never be able to fully participate in the real experiment. However, as it stands, the resource could equally easily exclude certain learners.

*Figure 2. Acid-base titration resource in virtual experiment*

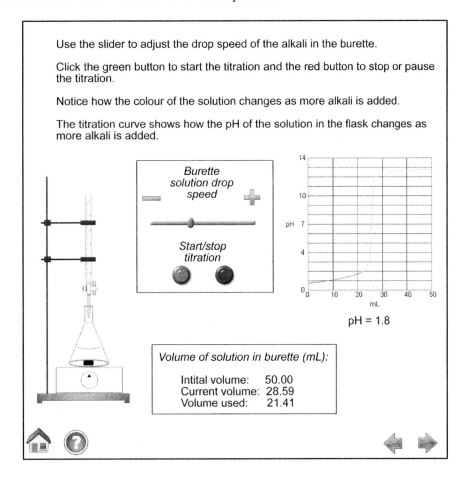

Thus, a blind or vision-impaired individual may be at a disadvantage if any of the following occurs.

- Synchronised equivalent alternatives to the visual aspects of the video and animation, in audio or text format, are not available.
- Different information is presented simultaneously on different parts of the screen (as is the case in this example).
- The visual content cannot be easily scaled or magnified.
- Colour is used exclusively to convey certain information (for example, in the instructions to "Notice how the colour of the solution changes" and "Click the green button to start... and the red button to stop").
- Being able to visually position a screen pointer is requisite for interaction (for example, the drag and drop exercise and rollover text).

A hearing-impaired individual may be excluded if an equivalent, and appropriately synchronised, alternative to the voice-overs is not available.

A mobility-impaired student may be excluded if navigation and interaction via alternative de-vices or voice-recognition software is not supported, and/or if very precise control of a pointer is required for navigation and interaction.

Users with certain cognitive or neurological difficulties may be adversely affected by the animated content. For example, flashing content may trigger seizures in people with photosensitive epilepsy, and users with attention deficit disorder or dyslexia can find any visual movement or animation extremely distracting, especially if it cannot be paused or disabled under their control.

## Who is Affected by Disability?

The number of students with a disability entering HE appears to be increasing on an international basis. For example, Figure 3 provides a breakdown of the UK Higher Education Statistics Agency's (HESA) data on the percentage of undergraduate and postgraduate students with a self-declared disability entering HE in the United Kingdom between 1994 and 2005. The number of undergraduates with a disability has increased from 1.18 to 5.11% during this period, while the number of postgraduates with a disability has increased from 3.11 to 6.38%.

Table 6 provides details on the specific disabilities declared by students entering UK HE

*Figure 3. Percentage undergraduate and postgraduate students with a self-declared disability entering HE between 1994 and 2005 (Source: HESA, 1994-2007)*

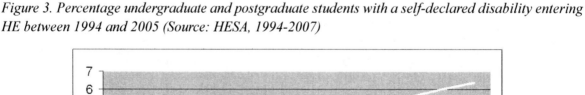
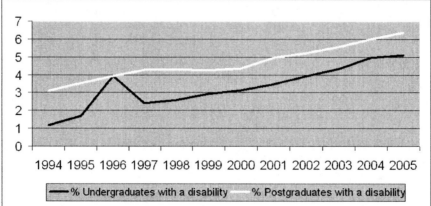

*Table 6. Specific disabilities declared by students entering UK HE in 2005 (Source: HESA, 2007a)*

| Self-Declared Disability | % Postgraduates | % Undergraduates |
|---|---|---|
| Dyslexia | 2.13 | 2.77 |
| Blind/Partially Sighted | 0.14 | 0.17 |
| Deaf/Hearing Impairment | 0.27 | 0.34 |
| Wheelchair User/Mobility Difficulties | 0.24 | 0.27 |
| Personal Care Support | 0.01 | 0.01 |
| Mental Health Difficulties | 0.21 | 0.35 |
| Autistic Spectrum Disorder | 0.03 | 0.06 |
| Unseen Disability | 1.14 | 1.08 |
| Multiple Disabilities | 0.31 | 0.58 |
| Other Disability | 0.64 | 0.75 |

in 2005. A significant number of recent entrants have cognitive, visual, hearing, or mobility difficulties that may impact their ability to interact with e-learning materials and activities. In fact, the actual number of students in UK HE with a disability may be greater than that indicated by the official statistics: Students are under no obligation to report a disability, and according to the HESA (2007b), in some cases data for some individuals may have been omitted.

It is difficult to make precise comparisons of disability-related statistics on an international basis because the definitions of disability vary significantly between jurisdictions. Nonetheless, it seems likely that the broad trends, as evidenced in this UK data, would be reflected in other comparable HE systems.

## What is Accessible Educational Multimedia?

Accessibility has been defined by numerous authors and organisations. For example, in its introduction to Web accessibility, the World Wide Web Consortium (W3C, 2007) succinctly states that "Web accessibility means that people with disabilities can use the Web." Some definitions

specifically address the accessibility of educational activities, materials, and environments. For example, the IMS Global Learning Consortium (2004) describes accessibility as "the ability of the learning environment to adjust to the needs of all learners. Accessibility is determined by the flexibility of the education environment (with respect to presentation, control methods, access modality, and learner supports) and the availability of alternative-but-equivalent content and activities." We define designing for accessibility in e-learning simply as the practice of ensuring that all teaching and learning materials and activities can be used by the widest possible range of potential students, regardless of any visual, aural, motor, cognitive, or neurological impairments. Designing for accessibility not only benefits students with disabilities: Students who access the e-learning resources via devices other than a typical desktop workstation will also generally benefit. These include students who access e-learning via devices with small display screens (mobile phones, personal digital assistants [PDAs], etc.), via low-bandwidth connections, via older computers, in noisy environments, where audio cannot be used, or whilst simultaneously engaged in other activities (whilst driving, for example). In addition, students with low literacy levels, and those who are accessing the multimedia via a language other than their first language will also generally benefit from accessible design.

## Assistive Technologies

Some commonly used assistive technologies are described in this section. Assistive technologies are specialist hardware and software that people with disabilities may use to interact with desktop applications and Web browsers. Although such technologies have the potential to generate opportunities for students with disabilities to participate more autonomously in HE, they are only useful if e-learning materials and activities are designed with an awareness of assistive technologies and how they are used in mind.

## Screen Readers and Text-to-Speech Software

Screen readers allow people who are blind or visually impaired to interact with desktop applications such as word processing software, spreadsheets, e-mail, and Web browsers typically via the keyboard or via voice recognition. The screen reader translates information presented on screen, such as text within a document or menus and dialog boxes within a software application, into audible format via a speech synthesiser. If text and other media are not designed so that they can be recognised and interpreted by a screen-reader user, then that content will be inaccessible. Screen readers also read out any author-supplied textual alternatives to nontextual visual media (images, video, animation, etc.); however, if such textual alternatives are not provided, then screen-reader users will generally be denied access to the information conveyed by the nontextual media.

Text-to-speech software is used by people who have difficulties reading on-screen text, or who prefer to listen to rather than read text, for example, students with low vision, dyslexia, or attention deficit disorder, or students for whom the text is not in their primary language. Typical functions include the ability to simultaneously visually highlight on-screen text and translate it into audible format.

## Braille Displays

A Braille display dynamically translates on-screen text into Braille format via a mechanical device that raises the appropriate combinations of dots on the display (see Figure 4). Braille displays may be used by students who are deaf and blind, and also by blind students instead of, or in conjunction with, a screen reader. As with screen readers, if text and other media are not designed so that they can be recognised and interpreted by the device, then that content will be inaccessible to users of Braille displays.

## Screen Magnifiers

Screen magnifiers allow users to enlarge screen content, such as text and images, by zooming into areas of the screen. Screen magnifiers are typically used by people who have some vision, but who have a visual impairment that makes it difficult for them to see the screen, such as low vision, glaucoma, or a cataract. If content becomes distorted or unreadable when magnified, then this may present a barrier to users of screen magnifiers.

## Keyboard and Mouse Alternatives

Many people cannot, or prefer not to, interact with computer software via the standard keyboard and mouse, for example, students with coordination problems or limited or no mobility in one or more limbs. These students may use alternatives to the mouse and keyboard including the following.

- Eye tracking devices: These allow learners to interact with the computer via their eye movements.

- Head tracking devices: These allow learners to interact with the computer via their head movements.
- Expanded and adapted keyboards
- Trackball
- Joystick
- Touch screen
- Foot-controlled mice and pedals
- Switches: These allow learners to interact with the computer by using a single switch that scans through on-screen options.
- Gesture-recognition systems: These allow the movement of a limb to be mapped to a particular command.
- Breathing pattern recognition ("sip and puff") devices: These allow inhalation and exhalation patterns to be mapped to particular commands.
- Speech-recognition software: This allows learners to input text and to interact with software applications via voice commands instead of a keyboard or mouse.

If e-learning content and activities are designed such that they can be controlled via keyboard commands, then, in general, they will also be accessible via the devices above. Content that requires the use of a mouse, for example, drag and drop exercises and rollovers that reveal hidden information, may not be accessible by users of these technologies.

## LEGISLATION, GUIDELINES, AND SPECIFICATIONS FOR ACCESSIBILITY

In this section, we outline the legislation, guidelines, and specifications relevant to the accessibility of e-learning in HE. We then discuss some of the common misconceptions regarding the implications of these for the design of educational multimedia in HE.

## Accessibility and the Law

Many jurisdictions now have explicit legal instruments that generically prohibit discrimination on the basis of disability. Examples include the U.S. Americans with Disabilities Act (ADA; U.S. Department of Justice, 1990), the UK Disability Discrimination Act (DDA; Her Majesty's Stationery Office [HMSO], 1995), and the Irish Equal Status Act (Government of Ireland, 2000). Some jurisdictions also have more specific legislation relating to equal access to education, such as the UK Special Educational Needs and Disability Act (SENDA; HMSO, 2001). Much legislation is presented in general terms of potential discrimination in the provision of any form of goods or services, and thus refers only implicitly to intangible products or resources such as educational multimedia. However, there are also examples of explicit regulation of such electronic goods and services, such as Section 508 of the U.S. Rehabilitation Act, which stipulates that electronic and information technology provided by federal departments and agencies is accessible (U.S. Department of Labor, 1973).

In addition to constitutional and statute law, there is also a small but growing body of case law. While many complaints of discrimination are settled out of court (i.e., without recording any precedent), there is at least one unambiguous and widely cited example of a successful complaint of discrimination on the basis of disability in the provision of a Web-based service. This is the case of Mr. Bruce Maguire vs. the Sydney Organising Committee for the Olympic Games (SOCOG). In a complaint lodged in June 1999, Maguire (who is blind) contended that significant parts of the SOCOG Web site were inaccessible to him, and that this was unnecessary and unreasonable. The complaint was upheld, and SOCOG was eventually fined $A20,000 (€12,800; Clark, 2004).

We will not attempt here any more comprehensive review of the legal implications of accessibility for the design of educational multimedia. More detailed discussion of the generic international situation, and the specific provisions in UK law, for example, are provided by Sloan (2001). The essential point is that the design of educational multimedia may well be subject to significant legal conditions on accessibility. Any professional developer of such resources should therefore be careful to be fully aware of, and to conform to, such conditions according to the specific local legislation and case law. Such conditions generally involve some interpretation and judgment, particularly in regard to what is practical or reasonable. However, we would suggest, as an absolute minimum, that a developer should always be able to demonstrate that due diligence has been completed, that is, that accessibility requirements have been properly and explicitly considered in the design, that the developed resources have been explicitly audited and/or tested for accessibility, and that if accessibility barriers remain, this should be due to explicitly identified reasons why it would be impractical or unreasonable to overcome them.

## STANDARDS AND GUIDELINES FOR E-LEARNING ACCESSIBILITY

### W3C Web Content Accessibility Guidelines

The W3C is responsible for the development of global standards for the World Wide Web. Although not specifically developed with e-learning in mind, given that the W3C's Web Content Accessibility Guidelines (WCAG 1.0) are recognised as the definitive guidelines in relation to Web accessibility, complying with these guidelines should, in theory at least, be the easiest method of creating accessible e-learning. Note that the WCAGs can be quite generally applied to multimedia resources even when using non-Web-based delivery (e.g., intranet, CD-ROM, DVD, etc.). In their current format, however, the WCAGs are ver-

bose and can be difficult for nontechnical readers to interpret (Version 2.0 promises improvements in this regard). The guidelines are also notoriously difficult to implement, especially where multimedia is concerned: As yet, the specific multimedia technologies endorsed by the W3C are much less prevalent than popular proprietary technologies widely employed in the development of educational simulations and animations for HE, such as Adobe™ Authorware, Flash™, and TechSmith Camtasia.

### E-Learning Accessibility Guidelines

Some countries and organisations have developed accessibility guidelines specific to e-learning. For example, the Skills for Access initiative, funded by the Higher Education Funding Council for England and the UK Department for Employment and Learning, has published guidelines for developing accessible materials via specific technologies (http://www.skillsforaccess.org.uk). The Le@rning Federation Accessibility Specification provides guidelines for the development of accessible educational curricula for the Le@rning Federation (2007), an initiative of the state and federal governments of Australia and New Zealand. The IMS Global Learning Consortium (2002) has published guidelines for developing accessible e-learning applications. Many HE institutions have developed local guidelines for developing accessible e-learning materials, for example, the University of Leeds in the United Kingdom (http://campus.leeds.ac.uk/guidelines/accessibility) and Deakin University in Australia (http://www.deakin.edu.au/dwm/accessibility).

### IMS Global Learning Consortium Technical Specifications

The IMS Global Learning Consortium develops open technical specifications for interoperable learning technology and promotes their adoption. It has developed two accessibility specifications for e-learning: The Accessibility for Learner Information Package (IMS ACCLIP; IMS, 2003) defines how learners' accessibility preferences can be specified and customised, while the AccessForAll Metadata (IMS ACCMD; IMS, 2004) provides a common metadata scheme or language that allows resources that match a learner's preferences to be described and identified (making it easier to locate suitable learning resources stored in learning-object repositories, for example).

## Myths and Misconceptions

Given the plethora of legislation, guidelines, and specifications, coupled with the possible difficulties in interpreting and implementing them, it is unsurprising that designers of e-learning may be confused or apprehensive about incorporating multimedia into their designs (Mirabella et al., 2004; D. Sloan & Stratford, 2004). In fact, as Seale (2006) points out, despite, or perhaps because of, the range of standards and guidelines that have emerged in recent years, there has not been a corresponding improvement in the accessibility of e-learning materials and resources in the HE sector.

Common concerns include the following.

- Inclusion of *any* multimedia will result in non-compliance with accessibility guidelines.
- Making multimedia accessible is not cost effective.
- Accessibility guidelines are too confusing to implement.
- Compliance with accessibility guidelines stifles innovative pedagogical design.

These concerns are misconceptions, however: Via careful and considered planning and design, it is possible to develop e-learning resources and activities that are both innovative and inclusive.

## SOLUTIONS AND RECOMMENDATIONS

### Developing Accessible Educational Multimedia

This section discusses the relative merits of two possible approaches to the accessible design of e-learning: universal design and alternative design. We then outline a four-step framework for best practice in the development of inclusive educational multimedia. Furthermore, specific advice for working with various media elements is provided in Appendix 1.

### Universal Design vs. Alternative Design

While one possible approach to accessibility might be to provide alternative resources for different groups of users, we contend that a universal design approach to e-learning is preferable, that is, a design approach that aims to develop e-learning resources and activities that can be used by as many potential students as is reasonably possible. In addition, we argue that an alternative design should only be provided if it is impossible, or too impractical, to provide a universal design. Universal design originated as an approach to building design that aims to ensure that physical spaces can be accessed and used by everyone. The term has subsequently been applied to other products and services including software applications. The architect Ron Mace, one of the first advocates of universal design, describes it as "the design of products and environments to be usable by all people, to the greatest extent possible, without the need for adaptation or specialised design" (Mace, 1997, para. 1).

However, as Vanderheiden (1996) acknowledges, in practical terms, there can be no totally universal designs: "There are <u>NO</u> universal designs; there are <u>NO</u> universally designed products. Universal design is a process which yields products (devices, environments, systems, and processes) which are usable by and useful to the widest possible range of people" (para. 5).

Taking Vanderheiden's (1996) definition into account, we can describe the universal design of educational multimedia as the design of e-learning activities and resources that avoids gratuitous barriers to access. While universal design aims for e-learning to be usable by the widest range of potential students, it does not equate to a "one size fits all" approach to e-learning design. Rather, it is a philosophy that offers learners a range of equivalent means in which to access a particular e-learning resource or activity integrated into a single cohesive package. Universal design benefits both designers and users of e-learning.

- It is more efficient as designers only need to create and maintain one design.
- It gives all learners more choice and flexibility in their learning experience. The provision of alternative formats may allow them to adapt media to their personal preferences and learning styles.
- It avoids stigmatising or singling out individuals; everyone uses the same design.

## Case Study

Recall the simulated laboratory experiment described earlier. Assuming that some additional elements are incorporated into the design, this resource could be accessible to a wider range of users.

- There will need to be alternatives to any static visual content used to convey information, such as photographs, charts, or diagrams. A synchronised equivalent alternative to any dynamic visual content, such as video or animation, will also be necessary.

- Captions providing an equivalent and appropriately synchronised alternative to the audio content will be required.
- Navigation and interaction via alternative devices or voice-recognition software should be supported.
- Learners should be able to control the various media elements; for example, they should be able to decide whether to watch a video with the audio on or off, or with or without captions describing audio or visual content, and they should be able to control the pace at which any animated or moving content is presented to them.

## A FRAMEWORK FOR BEST PRACTICE FOR THE DEVELOPMENT OF EDUCATIONAL MULTIMEDIA

This section outlines a framework for best practice in the development of inclusive educational multimedia. The framework is informed by universal design principles and is derived from the generic W3C guidelines for Web accessibility. As was noted earlier, the W3C guidelines can be difficult to interpret and implement. In addition, they are focused on the development of generic Web sites rather than on educational multimedia. The guidelines have therefore been adapted for educational multimedia, and distilled into four key steps that, when applied, will facilitate the design of e-learning materials, activities, and resources that are usable by the widest possible range of potential learners, avoid gratuitous barriers to access, and offer opportunities for user choice and autonomy.

## Use Multimedia Appropriately

There are many sound pedagogical reasons for using multimedia, and there are many circumstances where appropriate application of multimedia can enhance accessibility. However, there are also situations where the pedagogical or accessibility benefits are not sufficient to warrant development of a particular resource, or where accessibility barriers outweigh the perceived benefits. Before designing a new multimedia resource or activity, consider the following.

- What are the pedagogical aims of the resource?
- What are anticipated pedagogical benefits?
- Who will use the resource? How will they use it? Where will they use it?
- Are there any accessibility benefits? For whom? How might these be enhanced?
- Will the resource pose any accessibility barriers? For whom? How might these be mitigated?

## Choose the Most Accessible Technology for Your Circumstances

A key recommendation made by the W3C in WCAG 1.0 is the endorsement of W3C technologies, as opposed to proprietary ones: *"Checkpoint 11.1: Use W3C technologies when they are available and appropriate for a task and use the latest versions when supported"* (W3C, 1999).

W3C technologies relevant to multimedia include the following.

- XML (Extensible Markup Language): This is an underlying enabling technology for many other W3C developments.
- HTML/XHTML (Extensible Hypertext Markup Language): They are used for the structured markup of documents, separate from stylistic presentation.
- CSS (Cascading Style Sheets): The technology is used to define the style of the presentation separate from specific content.
- SVG (Scalable Vector Graphics): They are used for the representation of images and animations.

- SMIL (Synchronised Multimedia Integration Language): This is a critical W3C technology for handling multimedia resources, providing a generic framework for the definition and synchronisation of arbitrary multimedia elements.

A full discussion of these technologies is beyond the scope of this chapter; however, it is worth noting the W3C's own rationale for endorsing them in WCAG. W3C technologies undergo continual review to ensure that accessibility issues are considered during the design phase, and they are extensively evaluated and reviewed for accessibility prior to being endorsed by W3C. Consequently, W3C technologies consistently include built-in accessibility features. In some cases, these provide intrinsic accessibility benefits for any application of the technology; in other cases, they provide facilities for content developers to ensure accessibility in a content-specific way. In addition, the W3C's specifications are developed in an open, industry-consensus process. This maximises the opportunity for third-party development of support for these technologies, which, in turn, maximises support for the needs of relatively small-scale niche users, such as many disability groups.

Proprietary multimedia formats are numerous and include Adobe Flash™, Director, Authorware, and Captivate; TechSmith's Camtasia; Apple QuickTime; and Microsoft Advanced Systems Format (ASF) media file format. Although such proprietary technologies may include some accessibility features, they are generally deprecated on accessibility grounds because of the following.

- They typically require either plug-ins or stand-alone applications to be installed before they can be accessed. These are not always available for all platforms or on all devices that people use to access the Web. Users with disabilities are naturally more likely to be using specialist access technologies, which make all such extra requirements more burdensome.

- Their development is, in general, controlled by a particular vendor, or is open to third parties only on payment of royalties to the vendor. This may inhibit innovation for small and/or specialist markets, precisely the markets for users with particular disabilities.

So, should proprietary technologies never be used? Can proprietary technologies be accessible? At present, there are no definitive answers to these questions: The accessibility of a particular resource will depend on the technology used, and on how that particular technology is employed. We introduced this discussion in the specific context of WCAG 1.0 Checkpoint 11.1, which does quite generically deprecate the use of non-W3C technologies on accessibility grounds. However, we should also note that W3C itself is already revisiting this in the course of drafting a new version of WCAG (2.0), and this requirement may well be significantly modified as a result. Accordingly, at this time, we can only say that the appropriateness of any particular technology should continue to be very carefully evaluated on a case-by-case basis. Ideally, proprietary technologies should not be used if there is a functional W3C technology alternative available. That is, before using Flash™, for example, one should pause to ask whether the same effect would be possible using W3C technologies. At the time of writing, however, of the multimedia technologies recommended by the W3C, only HTML, XML, XHTML, and CSS are considered to be mainstream, being supported by current browsers and having development tools widely available. The more sophisticated W3C multimedia technologies, such as SVG and SMIL, are not yet as mature nor are they as well supported.

In some cases, creative use of a combination of the mainstream W3C technologies may produce the desired effect; in other situations, a less mainstream technology, such as SVG, would be

required, and, for the time being at least, it may be easier, more cost effective, or more practical to employ a proprietary technology. However, even in such cases, it is worth investigating available development tools to see if they support W3C technologies (in addition to proprietary ones), either already or as part of a development road map. This may allow relatively easy deployment of equivalent resources offering *both* proprietary and W3C technology versions in parallel with minimal additional development overhead.

## Exploit the Accessibility Features of the Technology you Choose

W3C technologies have built-in accessibility features; for example, when applied correctly, CSS will allow learners to adapt the visual presentation of content according to their preferences. In addition, W3C technologies generally allow for interaction via keyboard shortcuts, and thus via alternative control devices. Proprietary technologies are more unpredictable in the accessibility features offered. However, regardless of whether one is using a W3C or a proprietary technology, one should exploit *whatever* specific accessibility features it makes available.

As an example, consider one of the most popular proprietary multimedia development technologies: Adobe Flash™ (formerly Macromedia Flash). Up until the launch of Flash MX 2004, this technology was criticised for being inaccessible (Clark, 2000); however, subsequent releases are very much improved in terms of accessibility, and it is now possible to develop Flash™ artefacts that incorporate the following.

- Capabilities for keyboard accessibility
- Compatibility with some, but not all, screen readers
- Capabilities for provision of alternatives to auditory and visual content
- Magnification of movies

- Options for user control over dynamic content

Add-on tools for synchronised captioning of Flash™ movies, such as Hi-Caption™ and MAGpie, are also available. Comprehensive guidelines for developing accessible Flash™ are given elsewhere, for example, by Regan (2005), Smith (2004), and Skills for Access (2007).

## Mitigate, as Far as Possible, any Accessibility Limitations of the Technology you Choose

All multimedia technologies, whether W3C or not, have accessibility limitations. As far as is possible, attempt to mitigate these limitations. This will typically necessitate offering resources implemented via more than one technology.

## Limitations of Proprietary Technologies

- Most crucially, many proprietary technologies require plug-ins that are not available for all platforms or for all devices.
- It is not always possible to mark up and define document structure.
- It not always possible to add metadata to elements.
- It is not always possible to include provision for user definition or user manipulation of styles.
- In general, accessibility features are not incorporated by default in proprietary technologies: They must be enabled by the designer. For example, although it is possible to create Flash™-based resources that are accessible on some platforms and on some devices, inaccessible Flash™ content is the default.

## Limitations of W3C Technologies

W3C technologies are only accessible if they are used in accordance with W3C accessibility guidelines. In addition, although W3C technologies include many features that will improve accessibility, these features may not necessarily be implemented on older browsers or on all devices that people use to access the Web.

## FUTURE TRENDS

The area of accessibility of electronic information and services in general, and educational multimedia in particular, is undergoing continuing rapid development. This section summarises some important trends and issues that are already apparent.

WCAG 1.0 is now somewhat dated, having been formally adopted as a W3C recommendation in May 1999. At the time of writing (June 2007), W3C has been working on a major revision (WCAG 2.0) for an extended period of time. It is difficult to predict, as yet, when this new version will reach recommendation status; but when it does, this should provide a significantly improved basis for the design and development of accessible Web-based multimedia resources.

The so-called AJAX (asynchronous Javascript and XML) combination of technologies is being increasingly deployed to allow Web-based applications that support much richer interactive functionality. This is greatly facilitated by the growing availability of always-on broadband Internet connectivity, both wired and wireless. In this way, the long-anticipated thin-client, Web-based computing is finally arriving. This holds out the promise that users will be able to access their personalised data and applications in a fully mobile and portable way, no longer tied to a particular client PC or workstation. As with all major technological innovations, this offers both challenges and opportunities for the inclusion of people with disabilities. W3C is again attempting to be proactive in this domain with the launch of its Accessible Rich Internet Applications (ARIA) suite of technical documents (http://www.w3.org/WAI/intro/aria).

A related, but separate, development is the rise of what is informally called Web 2.0. This is not a specific, sharply delimited technology, but refers rather to a somewhat amorphous new style of Web-based service or interaction. It is typified by Web-mediated social networking and user-generated content. Prime examples include Wikipedia, the user-created encyclopaedia (http://www.wikipedia.org), Flickr for photo and image sharing (http://flickr.com), and YouTube for video sharing (http://www.youtube.com). As always, any such new service may, in the haste of rapid innovation, overlook the needs of (and opportunities for) people with disabilities and introduce new, yet eminently avoidable, barriers. It is important that anyone building educational activities or resources on top of such services should be proactive in identifying and mitigating any such unintended new barriers. Conversely, it is very worthwhile to support and encourage innovation that can enhance or extend inclusively, for example, by offering a wider variety of alternative, equivalent content and interactions.

There has been a resurgence of interest in so-called immersive virtual environments, with Second Life (http://secondlife.com) being the most prominent example. It is very much still an open question of how much this is simply a fad, and how much it will actually offer genuinely new functionality, particularly in education; however, it does appear that these innovations should offer significantly new opportunities for inclusion of people with disabilities.

The development of educational resources generally relies critically on being able to build effectively on prior creative works. These exist in a pool of shared human culture. This clearly interacts with the regime of copyright law and copyright technologies, such as digital rights management (DRM). There is a very active ongoing debate about whether the current copyright system continues to represent a fair and workable social contract, properly balancing the interests of content creators and the interests of the societ-

ies on which they rely (see, for example, Lessig, 2004). The DRM issue is particularly significant for accessibility, as DRM mechanisms frequently introduce new barriers and incompatibility with assistive technologies used by people with disabilities. Furthermore, the general experience of DRM is that it is, anyway, largely ineffective for its supposed purpose of preventing illicit copying. Accordingly, as a general principle, we would encourage developers of educational multimedia, where feasible, to release such resources under licenses that facilitate flexible reuse (such as those provided by the Creative Commons initiative, http://creativecommons.org), and especially to release such resources in a form that is not encumbered with DRM.

Finally, and perhaps most importantly, there is a clear trend of steadily increasing sensitivity to equality and accessibility issues on the part of governments, regulatory and funding agencies, educational institutions, and individual staff and students. In particular, in many countries, there is an explicit policy objective to increase participation by people with disabilities in HE. This will surely require the progressive elimination of historical barriers, and a systematic commitment to avoiding the creation of new ones (technological or otherwise); but, more positively, it should also involve even more proactive exploitation of technology to actually enhance access.

## CONCLUSION

Web-based educational multimedia provides an important opportunity to enrich learning experiences for all students in HE, and particularly including students with disabilities. We strongly encourage the incorporation of such content where it is pedagogically well motivated and designed. However, in any such multimedia innovation, there is also potential for accidental and gratuitous exclusion of some students with disabilities. We strongly encourage careful consideration at the earliest design stage of how effective and reasonable accommodations can be made to minimise or, ideally, eliminate, any such unintended outcomes. In this way, and reflecting an overall objective of this book, e-learning can most effectively meet the needs of a key stakeholder group, namely, learners affected by disabilities.

## FUTURE RESEARCH DIRECTIONS

This chapter has focused primarily on the technical issues arising in making multimedia resources of any kind as accessible as possible to users with disabilities. We suggest that this is appropriate in the current state of the art, where such attention to accessibility still appears to be the exception rather than the rule in the development of e-learning resources. However, as accessible design becomes better integrated in e-learning development processes, we can anticipate some fruitful new research directions.

- Investigation of how best to integrate accessible design directly into multimedia authoring tools will be valuable, and especially how to maximise the productivity of authors and designers when they are incorporating accessibility features into e-learning resources.
- Investigation of the practical experiences of learners with disabilities in using and learning with properly accessible e-learning resources should be carried out. In particular, this might test whether there are special features, important to accessibility in the context of learning, that are not adequately captured by generic accessibility guidelines.
- In principle, making e-learning resources available under open licensing conditions (e.g., Creative Commons, etc.) should facilitate accessibility because a wider community can potentially contribute to accessibility enhancements. However, to our knowledge, this has not been tested in any systematic

way, nor has there been any detailed research into how to maximise such collaborative, community-based adaptation.

## REFERENCES

Bradley, C., Haynes, R., & Boyle, T. (2005, September 6-8). Design for multimedia m-learning: Lessons from two case studies. In J. Cook & D. Whitelock (Eds.), *Exploring the Frontiers of E-Learning: Borders, Outposts and Migration. Research Proceedings of the 12th Association for Learning Technology Conference (ALT-C 2005)*, Manchester, United Kingdom (pp. 98-108).

Burbules, N., & Callister, T. (2000). Universities in transition: The promise and challenge of new technologies. *Teachers College Record, 102*(2), 271-293.

Cairncross, S., & Mannion, M. (2001). Interactive multimedia and learning: Realizing the benefits. *Innovations in Education and Teaching International, 38*(2), 156-164.

Clark, J. (2000). *Flash access: Unclear on the concept.* Retrieved June 12, 2007, from http://www.alistapart.com/articles/unclear/

Clark, J. (2004). *Reader's guide to Sydney Olympics accessibility complaint.* Retrieved June 12, 2007, from http://www.contenu.nu/socog.html

Coleman, J. (1971). Learning through games. In E. Avedon & B. Sutton-Smith (Eds.), *The study of games* (pp. 322-329). New York: John Wiley.

Downes, S. (2005). E-learning 2.0. *E-Learn Magazine.* Retrieved June 12, 2007, from http://www.elearnmag.org/subpage.cfm?section=articles&article=29-1

Fasli, M., & Michalakopoulos, M. (2005, August 30-September1). *Learning through game-like simulations.* Paper presented at the Sixth Higher Education Academy Information and Computer Sciences Conference (HEA-ICS), York, United Kingdom. Retrieved June 12, 2007, from http://www.ics.heacademy.ac.uk/italics/vol5iss2/MFasli.htm

Garris, R., Ahlers, R., & Driskell, J. (2002). Games, motivation, and learning: A research and practice model. *Simulation & Gaming: An International Journal, 33,* 441-467.

Gayeski, D. (1996). Multimedia packages in education. In T. Plomp & D. Ely (Eds.), *International encyclopaedia of educational technology* (pp. 440-445). New York: Elsevier.

Gil, L., Blanco, E., & Auli, J. (2000). The virtual laboratory concept applied to strain measurements. *European Journal of Engineering Education, 25*(3), 243-251.

Government of Ireland. (2000). *Equal Status Act.* Dublin, Ireland: Stationery Office. Retrieved June 12, 2007, from http://www.irishstatutebook.ie/2000/en/act/pub/0008/index.html

*Hi-Caption™ software.* (n.d.). Retrieved June 12, 2007, from http://www.hisoftware.com/hmccflash/index.html

Higher Education Statistics Agency (HESA). (1994-2007). *First year UK domiciled HE students by qualification aim, mode of study, gender and disability.* Retrieved June 12, 2007, from http://www.hesa.ac.uk

Her Majesty's Stationery Office (HMSO). (1995). *UK Disability Discrimination Act.* Retrieved June 12, 2007, from http://www.legislation.hmso.gov.uk/acts/acts1995/Ukpga_19950050_en_1.htm

Her Majesty's Stationery Office (HMSO). (2001). *UK Special Educational Needs and Disability Act.* Retrieved June 12, 2007, from http://www.legislation.hmso.gov.uk/acts/acts2001/20010010.htm

IMS Global Learning Consortium. (2002). *IMS guidelines for developing accessible learning applications V.1.* Retrieved June 12, 2007, from http://www.imsglobal.org/accessibility/accessiblevers/index.html

IMS Global Learning Consortium. (2003). *IMS learner information package accessibility for LIP best practice and implementation guide Version 1.0 final specification.* Retrieved June 12, 2007, from http://www.imsglobal.org/accessibility/acclipv1p0/imsacclip_bestv1p0.html

IMS Global Learning Consortium. (2004). *IMS access for all meta-data overview, version 1.0 final specification.* Retrieved June 12, 2007, from http://www.imsglobal.org/accessibility/accmdv1p0/imsaccmd_oviewv1p0.html

Le@rning Federation. (2007). *The Le@rning Federation accessibility specification V2.1.* Retrieved June 12, 2007, from http://www.thelearningfederation.edu.au/tlf2/sitefiles/assets/docs/specifications/Accessibility_Specification_V2.1.pdf

Lessig, L. (2004). *Free culture: How big media uses technology and the law to lock down culture and control creativity.* New York: The Penguin Press.

Mace, R. (1997). *The principles of universal design.* Retrieved June 12, 2007, from http://www.design.ncsu.edu/cud/about_ud/udprinciplestext.htm

McFarlane, A., Sparrowhawk, A., & Heald, Y. (2002). *Report on the educational use of games.* Teachers Evaluating Educational Multimedia. Retrieved June 12, 2007, from http://www.teem.org.uk/publications/teem_gamesined_full.pdf

*Media Access Generator (MAGpie) software.* (n.d.). Retrieved June 12, 2007, from http://ncam.wgbh.org/webaccess/magpie

Mirabella, V., Kimani, S., Gabrielli, S., & Catarci, T. (2004). Accessible e-learning material: A no-frills avenue for didactical experts. *The New Review of Hypermedia and Multimedia, 10*(2), 1-16.

Montgomery, S. (1995, November 1-4). Addressing diverse learning styles through the use of multimedia. In *Engineering Education for the 21st Century: Proceedings of the 25th Annual Frontiers in Education Conference* (pp. 3a2.13-3a2.21). Atlanta, GA.

Prensky, M. (2001). *Digital game-based learning.* New York: McGraw-Hill.

Regan, B. (2005). *Best practices for accessible Flash design.* Retrieved June 12, 2007, from http://www.adobe.com/resources/accessibility/best_practices/bp_fp.html

Seale, J. (2006). *Disability and e-learning in higher education: Accessibility theory and practice.* Oxford, United Kingdom: Routledge.

Shephard, K. (2003). Questioning, promoting and evaluating the use of streaming video to support student learning. *British Journal of Educational Technology, 34*(3), 295-308.

*Skills for Access Project.* (2007). Retrieved June 12, 2007, from http://www.skillsforaccess.org.uk

Sloan, D., & Stratford, J. (2004, January 29). *Producing high quality materials on accessible multimedia.* Paper presented at the ILTHE Disability Forum. Retrieved June 12, 2007, from http://www.heacademy.ac.uk/embedded_object.asp?id=21627&filename=Sloan_and_Stratford

Sloan, D., Stratford, J., & Gregor, P. (2006). Using multimedia to enhance the accessibility of the learning environment for disabled students: Reflections from the Skills for Access project. *Association for Learning Technology Journal (ALT-J), 14*(1), 39-54.

Sloan, M. (2001). Web accessibility and the DDA. *The Journal of Information, Law and Technology (JILT), 2.* Retrieved June 12, 2007, from http://www2.warwick.ac.uk/fac/soc/law/elj/jilt/2001_2/sloan

Smith, J. (2004). *Creating accessible Macromedia Flash content.* Retrieved June 12, 2007, from http://www.webaim.org/techniques/flash/?templatetype=3

Tuthill, G., & Klemm, E. (2002). Virtual field trips: Alternatives to actual field trips. *International Journal of Instructional Media, 29*(4), 453-468.

U.S. Department of Justice. (1990). *Americans with Disabilities Act of 1990 (ADA).* Retrieved June 12, 2007, from http://www.ada.gov/pubs/ada.htm

U.S. Department of Labor. (1973). *Section 508, Rehabilitation Act of 1973.* Retrieved June 12, 2007, from http://www.dol.gov/oasam/regs/statutes/sec508.htm

Vanderheiden, G. (1996). *Universal design... What it is and what it isn't.* Retrieved June 12, 2007, from http://trace.wisc.edu/docs/whats_ud/whats_ud.htm

World Wide Web Consortium (W3C). (1999). *Web content accessibility guidelines 1.0.* Retrieved June 12, 2007, from http://www.w3.org/TR/WCAG10

## ADDITIONAL READING

IMS Global Learning Consortium. (2002). *IMS guidelines for developing accessible learning applications V.1.* Retrieved June 12, 2007, from http://www.imsglobal.org/accessibility/accessiblevers/index.html

This work includes advice on developing accessible e-learning environments, authoring tools, and communication and collaboration tools.

*Media Access Generator (MAGpie).* (n.d.). Retrieved June 12, 2007, from http://ncam.wgbh.org/webaccess/magpie

This is a useful tool for creating captions and audio descriptions for rich media.

Seale, J. (2006). *Disability and e-learning in higher education: Accessibility theory and practice.* Oxford, United Kingdom: Routledge.

Seale gives comprehensive coverage of all aspects of e-learning and accessibility, including advice targeted at lecturers, learning technologists, student support staff, staff, and senior managers.

*Skills for Access Project.* (2007). Retrieved June 12, 2007, from http://www.skillsforaccess.org.uk

The Skills for Access initiative is funded by the Higher Education Funding Council for England and the UK Department for Employment and Learning. The Skills for Access Web site provides a wide range of resources relating to e-learning and accessibility, including case studies and practical advice for working with specific technologies.

TechDis. (n.d.). Retrieved August 14, 2007, from http://www.techdis.ac.uk

TechDis is a Joint Information Systems Committee funded advisory service that provides advice and guidance on disability and technology to the UK higher education sector. The TechDis Web site includes a range of publications, articles, and case studies relating to e-learning accessibility.

University of Wisconsin, Madison, Division of Information Technology. (n.d.). Retrieved August 14, 2007, from http://www.doit.wisc.edu/accessibility/video/Accessibility

The site links to a number of useful (and accessible) videos on Web accessibility.

University of Toronto Adaptive Technology Resource Centre. (n.d.). *Assistive technology glossary.* Retrieved June 12, 2007, from http://www.utoronto.ca/atrc/reference/tech/techgloss.html

The site gives a comprehensive overview of various assistive technologies, including descriptions, images, and links to manufacturers' Web sites.

World Wide Web Consortium (W3C). (1999). *Web content accessibility guidelines 1.0.* Retrieved June 12, 2007, from http://www.w3.org/TR/WCAG10

This gives the definitive Web accessibility guidelines.

## APPENDIX 1: TIPS FOR ACCESSIBLE MULTIMEDIA E-LEARNING DESIGN

These tips build on the framework for best practice and provide generic guidance based on WCAG 1.0 for working with various multimedia elements. We do not provide guidance for working with specific technologies, however: This information is subject to change as new versions of technologies and supporting applications are released, and is well documented elsewhere (see, for example, Skills for Access, 2007).

### General Tips for E-Learning Interface Design

A number of simple design considerations can help to make e-learning interfaces more accessible.

- Provide consistent and predictable screen layouts and navigation schemes.
- Provide information on navigation.
- Allow users to skip navigation elements.
- Warn users when new windows will open.
- Provide keyboard equivalents for all commands.
- Make content easy to read on screen: Use lists, headings, and so forth to organise information.

### Tips for Working with Text and Hypertext

Some students can get an overview of a Web page or educational resource by visually scanning the page content. Learners who are unable to do this typically view or access small sections of the page at a time instead. For example, users of screen readers and Braille displays read small chunks of the screen at a time. Similarly, users of screen magnifiers and users of devices with small displays (such as mobile phones and PDAs) view small sections of the whole screen at a time. Instead of scanning the page visually, users of screen readers and devices with small displays can obtain an overview of a page by reading extracts from the page, such as a list of all of the headings or hyperlinks on the page. Such information is only useful if text is consistently marked up according to its semantic meaning rather than solely according to presentation: If text is manually marked up as a heading, for example, by making it bold or a larger size, although visual users may recognise that the text is intended as a heading, nonvisual users will not since there is no way to distinguish it from the text surrounding it. Similarly, it may be confusing for nonvisual users if text that is not intended as a heading is marked as such. A list of hyperlinks is only useful if the hyperlinks make sense when read out of context; if hyperlink destinations are not explicit, then an assistive technology user might end up with a list of links that provides little or no useful information.

- Make content easy to read on screen: Use lists, headings, and so forth to organise information.
- Avoid hard coding the presentation of text into resources. Where possible, use a style sheet instead (a document that defines how elements such as headings, emphasis, and bulleted lists appear). This means, for example, that text marked as a heading will be visually presented according to the style sheet applied to the document by the Web page author or end user. Using styles also ensures that all content of a particular type are displayed consistently (for example, headings, text intended to

be emphasised, etc.) and allows the appearance (size, font colour, contrast) of text and background to be customised according to user preferences.

- Where available, mark up text according to structure; for example, mark up headings as headings rather than simply changing the appearance of the text (by making it bold, for instance).
- Create hyperlinks that link from a meaningful phrase rather than isolated words.
- Avoid creating multiple hyperlinks on the same page that link from the same repeated word or phrase, such as "Click here."
- In general, it is preferable not to use hyperlinks that cause new windows to appear or new applications to open without informing the user.

## Tips for Working with Images and Diagrams

Images (photographs, diagrams, graphs, etc.) can be very useful in enhancing comprehension and presenting information that would be very complex when conveyed only via text. However, such purely visual information may be difficult or even impossible for some users to properly perceive, for example, learners who are blind or have other visual impairments, or who are using devices with small displays.

- Provide an equivalent text-based alternative to information that is otherwise presented only in some image format, for example, photographs, diagrams, and graphs.
- In general, avoid using an image that simply conveys textual information; instead, just present the information as text in the first place. However, if there is some particular reason for using an image that simply conveys textual information, ensure that this information is also available as a proper text-based alternative.
- If an image is simply for visual decoration and does not actually convey any useful or significant information, then provide a *blank* text alternative. Do *not* provide text descriptions of such images; rather than serving as decoration for nonvisual users, they actually get in the way and slow down or confuse access to the real information.
- If an image conveys important information but this information is *already* available in the text around or adjacent to the image, then it is again appropriate simply to provide a *blank* text alternative for the image. Do *not* simply copy or duplicate information that is already in your text into the text alternative for the image.
- Ensure that, as far as is possible, images are still usable when magnified or scaled.

## Tips for Working with Audio and Video

Audio and video can be useful complements to the learning experience. For example, provision of media in audiovisual format can appeal to a range of learning styles, and can motivate and engage some students more effectively (Montgomery, 1995; Shephard, 2003). However, both audio and video may present barriers to students who cannot hear audio or see video, or who access these media via nonstandard devices.

- Provide an appropriately synchronised textual alternative to visual content.
- Provide an equivalent and appropriately synchronised alternative to audio content (including spoken and other sounds, such as background noises; music; and audio prompts).

- Provide an equivalent and appropriately synchronised alternative to audio alerts.
- Avoid incorporating flashing or flickering content, especially between 2 and 59 hertz (flashes per second).
- Provide prior warning before presenting any animated or flashing content.
- Ensure that, as far as is possible, video is still usable when magnified or scaled.
- Allow learners control to turn audiovisuals on or off and to control sound level via the keyboard.

## Tips for Working with Animations, Simulations, and Games

Animations and simulations have significant potential to enhance learning in HE (Cairncross & Mannion, 2001). Games have been used for many years to support teaching and learning (see, for example, Coleman, 1971). More recently, there has been interest in the potential of online multiplayer games, simulations, and virtual worlds for increasing students' motivation and developing their strategic thinking and problem-solving skills (Garris, Ahlers, & Driskell, 2002; Prensky, 2001).

- Provide an appropriately synchronised textual alternative to visual content.
- Provide an equivalent and appropriately synchronised alternative to audio content (including spoken and other sounds, such as background noises; music; and audio prompts).
- Avoid incorporating flashing or flickering content, especially between 2 and 59 hertz (flashes per second).
- Allow animated content to be turned off and its speed adjusted.
- Provide prior warning before presenting any animated or flashing content.
- Ensure that, as far as is possible, content is still usable when magnified or scaled.
- Where possible, allow the appearance of text and background to be modified, including the size, font, colour, and text and background contrast.
- Allow learners to interact via the keyboard.

## Tips for Working with Colour

Colour coding can be very useful in an educational context in order to distinguish between the various parts of a whole, for example, to explain sentence structure in language teaching or to highlight parts of a computer program. However, if colour is the *sole mechanism* for conveying information, many users may not be able to comprehend the information. The following users may experience difficulties.

- Users for whom it is difficult or impossible to differentiate between certain colours (for example, users who are blind or have visual impairments such as colour blindness)
- Users of devices that have noncolour or nonvisual displays

Colour contrast is also important: When foreground and background colours are too close, they may not provide sufficient contrast when viewed, especially for those who have difficulty distinguishing between certain colours (for example, colour-blind students) or who are accessing the information via small displays or noncolour displays.

- Ensure that all information conveyed with colour (both via text and images) can also be understood without colour.
- Ensure that foreground and background colour combinations provide sufficient contrast, and ideally allow students to customise colour and contrast according to their own preferences.
- When using colour to convey information, try printing out the page on a black and white printer to check that there is a reasonable degree of contrast even for someone without good colour discrimination.
- In any case, do not use colour *alone* to convey information; complement it by *also* conveying the same information with some distinct additional text or punctuation.

# Section III
# Designing E-Learning and E-Teaching Experiences

*The chapters of Section III cover the design of online courses and eLearning tools as well as appropriate pedagogical strategies and learning theories in relation to various topics and subject disciplines in higher education.*

# Chapter IX
# Enhancing Students' Transition to University through Online Preinduction Courses

**Ursula Wingate**
*King's College London, UK*

## ABSTRACT

*This chapter proposes online preinduction courses as an innovative method for preparing students for learning in higher education. It is argued that such courses would be most effective as components of a comprehensive learning support framework. One specific online preinduction course, which was created for undergraduate students of management, is presented. The design principles as well as the rationale and content of its five modules are discussed. The design of the course is based on constructivist, experiential, and situated learning theories, which determined the choice of subject-specific materials and authentic activities. The second part of the chapter focuses on the pilot study in which students were observed and asked to think aloud while working on the course's materials and tasks. Findings from the pilot study show that the instructional design principles were successful in helping students to achieve the various learning objectives.*

## INTRODUCTION

Online preinduction courses (OPICs) represent an e-teaching and e-learning approach that can considerably enhance individual and institutional learning. The courses give students the opportunity to reflect on epistemological issues, consider effective learning strategies, and gain insight into academic writing practices before their arrival at university. Thus, they provide necessary preparation for studying in higher education, a preparation that students entering university are commonly lacking.

In the United Kingdom, as elsewhere, widening participation has led to a diverse student population with different levels of preparation, different abilities, and different learning experiences. For most students, regardless of their background, the transition to university is challenging as new demands are placed on them as learners: They are expected to learn independently, to adapt to new epistemological understandings, to develop analytical and critical approaches, and to express their voice in presentations and writing. To cope with these requirements, students need careful induction and support at the beginning of the university course. However, high withdrawal levels are a persistent problem for departments (Edward, 2003; Hughes, 2007), which indicate that universities have not implemented adequate support schemes that cater to the diverse needs of students from different backgrounds. Instead, the remedial system that was aimed at the few problematic students in the previous selective system still prevails. To support all students, universities need to develop "learning to learn" frameworks that are both inclusive, that is, by reaching all students through embedding support in the curriculum, and comprehensive, by developing student learning with various complementary methods over time.

Online preinduction courses could be part of such a framework. They prepare students for studying at university before the start of their first term. This is done by using Web-based materials and tasks that provide information and develop learning skills. Students are given access to the OPIC upon admission, about 4 weeks before registration, and will have the opportunity to use the course throughout their first year.

In the next section, the learning needs of students entering higher education and current provision of learning support at UK universities are considered. This is followed by a brief discussion of a framework for learning support in which OPICs are the initial component. Then, the benefits of e-learning are considered in the context of

OPICs. In the main part of the chapter, a specific OPIC that was developed for an undergraduate management programme is described in terms of its teaching and learning strategies. Finally, the results of piloting this OPIC are presented, and the impact of OPIC's instructional design on student learning is analysed.

## BACKGROUND

## Students' Learning Needs and the Provision of Support

Unlike other countries, the United Kingdom's higher education system remained highly selective until the 1990s, and there was little demand for student preparation and learning support. The rapid expansion of the sector led to a far more diverse student population in which many students are not as prepared for the challenges of university study as their predecessors in the elite system (Ivanic & Lea, 2006). Research into the first-year experience reveals that there are currently insufficient support mechanisms for students' transition to university (Lillis, 2001, 2006). Yorke (2001) reported that about two thirds of withdrawals in UK universities happen during or at the end of the first year. The foremost factor for failure is the lack of preparation for learning in higher education (Drew, 2001; Ozga & Sukhnandan, 1998). The National Audit Office (2002) found that due to changes in the secondary system, most students from the traditional A-level route, having been "spoon-fed" at school, are not adequately prepared for the independent learning required at university. Based on their learning experience at school, they tend to regard knowledge as an "external, objective body of facts" (Gamache, 2002, p. 277) that they have to absorb. However, in most disciplines, students have to develop from dependent receivers of knowledge into active, independent learners who critically approach and contest knowledge in order to study successfully (Gamache). For this rather substantial transformation, effective induction to university as well as ongoing support is essential.

Both Edward (2003) and Tinto (1993) stress the importance of meaningful induction events for students' retention and progression. In most study programmes, students are required to attend induction events, ranging from a day to whole weeks of freshman activities. However, as Edward describes, these events are often "passive and dull" for students. They sit in the lecture theatre all day listening to speakers who "deliver their concentrated 20-minute talk on course structure, computer systems, Students' Association—and, what was most probably needed by the end of the day, counselling services" (p. 226).

Induction events would be far more beneficial if they helped students, through interaction and meaningful tasks, to become aware of the concepts of learning and knowledge in their discipline. The vast amount of information that is usually presented during induction might be retrieved more comfortably from leaflets and Web sites.

After induction, there are rarely any regular support activities that are embedded in the curriculum. Learning to learn at university is left to the students. Most universities still follow a remedial practice, offering support only to those students who show obvious signs of not coping with the requirements (Wingate, 2006). The lack of adequate support is particularly obvious in the area of academic writing, which is the "key assessment tool" (Lillis, 2001, p. 20), determining whether students pass or fail courses. Lillis explains that universities in the United Kingdom, unlike those in countries with a longer history of widening participation, have only "fragmented and limited additional provision" (p. 22) to help students develop their writing, usually in extracurricular study-skills courses.

Researchers in academic literacies (Lea & Street, 1998; Lillis 2001) emphasised the limitations of the skills approach. Reading and writing are cultural and social practices that depend on tutors' and students' assumptions of what constitutes knowledge, and clearly vary across disciplines, if not within subject areas themselves. Students need to understand the ways in which knowledge is constructed and contested in their specific discipline. Generic approaches to developing students' writing are therefore not effective. Cottrell (2001) has considered this issue and emphasises that study skills must be integrated into the curriculum instead of being "bolted on."

Given the complexity of learning at university, it is important to take approaches that support students over a period of time. A potential learning support framework that offers a variety of complementary support methods from preinduction to the end of the first term has been proposed elsewhere (Wingate, in press) and is briefly discussed in the next section.

## OPIC as Part of a Learning Support Framework

The proposed framework aims to provide inclusive and subject-specific learning support for students new to a study programme. Therefore, three of the framework's four components integrate learning development activities into regular programme events. These components are induction, personal tutorials, and lectures and seminars.

OPIC is the first component in the framework and has the following objectives: to prepare students for learning at university by (a) providing information to reduce information overload in induction events, (b) raising awareness of the nature of learning and knowledge in the higher education context, and (c) introducing students to academic writing in their discipline.

Some issues raised in OPIC will be taken up in the second component: induction. For instance, case studies concerned with common difficulties experienced by first-year students will be taken up again for role plays and discussions during induction. OPIC also offers a self-assessment questionnaire on academic skills that aims at laying the foundations for independent learning and personal development planning. Students are encouraged to assess their present abilities, set targets, and plan action for the improvement of these abilities. This process will be continued in the third component: the personal tutorial. Following up on the targets the students identified, the personal tutors will discuss possible action, how to monitor progress, and how to evaluate outcomes.

The fourth component is primarily concerned with writing. It requires subject tutors to allocate some of their regular teaching time to referring to epistemological issues of writing that were first raised in the OPIC. These issues involve a critical-analytical approach to reading, the development of an argument, and the expression of the writer's own voice. Some technical aspects of writing, for instance, spelling, grammar, and style, remain in the OPIC and can be revisited online anytime.

OPIC makes effective use of time before the term starts to give students initial preparation. This can take stress out of the first weeks at university, and may, for some students, relieve the anxiety they feel before their arrival.

Whilst OPIC could be offered as a stand-alone method for preparing pre-entry students for university, it is more effective when it is integrated in the learning support framework.

## E-Learning Affordances for OPIC

Integrating OPIC in the above framework follows the blended learning approach. Whilst there are various interpretations of blended learning, and Oliver and Trigwell (2005) even recommend abandoning the term altogether because of its inconsistency, it is understood here in its widely used sense as "the integrated approach of traditional learning with Web-based online approaches" (Whitelock & Jelfs, 2003).

Blending e-learning into traditional courses has resulted in improved student retention (Dziuban et al., 2004; Hughes, 2007) as the e-learning

component enhances deeper student learning (Fox & MacKeogh, 2003), provides more flexible learning opportunities (Conole & Fill, 2005), and increases "interaction between student-instructor, student-student, student-content, and student-outside resources" (Dziuban et al., p. 3). In the context of OPICs, another major benefit of the blended learning approach is the firm integration of student learning into the mainstream curriculum.

OPIC relies on the affordances of e-learning. From a practical point of view, it is the most effective method of reaching and engaging students before the start of their course. Furthermore, e-learning offers a learning environment that fosters constructivist learning. As Doolittle (1999, p. 1) points out, "online education provides the resources necessary for students to engage in rich and effective construction of knowledge." E-learning has the potential to provide "virtual environments in which one can simulate real-world events" (ibid.). As the next section will show, OPIC's theoretical underpinnings draw on constructivist, experiential, and situated learning. The online format affords these types of learning through the nonlinear presentation of links to essential information, audio and video files representing real-life student experiences, access to text and other students' writings through PDF (Portable Document Format) files, authentic study activities, and immediate feedback through pop-up windows. The design of some of OPIC's activities is explained in more detail below.

So far, the background for the development of OPICs was explained in terms of student needs, a framework for learning support, and the affordances of e-learning. The following main section discusses the OPIC that was created for an undergraduate degree course in management.

## THE MANAGEMENT OPIC

The management OPIC was designed in 2005 and 2006, piloted in 2006, and implemented for all students of the course in 2007. Its design principles are explained first, followed by a description of the components.

## Design of the OPIC

The management OPIC was the first of a series of OPICs to be developed for different subjects in the social sciences and humanities. It was created with a generic structure on the platform of WebCT Vista. The structure can be filled with subject-specific texts and tasks, and therefore easily be adapted to other subjects.

It was argued earlier that academic writing should be learned within the context of the discipline. In the OPIC, subject-specific materials were not only used in the modules concerned with academic writing, but throughout to make the course relevant and authentic for students.

The design principles of OPIC are based on constructivist and experiential learning theories. Constructivists regard learning as effective when (a) students construct their own knowledge through engaging in meaningful learning activities, and (b) teaching approaches provide chances for the students to be active and to find answers independently. Teaching approaches in which knowledge is transmitted do not give students the opportunity to construct knowledge (Biggs, 2003). Similarly, experiential learning requires learners to experience problems, reflect on them, and find and try out solutions (Kolb, 1984). Many Web sites on study skills transmit knowledge by presenting long lists of instructions on how to carry out academic tasks. Instructions were avoided in the OPIC. Instead, activities were designed in a way that students can find out principles, criteria, and concepts by themselves.

The theory of situated learning also informed the design of OPIC. It gave further support to the decision to use subject-specific materials and to avoid instructions. Situated learning is based on the understanding that abstract knowledge cannot be retrieved to solve real-life problems. In the context of OPIC, this means that instructions on

learning are unlikely to be translated into effective learning strategies when students have to solve specific learning problems. The theory of situated learning proposes that knowledge and skills are learned in contexts that reflect how the knowledge will be used in real life (Brown, 1997).

Lave and Wenger (1991) added the concept of "legitimate peripheral participation" to the theory of situated learning and explained how "apprentices" first observe the practices, and then gradually learn the language and culture of the "community of practice." For the development from apprentice to full member in the specific knowledge community, learners need "broad access to arenas of mature practice" (p. 110). Following Lave and Wenger's concept, OPIC provides access to mature writing in the discipline with links to journal articles written by academic staff in the students' department.

Herrington and Oliver (2000) drew on the principles of situated learning when designing a multimedia programme on assessment for teacher trainees. They found that the situated learning framework "appeared to provide effective instructional design guidelines for the design of an environment for the acquisition of advanced knowledge" (p. 23).

Herrington and Oliver (2000) provide a list with the essential instructional features for situated learning environments. The list includes "authentic contexts that reflect the way the knowledge will be used in real life" and "authentic activities" (p. 26). OPIC offers these features; for instance, authentic contexts are provided through case studies, interviews with students from the same course, or student essays annotated with teachers' comments. Many of OPIC's activities mirror those that students will have to do once they start the course, for instance, structuring and proofreading texts, writing references, or paraphrasing statements from the literature.

However, OPIC lacks some of the instructional features listed by Herrington and Oliver (2000), such as "collaborative construction of knowledge" and "coaching and scaffolding by the teacher at critical times" (pp. 26 -27).

The lack of peer collaboration and teacher feedback is due to the fact that OPIC is made available to those students who have been admitted to the course about 4 weeks before registration. However, before the students arrive at the university, due to concerns about personal data protection, it is not possible to set up peer groups for collaborative learning. Equally, during this period, no tutors may be available to provide feedback.

This makes the positioning of OPIC in a support framework even more important because the lack of collaboration and feedback will be compensated for by face-to-face activities in the other components. In several of OPIC's activities, students are informed that the issues will be revisited, and are encouraged to bring comments and questions back to induction week, personal tutorials, and teaching sessions. While they are working on their own with the OPIC materials, feedback is provided by model answers. These offer a variety of possible answers and remind students that there are no right or wrong answers, and that in case of doubt, they should consult their tutors once they are at the university.

## OPIC's Modules

OPIC consists of five modules: (a) Information Centre, (b) Learning to Learn at University, (c) Academic Writing, (d) Referencing, and (e) Avoiding Plagiarism. Appendix 1 shows the modules as they are presented on OPIC's front page.

The modules were chosen to address the most common learning needs that were identified at this particular university through a survey with teaching staff, programme leaders, and students. Much emphasis is given to academic writing, which was regarded by the participants in the survey as the major difficulty for first-year students. As writing is a complex topic, separate modules were created for related areas such as Referencing and Avoiding Plagiarism.

Below, there is a brief description of the modules, their objectives, and their methods, followed by a detailed discussion of the module Academic Writing.

## Information Centre

The main objectives are to reduce the information overload that students usually experience during induction week and to reduce anxiety by familiarising students with their new learning environment. Students can find out at their own pace about facilities, services, and their new department through Web links and additional explanations. The Information Centre introduces the academic and administrative staff members who are in charge of first-year students. The subsection Who is Who in the Department explains the specific roles of staff members, and advises students on whom to turn to in case of problems. Frequently Asked Questions offers information on the department's teaching and assessment methods and on expectations placed on students concerning attendance, deadlines, and workload.

Students are also given the opportunity to share the experiences of previous first-year students. The Information Centre presents interviews with two students who report on their start in university life, their initial worries, and how they overcame difficulties.

## Learning to Learn

The objectives of the module are to (a) raise students' awareness of the epistemological approach of the discipline, and what it requires from them as learners, and (b) develop their independent learning skills.

Case studies are one of the methods used to achieve these objectives. The case study of Fred, for instance, describes a hardworking student who uncritically absorbs vast amounts of facts, which he then regurgitates in exams. He feels unfairly treated when he receives low grades in his first exam in microeconomics. After seeking advice from his lecturer, he realises that he was expected to relate theories to each other instead of presenting a list of them.

The case studies are accompanied by tasks that invite students to analyse what went wrong, to formulate advice on how to study more effectively, and to describe differences between learning at school and learning at university. Rather than telling students how to study effectively, the tasks encourage them to find out by themselves.

Independent learners take control of their learning through metacognitive skills such as reflection, self-assessment, target setting, and action planning as well as evaluation of their progress (Fazey & Fazey, 2001). The self-profiling questionnaire that was mentioned earlier has the aim to initiate the process of independent learning. The task for students is to rate on a scale from 1 to 5 their skills in the areas of time management, task management, learning actively and effectively, and working with others. The first page of the questionnaire is shown in Appendix 2. The students are also asked to prioritise a number of skills that they want to improve, and to think of ways to improve them. They are invited to bring their questionnaires, targets, and action plans to the first meeting with their personal tutor.

The modules Referencing and Avoiding Plagiarism follow the same principle of encouraging students to identify and name relevant criteria. Table 1 shows an example from the module Referencing.

Another task requires students to fix incorrect references and to compare their answers with the correct versions. A series of scenarios is presented for students to judge whether in the particular circumstances plagiarism was committed. As Appendix 3 shows, the programme provides pop-up windows in which the correct answers are given. The colour of the pop-up window indicates whether the student answer was correct or not.

## Academic Writing

This module is the largest one in OPIC. The sequence of components is described below to demonstrate how experiential and constructivist learning is facilitated. The module's progression enables students to discover and apply the principles of academic writing.

1.  The first component presents two case studies of first-year students experiencing difficulties with their first writing assignments, such as time management, selecting relevant litera-

*Table 1. Task from the Module Referencing*

Like Andrew, many students do not fully understand what is expected from them. They believe that they must refer to the literature to prove to their lecturers that they have done some reading. Look at the following reference.

**Extract from an Essay Written by a First-Year Student**
*"For a full study of welfare economics, see Beggs, Chapter 16. This was the book I was recommended to use in my course. I used this book throughout the year. The text begins with a definition of welfare economics, followed by definitions of the terms equity and efficiency. The remainder of the chapter discussed more advanced topics."*

Imagine you were this student's tutor and write a brief comment on the reference using the Notes facility. You can then compare your comment with the Model answer.

ture, and synthesising their sources into a critical-analytical argument. The associated tasks require students to identify these problems and think of ways of avoiding them.

2.  The second component offers legitimate peripheral participation (Lave & Wenger, 1991) by presenting a journal article, authored by two lecturers of the management department. The aim is to introduce students to the new genre and the conventions of academic writing in their discipline. They are requested to skim the article and to identify features of academic writing.

3.  The next component aims to help students to identify and internalise the criteria for appropriate essay writing. They can draw on several sources to derive these criteria: One source is a list of comments by subject tutors who were asked in interviews what they consider as good or bad essays. Then follows a list of one lecturer's comments on 14 essays on a specific topic, together with the grades he assigned to these essays. Table 2 shows an excerpt from the list. The comments demonstrate some key criteria (focus, structure, argument) to students.

4.  Finally, another lecturer's PowerPoint presentation with feedback on a specific essay can

be viewed. The students are asked to compile their own list of guidelines for essay writing from these sources.

5.  The next step is to apply the criteria, complying with the concept of experiential learning, in which the reflection and planning stage is followed by action. For this purpose, PDF files show essays written by previous first-year students. The students are required to make comments, based on their list of guidelines, and compare them with the lecturer's feedback on the essays, which can be accessed in separate files.

The last component provides practical tasks to enhance technical writing skills. They include a proofreading exercise in which grammar, spelling, and expression errors in a weak student essay have to be identified and corrected; an exercise in which paragraphs have to be inserted in an unstructured text; and one in which overlong sentences have to be divided into shorter ones. The final exercise deals with presenting tables and figures accurately.

The evaluation and piloting of the management OPIC led to a number of amendments. In the spring of 2007, a couple of workshops were held to familiarise lecturers in the management

*Table 2. Tutor comments on student essays*

| **Grade: 38** |
| Key issues are not identified and you appear confused about issues to do with taxation and producer surplus. The discussion of the consumer surplus is flawed. Explanations of how tax affects economic welfare are needed to support your argument. |
| **Grade: 60** |
| The basics are good. Your essay would improve with a sharper focus, a concentration on key issues, and avoiding the use of so many unnecessary paragraph titles. Your understanding of the effects of the tax on the distribution of welfare losses is correct but needs further development. The conclusion needs to be developed. |
| **Grade: 80** |
| The key issues are clearly understood—notably the link between the absolute size of the change in surplus and the relative shares of consumers and producers. Your structure is coherent and logical, although there are some minor mistakes. A proper conclusion would help. |

department who teach first-year students with the materials. The course was implemented for the first-year cohort in autumn of 2007.

## EVALUATION AND PILOTING OF OPIC

### Evaluation

Each of OPIC's modules was evaluated by a management lecturer and a lecturer in higher education to get feedback on the adequacy of both the subject content and the pedagogical approach.

The lecturers were given a set of evaluation criteria, including instructional design, usability, multimedia utilisation, meeting of students' needs, and authenticity. For instance, lecturers were asked whether they found any sections too text heavy; whether they found task explanations, learning outcomes, and feedback clearly expressed; whether they regarded the subject content and the tasks as appropriate for first-year students; and whether they found the activities challenging and authentic.

The feedback was positive on the content and instructional approach. Suggested changes were mainly concerned with certain difficulties in navigating between the sections and a lack of signposting. Following the suggestions, more links between sections were installed, and suggestions on where to go next were added at the end of sections.

This evaluation with lecturers served the purpose of identifying weaknesses in the OPIC so that necessary changes could be made before the course was piloted with students. No claims can be derived from it about OPIC's effectiveness in developing and supporting students' learning. A comprehensive evaluation with quantitative and qualitative measures will be carried out with the first cohort in the academic year of 2007 to 2008.

### Piloting

The pilot study investigated the following questions.

1. Did the participants experience any problems when using the course?
2. Was the instructional design of the course successful in helping the participants to reach the learning objectives?
3. Did the participants find the materials and activities authentic and useful?

These questions could best be answered by observing the students while they were working on the OPIC. To identify if and how the students learn on the basis of the online materials and activities, it was necessary to capture the cognitive processes during their interaction with OPIC. For this purpose, the think-aloud method was used in which participants are encouraged to verbalise all their thoughts "unedited and unanalyzed" (Cohen, 1987, p. 84) while working on the tasks. For validity reasons, the think-aloud methodology requires the researcher to take a neutral role and interfere in the process only to give "contentless prompts" (Smagorinsky, 1994, p. 5), such as "What are you thinking now?" when the participant lapses into silence.

However, this requirement was not strictly observed in the pilot study, but the model of "participative evaluation" (Oliver, 2000, p. 21) was followed, in which evaluation is perceived as "a collaborative process of building mutual understanding." The researcher asked direct questions when the think-aloud procedure did not produce clear answers to the study's main questions. An example in which the researcher seeks further clarification on the student's understanding of a case study can be seen in Extract 1.

From the 2006 intake of management students, four volunteered to participate in the pilot study. They were given book vouchers as an incentive to participate. All four students had just completed secondary school. Two were overseas students (S1 and S2) from Asia who both had completed the international baccalaureate (IB) as entrance qualification to the university. The other two participants (S3 and S4) were UK school graduates with the traditional A-level qualification. The pilot study was carried out in the fourth and fifth weeks of the first term, shortly before the participants had to start working on their first assignments.

The four participants came individually to the researcher's office for three or four sessions, working in each session through one or two modules. Their thinking aloud was audio taped, while a video camera was directed at the computer screen to pick up any problems the students might experience when navigating through the components of the course. A few navigation problems were detected from the video recordings and consequently addressed. The audio taped think-aloud data were fully transcribed and analysed to answer Questions 2 and 3. The findings are presented below.

## The Impact of OPIC's Instructional Design on Student Learning

As explained earlier, a major design principle of OPIC was to give students the opportunity to discover concepts and criteria without giving them instructions. The following examples show how different learning objectives were achieved through OPIC's materials and activities. The first two examples illustrate how students learn from case studies.

## Example 1: Case Studies Challenging Epistemological Beliefs

One objective of the module Learning to Learn was to raise students' awareness of the epistemological approach in their discipline that is most likely to differ from the epistemological approach they experienced at school. Extracts

1 and 2 from the verbal protocols present the comments of one participant while reading one of the case studies.

## Extract 1

*S1: I think I am facing this problem that Andrew has.*
*I: What's that?*
*S1: This problem that they mention, that you are reading books and they keep on giving you lots of references to other books, and you want to read those books as well and when you start taking notes you find that you are copying down chunks of text and by the time you get around to actually going back and revising, it is almost as if you have to read the book again.*

The researchers' question prompted the student to describe in detail his difficulties in reading selectively, which he has in common with the person in the case study. His comments indicate that the case study made him fully aware of his own ineffective reading strategies. The next segment of the verbal protocol reveals that the student had also gained an understanding of the epistemological belief that leads to ineffective reading.

## Extract 2

*It's like…it's like Fred too, he's got the problem that he reads and learns just everything. Like, if something gets written in a book, it must be important, I must read it carefully, I must not miss anything. (Student 1)*

The extracts demonstrate that the case studies were an effective method to initiate the student's analysis of his own epistemological beliefs. They also reveal a particular strength of case studies: They facilitate experiential learning, particularly when students, as in this case, can relate them to their own experience.

The following example shows the effectiveness of case studies for developing writing strategies.

## Example 2: Case Studies Leading to the Identification of Writing Strategies

One of the objectives of the module on Academic Writing was to enable students to identify problems associated with academic writing and to think of strategies to avoid them. The extracts below show a number of difficulties that the students identified in the case studies. Extracts 3 and 4 identify the same problem, that is, selecting relevant information from the literature that Student 1 (Extract 1) recognised from the case studies in the previous module.

## Extract 3

*When you are taking notes you have the tendency to write down everything you see on the page. And I think that is the biggest challenge, of how you filter down that information and write down only what you need. (Student 2)*

## Extract 4

*Ok, I think he just used a bunch of information that didn't really pull together, he didn't really structure it that well and everything. (Student 3)*

## Extract 5

*Students tend to write when they actually find the information... it's almost like copy and pasting as I first said. That you've again just described everything, you haven't analysed what has been said. Or you haven't taken things from different sources and tried to relate them together. So I think those would be the main two problems. (Student 4)*

Students 3 and 4 have clearly learned important issues from the case studies: that academic writing requires the ability to analyse literature rather than describe it, and the ability to relate together information from different sources.

The case studies were accompanied by the task to write down some advice for effective writing. The notes of Student 4, presented in Table 3, indicate that she, in common with the other three students, derived useful learning strategies from the case studies.

The following examples demonstrate the value of giving students models of academic writing to develop their understanding of the requirements.

## Example 3: Learning from "Mature Practice." Identifying Features of Academic Writing

Following Lave and Wenger's (1991) concept of legitimate peripheral participation, one activity required the students to analyse a journal article

*Table 3. Notes for Task 3.2 of Student 4*

-Make sure you properly read and understand the essay question.
-Don't read books from the beginning to the end.
-Don't read too many books.
-Don't take too many notes.
-Don't copy text from books. Write notes in your own words.
-Don't just describe other people's claims. Write your own argument.

for typical features of academic writing. All four participants had not read an academic article before and had only vague ideas of this genre. The extracts below show that essential features were identified in the activity.

## Extract 6

*There's a clear statement in the title. And then at the beginning there's…a summary to say what you're going to be talking about, and what sources you're going to be using… (Student 1)*

## Extract 7

*And then there's an introduction. The structure, the headings, the subheadings, the references coming at the end and the specific title. They are to the point and very systematic, the way they've done it. Everything is always cited with citations to show that the ideas are actually someone else's but they are using it in their own words. (Student 2)*

## Extract 8

*Oh and they have very clear goals and aims for the paper. (Student 3)*

## Extract 9

*The impersonal style…yes, instead of saying, "we collected data" they say "data was collected." (Student 4)*

As explained earlier, the students had to compile a list of criteria for academic writing from this activity and other sources. The next activity required them to apply these criteria.

## Example 4: Learning by Applying Criteria

It was regarded as an indication of effective learning if students were able to assess other students'

essays (presented on PDF files) on the basis of the criteria they had previously derived from different sources. As the extracts below indicate, the participants from the pilot study were able to identify the strengths and weaknesses in the presented essays.

## Extract 10

*There's no conclusion. No headings. They didn't establish the points, they didn't establish what question they are answering. (Student 1)*

## Extract 11

*I think that these diagrams help in understanding what he is trying to say. They illustrate his argument. (Student 2)*

## Extract 12

*The paper is very descriptive, which is another thing. (Student 4)*

These comments demonstrate that the previous tasks had enabled the participants to understand and internalise essential requirements of academic writing. The verbal protocols contain many utterances that show that the activities in other components were equally effective for learning. The findings of the pilot study confirm that the OPIC's instructional design was indeed successful in helping the participants to construct knowledge about the requirements of learning at university, and particularly of writing in their chosen discipline.

The next question for which the pilot study sought answers was whether the participants found the materials and activities authentic and useful. The verbal protocols were therefore analysed for statements that expressed the students' perceptions of OPIC.

## Students' Perceptions of OPIC

According to situated learning theory, OPIC aimed to use "authentic contexts that reflect the way the knowledge will be used in real life" (Herrington & Oliver, 2000, p. 26) and authentic activities. Whilst OPIC's designer had tried to create authentic content, it was important to find out whether the participants in the pilot study had the same perception of authenticity, and therefore regarded materials and activities as relevant and useful.

In addition to the statements made by the students during the think-aloud procedure, their perceptions of OPIC were elicited by specific questions. When they completed a module, the students were asked whether and why they found the module useful, and which activities they found most useful. The components that all four students found relevant and useful were the case studies, the self-profiling questionnaire, the access to journal articles and student essays, and the practical exercises in the modules Academic Writing and Referencing.

The next three extracts show why the case studies were perceived as most useful: They were regarded as authentic as the students could identify with the characters and their problems.

### Extract 13

*I think they are very relevant, these studies, because, not only have I seen my own fellow students going through the same thing but myself as well. (Student 1)*

### Extract 14

*That sounds very familiar! I think that starting early would probably be the best turning point and then I think, as her teacher suggests, breaking it down into smaller subtasks. (Student 3)*

### Extract 15

*A lot of my friends experience the same thing and they get into trouble for plagiarism and everything, just because they don't understand. Like, it's unintentional but it just happens. (Student 4)*

Furthermore, the case studies were perceived as reassuring, as can be seen in the next extract.

### Extract 16

*Very useful for me as a foreign student. I feel much better knowing that all first-year undergraduates might have the same problems as me. (Student 2)*

The self-profiling questionnaire was considered as useful; Student 2 said, "It has reminded me exactly what I did wrong in school and how I never want to feel out of control of my work." The other participants regarded it as an indicator of their potential success at university as it helped them to identify their strengths and weaknesses. Two students found the questionnaire relevant because it made them understand what was expected from students at university.

Several practical exercises, for instance, correcting references and identifying incidents of plagiarism, were perceived as fun and at the same time as directly relevant to the students' impending first assignment.

While none of OPIC's activities was declared as irrelevant or not useful, some practical tasks were not liked by all participants. For instance, one student disliked the proofreading exercise. He has always had difficulties with spelling and felt that the exercise did not "cure" his problem. As a result, the introductory text for the exercise was changed. It now states that the exercise's objective is to make students aware of common mistakes and of the importance to pay attention to accuracy.

## DISCUSSION

The analysis of the think-aloud data has confirmed that the instructional design principles were effective in enabling the students to achieve the learning objectives of the different modules. Furthermore, the four participants clearly enjoyed working with OPIC and found the activities useful.

However, these are preliminary findings of a small-scale study that have to be treated with caution as the pilot study had several limitations. One limitation is obviously the small sample size that comes with the qualitative method chosen for the pilot study. While the think-aloud data gave some important insights into learning processes, no claims can be made as to how effective OPIC might be for other first-year students.

The second limitation was that the participants of the pilot study had already been at university for 5 to 6 weeks, and therefore had gained some understanding of learning in higher education. Therefore, they may have benefited more from the activities or found them more relevant than the intended user population, preinduction students, might. Furthermore, two participants had done received the international baccalaureate, which requires extensive essay writing. They may have found the tasks in the Academic Writing module less challenging than A-level students who usually are less experienced in writing essays. However, a difference in understanding the concepts of writing between the two participants with the IB qualification and the two A-level students was not obvious in the pilot study.

Third, the participants in the pilot study were bound to make positive comments. They were volunteers and as such perhaps more motivated and interested in their own learning than other students. In addition, they were making their comments in the presence of the researcher, from whom they had received an incentive to participate.

Valid claims about OPIC's effectiveness in preparing students for learning at university can only be made after a large-scale and long-term evaluation has been carried out. Such an evaluation will start after the implementation of the management OPIC in the autumn of 2007. It will include the following methods: (a) a measure of the uptake of OPIC over a few years, (b) a survey of users' perceptions of the effectiveness of OPIC, (c) a survey of lecturers' perceptions of improved learning abilities, and (d) the comparisons of the performance and achievements (e.g., results of first assignment) of those cohorts of students who used OPIC with those who did not. The long-term evaluation will also need to assess how effectively OPIC is linked to face-to-face activities during the first year.

## CONCLUSION

In this chapter, a subject-specific OPIC was described as a learning support tool for students of management. This final section considers the potential of OPIC as a widely used tool to prepare students for university. If the large-scale evaluation confirms the encouraging findings of the pilot study, OPIC, with its generic framework, could, from a designer's and technologist's point of view, easily be adapted to a range of disciplines and applied across universities.

There are two potential problems with the widespread use of OPIC. First, different universities, or indeed different courses, have different intakes of students. Whilst high-achieving students might enjoy the activities and benefit from them, lower achieving students might not cope and lose confidence. In such a context, the lack of peer collaboration and tutor feedback that was mentioned earlier would be particularly disadvantageous. In other words, the adequacy of OPIC would have to be evaluated for different user groups. In some contexts, OPIC might be better offered during and after induction week, when personal advice can be sought.

191

The second problem is that OPIC might be welcomed by university teachers and university managers as an easy support method that does not require the involvement and time of academic staff members. Thus, OPIC would be used in the same way as remedial support methods, that is, as something external to which the students can be referred without offering them the specific personal advice that most of them need. It was argued earlier that OPIC is less effective as a stand-alone method. To give students relevant support for the transition to university, OPIC should be part of a learning support framework that consists of several mutually reinforcing components and involves the people who are teaching and assessing the students.

## FUTURE RESEARCH DIRECTIONS

An important area for future research is the development and evaluation of learning support frameworks that help students during the transition period and enhance their progression at university. Support mechanisms are particularly needed for academic writing, which is the foremost problem for first-year students. There is a large body of literature concerned with academic writing, addressing genres (e.g., Swales, 1990), the specific literacies of different disciplines (e.g., Berkenkotter & Huckin, 1995), new literacy studies (e.g. Lankshear & Knobel, 2003), and the analysis of novice writing (e.g., Jones, Turner, & Street, 1999). These studies have led to various approaches in the teaching of writing, such as Writing across the Curriculum (WAC; e.g., Blumner, Eliason, & Fritz, 2001), and genre-based literacy pedagogy (e.g., Ellis, 2004). In the latter approach, the teaching-learning cycle of academic writing is divided in a modeling or deconstruction phase, a joint construction phase, and an independent construction phase. The deconstruction phase makes all aspects of the

genre explicit to the learners, while the next two stages are concerned with writing in the genre, first as a joined effort guided by the teacher and than independently (Drury, 2004). It seems that e-learning has an important role in this cycle as the deconstruction phase can be offered electronically by providing model texts and tasks for analysis. OPIC, for instance, has a component of model texts that are to be analysed by students. Ellis and Drury describe the use of electronic databases and on-screen presentation of academic texts to help students to analyse discipline-specific writing as a basis for constructing their own.

E-learning seems a highly suitable initial method for developing students' understanding of the epistemology and requirements of their discipline in general, and of academic writing practices in particular. However, for the development of successful learners and writers, it is important that this initial method is followed up by explicit advice, classroom interaction, and other activities during the study programme.

Further research should investigate how e-learning courses that prepare students for university, such as OPIC, can be most effectively followed up in the study programme and, particularly, which combination of methods works best for the development of academic writing. Within genre-based literacy pedagogy, research should further explore the potential of online learning for the deconstruction phase, and possibly as a complementary method for the other two phases. Finally, more research is needed on the question of how computer-mediated peer collaboration and student-teacher interaction can facilitate learning to learn and learning to write.

## REFERENCES

Berkenkotter, C., & Huckin, T. (1995). *Genre knowledge in disciplinary communication.* New York: Lawrence Erlbaum.

Biggs, J. (2003). *Teaching for quality learning at university* (2nd ed.). Buckingham, United Kingdom: Open University Press.

Blumner, J., Eliason, J., & Fritz, F. (2001). Beyond the reactive: WAC programs and the steps ahead. *The WAC Journal, 12*, 21-36.

Blythman, M., & Orr, S. (2002). A joined-up approach to student support. In M. Peelo & T. Wareham (Eds.), *Failing students in higher education* (pp. 35-47). Buckingham, United Kingdom: The Society for Research into Higher Education & Open University Press.

Brown, A. L. (1997). Transforming schools into communities of thinking and learning about serious matters. *American Psychologist, 52*(4), 399-413.

Brown, J. S., Collins, A., & Duguid, P. (1989). Situated cognition and the culture of learning. *Educational Researcher, 18*(1), 32-42.

Cohen, A. (1987). Using verbal protocols in research on language learning. In C. Faerch & G. Kasper (Eds.), *Introspection in second language research* (pp. 82-95). Clevedon, United Kingdom: Multilingual Matters.

Conole, G., & Fill, K. (2005). A learning design toolkit to create pedagogically effective learning activities. *Journal of Interactive Media in Education, 8*, 1-16.

Cottrell, S. (2001). *Teaching study skills and supporting learning*. Basingstoke, United Kingdom: Palgrave Macmillan.

Doolittle, P. (1999). *Constructivism and online education*. Retrieved August 16, 2007, from http://edpsychserver.ed.vt.edu/workshops/tohe1999/text/doo2s.doc

Drew, S. (2001). Student perceptions of what helps them learn and develop in higher education. *Teaching in Higher Education, 6*(3), 309-331.

Drummond, I., Nixon, I., & Wiltshire, J. (1998). Personal transferable skills in higher education. *Quality Assurance in Education, 6*(1), 19-27.

Drury, H. (2004). Teaching academic writing on screen: A search for best practice. In L. Ravelli & R. Ellis (Eds.), *Analysing academic writing* (pp. 233-253). London: Continuum.

Durkin, K., & Main, A. (2002). Discipline-based study skills support for first-year undergraduate students. *Active Learning in Higher Education, 3*(1), 24-39.

Edward, N. (2003). First impressions last. *Active Learning in Higher Education, 4*(3), 226-242.

Ellis, R. (2004). Supporting genre-based literacy pedagogy with technology: The implications for the framing and classification of the pedagogy. In L. Ravelli & R. Ellis (Eds.), *Analysing academic writing* (pp. 210-232). London: Continuum.

Fazey, D., & Fazey, J. (2001). The potential for autonomy in learning: Perceptions of competence, motivation and locus of control in first-year undergraduate students. *Studies in Higher Education, 26*(3), 345-361.

Fox, S., & MacKeogh, K. (2003). Can e-learning promote higher-order learning without tutor overload? *Open Learning, 18*(2), 121-134.

Gamache, P. (2002). University students as creators of personal knowledge: An alternative epistemological view. *Teaching in Higher Education, 7*(3), 277-293.

Gibbs, G. (1992). *Improving the quality of student learning*. Oxford, United Kingdom: Oxford Centre for Staff Development.

Gibbs, G. (1994). *Improving student learning: Through assessment and evaluation*. Oxford, United Kingdom: Oxford Centre for Staff Development.

Hendricks, M., & Quinn, L. (2000). Teaching referencing as an introduction to epistemological empowerment. *Teaching in Higher Education, 5*(4), 447-457.

Herrington, J., & Oliver, R. (2000). An instructional design framework for authentic learning environments. *Educational Technology Research and Development, 48*(3), 23-48.

Hughes, G. (2007). Using blended learning to increase learner support and improve retention. *Teaching in Higher Education, 12*(3), 349-363.

Ivanic, R., & Lea, M. (2006). New contexts, new challenges: The teaching of writing in UK higher education. In L. Ganobcsik-Williams (Ed.), *Teaching academic writing in UK higher education* (pp. 6-15). Basingstoke, United Kingdom: Palgrave Macmillan.

Jones, C., Turner, J., & Street, B. (Eds.). (1999). *Student writing in the university: Cultural and epistemological issues.* Amsterdam: John Benjamins.

Keenan, C. (2005). *Stepping stones 2HE: Students working to bridge the transition gap.* Unpublished manuscript.

Kolb, D. A. (1984). *Experiential learning.* NJ: Prentice Hall.

Laing, C., Robinson, A., & Johnston, V. (2005). Managing the transition into higher education. *Active Learning in Higher Education, 6*(3), 243-255.

Lankshear, C., & Knobel, M. (2003). *New literacies: Changing knowledge and classroom learning.* Maidenhead, United Kingdom: Open University Press.

Lave, J., & Wenger, E. (1991). *Situated learning: Legitimate peripheral participation.* Cambridge, United Kingdom: Cambridge University Press.

Lea, M. (2004). Academic literacies: A pedagogy for course design. *Studies in Higher Education, 29*(6), 739-756.

Lea, M., & Street, B. (1998). Student writing in higher education: An academic literacies approach. *Studies in Higher Education, 11*(3), 182-199.

Lillis, T. (2001). *Student writing.* London: Routledge.

Lillis, T. (2006). Moving towards an "academic literacies" pedagogy: Dialogues of participation. In L. Ganobcsik-Williams (Ed.), *Teaching academic writing in UK higher education* (pp. 30-45). Basingstoke, United Kingdom: Palgrave Macmillan.

McInnis, C. (2001). Researching the first year experience: Where to from here? *Higher Education Research & Development, 20*(2), 105-114.

National Audit Office. (2002). *Improving student achievement in English higher education: Report by the Comptroller and Auditor General, HC 486.* London: The Stationery Office.

Nisbet, J., & Shucksmith, J. (1986). *Learning strategies.* London: Routledge.

Northedge, A. (2003). Enabling participation in academic discourse. *Teaching in Higher Education, 8*(2), 169-180.

Oliver, M. (2000). An introduction to the evaluation of learning technology. *Educational Technology & Society, 3*(4), 20-30.

Oliver, M., & Trigwell, K. (2005). Can "blended learning" be redeemed? *E-Learning, 2*(1), 17-26.

Ozga, J., & Sukhnandan, L. (1998). Undergraduate non-completion: Developing an explanatory model. *Higher Education Quarterly, 52*(3), 316-333.

Smagorinsky, P. (1994). *Speaking about writing: Reflections on research methodology.* London: Sage.

Swales, J. (1990). *Genre analysis: English in academic and research settings.* Cambridge, United Kingdom: Cambridge University Press.

Thomas, L. (2002). Student retention in higher education: The role of institutional habitus. *Journal of Educational Policy, 17*(4), 423-432.

Tinto, V. (1993). *Leaving college: Rethinking the causes and cures of student attrition* (2nd ed.). Chicago: Chicago University Press.

Whitelock, D., & Jelfs, A. (2003). Editorial: Journal of Educational Media special issue on blended learning. *Journal of Educational Media, 28*(2-3), 99-100.

Winch, C., & Wells, P. (1995). The quality of student writing in higher education: A cause for concern? *British Journal of Educational Studies, 43*(1), 75-87.

Wingate, U. (2006). Doing away with study skills. *Teaching in Higher Education, 11*(4), 457-465.

Wingate, U. (in press). A framework for transition: Supporting "learning to learn" in higher education. *Higher Education Quarterly.*

Yorke, M. (2001). Formative assessment and its relevance in retention. *Higher Education Research and Development, 20*(2), 115-123.

## ADDITIONIONAL READING

Bach, S., Haynes, P., & Smith, J. (2007). *Online learning and teaching in higher education.* Maidenhead, United Kingdom: Open University Press.

An innovative approach to the topic was taken: The authors show how online learning and teaching is changing higher education policy and practice. The discussion of the impact of learning theories on the successful implementation of e-learning is useful. The book also considers practical aspects; Chapter IV, for instance, informs on the design of online learning environments and is accessible and helpful even to novices in online learning and teaching.

Berkenkotter, C., & Huckin, T. (1995). *Genre knowledge in disciplinary communication.* New York: Lawrence Erlbaum.

The authors propose a sociocognitive theory of genre based on 8 years of research into disciplinary genre. The book presents findings of research into scientific writing, useful insights into academic conventions, and gatekeeping, as well as into the ways in which students learn the curriculum genres at school and university.

Blumner, J., Eliason, J., & Fritz, F. (2001). Beyond the reactive: WAC programs and the steps ahead. *The WAC Journal, 12,* 21-36.

This article helps to understand the concept of Writing across the Curriculum (WAC) as facilitating learning to write and writing to learn. The authors criticise typical institutional approaches and discuss effective approaches to using WAC.

Christie, H., Munro, M., & Fisher, T. (2004). Leaving university early: Exploring the differences between continuing and non-continuing students. *Studies in Higher Education, 29*(5), 617-636.

The paper provides interesting evidence from a small quantitative study of a range of factors that lead to students' withdrawal from university. The authors stress the need for more research into the effectiveness of different retention and progression initiatives.

Drury, H. (2004). Teaching academic writing on screen: A search for best practice. In L. Ravelli & R. Ellis (Eds.), *Analysing academic writing* (pp. 233-253). London: Continuum.

Ellis, R. (2004). Supporting genre-based literacy pedagogy with technology: The implications for the framing and classification of the pedagogy. In

L. Ravelli & R. Ellis (Eds.), *Analysing academic writing* (pp. 210-232). London: Continuum.

Both Drury's and Ellis's chapters provide new insights into the development of academic writing by explaining how genre-based literacy pedagogy has helped students in higher education to understand the purpose and register of academic texts, as well as the type of knowledge needed to participate in the academic community. They demonstrate the application of technology (Ellis, scientific writing database; Drury, laboratory report-writing programme) to enhance student performance in the three-stage teaching and learning cycle.

Garrison, D., & Anderson, T. (2003). *E-learning in the 21st century.* London: Routledge.

The book is based on the authors' research into the implications of e-learning in higher education. It offers a helpful theoretical framework for understanding the application of new technologies for educational purposes.

Ganobcsik-Williams, L. (Ed.). (2006). *Teaching academic writing in UK higher education.* Basingstoke, United Kingdom: Palgrave Macmillan.

This book is the most recent update on theories, models, and practices of academic writing pedagogy and provides the target audience, UK writing practitioners, policy makers, and researchers, with important examples of academic writing projects in the United Kingdom.

Haggis, T., & Pouget, M. (2002). Trying to be motivated: Perspectives on learning from younger students accessing higher education. *Teaching in Higher Education, 7*(3), 323-336.

The authors present a case study of the experience of 13 students who were the first in their families to participate in higher education. They put forward valuable suggestions for approaches that help to better prepare and engage students who arrive at university with no conceptions of what is being expected from them.

Hewings, M. (Ed.). (2001). *Academic writing in context: Implications and applications.* Birmingham, United Kingdom: University of Birmingham Press.

The book deals with important themes in the area of writing at university. The chapter by A. Johns, "Preparing Diverse Students for the Challenges of University Text and Cultures," was particularly informative for the development of OPIC.

Hyland, K. (2004). *Disciplinary discourses: Social interactions in academic writing.* MI: The University of Michigan Press.

Hyland's book has important implications for writing instruction. His research into disciplinary writing revealed enormous differences between academic discourses. This reinforces the argument that writing needs to be taught within the specific discourse community or field.

Jones, C., Turner, J., & Street, B. (Eds.). (1999). *Student writing in the university: Cultural and epistemological issues.* Amsterdam: John Benjamins.

Some interesting case studies of students' and tutors' encounters with student writing are presented, and important cultural, epistemological, and identity issues of academic writing in higher education are discussed.

Lankshear, C., & Knobel, M. (2003). *New literacies: Changing knowledge and classroom learning.* Maidenhead, United Kingdom: Open University Press.

The introductory chapter is particularly useful for gaining background knowledge on the concept of literacy as social and cultural practice, and the development of new literacy studies. The book provides a number of examples of social practices and their literacies.

Lea, M., & Stierer, B. (Eds.). (2000). *Student writing in higher education: New contexts.* Buckingham, United Kingdom: The Society for Research into Higher Education & Open University Press.

Lea and Stierer's volume offers an excellent account of the demands that writing places on students in new or hybrid disciplines, and of other difficulties encountered by students. There are interesting examples of academic writing practice in various courses.

Mann, S. (2001). Alternative perspectives on the student experience: Alienation and engagement. *Studies in Higher Education, 26*(1), 7-19.

The paper puts forward various theoretical perspectives on the student experience and alienation in higher education, and offers useful suggestions for engaging students in learning in higher education.

Northedge, A. (2003). Rethinking teaching in the context of diversity. *Teaching in Higher Education, 8*(1), 17-32.

Northedge's argument is based on sociocultural theories of learning. The paper provides pertinent advice on how teaching can enable students to become participants in the knowledge and discourse community of their field.

Scott, M. (2000). Student, critic and literary text: A discussion of "critical thinking" in a student essay. *Teaching in Higher Education, 5*(3), 277-288.

Scott demonstrates in a case study the application of literacy criticism in essay writing and offers valuable views on the teaching of critical thinking.

Swales, J. (1990). *Genre analysis: English in academic and research settings.* Cambridge, United Kingdom: Cambridge University Press.

The book offers an excellent introduction to genre theory and analysis. Swales defines genre with a focus on the relevant discourse communities and the communicative purpose of the discourse. His work has led to useful genre-based frameworks for EAP and the teaching of academic writing.

Yorke, M. (1999). *Leaving early: Undergraduate non-completion in higher education.* London: Falmer Press.

Yorke, M. & Longden, B. (2004). *Retention and student success in higher education.* Maidenhead, United Kingdom: Open University Press.

Both books provide a range of theoretical perspectives on student departure, as well an account of the complex reasons for students' withdrawal from higher education based on large-scale surveys in the United Kingdom. The 2004 publication also takes an international perspective, looking at access and retention in other countries. It considers what institutions can do to retain students and enhance their success.

# APPENDIX 1

## Screenshot of OPIC's Front Page

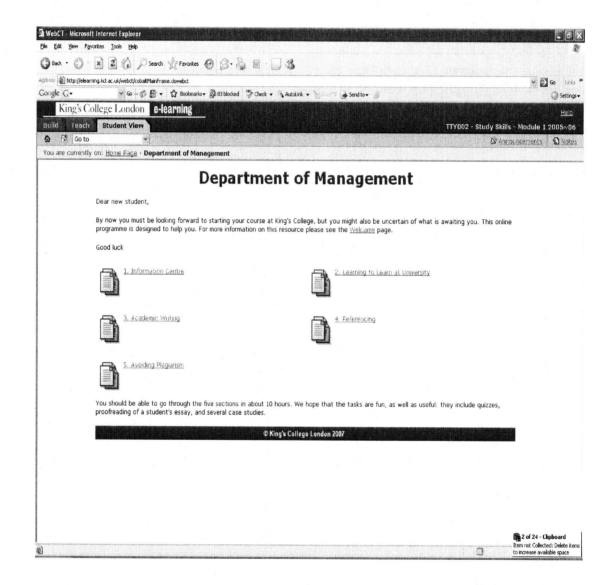

## APPENDIX 2

## First Page of Self-Profiling Questionnaire

**How good am I at...**

    5 = very good      4 = good     3 = satisfactory     2 = not good     1 = bad

**Which skills do I regard as most important for my first year at university and want to develop first?**

    5 = very important   4 = important   3 = important but not urgent   2 = not important

    1 = not at all important

| Skill | Rating | Priority |
|---|---|---|
| **1. Time management** | | |
| a.   Getting tasks finished for deadlines | | |
| b.   Getting down to work quickly | | |
| c.   Knowing how long it takes me to complete tasks | | |
| d.   Drawing up a weekly time schedule | | |
| e.   Keeping an effective diary | | |
| f.   Balancing work and leisure time | | |
| g.   Identifying priorities | | |
| h.   Using empty time (waiting in a queue, sitting on the train) for revision or for thinking about a problem | | |
| **2. Task management** | | |
| a.   Breaking large project into manageable tasks | | |
| b.   Setting myself targets that I can reach | | |
| c.   Devising plans on how to achieve the targets | | |
| d.   Analysing whether I am making good progress | | |
| e.   Evaluating whether I completed the tasks successfully | | |
| f.   Asking for help when necessary | | |
| g.   Starting the task rather than worrying about it | | |
| h.   Working steadily rather than leaving the work until the last minute | | |
| **3. Learning actively and effectively** | | |
| a.   Knowing at what times of the day, and in which environment I work best | | |
| b.   Knowing how I remember facts best | | |
| c.   Not waiting for instructions, but taking the initiative to do something | | |
| d.   Trying to assess my work myself, before I hand it in to the teacher | | |

# APPENDIX 3

# Scenario from Avoiding Plagiarism Module

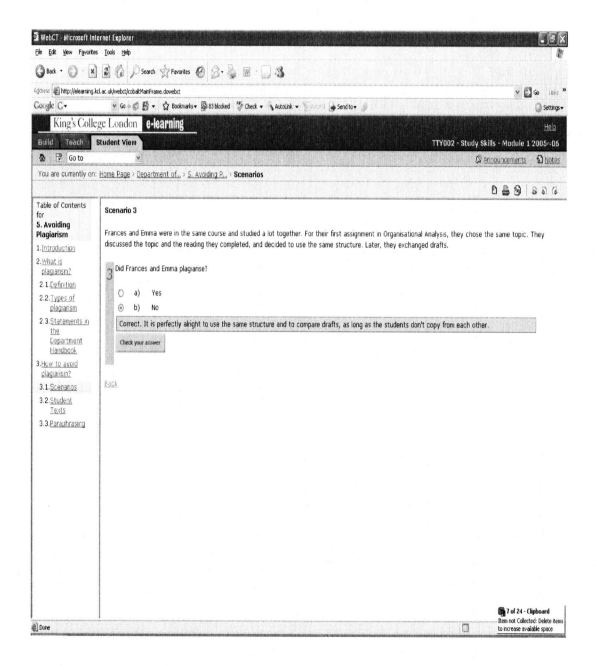

# Chapter X
# A Methodology for Integrating Information Technology in Software Engineering Education

**Pankaj Kamthan**
*Concordia University, Canada*

## ABSTRACT

*The discipline of software engineering has been gaining increasing significance in computer science and engineering education. In this chapter, the goal is to describe a systematic approach toward integrating information technologies in software engineering education (SEE), both inside and outside the classroom. A methodology for integrating IT is proposed and explored in the context of SEE, particularly related to the Internet and the Web; in this context, SEE supports a heterogeneous combination of objectivism and constructivism, and aims to be feasibility sensitive. In doing so, the prospects and concerns of incorporating IT in SEE are presented. The potential of integrating IT in SEE is illustrated by examples.*

## INTRODUCTION

There are various sectors of society where software plays an indispensable role. This calls for special attention in the way software is developed, maintained, and used. The discipline of software engineering (Ghezzi, Jazayeri, & Mandrioli, 2003) was born out of the need to introduce order and predictability in large-scale software develop-

ment. It advocates a systematic approach to the sustainable development of large-scale software that aims for high quality within the given organisational constraints.

In the last few decades, software engineering has been playing an increasingly prominent role in computer science and engineering curricula of universities around the world (Tomayko, 1998). Indeed, there has been a rise in programmes offering undergraduate and graduate degrees in software engineering (Rezaei, 2005; Surakka, 2007), including the establishment of such programmes at the author's institution.

As software engineering matures, the question of how its body of knowledge is communicated, transferred, and understood arises. Like other disciplines, software engineering education (SEE) needs to be sensitive to the variations and evolution of the social and technical environment around it. The changes in the technological environment, specifically that of information technologies, need to be reflected in education if it leads to viable opportunities and proven savings. There have been calls for a reform of SEE with a plea to give a prominent place to technology in general and IT in particular (Frailey, 1998). However, there has been little effort in the past toward precisely and objectively articulating the integration of IT in SEE, and it is this that provides the motivation for this current work.

The readership of this chapter is aimed primarily toward educators in software engineering and information systems engineering. In particular, it is therefore assumed that the reader has basic knowledge of phases, workflows, and activities in a typical software process.

The remainder of the chapter is organised as follows. First, the background necessary for later discussion is provided and the position that is taken is stated. This is followed by the introduction of a methodology for systematically integrating IT in SEE, labeled as IT4SE2. One of the steps of IT4SE2 includes the prospects and concerns of integrating IT both inside and outside the classroom. Next, some practical examples are presented, and then concluding remarks are given. Finally, challenges and directions for future research are outlined.

## BACKGROUND

In this section, previous work on integrating IT in SEE is discussed. When referring to IT in this chapter, this means the technologies for various activities related to information (such as acquisition, creation, communication, dissemination, processing, archival, retrieval, transformation, and so on) within the context of the Internet and the Web.

## Impact of Information Technologies on Software Engineering Education

There have been some previous instances where the use of IT has been found to be useful in areas related to SEE. The use of Internet forums for communicating with the client during requirements elicitation and for active learning has been suggested (Parsons & Fostert, 2000). The use of the extensible markup language (XML) for marking up software process documents (Mundle, 2001) and source code (Deveaux & La Traon, 2001) has been reported. The benefits of hypertext for relating and navigating through software artefacts have been shown (Bompani, Ciancarini, & Vitali, 2002). The use of Java applets in illustrating the dynamics of complex algorithms in a classroom has been emphasised (Kamthan, 1999). The unified modeling language (UML) has emerged as a standard language for modeling the structure and behaviour of object-oriented software systems, and its use in SEE is on the rise. However, these works are limited by one or more of the following issues: The focus has been on the specifics of respective technologies rather than on the learner or on the learning process, the approach to IT integration does not appear to be systematic, and the trade-offs are seldom discussed, if at all.

To (learn how to) develop software requires certain knowledge and skills. In past surveys (Lethbridge, 1998, 2000a), it was concluded that IT played a minor but relevant role in the software engineering curriculum. The prerequisite, generic, and specific skills required of a software engineer have been pointed out previously within the context of a specific research project (Seffah & Grogono, 2002). Although these skills include certain technologies, they do not include the use of the Internet or the Web in their potential, and these skills have not been placed into any known strategies of teaching or theories of learning. A recent survey at one university (Surakka, 2007) reflects a gap between the educators and students (including but not exclusive to software engineers) with respect to the topics and skills considered significant to the curriculum. Still, both classes of respondents do consider technologies related to the network in general and the Web in particular such as Java and XML as increasingly significant.

## Teaching Strategies and Learning Theories in Software Engineering Education

The two theories of learning on which pedagogical strategies are increasingly being modeled are objectivism and constructivism (Smith & Ragan, 1999). In an objectivist view, knowledge is external to an individual (and therefore objective). Hence, learning involves a transfer of knowledge from the instructor to the learner. In a constructivist view, knowledge is not external to an individual. Therefore, learning involves constructing one's own knowledge from one's own experiences. Constructivism has been broadly classified into the categories of individual, radical, and social. WebCT™ (commercial) and Moodle™ (open source) are learning management systems that support constructivism.

There has been much debate over the years in the educational community on the virtues and drawbacks of each (Jonassen, 1991). Each of the objectivist and the constructivist approaches has its advantages and disadvantages (Nunes & McPherson, 2003). For example, while objectivism focuses on the discipline (knowledge of the subject) and not on the learner, constructivism is hard to follow in today's classroom environment of increasingly large class sizes and invariable time constraints. However, there are signs of reconcili-

ation (Cronjé, 2006; Moallem, 2001). Indeed, the two views should be seen as complementary and in certain cases nonmutually exclusive rather than in conflict. It has been shown that the same instructional activity, whether supplantive or generative, can contain both objectivist and constructivist elements (albeit with varying emphasis if necessary) and can be carried out in a feasible manner (Cronjé). Therefore, it is the author's contention that in SEE a heterogeneous, integrated approach toward adopting the appropriate philosophy of education is desirable.

The different theories of learning provide the basis and motivation for the different instructional design models in use today. The objectivist instructional design models (Dick & Carey, 2004; Gagné, 1985; Gagné et al., 2005) are associated with behaviourism (by providing prescriptions about the correlation between learning conditions and learning outcomes) and cognitive science (by emphasising the learner's schema as an organised knowledge structure). The constructivist instructional design models (Duffy & Jonassen, 1992), on the other hand, are associated with cognitive science, social psychology, and social learning paradigms.

Like other disciplines, software engineering courses often have assignments to be conducted outside the classroom. However, a distinct aspect of SEE is often the presence of a required project component in courses that requires teamwork. These practices are in agreement with a constructivist approach. It is therefore necessary to consider the implications of integrating IT in SEE both inside and outside the classroom.

In recent years, both objectivism and constructivism have received attention in computer science education (Ben-Ari, 2001), in SEE (Hadjerrouit, 2005), and in e-learning (Moallem, 2001; Nunes & McPherson, 2003; Phillips, 1998). However, their ramifications with respect to the integration of IT in SEE have not been discussed.

## A SYSTEMATIC APPROACH FOR INFORMATION-TECHNOLOGY-BASED SOFTWARE ENGINEERING EDUCATION

In this section, we introduce IT4SE2, which is a methodology for integrating IT in SEE. IT4SE2 consists of a nonlinear and nonmutually exclusive sequence of steps as shown in Table 1.

The following characteristics of the steps in Table 1 can be noted. First, it is contended that the steps are necessary, but no claim is made on their sufficiency. Indeed, the steps are stated at a high level and could be granularised further if necessary. Second, Steps 1 to 3 are in a bidirectional cycle (Step 1 depends and is depended upon by Step 2, and so on), which is exited only when each step is adequately satisfied with respect to the others and is feasible. Third, Step 4 depends on Step 1. Each of the items of Table 1 are now discussed in detail.

### Step One: Deciding the Scope of Software Engineering Knowledge, Potential Information Technologies, and Educational Activities

In IT4SE2, it is assumed that the role of IT in SEE is twofold: (a) enhance concepts and topics within the body of software engineering knowledge, and (b) provide support to activities during teaching and/or learning.

The software engineering topics could correspond to the knowledge areas of the software engineering body of knowledge (SWEBOK) and software engineering education knowledge (SEEK). Tables 2 and 3 provide a relationship between common software engineering topics, IT, and educational activities.

### Step Two: Adopting a Learning Theory and a Teaching Strategy

It is suggested that a teaching approach (strategy) must be sensitive to the theories of learning that have been adopted and are currently in practice, but should not be constrained by any one of them. In particular, the teaching strategy must be agile (adaptive).

Classroom use of IT in SEE could be more objectivist than constructivist where the educator plays the role of an instructor. This could, for example, entail preparing IT-based lesson plans and lectures, and encouraging questions from students on a timely basis without severely interrupting the flow of the lectures. Project use of IT in SEE could be more socially constructivist than objectivist where the educator plays the role of a guide. This could, for example, entail providing a balance between discipline and flexibility to the students in carrying out a software project with minimal guidance and timely feedback by the educator when needed: The crucial aspect is that the students play the primary role and the educator plays the secondary role.

*Table 1. A feasibility-sensitive methodology for integrating information technologies in software engineering education*

| | |
|---|---|
| 1. Deciding the Scope of Software Engineering Knowledge, Potential Information Technologies, and Educational Activities<br>2. Adopting a Learning Theory and a Teaching Strategy<br>3. Identifying and Understanding the Participants<br>4. Selecting and Applying Suitable Information Technologies to a Software Engineering Education Context<br>5. Evaluating the Effectiveness of Integrating Information Technologies in Software Engineering Education | Feasibility |

*Table 2. A mapping of topics in software engineering and corresponding information technologies*

| Software Engineering Topic | Examples of Applicable Information Technologies |
|---|---|
| Software Configuration/Version Management | Web-Based Distributed Authoring and Versioning (WebDAV), Web-Based Version Control System (WVCS) |
| Formal Specifications | Extensible Hypertext Markup Language (XHTML) + Cascading Style Sheets (CSS) + Mathematical Markup Language (MathML), |
| Internal and External Software Documentation | DocBook XML + Extensible Stylesheet Language Transformations (XSLT) + XHTML + CSS, Doxygen |
| Software Models | UML, XML Metadata Interchange (XMI), XSLT, Scalable Vector Graphics (SVG) |
| Software Project Management | SourceForge |
| Software Quality Assurance | Web-Based Auditing Services, Web-Based Syntax Checking Services (W3C HTML Validator), Web-Based Accessibility Testing Services (Cynthia) |
| Software Reuse | Web Engineering Frameworks (asynchronous JavaScript and XML [AJAX], prototype, rails) |
| Software Domain Knowledge Acquisition | Internet/Web, Ontologies, Reasoning Services |
| Source Code Comprehension (Visualisation and Navigation) | Internet/Web, Hypertext Representation and Presentation (XHTML + CSS), Java |

*Table 3. (a) A mapping of educational activities inside the classroom and corresponding information technologies*

| Educational Activity: Inside Classroom | Examples of Applicable Information Technology |
|---|---|
| Real-Time Complements/Supplements to Lectures | Internet/Web, Moving Picture Experts Group Layer 4 (MPEG-4), RealMedia |
| Classroom Experiments (Demonstration of Concepts) | User Agents (Web Browsers), Java Applets, ECMAScript (JavaScript, JScript) VBScript Scripts |

*Table 3. (b) A mapping of educational activities outside the classroom and corresponding information technologies*

| Educational Activity: Outside Classroom | Examples of Applicable Information Technology |
|---|---|
| Student Access to Lectures | Internet/Web, RealMedia |
| Acquisition and Submission of Assignments | Internet/Web, XHTML Forms + Server-Side Programming (Active Server Pages [ASP], Common Gateway Interface [CGI], Java Server Pages [JSP], PHP Hypertext Preprocessor [PHP]) |
| Teacher-Student Communication | Blogs, Electronic Mail, Internet/Web, Syndication (Real Simple Syndication [RSS]) |
| Student-Student (Project Team) Collaboration and Communication | Blogs, Electronic Mail, Instant Messaging System (ICQ), Internet/Web, Peer-to-Peer Services (Gnutella), MediaWiki, News Groups (Yahoo! Groups), Social Bookmarking (citeulike, del.icio.us), Social Classification (Folksonomies), Social Networking (Ning) |

The modes of assessment could also take a heterogeneous approach where the teaching strategy could include a combination of both formative- and summative-type assessments. The problems and questions in the assignments could encourage the use of IT for experimentation and focus on group work instead of rote memorisation and recall. The place where the use of IT is likely to be less effective is paper-pen-based in-class tests. The issue of summative computer-based assessment is dealt in detail in one of the other chapters of this book.

## Pedagogical Patterns in IT4SE2

A pattern is an entity of knowledge based on past experience and expertise that provides a proven solution to a recurring problem in a given context (Appleton, 1997). A unique aspect of a pattern (as opposed to other entities of knowledge such as a guideline or best practice) is that it describes not just how but why a certain solution works, the scope within which it works, and both the positive and negative consequences of applying it.

There are pedagogical patterns available within the auspices of the Pedagogical Patterns Project, which attempts to capture expert knowledge of the practice of teaching and learning. There are patterns for teaching in general (Bergin, 2000; Eckstein, 2000), patterns for teaching software concepts in a classroom (Schmolitzky, 2007), and patterns for course projects (Hayes, Hill, Mannette-Wright, & Wong, 2006). For example, the CHALLENGE pattern (Eckstein) suggests ways in which students are encouraged to develop their own solutions, the CONSISTENT METAPHOR pattern (Bergin) suggests how to have the students see the big picture without getting lost in the details, and the TOY BOX pattern (Bergin) suggests ways for students to experiment with object-oriented technologies.

## Formulating Teaching and Learning Goals

It is crucial that there be both teaching and learning goals, that they be aligned with the rest of the curriculum, that they be based upon established strategies of teaching and theories of learning, and that they be feasible (attainable). Goals can be classified as hard or soft. A hard goal is either satisfied or not satisfied. A soft goal cannot be completely satisfied; it can only be satisfied to a certain degree, that is, "satisficed" (Simon, 1996). We contend that teaching and learning goals are soft goals, and therefore it is critical that they be feasible.

A simple teaching goal using an IT could be to be able to optimally use the available time to introduce a concept (while keeping the role of IT as transparent as possible). The factors that can impact setting and achieving the teaching goals include budget, infrastructure, class size, contact available time (lecture or otherwise), the background of students (lowest common denominator), the level of teacher training, the nature of the content, and the availability of suitable IT.

A simple learning goal using an IT could be to be able to understand and make use of a concept in the shortest time possible. The factors that can impact setting and achieving the learning goals include the nature of the content in the body of knowledge, the IT learning curve (compatibility of students with the selected IT), and modes of assessment.

## Step Three: Identifying and Understanding the Participants

Ultimately, any IT deployment in an educational context involves people. In an institution making use of IT in SEE, two broad classes of participants can be identified: teacher, teaching assistant, and student are the primary participants, while academic administrators (such as the department chairperson or the faculty dean) and system administrators could be viewed as secondary participants.

Studies in human psychology have shown that variations among people with respect to their predispositions, abilities, and knowledge need to be accepted and managed (Keirsey, 1998). Specifically, one size does not fit all: An understanding of the variations among students is important for integration of any technology in education (Harley, 2007), including SEE. This is also consistent with a constructivist approach to learning: The large range of individual differences between learners, including their prior knowledge and experiences or their physiological and cognitive abilities, can affect the learning outcomes and instructional techniques (Jonassen & Grabowski, 1993). For example, in courses on programming languages and software engineering over the years, the author has come across students with a variety of disabilities (such as attention deficit hyperactivity disorder [ADHD] and partial blindness or deafness), and appropriate adjustments needed to be a made to accommodate them.

There are a few practical approaches that could be taken to understand the variations among students. A common measure of (variations in) personality is the Myers-Briggs Type Indicator (MBTI; Keirsey, 1998) that measures an individual's preference on four bipolar dimensions: introversion/extraversion (I/E), intuition/sensing (I/S), feeling/thinking (F/T), and judgment/perception (J/P). An MBTI personality type consists of a four-letter code, such as ESTJ (extraverted, sensing, thinking, judging), to indicate the personality type of an individual. The possible combinations yield 16 different personality types, each with a distinct descriptive profile of characteristic behaviour patterns. An informal survey (interview or otherwise) for identifying the different MBTI personality types and for verifying prerequisites could be useful in assessing individual preferences, physiological and cognitive abilities, and the technological background of students.

## Step Four: Selecting and Applying Suitable Information Technologies to a Software Engineering Education Context

For a given concept in a problem domain, there may be more than one applicable IT, and they may not necessarily be equally suitable. The following criteria for the selection of IT are recommended: the nature of the information being communicated by the IT, alignment with teaching and learning goals, considerations for commercial (Learning Space, TopClass, and Blackboard™/WebCT™) vs. noncommercial (Moodle™) tools, maturity, availability, and the feasibility of different technologies. An objective third-party review of a candidate IT can also help in making the decision for adoption. There are numerous possibilities as well as obstacles in applying IT to SEE, all of which must be examined to make an informed decision. Each are now discussed in turn.

## Prospects of Integrating Information Technology in Software Engineering Education

The role of IT in SEE can be broadly classified into three categories: as means for teaching concepts, as means for learning concepts, and as means for performing tasks. This potential is further elaborated in the following.

**Necessary Alternative in a Classroom.** IT can give teachers alternative ways to discuss in the classroom the software engineering concepts that by nature are dynamic or nonlinear, and are difficult to present using traditional means. This is particularly the case with concepts related to complex structures (such as three-dimensional graphics) and evolving spatial-temporal behaviour (such as iteration or recursion) in a software system.

**Interactive Classroom Experiments.** IT can be a useful tool to foster an interactive environment in a classroom. A teacher could, for example, give a demonstration of a software system with a predetermined, fixed data set and ask questions based on the variations of the data set (that will lead to unpredictable behaviour of the system). In such a case, both correct and incorrect answers can contribute to the learning process. It is known that a discussion of the economics of software development is crucial in SEE to reflect the inevitable financial aspect of the subject. There are mature implementations of widely regarded cost-estimation models, such as COCOMO II, available for both the desktop and the Web. They could be used in the classroom as tools of inquiry (and possibly even to stimulate enjoyment for the students) in various realisable ways: investigating the variations in time and effort with respect to the number of team members or the selection of programming languages, observing the impact of input data that would lead to an output that could be theoretically possible but would likely never occur in a real-world corporate situation (such as an estimate of 100 years to complete a software project), and so on.

**New Horizons.** IT can open horizons for teachers and students to new activities and to ask and answer questions not (readily) feasible or even possible before. Using inexpensive and fast computers, it is now possible to carry out complex calculations and process very large data sets. This, for example, allows one to experiment and present the results involving software measurement in a short amount of time, thus befitting lectures and laboratory-based tests.

**New Means of Communication and Collaboration.** At times, students can find office hours insufficient or inconvenient. On the other hand, teachers may wish to keep in touch with students when they are away. For example, a teacher may need to travel for a conference during the spring break but would still like to be available for any questions from students on a software deliverable due at the end of the break. IT can provide alternative ways to teachers for communicating with their students outside the classroom synchronously or asynchronously and via client pull or server push. The proliferation of mobile phones with support for electronic mail and technologies for syndication has led to new opportunities for asynchronous communication. By collaborating amongst themselves, students can learn software engineering concepts as well as the traits of work ethics. Software projects make such collaboration a necessity, and appropriate use of IT can help facilitate that.

**Dissemination of Course Content.** IT can provide opportunities for teachers to make their lectures and related content available outside the classroom. This could, for example, be useful to students who for some reasons (such as absence on medical grounds or preparation for a test) would like to have access to the lectures.

**Rich Course Content.** IT can provide opportunities for teachers to complement or supplement their lectures with related material. For example, as part of the lecture on a topic, a video by an external expert could be shown in the classroom; as part of the response to a question by a student in the class, the teacher could point to a uniform resource locator (URL) where more information can be found; or in the classroom, using student-supplied input, the teacher could run a programme that could be started or stopped at arbitrary places to provide explanation if necessary.

**Reuse.** Being able to reuse existing knowledge, in part or in whole, in a justifiable way is critical for large-scale software development. IT can help make that a reality and enable prospects for different types of reuse. For example, the source code of software could be viewed graphically (by designers) or textually (by programmers). As another example, the presence of frameworks such as AxKit, Ajax, Prototype, and Rails allows a software engineer to not have to create everything from scratch, thereby accelerating the development of Web applications.

**Future Careers.** Being introduced to state-of-the-art IT could help students in their future career paths. Indeed, teachers could use market demand as one of the criteria for the selection of suitable IT, particularly for course projects.

**Rich Course Assignments.** The course assignments can be made available and submitted electronically over the Internet. This has several advantages over its paper-only counterpart: The content of the assignment problems and solutions can be richer (dynamic), which is closer to the nature of the discipline; a student does not need to be physically present for submission and therefore could submit the assignment from virtually anywhere, at any time (prior to the deadline); the teacher does not need to carry the paper load or be concerned about misplacing or losing any of the submissions; and the marking of assignments in certain cases becomes more natural, for example, when source code is part of the submission and needs to be checked for certain properties (like syntactic correctness or efficiency).

**Reducing Duplication.** It is well known that documentation is integral to software, and IT could be used to reduce redundancy in documentation. For example, a single source could be transformed into multiple formats and disseminated via the Web for, say, viewing on a desktop computer, viewing on a mobile device such as a personal digital assistant (PDA), and for printing.

## Concerns of Integrating Information Technology in Software Engineering Education

The integration of IT in SEE has its limitations, the details of which are outlined in the following.

**No Free Lunch.** There can be costs associated with training, administering, and/or purchasing software for processing the selected IT, which may need to be balanced with respect to budgetary constraints. For example, the cost involving infrastructure for streaming media remains prohibitive even for noncommercial purposes. Although the presence of open-source software (OSS) has alleviated some of the costs, there is

no a priori guarantee that a suitable OSS may be available for a chosen IT. Yet another option is the use of services like YouTube™, but the need for bandwidth and licensing conditions associated with media could pose challenges.

**Technology Fatigue.** There is a potential for technology overload or fatigue for both teachers and students, particularly in keeping up with the technologies that are deemed relevant but are either transient or moving targets.

**Quality Concerns.** Within this chapter, the notion of quality is assumed to be an aggregate of several attributes. The use of network-specific IT can pose a variety of quality-related challenges. It has been pointed out (Yee, Xu, Korba, & El-Khatib, 2006) that privacy and security are concerns for learners in e-learning environments, particularly those using mobile devices. Furthermore, in use of IT during critical times there is potential for issues related to reliability and robustness. For example, there exists the likelihood of device failure or low battery power during project demonstrations or class presentations, crashes of assignment servers in handling multiple simultaneous submissions around the time of the deadline, and so on. With the collective intelligence of Web 2.0 comes the possibility of participation and posting of information by virtually anybody, thus raising the issue of credibility (Fogg, 2003). This is particularly the case with the use of IT for collaboration, outlined in Table 3b.

**Shift of Focus.** In the rapidly evolving discipline of software engineering, where the teaching and learning environment is in a constant state of flux, it is crucial to ask for the invariant knowledge that is necessary (Lethbridge, 2000b). If applied well, IT can play a crucial role in facilitation and communication of this knowledge. However, there is a possibility of a shift of focus in the use of IT that may be undesirable. For instance, there could be considerable time spent in learning the intricacies of IT for subsequent use rather than the software engineering concept or topic at hand. The increasing emphasis on technologies like Java 2 Enterprise Edition (J2EE) rather than on the basics of high-level software design has been reported (Voelter, 2006). It also has been the author's experience that, instead of thoroughly understanding the underlying application domain, students start focusing on technological manipulations rather early in their software projects. An early and perhaps periodic reminder to the students may help circumvent this issue.

**Participation.** The mere availability of an IT does not in itself entail participation by the students. For example, the mere existence of a course-wide or project-team-wide electronic forum for collaboration does not automatically imply that all students will participate or do so with the same enthusiasm. Indeed, students' personalities vary and some students can become rather conscious when they realise that what they write is a matter of public record that is exposed both to the teacher and to the entire class (Moallem, 2001).

**Obfuscation of Concept with Information Technology.** There is a potential for students to exclusively associate a concept with the IT that is used to illustrate it. For example, there is a tendency to associate the notions of hypertext or markup with HTML and only HTML, unless suggested otherwise. This leads not only to linear thinking, but also to the potential for obsolescence if the IT in question loses support or becomes superseded.

**No Free Lunch: Reprise.** The introduction of an IT could lead to regression: Although one issue is resolved, other issues could arise from the mere presence of the IT leading to a cascade of problems. For example, as discussed previously, electronic submission of course assignments has many advantages over paper submissions. However, the computing environments of the teacher, teaching assistants, and students can vary tremendously. Therefore, it is not automatic that assignments created in one environment (that of students) will be readable or processable in another environment (that of the teacher or the teaching assistants).

It is noted that neither the aforementioned prospects nor the concerns are absolute. Furthermore, the same IT may have certain advantages and disadvantages, but may be suitable for adoption if the benefits outweigh the costs.

## Step Five: Evaluating the Effectiveness of Integrating Information Technologies in Software Engineering Education

The effectiveness of integrating IT in SEE should be evaluated against Step 2 and in light of Step 3. Some of the possible means for assessing that the use of IT has been successful are reduction in teacher and student effort (and/or increase in teacher and student productivity), improvements in outcomes of student assessments (say, the average class performance on presentations or on tests), and on average favorable response in anonymous student surveys. For survey data collection (Babbie, 1990), the use of questionnaires may be more effective and practical than conducting interviews due to the nature of the teacher-student relationship and due to time constraints. There is survey software available without cost for small surveys (in terms of the number of questions and number of respondents) available for academic purposes. For example, Survey Monkey uses a Web-based interface for designing questions, collecting responses to the questions, and performing elementary statistical analysis of the results.

It is noted, however, that such electronic surveys suffer the possibility of skewed results if not carried out simultaneously by all students and would therefore require time management.

## Feasibility of Steps in IT4SE2

The teaching and learning of software engineering needs to take real-world constraints into consideration in order to be practical. Therefore, all the Steps 1 to 5 from their initiation to their completion involving IT need to be feasible. If a step is not deemed feasible, there is need to revert back to it and move forward once the necessary modifications are made. This is essential as a variety of feasibility-related concerns can arise. For example, it may be useful to elicit as much background information on a student as possible, but privacy concerns may prevent one from doing so in its entirety; a high-level teaching and learning goal may make sense theoretically but may be practically unrealisable; the adoption of a specific learning theory may seem appealing and may even be the best pedagogical choice, but may not be within the scope of the given constraints of time and class size; a specific IT may be an attractive option, but the software available for processing it may be proprietary and not within the given budget; and so on. The feasibility study could be a part of the overall course management activity. Further discussion of this aspect is beyond the scope of this chapter.

# SCENARIOS OF INFORMATION TECHNOLOGY USE IN SOFTWARE ENGINEERING EDUCATION

In this section, scenarios of the use of IT in a classroom and outside the classroom are presented, namely, in a course project.

## IT-Supported Sorting in a Classroom

There are various ways of sorting data, and one must be able to decide which of these approaches is optimal. Figure 1 illustrates a snapshot taken from an animation implemented as a Java applet. It shows the relative speeds between two sorting algorithms, namely, Merge Sort and Quick Sort, for a fixed set of elements.

Following the SHOW IT RUNNING pattern (Schmolitzky, 2007), the author used the applet in an undergraduate class to demonstrate sorting with sets of elements with different cardinalities. The animation was complemented with occasional narration by the author and was stopped and restarted upon questions from students. It is noted

*Figure 1. The relative speeds of Merge Sort and Quick Sort algorithms for 40 elements*

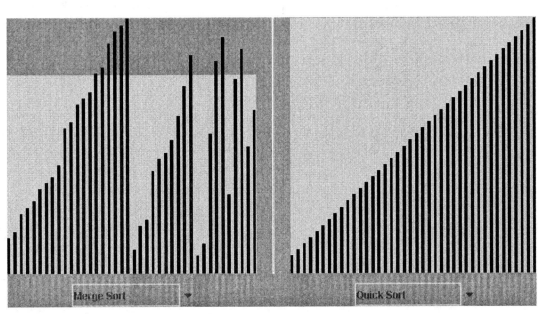

that this simple exercise would be rather difficult by traditional means (blackboard, whiteboard, paper, or slides with overhead projector). For the purpose of rigor, the animation was complemented with formal mathematical arguments.

The students were then, as part of an assignment, asked to repeat the exercise using other sorting algorithms such as Insertion Sort and Selection Sort, and presented the results in a comparison table. The learning outcomes and reactions of students were mixed. Some of the students were enthusiastic as they found various directions in which the functionality of the applet, including its user interface, could be improved. Those who did not attend the lecture faced technical and cognitive difficulties in carrying out the exercise on their own due to the lack of sufficient documentation outlining client-side requirements and due to the lack of the complete description of the applet.

## IT-Supported Course Project

It is known that learning by doing is one of the traits of social constructivism, and software projects provide an opportunity for students to realise that (Saliou & Ribaud, 2006). Also, there are various patterns (Hayes et al., 2006) that can be used to put course projects into practice. During one semester, the author supervised a project that required the students to build a book auction system as a Web application. The system would enable users to use the Internet to check books organised under different categories (art, fiction, science, and so on). A book could be found by navigating or searching in different ways (using the title, author's name, year of publication, starting price, etc.). Users who wish to bid would have to register and provide basic information about themselves. The system would enable administrators to add or delete a book entry in the database, modify the information on an existing book, and allow or prohibit a user from register-

ing or bidding (for example, based on past history of interaction).

The class of about 50 students was divided into teams of 10 each with one student acting as the team leader and liaison between the teacher and the members of the respective team. The students were given complete freedom of choice in the underlying technology except that the process artefacts would follow standards from the Institute of Electrical and Electronics Engineers (IEEE) and International Organisation for Standardisation/International Electrotechnical Commission (ISO/IEC), and the final system would have to be entirely based on OSS. The teams independently set up and used Yahoo! Groups to collaborate and used Concurrent Version Systems (CVS) for configuration management of process documents (specifically, project schedule, requirements, design, and test plan) in Open Office and models in UML.

For the final product, some teams used Amaya as the user agent on the client side and the Apache Web Server along with Apache Tomcat for dynamic delivery of resources on the server side. Others preferred the combination of the Mozilla FireFox user agent and MySQL/PHP Hypertext Preprocessor (PHP). This differential was attributed to the diverse background of courses that they had previously taken.

There were three main challenges faced during the project.

1.  Most students were not familiar with the application domain, namely, auctions. However, the presence of public auction systems available on the Web such as eBay™ was helpful in eliciting, understanding, and documenting the required knowledge.
2.  Since most of the industrial-strength software available currently for quality assurance and evaluation is commercial, addressing quality control posed another challenge. The students used the OSS tools from the World Wide Web Consortium (W3C) for automatically evaluat-

ing the quality of documents in XHTML and the style sheets in CSS. However, the evaluation was limited to conformance to syntax and checking for accessibility.

3. Due to security considerations, the students were not allowed to run any network software (and therefore the subsystems necessary for the project) on the university computer network. Although it raises another set of concerns, upon mutual agreement, the resolution found to this issue was that the running and testing of the executable software would be done on a notebook computer belonging to one of the students (preferably the team leader, if possible).

An anonymous survey led to the following conclusions. In general, the students found the project to be a worthwhile experience, albeit in different ways. While some saw the project as an opportunity to learn new IT, others saw it as a timely occasion to highlight their graphics design abilities, and yet others viewed it as means to accentuate their leadership skills (acquired from working in the industry). Although some students did not have the requisite background in the aforementioned technologies, they were (with the help of their peers and teaching assistants) willing to learn based on the likelihood that these technologies would be useful in other courses and their future careers.

## GUIDELINES FOR INTEGRATING INFORMATION TECHNOLOGY IN SOFTWARE ENGINEERING EDUCATION

It is important to ask specific questions about integrating IT in any educational context, and it is the author's contention that the same holds for SEE. In this section, a set of guidelines for educators is presented that could serve as a starting point for

the key questions regarding planning, executing, and reflecting when integrating IT in SEE.

**Including Administration as a Participant.** There are factors such as bureaucracy and apparent resistance to change that can impact the adoption of an IT at educational institutions. After all, reluctance to change when conditions are comfortable (Weinberg, 1992) is a basic human characteristic. For example, those who have been in senior positions for a long period of time and have been using nontraditional means may see the proposed inclusion of an IT such as XML as a threat, not necessarily as a welcome novelty to be embraced naturally. In general, it could be useful in the long term if the administration of the institution is kept informed and even involved when making an investment in an IT.

**Long-Term Planning.** In infrastructure planning, there needs to be provision not only for an enthusiastic entry (adopting a specific IT) but also for a graceful exit (retiring the adopted IT). There is cost associated with adopted and discarded technology: In the case of hardware technology, it takes up physical space; in the case of electronic information technology, it takes up disk space. In the author's experience, it is seldom the situation that acquisition, particularly that of hardware, includes a long-term consideration of its termination. Although removal of software from computer systems is straightforward, severing dependencies created over the duration of its use are not, and doing so can lead to side effects. There is value in the long run in being environment friendly, whether that environment is real (natural) or virtual (electronic).

**Careful Selection of IT.** During the selection of an IT for use in a software engineering course, the level of maturity, the extent of outreach (such as access to books, tutorials, and so on), and affordability (such as availability of inexpensive software support) are some of the critical factors. In general, novelty in itself does not imply stability or an improvement. During the selection of an IT, it may be useful to make a distinction between stable and evolving technology. An analysis based on independent and publicly available reviews of the corresponding IT can be useful in this regard.

**Learner-Centred Integration of IT.** It is unlikely that simply making a large amount of information or features available within an IT environment will automatically lead to the desired teaching or learning goals (Nam & Smith-Jackson, 2007). It is recommended that an IT environment for SEE making use of the Web should be user centred and, specifically in case of the students, learner centred. For that, equilibrium between the objectivist and the constructivist theories of learning is recommended. Furthermore, a systematic approach to the IT environment, for example, as advocated by Web engineering (Kappel, Pröll, Reich, & Retschitzegger, 2006), is desirable. Specifically, the following may need to be considered: accessibility and usability, the inclusion of a comprehensive help system, and the inclusion of a feedback system (to solicit comments for improvement).

**Technology not Just for Technology's Sake.** Introducing IT to software engineering students should be such that it leads to curiosity and activity, not passivity amongst them; it should not lead

to just answers but also to nontrivial questions. The *why* is very important to consider, not just the how. The students should be presented with an objective view of the IT that includes discussion of both its strengths and weaknesses. The introduction to IT could be driven by necessity. For example, it could be pointed out to students that certain topics in software engineering may be in more need for an IT treatment than others.

**More than Just Users.** There is much that software engineering has done and will likely continue to do to help advance state-of-the-art of IT. For example, software engineering principles such as abstraction, anticipation of change, incrementality, generality, and modularity have been a major inspiration in the design of programming languages and markup languages. Conversely, IT has helped put theoretical aspects of software engineering into practice in the real world (Dawson & Newsham, 1997). It could be instilled in students that their relationship with IT is symbiotic (Figure 2): They are not only the consumers of IT, but hopefully also as software engineering students, the future contributors and inventors of IT. Indeed, the weaknesses of a certain IT could be a starting point for motivation

*Figure 2. The symbiotic relationship between information technology and software engineering*

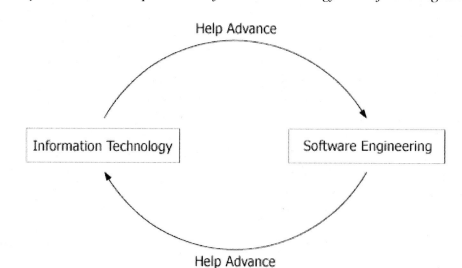

for improvement of that IT and even lead to the development of a new IT.

**Teaching How to Fish.** It is unrealistic for teachers to keep up with or introduce the students to every new and upcoming IT. Moreover, teachers are to some extent responsible for preparing students for their future career paths. Therefore, teachers should help train students how to judiciously select an IT for a given purpose. This knowledge is likely to stay with students even when a course is over and into the future when they have graduated.

## CONCLUSION

If evolution is about verifiable progress, then educational processes need to evolve with time, both out of necessity imposed by the variations in the social and technical environment in which they thrive and to avoid obsolescence. For SEE to continue to thrive, the software engineering programmes in higher education must adapt to the ecosystem in which they exist, remain "useful and applicable" (Parnas, 1999), and learn from the past lessons of successes and failures in other closely related programmes such as computer science (Patterson, 2005). Indeed, it has been pointed out (Frailey, 1998) that there are many similarities between the reengineering of software and the reengineering of education, and that technology can play a central role in recasting SEE for the benefit of all involved.

The selection, adoption, and inclusion of any IT is not automatic in any sector of society, and the same applies to the educational contexts of software engineering. To use IT to its full potential in SEE, a systematic approach and a coexistential balance between the objectivist and the constructivist theories of learning is necessary. IT4SE2 is one step in that direction.

In conclusion, the evolution of IT has reached a state that can be embraced or debated, but not ignored. The use of IT in SEE needs to be kept in perspective: There are issues inherent to SEE that apparently cannot be dealt with through any IT. Instead of being swayed by trends, the integration of IT in SEE should be driven by the need to solve real instructional and learning problems that are otherwise difficult to address by traditional means available at the time. To embrace such a change requires a reflection and reexamination of the current state of SEE. For that to come to a successful realisation, the current software engineering culture in educational institutions will need to evolve.

## FUTURE RESEARCH DIRECTIONS

The symbiosis between software engineering and IT is likely to remain active in the foreseeable future, and SEE will need to respond to this continuously changing environment. It is therefore also likely that the prospects and concerns of integrating IT in SEE that have been highlighted in Step 4 of IT4SE2 need to be revisited periodically.

The pedagogical patterns currently available tend to focus on computer science education in general, and tailoring them for use with IT4SE2 would be of interest. In particular, these patterns could contribute to formulating IT-specific teaching strategies, that is, Step 2 of IT4SE2, in a practical tried-and-tested manner.

IT4SE2 is also subject to improvement from realisations in academia and industry (corporate training). Indeed, it would be useful to present more case studies of both successes and of failures of the use of IT in SEE, and make them publicly available via the Web.

There have been predictions of the different directions of evolution of IT and the expected impact on education in general (Moursund, 1997). Three current directions with the common theme of flexibility and their anticipated impact within the context of IT4SE2 are considered.

The use of nonstationary devices such as notebook computers, PDAs, and mobile phones is likely to flourish as they become increasingly affordable and enter nonsaturated markets. They can be helpful to students during team meetings to discuss the software project (for example, for researching or taking minutes), for making class presentations and demonstrations, for communicating, and so on. Although this may improve the productivity of a team, examining the impact on the quality of the final product would be of interest.

OSS and indeed open content (nonexecutable open course material, open textbooks, and so on) will likely continue to play a key role in the proliferation of IT, particularly in situations when affordability is a primary concern. Taking into consideration the role of the open environment in SEE, it would be of interest to align IT4SE2 more closely with OSS and open content. However, the use of OSS in SEE brings its own set of issues (Kamthan, 2007) that would need to be taken into consideration and could be worth investigating in the future.

Finally, it is likely that the ascent of the Social Web (O'Reilly, 2005) will have a notable impact on education. To that regard, it could be useful to examine the prospects and assess the concerns of integrating the technologies underlying the Social Web, particularly those related to real-time collaboration and sharing, in SEE.

## ACKNOWLEDGMENT

The author would like to thank his students for their participation in course projects and the peer reviewers for feedback and suggestions for improvement.

## REFERENCES

Appleton, B. A. (1997). Patterns and software: Essential concepts and terminology. *Object Magazine Online, 3*(5), 20-25.

Babbie, C. (1990). *Survey research methods.* Belmont, CA: Wadsworth.

Ben-Ari, M. (2001). Constructivism in computer science education. *Journal of Computers in Mathematics and Science Teaching, 20*(1), 45-73.

Bergin, J. (2000, July 5-9). *Fourteen pedagogical patterns.* Paper presented at the Fifth European Conference on Pattern Languages of Programs (EuroPLoP 2000), Irsee, Germany.

Bloom, B. S., Englehart, M. B., Furst, E. J., Hill, W. H., & Krathwohl, D. R. (1956). *Taxonomy of educational objectives: The classification of educational goals. Handbook I: The cognitive domain.* New York: Longman.

Bompani, L., Ciancarini, P., & Vitali, F. (2002). XML-based hypertext functionalities for software engineering. *Annals of Software Engineering, 13*(1-4), 231-247.

Cronjé, J. (2006). Paradigms regained: Toward integrating objectivism and constructivism in instructional design and the learning sciences. *Journal of Educational Technology Research and Development, 54*(4), 387-416.

Dawson, R., & Newsham, R. (1997). Introducing software engineers to the real world. *IEEE Software, 14*(6), 37-43.

Deveaux, D., & La Traon, Y. (2001, May 15). *XML to manage source engineering in object-oriented development: An example.* Paper presented at the International Workshop on XML Technologies and Software Engineering (XSE 2001), Toronto, Canada.

Dick, W., & Carey, L. (2004). *The systematic design of instruction* (6th ed.). Boston: Allyn and Bacon.

Duffy, T. M., & Jonassen, D. H. (1992). *Constructivist and the technology of instruction: A conversation.* NJ: Lawrence Erlbaum Associates.

Eckstein, J. (2000, July 5-9). *Learning to teach and learning to learn: Pedagogical and social issues in education.* Paper presented at the Fifth European Conference on Pattern Languages of Programs (EuroPLoP 2000), Irsee, Germany.

Frailey, D. J. (1998). Opportunities for software engineering education. *Annals of Software Engineering, 6*(1-4), 131-144.

Fogg, B. J. (2003). *Persuasive technology: Using computers to change what we think and do.* San Francisco: Morgan Kaufmann Publishers, Inc.

Gagné, R.M. (1985). *The conditions of learning and theory of instruction* (Fourth Edition). Holt, Rinehart, and Winston.

Gagné, R.M., Wagner, W.W., Gloas, K., & Keller, J.M. (2005). *Principles of instructional design* (5th ed.) Wadsworth.

Ghezzi, C., Jazayeri, M., & Mandrioli, D. (2003). *Fundamentals of software engineering* (2nd ed.). Upper Saddle River, NJ: Prentice-Hall.

Hadjerrouit, S. (2005). Constructivism as guiding philosophy for software engineering education. *ACM SIGCSE Bulletin, 37*(4), 45-49.

Harley, D. (2007). Why study users? An environmental scan of use and users of digital resources in humanities and social sciences undergraduate education. *First Monday, 12*(1). Retrieved April 1, 2007, from http://firstmonday.org/issues/issue12_1/harley/index.html

Hayes, D., Hill, J., Mannette-Wright, A., & Wong, H. (2006, October 21-23). *Team project patterns for college students.* Paper presented at the 13th Conference on Pattern Languages of Programs (PLoP 2006), Portland, OR.

Jonassen, D. H. (1991). Objectivist vs. constructivist: Do we need a new philosophical paradigm? *Educational Technology Research and Development, 39*(3), 5-14.

Jonassen, D. H., & Grabowski, B. L. (1993). *Handbook of individual differences: Learning and instruction.* NJ: Lawrence Erlbaum Associates.

Kamthan, P. (1999, March 7). *Java applets in education: Internet related technologies (IRT. ORG).* Retrieved April 1, 2007, from http://www.irt.org/articles/js151/index.com

Kamthan, P. (2007). On the prospects and concerns of integrating open source software environment in software engineering education. *Journal of Information Technology Education, 6*, 45-64.

Kappel, G., Pröll, B., Reich, S., & Retschitzegger, W. (2006). *Web engineering.* NJ: John Wiley and Sons.

Keirsey, D. (1998). *Please understand me II.* Del Mar, CA: Prometheus Nemesis Book Company.

Lethbridge, T. C. (1998). The relevance of software education: A survey and some recommendations. *Annals of Software Engineering, 6*(1-4), 91-110.

Lethbridge, T. C. (2000a). Priorities for the education and training of software engineers. *Journal of Systems and Software, 53*(1), 53-71.

Lethbridge, T. C. (2000b). What knowledge is important to a software engineer? *Computer, 33*(5), 44-50.

Moallem, M. (2001). Applying constructivist and objectivist learning theories in the design of a Web-based course: Implications for practice. *Journal of Educational Technology and Society, 4*(3), 113-125.

Moursund, D. (1997). *The future of information technology in education.* Washington, DC: The International Society for Technology in Education.

Mundle, D. (2001, May 15). *Using XML for software process documents.* Paper presented at the

International Workshop on XML Technologies and Software Engineering (XSE 2001), Toronto, Canada.

Nam, C. S., & Smith-Jackson, T. L. (2007). Web-based learning environment: A theory-based design process for development and evaluation. *Journal of Information Technology Education, 6*, 23-43.

Nunes, M. B., & McPherson, M. (2003, July 9-11). *Constructivism vs. objectivism: Where is difference for designers of e-learning environments?* Paper presented at the Third IEEE International Conference on Advanced Learning Technologies (ICALT 2003), Athens, Greece.

O'Reilly, T. (2005). *What is Web 2.0: Design patterns and business models for the next generation of software.* O'Reilly Network, September 30, 2005.

Parnas, D. L. (1999). Software engineering programs are not computer science programs. *IEEE Software, 16*(6), 19-30.

Parsons, J., & Fostert, K. D. (2000). Using the Internet to build realism in teaching requirements analysis. *Journal of Information Systems Education, 11*(3-4), 141-145.

Patterson, D. A. (2005). Restoring the popularity of computer science. *Communications of the ACM, 48*(9), 25-28.

Phillips, R. (1998, February 4-5). *Models of learning appropriate to educational applications of information technology.* Paper presented at the Seventh Annual Teaching Learning Forum, Perth, Australia.

Rezaei, S. (2005, May 5-6). *Software engineering education in Canada.* Paper presented at the Western Canadian Conference on Computing Education (WCCCE 2005), Prince George, Canada.

Saliou, P., & Ribaud, V. (2006, November 9-10). *Learning by doing software engineering.* Paper presented at Informatics Education Europe, Montpellier, France.

Schmolitzky, A. (2007, July 4-8). *Patterns for teaching software in classroom.* Paper presented at the 12th European Conference on Pattern Languages of Programs (EuroPLoP 2007), Irsee, Germany.

Seffah, A., & Grogono, P. (2002, February 25-27). *Learner-centered software engineering education: From resources to skills and pedagogical patterns.* Paper presented to the 15th International Conference on Software Engineering Education and Training (CSEE&T 2002), Covington, KY.

Simon, H. (1996). *The sciences of the artificial* (3rd ed.). Cambridge, MA: The MIT Press.

Smith, P., & Ragan, T.J. (1999). Instructional Design (2nd ed.). John Wiley and Sons.

Surakka, S. (2007). What subjects and skills are important for software developers? *Communications of the ACM, 50*(1), 73-78.

Tomayko, J. E. (1998). Forging a discipline: An outline history of software engineering education. *Annals of Software Engineering, 6*(1-4), 3-18.

Voelter, M. (2006, July 5-9). *Software architecture: A pattern language for building sustainable software architectures.* Paper presented at the 11th European Conference on Pattern Languages of Programs (EuroPLoP 2006), Irsee, Germany.

Weinberg, G. M. (1992). *Quality software management: Vol. 1. Systems thinking.* New York: Dorset House.

Yee, G., Xu, Y., Korba, L., & El-Khatib, K. (2006). Privacy and security in e-learning. In T. Shih & J. Hung (Eds.), *Future directions in distance learning and communication technologies* (pp. 52-75). Hershey, PA: Idea Group, Inc.

## ADDITIONAL READING

The following publications provide details on the role of OSS in SEE by drawing the similarities and differences between conventional software engineering and open-source software engineering.

Attwell, G. (2005, July 11-15). *What is the significance of open source software for the education and training community?* Paper presented at the First International Conference on Open Source Systems (OSS 2005), Genova, Italy.

Liu, C. (2003, May 3). *Adopting open-source software engineering in computer science education.* Paper presented at the Third Workshop on Open Source Software Engineering, Portland, OR.

The following publications create a mapping between the personality types of people and the activities critical to software engineering such as problem solving and programming.

Bishop-Clark, C., & Wheeler, D. D. (1994). The Myers-Briggs personality type and its relationship to computer programming. *Journal of Research on Computing in Education, 26*(3), 358-370.

Boreham, N. C. (1987). Causal attribution by sensing and intuitive types during diagnostic problem solving. *Instructional Science, 16*, 123-136.

The following publications study potential opportunities for using the Web as a medium for instruction independent of any domain, and present guidelines and techniques to realise that successfully.

Adelsberger, H. H., Collis, B., & Pawlowski, J. M. (2002). *Handbook on information technologies for education and training.* Berlin, Germany: Springer-Verlag.

Brooks, D. W. (1997). *Web-teaching: A guide to designing interactive teaching for the World Wide Web.* New York: Plenum Press.

Khan, B. H. (1997). *Web-based instruction.* Englewood Cliffs, NJ: Educational Technology Publications.

The following publications discuss the significance of group work in course projects, and the role of IT in putting them to practice.

Layman, L., Williams, L., Osborne, J., Berenson, S., Slaten, K., & Vouk, M. (2005, October 19-22). *How and why collaborative software development impacts the software engineering course.* Paper presented at the 35th Annual Conference on Frontiers in Education (FIE 2005), Indianapolis, IN.

Martz, B., Shepherd, M., & Hickey, A. (2001). Using groupware in a classroom environment. *Journal of Information Systems Education, 12*(10), 31-41.

The following publication outlines potential directions of the evolution of SEE and in doing so makes modest suggestions toward the role of IT within it.

Shaw, M. (2000, June 4-11). *Software engineering education: A roadmap.* Paper presented at the 22nd International Conference on Software Engineering (ICSE 2000), Limerick, Ireland.

# Chapter XI
# Using Technology in Research Methods Teaching

**Gordon Joyes**
*School of Education, University of Nottingham, UK*

**Sheena Banks**
*School of Education, University of Sheffield, UK*

## ABSTRACT

*The focus of this chapter is on the use of technology in the teaching and learning of research methods in masters' and doctoral programmes in higher education, with particular reference to the field of educational research. The current challenges in research-methods teaching are taken up with the aim of, first, reflecting on questions about developing innovative and engaging flexible learning practices that are appropriate to the ways in which researchers (in particular, new researchers) can develop their skills, knowledge, and practice in diverse academic and professional settings. Second, the chapter explores how technology can be effectively used in the teaching and learning of research methods and how technology and pedagogy can be integrated to achieve a successful e-learning design. We explore these issues through a case study of the V-ResORT project (Virtual Resources for Online Research Training). Third, we describe an action research approach we have developed in the project to build an effective theoretical framework that underpins the production of video narratives and other online learning and teaching resources. Fourth, we present our approach to learning design and reusability as requirements to enable online materials to be embedded within course settings and across institutions using an "invented everywhere" approach. We present some practical examples of how our ideas have been translated into practice. Finally, we draw some conclusions from our action research study and present some ideas about trends for future developments of online research-methods learning and teaching.*

## INTRODUCTION

Recent trends in postgraduate education with the emergence of professional doctorates involving those new to research and the widespread provision of institutionally organized research training programmes have led to new debates about how researchers develop research expertise. Graduate provision in higher education in the United Kingdom now accounts for almost 25% of total student numbers, and the dominant model for the organization of research-methods teaching and support is the institutional graduate school (Woodward & Denicolo, 2004). There is greater diversity in the provision of research degrees, ranging across all subject disciplines, from professional and work-related doctorates to traditional PhDs, as well as greater diversity of research students. Much current provision is more appropriate for the full-time young career researcher than for the professionally employed off-campus researcher studying part time. Criticism of current practice has consequently addressed issues about the emphasis on skills training, the complexity of teaching research methods, epistemological concerns, and the role of technology. Powell and Green (2007), for example, in their critical analysis of doctorate programmes worldwide, state that the current emphasis on skills training for research students is "in danger of shifting the focus of doctoral education to a functionalist skills-led perspective" (pp. 258-259). There have been a number of calls for a review of research-methods learning and teaching, including from Birbili (2002), who states that there is a "pressing need for all those involved in (research methods training) to reflect on their current practice and introduce greater flexibility into its organization and provision." The UK GRAD Programme (2007) is the United Kingdom's main provider of personal and career management skills development for postgraduate researchers, and its Roberts Policy Forum calls for the coordination of examples of good practice in research-methods skills training.

Deem and Lucas (2006) examine questions around the relationship between teaching and research in higher education with reference to social science methods and particularly educational research. Their empirical data reveal confusion, particularly among master's students, about the nature of research and the need for support in "bringing together the abstract and more practical aspects of research" (p. 3). Both Birbili (2002) and Deem and Lucas identify the potential of technology to bring more flexibility into the learning and teaching of research methods.

## BACKGROUND

In this chapter, we highlight the problematic nature of how research methods are taught and how postgraduate students learn about research by presenting and reflecting on the outcomes of the three-year V-ResORT project (Virtual Resources for Online Research Training). We believe there is a need to change pedagogic approaches to the teaching of research methods to acknowledge educational research as complex, dynamic, and diverse, and our experience has given us some insight into how this can be achieved. V-ResORT has developed innovative, flexible learning materials that provide video narratives of researchers exploring key questions connected with their work. These online resources employ cutting-edge technologies to make the content accessible to both research students and their lecturers.

In the course of implementing the project, we have carried out action research into the design of a reusable Web site that incorporates an invented-everywhere principle. The process has involved a user needs analysis, expert panels, a literature review of transferability issues related to the reuse of resources, rapid prototyping, and the use of local mentors as part of ongoing dissemination and evaluation.

This work has been funded by the Higher Education Funding Council for England (HEFCE) through the Fund for the Development of Teaching and Learning (FDTL5) over a 3-year period from 2004 to 2007. It initially involved a University of Nottingham led consortium of four UK universities, including the University of Sheffield, Bath, and Canterbury Christ Church, yet it set out with the ambition of changing pedagogy in relation to research training much more widely. The aim of this project is to address the need to build capacity in UK research and to develop research-skills training that acknowledges educational research as a complex, dynamic, and diverse process. It aims to help universities in their support of research students through flexible learning approaches. The project incorporates an online multimedia framework for the teaching of research methods in masters' and doctoral programmes in educational studies through the use of online video narratives, where researchers explore key methodological questions connected with their work. These narratives are displayed using the MS Producer video-streaming software as a series of short 3- to 5-minute clips in high resolution alongside

PowerPoint slides and a transcript (see Figure 1). This enables the user to easily navigate through the complete narrative and provides him or her with support for the often complex language used within research methodology.

## THE ACTION RESEARCH APPROACH

The action research cycles within the project have extended the use of the project materials beyond the four project partner institutions and across the social sciences, and as part of the process, case studies to support reuse have been captured.

The key challenges faced in designing for the reuse of these resources were the following.

- *Pedagogic:* linking the content to a research framework and a context of use
- *Learning design:* bringing the pedagogy and the technology together to achieve required learning outcomes suited to a wide range of learning and teaching contexts

*Figure 1. A research narrative*

- *Technical:* choosing a technology that would achieve high visual impact and interactivity
- *Production:* developing a production process and protocol that effectively employed available production resources and led to the pedagogic outcomes we required
- *Reuse and repurposing:* understanding how to customise the learning resources for reuse and repurposing for the requirements of individual institutions and courses
- *Take-up and use of resources:* encouraging take-up and reuse of the resources within research-methods teaching in partner institutions and beyond
- *Staff development:* organising staff development opportunities to enable academic staff to understand and develop their expertise in using online video narratives and resources in their teaching
- *Sustainability:* ensuring the use of the resources and their continued development beyond the timescale of the project

An action research approach was taken to address these challenges, and the following discusses the rationale for this approach by considering our theoretical framework, some principles for effective project design, design for reusable e-learning, and the relationship between these. Key aspects of the six action research cycles within the project are then discussed.

## DEVELOPING A THEORETICAL FRAMEWORK

Our pedagogic approach to the development of the video narratives has been influenced by the work of Land and Hannafin (2000), who, in describing their principles of grounded design in e-learning, emphasise the need for a clear alignment of a defensible theoretical framework, assumptions and methods, the need for generalisability, and

an iterative approach to learning design where the theoretical framework can be tested and adapted. This process began for us as a result of earlier projects during 2002 to 2004: feedback from an Education Subject Centre (ESCalate) funded project at the University of Nottingham on the use of learning technologies in the teaching of research methods, and the evaluation of an interactive CD-ROM on educational research (e-research) at the University of Sheffield, which was subsequently evaluated through ESCalate funding.

The e-research CD-ROM contained video extracts, texts, and an interactive glossary covering a wide range of perspectives designed to represent real-world situations in which each researcher's understanding of educational research terms, concepts, processes, and activities could be uniquely nuanced and personalised. We agree with Barrett and Lally (2000), who in the development of an earlier CD-ROM, wished to "emphasise the personal nature of research and highlight the idea that a wide range of responses to problems of subject, structure and process is possible. The research process, we suggest, involves competing perspectives in which decisions are personal and therefore contestable" (p. 273).

In approaching the design of the e-research CD-ROM, there was a vision of engaging with a range of learning situations: individual, group, fully online, face to face, blended, and with an audience of national and international learners. The initial design emphasised nonlinearity and a flexible structure, where learner autonomy was encouraged (Winter, 2004). However, the evaluation showed that the resultant design was too loose and unstructured for the range of contexts and audiences envisaged and could not fully meet the original vision.

The evaluation data, nevertheless, supported our belief that video narratives with associated Web links offered a more interesting experience than reading an educational research textbook. Effective representation of the work of international researchers, good-quality video and audio, and multiple perspectives on research terminology and approaches were particularly valued features of the CD-ROM. However, more comprehensive coverage of research methods was needed, particularly in relation to quantitative methods, as well as improved navigation, a site map, and a search facility that would help to support learners in finding what they needed. It was also found that more scaffolding was needed for both staff and students to clarify the context of use, structure, purpose, tasks, and ways to engage with the narratives. The video narratives needed further development in terms of interactivity and instructional guidance. Users wanted breadth and depth in the video narratives. Interestingly, they wanted full transcripts of the video narratives to be displayed simultaneously. Finally, users wanted the materials to be Web-based so that online communication could be incorporated.

Our action research approach enabled us to build on these ideas at the beginning of the V-ResORT project. We did this by building a research framework. This has an underpinning key principle to take account of the learner or novice researcher's perspective. We approach issues in research methodology from the kinds of questions that novice educational researchers might have. Rather than beginning with abstract accounts of the different traditions and paradigms and then moving to the more specific research design and conduct issues, we have started with the more practical questions, issues, and dilemmas faced by researchers in education (and other social science disciplines). Then, through the narratives and supporting commentaries and materials, we begin to identify the various disciplinary, theoretical, conceptual, and methodological perspectives underpinning and informing research. We also consider the relationship between research projects, the kinds of knowledge being created, and the purposes for which research is undertaken. This has led to six main questions that have been used to guide the construction of research narratives and case studies.

1. Where did the ideas for research come from?
2. What is the aim and purpose of the research project?
3. Why were the theoretical and methodological approaches chosen?
4. How was the research project designed and conducted?
5. How was the research reported and communicated to a range of audiences?
6. What happened to the research after it was completed?

This conceptual framework was developed in collaboration with national experts: Professor Rosemary Deem of the University of Bristol, Louise Poulson of the University of Bath, and Professor Jerry Wellington of the University of Sheffield (the full framework can be viewed at http://www.v-resort.ac.uk). We have used this framework successfully to build the storyboard for the different video narratives.

Another pedagogic approach we were attempting to use is that of inquiry-based learning. This term has been adopted by CILASS (Centre of Excellence into Inquiry-Based Learning at the University of Sheffield) to refer to a spectrum of pedagogical approaches that are based on student-led inquiry or research (e.g., Brew, 2006, Levy, 2007). While it has always been true that learning at the postgraduate and doctoral levels involves inquiry-based learning, the wider adoption of the term through, for example, the CETL (Centres of Excellence in Teaching and Learning, funded by the Higher Education Funding Council for England) network has enabled us to think about how technology can be used to place inquiry at the centre of the learning experience, and how we can involve research students in rich interactions with peers and more experienced researchers and engagement with authentic examples and insights about practice. Our view of inquiry-based learning has also led us to ideas of advanced knowledge construction and situated knowledge where learners link new knowledge to their prior knowledge and actively construct new internal representations of the ideas being presented (Boekaerts & Simons, 1995).

In thinking through our theoretical framework, the situated and engagement view of learning outlined above points to the need to consider not just the learner, but also the context in which they learn. With learning technology, this will also include tools and resources that are present alongside learning content: the learning "surround." Perkins (1993, p. 90) claims "the surround—the immediate physical and social resources outside the person—participates in cognition, not just a source of input and a receiver of output, but as a vehicle of thought." He further suggests that the results of thinking remain not just in the mind, but in the arrangement of the surround, which should also be considered part of the learning. We are building tools and resources alongside the video narratives and believe these to be an integral part of the learner's experience. These will include communication tools for the building of online learning communities. We are also using the affordances of visual learning to tell a story and to convey real-life examples of practice with which learners can identify.

## DESIGN AND REUSABILITY

The search for effective pedagogy is of key importance since the need to excite learners' interests, retain them on courses and enable their progression is vital to institutions and practitioners as well as to the learners themselves. (HEFCE, 2004, p. 21)

The learning context is critical to whether learning technologies are successful (Laurillard, 1994), and an understanding of the learning context needs to influence the design. Developing this understanding is complex. Should the needs of the learners be sought and influence the design,

or should the institutional expectations of learner behaviours predominate? Learners' perceptions will be based on current and past experiences, and they are likely to be unaware of the need for particular requirements for learning within a new course, especially at a higher level. Moreover, there is research evidence that lecturers are not good at predicting learners' perceptions of their needs (Spratt, 1999), so these do need to be sought. It seems that the process of design needs to be one of working to develop an awareness of effective pedagogy within the community of potential users rather than assuming this is a known. Many projects that set out to influence practice across the higher education sector have failed to achieve this, encountering the "not invented here" barrier to reuse sometimes within the departments in which they were developed. A solution is to create a project design that takes an invented-everywhere approach, but this impacts on the design of the materials.

Design for learning has become an established term within e-learning (HEFCE, 2004). This recognises the complex process involved in designing e-learning materials that involves a partnership between the potential users, in this case, academics and research students, and the technologists who develop the materials: This is something learning or instructional design approaches did not often address. An invented-everywhere approach presents many challenges. How can the approach ensure that it does not become something invented everywhere, but suited to nowhere? How can the materials be designed so as to be universally usable and allow for some form of localisation (customisation)? How can the core materials be designed so that they are not only sustainable, but allow for additions to the resource?

Design for learning then not only refers to the materials design, but needs to influence the project design itself, that is, not only how it sets out to design the materials to allow potential users ownership of the materials, but how it engages those users in the design process. The latter is often referred to as ongoing dissemination, but design for reusable learning requires a new approach where dissemination is not simply letting the community know the project materials exist. Important though that may be, it is also about inviting and involving potential users from the start of the project to contribute to the development of the resource so that they develop a sense of ownership, localising this, and at the same time adding to the resource for all users. The action research approach to design was adopted to explore the context for use with potential users and develop a dissemination strategy that involved a professional development process in which academics were supported not only in understanding the ways the materials could be used within their learning and teaching contexts, but in understanding how they might add to the resource itself and link the resource to existing materials.

A summary of key points in the design for reusable learning or the invented-everywhere approach is provided below. The ways Points 1 to 3 were addressed in the V-ResORT project are then discussed.

The key features of the invented-everywhere approach are as follows.

1.  Strategically managed user engagement in the design process and the creation of the materials; it progressively engages a variety of stakeholders, that is, individual lecturers, students, schools, graduate schools, institutions, subject centres, CETLs, and the HEA (Higher Education Academy).
2.  Dissemination as a professional development process
3.  A pedagogic design that is flexible so that it engages both academics and students; it is used in lectures or seminars with a group of research students and yet is suited to individual self-study.

4.  An effective technical specification that ensures a high-quality resource that is motivating and fit for its purpose yet is robust

## Strategically Managed User Engagement

The first plan-act-review action research cycle started at the project planning stage. Before the project proposal was put together, a 1-day conference to discuss the use of new learning technologies in education studies was held (Joyes, 2002). This attracted representatives from 22 higher education institutions and revealed the rather traditional pedagogic approaches used to teach research methods. However, strong interest was shown in video materials in use online at the University of Nottingham and those developed on the e-research CD at the University of Sheffield. Evaluation of these materials (discussed earlier in this chapter) identified a need for Web-based materials and it was also clear that the resources would need to be used flexibly, that is, in teacher-led as well as student-centred settings. The evaluation data were used to conceptualise a more advanced concept, and this process also identified key partners, creating an inner circle of collaborators for the project. The outcome of this was a peer-reviewed project proposal submitted to HEFCE under the FDTL5 initiative.

The second action research cycle occurred once the project successfully gained funding, and this focused on work by the four project partners supported by the national steering group, consisting of senior representatives from partner university management including a graduate school and health studies, ESCalate, the Higher Education Academy, and an external evaluator. The key task was to create and evaluate an appropriate conceptual, pedagogic, and technical design that would encourage reuse and that would meet the needs of our users. The design was influenced by the approach to dissemination used within the project.

## Dissemination as a Professional Development Process

Drivers for change in integrating new learning technologies are locally sensitive.

It is important not to make assumptions about the willingness to use learning technologies in subject disciplines; for example, not all of the social sciences will be similarly receptive to new learning technologies. We should avoid caricaturing institutions as research and teaching led, making assumptions about receptiveness to new learning technology uptake (White, 2006). The third action research cycle involved two key elements.

1.  The creation of a functioning prototype resource on the project Web site incorporating the key pedagogic design features that acted as a test bed for the technologies and the approach for reuse. This was key in sharing the vision within the project and beyond.

2.  The identification of local mentors within the partner schools who were to use the materials. These were key academics with high status who not only acted as mentors within their institutions, but also with the project team to support understanding of the ways to engage with the local culture. The process involved contribution to the creation of one video narrative by each of the four partners. When these were incorporated in the Web site, local workshops were used to support the development of an understanding of effective pedagogy and to identify new resources to suit local reuse of materials across a range of courses. This approach identified the need for materials at the master's level as well as identifying quality existing resources that could be repurposed for the Web site. These were then incorporated.

The fourth and fifth cycles involved engaging the inner circle (a wider group of universities) and then the wider educational research community in

similar ways. The sixth cycle, building on the success of the earlier cycles, involves transferability across the social sciences, within health studies and within a graduate school cross-university programme. This action research approach allows each new dissemination engagement with the community of users to be problematised so that the local context is accommodated; as a result, not only does the community of users grow, but so does the resource.

## A Pedagogic Design that is Flexible

The innovative project materials have been made freely available on the Web site at http://www.v-resort.ac.uk, which provides video narratives of researchers exploring key questions connected with their work. Importantly, these online learning resources employ compelling cutting-edge technologies that have been made accessible to research students, their lecturers, and their supervisors. The video narratives include a range of perspectives including those of successful master's- and doctorate-level students as well as those of successful academics who explore influential nationally funded research projects. In addition, discussant video narratives are included that explore issues raised by the researcher narratives, providing a critical overview. A wide range of supporting resources are also included to help learners in making sense of the materials, such as key texts, Web resources, doctoral theses, project reports, and so forth. Skills training is provided that relates directly to skills referred to within the narratives, that is, the use of interviews, focus groups, and data analysis software. Learner pathways provide scaffolded support through the materials and a sophisticated search engine provides easy access to individual video clips.

Figure 2 provides a view of the main navigation page, showing the six key questions, the conceptual framework (referred to earlier in this chapter), that the researchers answered in describing their research journey. Learners can select a question, a researcher, and then one of the short video clips shown. Selection of one researcher and then questions will reveal a complete research journey. Selection of a question and then the researchers in turn enables comparisons between research narratives to be made. The main navigation page representing the research journey and the profile of one of the researchers featured in the narratives is shown in Figure 2. Figure 1 illustrated one of the video narrative clips for this researcher.

A key feature of the V-ResORT Web site is the way the materials are integrated into a meaningful learning resource. The complete research narratives are linked to reports, articles, data, thesis chapters, and other useful online and text-based resources. Skills training is provided that relates directly to skills referred to within the narratives, that is, the use of interviews, focus groups, and data analysis software. Figure 3 shows a skills-based training video clip covering approaches to writing at the research-degree level that is also used for the analysis of the conduct of focus groups.

Discussant narratives are also included that explore general methodological issues such as transferability and ethics that arise directly from the research narratives. This internal referencing was a deliberate pedagogic choice: The researcher narrative providing context and meaning for the learner is something research-methodology texts often fail to do.

In reality, academic users are able to adapt the materials to local contexts, and student users are able to personalise the materials (take individual learning pathways to meet individual learning needs). This is achieved through the use of navigation tools to support easy access to individual resources. The research journey navigation shown in Figure 2 is one approach. Another approach is the search facility that provides quick access to video clips on such issues as ethics, interviews, data analysis, and so forth. In addition, learning pathways are provided that lead the user through commonly accessed routes through the resources such as understanding the research process, developing research questions, ethical issues in educational research, and so on. In order to support localisation as part of the dissemination process,

*Figure 2. The research journey*

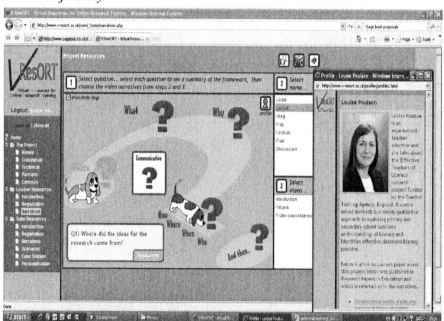

*Figure 3. Skills training: Discussing writing and analysing the focus group*

academics have been encouraged to suggest new learning pathways to suit their courses as well as to contribute new video narratives to the Web site, and this work is in progress. In addition, scenarios of use as well as case studies of actual use in a variety of courses are being captured to support the localisation process.

## FINDINGS

Evaluation has been ongoing as part of the action research process, and the following provides a snapshot of some of the evidence that supports the resource design principles, namely,

- student reaction on courses,
- take-up on courses within education studies and beyond, and
- localisation of the materials through contributions from the wider sector.

### Student Reaction: A Case Study

One example of use of the resource is within a campus-based master's programme in educational research methods at the University of Nottingham, United Kingdom. As part of the localisation approach, specific learning pathways were designed to scaffold the student experience. Fifteen students accessed the Web site through their 1-year course and took part in two online group discussion activities that supported the exploration of the researcher narratives. They were required to identify and share clips they found of most value and discuss how these contributed to their developing understanding of research. Reaction to the researcher narratives was positive, and in some cases very enthusiastic. One student explained that after having viewed one clip, she found herself "driven" to explore all 20 of the 4-minute clips to view the whole research story. She described how she listened to these at home whilst making and eating her evening meal. We have found this reaction quite typical, particularly once a student has found a clip that resonates with his or her area of research and/or situation. For example, the most popular video narrative for these master's students was one by an international PhD research student because they felt that her description of the challenges she had encountered was closest to their situation as beginning researchers. This narrative acted as an entry point to the other resources on the Web site and as a bridge to understanding the more formal and theoretical approaches used within the course texts. As a result of this evaluation and of the needs expressed by lecturers during the project dissemination activities, a discrete set of video narratives covering the master's degree dissertation journey has been developed for the Web site.

## Take-Up on Courses

Visitors to the V-ResORT Web site are required to register to use the resources for which there is no charge, but they need to agree to take part in any evaluation of the materials. For the academic year 2006 to 2007, students and lecturers from 90% of UK higher education institutions were registered, and the ongoing evaluation seeks to explore their experiences and develop case studies of use for inclusion on the Web site.

## Localisation of the Resource

The Web site has been consciously promoted through conference papers and demonstrations to small target groups to primarily attract education studies lecturers to localise the resource by suggesting and contributing video narratives. This has been supported by engagement with the UK ESCalate and through the Scottish Applied Educational Research network. This approach has been successful, and the resource has moved within a period of 2 years from the four initial video narratives contributed by the four partner institutions to a current resource of over 20 video narratives, with contributions from seven UK universities.

The project has received recognition from HEFCE through the award of additional transferability funding to extend the localisation work to support the integration of the V-ResORT resources into a virtual graduate school for use across the social sciences, the incorporation of

additional narratives from additional universities, and the development of the resource for use within nursing and health studies. This success leads us to believe that the materials are suited for academic use in a wide range of contexts, not just educational research.

## Implications

V-ResORT addresses key issues in relation to the uptake of new learning technologies in the teaching of research methods. The conscious design for the reusable learning approach adopted and the action research approach taken to dissemination and localisation of resources revealed some important tensions within the sector. These relate to academics' perceptions of student needs as well as the sharing of practice and resources. This has implications for the nature of professional development surrounding the teaching of research methods.

Laurillard, Swift, and Darby (1992) conducted research that found that academics, though interested in using software developed elsewhere, wanted to be able to customise this to their own courses. We found many academics willing to use the resources developed within the project without any form of localisation. This was to some extent due to the effective design of the materials, but also because of the effort it would take to customise them and because they were not able to take a student perspective (Spratt, 1999). Evaluation evidence within the project found that students were more critical and preferred resources customised to the needs of their particular courses. For example, research narratives related to school-based learning were felt to be less helpful for those students focusing on early childhood even though the generic research issues could be considered to be essentially the same, seemingly only for those with more experience. This highlights the importance of working closely with academics to help develop their understanding of the need to actually contribute to the resource as well as use it.

The project confirmed the findings of its earlier work that teachers of research methods at the master's and doctoral level as well as research supervisors tended to develop courses in isolation from each other, and although the notion of sharing practice was not seen as problematic, this was rarely achieved. V-ResORT has provided a catalyst for change in that it has promoted the sharing of practice and a debate about the nature of effective research training and of resources that can be used to support both training within taught modules and for supervision. As mentioned previously, in one institution this has led to the development of a virtual graduate school. It has to be recognised that without the external funding provided by HEFCE and the vision of the partner institutions to pursue the collaboration, the developments discussed in this chapter would not have occurred. V-ResORT will continue to develop, gathering further evaluation data, and should provide evidence of the need for a UK virtual graduate school serving the higher education research community.

## CONCLUSION

We believe that the innovative and engaging practices represented by V-ResORT in the way that the project has been able to bring pedagogy and technology together to achieve a successful learning design that can be repurposed and reused is strategically important for the higher education sector. Importantly, design for reusable learning has been envisioned within the project as a process that integrates continuing professional development alongside pedagogy and technology. This was an important element of the strategy developed to change pedagogic practice in the teaching of research methods, something we believe that we are beginning to succeed to do.

Universities sometimes misunderstand the needs of students in the way that they develop knowledge and practice in research methods, and there is a national need for more flexibility in the teaching of this topic. We have therefore made it a priority to work within the community of potential users to develop an awareness of effective pedagogy rather than assuming that this is known. In some ways, therefore, the project's strategy of working with local mentors, key academics with high status, to achieve ownership, localisation, and personalisation has been the most important aspect of the project. The development of the functioning prototype was also important in helping to share the vision and stimulate uptake.

## FUTURE TRENDS

We believe that the V-ResORT project has been strategic and timely in enabling us to implement innovative approaches to the use of technology in research-methods learning and teaching. The vision for V-ResORT was stimulated not only by our own experiences and observations of the problematic nature of research-methods learning and teaching, but also the opportunity offered by technology to enhance the learning and teaching of research methods that reflects current and future policy trends in higher education.

### Teaching-Research Nexus

Some of the key trends in higher education that will continue to have impact for the next decade relate to current debates about links between teaching and research. For example, a research report recently commissioned by the Higher Education Academy (Jenkins, Healy, & Zetter, 2007) has highlighted the "teaching-research nexus" as "central to higher education" (p. 2). Another key finding states that "effective teaching-research links" are not automatic and have to be constructed (p. 63). This chimes with our own experience in the V-ResORT project of having to make teaching-research practice explicit rather than tacit as part of the learning design process.

## Mainstream Impact of E-Learning and Technology

The second key trend, to state what seems to be obvious, is that e-learning and technology will continue to impact higher education research and teaching in ways that to some extent can be predicted, but in some ways may be unexpected. In some instances, for example, the implementation of e-learning means researchers and teachers have to rethink their existing practice in order to develop new practices that incorporate the challenges of technology. Price and Oliver (2007) highlight the complexity of this in their comment that "the move to teaching online renders the role of the teacher both the same *and* different simultaneously" (p. 24). It is also true that e-learning is only just becoming embedded in the learning, teaching, and research practice of higher education institutions because of the complexity of the drivers for the successful implementation of e-learning. There is not space here to discuss these drivers, but they include issues about quality, as identified by Littlejohn and Pegler (2007), and the influence of policy on practice where expectations of e-learning have often been unrealistic (Conole & Oliver, 2007).

## Reusability

The third key trend will be continuing developments and deeper understandings of reusability, which necessarily need to go beyond the rather restricted notions of reusability as defined by the reusable learning object (RLO) movement. There is a strong economic argument for reusable designs as online interactive materials are expensive to produce, and often the same or similar content is developed to be used in different contexts, using different technologies for delivery on different platforms. Metadata standards have been defined for RLOs and these standards define an RLO as "any entity, digital or non-digital, that

may be used for learning, education or training" (Institute of Electrical and Electronics Engineers [IEEE], 2002, p. 6). From an RLO perspective, it is considered that interoperability (content from multiple sources working equally well with different learning systems) and reusability (content developed in one context being transferable to another context) are essential for this localisation to occur. The reusability paradox presents an argument against RLOs being effective in supporting learning: "To make learning objects maximally reusable, learning objects should contain as little context as possible (however) the meaningfulness of educational content is a function of its context" (Wiley, 2004). Design for reusable learning will become increasingly important with the increasing expectations of online resources. These complex issues will increasingly be solved through open research approaches as outlined in the recent Kaleidoscope European network statement: Open research will need to operate at open outcomes, tools, and process levels (Laurillard, 2006).

## Pedagogic Planning Tools

As argued in this chapter, approaches to design for reusable learning will necessarily need to incorporate pedagogy, technology, and professional development. The V-ResORT project found that technologists, academics, and students had different understandings of the key pedagogic issues, yet effective design needs to be a collaborative endeavour. Professional development in which those responsible for the design develop a shared understanding of effective pedagogy suited to the context for learning needs to occur. Processes for developing this shared dialogue need to be explored that go beyond the use of rapid prototypes and early demonstrators as used in the V-ResORT project. These are useful later in the design process, but what is needed to support the necessary staff development at the beginning of the design process are analytic tools (Joyes,

2007) through which technologists, academics, and learners can develop a shared perspective of an effective learning design to suit a particular learning context and the use of appropriate technologies to support this. It is in this way that designs can be made reusable, and that reusable designs can be repurposed.

## Personalisation

A further trend will be the increasing use of technologies to support personalisation. New technologies have increased learner expectations; users want to be able to tailor their informal and formal learning to meet their needs, and want a shift to more learner-centred approaches in formal education. The V-ResORT material caters to this at several levels: It allows personal narratives of research to be explored, allows academics to include their own personal research accounts and perspectives, and allows learners to choose the ways they interact with materials. A key to this support for personalisation is in the sophisticated approach to navigation taken.

Web 2.0 technologies such as those incorporated in YouTube™ allow users to upload their own video narratives. Initial explorations into personal use of research methods such as illustrated by the focus group example in Figure 3 could relatively easily be uploaded, shared, and explored through incorporation of a discussion group or a blog. However, these tools to support personalisation, sharing, and knowledge construction need to incorporate private and safe spaces for collaborative working as well as the means to share understanding more widely. A tool that combines this functionality, the Virtual Interactive Player, is described at http://www.echina-uk.org and will eventually be used alongside the V-ResORT materials. Higher education is in a position to gain in this way from the repurposing and combining of Web 2.0 social networking tools to suit specific learning contexts.

## Internationalisation

Finally, we should draw attention to the fact that technology and e-learning are global phenomena that in the West are strategic elements of the marketisation and internationalisation of higher education. Middlehurst and Woodfield (2007), in their research for HEFCE on internationalisation, comment that the changing international context for higher education is linked to the impact of globalization. This in turn leads to policy development addressing the digital divide in technology, and strategies for flexible learning to overcome barriers of time and distance. E-learning is often seen as problematic because of high and unrealistic expectations of what it can achieve, which range from concepts around the knowledge economy to the digital divide, the gap between policy and practice and between the functionality of technology and educational expertise in the use of it. There are huge challenges in the internationalisation of e-learning, not only in achieving reusability of materials on a global basis, but also the challenge of differences in e-learning, including cultural and pedagogic differences. Middlehurst (2002, p. 3) discusses a concept of "borderless education" where technology is cutting across boundaries of levels and types of education, and removing barriers to education in relation to time, space, and distance. However, the issue of difference in e-learning is only just beginning to be identified.

Furthermore, the use of technology and e-learning can exacerbate difference, particularly cultural difference, which is frequently ignored in the design of e-learning. A number of writers in the e-learning field have identified this as an issue. Moore, Shattuck, and Al-Harthi (2005), for example, raise important questions about the complex relationship of e-teaching, learning, and culture in global online environments, with examples from American distance learning, to show how pedagogies based on Western beliefs might cause conflict with the cultural values of learners from other countries. Ziguras (2001, p. 8), while acknowledging that "educational imperialism" often occurs within transnational education, observes that the use of ICT has intensified the flow of "knowledge transfer" and therefore the concerns about cultural impacts of ICT. Collis (1999) identified the need to operationalise the accommodation of cultural difference into the design of e-learning by providing some design guidelines for flexibility that respond to multiple cultures. There are other substantive issues around the e-learning development in international settings, including a global need for effective e-tutor training and staffing for e-learning production and collaboration. There is no doubt that technology and e-learning are key drivers for achieving a knowledge economy and an HE system that is truly international.

## REFERENCES

Barrett, E., & Lally, V. (2000). Meeting new challenges in educational research training: The signposts for educational research CD Rom. *British Educational Research Journal, 26*(2), 271-290.

Birbili, M. (2002). *Teaching educational research methods.* Retrieved March 10, 2007, from http://escalate.ac.uk

Boekaerts, M., & Simons, P. R. J. (1995). *Leren en instructie: Psychologie van de leerling en het leerproces* [Learning and instruction: The psychology of the learner and his learning process]. Assen, The Netherlands: Dekker & Van de Vegt.

Brew, A. (2006). *Research and teaching: Beyond the divide.* Basingstoke, United Kingdom: Palgrave Macmillan.

Collis, B. (1999). Designing for difference: Cultural issues in the design of WWW based course support sites. *British Journal of Educational Technology, 30*(3), 201-215.

Conole, G., & Oliver, M. (Eds.). (2007). Introduction. In *Contemporary perspectives in elearning research: Themes, methods and impact on practice* (pp. 5-8). London: Routledge.

Deem, R., & Lucas, L. (2006). Learning about research: Exploring the learning and teaching/research relationship amongst educational practitioners studying in higher education. *Teaching in Higher Education, 11*(1), 1-18.

Higher Education Funding Council for England (HEFCE). (2004). *Effective practice with e-learning: A good practice guide in designing for learning.* Retrieved March 10, 2007, from http://www.jisc.ac.uk/uploaded_documents/ACF5D0.pdf

Institute of Electrical and Electronics Engineers (IEEE). (2002). *Draft standard for learning object metadata.* Retrieved November 4, 2006, from http://ltsc.ieee.org/wg12

Jenkins, A., Healy, A., & Zetter, R. (2007). *Linking teaching and research in disciplines and departments.* Retrieved November 27, 2007, from http://www.heacademy.ac.uk/ourwork/research/teaching

Joyes, G. (2002, June 7). *On-line learning and research methods: An ESCalate funded project.* Paper presented at the ESCalate Research Methods for Research Students Conference, London. Retrieved November 27, 2007, from http://www.escalate.ac.uk/diary/reports/7Junindex.php3

Joyes, G. (2006, June 7). *Generic e-learning materials: Exploring localisation and personalisation issues.* Paper presented at the Universitas 21 Elearning Conference, Guadalajara, Mexico. Retrieved March 11, 2007, from http://www.universitas21.com/elearning.html

Joyes, G. (2007). E-learning design for localisation and personalisation. *Malaysian Journal of Distance Education, 8*(2), 69-82.

Lally, V., Timmis, S., Jones, C., & Banks, S. (2004) *E-research: Using multimedia for research methods teaching and learning. ESCalate project report.* Retrieved November 13, 2006, from http://escalate.ac.uk/1132

Land, S., & Hannafin, M. (2000*).* Student-centred learning environments. In D. H. Jonassen & S. M. Land (Eds.), *Theoretical foundations of learning environments* (pp. 1-23). Mahwah, NJ: Lawrence Erlbaum.

Laurillard, D. (1994). How can learning technologies improve learning? *Law Technology Journal, 3*(2). Retrieved March 10, 2007, from http://www.law.warwick.ac.uk/ltj/3-2j.html

Laurillard, D. (2006). *Kaleidoscope: A scientific vision.* Retrieved March 11, 2007, from http://www.noe-kaleidoscope.org/public/pub/lastnews/images/kal_vision.pdf

Laurillard, D., Swift, B., & Darby, J. (1992). Probing the not invented here syndrome. *The CTISS File, 14.*

Levy, P. (2007). Exploring and developing excellence: Towards a community of praxis. In A. Skelton (Ed.), *International perspectives on teaching excellence in higher education.* Routledge.

Littlejohn, A., & Pegler, C. (2007). *Preparing for blended learning.* New York: Routledge.

Middlehurst, R. (2002). Variations on a theme: Complexity and choice in a world of borderless education. *Journal of Studies in International Education, 6*(2), 134-155.

Middlehurst, R., & Woodfield, S. (2007). *Responding to the internationalization agenda: implications for institutional policy and practice.* Retrieved June 10, 2007, from http://www.heacademy.ac.uk

Moore, M. G., Shattuck, K., & Al-Harthi, A. (2005). Cultures meeting cultures in online distance education. *Journal of E-Learning and Knowledge Society, 1*(2), 187-208.

Perkins, D. N. (1993). Person plus: A distributed view of thinking and learning. In G. Salomon (Ed.), *Distributed cognitions: Psychological and educational considerations* (pp. 88-110). Cambridge, United Kingdom: Cambridge University Press.

Powell, S., & Green, H. (Eds.). (2007). *The doctorate worldwide.* Maidenhead, United Kingdom: Oxford University Press & Society for Research into Higher Education.

Price, S., & Oliver, M. (2007). A framework for conceptualising the impact of technology on learning and teaching. *Journal of Educational Technology and Society, 10*(1), 16-27.

Spratt, M. (1999). How good are we at knowing what learners like? *System, 27,* 141-155.

UK GRAD Programme. (2007). *Report of proceedings UK GRAD Programme Roberts policy forum.* Retrieved November 27, 2007, from http://www.grad.ac.uk

White, S. A. (2006, September 17-22). *Critical success factors for institutional change: Some organizational perspectives.* In H. C. Davis & S. Eales (Eds.), *Proceedings of Critical Success Factors for Institutional Change: A Workshop of the European Conference of Digital Libraries (ECDL'06),* Alicante, Spain (pp. 75-89). Retrieved March 10, 2007, from http://eprints.ecs.soton.ac.uk/13225/01/Critical_Success_Factors_for_Institutional_Change_latest.pdf

Wiley, D. (2004). *The reusability paradox.* Retrieved November 11, 2006, from http://cnx.org/content/m11898/latest/

Winter, C. (2004, April 5-7). *The e-research project: Developing an IMM resource for supporting communities of learners through CSCL.* In S. Banks, P. Goodyear, V. Hodgson, C. Jones, V. Lally, McConnell, & C. Steeples (Eds.), *Fourth International Networked Learning 2004 Conference Proceedings.* Retrieved November 27, 2007, from http://www.networkedlearningconference. org.uk/past/nlc2004/proceedings/individual_papers/winter/htm

Woodward, D., & Denicolo, P. (2004). *Review of graduate schools in the UK*. Lichfield, United Kingdom: Council for Graduate Education.

Ziguras, C. (2001). Educational technology in transnational higher education in South East Asia: The cultural politics of flexible learning. *Journal of Educational Technology and Society, 4*(4), 8-18.

## ADDITIONAL READING

Andrews, R., & Haythornthwaite, C. (Eds.). (2007). *E-learning research handbook*. London: Sage.

This is a new publication with international case studies of research and practice, involving leading researchers who address substantive research issues on the theory and practice of e-learning.

Barron, B. (2003). When smart groups fail. *The Journal of the Learning Sciences, 12*(3), 307-359. Retrieved November 27, 2007, from http://www.stanford.edu/~barronbj/documents/Barron_JLS03.pdf

This reports research into how collaborative interactions influence problem-solving outcomes, indicating that how participants manage these interacting spaces is critical to the outcome of their work. Useful directions for future research are suggested.

Beetham, H., & Sharpe, R. (Eds.). (2007). *Rethinking pedagogy for a digital age: Designing and delivering e-learning*. London: Routledge.

The book by Beetham and Sharpe looks at different perspectives on how to design learning content and activities that are pedagogically sound. It demystifies learning design by showing how it is part of the educational process. There are useful case studies and appendices of tools and resources.

Castells, M. (2001). *The Internet galaxy: Reflections on the Internet, business and society*. Oxford, United Kingdom: Oxford University Press.

Castells is an American sociologist who writes in an accessible way about the social (rather than technical) implications of technology on the global society. He particularly focuses on the significance of the Internet for online business.

Collis, B., & Moonen, J. (2001). *Flexible learning in a digital world: Experiences and expectations*. New York: Routledge Falmer.

Collis and Moonen are experienced e-learning innovators and practitioners. They write about the role of technology in achieving flexible learning, linking theoretical knowledge with practical guidelines.

Conole, G., & Oliver, M. (Eds.). (2007). *Contemporary perspectives in elearning research: Themes, methods and impact on practice*. London: Routledge.

The development of e-learning research, particularly in providing evidence of good practice, has been very problematic. This book, which has chapters contributed by some very well-known names, offers a comprehensive review and analysis of the challenges of e-learning research and how it can impact practice.

Dillenbourg, P. (Ed.). (1999). *Collaborative learning: Cognitive and computational approaches*. Oxford, United Kingdom: Pergamon Press.

This book presents a multidisciplinary perspective to develop understandings of what collaborative learning is from the psychology, education, and computer science viewpoints. A range of authors from different disciplines have contributed chapters, and a powerful case for collaborative learning is critically explored and presented.

Downes, S. (2001). Learning objects: Resources for distance education worldwide. *The International Review of Research in Open and Distance Learning, 2*(1). Retrieved November 27, 2007, from http://www.irrodl.org/index.php/irrodl/article/view/32/378

This article presents a useful overview of learning objects. It covers the need for learning objects and their essential components, provides a theoretical perspective, and covers their development and use.

Garrison, D. R., & Anderson, T. (2002). *E-learning in the 21st century: A framework for research and practice.* London: Routledge.

Garrison and Anderson are Canadian researchers who have particular expertise in distance learning forms of e-learning. They draw on their expertise as educational researchers and practitioners to explore technical, pedagogical, and organizational aspects of e-learning. They offer models (frameworks) of practice rather than case studies.

Goodyear, P., Steeples, C., et al. (2001). *Effective networked learning in higher education: Notes and guidelines.* Retrieved November 27, 2007, from http://www.csalt.lancs.ac.uk/jisc/guidelines_final.doc

Produced by Professor Peter Goodyear and his team, then based at Lancaster University, United Kingdom, this combines authoritative theoretical aspects of e-learning with practical guidelines. The definition of e-learning as networked learning is important as it underpins an approach to e-earning that builds on communication between learners and teachers.

Green, H., Facer, K., Rudd, T., Dillon, P., & Humphreys, P. (2005). *Personalisation and digital technologies.* Retrieved November 27, 2007, from http://www.futurelab.org.uk/resources/publications_reports_articles/opening_education_reports/Opening_Education_Report201/

This provides a comprehensive and well-informed overview of issues related to the key e-learning concept of personalisation, that is, harnessing the potential of digital technologies to place the learner at the centre of education.

Harasim, L. M. (1995). *Learning networks: A field guide to teaching and learning online.* Cambridge, MA: MIT Press.

This is a guide to the use of new technologies to support learning networks at all levels of education by an experienced practitioner and academic.

Hartnell-Young, E., & Morriss, M. (2007). *Digital portfolios: Powerful tools for promoting professional growth and reflection* (2nd ed.). Thousand Oaks, CA: Corwin Press.

This book by leading researchers in the field provides a comprehensive analysis of the nature of portfolios and their potential for supporting professional growth and reflection. It also demonstrates how to develop high-quality portfolios that reflect personal vision, record professional growth, and celebrate achievements.

Jochems, W., van Merrienboer, J., & Koper, R. (2003). *Integrated e-learning.* London: Kogan Page.

Examines in some depth the issues of how new learning methods offered by the use of technology can be developed. The book takes a very systematic and practical approach to how to integrate pedagogy, technology, and organizational requirements to achieve high-quality e-learning. It is a good book for practitioners.

Kress, G. (2003). *Literacy in the new media age.* London: Routledge.

This important book considers the effects of the new media age in which the screen has replaced the book as the dominant medium of communication; it is a revolution that has radically altered the relationship between writing and the book.

Koschmann, T. (1996).*CSCL: Theory & practice of an emerging paradigm.* NJ: Laurence Erlbaum Associates.

Tim Koschmann is a leading American expert in the theory and practice of computer-supported collaborative learning (CSCL). CSCL is obviously a very specialized area of e-learning. This book emphasises in some depth the theory rather than the practice of CSCL. Tim Koschmann has been working in this field for some time, and this book is very authoritative.

Laurillard, D. (2001). *Rethinking university teaching.* New York: Routledge Falmer.

Professor Laurillard's book has had a major impact on the development of e-learning theory and practice in the United Kingdom, and is one of the most cited publications in e-learning research. The conversational model drawn from distance learning practice at the Open University seems to have universal applications to e-learning practice.

Lave, J., & Wenger, E. (1991). *Situated learning: Legitimate peripheral participation.* Cambridge, United Kingdom: Cambridge University Press.

This book has had a seminal influence on the development of e-learning. It promotes in a theoretical way the notion of learning as a social process that enables participants to move toward a community of practice. Examples of communities of practice are given (e.g., midwives). It is another widely cited source in e-learning research.

Levy, P. (2003). A methodological framework for practice-based research in networked learning. *Instructional Science, 3*, 87-100.

Dr. Levy comes from an information science background and has developed this model from the experience of running a postgraduate professional online course for information professionals. The paper is very authoritative about both theory and practice, but is a good read, and there is much here for both e-learning researchers and practitioners.

Lipponen, L. (2002, January 7-11). Exploring foundations for computer-supported collaborative learning. In G. Stahl (Ed.), *Computer Support for Collaborative Learning: Foundations for a CSCL Community. Proceedings of the Computer-Supported Collaborative Learning 2002 Conference* (pp. 72-81). Hillsdale, NJ: Erlbaum. Retrieved November 27, 2007, from http://www.helsinki.fi/science/networkedlearning/texts/lipponen2002.pdf

This paper provides a useful overview of research into computer-supported collaborative learning that contributes to the theoretical as well as empirical understanding and development of the area.

Littlejohn, A. (2003). *Reusing online resources: A sustainable approach to e-learning.* London: Kogan Page.

Professor Littlejohn's book is an excellent introduction to e-learning as it focuses on the starting point of most practitioners in developing e-learning: the reuse of online resources. She covers theory, but the strength of the book is its accessibility and emphasis on practice.

McConnell, D. (2000). *Implementing computer supported cooperative learning.* London: Kogan Page.

This much cited book is about the use of computers to facilitate cooperative learning among groups of isolated individuals; its central tenet is that people learn best when they have the opportunity to work with others. The book covers technologies, cooperative learning design, and tutoring.

McConnell, D. (2006). *E-learning groups and communities.* Maidenhead, United Kingdom: SRHE/Open University Press.

Professor McConnell has many years of experience in researching and developing e-learning groups and communities, and this is reflected in this authoritative book that also gives some guidelines for implementing and tutoring online learning communities.

McDonald, J. (2006). *Blended learning and online tutoring: A good practice guide.* Aldershot, United Kingdom: Gower.

A practical guide to how to develop blended learning (learning that combines face-to-face methods with the use of online media) in a wide range of learning and teaching contexts. There are international examples of practice.

Mason, R., & Rennie, F. (2006). *Elearning: The key concepts.* London: Routledge.

This is a useful book that provides concise and user-friendly definitions of the crucial terms used in the e-learning field.

Mayes, T., & de Freitas, S. (2004). *Review of e-learning frameworks, models and theories.* Retrieved November 27, 2007, from http://www. jisc.ac.uk/uploaded_documents/Stage%202%20 Learning%20Models%20(Version%201).pdf

This is a comprehensive overview of fundamental learning theories and concepts that have contributed to the development of e-learning, and some critical assessment of how they can be used in the design and development of e-learning.

Rheingold, H. (2000). *Tools for thought: The history and future of mind-expanding technology.* Cambridge, MA: MIT Press. Retrieved November 27, 2007, from http://www.rheingold. com/texts/tft

*Tools for Thought* traces the visionary work that led to the personal computer, the Internet, and so forth. It pieces together how Boole and Babbage, and Turing and von Neumann created the foundations that the later tool builders stood upon to create the future we live in today.

Salmon, G. (2000). *E-moderating: The key to teaching and learning online.* London: Kogan Page.

Salmon's authoritative book about online learning and teaching has had a big impact on higher education. It is a clear and accessible read.

Sharples, M. (Ed.). (2006). *Big issues in mobile learning: Report of a workshop by the Kaleidoscope Network of Excellence Mobile Learning Initiative.* Nottingham, United Kingdom: University of Nottingham. Retrieved November 27, 2007, from http://www.nottingham.ac.uk/lsri/ msh/Reports/Big%20Issues%20in%20mobile%2 0learning%20report.pdf

Mobile learning is not just about learning using portable devices, but learning across contexts. With technology getting smaller, more personal, more ubiquitous, and more powerful, it better supports a mobile society. This report represents current thinking about mobile learning by leading experts.

Snyder, I. (Ed.). (2002). *Silicon literacies: Communication, innovation and education in the electronic age.* London: Routledge.

Written by leading international scholars from a range of disciplines, this book explores the social, cultural, and educational impact of electronic communication literacy practices.

Somekh, B. (2007). *Pedagogy and learning with ICT: Researching the art of innovation.* London: Routledge.

Professor Somekh is an experienced researcher and evaluator of ICT in education. Her book gives an extended overview of the key processes of change required for effective implementation of ICT in education, particularly highlighting the impact on teachers, schools, and education systems. It clarifies in a straightforward way what the art of innovation really means and its impact on practice.

Steeples, C., & Jones, C. (2001). *Networked learning: Perspectives and issues.* London: Springer Verlag.

This is an authoritative collection of chapters from researchers who address the problems and complexities of effective development of networked learning. A wide range of issues are analysed, reflecting many different social and institutional perspectives. The implications of adopting different approaches to learning design and the use of different technologies in networked learning are examined in depth.

Turkle, S. (1995). *Life on the screen: Identity in the age of the Internet.* New York: Touchstone.

This is an ethnographic study of the Internet that explores different modes of conceptualising notions of the self. This book is important in that it locates a discourse at the individual or phenomenological level.

Wenger, E. (1999). *Communities of practice: Learning, meaning, and identity.* Cambridge, United Kingdom: Cambridge University Press.

This is another essential book for e-learning researchers. It develops further, in a systematic and thorough way, the idea of learning as a social participation process that is achieved through a community of practice. Wenger has had a big impact on the theory and practice of e-learning, and this is an important book.

# Chapter XII
# Instructional Design for Class–Based and Computer–Mediated Learning:
## Creating the Right Blend for Student–Centered Learning

**Richard Walker**
*E-Learning Development Team, University of York, UK*

**Walter Baets**
*Euromed Marseille École de Management, France*

## ABSTRACT

*Blended learning occupies a prominent place within higher education teaching strategies, yet there is no clear definition for what we mean by this term as an instructional approach. In this chapter, we present a working definition for blended learning that is based around a learner-centred framework, and outline three instructional models for blended course design in support of student-centred learning. We have applied these models to a series of course experiments that were undertaken at two international business schools: Nyenrode Business University (The Netherlands) and Euromed Marseille École de Management (France). Common to each course design was the use of e-tools to solicit and share knowledge for the out-of-class phase of student learning. We discuss the reception of these models by students and their relevance to Net Generation learners in promoting socially active learning through collaboration and experience sharing. Drawing together the lessons learned from these experiments, we present an instructional framework for course designers, focusing on the key phases in the delivery of a blended course and the accompanying instructional responsibilities that underpin this instructional approach.*

## INTRODUCTION

Technological change has brought with it new opportunities for teaching and learning within higher education (HE). E-learning, so often associated with distance education, is now assuming an important role in the way that instructors interact with campus-based students. Over recent years, the adoption of e-learning tools by instructors has become widespread within higher education, and course innovation along these lines has underlined the potential for new ways of teaching and learning. Impressive claims have indeed accompanied these changes. Computer-mediated learning offers educators the opportunity to transform pedagogic practice, shifting instruction from the physical to the virtual classroom (Hiltz, 1994). The introduction of technology also provides the scope for enriched learning opportunities, facilitating the sharing of knowledge and understanding among members of a group, increasing interaction between students, and supporting higher order learning (Harasim, 1989; Jarvela & Hakkinen, 2002; Meyer, 2003; Salmon, 2000a).

Whilst the case for e-learning on an institutional level is now firmly established, and online activity occupies a prominent place in campus-based teaching strategies, there is still no commonly agreed definition for what we mean by blended learning: the combination of computer-mediated and face-to-face learning. The plethora of terms (hybrid, mixed mode) reflects the confused status of this instructional approach and the pedagogic properties that underpin it. Poor definition has hampered the development of instructional models and frameworks that can be applied to blended course design and delivery, and the dearth of research literature reflects this state of affairs. Furthermore, the evidence suggests that instructional design methodology has been slow to realise the benefits of student-centred learning, with traditional teaching models applied to online activity, supporting an e-teaching rather than e-learning design approach. In our view,

current practice in the design of blended courses runs counter to Net Generation study patterns and the interrelationship between formal and informal learning activities, where students control the pace of learning. It is timely, therefore, to consider instructional models that are appropriate for today's learners, and that emphasise the responsibility of individuals in managing their own learning.

In this chapter, we seek to address these issues by positioning blended learning within a learner-centred pedagogic framework. We present a series of instructional models that employ e-learning tools to engage course participants in sense making and knowledge building through self-directed and collaborative learning activities. The models have been applied to a series of blended modules that were delivered to management students at Nyenrode Business University (The Netherlands) and Euromed Marseille Ecole de Management (France). We report on the results from these courses and draw together the lessons learned in course delivery from these institutional experiences.

This chapter therefore offers course designers and instructors a selection of models for blended course delivery that may be applied to other disciplines that place the control of the content and pace of learning in the hands of students, a variation from traditional e-teaching pedagogy. The lessons learned from the blended modules are presented in the form of an instructional framework, which is intended to serve as a practical guide for course designers and instructors who are preparing to deliver their own courses. The guide draws on our own experiences in blended course design, with our observations on student learning referenced against the emerging literature in this field.

In summary, this chapter addresses the following objectives.

1.  To provide a working definition for blended learning as an instructional approach that is learner centred in focus and relevant to Net Generation students

2. To explore approaches to blended learning and appropriate course design models that are based on a learner-centred pedagogic framework
3. To present an instructional design and delivery framework for blended learning, drawing on the lessons learned from the course experiments described in this chapter, which will offer a practical guide on how to design and deliver a blended course, addressing the responsibilities of course designers and instructors

## BACKGROUND

## Trends and Current Practice in Blended Learning

The Bologna process has supported a strong drive toward the adoption of e-learning developments across Europe through the emphasis on student mobility and the complementary expertise of institutions in delivering education (EADTU, 2004). Most standard instructional practices in universities across Europe now involve a mixture of traditional and online instructional approaches, such as the blending of resources and location, and mixtures of face-to-face and online learning activities (Rothery, Dorup, & Cadewener, 2006).

Within the United Kingdom, e-learning developments have become synonymous with the deployment of virtual learning environments (VLEs) as institutional platforms and enterprise-wide learning systems. A joint JISC-UCISA[1] study (Joint Information Systems Committee-Universities and Colleges Information Systems Association) recently reported that 95% of HE institutions now use such a system to deliver teaching to campus-based and distance learners (JISC, 2005). In recent years, we have witnessed the emergence of enterprise-wide learning systems such as Blackboard™ and WebCT™ (Intrallect, 2004), supporting online activity for an ever-

increasing number of campus-based students. The JISC report of 2005 noted that 20% of new universities in the United Kingdom[2] now support an excess of 20,000 active users on their institutional VLEs. Whilst we may question the scale of deployment of these learning systems and the range of activities that are supported online, the figures do suggest that e-learning is becoming an accepted and established component of the learning experience for campus-based students within higher education. In parallel, we observe a growing interest in companies applying e-learning approaches within so-called corporate universities, and this is often linked to knowledge management approaches (Baets, Browaeys, & Walker, 2001; Baets & Van der Linden, 2003).

The case for e-learning at an institutional level appears to be well established, but to what extent has the introduction of technology transformed the way that students learn and established new pedagogic approaches? The evidence suggests that the drivers for e-learning have been top-down, with pedagogic changes much slower to evolve. Current practice in the use of technology appears still to be wedded to traditional pedagogic models. Sharpe, Benfield, Roberts, and Francis (2006), in their study of the undergraduate experience of blended e-learning within UK higher education institutions, found that the most common type of blended learning is "the provision of supplementary resources for courses that are conducted predominantly along traditional lines through an institutionally supported virtual learning environment" (p. 2).

Sharpe et al. (2006) found "far fewer impressive examples of transformative course level practices underpinned by radical course designs" (p. 2). This finding has been replicated in other studies (Bricheno, Higgison, & Weedon, 2004; Browne, Jenkins, & Walker, 2006; Garrett & Verbik, 2004; Hara & Kling, 2000), where online learning has been commonly used by instructors as a supplement to teacher-centred curricula rather than as a means to introduce new methods of learning that empower the student. The mere introduction of technological features to course design will not ensure that effective communication and community-based interaction will take place. While the attributes of networks enable significant advantages for human communication, they are not a guarantee (Clark, 1994; Harasim, 1993). Much will depend on the course design and type of activities to be performed online, as well as the individual characteristics of learners and instructors, such as their backgrounds and attitudes.

The evidence suggests that the embedding of e-learning practices across higher education institutions is yet to have a significant impact in changing the instructor's role. Indeed the JISC survey (2005) reinforces this picture, with respondents indicating that access to resources and course materials continues to account for the greatest use of institutional VLEs. As Browne et al. (2006) note, though, it is not really surprising that the transformative impact of centrally managed VLE systems has yet to be realised: The institutional adoption and deployment of systems is far easier to implement than the cultural changes in the way that teaching and learning activities are delivered.

## REVIEW OF LITERATURE: DEFINITIONS OF BLENDED LEARNING AND GUIDANCE ON INSTRUCTIONAL DESIGN

Technological changes appear to have run ahead of pedagogic development, and a symptom of this trend has been the slow development of instructional design frameworks to embrace this way of teaching and learning. The existence of so many names (hybrid, blended, and mixed-mode instruction) for the combination of class-based and computer-mediated learning indeed reflects the absence of a dominant model for course design and delivery (Dziuban, Hartman, & Moskal, 2004).

In fact, blended learning as a term has been around for a long time, and has been used to describe the mixing of delivery methods to students (distance and face to face, face to face and independent learning) as well as the combination of face-to-face instruction with various types of nonclassroom technology-mediated delivery (e.g., instructional television). In its current guise, blended learning is most commonly associated with the combination of face-to-face and fully online components of a course (Rooney, 2003; Young, 2002), yet the term has also been used to describe the combination of media and tools employed in an e-learning environment, as well as the combination of a number of pedagogic approaches within one course design, irrespective of learning technology use (Driscoll, 2002; Oliver & Trigwell, 2005). Sharpe et al. (2006) have indeed identified eight dimensions in which learning may be blended, encompassing "delivery mode, technology, chronology, locus, roles, pedagogy, focus and direction" (p. 21).

Such diverse interpretations underline the confused understanding that we share toward blended learning as a pedagogic concept. However, the lack of definition has provided the potential for practitioners to explore the reconceptualisation of instructional methods using technology, in particular the shift in emphasis from teacher-centred to student-centred learning paradigms (Barr & Tagg, 1995). Accompanying this trend have been increasing interest in theories of learning such as social constructivism and collaborative models of teaching and learning, which have been associated with an educational transformation or paradigm shift (Baets & Van der Linden, 2000, 2003; Dziuban et al., 2004). From this perspective, the introduction of online learning to campus-based teaching may offer us the potential to transform the way that students learn, shifting the emphasis from lecture-driven to student-centred instruction, and enabling students to become socially active and interactive learners (Collis, Bruijstens, van der Veen, 2003). Learning is the product of a cooperative learning experience rather than provided knowledge to be systematically applied by students.

This chimes with our conception of blended learning (Walker & Baets, 2000, 2002) and the need for pedagogical redesign with students recast in the role of socially active and collaborative learners so that they are engaged in sense making through internal reflection and external dialogue in both formal and informal learning activities. The acknowledgement of prior experience and the connection between tacit knowing and explicit knowledge are important features of this approach, with dialogue central to making knowledge explicit. We may therefore define blended learning as representing the combination of class-based and virtual learning, where the virtual learning space is used to represent a medium for idea sharing and knowledge building. In this way, technology is employed to support a learner-centred instructional model in which students solicit and share knowledge while developing common ground with their peers and instructor.

Table 1 offers a representation of instructional approaches and a means by which we may posi-tion our interpretation of blended learning. The approaches on the left-hand side of the table (instructional information processing and in-structional behaviourism) are compatible with e-teaching methods in our estimation. The process of instruction is directed toward the presentation of knowledge in such a way that it can be accurately acquired and reproduced. Our vision is based on the use of technology to support discourse among learners, with learning constructed relative to a social context (Winn, 1993). This is best captured by the social constructivist philosophy, which may inform the way that we design virtual spaces, as reflected by the right-hand column of Table 1.

We envisage students using their virtual space to negotiate meaning, share ideas and experiences, collect information, and solve problems. There is a wide variety of tools available to support this activity, from Web 2.0 tools such as wikis and blogs to discussion boards. Collaborative tools indeed support participant models of contact and interaction, enabling groups of students to construct their own sense of meaning (Aram & Noble, 1999).

*Table 1. Instructional approaches and their consequences for e-learning*

|  | Instructional Information Processing | Instructional Behaviourism | Personal Constructivism | Social Constructivism |
|---|---|---|---|---|
| Philosophy | Knowledge as reproduced cognition | Knowledge as modified behaviour | Knowledge as personally constructed meaning | Knowledge as socially constructed meaning |
| How to Learn? | Learning is processing information (computer metaphor) | Learning is a response to stimulus | Learning is experiencing and reflecting autonomously | Learning is experiencing and reflecting relative to a social context |
| Electronic Support | *E-Teaching:* Classroom-based learning environments (virtual classrooms, videoconferencing)<br><br>Technologies used as tools in support of classroom activities | *E-Teaching:* Web-assisted instruction (computer-aided instruction environments) | *E-Learning:* Set of manageable content-rich tools (e.g., simulations, microworlds) | *E-Learning:* Set of manageable, content-rich tools and knowledge-sharing and collaboration tools (e.g., wikis, blogs, forums) |

## Implications for Instruction

We have described a transformational model of instructional design that is at odds with e-teaching methods and the use of Web technology to disseminate information to students. The potential of blended learning is employed instead to deliver a variation in the experience of the learner, with the computer-mediated component of a blended course enabling students to experience a different way of learning that is self-directed rather than instructor driven (Oliver & Trigwell, 2005). This brings with it new responsibilities for the instructor, who becomes a facilitator and participant in a sense-making process for the online activity, committed to producing learning rather than delivering instruction (Barr & Tagg, 1995). For collaborative learning models, this may require the instructor to play an active role online, engaging as a participant in a many-to-many rather than one-to-many communication process.

The challenge arises as to how to structure learning in this way, and to this end, the literature is largely silent. Perhaps too much attention has been drawn to Gilly Salmon's (2000b) five-stage model of teaching and learning online as a framework for online learning in higher education. Whilst useful as a design model for e-moderated course delivery and a guide for e-moderators to support student engagement and learning online, it is not appropriate to serve as a template for blended learning. In our estimation, it represents a linear model of learning, driving students through progressive stages of group work. Indeed, as Moule (2007) observes, the model does not address the use of e-learning as part of an integrated approach that includes face-to-face delivery. Her own e-learning ladder offers a different way of conceptualising e-learning activity through a combination of instructivist and constructivist learning approaches. Whilst valuable as a conceptual model, this does not address course design issues, notably the structuring and presentation

of the virtual learning environment to students and its integration with class-based learning, nor does it address the challenges in guiding students through the transformation from traditional to learner-centred curriculum design, notably the cultural shift in relationships between learner and instructor bringing with it greater involvement and responsibility for the learner. In short, there is a lack of guidance on how we design for blended learning and address approaches to the way we integrate online and class-based learning for campus-based students.

With these issues in mind, we have embarked on a series of course experiments that focus on learner-centred models for blended learning and the effective combination of face-to-face and online learning components with the aim of teasing out the key instructional responsibilities bound up with this approach.

## RESEARCH REVIEW: CASE STUDY ACCOUNTS OF BLENDED LEARNING

## Introduction

In this section, we report on a series of blended course experiments that were conducted at Nyenrode Business University, The Netherlands, and Euromed Marseille Ecole de Management, France. Our research was based on the introduction of an e-learning component to established management courses with the aim of transforming the instructional process by fostering learner-centred activity, supported through the use of e-learning tools. The course experiments were devised for master's in management and MBA students, combining class-based teaching with the use of a VLE and associated e-learning tools for the Nyenrode students, and the use of wiki and blog technology for the Euromed students.

## Institutional Contexts and Drivers for E-Learning

Nyenrode Business University remains the only private university in The Netherlands and was the first business school to be established in the country. Nyenrode offers a wide range of degree programmes for management students, including the full-time international MBA (IMBA) and international modular MBA (IMMBA) programmes, and a part-time accountancy programme (PDCO). The majority of students following these programmes hold middle-management positions, with several years work experience, and expect to present and reflect on their work experiences in class. There is a strong emphasis on experiential learning: the critical reflection on work-based practices combined with the social role of learning in exchanging insights and building knowledge through collaborative activities. Consequently, the application of online activities that promote reflection and knowledge sharing have been judged to be appropriate for this group of students and applicable to the class-based and preparatory (off-campus) phases of their learning (Walker, 2003).

Euromed Marseille Ecole de Management is a French grande ecole (business school) and offers a wide range of academic programmes, meeting the needs of undergraduate, graduate, and executive students. The teaching approach has two key dimensions focusing on the strategic challenges that companies face today and on the application of a project-based pedagogical model. The school offers a range of programmes including a generalist master's in management degree (ESC programme, Diplome de Grande Ecole), a number of MS programmes, and specialised master's degrees (recognised by the Conference des Grandes Ecoles). The programmes each share high academic standards with a strong multicultural focus (the Euromed Marseille dimension) and an emphasis on professional expertise.

We may draw parallels between the two institutions in terms of the work experience and profile of the students attending these schools, and the pedagogy they are exposed to, which focuses on the transfer of knowledge, education, and development through a competence-oriented instructional approach. In our estimation, students are therefore open to the introduction of active learning methods, with a particular emphasis on internal reflection on individual experiences and work practices, and collaborative knowledge building based on the sharing of these experiences and formulation of conceptual knowledge (Baets & Van der Linden, 2000). These activities may indeed be supported by the introduction of an e-learning component that represents the focus of the course experiments described below.

## Experimental Design & Blended Models

For the experimental phase of our research, we selected five courses at Nyenrode and two from Euromed Marseille that were redesigned to support a blended delivery approach. The online component of each of these courses was designed around a learner-centred instructional model, placing much of the control of the content and pace of learning in the hands of the students, not the instructor—a marked shift in the learning process. Students were encouraged to become part of the knowledge creation process, with the instructor serving as a mediator rather than a dictator of the learning process for the online component of the course. The e-learning models employed in these course experiments reflected a range of tools that were intended to support individual knowledge building and collaborative learning activities, in line with the learner-centred principles that were identified for these courses. Jonassen's (1996) classification of "mindtools" was helpful in guiding us in the tool selection process for each model.

247

## Model 1: Group-Based Discussion

In Model 1, we introduced conversation tools to support a simple discourse approach for student learning. These tools were intended to be used by students to support work-based and collaborative group discussion on organisational case examples related to information systems management. Students following the Nyenrode IMMBA course on management information systems (MIS) were presented with a combination of synchronous and asynchronous communication tools (group chat box and discussion forum). These tools were intended to support pair and group-based discussion and collaborative learning in the performance of a series of preparatory assignments that introduced students to foundation concepts for the course prior to the face-to-face seminars on campus. For the course entitled Complexity and the Networked Economy, Euromed master's in management students were presented with a group blog tool[3] that was used by students to prepare weekly assignments. Students recorded their assignment discussions online prior to the submission of a hard copy to the course instructor.

## Model 2: Knowledge Sharing and Discussion

In Model 2, we experimented with a combination of conversation and knowledge construction tools to support the processes of discussion and knowledge building between students. The Nyenrode IMBA students were presented with a discussion board and digital archive, which they were encouraged to use to publish group presentations and case reports, and engage in critical discussion on their work beyond the physical classroom. Euromed students of the master's in management programme were presented with a wiki tool[4] that was intended to be used as a forum for weekly discussion on aspects of the Euro-Mediterranean management approach and a location for collaborative writing on these themes. The

pedagogical aim was to foster a learning-by-doing approach by engaging students in the cocreation of understanding through their discussion and writing activities.

## Model 3: Knowledge Acquisition, Communication, and Discussion

This model represented a further extension of the discussion and knowledge-building activities described in Model 2. Nyenrode IMMBA students and participants following the PDCO accountancy programme were presented with communication and knowledge-sharing tools in the form of discussion boards, synchronous discussion tools (e.g., chat boxes), and a digital archive for group work and plenary usage. In addition to this, students were also presented with information resources in the form of a virtual library of hypertext-linked management concepts, which covered the knowledge base for the course. The tools were used to support individual and group-based research tasks, in line with an active learning approach.

The e-learning models and experimental courses are summarised in Table 2.

## Research Approach

We selected an exploratory case-study design (Robson, 1993; Yin, 1993) in order to research the experiences of the participants following the experimental courses. The study aimed at revealing student attitudes toward the blended delivery methods (virtual and class-based learning modes). The investigation also considered the contribution of the e-learning tools and course design model to student learning: to what extent the tools and resources added value to their learning experiences. Student perceptions of the blended learning experience were recorded using a combination of questionnaires, interviews, and activity logs.

*Table 2. E-learning models for the course experiments*

| Model 1 | Model 2 | Model 3 |
|---|---|---|
| **Group-Based Discussion** | **Knowledge Sharing and Discussion** | **Knowledge Acquisition, Communication, and Discussion** |
| *Tools supporting collaborative learning for individuals working within study groups. Nyenrode students used a combination of forums and chat boxes to complete group-based discussion activities. EuroMed students used group blog tools.* | *Tools supporting knowledge sharing via the uploading of group and individual work to the environment. Nyenrode students used group and plenary discussion boards to post feedback and discuss assignments and course issues. Documents were uploaded via a digital archive. EuroMed students used group wiki tools.* | *Tools supporting knowledge acquisition, knowledge building, and collaborative discussion activities. Nyenrode students used a virtual library of management concepts, group and plenary bulletin boards, NetMeeting tools, and a digital archive hosted within a VLE.* |
| **Management Information Systems IMMBA (Nyenrode)** | **International Money & Finance IMBA (Nyenrode)** | **Management Information Systems IMMBA (Nyenrode)** |
| Work-based discussion and collaboration activities | Group-based research assignments | Work-based discussion, collaboration and knowledge-building activities |
| **Complexity & Networked Economy: Master's in Management (Euromed)** | **Business Ethics IMBA (Nyenrode)** | **Information Management PDCO (Nyenrode)** |
| | Case-based discussion on ethical dilemmas | Work-based discussion, collaboration and knowledge-building activities |
| Group-based discussion | **Euro-Mediterranean Management Approach (Euromed)** | |
| | Group-based knowledge building | |

## Outcomes from the Course Experiments

### Model 1: Group-Based Discussion

Nyenrode IMMBA students following the MIS course recorded mixed responses to the use of e-tools. By the end of the course, 60% of participants believed that the e-learning approach contributed to higher levels of collaborative learning and idea sharing amongst students via the pair-work and group activities compared to traditional group-work activities they had experienced in the IMMBA study programme. Students highlighted, though, the technical problems in using synchronous chat tools effectively, and remarked on the discontinuity between the e-learning work and the class sessions in terms of the way that the course was presented to students. The two phases dealt with "different subjects" with the online preparatory work "not used during class sessions."

For Complexity and Networked Economy, Euromed students were presented with a group blog tool for the first time and were encouraged to use it to support group work over a 3-month period. Whilst the output from the blogs reflected some interesting and valuable discussions, the participation rate in terms of individual contributors remained rather low. Over the period of the course, we recorded 70 active contributors out of a cohort of 300 students. Student feedback was mixed over the use of the blog tool, with a third of the cohort valuing the opportunity to negotiate their understanding of the concepts of the course. However, the majority of participants remained unconvinced with this approach, which represented a departure from established study patterns within their programme of study.

## Model 2: Knowledge Sharing and Discussion

Nyenrode students following the International Money and Finance course and Business Ethics module responded in similar ways to the virtual tools in their postcourse feedback. The tools offered groups the opportunity to publish their reports and cases within an open forum, and invited feedback and multiple perspectives on their work. The participation of the instructor in providing feedback online was particularly welcomed, but students remarked that the quality of contributions from peers could not be guaranteed and that the level of interaction online was not evenly distributed across the class. This frustrated some students, as evidenced in the survey response of one Business Ethics participant: "The responses for the individual cases were quite varied, with some cases receiving no responses and others receiving six replies. It was difficult to distribute the comments evenly. Some students really wanted feedback but didn't get it."

For the Euro-Mediterranean Management Approach course, wiki usage was monitored over a 4-month period, which was deemed to be a sufficient period for groups to generate a virtual community of practice. We noted that out of a cohort of 300 students and 60 groups, 18 groups adopted the wiki to produce reports of excellent quality, 30 wiki sites were good, and 12 were unsatisfactory. Through the interview feedback, students revealed that while the technical functionalities of the wikis were easy to master, they encountered greater challenges in managing the collaborative group-work processes, which required them to publish work directly on to the wiki and edit the work of others. One group reverted to traditional study methods rather than engage with the wiki: "We do not manage to work directly

on the wiki. We have to meet two or three times a week to discuss work." Contrary to the aims of the course, participants perceived the wiki as a public place for publishing rather than drafting work: "We have not published our interpretation because it is not completely finished, and we prefer to wait....We don't want to be assessed on incomplete work." Students also struggled with the virtual cocreation of their work, which was visible to the other groups following this course, and some groups refused to present their work in progress through fear of plagiarism: "Why work for others?"

## Model 3: Knowledge Acquisition, Communication, and Discussion

Nyenrode students following the MIS course encountered communication, knowledge-sharing tools, and online information resources for the first time in their MBA programme. In their postcourse feedback, they highlighted the convenience of accessing resources in one central place, the virtual environment, which was easily accessible. Technical problems, however, hampered the use of the synchronous communication tools, and students felt that the workload and time investment to engage in collaborative tasks online outweighed the benefits of this study approach: "The collaboration was primarily based on sharing the workload, not sharing ideas." Interestingly, we observed that some students set up their own free shareware to exchange documents and opinions on the course in parallel to the official course environment, illustrating their willingness to use collaborative tools to support their learning.

PDCO students noted that their work commitments got in the way of their study time, restricting what they could do in terms of exploring the contents of the hypertext library, digital archive, and other information resources contained within the environment. They felt that the e-learning opportunities were not fully exploited in this course and opted for traditional media (e-mail and telephone) to support peer discussion activities: "At the beginning the site was used, but later everyone reverted to email. Interaction was not really there within the website." Another student commented, "If the virtual approach were compulsory, things would work better. You have to force students to use the platform, otherwise they will choose other ways of working."

## Summary of Findings

Reviewing the evidence from the experimental courses, there appears to be no automatic link between the introduction of e-learning tools and the adoption of active learning strategies as we had posited at the outset of these experiments. The combination of virtual and class-based methods by itself does not appear to motivate students to take control over their own learning or to actively engage learners in knowledge building and experience sharing. Nyenrode students identified the poor technical performance of the synchronous chat tools as an obstacle to effective communication. More generally, they pointed to the time investment that was necessary to master the collaborative tools and employ them in effective collaborative activities. We also observed that the introduction of tools such as the group wiki presented challenges to working patterns that had been established during the study programme, with some groups of Euromed students struggling to come to terms with a new learning approach. As a general rule, we observed that students needed to be triggered into the adoption of e-tools for formal learning activities and required support to master the competencies governing effective collaboration online.

However, it would be wrong to discount altogether the potential of blended study methods to support learner-centred outcomes and complementary knowledge-building processes. The e-tools helped students to reflect on their individual work experiences and make effective use of their tacit knowledge in knowledge-shar-

ing and knowledge-building tasks. The mixed reception of these methods reinforces the view that the learning conditions and instructional responsibilities for formal study activities need to be carefully managed by course instructors, with attention paid to the engagement of students with the online activities. In the final part of this chapter, we therefore sum up the instructional responsibilities that appear to be central to the effective delivery of a blended course.

## INSTRUCTIONAL DESIGN FRAMEWORK FOR BLENDED LEARNING

Reviewing the feedback from the experimental courses, we observed a number of issues that students identified as being important to their learning and central to effective knowledge building and sharing. Drawing together the lessons learned and referencing them where possible to the emerging research literature in this area, we propose a framework of responsibilities that appear significant to the design and delivery of a blended course. This represents an updated version of the findings presented for our experiments at Nyenrode (Walker, 2003, 2005), taking account of the combined experiences and reflections of students at both Nyenrode and Euromed Marseille.

We focus here on the actions of the instructor, and how the presentation of virtual tools to students may influence adoption patterns. This involves a discussion on the presentation of the instructional setting to participants and its management by the instructor. The instructional setting is an all-inclusive term, covering the presentation of the blended course design, study methods, and learning environment to individuals. Our framework of instructional responsibilities also focuses on the management of the learning process: the actions by which the instructor facilitates individual learning from the early stages right through to the end of the cycle.

The instructional responsibilities that we have identified may be grouped into the following categories. The categories represent five distinct phases in the design and delivery of a blended learning pathway.

a.  **Preparing the blended learning pathway (design phase):** This involves establishing the pedagogical process and aligning the pedagogical objectives with the delivery methods. It also requires integrating the virtual and class-based components within one learning design, and developing a suitable assessment policy that matches the new learning approach and acts as a driver for student participation online (pedagogic).

b.  **Socialising learners (start of the learning pathway):** Here the instructor should prepare students to conduct their learning online by articulating the rationale, goals, and benefits of the blended approach. Modeling and inducting students in new learning activities, and addressing technology and new study patterns will help with the cultural shift in learning (attitudinal, technical, learning variables).

c.  **Supporting online participation (early stages):** This requires establishing a virtual presence online and a framework of support, feedback, and activity for course participants. Also important is making connections between the virtual and class-based learning components, and reflecting on a holistic approach to student learning (technical, pedagogical, and learning variables).

d.  **Sustaining online interaction (later stages):** Sustaining interaction involves supporting individuals in their online activities, especially knowledge sharing and knowledge building. Student participation online can be motivated through extrinsic benefits and assessment drivers (technical, pedagogical, motivational variables).

e.  **Summing up the learning outcomes (end of the learning trajectory):** Here we identify the lessons learned, emphasising the link between the virtual and class-based phases of the learning (pedagogical and learning variables).

## Preparing of the Blended Learning Pathway: Design Phase

In this design phase, the instructor should establish the pedagogical vision for the learning trajectory, identifying the objectives and targeted learning behaviour. These decisions should then determine the choice of study activities and the selection of e-learning tools that will be used in the learning design. At this stage, it is important to take account of the profile of students and the technical and learning competencies that they will need to master to ensure that the learning design is practical. As previous research has shown, student characteristics will influence the nature and extent of online participation and activity (Hwang & Wang, 2004; Rovai, 2002).

The alignment of the tools with the tasks and learning objectives is of particular importance. Critics in the experimental courses commented on the artificiality of the interaction online, saying that the medium of virtual communication was not really essential for the performance of the coursework and fulfillment of the targeted online learning activities. As one campus-based student following the International Money and Finance course remarked, "The website forces people to communicate. It's just a shift of communication medium, and in fact, a less interactive one." This suggests that the design of the experimental courses and particularly the learning activities could have been strengthened in order to link them more closely with the use of the asynchronous communication tools. From a user's perspective, the effectiveness of the tools and the virtual approach appear related to their fitness for purpose: their alignment with the targeted learning processes

(Chee, 2002; Collis, 1995; Leidner & Jarvenpaa, 1995). Indeed, as the MIS course (Model 3) demonstrated, where students are unconvinced by the match-up between the learning activities and online environment, they may introduce their own tools to support collaborative learning activities, a practice that is consistent with the profile of Net Generation students (Oblinger & Oblinger, 2005) and one that we may expect to grow in years to come. Another key responsibility is to establish an assessment policy that will complement the course and act as a driver for student participation online, a priority identified in previous studies (Gerbic, 2006; Laurillard, 2002; Ramsden, 2003) and a recurring theme in student feedback from the experimental courses. Note the comments from PDCO students (Model 3) on this theme: "If you want people to use the tools—make it obligatory to upload documents." According to another, "Stimulate interactiveness more or make it a necessity. Force people to use it—then it will be a real innovative learning."

## Socialising Learners (Start of the Learning Pathway)

In this opening phase of the course, the instructor should focus on the effective presentation of the new study methods and tools to students. The evidence suggests that the instructor's presentation methods and teaching style will influence attitudes within the class toward the learning tools, a finding consistent with previous studies (Webster & Hackley, 1997). A common finding from the experimental courses was that participants received only a limited orientation from the instructor on the e-learning study methods to be used. Based on the interview feedback, respondents highlighted a range of factors that indicated they were not properly prepared to embrace e-learning methods. Here we refer to affective issues such as the reasons for adopting a new way of learning, the rationale for a new course design using e-learning, and its

introduction so late within the study programme. MIS participants noted the following.

*"The biggest weakness of the class was the lack of expectation setting before the whole concept was introduced."*

*"[The VLE] can be an effective way of delivering management education, but you can't just put it in front of a group and expect them to accept it fully."*

*"The design needs to compensate for the resistance that some students have toward using certain computer technology, such as groupware."*

This finding has been replicated in other studies (Armatas, Holt, & Rice, 2003) where student expectations are related to traditional teaching approaches, and students are not disposed to embrace online learning activities without clear articulation of the benefits of working in this way.

We also observed a technical barrier to the adoption of the virtual tools. Some participants encountered problems using the synchronous chat tools effectively. This finding suggests that new users need time to familiarise themselves with the virtual tools. In particular, we refer here to first-time users (IT novices) who require the space to develop the technical skills to function effectively online, a conclusion drawn in other studies of virtual learning (e.g., Hara & Kling, 2000; Mason, 1998; Renzi & Klobas, 2000). The evidence from the courses suggests that user friendliness and accessibility for computer tools are important determinants of learning effectiveness, particularly regarding IT novices' affective reaction to virtual learning, a finding replicated in previous studies (Hiltz, 1993; Webster & Hackley, 1997).

Other participants appeared to lack the requisite learning skills and competencies to work effectively online. They appeared unaware of how to get the best out of the discussion forum as a communication medium: to relate their postings to other comments online and build a discussion thread. The wiki experiment indeed highlighted the unwillingness of students to engage in the virtual cocreation of work; they were reluctant to edit and construct reports using a common tool with group leaders exercising control over individual contributions. As one group leader noted, "I prefer that the others send me their work or their comment before that I put them online. It allows me to check the content. And often I must start again." This comment reflects a lack of trust and awareness of how to work in this way, and we indeed observed some students reverting to traditional study methods (face-to-face meetings) while others opted out of the group activity altogether. This finding concurs with the research of Salmon (2000a) and Knoll and Jarvenpaa (1995), who have argued that users need time at the beginning of a course to learn how to work collaboratively online before tackling content-related activities. Turoff (1989) has indeed argued for users to receive grounding in netiquette for communication and expression online prior to commencing virtual learning activities. Turoff sets out a four-stage competency model, focusing on key competencies such as learning system mechanics, learning how to communicate, learning how to work electronically within a group, and learning how to adapt and develop the system to maximise utility.

Beyond these motivational and technical concerns, the evidence from the experimental courses suggests that students need to generate a common sense of purpose in order to work collaboratively online. This sense of shared purpose is difficult to achieve when students are accustomed to traditional study methods (Collis & Moonen, 2001; Molesworth, 2004). Indeed, as the results from the Euromed Management Approach course demonstrated, even when participants are familiar with the technical concerns related to online collaboration, there is no automatic trend toward the adoption of virtual learning methods. Users need time to recognise virtual learning

environments as spaces for ideas and information sharing and the adoption of collaborative work patterns. Jarvenpaa, Knoll, and Leidner (1998) emphasise the need for students to build new social relationships and trust for online learning. The sense of "common ground" (Preece, 2000) or shared purpose also requires a collective commitment from participants to invest time and effort in this way of learning. Levin, Kim, and Riel (1990) describe this dynamic as a shared sense of responsibility to the online group, a key factor in the successful functioning of a network community. Evidence from the experimental courses suggests that this might be easier to establish at the beginning of the programme of study rather than at a later stage for one specific course. Renzi and Klobas (2002) have demonstrated how this might be achieved by organising face-to-face activities prior to the commencement of virtual activities, which helps students to develop skills for participation and engagement in community building. They also argue for the inclusion of community building activities among the initial online course exercises.

## Supporting Online Participation: Early Stages

Based on the feedback from the experimental courses, participants require a degree of guidance and support in the early stages of an online learning experience. The virtual presence of the instructor and tutors is important in this respect in welcoming students to the online space, providing a framework of support and establishing a culture of activity that will engage them. We observed from the course experiments that the instructor could elicit contributions by pushing students to respond to comments within the online forum. The instructor could also play a proactive role by modeling targeted learning behaviour online (e.g., by posting new discussion themes, responding or referring to postings online, integrating student responses, etc.). There is indeed an extensive list of studies advocating intervention by course instructors along these lines, that is, a managed process of teaching and learning, establishing study norms for online learning (e.g., Collis, 1996; Renzi & Klobas, 2000; Salmon & Giles, 1997). The evidence suggests that structured discussion activities will lead to higher levels of complex and critical thinking by course participants (Aviv, Erlich, Ravid, & Geva, 2003).

During the startup phase of the learning activities, students may require technical support and guidance on the collaborative processes in conducting their work online. Another key responsibility for the instructor at this stage is to make explicit the links between the virtual and face-to-face components of the course so that students understand the interrelationships between the learning activities they are engaging in and receive a holistic picture of the learning process. Feedback from students following the MIS course in particular highlighted the disconnection between the e-learning and class-based sessions, which impacted their acceptance of the learning activities. We conclude from this that the relationship between the learning activities taking place within the physical and virtual domains needs to be recognised and referred to at an early stage in the course, with procedural feedback directed to course participants over the duration of the course.

## Sustaining Online Interaction: Later Stages

In the later stages of the experimental courses, we noted a greater degree of confidence from students, who required less support in the performance of their online activities. The visibility of the instructor online appeared to be less important, a finding consistent with previous studies of virtual courses (e.g., Nixon & Salmon, 1995). However, we observed that the course instructor still needed to remain vigilant, monitoring the learning processes online and ensuring that the

interest of students in the course was maintained. For instance, Nyenrode students following the International Money and Finance course remarked on the lack of significant pull factors to use the virtual environment and e-learning tools. Individuals noted that they would have been more interested in visiting the site if there had been new articles and resources included on the site, which could add value to their learning. This finding is consistent with published research on high-ability students, who are believed to benefit from pull-based learning (Bovy, 1981). Respondents also noted that there was no extrinsic reward or recognition for active participation online, that is, discussing and responding to the comments of others, or referring to these comments when completing feedback obligations. The assessment policy was directed toward evaluation comments that could be delivered on a one-shot basis. A change in assessment policy might have stimulated greater online interaction between students, a conclusion reached by students following the Business Ethics course, as evidenced in the following survey response: "There should be some form of data regulation, so participation is part of your grade. This would encourage more interaction. The professor could force this." Aligning the assessment policy with targeted learning behaviour is therefore important in this respect and in encouraging students to participate online. This appears to limit the scope for opting out, motivating students to meet the participation requirements for the course (Johnson & Howell, 2005).

## Summing up the Learning Outcomes: End of the Learning Trajectory

Participants agreed that there should be a significant concluding phase to blended study trajectories. They expected the instructor to identify the key outcomes of the class-based and virtual learning, tying together the loose ends of the learning experience. This was found to be important in two respects: The summing-up process would help to present a coherent learning experience to participants whilst emphasising the complementary nature of the virtual and class-based learning processes. In this way, the final class sessions could reinforce the lessons learned from the virtual phase of the course. Outstanding issues from these assignments could be dealt with in the final class sessions, with the instructor providing feedback on the research and collaborative learning activities. Students would therefore complete the course with a clear understanding of the learning outcomes and the relationship between the virtual and class-based learning processes.

## CONCLUSION

In this chapter, we have set out an interpretation of blended learning that is directed toward the use of e-learning tools to support a transformational approach to instructional design, with a focus on student-centred learning activity. The course experiments conducted at Nyenrode Business University and Euromed Marseille were designed with this approach in mind using a variety of e-learning tools and models to support knowledge building and discourse amongst communities of learners. The experiments represent first steps in the design of learner-centred courses, and serve as contributions to the emerging research literature in this area. Whilst the experiments highlight limitations in the adoption of the targeted study methods by students, the feedback we have gathered from students reveals a range of variables that may influence the reception of blended course design and delivery methods. Central to the acceptance of active learning methods by students appears to be a necessary shift in mind-set, with students assuming ownership and responsibility for the virtual spaces in which they conduct their learning, and the instructor facilitating the learning activities and drawing together the outcomes

from the online and face-to-face components of the course.

The instructional framework for blended learning represents the key finding from our course experiments based on our observations and the accumulated feedback from management students from two international business schools, which we have referenced against the research literature. We present these results as a preliminary pedagogical framework for course instructors in higher education who wish to deliver blended courses, and the framework is intended to be used as a guide for design approaches that enhance the student learning experience. We recognise, though, that empirical tests are required to verify the significance of the variables we have identified, with testing applied to different disciplinary domains.

## FUTURE RESEARCH DIRECTIONS

Drawing on the lessons learned from these experiments, we identify three possible research directions.

1.  Further research is required on the suitability of blended course design within different educational domains. Does the subject matter influence student responses to a blended course offering, and how significant is the student profile in responding to this way of learning? It is also worth considering the extent to which blended methods and the learner-centred approach may be applied to adult and school education, as well as to formal and informal educational settings.
2.  With the emergence of the Net Generation, scope arises for further studies of the way in which students use e-tools to conduct their learning. In particular, we refer here to research on how students make use of their own technology and blend informal learning methods with the formal tools that are

provided for them to drive individual and collaborative learning, and how this relates to the class-based learning experience. It would be helpful to have a wider experience base, describing the ways in which students navigate between informal and formal learning spaces.

3.  Eventually, research should be undertaken with completely blended programmes of study, where the researched approach is the design principle for the entire curriculum. As argued earlier in the chapter, most academic institutions are not yet ready for that due to the cultural challenges in transforming established teaching and learning practices. However, a completely hybrid learning format might and should resolve a number of the hurdles suggested by the students. The launch and follow-up of such a blended learner-centred degree programme is most certainly an interesting research project for the future.

## REFERENCES

Aram, E., & Noble, D. (1990). Educating prospective managers in the complexity of organizational life. *Management Learning, 30*(3), 321-342.

Armatas, C., Holt, D., & Rice, M. (2003). Impacts of an online-supported resources-based learning environment: Does one size fit all? *Distance Education, 24*(2), 141-158.

Aviv, R., Erlich, Z., Ravid, G., & Geva, A. (2003). Network analysis of knowledge construction in asynchronous learning networks. *Journal of Asynchronous Learning Networks, 7*(3). Retrieved March 10, 2007, from http://www.sloan-c.org/publications/jaln/v7n3/index.asp

Baets, W., Browaeys, M., & Walker, R. (2001). *ADAGIO: A methodology for designing corporate virtual universities.* Breukelen, The Netherlands: Nyenrode University Press.

Baets, W., & Van der Linden, G. (2000). *The hybrid business school: Developing knowledge management through management learning.* Amsterdam: Prentice Hall.

Baets, W., & Van der Linden, G. (2003). *Virtual corporate universities: A matrix of knowledge and learning for the new digital dawn.* Boston: Kluwer Academic.

Barr, R., & Tagg, J. (1995). From teaching to learning: A new paradigm for undergraduate education. *Change, 27*(6), 13-25.

Bricheno, P., Higgison, C., & Weedon, E. (2004). *The impact of networked learning on education institutions.* Bradford, United Kingdom: UHI Millennium Institute & Bradford University, INLEI Project. Retrieved March 17, 2007, from http://www.sfeuprojects.org.uk/inlei/Final_Report.pdf

Browne, T., Jenkins, M., & Walker, R. (2006). A longitudinal perspective regarding the use of VLEs by higher education institutions in the United Kingdom. *Interactive Learning Environments, 14*(2), 177-192.

Bovy, R. (1981). Successful instructional methods: A cognitive information processing approach. *ECTJ, 29*(4), 203-217.

Chee, Y. (2002). Refocusing learning on pedagogy in a connected world. *On The Horizon, 10*(4), 7-13.

Clark, R. (1994). Media will never influence learning. *Educational Technology Research & Development, 42*(2), 1042-1069.

Collis, B. (1996). *Telelearning in a digital world: The future of distance learning.* London: International Thomson Computer Press.

Collis, B., Bruijstens, H., & van der Veen, J. K. (2003). Course redesign for blended learning: Modern optics for technical professionals. *International Journal of Continuing Engineering Education and Lifelong Learning, 13*(1/2), 22-38.

Collis, B., & Moonen, J. (2001). *Flexible learning in a digital world.* London: Kogan Page.

Driscoll, M. (2002, March 1). Blended learning: Let's get beyond the hype. *LTI Newsline.* Retrieved March 20, 2007, from http://www.lti-magazine.com/ltimagazine/article/articleDetail.jsp?id=11755

Dziuban, C., Hartman, J., & Moskal, P. (2004, March 30). Blended learning. *Educause Center for Applied Research, Research Bulletin, 7.* Retrieved March 15, 2007, from http://www.educause.edu/LibraryDetailPage/666?ID=ERB0407

EADTU. (2004). *Report of the eLearning Programme of Education and Culture, European Commission.* Retrieved March 15, 2007, from http://www.eadtu.nl/files/EADTUstatementEC.final.doc

Garrett, R., & Verbik, L. (2004). *Online learning in Commonwealth universities: Selected data from the 2004 observatory survey: Part 2* (Rep. No. 21). London: The Observatory on Borderless Higher Education.

Gerbic, P. (2006, December 3-6). To post or not to post: Undergraduate student perceptions about participating in online discussions. In *Proceedings of the 23rd Annual Ascilite Conference: Who's Learning? Whose Technology?* (pp. 271-281). Retrieved May 15, 2007, from http://www.ascilite.org.au/conferences/sydney06/proceeding/pdf_papers/p124.pdf

Hara, N., & Kling, R. (2000). Students' distress with a Web-based distance education course: An ethnographic study of participants' experiences. *Information, Communication and Society, 3*(4), 557-579.

Harasim, L. (1989). On-line education: A new domain. In R. Mason & A. Kaye (Eds.), *Mindweave: Communication, computers and distance education* (pp. 50-62). Oxford, United Kingdom: Pergamon Press.

Harasim, L. (1993). Collaborating in cyberspace: Using computer conferences as group learning environments. *Interactive Learning Environments, 3*(2), 119-130.

Hiltz, S. (1993). Correlates of learning in a virtual classroom. *International Journal of Man-Machine Studies, 39,* 71-98.

Hiltz, S. (1994). *The virtual classroom.* Norwood, NJ: Ablex Publishing Corporation.

Hwang, W., & Wang, C. (2004). A study of learning time patterns in asynchronous learning environments. *Journal of Computer Assisted Learning, 20,* 292-304.

Intrallect. (2004). *Learning objects repositories in UK universities: A survey.* Author.

Jarvela, S., & Hakkinen, P. (2002). Web-based cases in teaching and learning: The quality of discussion and stage of perspective taking in asynchronous communication. *Interactive Learning Environments, 10,* 1-22.

Jarvenpaa, S., Knoll, K., & Leidner, D. (1998). Is anybody out there? Antecedents of trust in global virtual teams. *Journal of MIS, 14,* 29-38.

Jenkins, M., Browne, T., & Walker, R. (2005). *VLE surveys: A longitudinal perspective between March 2001, March 2003 and March 2005 for higher education in the United Kingdom.* UCISA. Retrieved March 20, 2007, from http://www.ucisa.ac.uk/groups/tlig/vle/index_html

Johnson, G., & Howell, A. (2005). Attitude toward instructional technology following required vs. optional WebCT usage. *Journal of Technology and Teacher Education, 13,* 643-654.

Joint Information Systems Committee (JISC). (2005). *Study of environments to support eLearning in UK further and higher education.* Retrieved March 18, 2006, from http://www.jisc.ac.uk/uploaded_documents/eLearning_survey_2005.pdf

Jonassen, D. (1996). *Computers in the classrooms: Mindtools for critical thinking.* Columbus, OH: Prentice Hall.

Knoll, K., & Jarvenpaa, S. (1995, January 3-6). Learning to work in distributed global teams. In *Proceedings of the 28th Hawaii Conference on Systems Sciences* (Vol. 4, pp. 92-101).

Laurillard, D. (2002). *Rethinking university teaching: A framework for the effective use of learning technologies* (2nd ed.). London: Routledge.

Leidner, D., & Jarvenpaa, S. (1995). The use of information technology to enhance management school education: A theoretical view. *MIS Quarterly, 19*(3), 265-292.

Levin, J., Kim, H., & Riel, M. (1990). Analyzing instructional interactions on electronic message networks. In L. Harasim (Ed.), *Online education: Perspectives on a new environment* (pp. 185-214). New York: Praeger.

Mason, R. (1998). *Globalising education: Trends and applications.* London: Routledge.

Meyer, K. (2003). Face-to-face versus threaded discussions: The role of time and higher-order thinking. *Journal of Asynchronous Learning Networks, 7.* Retrieved April 20, 2007, from http://www.sloan-c.org/publications/jaln/v7n3/index.asp

Molesworth, M. (2004). Collaboration, reflection and selective neglect: Campus-based marketing students' experiences of using a virtual learning environment. *Innovations in Education and Training International, 41*(1), 79-92.

Moule, P. (2007). Challenging the five-stage model for eLearning: A new approach. *ALT-J, Research in Learning Technology, 15*(1), 37-50.

Nixon, T., & Salmon, G. (1995, December 12-14). *Spinning your Web: Interactive computer-mediated conferencing its potential for learning and teaching in higher education.* Paper presented at the Society for Research into Higher Education Annual Conference, Edinburgh, United Kingdom.

Oblinger, D., & Oblinger, J. (2005). Is it age or IT: First steps towards understanding the Net generation. In D. Oblinger & J. Oblinger (Eds.), *Educating the Net generation.* Boulder, CO: Educause. Retrieved March 19, 2007, from http://www.educause.edu/content.asp?page_id=6058&bhcp=1

Oliver, M., & Trigwell, K. (2005). Can "blended learning" be redeemed? *ELearning, 2*(1), 17-26. Retrieved March 10, 2007, from http://www.wwwords.co.uk/pdf/viewpdf.asp?j=elea&vol=2&issue=1&year=2005&article=3_Oliver_ELEA_2_1_web&id=144.32.128.113

Preece, J. (2000). *Online communities: Designing usability, supporting sociability.* Chichester, United Kingdom: John Wiley & Sons.

Ramsden, P. (2003). *Learning to teach in higher education* (2nd ed.). London: Routledge Falmer.

Renzi, S., & Klobas, J. (2000). First steps toward computer-supported collaborative learning in large classrooms. *Educational Technology & Society, 3*(3), 317-328.

Robson, C. (1993). *Real world research: A resource for social scientists and practitioner-researchers.* London: Blackwell.

Rooney, J. (2003). Blending learning opportunities to enhance educational programming and meetings. *Association Management, 55*(5), 26-32.

Rothery, A., Dorup, J., & Cadewener, B. (2006). *EUNIS ELearning snapshots.* Retrieved March 10, 2007, from http://www.au.dk/elearning/ikt/publikationer/euniselearningsnapshots.pdf

Rovai, A. (2002). Sense of community, perceived cognitive learning, and persistence in asynchronous learning networks. *Internet and Higher Education, 5,* 319-332.

Salmon, G. (2000a). Computer-mediated conferencing for management learning at the Open University. *Management Learning, 31*(4), 491-502.

Salmon, G. (2000b). *EModerating: The key to teaching and learning online.* London: Kogan Page.

Salmon, G., & Giles, K. (1997, October 29-31). Moderating online. In *Proceedings of the Online Educa Conference*, Berlin, Germany. Retrieved March 10, 2007, from http://www.atimod.com/research/presentations/Mod.doc

Sharpe, R., Benfield, G., Roberts, G., & Francis, R. (2006). *The undergraduate experience of blended eLearning: A review of UK literature and practice undertaken for the Higher Education Academy.* Retrieved February 20, 2007, from http://www.heacademy.ac.uk/4884.htm

Turoff, M. (1989). The anatomy of a computer application innovation: Computer mediated communications (CMC). *Technological Forecasting and Social Change, 36*, 107-122.

Walker, R. (2003). *An investigation into virtual learner-centred solutions for competency-based management education.* Groningen, The Netherlands: Gopher Publishers.

Walker, R. (2005). Virtual learner-centred solutions for management education and training. In W. Baets (Ed.), *Knowledge management and management learning* (pp. 143-164). New York: Springer.

Walker, R., & Baets, W. (2000). Designing a virtual course environment for management education: A learner-centred approach. *Indian Journal of Open Learning, 9*(3), 299-317.

Walker, R., & Baets, W. (2002, June 6-8). Introducing "conversational" eLearning to management education: A comparison of student experiences from two MIS courses. In *Proceedings of the 10th European Conference on Information Systems*, Gdansk, Poland (pp. 1400-1409). Retrieved March 18, 2006, from http://is2.lse.ac.uk/asp/aspecis/20020130.pdf

Webster, J., & Hackley, P. (1997). Teaching effectiveness in technology-mediated distance learning. *Academy of Management Review, 40*(6), 1282-1309.

Winn, W. (1993). A constructivist critique of the assumptions of instructional design. In T. Duffy, J. Lowyck, & D. Jonassen (Eds.), *Designing environments for constructive learning.* New York: Springer.

Yin, R. (1993). *Applications of case study research: Design and methods.* Newbury Park, CA: Sage Publications.

Young, J. (2002). "Hybrid" teaching seeks to end the divide between traditional and online instruction. *Chronicle of Higher Education*, p. A33. Retrieved February 20, 2007, from http://chronicle.com/free/v48/i28/28a03301.htm

## ADDITIONAL READING

Scholze, T., & Wiemann, S. (2007). Successful blended learning projects in 2006: Experiences in different formal, non-formal and informal learning environments. *ELearning Papers, 3*, 1887-1542. Retrieved May 21, 2007, from http://www.elearningeuropa.info/files/media/media11897.pdf

Scholze and Wiemann have reviewed a range of European blended learning projects that reflect mixed learning methodologies with a focus on intercultural learning. The case examples will be of interest to course designers, and there is a useful discussion on multicultural approaches to e-learning.

Laster, S. (2004). Model driven design: Systematically building integrated blended learning experiences. *Elements of Quality Online Education: Into the Mainstream, 5*, 159-174.

For an institutional view of blended delivery and its integration across the curriculum, the report by Stephen Laster on Babson College's approach is insightful.

Bonk, C., Kim, K., & Zeng, T. (2006). Future directions of blended learning in higher education and workplace settings. In C. Bonk & C. Graham (Eds.), *Handbook of blended learning: Global perspectives, local designs.* San Francisco: Pfeiffer Publishing.

Bonk and Zeng offer an excellent overview of future directions in blended learning within higher education.

Van Baalen, P. J., & Moratis, L. T. (2001). *Management education in the networked economy: Its context, content, and organization.* Boston: Kluwer Academic Publishers.

For readers with a specific interest in e-learning solutions applied to management education, the book by Van Baalen and Moratis is a good starting point, with discussion on the networked economy and its impact on the way that business education is designed and delivered.

## ENDNOTES

[1] The Joint Information Systems Council (http://www.jisc.ac.uk) is a UK agency that supports further and higher education by providing strategic guidance, advice, and opportunities to use ICT to support teaching, learning, research, and administration. The Universities and Colleges Information Systems Association (http://www.ucisa.ac.uk) is a UK association that represents the whole of higher education, and increasingly further education, in the provision and development of academic, management, and administrative information systems, providing a network of contacts and a powerful lobbying voice.

[2] Post-92 institutions are former polytechnics that were awarded university status as a result of the Further & Higher Education Acts of 1992.

[3] See http://Euromed.blogs.com for an example of the blog tool used for this activity.

[4] See http://www.xwiki.org/xwiki/bin/view/Main/WebHome for information on the XWiki tool used for this course.

# Chapter XIII
# Online Communities of Inquiry in Higher Education

**Ann Donohoe**
*School of Nursing, Midwifery and Health Systems, University College Dublin, Ireland*

**Tim McMahon**
*Centre for Teaching and Learning, University College Dublin, Ireland*

**Geraldine O'Neill**
*Centre for Teaching and Learning, University College Dublin, Ireland*

## ABSTRACT

*The primary purpose of this chapter is to explore how online communities of inquiry can be developed to facilitate students to engage in reflective practice. The discussion begins with a critical review of the literature, examining the role of educational technology within higher education and the need to develop pedagogical frameworks for its use in practice. An overview of an action research study is presented that used communities of inquiry to facilitate registered nurses to critically reflect on clinical practice. The preliminary findings from focus group interviews indicate that learners viewed their participation in online communities of inquiry as a beneficial aid to reflection. The chapter concludes with recommendations for practice and for further research in the area of online communities of inquiry.*

## INTRODUCTION

There has been intense interest and speculation in the ways that technology can be used to support student learning in higher education (Issroff & Scanlon, 2002; Rogers, 2000). Universities are seeking to integrate technology into classroom teaching practice due to the widespread integration of the Internet into society (Issroff & Scanlon), the expanding capabilities of educational technology (Surry, Ensminger, & Haab, 2005), and ubiquitous personal computing and communication (McCredie, 2000). Although education has novel technological tools at its disposal, Salmon (2002) cautions that many of these applications are devoid of empirical, instructional, or pedagogical underpinnings to justify their employment. Therefore, it is imperative that educators develop educational theory and practice to guide the utilisation of technology within university teaching practice. In this regard, this chapter examines the role of educational technology within higher education, focusing specifically on how communities of inquiry can be developed within an online environment. The objectives of this chapter are

- To explore the role of technology within higher education,
- To examine what is meant by the term community of inquiry,
- To consider how a community of inquiry can be developed within an e-learning environment,
- To examine how a community of inquiry can be used to facilitate reflective practice within the context of nurse education.

In addition, this chapter demonstrates how online communities provide a valuable opportunity for educationalists to empirically examine how technology can be utilised in the development of teaching and learning interventions within higher education.

## EDUCATIONAL TECHNOLOGY IN HIGHER EDUCATION

*"Let the main object of this, our didactic, be as follows: to seek and to find a method of instruction, by which teachers may teach less, but learners may learn more"* (John Amos Cornelius, a 16th century scholar, as cited in Lusty, 1969, p. 53).

Down through the ages, a variety of instructional methods have been proposed by educational luminaries, ranging from Socrates, Abelard, Aquinas, and Bell, to Dewey, Montessori, Lewin, and Skinner; however, the search for the perfect method of instruction remains an illusive quest (Lusty, 1969). This quest continues within contemporary higher education, where there is a growing recognition that traditional university teaching methods have served the interests of lecturers and educational institutions more than those of students (Milliken & Barnes, 2002). This disparity has resulted in ever-increasing calls for greater accountability and quality assurance within the realm of educational delivery (Pennington & O'Neill, 1994; Ruth, 1997). In response, several countries have established agencies to develop the teaching function of universities and to explore various mechanisms aimed at examining the scholarship of teaching in academia (Healey, 2003). Traditionally, efforts designed to improve learning in higher education have focused on teaching and the ways in which learning activities are organised. As the international debate develops, significance is being given to understanding the mechanisms by which students learn (Milliken & Barnes). While the process of facilitating effective student learning is multifaceted, educational technology is increasingly being recognised as an instrument that may enhance the teaching and learning transaction (Garrison & Anderson, 2003; Laurillard, 1993; Salmon, 2000). Consequently, stakeholders who are interested in improving the quality of teaching in higher education are beginning to look toward new technology as a mechanism through which improvements can be realised.

Academia has responded to the use of ICT by conducting research on how tools such as the computer and the Internet can be used to accelerate university students' learning, to enhance and democratise access to educational opportunities, and to support interactivity, interaction, and collaboration (Selwyn, 2007). In addition, universities worldwide are investing heavily in various applications of educational technology with commercial interests often driving the hype about the benefits of educational technology for teaching and learning. In his review of computer technology in higher education, Selwyn suggests that the use of virtual learning environments such as WebCT™, Blackboard™, and Moodle™ is so prevalent that the concept of the university campus is moving away from bricks and mortar to "clicks and mortar" (p. 2).

While there is an apparent rush to treat the ills of higher education with a quick technical fix (Robins & Webster, 1989), many commentators are questioning the precise role and function of technology within academia (Feenberg, 2001; Privateer, 1999; Spector, 2001). Watson (2001) and Ascough (2002) both call for pedagogy to be placed firmly before technology, while McMullin (2005) highlights that the potential of technology to enhance learning lies primarily in its ability to act as an instrument of pedagogical change. Bielaczyz (2001) emphasises the importance of building the right kind of social infrastructure to encourage, enable, and support learners in their use of modern communication technology. The argument that it is more important for educational technology to provide new ways to build communities of learning rather than new ways to access knowledge is supported by Lipponen and Lallimo (2004), who go further and suggest that building social infrastructures should be regarded as the primary objective of teachers using new technology.

Despite the rhetoric, in reality, many educators are struggling to make effective use of these new technologies to enrich the teaching and learning environment (McAlpine & Gandell, 2003). In attempting to explain the reasons for this struggle, Garrison and Anderson (2003) propose that the adoption of ICT in academia has outpaced our understanding of how to use such technologies to support educational experiences. Similarly, Salmon (2000) notes that millions of words have

been written about educational technology and its potential, but significantly less has been written about what teachers and learners actually do online. As we look to the future, it is important to heed Feenberg's (2001) warning that whenever a new educational technology is introduced, we ought to be wary lest reformers configure it in a way that closes off the process of intellectual exchange. Therefore, it is imperative that educationalists drive future research, development, and application of ICT within higher education (Eynon, 2005) and ensure that pedagogy is placed firmly before technology (Watson, 2001). While there is a myriad of technological applications being explored and investigated, the development of online communities of inquiry is an area that is particularly worthy of further investigation.

## COMMUNITIES OF INQUIRY IN HIGHER EDUCATION

The term *community* is becoming a significant factor in contemporary educational practice with the notion of community being operationalised in numerous ways within educational discourse. For example, phrases such as "community of practice" (Wenger, 1998), "learning community" (Peterson, 1992), "community of learners" (Rogoff, Matusov, & White, 1996), and "classroom community" (Bridges, 1995) are indicative of some of the constructs evident within the literature (Paradales & Girod, 2006). While this variation in how community is operationalised may reflect the increasingly pervasive nature of the construct within academia, it also suggests that the term *community* can be interpreted in a variety of ways depending on the context. Thus, for the purposes of this discussion, the use of the term *community* will be limited to its application within the phrase "community of inquiry."

Community inquiry theory is rooted in pragmatism, a tradition of philosophy and social action that rose to prominence at the turn of the

20th century (Bishop et al., 2004). Charles Sanders Pierce, a noted scientist and philosopher, is credited with developing the term *community of inquiry* and used the phrase to refer to a group of individuals (most often scientists) employing an interpersonal method for arriving at results (Paradales & Girod, 2006). While Dewey wrote extensively about the way knowledge is shaped through active engagement within a community (Bishop et al.), it was Matthew Lipman and Ann Sharp, founders of Philosophy for Children, who adapted Pierce's work to represent the classroom as a community of inquiry (Paradales & Girod). They viewed the classroom as a community where students and teachers could inquire into topics of mutual interest with the purpose of reconstructing experience and knowledge through critical analysis, questioning, and the challenging of assumptions (Lipman, 1991). Although, a variety of authors have attempted to explore the essence of these educational structures (Bishop et al.), Lipman's view that learning is "persistently exploratory" (p. 19) remains prominent.

The relatively recent development of educational technologies has revitalised the debate around the potential for communities of inquiry to facilitate learning within the context of higher education. Educational technologies, which allow for synchronous and asynchronous collaborative communication, are presenting possibilities for the community-of-inquiry process that would not have been imaginable in the time of Pierce and Dewey. In addition, these technologies are reflective of social constructivism (Vygotsky, 1978), one of the most accepted epistemological positions associated with online learning, which advocates that knowledge is generated through social intercourse; it is through this interaction that advances in levels of knowing are accumulated (Kanuka & Anderson, 1998). The body of literature relating to online communities of inquiry is growing rapidly, and research is beginning to document the role that communities of inquiry play in developing shared knowledge

(Garrison, Anderson, & Archer, 2000; Kanuka & Anderson).

The creation of communities of inquiry within a virtual text-based environment presents major challenges for educators (Garrison and Anderson, 2003). A limited number of models are beginning to emerge that have been developed specifically for online inquiry-based learning. Among the most prominent models are open learning environments (Hannifin, Land, & Oliver, 1983), online inquiry-based learning environments (Lim, 2004), and the community-of-inquiry framework (Garrison et al., 2000). While open learning environments are structured to encourage personal inquiry, they are generally considered unsuitable for learners trying to resolve issues as a group or community. Online inquiry-based learning environments are designed to encompass all course activities into an integrated system and incorporate a variety of learning activities, including a community of inquiry for collaboration and support. The community-of-inquiry model devised by Garrison (2002) provides a well-designed conceptual framework specifically developed to guide the use of computer conferencing to support critical thinking in higher education (Rourke, Anderson, Garrison, & Archer, 2001). Garrison et al. (2000) propose that the community-of-inquiry framework can be applied to any educational experience, and consider the revaluing of the traditional ideal of a community of learners to be at the heart of the e-learning transformation.

## COMMUNITY OF INQUIRY FRAMEWORK

The community-of-inquiry framework (Garrison, et al. 2000) has its genesis in the work of John Dewey and is consistent with constructivist approaches to education; it is a conceptual model that facilitates the development of online communities within the context of higher education (see Figure 1). In the community of inquiry model, deep and meaningful learning, the raison d'etre of higher education, occurs within online communities where instructors and learners are the key participants in the educational process. The model assumes that, in an online community, learning occurs through the interaction of three complementary and partially overlapping elements: cognitive presence, teaching presence, and social presence.[1]

## Elements in the Community-of-Inquiry Framework: Cognitive Presence, Teaching Presence, and Social Presence

Cognitive presence is defined as "the extent to which the participants in any particular configuration of a community of inquiry are able to construct meaning through sustained communication" (Garrison et al., 2000, p. 89). In essence, cognitive presence, a condition of higher order thinking and learning, is operationalised through the practical inquiry model (Garrison et al.). This cycle, largely derived from Dewey's (1933) work on reflective thinking, consists of four phases: the triggering event, exploration, integration, and resolution. The educational goal and challenge is to move the inquiry process through all four phases of the model to ensure a successful outcome (Garrison, Anderson, & Archer, 2001).

Teaching presence refers to "the design, facilitation and direction of cognitive and social processes for the purpose of realising personally meaningful and educationally worthwhile learning outcomes" (Anderson, Rourke, Garrison, & Archer, 2001, p. 5). This element considers the roles and functions of all participants in creating and maintaining a dynamic learning community (Vaughan & Garrison, 2005).

Social presence pertains to "the ability of participants in a community of inquiry to project themselves socially and emotionally as real people through the medium of the communication being used" (Garrison et al., 2000, p. 94). The function of this element is to support the cognitive and affective objectives of learning. Social presence creates a sense of belonging that promotes meaningful inquiry and provides a context that facilitates critical discourse and reflection (Vaughan & Garrison, 2005).

When social presence is combined with appropriate teaching presence, a high level of cognitive presence leading to fruitful critical inquiry can result (Garrison et al., 2000). For further information on this model, please refer to Garrison and Anderson (2003).

Research indicates that the community-of-inquiry framework provides significant insights and methodological solutions for studying online learning (Garrison, Cleveland-Innes, Koole, & Kappelman, 2006; Perry & Edwards, 2005) and is effective for guiding successful educational experiences in a variety of online learning environments (Garrison et al., 2001; McKlin, Harmon, Evans, & Jones, 2001; Meyer, 2003; Pawan, Paulus, Yalcin, & Chang, 2003; Vaughan & Garrison, 2005). Research has been conducted into each of

*Figure 1. Community of inquiry*

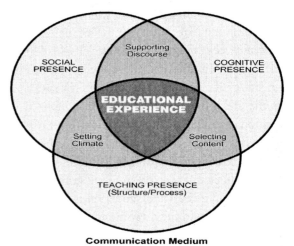

*Source: Garrison et al. (2000; reproduced with permission from Elsevier Science Inc.)*

the three elements of the model: cognitive presence (Garrison, et al., 2001; Kanuka & Garrison, 2004), teaching presence (Anderson et al., 2001; Shea, Pickett, & Pelt, 2003), and social presence (Rourke et al., 2001). In addition, the structure of the community-of-inquiry framework has been confirmed through factor analysis (Garrison, Cleveland-Innes, & Fung 2004).

Garrison and Anderson (2003) propose that the community-of-inquiry framework provides a coherent model with the potential to structure, guide, and assess e-learning approaches, strategies, and techniques within higher education. However, they note that research relating to the community-of-inquiry framework remains in its infancy and call for the model to be tested in a variety of settings. It is against this background that the current research study was devised, with the aim of exploring the potential of the community-of-inquiry framework to facilitate nurses to reflect on practice. In order to understand the context of this study, the discussion includes an exploration of the role of reflective practice within contemporary nurse education and proceeds with an overview of the design, delivery, and evaluation of the online reflective practice resource.

## REFLECTIVE PRACTICE AND NURSE EDUCATION

The concept of the reflective practitioner has been widely embraced, and innumerable professional courses in many disciplines and countries claim to use this approach (Bulman & Schutz, 2004). The seminal work of Donald Schön is of particular relevance in this regard as he developed an alternative theory of the professional as a reflective practitioner, a person who uses reflective processes to critically analyse, reappraise, and learn from experiences (Bulman & Schutz). Schön's views are heavily influenced by theorists such as Dewey, Freire, and Mezirow, all of whom

played important roles in developing a view of learning as a transformative process through which individuals are encouraged to critically examine and learn from their interpretations of experience (Redmond, 2004).

Literature relating to reflective practice can be found in professional areas as diverse as public planning and policy making, teaching and education, organisational psychology and psychotherapy, health services and social work (Redmond, 2004). Reflective practice is deemed relevant for nursing as the profession is primarily practice based, and reflection has the potential to provide a vehicle through which the importance of practice knowledge can be communicated (Bulman & Schutz, 2004). However, *reflective practice* remains poorly defined and there are significant inconsistencies as to what exactly constitutes the term (Teekman, 2000). This lack of clarity has prompted Atkins and Murphy (1993) to question whether authors share a common understanding of reflective practice, while Eraut (2004) notes that the term *reflection* is now in such common use in professional education that there is considerable danger of it being taken for granted rather than being treated as problematic. The most overwhelming criticism of reflective practice relates to its evidence base, which predominantly centres on theoretical debate as opposed to empirical research (Bulman & Schutz; Paget, 2001; Teekman). Consequently, theorists in many professional fields are calling for reflective practice to be subjected to closer critical examination (Bulman & Schutz; Redmond, 2004).

Reflective practice poses similar problems for the nursing profession, where the idea of reflection has been widely accepted, despite its controversial position. While claims as to the benefits of reflective practice to nursing are evident in the literature, Teekman (2000) argues that some claims are unsubstantiated. Many European countries advocate the need for a more reflective nurse and indicate that nurse education programmes should lead to students being able to demonstrate the development of reflective practice skills (An Bord Altranais, 2000). However, evidence-based strategies demonstrating how reflection can be facilitated in both education and practice are exceptionally limited (Bulman & Schutz, 2004; Nicholl & Higgins, 2004).

At this juncture, it is important to recognise that academics are also grappling with how to facilitate reflective practice within an educational milieu. Reflective practice is viewed as the way forward for both students and academics alike (Davis, 2003), and there is a growing aspiration that higher education should be involved in facilitating students to become critical reflective thinkers who are able to cope with a rapidly changing world. Jonassen, Mayes, and McAleese (1993) advocate that the goal of universities should be to produce reflective practitioners and suggest that technology can be used to enhance the reflective process. They propose that computers can provide a conversational environment in which learners can apply knowledge to problems and consider their actions as reusable events. With the assistance of appropriate technological support, learners can be facilitated to control their learning, to learn from others, and to develop reflection in action and reflection on action as metacognitive skills (Jonassen et al.). Some studies have been conducted that focus on the use of computer-mediated communication (CMC) to promote reflective and critical thinking through debate (Barnes, 1998; Bodzin & Park, 2002; Selinger, 1998). Referring specifically to teacher education, Harrington and Hathaway (1994) and Galanouli and Collins (2000) argue that CMC can be structured to foster critical reflection. However, Bautista (1998) and Admiraal, Veen, Korthagen, Lockhorst, and Wubbels (1999) report that the nature of such communications relate to technical and practical matters as opposed to critical reflection on practice. A study undertaken by Seale and Cann (2000) provides some evidence that CMC technologies help to facilitate reflection for some students. Overall, however, the literature indicates that research examining the role of educational technology in facilitating reflective practice is in the initial phase of development. Consequently, it is imperative that a variety of empirical investigations are undertaken to examine the synergy between educational technology and reflective practice if its true potential as a reflective catalyst is to be realised.

In summary, reflective practice is destined to remain a central tenant of professional education. Therefore, it is incumbent on professions such as nursing to investigate the content, methodologies, and resources required to teach reflective practice effectively (Nicholl & Higgins, 2004). Interestingly, some educationalists view technology as a potential mechanism by which the problems associated with facilitating reflection can be addressed. The following study was designed to contribute to this discourse by demonstrating how an online resource can be used to facilitate reflective practice in nursing.

## BACKGROUND TO THE STUDY

The following section provides an overview of the development, delivery, and evaluation of a reflective practice resource that was pedagogically designed to facilitate registered nurses to critically reflect on practice. The discussion begins with an account of how the resource was developed and delivered using the community-of-inquiry framework devised by Garrison et al. (2000). Preliminary findings from the analysis of three focus-group interviews are presented, followed by an interpretation of these findings within the context of the community-of-inquiry framework. The discussion includes recommendations as to how a similar online resource can be improved and used within the context of an online learning experience.

## Design and Delivery of the Online Reflective Practice Resource

The Bachelor of Science in Nursing Modular Programme at University College Dublin (UCD) is a 1-year part-time degree programme designed specifically for registered nurses. It is comprised of six core modules; each module is 72 hours in duration with 36 hours representing direct student contact. The reflective practice resource was developed for use on the degree module entitled Issues in Professional Practice. This module consisted of three units of study: (a) Teaching and Assessing in the Clinical Setting (12 hours), (b) Reflective Practice (12 hours), and (c) Professional Care (12 hours). As the degree programme was a part-time course, the students attended face-to-face lectures on reflective practice for 3 hours on four separate occasions during the first semester. The lecturer, who was also the researcher in this investigation, delivered 12 hours of lectures on reflective practice and designed the online reflective practice resource to supplement the face-to-face teaching sessions.

The community-of-inquiry framework (Garrison et al., 2000) and the corresponding guidelines for practice devised by Garrison and Anderson (2003) were used in the design and delivery of the resource. As previously stated, the community-of-inquiry model features three complementary and partially overlapping elements: social presence, cognitive presence, and teaching presence. It is important to note that Garrison and Anderson suggest that the framework is operationalised from the perspective of teaching presence and its three dimensions: instructional design and organisation, discourse facilitation, and direct instruction. The issues pertaining to social and cognitive presence are addressed as they relate to each of the three dimensions of teaching presence. While these elements are presented separately, some of the activities identified may relate to more than one presence or dimension of the model.

## Design and Organisation

The first element of teaching presence, instructional design and organisation, involves developing the macro structure and processes of an online learning experience. The reflective practice resource was devised using Blackboard™ as the virtual learning environment and was operational for the duration of the 12-week semester. In addition to the standard features of Blackboard, such as announcements, course documents, and course information, additional categories linking directly to the communities of inquiry and a reflective corner were created. Ten separate communities of inquiry were created, each consisting of between five to seven students. Each student was given the opportunity to select the community they wished to join; students who did not express a preference were allocated to a community by the course moderator. Students were required to complete eight individual learning activities and contribute to three sequential discussion forums. The learning activities and discussion forums were closely aligned with the summative assessment for the module. An overview of the learning activities and the discussion forums is presented in Figure 2.

Strategies to facilitate social presence were specifically incorporated into the reflective practice resource. For example, Learning Activity 1, Create Your Own Home Page, and Learning Activity 2, Join a Community of Inquiry, were devised to foster the development of social presence. Students were required to create a home page within Blackboard to introduce themselves to the class and to detail their area of clinical practice. They were then invited to review the home pages of their fellow students and select four to seven people with whom they wished to form a community of inquiry.

With regard to cognitive presence, an additional space, called the reflective corner, was created to provide further insights into the reflec-

*Figure 2. Learning activities and discussion forums in the reflective practice resource*

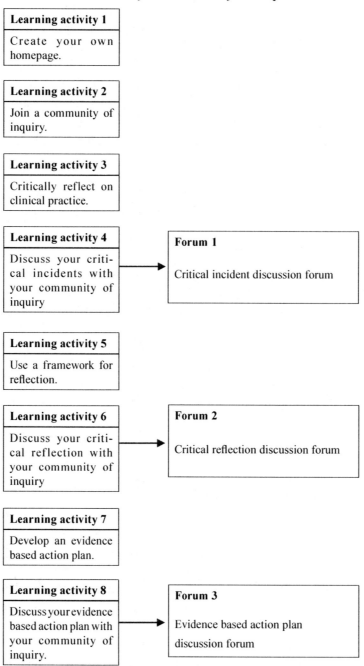

tive process. This facility offered direct access to relevant literature, such as articles on reflective practice, Web pages of relevant authors, and information on the community-of-inquiry framework. The reflective practice resource also contained direct links to library databases and step-by-step instructions detailing how to use the various components. A proportion of the face-to-face lectures were undertaken in the computer room, which facilitated the students to become familiar with using the resource.

## Facilitating Discourse

The second element of teaching presence, facilitating discourse, recognises the community of inquiry as a mechanism for enabling and encouraging the construction of personal meaning as well as shaping and confirming mutual understanding (Garrison & Anderson, 2003).

With regard to facilitating social presence through discourse, the lecturer acting as the online moderator modeled various open communication strategies. These communication strategies ranged from acknowledging and welcoming participants as they entered the discussion to being encouraging, polite, and supportive. In addition, clear instructions were given to students on how to engage in the discussion forums. For example, in each forum, students were advised to end each posting with a question and to respond to the postings of at least one of their peers. Students were also given specific directions about maintaining confidentiality when discussing issues relating to clinical practice.

Regarding cognitive presence, each of the three discussion forums were designed to prompt the student to move through the four phases of practical inquiry as described by Garrison et al. (2000): the triggering event, exploration, integration, and resolution. In Forum 1, Critical Incident Discussion Forum, the students were invited to post summaries of incidents from their own clinical practice experience for discussion within their relevant community of inquiry. This forum was designed to act as the triggering event to prompt the student to engage with the reflective practice resource and to interact with other students online. Forum 2, Critical Reflection Discussion Forum, was related to exploration, the second stage of the practical inquiry model. Students were asked to discuss a specific incident from their clinical practice with their community of inquiry. The purpose of this reflective activity was to use the discussion forum as a mechanism to gain an understanding of the nature of a specific clinical issue

through discussion with community of inquiry peers. Students were required to substantiate their discussions by incorporating relevant literature and by including hyperlinks to relevant articles where possible. Forum 3, Evidence Based Action Plan, involved integration and resolution, the final two phases of the practical inquiry model. In this third forum, the students were invited to conclude the reflective process by developing an evidence-based action plan aimed at addressing and resolving the clinical issue they had explored in Forum 2.

## Direct Instruction

Direct instruction goes beyond that of a facilitation role and is most often associated with specific content issues such as diagnosing misconceptions (Garrison & Anderson, 2003).

Social presence was facilitated by ensuring that the lecturer who delivered the face-to-face content of the course also moderated the communities of inquiry and all online interactions. Thus, the students received consistent intellectual and pedagogic leadership throughout their educational experience on the module. This dual role permitted the lecturer to provide prompt individual feedback and to direct student learning in a constructive and encouraging manner. The overall aim was to develop social presence to a degree where students perceived their community of inquiry as an environment in which they could reflect with their fellow students and the lecturer in a supportive and informative way.

With regard to cognitive presence, the purpose of the resource was to facilitate students to engage in reflective practice. This goal was achieved by designing learning activities that were reflective in nature and that prepared the student to engage effectively in the discussion forums. These discussion forums prompted the student to progress through each phase of the practical inquiry model and were closely aligned with the summative reflective assignment for the module.

Consequently, students could use the feedback that they received in the discussion forums to inform the development of their course work.

In summary, the community-of-inquiry framework (Garrison et al., 2000) and the corresponding guidelines for practice (Garrison and Anderson, 2003) provided a comprehensive model that facilitated the design and delivery of the reflective practice resource. The resource remained inherently flexible and was continuously modified and constructed as the module progressed in response to the needs of the students and the lecturer.

## PRELIMINARY FINDINGS FROM THE FOCUS-GROUP INTERVIEWS

The reflective practice resource was evaluated using focus-group interviews, an end-of-semester student survey, and analyses of online discussions for evidence of the development of reflective ability. Sixty-one students were registered for the module. Each student had access to the reflective practice resource; 37 (60.6%) students posted to the various discussion forums, with an average of 6.3 postings per student. A total of 16 students participated in three focus-group interviews, and each group consisted of between five to six students. As the analysis is ongoing, the following discussion will be limited to the preliminary findings from the focus-group interviews.

Focus groups were selected for use in this study because they provide a form of group interview that capitalises on communication among research participants in order to generate data (Kitzinger, 1996). This emphasis on interaction and data generation is central to the focus-group methodology (Morgan, 1996) and is particularly pertinent to this investigation as it allows the researcher to explore the participants' initial attitudes toward the use of the reflective practice resource, both individually and collectively. After an introduction to the study, potential participants were invited to take part in the focus-group interviews and

were provided with written documentation about the study, including the right to withdraw at any time. Formal ethical approval was obtained from the university's human research ethics committee, and strategies were put in place to ensure the confidentiality of individuals' contributions. A series of questions aimed at ascertaining how the reflective practice resource had impacted the students' learning were developed from the literature. These questions focused specifically on identifying the elements of the resource that facilitated or inhibited engagement in critical reflection. The focus groups were audio taped and transcribed verbatim. Qualitative thematic analysis was used to draw themes from the data. A qualitative data software package, MAXqda, was used to assist with storage and retrieval of data. Five main themes were identified: working within a community of inquiry, becoming an online learner, the role of the moderator, writing online, and assessment.

### Working within a Community of Inquiry

The students' experiences of working within their respective communities of inquiry varied. Many of the students commented on the important role that group discussion played within the online environment. For example, Jack said,

*I'd say that's just the most beneficial part of it altogether really is the group discussion—discussion with other people and discussion with the lecturer. It's just getting used to that form of communication...you know online communication, because I certainly wouldn't be that familiar with it.*

Students reported that they found it interesting to hear about clinical issues and experiences from other members of their community of inquiry and expressed that their online communities were supportive environments. They also found it beneficial to be in a community with students who had similar clinical backgrounds and with whom they were already familiar. Jane stated,

*It's good to have kind of a support base as well, because otherwise it can be very impersonal, and by doing the community of inquiry you actually do get to know other people that are within the groups. It provides a focal point for talking.*

Generally, the students that commented positively on the resource were those who had been members of communities that were active and where participation rates were high. However, some students experienced inactivity within the groups when members of their community did not respond to postings. While students in an inactive group were given the option to leave their group and join a more active one, many reported that they just stopped posting. This inactivity caused the students to feel de-motivated. For example, Amy explained, "You weren't getting any feedback, so why would you want to spend time providing feedback to people that aren't supplying feedback to you. So I kind of got a little bit disillusioned and just didn't bother then in the end.

## Becoming an Online Learner

For most of the students, this was their first time engaging in any form of online learning. The students were conscious of the fact that communicating with one another online is very different from communicating face to face and that this type of interaction required a period of adjustment. They also identified disadvantages to the process, which were primarily related to the difficulties involved in moving from face-to-face to online communication. This disadvantage of online communication is encapsulated in the words of Jill:

*I feel if you are verbally communicating with somebody you can get your point across and you can get your answer kind of and explore more;*

*but personally I found it difficult to type in and try and communicate when I actually couldn't see the course coordinator or whatever, so in my opinion I just found it quite difficult to change, going from face to face to typing online and not seeing.*

Students also felt that the process was time consuming since they had to post several times to be understood clearly, as described by Jack:

*Whereas if I was having a discussion with [Jill] or with yourself or whatever, you know you could rattle out the points and be done with it and find out exactly what you want to know; whereas online you might exchange three or four different e-mails and you still might not have the exact information that you are looking for.*

Students noted that their lack of computer skills adversely affected their ability to engage with the reflective practice resource. In many cases, this was compounded by limited access to a home computer with an Internet connection. Other students reported that they spent more time learning how to use the resource than actually learning from the resource. It is interesting to note that the use of computers in nursing education is at a developmental stage, and that many students found online learning a significant change from their traditional learning experiences. Noreen's response highlighted this deficit:

*Just the fact that nursing is never—you never had a computer class. Like, during my 3 years diploma training we never actually had computer classes or anything like that; we never got to expand any computer skills in diploma training, so I found it good that you could do that in this class.*

However, other students noted that they felt that engaging in the process helped them to develop their computer skills. In addition, these students agreed that class time spent in the computer laboratory to learn how to use the reflective practice resource was particularly beneficial.

## Role of the Moderator

The dual role of the instructor as lecturer and moderator for each of the communities of inquiry was viewed very positively; the students appreciated being able to contact the lecturer directly, to receive individual feedback to their postings, and to read the postings of others. The prompt nature of the instructor's responses was identified as particularly significant as some students felt that this facilitated interaction with their community. For example, Tom said, *"I suppose if the responses weren't flying fast, you'd be less inclined to post. At least you knew, well it's posted today and I'll have a reply by tomorrow evening or the next day at the latest. That, like, compelled you."*

However, the students stated that the feedback from their peers was not as helpful as that of the moderator; they tended to value the responses from the moderator more highly than those of the other students. The preference for the moderator's feedback is captured in Catherine's statement: *"So it's the ability to ask the questions to the person that's able to tell you the answer, not that your group of people can't but...I suppose you're looking for the answer from the course leader."*

The students indicated that peer moderation would not be a welcome addition due primarily to the time pressures associated with their status as part-time students. However, the students could see the potential of peer moderation in future iterations of the reflective practice resource, specifically if they developed their computer skills.

## Writing Online

The students stated that the act of writing in the online community in inquiry discussion forums was beneficial. In particular, the students felt that writing helped them think more about what they wished to say. They could also see the development of their reflections by referring back to the message transcripts. For example, Amy said,

*I suppose if you have things written down that you can refer back to, you have the theme to start with and then you get a reply and another reply within that section. Then you can refer back to that and see where your original thought stemmed from and then see where you're now thinking of that problem: It's the progression.*

Many of the students noted that the act of writing prompted them to think in different ways and felt that the links to the library databases and the reflective corner were helpful in facilitating reflection. As Catherine explained,

*Having the links [to library databases] put there... was great, and also having the reflective corner where [the lecturer] had posted articles as well. So if you had the time certainly or the means, the use of the computer, it was good that it was there already; it makes it so much easier.*

## Assessment

The reflective practice resource included a number of learning activities and discussion forums that were aligned with the summative assignment. This element of the resource provided the students with an opportunity to present elements of their work to members of their community of inquiry, and to receive formative feedback as they progressed through their assignment. Many students reported that they found this process helpful in completing their course work. For example, Jane said, *"You had to look for research and you had to get backing for what you were going to say in your assignment, so it encouraged you to delve a bit more and seek out more information."*

While the structure and function of the resource and its relevance to the assignment were clearly explained, some students did not readily recognise the connection between the assignment and the reflective practice resource. Others students recognised the relationship between the two entities only in retrospect, as indicated in Jack's statement:

*I personally didn't really understand the concept of [the community of inquiry] in the beginning—that it was going to aid...the reflection process, but in doing that it was going to aid you to do the assignment—but I didn't really understand that at the beginning.*

This inability to recognise the interrelated nature of the activities might be explained by the fact that this was a new method of learning for many of the students.

## DISCUSSION

Garrison et al.'s (2000) community-of-inquiry framework was used to interpret the findings from the study as the model had been instrumental in guiding the design and delivery of the reflective practice resource. The findings are discussed below as they relate to the three primary elements of this framework: social presence, cognitive presence, and teaching presence. Due to the inherent interaction of these processes within the framework, many of the issues addressed in the discussion may relate to more than one element.

### Social Presence

The purpose of social presence is to create a sense of belonging that promotes meaningful inquiry, while also creating a context that facilitates critical discourse and reflection (Vaughan & Garrison, 2005). The findings relating to working within a community of inquiry and becoming an online learner suggest that the students felt a degree of social presence within this online environment.

The students stated that they found working within their respective communities of inquiry to be a beneficial experience. In fact, many of the participants used the terms *our* and *we* to

describe their community of inquiry. The students also stated that they enjoyed interacting with others from similar clinical backgrounds, and noted that engaging with persons that they already knew appeared to facilitate the learning process. As Moule (2006) found, having group participants with prior knowledge of one another was an important factor in facilitating effective group work. However, it is important to note that some students did not engage with the resource or only did so on a limited basis. While the exact reasons for this lack of engagement are unclear, the difficulties in adjusting to online learning may have been a contributing factor. For many students, it was their first time participating in any sort of online educative process and, consequently, this lack of experience may have had a negative impact on their ability to communicate online. For example, a number of students noted that engaging with the reflective practice resource was time consuming and laborious. Students' concerns relating to the time it takes to engage in online activities are expressed in the literature (Gillis, Jackson, Braid, MacDonald, & MacQuarrie, 2000; Steele, Johnson Palensky, Lynch, Lacy, & Duffy, 2002). In addition, in this study, the participants appeared to be concerned with learning how to use the technology rather than actually learning from the resource. This finding is consistent with those reported by Moule. The students also stated that they missed the interaction of face-to-face discussion and found adjusting to the online discussion forums challenging. Similar findings have been reported in previous research (Stodel, Thompson, & MacDonald, 2006; Thomas, 2002). Difficulties with computer skills and computer access in relation to e-learning are widely acknowledged in the literature (Geibert, 2000; Moule).

During the design and delivery of the resource, significant efforts were made to create an online environment that could facilitate social presence. However, it is clear from the findings that more is required to foster social presence. The inclusion of nontask contexts and collaborative learning activities, together with the use of innovative communication technologies are some of the areas that could be developed further in order to foster social presence.

Social interaction in the reflective practice resource was achieved primarily through the medium of specified online tasks; for example, students created home pages and contributed to discussion forums. Kreijns, Kirschner, and Jochems (2003) and Wheeler (2005) suggest that the use of nontask contexts, which tend to be characterised by informal and casual conversations and allow participants to become acquainted in a more casual way, such as an online coffee shop or interactive space, may help foster social processes more than task contexts alone. However, Gunawardena (1995) argues that if social presence is to be created effectively within online environments, the participants must have specific training in the mechanisms of creating social presence. In addition, Rovai (2000) highlights the importance of class size, noting that when the student-instructor ratio is higher than 30:1, it is difficult to establish and maintain social presence.

Collaborative learning activities can also facilitate the development of social presence (Rovai 2000). Collaborative learning must be carefully designed into online environments and the incentive to collaborate specifically structured within the online groups (Kreijns et al., 2003). In this study, collaborative learning was limited to online discussion forums, thus, the incentive for students to work together was quite circumscribed. While collaborative activities, such as group work, group assignments, and group projects, have the potential to facilitate social presence, developing effective collaborative activities is challenging. In particular, fostering group cohesion to a level where members are willing to help one another is especially difficult within an online environment (Kreijns et al.). Nonetheless, initiatives to consider in future iterations of the reflective practice resource include incorporating a collaborative component into the summative

assignment or allocating credit for online collaborative activities.

As educational technology continues to develop, it is important to consider how such technologies can be used to facilitate social presence in online environments. Stodel et al. (2006) propose a range of emerging technologies with the potential to facilitate social presence, ranging from interactive voice response (IVR) systems that will type the spoken word to the integration of audio and video technologies that allow for the creation of richer communication media. While it is important to embrace novel technological advancements, it is imperative that such advances are deployed in ways that are pedagogically valid and cognizant of the students' ability to use and gain access to such technologies. Research that investigates the use of software to foster social presence and enhance online learning is urgently required.

## Cognitive Presence

Cognitive presence is the element within a community of inquiry that reflects the focus and success of the learning experience (Vaughan & Garrison, 2005). The findings of this study pertaining to writing online and assessment suggest that a degree of cognitive presence was developed within the resource.

Students in the current study noted that the act of writing online in the discussion forums was beneficial to their learning. In particular, the students stated that writing helped them to think more about what they wished to say. As Lapadat (2002) suggested, the act of writing in online conferences may foster higher order thinking for reasons pertaining to the relationship between writing and cognition. As participants struggle to express and defend their points of view, they tend to use higher order thinking processes such as analysis, synthesis, and evaluation (ibid.). Within an online environment, these higher order thinking processes are further enhanced through the medium of writing (Harasim, 1993). Writing enables people to say and to think things that they could not say, or at least had not said but thought, without writing (Olson, 1995). In this study, the students also noted that they could see the development of their reflection and learning by referring back to the message transcripts. Reflection and sense making are facilitated by assisting an individual in planning his or her own path through the educational material and revisiting chosen portions (Lapadat). Many students recognised that the feedback they received online facilitated their completion of the summative assessment for the module. A crucial element in encouraging students to use this reflective practice resource was ensuring alignment between the reflective practice resource and the summative assessment. Salmon's (2004) view that many course designers find that assessment is the engine that drives and motivates students is supported by Moule (2006), who argues that the use of an assessment-driven focus that marries outcomes to online activities is an important element in the design of online courses.

However, it is important to note that, despite aligning the learning activities and discussion forums in the reflective practice resource with the summative assessment for the module, some students chose not to use the resource or used it in a limited way. While some students expressed difficulty in understanding how the reflective practice resource contributed to their learning, others did not readily recognise the link between the online activities and the summative assessment. In addition, some students noted that their communities became inactive when students did not post to the discussion boards or did not respond to postings. Consequently, it is necessary to consider ways to improve the cognitive element of this online environment, for example, by increasing metacognitive awareness and encouraging self-assessment.

Schraw (2001) has described two components of metacognition: knowledge of cognition and

regulation of cognition. Knowledge of cognition refers to knowledge of oneself and one's own cognitive strategies, while regulation of cognition pertains to a set of activities that facilitate students in controlling their learning. Garrison (2002) suggests that metacognitive awareness can be greatly assisted by explicitly sharing a model of the learning process with students. In this study, the lecturer used Garrison et al.'s (2000) community-of-inquiry model to structure the development of the online discussion forums, but did not explicitly refer to the model when engaging with students. Garrison et al. suggest that sharing underlying models and processes with students facilitates them to gain insight into their own learning; the incorporation of strategies that develop metacognitive awareness is likely to be an important tool in facilitating students to act confidently and effectively when using reflective practice resources.

The need to move toward aligning assessment strategies with online teaching approaches is a significant and immediate challenge for the online educator (Moule, 2006). In this study, while the task requirements in the online reflective practice resource and the summative assessment were closely aligned, it became apparent that additional measures were needed to strengthen cognitive presence. The process of assigning a portion of the assessment grade for online participation is the subject of much debate in academic circles. For example, Palloff and Pratt (2000) argue that participation must be evaluated and rewarded if online communities are to develop, while Cheng and Vassileva (2005) caution that designing incentives to ensure participation in online communities is one of the most challenging problems in social computing. Anderson (2004) adopts a moderate approach by suggesting that an assessed learning activity be used, where students are required to use online postings to demonstrate their understanding of content and intellectual growth. Assessed learning activities involve student self-assessment, a process where learners take responsibility for making judgments about their own work. Self-assessment in collaboration with the lecturer can improve the quality of online work and facilitate students to take greater responsibility for their own learning (Kanuka & Garrison, 2004). Self-assessment is a strategy that is of particular relevance to this study as it is essentially a reflective process that has the potential to contribute to student understanding and metacognition.

## Teaching Presence

Teaching presence considers the roles and functions of all participants in creating and maintaining a dynamic learning community (Vaughan & Garrison, 2005). The findings of this study indicate that the category pertaining to moderation is particularly relevant to the development of teaching presence.

Most of the students agreed that effective online feedback from the course moderator was one of the most helpful aspects of the online environment, and stated that the prompt nature of the responses was central to their decision to interact with their community. Effective feedback is viewed as essential to student learning (Driscoll, 2000) and may be even more important within an online environment. Salmon (2004) stresses the significance of effective feedback, stating that students view the quality and quantity of feedback on their work as an important part of the relationship with their educational provider. In the present study, the participants valued the responses of the moderator more than those of their peers; this finding is similar to those reported by other researchers (Ertmer, Richardson, Belland, Camin, Connolly, & Coulthard, 2007; Topping, 1998), who found that students perceive that their peers lack the necessary skills to provide valuable feedback. In an effort to address this undervaluing of peer feedback, some educators recommend that well-devised peer feedback strategies are used (Ertmer et al.).

In this study, the students also noted that the opportunity to engage in online discussion within their respective communities of inquiry was particularly useful. This finding is similar to others presented in the literature that suggests that learning through discussion is an important educational strategy for students (Wang & Woo, 2007). Online discussion forums reflect the conversational mode of learning (Laurillard, 1993) that is associated with increased motivation and engagement in the learning task, deeper levels of understanding, increased metacognition, and the development of higher order thinking skills (Thomas, 2002). However, for online educators, developing discussion forums that facilitate the necessary level of interactive dialogue is a difficult challenge (Stodel et al., 2006; Thomas). In this study, some of the students felt that the lack of online interaction adversely affected their ability to engage with their community of inquiry.

While the findings of this study reveal that the online moderation and discussion boards were particularly useful aspects of this resource, it is important to consider additional means by which teaching presence can be enhanced. Strategies that facilitate effective moderation, including peer-to-peer moderation, are especially relevant.

The effective moderation of online interaction is an essential component in facilitating teaching presence. However, the mechanisms by which effective moderation can be achieved are the subject of much discussion. Garrison and Anderson (2003) call for moderation to be carried out by experienced, responsible teachers who can identify material worthy of study, organise learning activities, and guide the online discourse. They question the validity of the "guide on the side" concept that can limit the teacher's role in online conferencing to that of facilitator of learning. Salmon (1998) argues that training to teach online is essential and that tutors need to be exposed to real but risk-free online environments before they assume the role of moderator.

The use of peer-to-peer feedback (Ertmer et al., 2007) is another strategy designed to facilitate effective online moderation that has the potential to humanise the learning environment, build a sense of community, and provide learning opportunities for both givers and receivers of feedback (Corgan, Hammer, Margolies, & Crossley, 2004). However, Pawan et al. (2003) caution that students require training and modeling by instructors before they can assume the role of facilitator in an effective manner. Similarly, Rourke and Anderson (2002) suggest that educators need to ensure that learners have the requisite skills and/or support to lead online discussions if they are being required to take on this role. Thus, it is apparent that the most effective mechanism to facilitate online moderation invariably depends on the nature and design of the learning experience. It is vital that the lecturer retains overall responsibility for the learning process and ensures that the appropriate mechanisms are in place to facilitate optimum online moderation.

In summary, overall, the preliminary findings from this study indicate that students viewed the online reflective practice resource as a beneficial aid to their learning. The findings also demonstrate that the community-of-inquiry framework (Garrison et al., 2000) and the corresponding guidelines for practice (Garrison & Anderson, 2003) provide a comprehensive model that facilitates the design, delivery, and evaluation of the reflective practice resource. The interpretation of the findings through the lens of the community-of-inquiry framework revealed that a variety of strategies can be employed to improve the efficacy of this resource. These include the following.

- Fostering social presence by incorporating nontask contexts, collaborative learning activities, and innovative communication technologies
- Developing cognitive presence by increasing the students' metacognitive awareness and encouraging self-assessment

- Strengthening teaching presence by developing appropriate and effective online moderation processes for students and lecturers

Finally, this study reinforces the pivotal role that the lecturer must play in the provision of successful and effective online learning experiences.

## FUTURE RESEARCH DIRECTIONS

Research on the use of online communities of inquiry to facilitate reflective practice is at a developmental stage. Further research is required to examine how online communities can be configured in order to assist student engagement in the reflective process. In addition, it is particularly important to examine those factors that assist and inhibit reflection within an online environment. In particular, emphasis is needed on how social presence, cognitive presence, and teaching presence influence the reflective process.

Moving beyond the confines of this investigation, an understanding of learners in online environments is required, and the impact of online learning on behaviour and knowledge development should be examined closely. It is also important to identify the factors that facilitate lecturers to deliver effective online learning experiences and to elucidate the role of educational institutions in the provision of appropriate infrastructures and supports.

Finally, as noted by Garrison and Anderson (2003), we are on the cusp of fully discovering the unique properties of e-learning and its impact on the educational system. If we are to harness the potential of online learning and create a higher education system of the future, it is incumbent on all stakeholders, educationalists, and students to embrace the research agenda actively.

## CONCLUSION

Educational technology provides a variety of challenges and opportunities for those working to improve teaching and learning within higher education. Currently, we are witnessing what Selwyn (2007) terms the "digital disconnect" (p. 2) between the enthusiastic rhetoric and the rather more mundane reality of technology utilisation within the university sector. Educationalists are charged with the daunting task of harnessing the benefits of state-of-the-art technological innovations while simultaneously ensuring that they are applied in a pedagogically and empirically appropriate fashion. Consequently, the publication of this book is most apposite as one of its principal aims is to support academic staff in the development and implementation of effective e-learning strategies within higher education. Accordingly, this chapter is designed primarily to offer some practical insights into the use and development of online communities of inquiry. Contemporary educational discourse suggests that there may be distinct advantages to creating online communities of inquiry, particularly within the context of facilitating reflective practice. To this end, the community-of-inquiry framework devised by Garrison et al. (2000) offers a comprehensive conceptual model that has the potential to foster critical thinking that includes the processes of higher order reflection and discourse (Garrison & Anderson, 2003). While further research in this area is urgently required, the community-of-inquiry framework provides a useful guide to structure and assess online resources. Finally, it is anticipated that the issues addressed in this chapter will contribute to the ever-evolving debate on the role and development of e-teaching within the context of higher education.

## REFERENCES

Admiraal, W., Veen, W., Korthagen, F., Lockhorst, D., & Wubbels, T. (1999). Tele-guidance to develop reflective practice: Experiences in four teacher education programmes across Europe. *Journal of Information Technology for Teacher Education, 8*, 1-21.

An Bord Altranais (2000). *Review of scope of practice for nursing and midwifery – Final report.* Dublin: An Bord Altranais.

Anderson, T. (2004). Teaching in an online learning context. In T. Anderson & F. Elloumi (Eds.), *Theory and practice of online learning* (pp. 271-294). Athabasca: Athabasca University. Retrieved September 1, 2007, from http://www.cde.athabascau.ca/online_book.

Anderson, T., Rourke, L., Garrison, D., & Archer, W. (2001). Assessing teaching presence in a computer conferencing environment. *Journal of Asynchronous Learning Networks, 5*(2). Retrieved September 1, 2007, from http://www.aln.org/alnweb/journal/jaln-vol5issue2v2.htm.

Ascough, R. S. (2002). Designing for online distance education: Putting pedagogy before technology. *Teaching Theology and Religion, 5*, 1-17.

Atkins, S., & Murphy, K. (1993). Reflection: A review of the literature. *Journal of Advanced Nursing, 18*(8), 1188-1192.

Barnes, A. (1998). Email as a non-directed means of developing independent reflection in beginning teachers of foreign languages. *Journal of Information Technology for Teacher Education, 7*, 189-206.

Bautista, A. (1998). A study of the possibilities of teacher education with computer-based telecommunications systems. *Journal of Information Technology for Teacher Education, 7*, 207-230.

Bielaczyc, K. (2001). Designing social infrastructure: The challenge of building computer-supported learning communities. In P. Dillenbourg, A. Eurelings, & K. Hakkarainen (Eds.), *European Perspectives on computer-supported collaborative learning.* (pp. 106–114). Maastricht: Maastricht McLuhan Institute.

Bishop, A. P., Bruce, B., Lunsford, K. J., Jones, M.C., Nazarova, M., Linderman, D., Won, M., Heidorn P. B, Ramprakash, R., & Brock, A. (2004). Supporting community inquiry with digital resources. *Journal of Digital Information, 5*(3). Article No. 308. Retrieved September 1, 2007, from http://jodi.tamu.edu/Articles/v05/i03/Bishop/.

Bodzin, A., & Park, J. P. (2002).Using a nonrestrictive web-based forum to promote reflective discourse with preservice science teachers. *Contemporary Issues in Technology and Teacher Education, 2*, 267-289. Retrieved September 1, 2007, from http://www.citejournal.org/vol2/iss3/science/article1.cfm.

Bridges, L. (1995). *Creating your classroom community.* New York: Stenhouse.

Bulman, C., & Schutz, S. (2004). *Reflective practice in nursing* (3rd ed.). Oxford: Blackwell.

Cheng, R., & Vassileva, J. (2005). Adaptive reward mechanism for sustainable online learning community. Proceedings *of the International Conference on Artificial Intelligence in Education* (pp.152-159). Retrieved September 1, 2007, from http://julita.usask.ca/Texte/aied2005-final.pdf

Corgan, R., Hammer, V., Margolies, M., &Crossley, C. (2004). Making your online course successful. *Business Education Forum, 58*(3), 51–53.

Davis, M. (2003). Barriers to reflective practice: The changing nature of higher education. *Active Learning in Higher Education, 4*(3) 243-255.

Dewey, J. (1933). *How we think. A restatement of the relation of reflective thinking to the educative process.* Boston: D. C. Heath.

Driscoll, M. (2000). *Psychology of learning for instruction* (2nd ed.). Boston: Allyn and Bacon.

Eraut, M. (2004) The practice of reflection. *Learning in Health and Social Care, 3*(2), 47–52.

Ertmer, P. A., Richardson, J. C., Belland, B., Camin, D., Connolly, P., & Coulthard, G. (2007). Using peer feedback to enhance the quality of student online postings: An exploratory study. *Journal of Computer-Mediated Communication, 12*(2), 412-433.

Eynon, R. (2005). The use of the Internet in higher education: Academics' experiences of using ICTs for teaching. Aslib Proceedings: *New Information Perspectives,57*(2), 168-180.

Feenberg, A. (2001). Whither educational technology? *International Journal of Technology and Design Education, 11*(1), 83-91.

Galanouli, D., & Collins, J. (2000). Using unmediated computer conferencing to promote reflective practice and confidence-building in initial teacher education. *Journal of Information Technology for Teacher Education, 9*(2), 237-254.

Garrison, D. R. (2002). *Cognitive presence for effective asynchronous online learning: The role of reflective inquiry, self-direction and metacognition.* Paper presented at the Fourth Annual Sloan ALN Workshop, Boltons Landing, NY. Retrieved September 1, 2007, from http://www.communitiesofinquiry.com/documents/SLOAN%20CP%20CHAPTER%202003.DOC

Garrison, D. R., & Anderson, T. (2003). *E-learning in the 21st century: A framework for research and practice.* London: RoutledgeFalmer.

Garrison, D. R., Anderson, T., & Archer, W. (2000). Critical inquiry in a text-based environment: Computer conferencing in higher education. *The Internet and Higher Education, 2*(2-3), 87-105.

Garrison, D. R., Anderson, T., & Archer, W. (2001). Critical thinking, cognitive presence, and computer conferencing in distance education. *American Journal of Distance Education, 15*(1), 7-23.

Garrison, D. R., Cleveland-Innes, M., & Fung, T. (2004). Student role adjustment in online communities of inquiry: Model and instrument validation. *Journal of Asynchronous Learning Networks, 8*(2), 1-7.

Garrison, D. R., Cleveland-Innes, M., Koole, M., & Kappleman, J. (2006). Revisiting methodological issues in transcript analysis: Negotiated coding and reliability. *The Internet and Higher Education, 9*(1), 1-8.

Geibert, R. (2000). Integrating web-based instruction into a graduate nursing program taught via videoconferencing: *Challenges and solutions. Computers in Nursing 18*(1), 26-34.

Gillis, A., Jackson, W., Braid, A., MacDonald, P., & MacQuarrie, M. (2000). The learning needs and experiences of women using print-based and CD-ROM technology in nursing distance education. *Journal of Distance Education 15*(1), 1–20.

Gunawardena, C. N. (1995). Social presence theory and implications for interaction and collaborative learning in computer conferences. International *Journal of Educational Telecommunications, 1*(2/3), 147-166.

Hannifin, M., Land, S., & Oliver, K. (1983). Open learning environments: Foundations, methods, and models. In C. M. Reigeluth (Ed.), *Instructional design theories and models.* (pp. 115-140). Hillsdale, NJ: Lawrence Erlbaum.

Harasim, L. (1993). Collaborating in cyberspace: Using computer conferences as a group learning

environment. *Interactive Learning Environments, 3*(2), 119–130.

Harrington, H. L., & Hathaway, R. S. (1994). Computer conferencing, critical reflection, and teacher development. *Teaching and Teacher Education, 10*(5), 543-554.

Healey, M. (2003). Promoting lifelong professional development in geography education: International perspectives on developing the scholarship of teaching in higher education in the twenty-first century. *The Professional Geographer, 55*(1), 1-17.

Issroff, K., & Scanlon, E. (2002). Using technology in higher education: An activity theory perspective. *Journal of Computer Assisted Learning, 18*(1), 77-83.

Jonassen, D., Mayes, T., & McAleese, R. (1993). A manifesto for a constructivist approach to uses of technology in higher education. In T. M. Duffy, J. Lowyck, & D. H. Jonassen, Designing *environments for constructive learning* (pp. 231-247).Berlin: Springer.

Kanuka, H., & Anderson, T. (1998). Online social interchange, discord, and knowledge construction. *Journal of Distance Education, 13*(1), 57-74.

Kanuka, H., & Garrison, D. R. (2004). Cognitive presence in online learning.*Journal of Computing in Higher Education, 15*(2), 30-48.

Kitzinger J. (1996). Introducing focus groups. In N. Mays & C. Pope (Eds.), *Qualitative research in health care* (pp. 36-45). London: B. M. J. Publishing Group.

Kreijns, K., Kirschner, P., & Jochems, W. (2003). Identifying the pitfalls for social interaction in computer-supported collaborative learning environments: A review of the research. *Computers in Human Behaviour, 19*(3), 335-353.

Lapadat, J. (2002). Written interaction: A key component in online learning. *Journal of Com-*

*puter-Mediated Communication, 7*(4). Retrieved September 1, 2007, from http://jcmc.indiana. edu/vol7/issue4/lapadat.html.

Laurillard, D. (1993). *Rethinking university teaching: A framework for the effective use of educational technology.* London: Routledge.

Lim, B. (2004).Challenges and issues in designing inquiry on the Web. *British Journal of Educational Technology, 35*(5), 627–643.

Lipman, M. (1991). *Thinking in education.* Cambridge: Cambridge University Press.

Lipponen, L., & Lallimo, J. (2004). From collaborative technology to collaborative use of technology: Designing learning oriented infrastructures. *Educational Media International, 41*(2), 111-116.

Lusty, S. (1969). Educational technology. *Peabody Journal of Education, 47*(1), 53-56.

McAlpine, L., & Gandell, T. (2003). Teaching improvement grants: What they tell us about professors' instructional choices for the use of technology in higher education. *British Journal of Educational Technology, 34*(3), 281-293.

McCredie, J. W. (2000). Planning for IT in Higher Education: It's not an oxymoron. *Educause Quarterly, 23*(4), 14-21.

McKlin, T., Harmon, S., Evans, W., & Jones, M. (2001). Cognitive presence in web-based learning: *A content analysis of student's online discussion.* IT Forum, 60, Retrieved May 10, 2006, from http://eric.ed.gov/ERICDocs/data/ericdocs2sql/ content_storage_01/0000019b/80/1a/86/0b.pdf.

McMullin, B. (2005). Putting the learning back into learning technology. In G. O'Neill, S. Moore, & B. McMullin (Eds.), *Emerging issues in the practice of university learning and teaching* (pp. 67-76). Dublin: AISHE.

Meyer, K. A. (2003).Face-to-face versus threaded discussions: The role of time and higher-order

thinking. *Journal of Asynchronous Learning Networks, 7*(3), 55-65.

Milliken, J., & Barnes, L. (2002). Teaching and technology in higher education: Student perceptions and personal reflections. *Computers & Education, 39*(3), 223-235.

Morgan, D. L. (1996). Focus groups. *Annual Review of Sociology, 22*, 129-152.

Moule, P. (2006). E-learning for healthcare students: *Developing the communities of practice framework. 54*(3), 370-380.

Nicholl, H., & Higgins, A. (2004).Reflection in pre-registration nursing curricula. *Journal of Advanced Nursing, 46*(6), 578-585.

Olson, D. R. (1995). Conceptualizing the written word: An intellectual autobiography. *Written Communication, 12*(3), 277–297.

Paget T. (2001). Reflective practice and clinical outcomes: Practitioners' views on how reflective practice has influenced their clinical practice. *Journal of Clinical Nursing, 10*(2), 204-214.

Palloff, R., & Pratt, K. (2000). *Making the transition: Helping teachers to teach online.* Paper presented at EDUCAUSE: Thinking it through. Nashville,TN. Retrieved September 1, 2007, from http://168.144.129.112/Articles/Helping%2 0Teachers%20to%20Teach%20Online.pdf.

Paradales, M., & Girod, M. (2006). Community of inquiry: Its past and present future. *Educational Philosophy and Theory, 38*(3), 299-309.

Pawan, F., Paulus, T., Yalcin, S., & Chang, C. (2003). Online learning: Patterns of engagement and interaction among in-service teachers. *Language, Learning and Technology, 7*(3), 119-140.

Pennington, G., & O'Neill, M. (1994). Enhancing the quality of teaching and learning in higher education. *Quality Assurance in Education, 2*(3), 13-18.

Perry, B., & Edwards, R. N. (2005). Exemplary online educators: Creating a community of inquiry. *Turkish Online Journal of Distance Education, 6* (2). Retrieved May 12, 2006, from http://tojde. anadolu.edu.tr/tojde18/articles/article6.htm.

Peterson, D. (1992). *Life in a crowded place: Making a learning community.* Portsmouth: Heinemann Educational Books.

Privateer, P. M. (1999). Academic technology and the future of higher education: *Strategic paths taken and not taken. The Journal of Higher Education, 70*(1), 60-79.

Redmond, B. (2004). *Reflection in action: Developing reflective practice in health and social services.* Aldershot: Ashgate Publishing.

Robins, K., & Webster, F. (1989). *The technical fix: Education, computers, and industry.* Basingstoke: Macmillan.

Rogers, D. L. (2000). A paradigm shift: Technology integration for higher education in the new millennium. *Educational Technology Review, 1*(13), 19-33.

Rogoff, B., Matusov, E., & White, C. (1996). Models of teaching and learning: Participation in a community of learners. In D. R. Olson & N. Torrance (Eds.) *The handbook of education and human development* (pp. 388-413). Oxford: Blackwell.

Rourke, L., & Anderson, T. (2002). Using peer teams to lead online discussions. *Journal of Interactive Media in Education, 1.* Retrieved September 1, 2007, from http://www-jime.open. ac.uk/2002/1/rourke-anderson-02-1.pdf.

Rourke, L., Anderson, T., Garrison, D., & Archer, W. (2001). Assessing social presence in asynchronous, text-based computer conferencing. *Journal of Distance Education, 14*(2), 51-70.

Rovai, A. P. (2000). Building and sustaining community in asynchronous learning networks. *The Internet and Higher Education, 3*(4), 285-297.

Ruth , S. (1997). Getting real about technology-based learning: The medium is NOT the message. *Educom Review, 32*(5), 32-37.

Salmon, G. (1998). Developing learning through effective online moderation. *Active Learning, 9* (December), 3–8.

Salmon, G. (2000). *Emoderating: The key to teaching and learning online.* London: Kogan-Page.

Salmon, G. (2002) Mirror, mirror, on my screen: Exploring online reflections. *British Journal of Educational Technology, 33*(4), 379-391.

Salmon, G. (2004). *Emoderating: The key to teaching and learning online.* London: Taylor and Francis Group.

Schraw, G. (2001). Promoting general metacognitive awareness. In H. J. Hartman (Ed.), *Metacognition in learning and instruction: Theory, research and practice* (pp. 3-16). Boston: Kluwer.

Seale, J. K., & Cann, A. J. (2000). Reflection online or off-line: The role of learning technologies in encouraging students to reflect. *Computers and Education, 34* (3-4), 309-320.

Selinger, M. (1998). Forming a critical community through telematics. *Computers and Education, 30*(1), 23-30.

Selwyn, N. (2007). The use of computer technology in university teaching and learning: A critical perspective. *Journal of Computer Assisted Learning, 23*(2), 83-94.

Shea, P., Pickett, A., & Pelt, W. (2003). A follow-up investigation of teaching presence in the SUNY learning network. *Journal of the Asynchronous Learning Network, 7*(2). Retrieved May 1, 2007, from http://www.aln.org/publications/jaln/v7n2/ v7n2_shea.asp.

Spector, J. M. (2001). An overview of progress and problems in educational technology. *Interactive Educational Multimedia, 3,* 27-37.

Steele D, Johnson Palensky J, Lynch T, Lacy N, Duffy S (2002). Learning preferences, computer attitudes and student evaluation of computerized education. *Medical Education, 36*(3), 225–232.

Stodel, E. J., Thompson, T. L, & MacDonald, C. J. (2006). Learners' perspectives on what is missing from online learning: Interpretations through the community of inquiry framework. *The International Review of Research in Open and Distance Learning, 7*(3). Retrieved September 1, 2007, from http://www.irrodl.org/index.php/irrodl/article/viewArticle/325/743

Surry, D. W., Ensminger, D. C., & Haab, M. (2005). A model for integrating instructional technology into higher education. *British Journal of Educational Technology, 36*(2), 327-329.

Teekman, B. (2000) Exploring reflective thinking in nursing practice. *Journal of Advanced Nursing, 31*(5), 1125-1135.

Thomas, M. J. W. (2002). Learning within incoherent structures: The space of online discussion forums. *Journal of Computer Assisted Learning, 18*(3), 351-366.

Topping, K. (1998). Peer assessment between students in colleges and universities. *Review of Educational Research, 68*(3), 249-276.

Vaughan, N., & Garrison, D. (2005). Creating cognitive presence in a blended faculty development community. *The Internet and Higher Education, 8*(1), 1-12.

Vygotsky, L. (1978). *Mind in society: The development of higher psychological processes.* Cambridge: Harvard University Press.

Wang, Q., & Woo, H. L. (2007). Comparing asynchronous online discussions and face-to-face discussions in a classroom setting. *British Journal of Educational Technology, 38*(2), 272-286.

Watson, D. (2001). Pedagogy before technology: Re-thinking the relationship between ICT and teaching. *Education and Information Technologies, 6*(4), 251-266.

Wenger, E. (1998). *Communities of practice: Learning, meaning, and identity.* Cambridge: Cambridge University Press.

Wheeler, S. (2005). *Creating social presence in digital learning environments: A presence of mind?* Featured paper for the TAFE conference, Queensland, Australia. Retrieved September 1, 2007, from http://videolinq.tafe.net/learning2005/papers/wheeler.pdf.

For theoretical and practical value, Garrison, et al. (2000) constructed a template of categories and indicators for each of the three core elements. This template, with its elements, categories, and indicators, has been used in the analysis of computer transcripts and the coding of messages in terms of cognitive presence, social presence, and teaching presence.

## ADDITIONAL READING

Connolly, T. M., MacArthur, E., Stansfield, M. H., & McLellan, E. (2007). A quasi-experimental study of three online learning courses in computing. *Computers and Education, 49*(2), 345-359.

This study investigates the extent to which the teaching and learning of three master's courses in computing were enhanced by being developed and delivered in an online format as compared to face-to-face, full-time, and part-time delivery. The results show that the online students consistently performed better than the face-to-face students.

Dearnley, C., Dunn, G., & Watson, S. (2006). An exploration of on-line access by non-traditional students in higher education: A case study. *Nurse Education Today, 26*(5), 409-415.

This paper discusses a case study that sought to identify the extent to which nontraditional students accessed online learning facilities in higher education. The findings indicate that the greatest obstacle to nontraditional students accessing and using university online learning resources is skill deficit.

Diekelmann, N., & Mendias, E. (2005). Being a supportive presence in online courses: Knowing and connecting with students through writing. *Journal of Nursing Education, 44*(8), 344-346.

This paper explores how teachers can act as a supportive presence by focusing on the meaning and significance of language in online learning environments.

Eom, S. B., Wen, H. J., & Ashill, N. (2006). The determinants of students' perceived learning outcomes and satisfaction in university online education: An empirical investigation. *Decision Sciences Journal of Innovative Education, 4*(2), 215-235.

This study examines the determinants of students' satisfaction and their perceived learning outcomes in the context of university online courses. The findings suggest online education can be a superior mode of instruction if it is targeted to learners with specific learning styles (visual and read/write learning styles) and includes timely, meaningful instructor feedback of various types.

Garrison, R., & Vaughan, N. (2008). *Blended learning in higher education: Framework, principles, and guidelines.* San Francisco: Jossey-Bass.

This book offers a practical guide to the application of blended learning in higher education and demonstrates how a blended learning approach can embrace the traditional values of face-to-face teaching while integrating the best practices of online learning.

Ginns, P., & Ellis, R. (2007). Quality in blended learning: Exploring the relationships between online and face-to-face teaching and learning. *The Internet and Higher Education, 10*(1), 53-64.

This study evaluates the quality of learning arising from learning experiences that involve both face-to-face and online contexts. It represents the beginning phase in the development of a student-centred approach to quality improvement and evaluation of learning in a blended learning context.

Hannan, H. (2005). Innovating in higher education: Contexts for change in learning technology. *British Journal of Educational Technology, 36*(6), 975-985.

This paper draws on three research projects that have examined innovation in learning and teaching methods in UK higher education; it considers the kinds of institutional structures and cultures that make innovation possible.

Hiltz, S. R., & Turoff, M. (2005). Education goes digital: The evolution of online learning and the revolution in higher education. *Communications of the ACM, 48*(10), 59-64.

This paper argues that the current evolutionary changes in educational technology and pedagogy will result in revolutionary changes to the nature of higher education as a process and as an institution.

Ling, L. H. (2007). Community of inquiry in an online undergraduate information technology course. *Journal of Information Technology Education, 6*, 153-168.

This paper presents a case study on the instructional application of online synchronous interaction in a distance IT undergraduate course and focuses on identifying cognitive, social, and teaching presences from the analyses of student experiences and chat exchanges during moderated virtual tutorial discussions.

Mupinga, D. M., Nora, R. T., & Yaw, D. C. (2006). The learning styles, expectations, and needs of online students. *College Teaching, 54*(1), 185-189.

This study explores the learning styles, expectations, and needs of students taking an online course.

Ng, K. C. (2007). Replacing face-to-face tutorials by synchronous online technologies: Challenges and pedagogical implications. *The International Review of Research in Open and Distance Learning, 8*(1), 1-15.

This paper reports on a study that investigated the implementation of a synchronous e-learning system for online tutorials in an information technology course. Issues concerning students' participation and interaction, and tutors' roles in real-time conferences are discussed.

Redmond, B. (2004). *Reflection in action: Developing reflective practice in health and social services.* Aldershot, United Kingdom: Ashgate Publishing.

This book outlines a reflective teaching and learning model that can be used with single- or multidisciplinary groups of students and professionals.

Rourke, L., & Anderson, T. (2004). Validity in quantitative content analysis. *Educational Technology Research and Development, 52*(1), 5-18.

The paper addresses the use of quantitative content analysis in the study of computer-mediated communication within an educational setting.

Salmon, G. (2002). *E-tivities: The key to active online learning.* London: Kogan Page.

This book, based on action research, provides a practical guide for teachers and learners in both higher education and corporate training who are seeking to develop interactive online programmes.

Shea, P. J. (2006). A study of students' sense of learning community in online learning environments. *Journal of Asynchronous Learning Networks, 10*(1). Retrieved September 1, 2007, from http://www.sloan-c.org/publications/jaln/v10n1/v10n1_4shea_member.asp

This paper examines the epistemological, philosophical, and theoretical assumptions that are foundational to student-centred, interactive online pedagogical models.

Shea, P., Sau Li, C., & Pickett, A. (2006). A study of teaching presence and student sense of learning community in fully online and Web-enhanced college courses. *The Internet and Higher Education, 9*(3), 175-190.

This study investigates the link between teaching presence in higher education classroom-based and online learning environments, and the learner's sense of community in these different settings.

Sieber, J. E. (2005). Misconceptions and realities about teaching online. *Science and Engineering Ethics, 11*(3), 329-340.

This article is designed to act as a guide for online course developers and teachers and includes a variety of recommendations aimed at delivering effective online educational experiences.

Swan, K., Shen, J., & Hiltz, S. R. (2006). Assessment and collaboration in online learning. *Journal of Asynchronous Learning Networks, 10*(1), 45-62.

This paper discusses three sorts of online collaborative activity: collaborative discussion, small-group collaboration, and collaborative exams. Theoretical grounding and practical advice for assessing collaboration in online courses is also provided.

Tallent-Runnels, M. K., Thomas, J. A., Lan, W. Y., Cooper, S., Ahern, T. C., Shaw, S. M., et al. (2006). Teaching courses online: A review of the research. *Review of Educational Research, 76*(1), 93-135.

This review of the literature examines research on online teaching and learning and focuses specifically on course environment, learners' outcomes, learners' characteristics, and institutional and administrative factors.

Wallace, R. M. (2003). Online learning in higher education: A review of research on interactions among teachers and students. *Education, Communication and Information, 3*(2), 241-280.

This paper provides an overview of the existing literature in communications, distance education, educational technology, and other education-related fields, and examines what is currently known about online teaching and learning.

Whipp, J. L. (2003). Scaffolding critical reflection in online discussions: Helping prospective teachers think deeply about field experiences in urban schools. *Journal of Teacher Education, 54*(4), 321-333.

This paper explores how a teacher educator used the methodology of a design experiment to compare patterns and levels of reflection in two semesters of her students' e-mail discussions about field experiences in urban schools.

Whitehead, T. D., Brown, J. W., & Kearns, S. P. (2007). Point and click! Review of the literature on utilization of online materials in nursing education programs. *Teaching and Learning in Nursing, 3*(1), 22-26.

This article provides an introduction to the history of Web-based teaching, learning, and assessment. The development of the field of distance education and its relevance to nurse education is also explored.

Wise, K., Hamman, B., & Thorson, K. (2006). Moderation, response rate, and message interactivity: Features of online communities and their effects on intent to participate. *Journal of Computer-Mediated Communication, 12*(1), 24-41.

This paper examines how moderation, response rate, and message interactivity affects people's intent to participate in a Web-based online community. These results indicate that both the structural features of interfaces and the content features of interactions affect people's intent to participate in online communities.

Yang, X., Li, Y., Tan, C. H., & Teo, H. H. (2007). Students' participation intention in an online discussion forum: Why is computer-mediated interaction attractive? *Information and Management, 44*(5), 456-466.

This paper explores the motivational behavioural factors that influence a student's intention to participate in an online discussion forum.

## ENDNOTE

[1]    For theoretical and practical value, Garrison et al. (2000) constructed a template of categories and indicators for each of the three core elements. This template, with its elements, categories, and indicators, has been used in the analysis of computer transcripts and the coding of messages in terms of cognitive presence, social presence, and teaching presence.

# Chapter XIV
# Using Multipoint Audio–Conferencing with Teaching Students:
## Balancing Technological Potential with Practical Challenges

**Nick Pratt**
*University of Plymouth, UK*

## ABSTRACT

*The aim of this chapter is to explore e-learning and e-teaching from a social perspective in order to show how the use of new technologies, like older technologies before them, must be considered in the light of human activity. It is hoped that such a perspective will allow the reader to better understand how, in one example at least, the use of new technology and the context of that use are integral to each other. The chapter considers how multipoint (i.e., multiple people) audio-conferencing might be used with higher education (HE) students undertaking work- or placement-based learning at a distance from their university base.*

## INTRODUCTION

Much of what is written about the use of new technologies in educational settings has focused on the technology itself and what the hardware and software offer users (often potentially) the opportunity to do. Much less emphasis has been placed on the way in which such technologies form part of a wider set of resources used in social settings by people. In part, this is because of the prevalence of a cognitive perspective on learning theory in general in which resources and the practical, emotional, and attitudinal aspects of their use are separate. Though such a cognitive approach can be of use, it often loses the complexity of the interconnections between the people, objects, and situation.

The exploration of e-teaching and e-learning from a social perspective is illustrated by an example taken from an initial teacher training (ITT) course in the southwest of England. This course is, to a large extent, focused on placement-based learning, in which student teachers are involved in practical teaching in schools to develop their professional expertise. Extended placements mean that students live and work away from their campus and must be taught at a distance; the nature of this learning is the development of professional, rather than academic, knowledge. By describing how the audio-conferencing process was used, the chapter illustrates the potential, but also the dilemmas, of such an approach, and shows how technology needs to be considered by educators as just one element in a complex social network. To this end, it aims to be pragmatic in that it illuminates some practical aspects of the use of e-conferencing. Though taking teacher training as the focus, much of what is said can be seen as common to other work-based learning situations, and the chapter will be of interest to anyone involved in such work.

## BACKGROUND CONTEXT

Students training to work in primary (elementary) schools in England must work toward national standards of competence (Training and Development Agency [TDA] for Schools, 2007) to achieve their qualified teacher status (QTS). For school-based elements of their course, they are usually placed with a particular class and hence a particular teacher. In addition to the ongoing support of this professional, the teaching of students on school-based placements is also undertaken by having school staff, who are trained by the university as mentors, with university link tutors supporting them. The project reported here aimed to supplement this link support through remote desktop audio-conferencing, which meant that in addition to making just a few visits to individual

schools, a group of students could also meet with a university tutor every week in a virtual conference.

The technology (both hardware and software) used for these meetings created a distinctive virtual environment within which the students and the tutor could learn together. However, this environment is situated within a number of other environments in the real world and must interact with them. As John and Sutherland (2005) have pointed out, any learning is not a function solely of the technology, nor can any technology "automatically guarantee learning" (p. 406). On the other hand, users are not independent of the features of the technology in use since, as Adams (2007) demonstrates, the internal structures of any technology are "quietly and persistently informing our every digitally-enhanced action and experience" (p. 232). Understanding how new technologies can be used to the best effect may be supported by theoretical models, but what is also necessary is "describing and reflecting on the lived experiences of teachers and students engaged in technology-enriched environments" (ibid.). In the context of work-placement learning, one cannot simply articulate how multipoint conferencing supports students' thinking since it is implicitly tied to a consideration of (at least) how learning might be understood in general and the features of the particular context (schooling, national standards for a teaching qualification, higher education [HE], etc.) within which the work is being undertaken. Just as importantly, studies of teaching and learning situations have shown that simply enacting superficial features of teaching does not necessarily change underlying patterns of learning behaviour (e.g., Pratt, 2006; F. Smith, Hardman, & Higgins, 2006; H. Smith & Higgins, 2006), which are often deeply historically and culturally embedded (e.g., Alexander, 2000) and strongly tied to the perceived aims of the programme, particularly the assessment regime (e.g., Rust, 2002).

## LEARNING IN (TEACHING) WORK PLACEMENTS

There are many models of learning, each of which has something different to offer in illuminating a process that is too complex to understand in its entirety. One feature of learning in work placements, including students of teaching, is that the learner is developing expertise in practice. Note the multiple meaning here: the learner is developing his or her knowledge of the practice in which he or she is involved and developing this expertise through the act of practicing. Furthermore, this expertise can be understood as residing in the practice itself; expertise is not a matter of being able to talk about the practice alone, but is seen through the professional's action in actually carrying out their work.

To understand how learning happens in this professional context Schön's (1983, 1987) notion of reflective practice is useful in suggesting that professionals develop expertise through reflection in action. This is the process of perceiving tensions and dilemmas in one's work and using the sense of discomfort associated with these as the stimulus to reconsider, and potentially change, one's actions. Much of this process may happen subconsciously. In addition, there is the process of reflection on action: deliberate reflection undertaken post hoc in order to make sense of what one did and, hopefully, to provide a possibility for acting differently next time.

As Billet (2001) has argued, "views about [vocational] expertise have largely been a product of theorising within cognitive psychology" (p. 431). In England, government models of professional expertise have certainly been dominated by this perspective, one which views knowledge as a commodity acquired and owned by the individual. The focus on acquisition implies that professionals need to gain "competencies" or "skill sets," which can then be "applied" to professional situations at will. Whilst such a model may sometimes be of

value, not least because it allows for the kinds of measurable accountability that is a feature of much current policy, it has considerable limitations. In particular, it does not account for the specific nature of the practices of the community within which the students are working (Wenger, 1998): how the community structures what is "normal practice" and how meaning is constituted between participants through this practice. Taking these things into account requires a perspective that focuses on social, cultural, and historical aspects of practice. From this viewpoint, knowledge is tied to the context in which it is developed since learning is not the acquisition of more things known but is the increased expertise that develops through participation in the practices of the community. As Kelly (2006, p. 509) describes it, in relation to teaching,

*in this [more complex, socially situated] view expertise no longer concerns the application of a richly indexed body of knowledge to solve problems. Rather it is the constant and iterative engagement in constructing and reconstructing professional knowledge using various perspectives including teacher research with the aim of conceptualising and addressing problems. Here teachers have an active and productive relationship with their professional knowledge base. They construct their own knowledge base for teaching, in their own particular circumstances, with a view to addressing the particular problems which they have identified.*

For teacher training in England, even if tutors and students adopt this complex view of professional learning, both parties are required to work within a very different and strongly competence-based model of expertise laid down and inspected by the government. Through their programme, they must demonstrate competence in nearly 40 different standards for qualified status. This is a very demanding task, particularly for postgraduate certificate of education (PGCE) students who, as graduates, undertake a training programme of just 9 months.

Inevitably, for students, the need to justify their attainment against standards is in tension with more complex, critical versions of professional development since the former demands compliance and therefore discourages the kind of risk taking and nonconformity that is essentially for the latter (Hayes, 2001). Power dimensions are important in this, playing out in terms of students' relationships and status in the placement community. Where they stand in relation to pupils, class teachers, and school-based and university-based mentors is often in question, illustrating again how professional learning is situated in the learning context and is very much an issue of identity (Kelly, 2006; Wenger, 1998).

## WHAT NEW TECHNOLOGIES MIGHT OFFER

The last few years have seen massive investment in new technologies for education in England, both in schools and in higher education. For example, around the turn of the millennium, the New Opportunities Fund (NOF) made £180 million available to English schools for ICT training, equipment, and broadband connections. Similarly, in 2004 to 2005, the TDA, which oversees teachers' initial training and continuing development in England, gave ITT providers £6.2 million to develop e-learning communities and around £1 million for online curriculum materials and interactive whiteboards. This commitment to investment is based on assumptions about the positive effects of ICT, which have yet to be fulfilled in practice. For schools in which ITT students are learning how to teach, significant change is very hard to deliver in education because of the deep cultural and historical nature of practices (Alexander, 2000; Earl, Watson, Levin, Leithwood, Fullan, &

Torrence, 2003). What is more, Somekh (2004) has suggested that this may be particularly true where new technology is concerned because of the particular way in which it challenges some of the orthodoxies of formal schooling, including increasing the autonomy of the learner. She argues that easy access to knowledge through, for example, the Internet and rapid and immediate communication, changes the relationships on which teaching and learning is founded. Add to this situation more pragmatic issues such as technical expertise and support and confidence that affect the uptake of ICT (Abbott, Grosbois, & Klein, 2005), and one can begin to understand why investment alone may not be making a substantial difference to practices in schools.

The arguments above apply equally to HE, with many institutions experimenting with technology but failing to embrace it fully enough to effect significant change in teaching and learning practices (Salmon, 2005). In both contexts, school and university, the integrated use of new technologies needs to be addressed in a range of ways. Surface-level technical issues need to be overcome but, alongside this, new technologies need to be part of significant changes to pedagogy so that the way teaching and learning is undertaken becomes different, as opposed to simply using technology as a new (not even necessarily better) way of doing what was always done (Salmon; Somekh, 2004; Webb & Cox, 2004). In other words, one significant question is how new technologies can be used in the design of teaching and learning experiences that are fundamentally different, taking into account both how learning happens and what new technologies offer.

Laurillard (2002) offers a model for this in the context of HE students. This model is based on the development of what she calls academic knowledge, which always involves dealing with "descriptions of the world"; one might therefore argue about how this relates to knowledge in practice, which is the focus of teaching students.

Nevertheless, her central point, that teaching and learning should essentially be an iterative dialogue between tutor and student, is relevant for student teachers and matches Kelly's (2006) perspective on professional learning. Laurillard (2002) argues that central features of this dialogical approach are that it should be

- discursive, with tutors providing an environment within which conceptions are accessible to others,
- adaptive to the changing needs of the student,
- interactive, in providing and using feedback for concept development, and
- reflective, such that feedback is used to reconsider and develop ideas.

Whereas Laurillard sees these as features of all effective teaching events, Vallance and Towndrow (2007, p. 223) offer a list of attributes of ICT that, in their view, make it likely to add value to learning. These include

- making possible activities not accessible without ICT,
- allowing greater flexibility for when and where learning takes place,
- increasing the range of available information,
- providing "socially-orientated contexts" for "knowledge construction,"
- encouraging discussion and interaction, and
- "providing a channel for feedback and assessment."

Though the latter are proposed specifically in relation to ICT, one can see considerable overlap between the two lists and both reflect the kinds of constant and iterative engagement with professional knowledge that Kelly (2006) describes.

## USING MULTIPOINT AUDIO-CONFERENCING TO SUPPORT PLACEMENT STUDENTS

How then does the discussion above relate to student placements and in particular to teaching students in primary schools? In the southwest of England, geographical issues dictate that primary schools are often small and relatively isolated. This means that students can often find themselves placed on their own with little or no contact with peers. What is more, on school placements generally, though there may be ongoing opportunities for discussion about practice with the host class teacher, opportunities to talk to the school mentor and the university link tutor are limited: usually once a week in the first case and only every few weeks in the latter. The immediacy of chances to reflect on incidents and discuss alternatives may be limited. In addition, the standards-driven agenda for success means that these opportunities are usually limited to discussion only about very specific aspects of practice and offer less opportunity to talk more generally about teaching and learning. Finally, one of the advantages of having a mentor on the spot is that he or she understands the local context and can help the student to make sense of this in a way that a visiting tutor cannot. This has been one of the central arguments for school-based tutoring, along with the claim that university tutors may not be in touch with current practice. Whether such claims are true or not, the very fact that the university tutor brings a different perspective, often based on a wider range of mentoring experiences than the school tutor, is potentially a considerable advantage. Thus, the breadth of experience and vision is a significant issue in placement supervision, with university tutors likely to bring a more global, less site-specific version of practice to a discussion.

These ideas allow us now to consider what one new technology, multipoint audio-conferencing, might offer teaching students working at a distance from their university base. A range of audio-conferencing software packages are now available. The one used in the project described here was commercially available on the Internet through Webex (http://www.webex.com) and allows multiple users to meet online with an Internet phone connection for two people at any one time with the others listening (see Figure 1). In addition to audio, it has a chat area for near-synchronous written comments (bottom-right corner) and a larger data area in which video, documents, and live presentations can also be shared synchronously. Other functionality of this software includes the ability for participants to indicate a desire to speak using a hand icon and the use of highlighting, pointing, and text creation in the data area so that documents can be annotated live. Being Web-based, it can potentially be used in any location in which there is Internet access.

It seems apparent that this software has the potential to afford all the items in Vallance and Towndrow's (2007) list. In terms of the specific case of (teaching) placement students outlined in the paragraphs above, we might expect audio-conferencing software to support them in particular in overcoming the difficulty of physical isolation from each other and in providing more immediate opportunities to make sense of the placement experience. What is more, because it affords the opportunity for the university tutor to be present on a more regular basis, it might also balance the potentially site-specific view of the school-based mentor, offering the students the best of both worlds: a local view and a global one together. In addition, this particular technology also affords the four features of effective teaching advanced by Laurillard (2002), offering an environment that can be discursive, adaptive, interactive, and reflective.

Two points are worth making at this juncture. First, saying that the technology affords these

*Figure 1. Screenshot of the Webex conference environment*

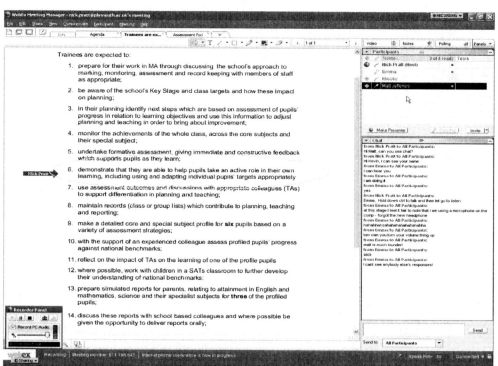

things this does not mean that they will happen, both because the technology itself may not function as planned and because it is only part of the wider, more complex social network within which it is being used. Second, the idea that something is afforded does not make this a good thing per se. The opportunity to think in a more global, less site-specific way may not be helpful for a student who wants to take a strategic approach to their learning (Entwistle, 1997), focusing perhaps on only those things that matter in the assessment of their practice and not on developing a wider view of professional practice. Conversely, constraints imposed by aspects of a system may also be helpful, for example, in limiting the number of choices one has to make at any one time. These are social and cultural issues related to the functioning of the community of practice within which placement students are operating.

## Illustrations from the Audio-Conferencing Project

Having outlined the main theoretical ideas that might pertain to placement learning situations, I continue my analysis through describing some practical examples from an audio-conferencing project involving student teachers on school placements. The project took place over 2 years and involved 33 students and 21 schools at various times during different phases. Though I draw broadly on all these experiences, examples are taken from one particular phase of the project with the focus on just four students. As a case study, this phase offers examples of practices that seem particularly important in making the use of multipoint conferencing positive and useful for participants.

Data were gathered across the 2 years of the project through student logs maintained during their school placements, group interviews after each school experience, and, for the four students reported here, an individual interview with each one at the end of their course. In addition, the conferencing software allows each conference to be recorded digitally in full and replayed later, meaning that recordings of the 10 conferences (audio, chat, and dynamic on-screen action) carried out with this group were also available for analysis. Transcription and careful listening and replaying of interviews, logs, and conferences led to the development of grounded theory through a constant-comparative approach of the kind described by Strauss and Corbin (1990). In outline, this involves assigning meaning to data and searching for patterns in this meaning. Once patterns are developed, the data are reexamined repeatedly, with categories altered and adjusted until they become distinct and satisfy all the data. It is then these categories and the meaning that they convey that are used to develop new theoretical ideas.

The aim here was not to quantify the effects of technology on participants in any way but, rather, to see the use of the technology in the wider picture of the students' experience on their placements and to provide the reader with some kind of access to how this felt for them. Such an analysis is in line with the main thesis of this chapter: that technology use can only be understood in terms of the social situations in which it takes place and the ways in which participants experience this use as part of their ongoing practice. Inevitably, such an analysis is a construction on the part of the researcher but in line with accepted practices in qualitative case-study research (Bassey, 1999; Maykut & Morehouse, 1994). Trustworthiness was sought through validation with participants who were provided with drafts of analysis for comment. Furthermore, findings were shared with peers through faculty seminars and considered carefully in light of previous research.

### Initial Stages

The four focus students were on a 9-month PGCE course and were all working in primary schools. Significantly, they were a self-selected group who had volunteered to take part in the course as a research project and to do so throughout the programme so that the use of conferencing could be developed fairly gradually over two extended placements. In all, 10 conferences were undertaken with the group: three on the shorter (5-week) first placement and seven on the longer (9-week) second placement. Though all four were reasonably computer literate, none were highly skilled technically or experienced in the use of Internet conferencing. On the other hand, their involvement was given willingly, and this was almost certainly significant in terms of their resilience, sticking with the project even when challenged by technical and pedagogical difficulties. Mark, for example, commented that he "quite like being involved in things…it's nice to feel a part of something, especially when you're doing it for a reason [being part of a research project], so it's kind of exciting then to be part of that" (Mark, personal interview).

Evie stated that "it was just nice to be doing something different from what you were doing in school" (Evie, personal interview).

It is worth noting that such resilience was not a feature of an early phase of the project, in which students had been selected to take part on the basis of the schools they were placed in. Though some worked enthusiastically to overcome difficulties, the many small challenges that new technologies tend to confront the user with offered perfect excuses for others to neglect the project. What matters here in terms of the development of e-learning projects is the way in which these student behaviours are constructed. It is tempting to see unwillingness to participate as a form of deficiency on their part—a sense of student apathy. However, from the perspective of the student, whose motivation is to be successful in the programme or at least to get by, the benefit of taking part in e-learning experiences needs to outweigh any cost to them in terms of effort and time. Generally, there tend to be considerable costs during the initial stages of any new development

before much is gained, and finding ways to make this seem worthwhile appears to be important. This was certainly the case here. The four students involved experienced many difficulties, not really getting the most from the experience until some way into their second school placement. Indeed, though none of them commented directly on why they stuck with it, there was a sense that it was a feeling of being committed to the research project that carried them over the initial entry cusp into useful participation.

## The Experience of Audio-Conferencing

The effort involved in this transition between cost and benefit might be thought of as overcoming technical challenges through training and repeated use: Things become easier once participants have simply learned what to do. However, a more complex picture was apparent in practice, with effort referring as much to the emotional response involved as to any technical knowledge. For example, Evie described the experience of attempting to log on to the conference through the host software, a process that she clearly knew how to do, noting that "it's that initial boom, boom; you know your heart's going when you try to get on. You're thinking, is it going to work, is it going to work?" (Evie, personal interview).

Keith claimed that the functionality of the conferences was smoother toward the end of the project, but an analysis of them from the digital recordings suggests that this was not the case and that this was simply Keith's perception. Such observations illustrate the way in which professional (placement) knowledge is more than simply know-how but is rather the kind of knowledge in practice suggested by Schön (1983, 1987) in which emotional and cognitive aspects of knowing are not seen as separate but as inseparable parts of coming to know something. They also suggest that, though training students in advance how to use technology may be very helpful, it may not relieve the need for fairly long lead-in times before practices become embedded.

Though the focus of this chapter is on the successes of audio-conferencing, there were, in practice, a considerable number of challenges to easy participation. Though space prevents an extended description, these related largely to lack of technical support and infrastructure and the working practices of teachers and schools, in particular the perceived value of new ways of working that challenge traditional approaches to the supervision of teaching students (Pratt, in press). Indeed, it was not until early in the second placement that students were reporting that conferences had become useful aspects of their professional development. Because the conferences aimed to supplement the more structured and formalised aspects of students' placement experiences, the format for them was relatively loose. Each one ended with the student agreeing on a date for the next meeting, and a few days prior to this an e-mail was sent out to each student asking what the focus might be. Consequently, some kind of activity was devised as the focus of the conference, usually in the form of an electronic document (in Word or PowerPoint) that could be shared synchronously as the focal point of the meeting. This way of working was an attempt to respond to students' needs with some degree of immediacy. It was also a deliberate attempt to provide a global perspective, moving away from the imperative of achieving the standards for qualified status that dominated students' attention. This was not because participants wanted to (or should) neglect these standards, but because it was considered useful to complement the tendency for inward-looking assessment with a more outward-looking and reflective approach. Rather than asking what had been achieved, the aim was to ask what might be significant and how this might relate to one's own situation.

Reaction to this way of working was very positive. In particular, all the students spoke positively of the opportunity to share with peers aspects of their practice that were difficult.

*"I really enjoyed it actually. I really appreciated it. The facility to actually talk to someone else going through the same sort of thing was really beneficial" (Keith, personal interview).*

*"It was nice sitting listening to other people having the same problems, and thinking I'm not just the only one" (Val, personal interview).*

Moreover, as well as this opportunity for peer reassurance, the access to expert advice at the point of need and flexibility to be able to deal with issues as they arose was highlighted: "It was nice that you [tutor] were confident and comfortable enough to take an issue which maybe you didn't know exactly what it was going to be but then kind of run with it" (Mark, personal interview).

In saying that this flexible approach was successful, I do not wish to imply that it represents some sort of magic formula for placement supervision. Indeed, the success I am describing is being constructed post hoc, not in the sense that people were not positive about it at the time, but in the sense that it was simply what we did (albeit based on principled decisions). My conjecture is that other ways of working might have been equally well received by students and this, I think, is very significant in arguing that e-learning and e-teaching are like all other forms of learning and teaching: highly dependent on the intent that lies within the human relationships at a deep level, not on the surface level of the learning task and the teacher's actions. What is brought to the fore by this observation is Laurillard's (2002) point about both the promise and the dangers of audio-conferencing (and other technologies). Just using technology is not enough and neither is simply analysing the task involved since what is equally crucial is the way in which the tutor uses this task to allow students to feel able to operate discursively, how he or she adapts the focus to the needs of the students, how reflection is encouraged, and how feedback is given in a way that promotes rather than prevents further thinking.

These elements of practice are functions of the relationships developed between participants, not least the power dynamics inherent in their identities. Much of students' experience in school placements is dominated by more powerful figures and by the agenda of the standards against which they must demonstrate competence by the end of their visit. Laurillard's (2002) suggested framework, on the other hand, demands a more democratic, less authoritative approach, which appeared to be provided, to some extent at least, by the conferences in this project. What then, we may ask, shaped this situation?

## Shaping Successful Learning

Though not enough on its own, the nature of the task that forms the focal point for conferencing is clearly important in shaping success. Though it states the obvious, for discursive interaction there needs to be something to discuss, and this means having a task that is open to interpretation in some way and provocative enough to generate different perspectives. Because the Webex software used here allowed for synchronous viewing of electronic documents, key questions relating to a topic could be prepared in advance and used as prompts for discussion. Statements offering alternative perspectives on the focus topic were also found to be useful and, as research has suggested (Dillon, 1990), were often better at generating productive discussion. Hence, for one conference, quotes from a course text were used as comparative statements for students to consider their own practice against. Alongside these, materials that had previously been used in faculty-based sessions, such as PowerPoint presentations and handouts, could be shown again to the students, helping them to make links between work undertaken in both settings and allowing them not just to reflect on their practice, but to

do so in the light of a theoretical framework. The effect of bringing frameworks to the placement is reflected in Keith's view that a conference

*actually has the potential to continue professional development input, study and reflection during a practice rather than doing a bit of professional development in college, going away from it for 3 weeks when you are on school experience and then coming back.... The benefit for me was actually bringing a document from outside—and how do you reflect on this document in the light of what you are doing? Is this helpful, you know, are you using bits of that, are you not? I think that was the benefit rather than "let's tutor [the school experience] through this." (Keith, personal interview)*

In addition to the task used in conferencing, the situation was deliberately designed to be less authoritative and more discursive than the students' usual school experience. Crucially, the tutoring role was set up as a "critical friend" rather than an assessor, meaning that students were not caught in the potentially fatal tension between having to justify their progress whilst simultaneously discussing their limitations. Without this freedom from assessment, deeply reflective interaction is challenging and feedback is less likely to lead to adaptation of practice because it will inevitably be seen as summative judgement. Evie, for instance, compared the more formal discussion that occurred when her tutor went to watch her teach with the opportunity for "more informal chat," which "was easier this time" because of the conferences. For her, discussion between peers and tutor "highlights the fact that you're all very different in different ways and you've got benefits that different people don't have, but it's not a bad thing. It was a real eye-opener to see what people's difficulties were [and to share one's own]" (Evie, personal interview).

Moreover, the freedom from assessment meant that foci could be chosen by students, who then had the power to further adapt them during the conference by bringing issues of immediate importance to the agenda as it began. For example, at one point, students had asked to discuss the assessment of pupils' work (a key target for them in meeting the standards) at the next conference, and Evie began this meeting by identifying what the issues were for her, as follows

NP: Ok, shall we just hear from everyone how things are going, generally? Evie, do you want to tell us how things are going?

E: Everything's going really well. I've taught the whole day today and over 75% of last week. So, volume-wise, it's all going really well. Um, I'm a bit worried about getting all of my assessment done. I've only just figured out that it's next Thursday, or the Thursday after the half term [holiday] that our files go in [to be moderated by tutors]. Is that right?

NP: Yes, I think so.

E: The first week back after half term is assessment and trips. There's not that much planning and teaching to do so it's quite a good time at the beginning of that week [to focus on assessment].

NP: Good, ok, well we're going to talk a bit about assessment tonight, I hope. That's what people asked for last week and so I've got some suggestions for assessment and we can perhaps talk about what each of us are doing.
(Conference transcript)

Despite this freedom to set the agenda, for all the students, practical issues had a bearing on what they could say, not least because conferences were usually carried out in the public arena of the school classroom, and hence, "one of the downsides is that sometimes it's difficult to speak about some of the things you want to talk about because you don't know who's listening in" (Keith, personal interview).

A third dimension of the shape of successful online practice, after situation and task, was the software itself. This was predominantly centred on the vocal mode of the two-way audio, which allowed for the conference presenter (usually the tutor) and one student to talk at any one time, with the other participants able to hear this conversation. To change the second speaker, the presenter had to "pass" the microphone to another person by clicking on an icon. This two-way structure affords specific patterns of communication, in particular, tending to create the familiar initiation-response-feedback (IRF) sequence that is well documented in classroom interactions (e.g., Mercer, 1995; Wells, 1993). In this IRF sequence, tutor-initiated questions are responded to by the student, and this response is then evaluated in feedback by the tutor before the cycle starts again. Though evident in conference recordings, students soon learnt to use other affordances of the software to gain access to the discussion. The use of a hand icon to indicate that they wanted to speak allowed them to gain the presenter's attention and interject, but more commonly, the facility to chat using asynchronous text was used by students to comment on what was being said. Annotation of shared documentation with arrows and highlighting led to a third layer of discussion, too, so that at any one time the proper conversation between tutor and student simultaneously involved the audio discussion, written comments, and visual prompts. This led to a richer discussion than might be imagined; indeed, students soon began to subvert the situation to their own ends, often carrying on peripheral conversations by text at the same time as engaging in the central focal discussion, using the kind of shortened, informal language common to phone texting that they were clearly familiar with. For Val, this seemed "almost like body language," and thus, whilst the software ostensibly afforded a two-way conversation, students found ways to contribute to this in some of the same ways that they would in a conventional face-to-face conversation.

Whilst the paragraphs above have pointed to task, the social context of the learning situation, and the affordances of the software as if they were separate dimensions of successful learning, it is their interdependence that I want to draw attention to and the observation that none would have worked the same way without the others. Setting the tutor up as a critical friend relies on creating a social situation in which power relationships are relatively level so that "we could discuss it almost on an equal footing" (Keith). Though direct statements were made at the start that this was how things were intended to be, this relationship was afforded more by both the open, nonjudgemental tasks used and by the software structure and the informality of its text-based chat. The latter, unlike the more carefully thought out and public contributions made vocally, allowed students to explore tentative ideas. According to one student, this was true

*because you could affirm things. You wouldn't want to say blatantly that you disagree with something anyway, but to be able to say [i.e., text chat] "oh yeah, definitely," or "that's the same for me," or "that's the same but this is slightly different," or trying to make a point that is maybe adding something, was useful. (Matt, personal interview)*

Just as relationships then were constituted in software, tasks, and the physical environment, so the tasks used were not in themselves open. It was their design, coupled with the ways in which the software afforded students' interaction and the social positioning and physical privacy of each participant that afforded or constrained the opportunity for discussion, feedback, adaptation, and reflection.

## PRACTICAL CHALLENGES AND TECHNOLOGICAL POTENTIAL

In the analysis that preceded the examples drawn from this project, I noted that new technologies afford, but do not guarantee, effective learning patterns, and that even when affordances are realised, this still may not be a good thing for learners per se. It is both these points that are, I think, sometimes missed in the analysis of new technologies, explaining why projects are often less successful in practice than hoped (Abbott et al., 2005). How affordances can be realised and understanding their impact on learning are both issues that relate as much to the social world of the users as to the technical world of the software and hardware. Moreover, taking a sociocultural perspective on new technologies suggests that these two worlds cannot be separated as if they were independent. People do not just carry their use of technology into the social world. Use and the social world are mutually defined by each other.

In light of the points above, the models offered by Vallance and Towndrow (2007) and by Laurillard (2002) are valuable, but, I would argue, need also to be seen within a wider, social perspective on the e-teaching and e-learning situation. Such an assertion is not new (for example, Adams, 2007); however, the brief examples given above have, I hope, illustrated this social interdependence by demonstrating the interaction between the relationships of participants, the tasks offered for learning, the physical environment within which this takes place, and the structure of the technology. From this perspective, my assertion is that the use of new technologies to support professional learning on placements presents a number of practical challenges for tutors and students, as follows.

First, though largely beyond the scope of this chapter, there remain many technical issues relating to compatibility, connectivity, and smooth functioning of hardware and software. The nature and extent of these will be different between differing professional contexts, with each presenting its own challenges. Schools, for example, require protective filters on Internet access that can also interfere with legitimate use. Funding may be limited and the historical nature of teaching practices may prevent necessary expertise from developing.

Second, the way in which participants are prepared for, and respond to, the frustrations that are presented by the inevitable unreliability of these technical issues needs to be considered and designed into the teaching programme. As the examples above demonstrate, though training a priori is useful, it is unlikely to prevent long lead-in times for smooth use since this appears to be as much about the way it feels to work with a new technology as it is about technical know-how. Participants must become comfortable with the use of the technology in context, not just with its functionality. Furthermore, whilst the events described here involved volunteers who were willing to persevere when things got difficult, the experience of earlier phases of the project suggest that technical difficulties provide perfect excuses to opt out for those not committed to it. Scaling up small projects to whole cohorts of students remains an issue therefore, and there will be a need for tutors to help potential participants to understand the value of the new technology in terms of how it will support learning. This, in turn, implies the need to be clear about the models of learning that are being used in their education and to help students to understand these too.

Third, and coming out of the second point above, there is a need to understand fully the nature of the community of practice (Wenger, 1998) within which the student will be working and the way in which the technology integrates with the norms, practices, and relationships that define this community. What is more, in work placements, there are multiple communities involved: the school (or other workplace) community, the university (or other overseeing organisation)

community, the student community, and so forth. How the use of the technology by the student will be viewed, how this use fits with the models of teaching and learning being used elsewhere (in school and in university, say), and how others will view this use and how it fits into established working practices are all questions that might be considered. From this need to understand the working practices clearly comes a fourth challenge. The planning and implementation of the use of the technology by tutors and students within this community will need to be carefully thought through, not just in advance but on an ongoing basis as the use of the technology itself changes established practices in a reciprocal way.

Though identified separately, as we have seen, these four challenges are very much interdependent, with each one holding implications for the others. This interdependence creates a complexity that perhaps belies the apparent simplicity of Vallance and Towndrow's (2007) list of valuable attributes of ICT, for whilst these are easy to describe retrospectively, they appear harder to control in practice. So, for example, whilst we might desire to use ICT to create socially orientated contexts for "knowledge construction" and for "providing a channel for feedback and assessment" (ibid., p. 223), the exact nature of the context and the channel created as vehicles for learning will be dependent on a great many factors. New technologies cannot therefore be dropped into established situations as if they will simply add a new choice for participants' working practices. The mutual interdependence of tools and practices means that participants may need to become more aware of well-established working habits and be open to analysing underlying assumptions and beliefs with a view to change. For example, in replacing traditional forms of individual, written reflection with group oral reflection through the introduction of audio-conferencing, some of the norms for students' work were upset. The idea that students recorded less and talked more had implications for assessment, traditionally carried out to a certain degree through student files. Similarly what, to the student, was time well spent online in consultation with a tutor was seen as time wasted by some teachers whose values lay in the practice of "getting on with it."

Despite these challenges, the chapter has illustrated the potential of desktop audio-conferencing in supporting students in work placements. In summary, its potential lies in affording the kind of dialogical approach to teaching and learning advocated by Laurillard (2002; being discursive, adaptive, interactive, and reflective), but also, in the context of the workplace, offering support that is both immediate in time and global in outlook. As Keith describes it, its value perhaps lies in

*the setting of the experience in a bigger context, both in terms of hearing how other students are coping with similar problems and different problems, and how it was for them, and also having the opportunity to share reflections on a more global scale rather than "This is what I'm doing this week." How's this actually helping me? (Keith, personal interview)*

## FUTURE RESEARCH DIRECTIONS

The study undertaken here was with ITT students in primary schools. As noted, many difficulties were encountered in setting up and sustaining conferences in relation to lack of technical support and infrastructure and the working practices of teachers and schools. Future work might usefully explore the following.

- Ways to support school-based mentors and teachers in e-conferencing so that they can take a more active part in the joint supervision of students. This would imply studying the ways in which participants renegotiated some of the norms and practices of supervision and their underlying assumptions.

- Ways to overcome some of the technical difficulties, particularly those associated with tight Internet security and the requirements and constraints of Internet service provision to schools

- Examples of materials, tasks, and approaches that have provided rich conferences (noting that an original aim of the project here was to share video of each student teaching for discussion as a group, an aim that became too difficult to realise in practice for both technical and ethical reasons; Pratt, 2008)

Though drawing its examples from schools, a central issue emerging from this chapter has been the situated nature of the use of technology, audio-conferencing in this case, and the way in which a sociocultural perspective helps to illuminate the interconnectedness of technology and social space. Given this point, a second important direction for future research is to better understand how use of the same technology is manifested in a range of different situations. Questions for further study are as follows.

- How might novice professionals make use of audio-conferencing in other professional situations (for example, medical students in hospitals or trainee social workers on placement)? What might we learn from each situation, recognising that vivid descriptions may offer as much as theoretical models?

- How do the situational issues, didactical approaches, and technological affordances interact in use? What benefits and costs do these have for participants, and do principles for increasing benefits emerge?

- How can any such principles feed back into the design of better technology and better didactical approaches (tasks, interrelationships, etc.)?

A third direction for research is in the nature of professional learning itself. Whilst the workplace has provided the context for insights into technology use in this chapter, so, equally, the latter provides insights into the way in which professional learning takes place. We might therefore ask the following.

- What can studies of the use of placement-based audio-conferencing (or other new technologies) tell us about the working practices of professional workplaces and the way in which these are maintained and constantly renegotiated by participants?

The thrust of this chapter has been on the need to consider new technologies in a broader manner than is commonly undertaken, focusing on the social practices within which they are being introduced. In part, this means a realisation that changes to the way in which technology is being used cannot be independent of the social, cultural, and historical practices already embedded in the context of this use. Put another way, any developing understanding of e-learning and e-teaching in educative contexts must focus on the interrelationship between both the *e* and the *learning* and *teaching*. Furthermore, though cognitive models and experimental studies will offer useful insights into such situations, sociocultural perspectives may well complement these studies in ways that offer different viewpoints. Indeed, since learning situations intrinsically involve social practices, the combination of both perspectives may offer the best chance of effecting significant and long-lasting change in the practice of teaching and learning with new technologies.

## REFERENCES

Abbott, C., Grosbois, M., & Klein, M. (2005). A beautiful house built on sand: What makes e-communication projects succeed—and why are they so rare? *Technology, Pedagogy and Education, 14*(2), 225-239.

Adams, C. (2007). On the "informed use" of PowerPoint: Rejoining Vallance and Towndrow. *Journal of Curriculum Studies, 39*(2), 229-233.

Alexander, R. J. (2000). *Culture and pedagogy: International comparisons in primary education.* Oxford, United Kingdom: Blackwell Publishers.

Bassey, M. (1999). *Case study research in educational settings.* Buckingham, United Kingdom: Open University Press.

Billett. (2001). Knowing in practice: Re-conceptualising vocational expertise. *Learning and Instruction, 11*(6), 431-452.

Dillon, J. T. (1990). *The practice of questioning.* London: Routledge.

Earl, L., Watson, N., Levin, B., Leithwood, K., Fullan, M., & Torrence, N. (2003). *Watching and learning: Final report of the external evaluation of England's national literacy and numeracy strategies.* London: DfES Publications.

Entwistle, N. J. (1997). Contrasting perspectives on learning. In F. Marton, D. Hounsell, & N. Entwistle (Eds.), *The experience of learning: Implications for teaching and studying in higher education* (pp. 3-22). Edinburgh, United Kingdom: Scottish Academic Press.

Hayes, D. (2001). Professional status and an emerging culture of conformity amongst teachers in England. *Education, 3*(13), 43-49.

John, P., & Sutherland, R. (2005). Affordance, opportunity and the pedagogical implications of ICT. *Educational Review, 57*(4), 405-413.

Kelly, P. (2006). What is teacher learning? A socio-cultural perspective. *Oxford Review of Education, 32*(4), 505-519.

Laurillard, D. (2002). *Rethinking university teaching: A conversational framework for the effective use of learning technologies* (2nd ed.). London: Routledge Falmer.

Maykut, P., & Morehouse, R. (1994). *Beginning qualitative research: A philosophic and practical guide*. London: Falmer Press.

Mercer, N. (1995). *The guided construction of knowledge*. Clevedon, United Kingdom: Multilingual Matters Ltd.

Pratt, N. (2006). Interactive teaching in numeracy lessons: What do children have to say? *Cambridge Journal of Education, 36*(2), 221-235.

Pratt, N. (2008). Multi-point e-conferencing with initial teacher training students in England: Pitfalls and potential. *Teaching and Teacher Education, 24*(6), 1476-1486.

Rust, C. (2002). The impact of assessment on student learning: How can the research literature practically help to inform the development of departmental assessment strategies and learner-centred assessment practices? *Active Learning in Higher Education, 3*(2), 145-158.

Salmon, G. (2005). Flying not flapping: A strategic framework for e-learning and pedagogical innovation in higher education institutions. *ALT-J, Research in Learning Technology, 13*(3), 201-218.

Schön, D. (1983). *The reflective practitioner: How professionals think in action*. New York: Basic Books.

Schön, D. (1987). *Educating the reflective practitioner: Toward a new design for teaching and learning in the professions*. San Francisco: Jossey-Bass.

Smith, F., Hardman, F., & Higgins, S. (2006). The impact of interactive whiteboards on teacher-pupil interaction in the national literacy and numeracy strategies. *British Educational Research Journal, 32*(3), 443-457.

Smith, H., & Higgins, S. (2006). Opening classroom interaction: The importance of feedback.

*Cambridge Journal of Education, 36*(4), 485-502.

Somekh, B. (2004). Taking the sociological imagination to school: An analysis of the (lack of) impact of information and communication technologies on education systems. *Technology, Pedagogy and Education, 13*(2), 163-180.

Strauss, A., & Corbin, J. (1990). *Basics of qualitative research: Grounded theory procedures and techniques*. London: Sage Publications.

Training and Development Agency for Schools. (2007). *Professional standards for teachers*. London: Author.

Vallance, M., & Towndrow, P. A. (2007). Towards the "informed use" of information and communication technology in education: A response to Adams' "PowerPoint, habits of mind, and classroom culture." *Journal of Curriculum Studies, 39*(2), 219-227.

Webb, M., & Cox, M. (2004). A review of pedagogy related to information and communications technology. *Technology, Pedagogy and Education, 13*(3), 235-286.

Wells, G. (1993). Re-evaluating the IRF sequence: A proposal for the articulation of theories of activity and discourse for the analysis of teaching and learning in the classroom. *Linguistics and Education, 5*(1), 1-37.

Wenger, E. (1998). *Communities of practice: Learning, meaning and identity*. Cambridge, United Kingdom: Cambridge University Press.

## ADDITIONAL READING

Beaty, L. (2003). Supporting learning from experience. In H. Fry, S. Ketteridge, & S. Marshall (Eds.), *A handbook for teaching & learning in higher education: Enhancing academic practice* (2nd ed.). New Delhi, India: Crest.

Beaty provides a good background to experiential learning in higher education, including work placements, the role that experience plays, and the forms of learning that might result.

Beck, C., & Schornack, G. (2004). Theory and practice for distance education: A heuristic model for the virtual classroom. In C. Howard, K. Schenk, & R. Discenza (Eds.), *Distance learning and university effectiveness*. London: Information Science Publishing.

This is a useful chapter providing background to the challenges of managing technological change in higher education, particularly for distance learning. It argues for a wide-ranging consideration of how technologies will change higher education, and against a simplistic cost-effectiveness model.

Beetham, H. (2005). E-learning research: Emerging issues? *ALT-J, Research in Learning Technology, 13*(1), 81-89.

This is an article that usefully discusses the potential foci for future research in e-learning in the United Kingdom. It draws from the early stages of a UK Joint Information Systems Committee funded programme, providing a clear list of possible research questions in the area of e-learning and e-teaching. These are themed under two categories: research into learning and teaching practice, and research into how learners learn with technologies.

Bracher, M., Collier, R., Ottewill, R., & Shephard, K. (2005). Accessing and engaging with video streams for educational purposes: Experiences, issues and concerns. *ALT-J, Research in Learning Technology, 13*(2), 139-150.

The article provides a consideration of how the "softer aspects of technological development" should be considered with as much care as the "harder" ones in developing technological solutions to teaching and learning. It uses a case study illustrating how undergraduate health care students interacted with a streamed video about back care, and notes, like this chapter here, how technical and personal issues are integrally tied together in students' IT practices.

Brockbank, A., & Mcgill, I. (2006). *Facilitating reflective learning through mentoring & coaching*. London: Kogan Page.

The title is self explanatory and the book provides ideas for developing reflective mentoring. It would be a useful text for those beginning to undertake mentoring roles, perhaps as part of work-based learning programmes.

Castleton, G., Gerber, R., & Pillay, H. (2006). *Improving workplace learning: Emerging international perspectives*. New York: Nova Science Publishers.

This is an excellent general text for those wanting to explore workplace learning. Chapters cover a range of issues in four categories: the impact of contextual issues on workplace learning, the forms of knowledge needed for work, existing models for practice, and directions for future consideration.

Chaiklin, S., & Lave, J. (Eds.). (1996). *Understanding practice: Perspectives on activity and context*. Cambridge, United Kingdom: Cambridge University Press.

This is an excellent general text for those wanting to understand more about social practice. It includes useful introductory chapters on the use of social practice theory.

Crawford, L., Sharpe, L., Moo, S. N., Gopinathan, S., & Wong, A. (2001). Multipoint desktop videoconferencing in teacher education: Preliminaries, problems and progress. *Asia-Pacific Journal of Teacher Education, 30*(1), 67-78.

This is a useful paper in support of this chapter exploring the practical difficulties in setting up DVC (desktop videoconferencing) with teaching students in a Singaporean context. The project reported made use of video streaming of classroom teaching episodes as a vehicle for online tutorials and discussion about teaching practices. The paper reports the challenges and advantages of this approach.

D'Andrea, V., Gosling, D., & Society for Research into Higher Education. (2005). *Improving teaching and learning in higher education: A whole institution approach.* Maidenhead, United Kingdom: Society for Research into Higher Education & Open University Press.

This is a good general reader relating to teaching and learning in higher education, including chapters on the effect of learning technologies on institutional change and building inclusive learning communities.

Department for Education and Skills. (2005). *Harnessing technology: Transforming learning and children's services.* Nottingham, United Kingdom: DfES Publications.

This is a position paper of the UK government explaining the context and aims for introducing technology into English schools. It provides a good general overview of the official government position in relation to IT at this particular point in time.

Fox, S., & Mackeogh, K. (2003). Can elearning promote higher-order learning without tutor overload? *Open Learning, 18*(2), 121-134.

This is a useful paper evaluating a number of approaches to online discussion with a particular focus on whether or not students can be encouraged to engage in higher order learning. It also focuses on the issue of tutor time and concludes that, with careful design, these higher order learning achievements can be managed without overburdening the tutor.

Furr, P., & Ragsdale, R. (2002). Desktop video conferencing: How to avoid teacher and student frustration. *Education and Information Technologies, 7*(4), 295-302.

The article details how, for postgraduate students in the United States who used desktop videoconferencing as part of their course, the experience led to considerable frustration. It goes on to suggest approaches to reducing this situation.

Hargreaves, A. (1994). *Changing teachers, changing times: Teachers' work in postmodern times.* London: Cassell.

This is a commonly referenced text that is acknowledged as describing in good detail the nature of teachers' working lives during a period of considerable change in English education. It is a useful background text for thinking about the English education system.

Hayes, D. (2003). Emotional preparation for teaching: A case study about trainee teachers in England. *Teacher Development, 7*(2), 153-171.

Hayes' article usefully sets up the background issues in terms of teaching students' emotional experiences in school placements.

Hearnshaw, D. (2000). Effective desktop videoconferencing with minimal network demands. *British Journal of Educational Technology, 31*(3), 221-228.

This is a paper exploring the relationship between the quality of video images and the quality of dialogue in DVC. It concludes that the former has no measurable effect on the latter, supporting the view in this chapter that the quality of learning is a complex sociocultural issue and not the product of technology alone.

Hu, C., Sharpe, L., Crawford, L., Gopinathan, S., Khine, M. S., Moo, S. N., & Wong, A. (2000). Using lesson video clips via multipoint desktop video conferencing to facilitate reflective practice. *Journal of Information Technology for Teacher Education, 9*(3), 377-388.

Hu et al. focuses on how reflective practice developed in a DVC project with teaching students in Singapore. The project formed the template for the work undertaken in this article and offers a useful cultural comparison between two international contexts.

Lave, J., & Wenger, E. (1991). *Situated learning: Legitimate peripheral participation.* Cambridge, United Kingdom: Cambridge University Press.

This is a seminal text in the field of social practice theory and the precursor to much that has been written in the field since. Lave and Wenger develop the idea of communities of practice and of learning as "apprenticeship," whereby learners work as "legitimate peripheral participants" in a community in order, eventually, to become experts. This forms an alternative to the cognitive metaphor for learning and is useful in conceptualising learning situations in nonformal, or workplace, situations.

Morgan, C., & Smit, A. (2001). Innovation in open and distance learning. In F. Lockwood & A. Gooley (Eds.), *Mentoring in open and distance learning.* London: Kogan Page.

The title of this text is self-explanatory; the work explores innovative approaches in open and distance learning contexts.

Martin, M. (2005). Seeing is believing: The role of videoconferencing in distance learning. *British Journal of Educational Technology, 36*(3), 397-405.

Martin's paper includes a brief survey of DVC projects and their effects. It goes on to discuss the need to fundamentally reconsider pedagogical approaches if DVC is to be used more effectively. In particular, it points to the lack of appreciation of the potential of DVC, and of research in its use, in primary and secondary schooling.

Palloff, R. M., & Pratt, K. (2005). *Collaborating online: Learning together in community.* San Francisco: Jossey-Bass.

The title of this text is self-explanatory. Palloff and Pratt explore how learning communities might work in online environments.

Peters, O. (1998). *Learning and teaching in distance education: Analyses and interpretations from an international perspective.* London: Kogan Page.

This is a useful guide to issues in distance learning.

Preston, C. (2004). *Learning to use ICT in classrooms: Teachers' and trainers' perspectives.* London: TTA/MirandaNet.

This is a guide from the body responsible for teacher training in England that discusses practice in the use of technologies in classrooms.

Salmon, G. (2002). *E-tivities: The key to active online learning.* London: Taylor & Francis.

Salmon explores ways to promote online learning that are active and engaging for students through careful consideration of learning activities and context of their implementation.

Salmon, G. (2002). Mirror, mirror, on my screen... Exploring online reflections. *British Journal of Educational Technology, 33*(4), 379-391.

This paper promotes the idea that reflection on practice in online environments is helpful for students' learning, and includes a discussion of how such reflection can be built into online courses.

Selwyn, N., Gorard, S., & Furlong, J. (2006). *Adult learning in the digital age: Information technology and the learning society.* London: Routledge.

This is an informative book describing "the ways in which adults in the 21st century interact with ICTs for learning at home, work and within the wider community," and considering the issues resulting from a large-scale study in this area.

Sharpe, L., Hu, C., Crawford, L., Gopinathan, S., Khine, M. S., Moo, S. N., et al. (2003). Enhancing multipoint desktop video conferencing (MDVC) with lesson video clips: Recent developments in pre-service teaching practice in Singapore. *Teaching and Teacher Education, 19*(5), 529-541.

This is a journal article reporting on a video-conferencing project carried out in Singapore in which teacher education students worked with tutors at a distance during school experiences. It formed the basis for some of the work undertaken in this chapter.

Smyth, R. (2005). Broadband videoconferencing as a tool for learner-centred distance learning in higher education. *British Journal of Educational Technology, 36*(5), 805-820.

Smyth's paper considers the situated nature of distance learning and the potential of DVC to support students working in a range of contexts. The need to match pedagogy and technology carefully is a useful and interesting focus.

Wheeler, S., Kelly, P., & Gale, K. (2005). The influence of online problem-based learning on teachers' professional practice and identity. *ALT-J, Research in Learning Technology, 13*(2), 125-137.

This paper takes a sociocultural perspective in describing the experiences of six teachers in an online master's programme in the United Kingdom. It usefully exemplifies the use of such a perspective in considering professional practice and identity, but also suggests a strong divide between the online community and real-world practice in classrooms.

Westera, W. (2004). On strategies of educational innovation: Between substitution and transformation. *Higher Education, 47*, 501-517.

Westera explores the nature of innovation and change in the introduction of technology to educational arenas. The paper notes that the apparently self-evident nature of innovation might need to be reconsidered in educational contexts if the potential of new technologies is to be realised.

Zumbach, J., Hillers, A., & Reimann, P. (2004). Supporting distributed problem-based learning: The use of feedback mechanisms in online learning. In T. Roberts (Ed.), *Online collaborative learning: Theory and practice*. London: Information Science Publishing.

This chapter explores the use of feedback in online learning situations and discusses ways to improve the use of such feedback.

# Chapter XV
# The Alliance of Problem-Based Learning, Technology, and Leadership

**Timo Portimojärvi**
*University of Tampere, Finland*

**Pirjo Vuoskoski**
*Mikkeli University of Applied Sciences, Finland*

## ABSTRACT

*This chapter will illustrate a combination of problem-based learning (PBL), information and communication technologies (ICT), and leadership in the context of health care education. It is argued that they form a coherent alliance that meets the challenges of education and leadership in health care. The topic and the research questions have emerged from expanding criticism against traditional educational programmes, and our own experiences of the research and development work in the context of problem-based pedagogy and the use of information and communication technologies in Finnish higher education.*

## INTRODUCTION

Recently there has been a growing interest in problem-based learning (PBL) and ICT among educational researchers. The relationship between PBL and ICT (Dennis, 2003; Donnelly, 2004, 2005; Donnelly & Portimojärvi, in press; Portimojärvi, 2006) or PBL and leadership (Bridges & Hallinger, 1997; Palmer & Major, 2004) has

been previously studied by several researchers. Furthermore, traditional educational programmes and methods of instruction have been criticised for not proving effective in helping students to develop leadership skills and abilities (Bridges & Hallinger; Costello, Brunner, & Hasty, 2002; Palmer & Major). However, to date, there has been little in the way of research on the integration of all three perspectives.

This chapter is positioned in the context of higher education, pedagogical innovations, and the use of information and communication technologies in learning and teaching. The research project at the heart of this chapter took place in two undergraduate-level leadership courses offered to second-year health care students at Mikkeli University of Applied Sciences in Savonlinna, Finland.

The goal of the study is to provide teachers and educational developers with a model of developing and exploring pedagogy, technology, and subject disciplines in parallel. Proceeding this way, e-learning and e-teaching cannot be driven only by technology, or any of its aspects, but by challenging the pedagogical practices and the technological solutions.

## BACKGROUND

This study is positioned in the context of a changing information and network society, where globalization, digitalization, and new sociocultural phenomena co-occur (Castells, 2000). Dispersed teams and organizations, the rich use of information and communication technologies, and a growing demand for pedagogical innovations such as PBL are realizations of this broad process of change.

Problem-based learning has been described as one of the most important pedagogical innovations in higher education in the last few decades. It was thought to have started in the 1960s in medical education in Canada. Since then, it has spread throughout the world in different variations whilst still preserving its foundations (Boud & Feletti, 1997). The context for this research is in Finnish higher education, where PBL was first adopted in medical and physiotherapy education in the 1990s (Poikela & Nummenmaa, 2006).

PBL is a comprehensive approach to learning environments, curriculum, learning, studying, and teaching. It is grounded in experiential, collaborative, contextual, and constructivist theories of learning, and it has a clear point of convergence with informal learning and action processes. PBL aims at the integration of different subjects and branches of knowledge so that it is possible for the student to achieve the necessary professional competence and growth during his or her education (Savin-Baden & Major, 2004).

It has been described as a transformative educational process that aims at student empowerment (see Costello et al., 2002). The role of a traditional teacher is replaced by the role of a tutor and group leader. Group-intensive learning activities utilize taking turns at roles such as discussion leader, recorder, and observer. The action among the group forms joint responsibility. Learning is seen as a participative, creative, collaborative but also individual process (Boud & Feletti, 1997; Poikela & Poikela, 2006a; Savin-Baden, 2000).

PBL in health care education aims to produce reflective professionals who often work as team members, leaders, and managers (Abrandt, 1997; Broberg et al., 2003; Paukkala, Pelkonen, Olkkonen, Jaroma, & Tossavainen, 2001; Solomon 2005). The learning activities and continuous process assessment in PBL can be seen as tools to develop the skills needed for leadership in the health care profession and practice. Self-management and team leadership are needed for effective and evidence-based work (Lorensen et al., 2001). Contemporary health care aims at patient empowerment and participation, which can be achieved with a communicative, collaborative, and reflective approach to treatment and counseling. The whole chain of links—from the work of tutors and the activities of students to the work of health professionals and the actions of patients—forms a coherent process of continuous empowerment.

ICT in education, especially in online learning, has been one of the most studied perspectives during the last decade. However, online learning is based on more common pedagogical contexts such as views of student-, knowledge-, and assessment-centred learning and communities of learning (Anderson, 2004). The environment that is built upon computers, networks, and software is often seen as a constructivist learning environment that enables collaboration with other students. The students are supposed to enhance each others' learning while using various tools and resources during supported problem-solving processes (Wilson, 1996). Online learning is expected to be active, collaborative, interactive, reflective, authentic, goal oriented, and constructive (Jonassen, 1995) in spite of the use of technical equipment and software that require learning to use them, and that are limited in their capabilities.

Globalization and virtuality are common trends in work and education today. Information and communication technology has a central role in the postmodern society. Working in geographically dispersed groups requires effective computer-mediated communication tools to enable group action in spite of the distance involved (Hildreth, Kimble, & Wright, 2000; Portimojärvi, Forthcoming; Vartiainen, Kokko, & Hakonen, 2003).

Dispersed groups and distributed teamwork can be described with the aspects of place, time, diversity, and modes of communication. The members of a dispersed group may work in the same place or be geographically separated. Additionally, distributed work may occur in fixed or mobile surroundings, in which case it can be described as mobile work. Even short distances contribute to the amount of interaction and communication. The teamwork can be based on synchronous or asynchronous communication, and the groups can be permanent or temporary by nature. Diversity in a group may appear as cultural, organizational, or educational differences in the backgrounds and the practices of the group members. Communication may take place face to face or it may be mediated with various technological systems. Few groups operate at the extreme ends of these aspects. Instead, virtuality is usually partial, and the strength of different aspects (place, time, diversity, and mode of communication) varies. Distributed teamwork itself requires many skills. Continuous changes in communication technology and practices create challenges that are typically responded to with competence mapping, development discussions, and arrangements for education (Vartiainen et al., 2003).

The ongoing social changes form a noteworthy context for the examination of leadership in the health care sector. Recently, there has been an increasing demand for evidence-based work and leadership practices. Leaders' up-to-date competency and ability for the constant renewal of practices have been described as prerequisites for continuous organizational-level development and change in health care. On the other hand, leadership practices have to serve the fundamental duty of health care delivery as well (Sinkkonen & Taskinen, 2002; Sydänmaanlakka, 2004).

Leadership and management are often used interchangeably when defining leadership. Management has been described as administrative implementation involving rational decision making on functions, and leadership as organizing people in complex relationships, that is, between superiors and employees (Sydänmaanlakka, 2004; Viitala, 2004a). However, the use of the two concepts is not always clear. Among others, Bennis and Nanus (1985) have defined management as producing and performing, being responsible, and doing one's duty, and leadership as affecting and steering toward a certain direction, function, or opinion.

## BLENDED AND ONLINE PBL COURSE ON LEADERSHIP

The research project at the heart of this chapter took place in two undergraduate-level leadership courses offered to second-year health care students at Mikkeli University of Applied Sciences in Savonlinna during the winter of 2005 and 2006.

Mikkeli University of Applied Sciences offers a broad range of higher education programmes in eastern Finland. There are five campuses located in Mikkeli, Pieksämäki, and Savonlinna. The campus of Savonniemi in Savonlinna offers undergraduate-level degree programmes in design, tourism, business, and health care. Previously, all undergraduate-level students in the campus were learning leadership abilities based on a more traditional curriculum and course design. However, there has been expanding criticism against traditional educational programmes and methods of instruction for not proving effective in helping students to develop leadership skills and abilities (Bridges & Hallinger, 1997; Costello et al., 2002; Palmer & Major, 2004). Additionally, the statistics given in nursing and physiotherapy students' feedback has shown high rates of dissatisfaction with the leadership course delivery, learning and teaching methods, and outcomes.

The 3.5-year bachelor-level physiotherapist degree programme in Savonlinna has been a totally integrated PBL curriculum since 1998. Integrated blocks of academic study units, alternating with practical training periods of 3 to 8 weeks in related content areas, have been designed to enhance the integration of academic and clinical learning. Academic study units are composed of weekly tutorials and there is usually one tutorial in the middle of each clinical period. In the nursing department, PBL has been mainly applied by individual teachers to their own courses or modules within a more traditional subject-based curriculum. Lately, there has been a shift toward more active and collaborative approaches of learning and teaching in the nursing department, and a range of electronic resources and online communication tools have been introduced to the staff and the students in both departments. This research project was launched to develop new ways of learning and teaching leadership in health care by exploring the integration of PBL, ICT, and leadership.

The implementation of the course was based on the development of blended and online PBL (Donnelly & Portimojärvi, in press), which combines ICT-enriched face-to-face settings with synchronous and asynchronous online learning. Before the course, the students could choose between face-to-face and online PBL tutorials, depending on their own needs at the period in question. The online delivery took the form of using desktop-conferencing software called Marratech (http://www.marratech.com) for enabling synchronous collaboration and shared knowledge construction in online tutorials. In face-to-face tutorials, students used computers for collaborative knowledge construction and documentation. Between the tutorials, all students used the virtual learning environment Moodle™ (http://www.moodle.org) for asynchronous collaboration and information delivery. Each of the phases of the PBL tutorial process has specific forms of action and communication. In particular, these characteristics should be resolved and understood before being utilized within online environments.

The activities in the group were guided by a tutor, and during the PBL process the group members took on the typical roles of discussion leader, recorder, or observer. The discussion leader was charged with ensuring full participation from all group members, and moderating individuals who may try to dominate the group discussion. The recorder's task was to keep track of unresolved issues, record group strategies, and maintain the archives of all work sheets and electronic files. The observer gave feedback to group members and led the group into assessment discussion at the end of each tutorial session. In addition, some temporal roles were used to promote certain aspects like productivity, critical thinking, or group dynamics. The roles were rotated, thus providing all group members an opportunity to practice group leadership. The tutor's role was to promote students' individual and group learning processes, problem solving, and functioning in different roles.

The delivery of the course was based on three PBL tutorial processes, with each process starting from an authentic problem related to a content theme concerning leadership in the health care sector. These content themes were (a) leadership and organizations, (b) leadership styles and qualities, (c) future leadership. The problems (phone-call discussion, picture collage, narrative story) were presented in multimedia format by using a data projector in face-to-face settings and the whiteboard tool of the Marratech™ desktop conferencing software (Figure 1) in online settings.

In the opening tutorial, the group recognised and elaborated their individual and shared prior knowledge on topics in the course. This was done by brainstorming and discussion. The online group used the conferencing software with multipoint full audio, Web-cam video, and shared writing and drawing tools to make the situation as real as possible. It is on these grounds that the group formulated a shared learning task and reached agreement on searching for information.

This was followed by a knowledge acquisition phase, during which the students were expected to research information from books, experts, and digital archives. No lectures were offered to the students during the course. Students reported and discussed their learning outcomes immediately after they found relevant information and if necessary adjusted their problem-solving strategy. This was done in the Moodle™ discussion forum, and the tutor commented on and guided this discussion. Without the forums, the students would have had to wait for the next group meeting. Thereby, in this online PBL course, the information retrieval process was combined with the final discussion phase of the traditional PBL process.

However, the closing tutorial in the form of either a synchronous face-to-face tutorial or a videoconference meeting was regarded to be important for the final synthesis of the learning issues. The outcome of the second tutorial was to be a shared, best possible understanding of the matter under discussion. For reaching this,

*Figure 1. A screenshot from a recorded meeting of Group A*

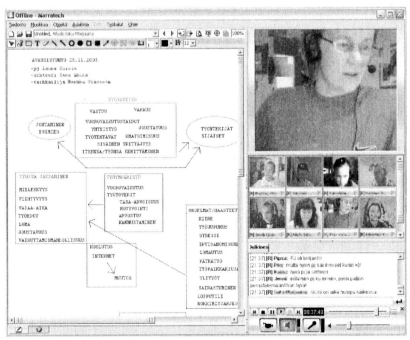

the groups were advised to create a joint concept map. This was done in face-to-face settings with the CmapTools (http://cmap.ihmc.us) concept mapping software and in online settings with the interactive tools of Marratech™.

At the end of every PBL process, students were to deliver their individual learning documents to Moodle™. In the learning documents, students were expected to demonstrate and reflect on their own learning and knowledge on related content themes, the usage of information resources, the group function, and their own actions during the PBL process. At the end of the course, they were asked in their final essays to evaluate the delivery and content of the course, and the suitability of the pedagogical and technological design for learning leadership. In this way, students were constructing their own learning portfolios that were commented on by peers and the tutor in the same forum. The course was graded as passed or failed.

From these two courses we formed three target groups for data collection. Group A (*n*=7), consisting of physiotherapy students, was an online PBL group alternating synchronous and asynchronous collaborative online learning and self-study. Two of the students were male, and the remainder female. Group B (*n*=6) and Group C (*n*=8) were traditional PBL groups consisting of female nursing students. They were using computers for collaborative knowledge construction and documentation in face-to-face tutorials, and asynchronous online collaboration between the tutorials. Later, we combined Groups B and C. This combined group will be called Group BC in this chapter.

All the groups used the virtual learning environment Moodle™ for asynchronous collaboration between the tutorials, mainly as a channel for discussion and information delivery. Group A was using Marratech™ for enabling synchronous audiovisual collaboration and shared whiteboard use in online tutorials. The desktop conferencing software, Web cameras, and headphones used in the tutorials enabled equal possibilities for

participation in group work and observing others visually and aurally. Group BC used CmapTools for conceptualization and documentation in face-to-face tutorials. In addition, all students used standard office application software.

## Exploring the Combination of PBL, ICT, and Leadership

The research project started with a speculation and the question of whether problem-based learning, information and communication technology, and leadership form a coherent combination that would meet the challenges of educational development, leadership in health care, and the empowering process of the patient. To examine this assumption, we formed four main research questions.

1. How do the students describe problem-based learning?
2. How do the students describe the use of information and communication technology?
3. How do the students describe leadership in health care?
4. What are the connections between the descriptions of PBL, ICT, and leadership?

The research used a qualitative case-study method. The textual data consist of short learning reports, written presuppositions, and a final essay from each student. All of them include issues of the learning content and reflective notions of their own and the group's collaborative learning process. The recorded data contain all the audiovisual and textual data produced in the tutorials. The 7 hours of video data were recorded during the online tutorials with the same software used for personal desktop conferencing. The textual data, consisting of approximately 26,000 words, were coded and analysed with QSR nVivo software. The recorded data was used to increase the level of objectivity of our findings from the textual data.

In the textual data analysis, we used methods of conventional qualitative content analysis (Hsieh & Shannon 2005) to portray how students describe and define leadership, PBL, and ICT in the context of the undergraduate-level leadership course in health care education. After creating an overall impression, the data were read more carefully to derive codes that appear to present the key thoughts or concepts. To reassert the reliability of analysis, the data were first coded by both researchers independently. The codings were then compared and analysed with QSR nVivo software. This showed if both or one of the researchers had made the same, overlapping codings.

The analysis then continued with the strong codings that were accepted by both researchers, and the results were checked by comparing them to the weak codings done by each researcher. Codes were then sorted into categories based on how different codes were related and linked. These emergent categories were used to organize and group codes into meaningful clusters. A tree diagram was developed to help in organizing these clusters, categories, codes, and their definitions into a hierarchical structure. QSR nVivo software was again used to check and validate the process, and to select exemplars for each code and category for reporting.

All the students from Groups A (5/7), B (4/6), and C (4/8) who returned their reports by the agreed deadline were accepted as the informants of this research (total 13/21). The reports that were returned after the deadline appeared to be of the same nature.

## How do the Students Describe Problem-Based Learning?

The students described PBL as a procedure or a method. For some of the students, PBL appeared to be an already known way of learning while others became acquainted with it during the course. Due to previous experiences, they voiced their presumptions of PBL. Some of the students chose this course because of PBL and some in spite of it. It seems that the clear procedure of the course has changed the negative opinions of PBL to be more positive: "*Our group really had to relearn the whole PBL-method. We had all been using problem-based learning earlier, but in a slightly different way. Our previous course of action was much the same, but not as clear as this*" (Student B1, final essay, translated).

*Before this course I was very nervous because my previous experiences of PBL-tutorials were poor, but this experience was good. This kind of learning is very rewarding and interesting. Now, when I have understood the functioning of the PBL-method, I think it would be very useful in other courses too.* (Student B2, final essay, translated)

In addition to the general descriptions, PBL appears more detailed in the students' expressions on the activities and participation. PBL is described as a meaningful and challenging way of learning, in which the central points are responsibility, engagement, fluency of collaboration, and decency in the acquisition of information. The tutor is seen in the role of a learning manager who helps the group in problematic situations and identifies the learning issues.

*For me the most challenging aspect of this PBL-method is finding relevant information and negotiating a common goal for the group. (Student B4, final essay, translated)*

*The PBL-method is a very efficient and pleasant way of learning. (Student C4, final essay, translated)*

*I think every member of the group was highly motivated and committed, which made everyone do one's share of the job. (Student C2)*

*The difficulties we encountered during the tutorials were solved with the assistance of the tutor, who was directing the course of action when necessary. (Student A3, final essay, translated)*

Students described the PBL process and the phases within it according to the PBL cycle model (see Poikela & Poikela, 2006). Detailed and varying phases and variations form three main phases: (a) the group's shared opening tutorial, (b) a more individual phase of information acquisition, and (c) the group's shared closing tutorial. Students' commitment to the shared learning task, information seeking, and discussion, played a central role in their descriptions related to the PBL process. The students in Group A (online group) highlighted the attainment of mutual understanding, while the students in Group BC (face-to-face groups) emphasize the completion of the problem-solving process.

The opening tutorial starts with a problem, which is presented as text, image, video, or audio. This leads the group to brainstorming, grouping ideas, and negotiating a shared learning task. A good learning task is illustrated to be a basic prerequisite for a successful phase of information acquisition, which shows up as a fragile and multifaceted process with the use of various information sources. Most of the group members did this separately. The students stressed the usefulness of the virtual environment in sharing the information reports with the other group members. This is considered to be important for the success of the closing tutorial:

*In this tutorial the problem was presented as a picture, and we had to stop and think before really understanding it. Although we did find the problem quite challenging, we were able to start the brainstorming phase quite easily. (Student A1, learning report, translated)*

*We were able to construct a concept map which we then used as a base for formulating the infor-*

*mation search task. (Student A2, learning report, translated)*

*We put the outcomes of our information search to Moodle™ to be shared with others before the closing tutorial...we have never done this before and I have always found my knowledge vague and scattered. Without this shared knowledge I would not have learned as much as I did now. (Student B1, learning report, translated)*

The students described the closing tutorial as a forum for discussion and negotiation, which included the presenting, comparing, and combining of different sources and findings of information retrieved. The descriptions often included notions about the closing tutorial being the place for insights, innovations, and deep learning. This is due to a combination of one's own and others' prior and new knowledge. Accurate, shared synthesis is seen as a culmination for the negotiation as well as a tool for understanding the original problem (Alanko-Turunen, 2005).

*It was the very first time in this tutorial that we were able to construct a proper group synthesis quite easily. I think this was due to the collaboration during the phases of the learning task formulation and information search....When the group is functioning well, it is easy to create a lively discussion and get new insights for the problem in the closing tutorial. (Student B4, final essay, translated)*

*The final synthesis was a useful addition to the group process because we had to form a visual description of our mutual understanding. (Student A1, final essay, translated)*

The activities in PBL are viewed from the perspective of the individual or the group, but also through the role of the tutor. Subjective and collective expressions overlap in the data. One's own activities are often reflected in the group's collaboration or in the roles of discussion leader or recorder. The students examined personal activities and collaboration critically. There were some significant expressions of satisfaction in their personal activities. The experiences of success were connected to the task roles or relevant information sources. The positive feedback from the others was also regarded as important. Difficulties in knowledge acquisition or in participating in the group discussion caused feelings of dissatisfaction. When describing the group's activities, the students were satisfied with the high motivation of the group members' active and equal participation and commitment to the shared learning task and information seeking. Notions of low activity or participation were expressed as reasons for dissatisfaction.

## How do the Students Describe the Use of Information and Communication Technology?

The students' descriptions on using information and communication technology were divided into three main categories: experiences, use of technology, and arguments. As experiences, they wrote about their feelings of satisfaction and dissatisfaction with the implementation of the course. They also described their experiences of high or low success. At its worst, e-learning can be disempowering and de-motivating for learners, leaving them lost and unsupported (Donnelly, 2006). Group A presented common views of online learning and their overall satisfaction with the ways the course proceeded, but they did not define details. The satisfaction was related to their motivation for having online courses in the future. A single negative comment on instruction was presented:

*From my opinion the course realization and courses of action were successful, though there seemed to be some uncertainty about returning*

*the learning reports. (Student A1, final essay, translated)*

A typical aspect in the data of Group BC was the added value of ICT in documenting and sharing knowledge. The members also described the workload involved and weak results of Internet searches. On the other hand, the data include single notions on the positive effect of ICT in face-to-face PBL tutorials, and the unsuccessful information seeking was related to the problems of controlling time and information.

*The use of the concept-mapping software supported our group-work and made it easier for the recorder to participate in the group discussion, and it made grouping of ideas clearer too. It was also good to have all the tutorial documents in Moodle™. We were able to go back to see them, which made it easier to construct the final learning report. (Student B4, final essay, translated)*

*One problem was the lack of time. When doing the search on the Internet you can find so much interesting information to read, and then there is no time left for the books. (Student B3, final essay, translated)*

The students illustrated their experience of technology by describing the ways of using different software and hardware, and by considering the requirements for the users. The most commonly described example of computer use was Google's search engine. They also describe Moodle™ as a tool for sharing information with each other. Additionally, they mention Marratech™ (Group A) and CmapTools (Group BC) software, which were used during the tutorials. The students argued the importance of online studies as an alternative form of study, especially the members of Group A. They described the fully online solution as being the only possible solution for them to participate in this course. Some of the students lived in another city and three of the students had their clinical practice period during the course. However, the students noted that distributed learning in a group demands high engagement and motivation:

*We had to deliver the outcomes of the information search to each other in Moodle™. It made us collaborate during the information acquisition phase, and that was a good thing. (Student B1, final essay, translated)*

*This course was implemented completely online which made it possible for some of us to be involved in spite of the ongoing period of clinical practice. (Student A5, final essay, translated)*

## How do the Students Describe Leadership in Health Care?

The students described leadership and management according to the theories, models, and styles that they have found in the literature. The descriptions emphasized on one hand the leader's abilities to work as a manager of change and a manager of situations, and alternatively the obligations to educate and develop themselves. Styles and habits of leadership are described as connected to personal characteristics, methods, and attitudes. Leadership and the decisions that it demands are seen as situation bound. The students described the challenges of leadership, especially in the health care sector, and emphasize the domination of women, rapid technological development, richness in teamwork, and the employees' responsibility in decisions.

A leader is illustrated as a superior who has authority over decisions and their execution, but who is also responsible for the work community, employees' well-being, and the working atmosphere. The students also defined the positive characteristics of a leader and the similarities and differences between male and female leaders. Skills in both managing tasks and leading personnel were seen as common characteristics.

When describing leadership from the working community's point of view, the students stressed the continuity of collaboration and success of interaction. The most appreciated characteristics of employees were shared responsibility and commitment to the work community and to continuing personal development:

*In the health care sector a good leader must have wide expertise and know-how. It is important to be able and willing to encourage cooperation and to manage situations independently at the same time. Besides, a leader must have a good sense of responsibility and be committed to continuous self-development. (Student A1, learning report, translated)*

*A good leader needs a high level of communication skills. They must be able to act as a mediator in conflict situations and to treat people in a decent manner. (Student C4, learning report, translated)*

These same aspects were emphasized when the students described their own activities as a member or the discussion leader of the group. Working in an active and committed group was described as an easy task. For the discussion leader, it was seen as challenging to control the time schedule and to activate and help the less engaged members to participate in the shared tasks.

*I think one of the aims was to get a personal touch of leadership by acting as a discussion leader in the tutorial group. Additionally we had other roles and tasks in the group. The discussion leader was leading the conversation and taking account of everyone's opinion at the same time by listening, posing questions and negotiating all possible solutions for the common goal. (Student B3, final essay, translated)*

*It was quite easy to be a discussion leader when everybody was participating, but it was really hard to stay on schedule. It was difficult to decide how much time to spend in each phase. (Student B4, final essay, translated)*

## What are the Connections between PBL, ICT, and Leadership?

A notable portion of the textual data included expressions, which were categorized in the analysis according to several perspectives (PBL, ICT, leadership). As expected, the coding of the data included several co-occurrences of the perspectives. The students' expressions were often related to two of them. However, there was only one explicit expression that was coded according to all of them:

*All participants of the course were motivated with the subject, maybe the future leaders? A special great honour of the success of this course belongs to the fellow students and to the tutor-teacher. In my opinion, this kind of online learning demands motivated and enthusiastic students, and that is how we can achieve good outcomes. Personally I am a strong supporter of online learning. (Student A2, final essay, translated)*

In the connections between Questions 1 (PBL), 2 (ICT), and 3 (leadership), and their appearance in the recorded tutorials (of Group A), the congruence between the textual and recorded data is noteworthy. The issues that appeared during the recorded speech and activities in the tutorials have been plausibly described in the textual data, but the recorded data are more explicit with small nuances and observations.

In the textual data, the connection between leadership and PBL focused on the functional roles (discussion leader, recorder, observer) used in the PBL tutorials. Particularly the role of the discussion leader appeared to be a concrete form of practicing leadership, and rotation of the roles inside the tutorial group put distributed or alternate leadership into practice. The importance of the role

of the discussion leader was related to the mastery of group function and time consumption. Also, in the video data, the discussion leaders seemed to have a clear regard for negotiated decisions and equal participation inside the group.

In the textual data, the tutor was seen in the role of a learning manager who helps the group in problematic situations and sees what learning issues are important. In the video data, the tutor strove to support the group action and learning by posing directive questions and comments. In more problematic situations, students themselves often asked advice from the tutor. Particularly in the video data, reflective discussion was present about the chosen course of action and behaviour of the discussion leader in the recorded tutorials. Notable was a single request from one student for the discussion leader to examine one's own leadership style and manner in the tutorial.

The connective link between PBL and ICT turned out to be the group, namely, the collaboration, mutual understanding, and joint responsibility within the group. In fostering the elements for group dynamics, students described the procedure of PBL, the online discussion, the software supporting shared understanding in face-to-face tutorials (in group BC), and the online tutorials (in Group A). The connective links (group, collaboration, mutual understanding, and joint responsibility) played a central role in the recorded data as well. During the tutorials, students strove for active participation through constant discussion and negotiation, asking and answering questions, and gaining and delivering information. Students indicated their dissatisfaction, especially at the beginning of the course, with the sparse asynchronous communication between the tutorials.

In the online tutorials, communication technology was used as an almost imperceptible tool for distributed teamwork. The students paid very little attention to the information and communication technology in their group discussion, and they did not judge the technology positively or negatively.

The presence of the technology appeared in the tutorials as single comments about the usefulness of some specific tool in collaboration, and about saving the group's output and adjusting the audio settings. In addition, the tutorials contained short sequences of discussion where the students agreed about the usage of technology.

The connection between ICT and leadership was limited to instrumental meaning and related to discussion and instruction, recording, and searching and sharing information. This appeared in the recorded data, too. Additionally, the use of technology was highlighted in constructing and visualizing the shared understanding and knowledge. In the tutorials, students were simultaneously using several channels (speech, text-based chat, and shared whiteboard) for discussing and constructing shared meaning. The recorder had a central role in documenting the discussion and knowledge construction on the whiteboard.

In addition to multipoint conferencing, Marratech™ also enables one-to-one communication, which can be used for directing group work by the tutor or the discussion leader. In the recorded data, the use of these private messages appeared in relation to the need for the tutor's involvement in a group function and/or time management. The software also enables limited user rights for teachers, students, and hosts, which were not used during this course. Instead of using technologically defined hierarchical rights, the roles and responsibilities of discussion leader, recorder, and participants were divided by agreement within the group in the beginning of each tutorial process.

## DISCUSSION

The comprehensiveness of problem-based pedagogy is not explicit in the students' descriptions. Instead, students highlighted the process and method of PBL. However, the expressions related to the principles of PBL and the congru-

ence between the content to be studied include notions of learning motivation, competencies, and knowledge in relation to future professional expectations. This supports the need for the practice of education and work to be congruent with each other (Poikela & Poikela, 2006b).

The results are compatible with other considerations about PBL students being active in information acquisition and in the usage of information technology (Blumberg, 2000), and about PBL fostering the students' motivation and awareness of their own action and learning (Blumberg; Hmelo & Evensen, 2000). PBL requires effort from both the students and the tutors, but it especially challenges students to assume ownership of their learning. This has been described as one of the key elements in student empowerment (Costello et al., 2002). The students described the tutor as a leader or mentor whose importance was emphasized in problem situations of knowledge seeking or group dynamics. The tutor's role appeared in the data as a supporter in problematic situations and an examiner of the content to be learned. This supports the need for the PBL tutor to be an expert of content with adequate pedagogical skills as described in different studies (Dolmans, Gijselars, Moust, de Grave, Wolfhagen, & van der Vleuten, 2002).

The formation and maintenance of sufficient, group-intensive interaction (Donnelly, 2004), and the alignment of communicative activities and technological solutions (Portimojärvi 2007) have been described as the challenges of online PBL. In the data, students' commitment to the shared learning task, information seeking, and discussion plays a central role. In their descriptions related to the PBL process, the students in Group A (online group) highlighted the attainment of joint understanding, while the students in group BC (face-to-face groups) emphasized the completion of the problem-solving process. The use of the virtual learning environment appeared as an important forum for retrieving and delivering information and building shared understanding in both groups. This supports the view of traditional face-to-face problem-based learning being enhanced by asynchronous online collaboration (Donnelly, 2004, 2005; Portimojärvi).

There are various ways and levels of online learning and using ICT in education. They can be illustrated from a material-oriented to a process-oriented view and from blended solutions to totally virtual courses. For both of the groups, this course was process oriented. Group A has worked totally virtually and Group BC has been using technology to supplement face-to-face meetings. Jonassen (1996) defines three different relations between learning and computers. Computers and media can be seen as substances (learning about media), or they may be sources or tools for retrieving information (learning from media), or they can be considered as mindtools (learning with media). The data include descriptions of the role of ICT as a source and a tool for learning. Group BC emphasized the use as a source, and Group A stressed the use as a tool. However, Group A used ICT more for interpersonal communication than for personal cognitive processes.

Learning and studying are based on interaction. This creates the need for understanding communication processes and media. Interaction can be examined as relations between students, teacher, and learning materials (Anderson, 2004). The main relationship in these data was the interaction among the students in synchronous or asynchronous face-to-face or virtual meetings. The students' descriptions do not include clear expressions of collaborative knowledge construction in the discussion forums, and the asynchronous discussions are narrowly described. The closing tutorial, face to face or mediated, is described as a situation for knowledge construction.

The discourse for describing leadership is different from the discourse for describing PBL or CMC. Leadership has been the course content while PBL and CMC are more instrumental aspects of the hidden curriculum. The students' descriptions about leadership are based on formal literature and other information sources, such as the interviews of health care professionals. The studies of leadership in Finnish health care have largely been focused on the connections of leadership behaviour with organizational productivity and success, employees' work performance, and the efficiency and outcomes of work. There has been research about the relationship between the leader's behaviour and the well-being of employees and the work community (Kanste, 2005). In these data, students describe the qualities of a good leader as being capable of directing people and business, and adapting with the situation to the role of expert or director, or as contributor for inspiration and development.

One of the main organizational-level problems is how to make use of human resources to improve productivity and competition. For managers, this involves a continuous challenge for directing and supporting collective learning and development in the work community (Viitala, 2004b). In these data, students emphasized collaborative and collective leadership and joint responsibility for the continuous development of practices. This supports the emphasis on leadership-oriented managerial approaches when there is an attempt to control and benefit ongoing changes (Heikkilä & Heikkilä, 2001), but also the empowerment of workers, shifting responsibility for decision making from upper level management to the workers themselves (Costello et al., 2002).

On the basis of the results, problem-based learning seems to enable student empowerment. The group functions and roles of the tutor and the discussion leader seemed to enable and support the personal and social empowerment processes. In particular, empowerment appears connected with the individual's well-being, and this plays a central role from the health care viewpoint. The results do not justify any conclusions for the students' behaviour at work. However, the research process confirms our presumption about PBL forming a coherent process of continuous empowerment, which could be transformed from the work of tutors and the activities of students to the work of health professionals and the actions of patients.

The research results are affected by the fact that the three considered perspectives had different functions or levels in the course. While leadership was the course content, PBL showed up as a method or a pedagogical approach and ICT as enabling tools. Therefore, leadership was described in a formal and theoretical way, ICT in a descriptive way, and PBL in a more reflective way. However, learning occurred in all of these levels, which is a relevant discovery to be considered when planning courses. In particular, when designing an online course, goals and processes of learning at all levels should be taken into account.

Students also evaluated the course implementation as compatible with the course content. This is apparent especially from the students' descriptions and actions connected with self-management and teamwork, information delivery, and knowledge construction.

## CONCLUSION

The research results endorse our premise that the combination of problem-based learning, information and communication technologies, and leadership form a coherent alliance that can meet the challenges of education and leadership in health care today. Problem-based learning enables student empowerment, and the students themselves support the importance of online studies as an alternative form of study for being compatible with the leadership course content. The results do not explicitly prove or disprove that PBL and ICT would form an effective tool for distributed teamwork and leadership. The textual data did not contain any expressions about health care telework, or the continuum between education and work. However, the results indicate PBL is a suitable pedagogical design for learning and

teaching leadership, and the usage of ICT enriches the group-orientated learning processes.

The results of this study are compatible with other research findings. According to Charlin, Mann, and Hansen (1998) and Palmer and Major (2004), PBL forms a safe and authentic environment for practicing and developing leadership skills. Donnelly (2004, 2005) and Portimojärvi (2006, forthcoming) have described the reciprocal positive impact between the usage of communication technology and problem-based learning.

The results of this research illuminates Barrows' (2002) question on whether the realization of distributed problem-based learning is really possible. In particular, the recorded data reveal the similarities of action and collaboration in both the online and face-to-face tutorials. The personal desktop conferencing software, shared whiteboard, Web cameras, and headphones used in online tutorials enabled equal possibilities for visual and aural observation of each others' collaboration and participation in the teamwork. The students formed a distributed community of shared action and learning with shared goals, distributed tasks, and rich synchronous collaboration.

## FUTURE RESEARCH DIRECTIONS

This study is positioned in the context of higher education, pedagogical innovations, and the use of information and communication technologies in learning and teaching. Dispersed teams and organizations, the rich use of ICT, and the growing demand for pedagogical innovations such as problem-based learning can be seen as realizations of the changing information and network society (Castells, 2000). This rapid evolution of the field requires constant research on the codevelopment of practices, technologies, and learning contexts.

This chapter illustrates a combination of PBL, ICT, and leadership in the context of health care education. The study suggests three points of interest for further research. First, it would be interesting and also challenging to examine more closely the combination of the three perspectives (PBL, ICT, leadership) considered in this study in a work community where the action is based on distributed teamwork, similar to problem-based learning and collaboration. Second, because of the transdisciplinary nature of leadership, it would be useful to explore and compare experiences of the combination in mixed small groups of students from different disciplines. Third, when combining the empowerment of students and workers in education and work with the empowerment of patients in health care, it could be beneficial to combine all these interests and build up networks of health care service providers, health care educators, and scientists for future development and research.

## REFERENCES

Abrandt, M. (1997). Learning physiotherapy: The impact of formal education and professional experience. *Linköping Studies in Education and Psychology Dissertations, 50.*

Alanko-Turunen, M. (2005). *Negotiating inter-discursivity in a problem-based learning tutorial site.* Unpublished doctoral dissertation, University of Tampere, Finland.

Anderson, T. (2004). Toward a theory of online learning. In T. Anderson & F. Elloumi (Eds.), *Theory and practice of online learning* (pp. 33-60). Athabasca, Canada: Athabasca University.

Barrows, H. (2002). Is it truly possible to have such a thing as dPBL? *Distance Education, 23*(1), 199-122.

Bennis, W. G., & Nanus, B. (1985). *Leaders: The strategies for taking charge.* New York: Harper & Row.

Blumberg, P. (2000). Evaluating the evidence that problem-based learners are self-directed learners: A review of the literature. In D. H. Evensen & C. E. Hmelo (Eds.), *Problem-based learning: A research perspective on learning interactions* (pp. 199-226). Mahwah, NJ: Lawrence Erlbaum Associates.

Boud, D., & Feletti, G. (1997). Changing problem-based learning: Introduction to the second edition. In D. Boud & G. Feletti (Eds.), *The challenge of problem-based learning* (pp. 1-14). London: Kogan Page.

Bridges, E., & Hallinger, P. (1997). Using problem-based learning to prepare educational leaders. *Peabody Journal of Education, 72*(2), 131-146.

Broberg, C., Aars, M., Beckmann, K., Emaus, N., Lehto, P., Lähteenmäki, M.-L., et al. (2003). A conceptual framework for curriculum design in physiotherapy education: An international perspective. *Advances in Physiotherapy, 5,* 161-168.

Charlin, B., Mann, K., & Hansen, P. (1998). The many faces of problem-based learning: A framework for understanding and comparison. *Medical Teacher, 20,* 323-330.

Costello, M. L., Brunner, P. W., & Hasty, K. (2002). Preparing students for the empowered workplace. *Active Learning in Higher Education, 3*(2), 117-127.

Dennis, J. K. (2003). Problem-based learning in online vs. face-to-face environments. *Education for Health, 16*(2), 198-209.

Dolmans, D., Gijselars, W., Moust, J., de Grave, W., Wolfhagen, I., & van der Vleuten, C. (2002). Trends in research on the tutor in problem-based learning: Conclusions and implications for educational practice and research. *Medical Teacher, 24*(2), 173-180.

Donnelly, R. (2004). The effectiveness of teaching "online learning" in a problem-based learning classroom environment. In M. Savin-Baden & K. Wilkie (Eds.), *Challenging research into problem-based learning*. Buckingham, United Kingdom: SRHE/Open University Press.

Donnelly, R. (2005). Using technology to support project and problem-based learning. In T. Barrett, I. Mac Labhrainn, & H. Fallon (Eds.), *Handbook of enquiry & problem-based learning* (pp. 157-177). Galway, Ireland: CELT.

Donnelly, R. (2006). The academic developer as tutor in PBLonline in higher education. In M. Savin-Baden & K. Wilkie (Eds.), *Problem-based learning online* (pp. 79-97). Buckingham, United Kingdom: Open University Press.

Donnelly, R., & Portimojärvi, T. (in press). Online problem-based learning in higher education: Shifting perceptions. In C. Howard, P. Rogers, J. Boettcher, G. Berg, L. Justice, & K. Schenk (Eds.), *Encyclopedia of distance learning* (2nd ed.). Hershey, PA: Idea Group Inc.

Heikkilä, K., & Heikkilä, J. (2001). *Innovatiivisuutta etsimässä: Irtiottoa keskinkertaisuudesta* [Searching for innovation: Letting go of the average]. Jyväskylä, Finland: Gummerus.

Hildreth, P., Kimble, C., & Wright, P. (2000). Communities of practice in the distributed international environment. *Journal of Knowledge Management, 4*(1), 27-37.

Hmelo, C., & Evensen, D. (2000). Problem-based learning: Gaining insights on learning interactions through multiple methods of inquiry. In C. Hmelo & D. Evensen (Eds.), *Problem-based learning: A research perspective on learning interactions* (pp. 1-16). Mahwah, NJ: Lawrence Erlbaum.

Hmelo, C., & Evensen, D. (Eds.). (2000). *Problem-based learning: A research perspective on learning interactions*. Mahwah, NJ: Lawrence Erlbaum.

Hsieh, H., & Shannon, S. (2005). Three approaches to qualitative content analysis. *Qualitative Health Research, 15*(9), 1277-1288.

Jonassen, D. (1995). Supporting communities of learners with technology: A vision for integrating technology with learning in schools. *Educational Technology*, pp. 60-63.

Jonassen, D. H. (1996). *Computers in the classroom: Mindtools for critical thinking*. Columbus, OH: Merrill/Prentice-Hall.

Kanste, O. (2005). *Moniulotteinen hoitotyön johtajuus ja hoitohenkilöstön työuupumus terveydenhuollossa* [Multidimensional nursing leadership and burn-out among nurses in health care]. Unpublished doctoral dissertation, University of Oulu, Finland.

Lorensen, M., Sinkkonen, S., Lichtenberg, A., Jensdotir, A. B., Hamran, G., Johansson, B., et al. (2001). *Knowledge and skill requirements for nurse leaders in the primary health care service6s in the Nordic countries*. Oslo, Norway: Det Medisinske Fakultet, Institutt for sykepleievitenskap, Universitetet i Oslo.

Palmer, B., & Major, C. (2004). Learning leadership through collaboration: The intersection of leadership and group dynamics in problem-based learning. In M. Savin-Baden & K. Wilkie (Eds.), *Challenging research in problem-based learning* (pp. 120-132). Maidenhead, United Kingdom: Open University Press.

Paukkala, M., Pelkonen, M., Olkkonen, A., Jaroma, A., & Tossavainen, K. (2001). Hoitotyön johtamiskoulutus: Haasteena muuttuva toimintaympäristö ja uudet osaamisvaatimukset [Innovative approaches in education to improve modern nursing leadership and management skills]. *Sairaanhoitaja, 74*(4), 26-29.

Poikela, E., & Nummenmaa, A. R. (2006). Introduction. In E. Poikela & A. R. Nummenmaa (Eds.), *Understanding problem-based learning* (pp. 9-10). Tampere, Finland: Tampere University Press.

Poikela, E., & Poikela, S. (2006a). Learning and knowing at work: Professional growth as a tutor.

In E. Poikela & A. R. Nummenmaa (Eds.), *Understanding problem-based learning* (pp. 183-207). Tampere, Finland: Tampere University Press.

Poikela, E., & Poikela, S. (2006b). Problem-based curricula: Theory, development and design. In E. Poikela & A. R. Nummenmaa (Eds.), *Understanding problem-based learning* (pp. 71-90). Tampere, Finland: Tampere University Press.

Portimojärvi, T. (2006). Synchronous and asynchronous communication in online PBL. In E. Poikela & A. R. Nummenmaa (Eds.), *Understanding problem-based learning* (pp. 91-104). Tampere, Finland: Tampere University Press.

Portimojärvi, T. (Forthcoming). *Ongelmaperustainen oppiminen verkossa* [Problem-based learning networked]. Unpublished doctoral dissertation, Tampereen Yliopisto, Finland.

Savin-Baden, M. (2000). *Problem-based learning in higher education: Untold stories.* Buckingham, United Kingdom: SRHE & Open University Press.

Savin-Baden, M., & Major, C. (2004). *Foundations of problem-based learning.* Berkshire, United Kingdom: Open University Press.

Sinkkonen, S., & Taskinen, H. (2002). Johtamisosaamisen vaatimukset ja taso perusterveydenhuollossa hoitotyön johtajilla [Leadership and management competencies of nurse leaders in primary health care settings]. *Hoitotiede, 14*(3), 129-141.

Solomon, P. (2005). Problem-based learning: A review of current issues relevant to physiotherapy education. *Physiotherapy Theory and Practice, 21*(1), 37-49.

Sydänmaanlakka, P. (2004). *Älykäs johtajuus: Ihmisten johtaminen älykkäissä organisaatioissa* [Smart leadership: Human management in smart organizations]. Hämeenlinna, Finland: Karisto.

Vartiainen, M., Kokko, N., & Hakonen, M. (2003, July 25-27). Competences in virtual organizations. In *Proceedings of the Third International Conference on Researching Work and Learning* (Vol. 1, pp. 209-219). Tampere, Finland.

Viitala, R. (2004a). *Henkilöstöjohtaminen* [Personnel leadership]. Helsinki, Finland: Edita.

Viitala, R. (2004b). *Osaamisen johtaminen esimiestyössä* [Knowledge leadership]. Unpublished doctoral dissertation, University of Vaasa, Finland.

Wilson, B. (1996). What is a constructivist learning environment? In B. G. Wilson (Ed.), *Constructivist learning environments: Case studies in instructional design* (p. 38). Englewood Cliffs, NJ: Educational Technology.

## ADDITIONAL READING

In addition to the references in the chapter, some further reading might be useful. The chapter is strongly linked with the recent developments of problem-based learning online. The books edited by Savin-Baden and Wilkie (2006) and Uden and Beaumont (2005) offer the most recent and comprehensive review on the development of the field. Earlier stages of the evolving research field were collected into the themed issue of *Distance Education* (Koschmann, 2002).

Savin-Baden, M., & Wilkie, K. (2006). *Problem-based learning online.* Maidenhead, United Kingdom: Open University Press.

Uden, L., & Beaumont, C. (2005). *Technology and problem-based learning.* Hershey, PA: Information Science Publishing.

Koschmann, T. (2002). Introduction to special issue on studying collaboration in distributed PBL environments. *Distance Education, 23*(1), 5-9.

Problem-based learning is constantly under discussion and redefinition, and there are many interpretations of the theory and practice of PBL as Maudsley (1999) points out. However, the early strong statements from scholars like Barrows and Tamblyn (1980) and Schmidt (1983) are highly valued.

Maudsley, G. (1999). Do we all mean the same thing by problem-based learning? A review of the concepts and a formulation of the ground rules. *Academic Medicine, 74*(2), 178-184.

Barrows, H., & Tamblyn, R. (1980). *Problem-based learning: An approach to medical education.* New York: Springer.

Schmidt, H. (1983). Problem-based learning: Rationale and description. *Medical Education, 17*, 11-16.

Several aspects in this chapter, such as empowerment and "soft" leadership, can be linked with theoretical constructions drawn from the ideas of Paolo Freire. Barrett (2001) explores problem-based learning as a subset of Freirian problem-posing education.

Barrett, T. (2001). Philosophical principles for problem-based learning: Freire's concept of personal development and social empowerment. In P. Little & P. Kandlbinder (Eds.), *The power of problem-based learning* (pp. 9-18). Newcastle, Australia: Problarc.

The course examined in the chapter relies strongly on collaboration and student-centred practices, and the constant presence and blended use of technology (see Bonk & King, 1998). However, collaboration as a concept is still under discussion (Dillenbourg, 1999). The strong and common emphasis on collaboration has recently been linked with new technologies.

Bonk, C. J., & King, K. S. (Eds.). (1998). *Electronic collaborators: Learner-centered technologies for literacy, apprenticeship, and discourse.* Mahwah, NJ: Erlbaum.

Dillenbourg, P. (1999). Introduction: What do you mean by collaborative learning? In P. Dillenbourg (Ed.), *Collaborative learning: Cognitive and computational approaches* (pp. 1-19). Oxford, United Kingdom: Pergamon.

Collaboration and communication are tightly interwoven. Preece (2000) offers a broad view on theories and practices regarding mediated communication in online communities. In addition, Wainfan and Davis (2005) review comprehensively the history and presence of virtual collaboration.

Preece, J. (2000). *Online communities: Designing usability, supporting sociability.* New York: Wiley.

Wainfan, L., & Davis, P. K. (2005). *Challenges in virtual collaboration: Videoconferencing, audioconferencing and computer-mediated communication.* Santa Monica, CA: Rand Corporation.

# Section IV
# Online Assessment

*As assessment is an integral part of learning in higher education a discussion of e-learning and e-teaching would not be complete without examination of this topic. The two chapters in this section discuss formative and summative online assessment.*

# Chapter XVI
# The Use of Online Role Play in Preparing for Assessment

**Steve Millard**
*School of Business and Management, Buckinghamshire New University, UK*

## ABSTRACT

*This chapter sets out a number of ways in which effective use of the online discussion board in a virtual learning environment can contribute to the preparation of assessment tasks. In particular, it examines the specific advantages of the use of online role play as a means of effective task preparation, and reviews various examples of its application in different academic areas and contexts. The primary emphasis of this chapter is the use of the VLE in general, and the use of role play within the discussion board in particular, as a means of preparing assessment rather than undertaking assessment online using a series of automated processes.*

## INTRODUCTION

The expectation that, one day, the virtual learning environment (VLE) may be able to handle all forms of assessment and be able to scan and grade essays online much as multiple-choice questions are automatically marked today is perhaps drawing attention away from the more pragmatic and effective uses of the VLE when it is combined with other forms of learning. Whilst some interesting advances have been reported in this area, the general consensus appears to be that a totally reliable online automatic marking facility is still a long way off, and may even be regarded as unhelpful in an educational context where the role of the tutor is to establish a relationship with students that might be impaired if assessment of discursive material is undertaken by a third party in the form a machine that automatically grades it.

Such limitations in the ability of the current state of technology to provide reliable summative assessment beyond the range of multiple-choice questions and similar closed interrogative methods has sharpened the focus on blended learning, which is here simply defined as combining virtual with other forms of learning and assessment.

There are a number of well-documented ways in which assessment can be assisted and prepared within a virtual learning environment. The assessment itself could be partially or even completely conducted online in the form of Web-based assignments, reflective journals, e-portfolios, and so forth, or could equally remain as the traditional essay, report, or presentation, but the means of preparing the task assigned could be more effectively assisted by a variety of uses of the tools on offer in the VLE.

## BACKGROUND AND LITERATURE REVIEW

Linser and Ip (2002), in their review of the applications of online role-play simulations, illustrate the range and potential value of the various forms of this approach, and emphasise that the use of discussion boards in a VLE provide new modes of interaction that are not, and should not, set out to be virtual replications of the social interaction of the classroom.

Gilroy (2001) stresses the importance of the social dimension of the discussion board and its encouragement of collaborative learning when participants engage in role-play simulations.

Deeper learning, empathy, and an understanding of attitudes are outcomes that have emerged in some of the simulations as reported by Fetherston (2001), and in particular by Vincent and Shepherd (1998) in their reporting of Middle East politics simulations in a pedagogic context.

Role play itself is a well-established technique of learning, and it has been used by a number of educational practitioners effectively to promote and deepen learning. Bollens and Marshall (1973) and Ladousse (1987) have attested to the benefits of role play in teaching and learning in the pre-Internet era, and its subsequent online applications are also well documented. In some instances, as will be discussed, the online role-play activity itself has formed the central element of the as-

sessment task, but it is its particular function in preparing assessment that forms the focal point of this chapter.

Linser and Ip (2002) highlight the limitations of e-learning environments that have simply transferred content from the classroom, but go beyond this to question the viability of simply transferring the traditional assumptions and strategies from the classroom or lecturing environments into e-learning. Gilroy (2001) has similarly indicated the importance of the social space provided by online interaction, which transcends the function of VLEs as a repository for course content. Similar criticism of a straight transfer of content from classroom to an online environment has been made by Stills (2001), who endorses a thorough and systematic preparation of customised online material. Linser and Ip question the appropriateness of transferring the social space of learning in the traditional learning environment to an online environment for two basic reasons. First, the two learning spaces may not be reconcilable, and second, there is the technical difficulty of transferring "the dynamic intimacy of face-to-face interaction" to an online environment. Given the constraints of such transfer, they endorse creating a "simulated social space in hyper reality to bring to life the course-content itself."

Naidu, Ip, and Linser (2000) develop the concept of dynamic goal-based learning, which broadly refers to the notion of learning through achieving the objectives as set by the participants in the game or online role-play exercise, and they argue that this adaptive and constructivist approach is particularly well-suited to asynchronous online discussion conducted in the form of a role-play simulation. The main thrust of their proposal is the importance of enabling participants to act out a role in character, and to react to others in their respective roles, thereby having to acquire more information, reflect, and adjust to their changing situations. As various subsequent examples will demonstrate, one of the principal aims of such an approach might well be to influence and broaden the attitudes and perceptions of the participants themselves so that they can better understand and appreciate viewpoints and perspectives that might be contrary to their own.

Its pedagogic value in realigning participants' perspectives and attitudes has been developed online. In a postgraduate programme with students from several countries including the Middle East, for example, Vincent and Shepherd (1998) observe the improved empathy students appear to have gained by taking part in a role-play simulation exercise in which the participants are ascribed roles in which they frequently had to pursue political agendas strongly opposed to their own. This aspect of role play is not exclusive to online simulations and was an attribute noted long before the existence of the Internet in its present form by Bollens and Marshall (1973), underlining the use of role play as a means of enhancing participants' empathy with contrary viewpoints and attitudes.

In another example of role play that predates the use of the Internet, Thompson (1978) specifically notes this increased empathy in the context of people adopting the role of the opposite gender, and role plays have also offered benefits for shy students (Ladousse, 1987) by developing a persona that enables them to interact more readily with others. One further attribute of role plays in general, adduced by Ladousse, is that they can be fun, which may be a factor in increasing student learning.

Online interaction offers several possibilities for improvement over face-to-face role plays. Anonymity can be used to overcome some of the concerns with possible face-to-face conflict and asynchrony allows students more time to reflect on the appropriate response for their role as demonstrated by Connolly, Jessup, and Valacich (1990), who found that in a computer-mediated group, more and better ideas were generated where the group members were anonymous and had a critical member who challenged ideas.

Olaniran, Savage, and Sorenson (1996) found that, despite some student resistance to their initial experience, computer-based groups, using the facility of the discussion board, produced significantly more ideas than face-to-face groups. This could well have been for a number of reasons, not least because of the greater opportunity for participation not always possible where some individuals may dominate live discussions. Asynchronous online discussion also adds the evident benefit of enabling a discussion or debate to be revisited and extended after appropriate contemplation and possible further research into the arguments.

## REPORTED CASES OF ONLINE ROLE PLAY

An interesting example of online role play is provided by Pavey (2003) working with the Department of Geography at Durham, where small groups prepared background research and material for a presentation and debate. In this exercise, each group represented a stakeholder in a scenario where a large industrial company wished to build a new factory on an environmentally sensitive site. The groups—the company, environmental activists, local government and planning officials, and local residents—undertook the final debate in front of an invited representative from government or enterprise. The students engaged to a high degree, and the large amount of work they did in preparation is clearly visible in the discussion-board activity.

In the Durham University example, role play formed the nature of the exercise and assessment, where use of the VLE assisted the preparation for a live staged debate as the climax of the assessment activity. Student participants familiarised themselves with their roles by means of engaging in online activity prior to the staged and assessed debate as a means of getting into the part. In this instance, therefore, the online role play facilitated rehearsal of a part as well as the enlargement of a back story to each of the participants, who were progressively more at ease with their own adopted persona and function in the exercise and became familiar with those adopting other parts within the debate. The online exchanges naturally did not fully prepare the participants for the more formal and possibly daunting experience of a live debate, but the background and attitudinal positions were at least rehearsed so that there was a familiarity with the arguments. Whilst such preparation could have been undertaken face to face, it might well have been more time consuming if undertaken in scheduled classes and more difficult to arrange outside timetabled programmes than it was to organise via a discussion board, where contributions could be added at any time. This demonstrates a situation where a properly constructed online exercise, with motivated participants, can be so helpful in preparing assessment and is much more than a computerised version of a face-to-face exercise.

Another documented example and type of online role play does in fact include the element of online assessment, but this was undertaken by the tutors monitoring the exercise and involved the sustained simulation of a particular event or activity to which students needed to respond in their allocated roles online. In this exercise undertaken by Freeman and Capper (1999) in the Department of Economics at the University of Sydney, students were given roles involved in the deregulation of the Australian securities market. The students' true identities were not revealed, so the whole exercise was conducted anonymously with only their role and function within the simulation being apparent. They then had a week to research the role that they were to play and then posted on the discussion board their profile, which was to include their perceptions of the concerns, ambitions, and strategies of their role so that they had time to absorb and reflect upon the implications and expectations of the adopted persona. Over a period of 10 days they would then have to respond online in character to a series of events.

Press releases, preconstructed by the monitoring tutors, were developed to ensure realistic and relevant situations, problems, and dilemmas that allowed all roles some chance of participating. The students could respond in role through the public discussion board, or could approach each other privately in role via e-mail. Students were assessed on their role profile and their private and public messages. To reward participation in the role play, 15% of marks were allocated to the role play (5% each to the role profile, quantity, and quality of input). In contrast to the Durham University example, part of the assessment was based upon participants' online performance, which in this case, as with many online evaluations, would have been deemed necessary in the construction of the activity in order to provide some of the necessary motivation for sustained participation.

The case also demonstrates a particular advantage of conducting the role play online in that the exercise can fruitfully be extended over a period of time in a way that would perhaps not be sustainable in a face-to-face context, where there might well not be sufficient impetus or energy to undertake more than two or three live interactive meetings.

McLaughlan (2004) conducted a similar exercise involving students from a wide geographical area in South East Asia, the aim of which was to develop a range of social and other related communication skills. Over 140 geography and engineering students from across Australia and overseas spent 4 weeks participating in an online role play and simulation set in the Mekong region of South East Asia. The specific subject area of the simulation and associated role-play exercise involved subjects related to technology assessment, environmental engineering, or Asia Pacific development studies, but its main purpose seems to be the development of the softer interpersonal skills and is therefore an example of role play designed to develop skills beyond those within the subject discipline itself, which then appear not to be explicitly tested or assessed, but which are deemed important as an educational rounding of undergraduate skills currently the focus of the ubiquitous personal development programmes within the UK academic and professional development context. As with the previous example, it could well be the case that the South East Asian preponderance in this type of exercise may be due to the geographically disparate nature of its students who are nonetheless linked by a common language. In fact, the Mekong e-Sim, the software used in this instance, can sit within a VLE such as Blackboard™ and is used to stage a range of simulations within a variety of academic disciplines.

Evaluating the quality of the online role play will entail issues of objectivity and appropriate assessment criteria, but this is perhaps no more problematic than the assessment of formal student presentations, where aspects of the presentation itself are evaluated. In fact, the advantage of online role play in this context is the logging of the contributions, which can be reviewed by several tutors, and which remains after the assessed event for review and possible moderation.

Integrating this type of exercise into a broader programme that uses online discussion boards as part of the teaching programme will obviously make it easier to implement when the assessment part of the programme is undertaken.

There is some interesting and pioneering work being done with discussion boards in general by one of the United Kingdom's leading economics authors, John Sloman, at the University of West England.

In a brief case review, Sloman (2002) outlines his construction of parallel online and live seminar groups, and highlights the value and potential contribution of the blended approach to the issue of online assessment and the design of a whole teaching programme illustrated here, which integrates online discussion as part of the overall assessment package and gives a clear indication of how effective use of online discussion contrib-

utes to overall assessment. The online seminar programme does include elements of role play where students are expected to post in character on macroeconomic matters. Sloman makes a number of incisive comments about the nature of economic material, which tends to work best in an online-conducted syllabus.

Sutcliffe (2002), again within the field of economics, also gives some clear advice on preparing groups of students for online role-play simulations and stresses the importance of enquiring the students about what they believe they have learned from their experience in the role play. Within the various online cases and scenarios, he underlines the importance of enabling the students at the end of the simulations to review and evaluate their actions and performances within their adopted roles, believing this to be a sound means of assessing the learning that has taken place. There is a particularly good example of the use of online role play to prepare tasks that are to be presented off line in the third of the cases demonstrated entitled Press Briefing, where teams interact within VLE discussion-board groups in order to prepare three constituent tasks.

Another online role play conducted by Possajennikov (2005) at Nottingham University explores the relationship between the success in final examinations and the type of formative assessment as practised in a virtual learning environment, which involves role play as one activity amongst others. This particular case does focus more on the relationship between success in final assessment and the role-play participation, which involves students playing the role of managers within a company and making decisions that lead to profit for their firms. Significantly, with regard to correlation between the role-play exercise and later examination success, Possajennikov observed much higher correlation between participation and subsequent examination success than between the profit made within the exercise and the examination results.

The use of role play online would therefore appear to offer useful opportunities to prepare for subsequent assessment, whether this is conducted online or in traditional format. In Sloman's (2002) case, a range of supplementary preparatory routes is offered to undergraduate students, which includes seminar discussion online, and his approach has enabled him to evaluate the relative merits and success of each.

## CASE STUDY: INFORMATION "DRIP-FEED" ROLE-PLAY EXERCISE

Assigning particular roles to students and casting the tutor as an information-provider is another variation of this general theme whereby the tutor sets up an online role-play exercise as a precursor to a written assignment and releases information when asked questions in the discussion board.

Within the School of Business and Management at the Buckinghamshire New University, I have recently experimented using this method with a group of 48 mature students aged between 28 and 47 currently in the Chartered Institute of Personnel and Development programme.

The year-long module is entitled Managing in a Strategic Business Context and explores the economic, political, social, international, and legal influences on UK private- and public-sector organisations.

Over a 2-week period, they were asked to make contributions to the discussion board prior to submitting a related assessment. My adopted role in the exercise was to act as a party political spokesman, representing the Labour or Conservative Party, and to reply to specific questions related to party policy that may have some bearing on their own companies or organisations, answers to which would be of immediate relevance to the questioner but might also be of use to the wider group, so this would thereby encourage their scrutiny of all the postings. This formed a sig-

nificant part of the preparation for an element of coursework that required participants to explore and report on an element of government policy that might impinge upon the commercial activities of their employers.

## These were the Instructions Issued

A General Election is looming and your line manager has set you the task of contacting your local MP or the spokesperson of a named mainstream UK political party and to frame specific questions about the intentions and policies of the political party which have some bearing on your firm or organisation. You therefore need to indicate the name of your firm and what it does, if that's not obvious or already well-known, and to indicate whether you are addressing the Labour or Conservative office. (I can only play one role at a time!)

Some of your questions may be addressed by my answers to other questions in the group, and so it would be valuable to monitor the general Discussion Board as the exercise progresses, but it is more likely that you will get specific information or commentary about specific areas of concern or interest to your firm.

At the end of this, you should summarise any relevant help and information that you have managed to solicit from the spokesperson in the form of a brief one-page memo to your line manager.

All students in this class work in human resource management (HRM) positions within companies located in the vicinity of the university, and are therefore clearly familiar with policies and laws relating to their own organisations in particular, and to HRM issues in general. The basic objective of the exercise was that participants should consider the possible impact on their own organisation of another party coming to power after a general election, or indeed, to refresh their awareness of the impact of the current government continuing in office. Their task was to draft a memo and submit it to me as if to their line manager who had requested them to summarise some likely outcomes of a change of party. The role that they adopt in this context is probably not the one that they would normally hold within their organisation, although it is possible that they might hold such a position. In some instances, therefore, the participants would adopt a slightly different role than the one that they held in their professional positions at their place of work.

Clearly the sort of questions they could pose would vary from the very specific, relevant only to their own organisation, to the more general, which might well be relevant to a wider range of companies represented by their class colleagues. The value of the exercise emanates from the diversity and quality of the questions asked, their relevance to the organisation, and the quality of the information gleaned from the online party political spokesman, who made use of a variety of online and other resources in order to supply this information.

An interesting aspect of this particular task was that some of the information provided by the tutor could have proved useful to others within the group so that certain information could be classified as specific to a particular company whilst other information could prove relevant to a range of companies. Proposed policies on educational reforms, for example, might affect a range of companies as might other areas of economic policy or taxation reform, or policies designed to reduce carbon footprints. Therefore, this was not a case of one-to-one communication between student and tutor as some of the information could prove useful to a wide range of participants seeking to prepare a particular assessment exercise. For this reason, the use of a discussion board would prove more useful and efficient than an exchange of e-mail between tutor and participants because the board would provide a display of all of the information provided once it had been accessed. This was not a competitive exercise or a zero-sum game where

one person's acquisition of information came at the expense of another's.

It is interesting to note that the exercise was by no means competitive, and, although it was also not overtly collaborative, participants were encouraged to provide answers to others' queries where such opportunities did arise, which in turn led to a more fruitful exercise. The contribution made by colleagues answering others' queries demonstrates the emerging collaborative nature of the exercise, and the particular importance and advantage of using a discussion board. Unlike a live debate, where there can only be one topic of discussion at a time, the board offered a growing variety of topics to which any other member of the class could contribute, and to which any member could return or refer to at a later stage. Indeed, several class members maintained and extended contributions to several threads.

The brevity of the exercise maintained a reasonably high level of interest and focus on the preparation of a specific task. However, Berge (1995) points out that more intensive periods of online role-play activity may tend to encourage greater participation.

In some cases, there was direct interaction between participants where one or more students were able to answer the query of another, in what thereby emerged as a truly collaborative exercise. This particular cohort of students was already reasonably well motivated but did have the extra incentive of needing to draft a memo as part of their formal assessment based upon the information that they were able to glean from participation in the discussion board. Every member of the class did contribute, due largely to the nature of the exercise and its participants who were free to phrase and present questions and queries on whatever way they wanted (within reason), but had to follow the appropriate protocol of ascribing a subject. A small sample of the contributions is reproduced in Figure 1.

*Figure 1. Extracts from "Drip-Feed" online role-play exercise*

---

**Forum:** Political party consultation exercise

Times Read: 80

**Date:** Thu Feb 09 2006 10:03

**Author:** <c0601299@bcuc.ac.uk>

**Subject:** Education - Qualification Standards

(Pharmaceutical Industry)

As a representative of the current government, what guarantees/policies are in place to ensure that the 50% of the population, who will be entering further/higher education, will qualify in subjects that are required by businesses in the UK ? Our organisation finds it increasingly difficult to find highly qualified employees with qualifications in the sciences, business management and commercial finance. Figures from the NSO support the fact that HE/FE places have doubled in the last 15 years, but the more academic (or could I suggest costly) places have halved. What proof is there that current education policies support the current and future needs of the UK economy ?

( Reply )

---

**Forum:** Political party consultation exercise

Times Read: 68

**Date:** Thu Feb 09 2006 11:03

**Author:** Millard, Stephen <smilla01@bcuc.ac.uk>

**Subject:** Re: Education - Qualification Standards

( Modify ) ( Remove )

We in the Labour Party are concerned to maintain and enhance the quality of our higher education provision as well as the number of students who are able to profit from this. To that end we are monitoring quality within the sector via the Quality Assurance Agency who periodically inspect universities and also award finances to those universities who are able to demonstrate a good track-record of fruitful research via the annual Research Assessment Exercises, the results of which determine levels of financial support that universities can expect to receive from Central Government. Teaching and Learning enhancement is monitored, encouraged and developed under the auspices of the Higher Education Academy, a body that encompasses academics across the sector.

( Reply )

*continued on following page*

*Figure 1. continued*

**Forum:** Political party consultation exercise

Times Read: 66

**Date:** Thu Feb 09 2006 15:20

**Author:** <c0526541@bcuc.ac.uk>

**Subject:** NHS financial deficits and increased patient choice

Hospitals NHS Trust

Addressing Conservative representative:

Local NHS Trusts are continuing to under-perform financially, with increasing financial deficits, as a result of both historic Conservative and current Labour healthcare policies.

Against this background, how will you support the implementation of increased patient choice and the provision of more competitive healthcare services, when this will require further investment in the NHS?

( Reply )

---

**Forum:** Political party consultation exercise

Times Read: 56

**Date:** Thu Feb 09 2006 16:42

**Author:** Millard, Stephen <smilla01@bcuc.ac.uk>

**Subject:** Re: NHS financial deficits and increased patient choice

( Modify ) ( Remove )

In reply to this, I include this extract from the Conservative Party manifesto:-
"6 **ACTION ON HEALTH**
We believe that a combination of freedom for professionals and patients' Right to Choose care from the public or independent sector will mean no needless waits for hospital treatment by the end of the next Parliament.
Waiting lists as we know them will become a thing of the past.

Currently, patients in need of hospital treatment must join the waiting list at the hospital chosen for them. Under a Conservative Government, patients will have the Right to Choose the hospital or care provider that is best for them.
All patients will have a choice of treatment at any hospital – NHS or independent – which can perform their operation to NHS standards at NHS costs. No-one will be required to pay for NHS treatment or NHS operations.
Patients will receive information on hospitals' infection rates, waiting times, treatment outcomes and patient experience surveys.
They will make decisions with their GP on the best and most convenient hospital and specialist for their needs.

Under a Conservative Government, funding will follow the patient, and go directly to front-line care. We will invest an additional £34 billion a year by the end of our first Parliament, over and above the level that we inherit from Labour.
The 28 Strategic Health Authorities will be abolished. The number and functions of Primary Care Trusts will be reduced, saving over £1.25 billion for front-line care. The quangos and inspectorates which currently dominate the NHS will be cut. By slimming down the Department of Health, by halving the number of quangos through eradicating waste and by scrapping a tier of health bureaucracy completely, we will ensure that, in addition to the growth in the NHS budget, billions of extra pounds will get through to front-line services.

## Comment on Exercise

The extract in Figure 1 is a small selection of the interaction that took place, but should be sufficient to demonstrate the nature of the contributions and the author's replies, which did involve the need to apply some role play.

This exercise appeared to work well and included a live session in a computer room in the teaching block after 1 week of contributions. Generally speaking, this is advisable to do at the beginning of the exercise to start the process and to familiarise students with the processes of adding new threads, and the general protocol of using a discussion board. In this particular case, however, these processes were demonstrated in class, but then the participants were left to make contributions outside class, and the level of interest generated in the exercise was monitored.

Approximately 75% of the students contributed to the board in the time between classes, which is a relatively high percentage of contributions in discussion boards, and there were a number of "lurkers," those who read the postings but did not contribute any themselves. When the groups were gathered into the computer room to view the postings, there was a general willingness to contribute further to the existing forums, which should engender interest in future boards that will be set up in support of forthcoming assessments. As a mechanism for boosting interest in online participation, this appeared to work well, particularly as participants could see that peers had already begun to contribute. Feedback from students was very positive. Responses in 36 out of the 48 end-of-module review questionnaires singled out this particular exercise as being one of the most informative and interesting pedagogic activities of their courses to date. More recently, a CIPD external validation conducted in June 2007 also specifically commended this activity.

The link between assessment and discussion-board contribution is clearly intended to encourage a higher level of active participation. In this particular group, interest already appeared to be reasonably high, but participation in a more general discussion board had hitherto been much lower, suggesting that the focused assessment-related exercises did encourage them to come online more often and post their questions.

The clear nature of the task was also helpful. They were to pose questions, the formation of which is a reasonably well-established technique of clarifying thought on any discursive topic, evidenced by the growth of inquiry-based learning techniques, which, as Palmer (2002) indicates, is highly constructive in establishing analytical technique and deeper learning. The collaborative aspect of this research can also enhance the breadth of knowledge acquired as well as demonstrate the value of the discussion board as a means of sharing knowledge.

As the associated summative assessment task was new, it is not feasible to compare assessment performance with the equivalent assignment prepared in a traditional way. However, students did indicate a high level of satisfaction with this form of exercise in the module review at the end of the academic year, and indicated quite strongly that they would appreciate more exercises that were undertaken this way.

One tentative conclusion that might be drawn from this reaction is that the initial exposure to this methodology has initiated some interest in repeating the experience using different scenarios and objectives but engaging in a similar kind of online collaborative activity. Part of the reluctance to engage in online discussion is arguably due to a lack of familiarity with the format. This exercise tends to introduce students to collaborative activity in a nonthreatening way, which is unlikely to lead to any humiliating exposure or ridicule which might deter others from becoming involved in the process. This is largely due to the fact that the participants are essentially engaging in a one-to-one dialogue with the tutor, in this instance, in order to prepare a task that is customised to their own organisation's operating environment, so clearly they will be familiar with the subject in question. However, rather than posting comments about this, as is the case with some online discussions embedded in work-based online interactions, this one requires the framing of relevant questions designed to elicit specific information. The element of role play in this particular exercise did not require the participants to move widely away from their normal working role in so far as they would probably be familiar with the organisation's range of commercial activities and interests, although in the case of a larger company, this might not necessarily be the case.

Some of the other studies cited in this chapter have focused upon the specific advantages of adopting a role that facilitates greater online participation and involvement by either taking participants outside their normal role, or by requiring them to become familiar with the functions and responsibilities of their adopted role as a main learning outcome.

## FUTURE RESEARCH DIRECTIONS

Following this last point, further projects based on this experience would involve a greater degree of role play over a longer period so that students could absorb the part more fully, thus developing and enlarging this online enquiry-based learning technique. Students working alone or in small teams could be cast in the role of consultants seeking to diagnose the causes of a particular company problem. Only by asking probing, intelligent, and relevant questions can an appropriate diagnosis be made and an acceptable assignment drafted. This is akin to the questioning technique of a detective, lawyer, or doctor, all of whom need to be sufficiently prepared and briefed with appropriate questions in their examinations of their subjects.

This could follow a particular set of cases practised in class and also possibly precede a more rigorous written examination that uses case-study analysis. In fact, this technique could be a valuable adjunct to a large case-study analysis building up to final assessment. Case-study analysis is a popular technique as a means of gaining insight into specific problems as well as more fully understanding the application of theoretical concepts.

Tutors in this situation are not really providing answers but furnishing pieces of information that might then lead to a greater insight into the causes of the problem, thereby helping the diagnosis by offering up more significant pieces of a jigsaw as a reward for probing and intelligent questioning. It requires further insight and thought to fashion the information into some sort of diagnosis, so that the more able student will process and interpret information appropriately.

This reflects the idea of collaborative learning as outlined by Gilroy (2001), and the synergies that evolve from that process, where all participants buy into the idea that learning can be better enhanced when underpinned by a degree of cooperation. This will obviously work well with a group of learners that share common attitudes toward learning, where there is less likely to be a "free-rider" problem, and most if not all members are willing and able to contribute. The free-riding problem has been well documented within online learning. One potential difficulty might therefore be that, in an open forum, one student might profit from answers provided by the tutor to the question of another student, obtaining something for nothing.

Experience would, however, tend to suggest that, whilst a certain degree of theft or involuntary information acquisition might take place, it is the act of interrogation that is suitably encouraged here. Students' insight and subsequent ability to identify the relevant issues and diagnose the problems will emerge through the accumulation of responses from the tutor. Those who are collectively asking the more germane questions will on balance be those that have, or can readily develop, powers of critical thinking, and who are then better able to process and interpret the information that is duly provided. This could and should obviously be encouraged in the background briefing to the exercise.

As with many such collective exercises of this nature, some degree of increasing involvement tends to evolve as peers perceive their colleagues to be getting involved. Such active involvement in learning has long been underlined by Stiles (2000) and others as a major advantage of the VLE discussion board. The emboldening nature of online asynchronous discussion can also lead to online involvement in the participants' own good time, whereas dominant speakers tend to keep more reluctant group members out of the proceedings in live situations as attested by Boardman (2002).

It is also interesting to speculate on the added educational value of the act of changing or even exchanging the traditional roles of student and tutor within the discussion area of a VLE, particularly in the context of role play. The framing of appropriate questions within a particular role can develop more generic skills of research and interrogation than other research sources, and the sustained experience of adopting such a role over a protracted period of time in a lengthier online role-play exercise would develop these more than might be the case in a single role-play simulation conducted live, which would perhaps not extend realistically to a second iteration.

Goodyear (2001) notes the flexibility and fluidity of roles that may develop during information exchanging role-play exercises where traditional inquisitor and information provider roles may be exchanged or be subtly blended. In the exercise conducted, participants were beginning to offer responses to questions posed to the tutor according to their own familiarity with the question-topics based upon their professional experience. Klemm and Snell (1996) claim that collaborative online learning thereby leads to a deeper learning experience through adopting a different perspective and through the act of collaboration itself.

The proposed consultative exercise outlined above could, however, contain a more competitive element than the open forum of the CIPD political consultation exercise. Using the Groups facility that most proprietary VLEs contain, participants could be divided into competing teams, each of which seeks to prepare the common task more effectively by asking suitable questions online to the tutor, who adopts one or more roles and provides information only when prompted to do so by the appropriate online interrogation. This would combine the competitive approach as demonstrated in the case devised and presented by Sutcliffe (2002) above with this interrogative approach.

The overall aim of each team would be to obtain more appropriate information and insight into the case-study situation and thereby produce a more effective report; those teams that perform better in this way should be suitably rewarded with the higher grade. This competitive variant of the online "drip-feed" interrogative model would of course still require collaboration amongst team members who, in addition to face-to-face meetings, could make use of the small-group discussion board in preparing their questions.

There are two interrelated themes from this research in the general area of collaborative online learning that warrant further exploration, and a further element that would explore a more competitive approach.

The first theme incorporates further investigation into the greater use of collaboration within the role-play exercise. In this brief exercise, and in some of those cited in the literature, the specific aim was to prepare participants to produce a piece of coursework that would be presented in hard copy, so the online role-play exercise thereby formed a significant part of the preparatory work. Cooperation amongst the participants was encouraged, but the level of collaboration was limited, and outcomes did not depend heavily upon such collaboration taking place, although it was apparent that the level of collaboration amongst participants did grow as the exercise progressed.

The first strand of further research, therefore, would be to establish an online exercise involving role play, but with a greater element of collaboration necessary to accomplish the learning goals. Encouraging cooperation amongst participants where elements of acquired information are to be shared would enhance the valuable collaborative nature of the activity. Allied to this would be further specific investigation into the enhanced learning motivation that might be an adjunct of such a collaborative approach.

A second strand would be to investigate further the role of the tutor or online moderator in this exercise. In this prototype exercise, the tutor played the role of principal information provider. Clearly, this does place a considerable burden on the tutor, and it was confirmed in a second iteration of this exercise that has subsequently occurred that the workload is considerable, albeit very rewarding. However, the second iteration did appear also to yield a greater degree of spontaneous collaboration amongst the participants, whereby answers to queries posted were in fact provided by fellow participants to a greater degree than had been the case in the first iteration. Whilst this cooperation was encouraged prior to the exercise in both cases, it was never a specific requirement. It became apparent that a future exercise could therefore be set up to require participants to ask and answer others' queries on a more systematic basis.

The continuity of this exercise from one cohort to the next might well facilitate a swifter assimilation of the main idea and potential benefits of the activity. The second iteration of the exercise was under way much more quickly than the first, largely because the contributions of the participants of the previous group, together with the tutor's replies, were archived on the discussion board. This may well have engendered a competitive element as the second cohort wanted to be seen to be at least as prolific as the first group.

It is to be hoped that the outcome of such a modification should be to encourage further the degree of effective collaborative learning, though it would also have the added secondary effect of easing the moderator's workload. This would naturally depend upon the levels of relevant knowledge that could be transferred between the participants, but in the principal demonstrated example, where there is a common professional link, the encouragement of further knowledge providers could actively develop the collaborative element.

Whilst this research and general approach has concentrated upon the fruitfulness of a collaborative approach to online learning, there is an alternative competitive approach, outlined briefly above, whereby participants, divided into teams online, are rewarded by collectively asking appropriate questions and eliciting suitably informative answers, helping the team to produce a more effective report. This is an area that will form the basis of future investigation.

In addition to the above suggested developments, future iterations of the same exercise undertaken with CIPD students and any new exercises will include a more detailed reflective journal to be completed at the end by the participants themselves. Whilst some helpful comments were made in the module questionnaires, these could be more focused if applied exclusively to this particular activity, with any recommendations for modification.

## CONCLUSION

The virtual learning environment can clearly facilitate assessment in a number of ways. There is a gradually growing range of fruitful initiatives to extend the ways in which assessment can be undertaken online, but the relationship between online preparation and off-line assessment is an area worth noting. Quite apart from enabling assessment to be tackled in a more informed manner, the encouragement to use the discussion board can itself set up effective learning patterns as it can encourage a collaborative approach to learning if appropriately prepared. Playing a role online is a means of achieving such an approach, but this technique also does offer other potential advantages as demonstrated by the cited cases. These include being able to understand the attitudes and perspectives of others, feeling more emboldened to make contributions when not intimidated by dominant speakers and when adopting another persona online, as well as monitoring the contributions of others across a range of linked themes. The short study outlined as a case study and the proposed development of this to incorporate the discussion board more explicitly to prepare summative assessment has a number of intended outcomes. The enticement to use it is initially set up by establishing it as a resource that can be used to acquire the knowledge and information that can help tackle a particular piece of coursework. Then, when this immediate aim is achieved, and subsequent threads or forums are started by the tutor, there tends to be a stronger chance that it will be used to continue to help in learning.

A module assessment programme based upon a series of exercises and tasks that require significant input resulting from online discussion can thereby encourage the habit of productive participation using this powerful learning tool. Assigning defined roles to all participants can demonstrably encourage its use and its effectiveness in preparing for assessment.

## REFERENCES

Berge, Z. (1995). Facilitating computer conferencing: Recommendations from the field. *Educational Technology, 35*(1), 22-30.

Boardman, K. (2002). *How to use a discussion board.* UK Centre for Legal Education. Retrieved December 14, 2000, from http://www.ukcle.ac.uk/resources/trns/discussions/index.html

Bollens, J. C., & Marshall, D. R. (1973). *A guide to participation: Fieldwork, role-playing cases and other forms.* Englewood Cliffs, NJ: Prentice-Hall.

Connolly, T., Jessup, L. M., & Valacich, J. S. (1990). Effects of anonymity and evaluative tone on idea generation in computer-mediated groups. *Management Science, 36*(6), 689-703.

Fetherston, T. (2001). Pedagogical challenges for the World Wide Web. *Educational Technology Review, 9*(1), 25-32.

Freeman, M., & Capper, J. (1999). Exploiting the Web for education: An anonymous asynchronous role simulation. *Australian Journal of Educational Technology, 15*(1), 95-116. Retrieved August 14, 2007, from http://www.ascilite.org.au/ajet/ajet15/freeman.html

Gilroy, K. (2001). Collaborative e-learning: The right approach. *ArsDigita Systems Journal.*

Goodyear, P. (2001). Teaching online. In N. Hativa & P. Goodyear (Eds.), *Teacher thinking, beliefs and knowledge in higher education* (pp. 79-101). The Netherlands: Kluwer.

Klemm, W. R., & Snell, J. R. (1996). Enriching computer-mediated group learning by coupling constructivism with collaborative learning. *Journal of Instructional Science and Technology.* Retrieved August 14, 2007, from http://www.usq.edu.au/electpub/e-jist/docs/old/vol1no2/article1.htm

Ladousse, G. P. (1987). *Role play.* Oxford, United Kingdom: Oxford University Press.

Linser, R., & Ip, A. (2002, October 15-19). *Beyond the current e-learning paradigm: Applications of role play simulations (RPS). Case studies.* Paper presented at E-Learn 2002, AACE Conference, Montreal, Canada. Retrieved July 17, 2007, from http://www.simplay.net/papers/E-Learning.html

McLaughlan, R. G. (2004). Using online role-play/simulations for creating learning experiences. *CAL-laborate, 7*. Retrieved August 14, 2007, from http://science.uniserve.edu.au/pubs/callab/vol7/mclaugh.html

Naidu, S., Ip, A., & Linser, R. (2000). Dynamic goal-based role play simulation on the Web: A case study. *Educational Technology & Society, 3*(3), 190-202.

Olaniran, B. A., Savage, G. T., & Sorenson, R. L. (1996). Experimental and experiential approaches to teaching face-to-face and computer-mediated group discussion. *Communication Education, 45*(3), 244-259.

Palmer, S. (2002). Enquiry-based learning can maximise a student's potential. *Psychology, Learning and Teaching, 2*(2), 82-86. Retrieved April 18, 2007, from http://www.psychology.heacademy.ac.uk/docs/pdf/p20030617_22palmer.pdf

Pavey, J. (2003). *Collaborating with communities.* Retrieved July 14, 2007, from http://www.heacademy.ac.uk/resources/detail/id216_leap_casestudy14_pavey

*Possajennikov, A. (2005). Using formative assessment and role-playing as means of enhancing learning.* Retrieved July 14, 2007, from http://www.nottingham.ac.uk/teaching/resources/methods/assessment/usingfor316

Sloman, J. (2002). *Case study: The use of lecture time for workshops.* Retrieved April 17, 2007, from http://www.economicsnetwork.ac.uk/showcase/sloman_workshop.htm

Stiles, M. J. (2000, April). *Effective learning and the virtual learning environment.* Keynote paper presented at EUNIS 2000: Towards Virtual Universities, Pozan, Poland.

Sutcliffe, M. (2002). *Simulations, games and role-play.* Retrieved April 14, 2007, from http://www.economicsnetwork.ac.uk/handbook/games

Thompson, J. F. (1978). *Using roleplay in the classroom.* Bloomington, IN: Phi Kappa Delta Educational Foundation.

Vincent, A., & Shepherd, J. (1998). Experiences in teaching Middle-East politics via Internet role-play simulations. *Journal of Interactive Media in Education, 11*. Retrieved April 18, 2007, from http://www-jime.open.ac.uk/98/11/vincent-98-11-paper.html

## ADDITIONAL READING

Aggarwal, A. (Ed.). (2000). *Web-based learning and teaching technologies: Opportunities and challenges.* Hershey, PA: Idea Group Publishing.

This book explores general pedagogic applications of Web technology and examines the steps involved in Web education. The perspectives of three major stakeholders, namely, the tutors, the student, and the technical personnel, are explored, and ways of providing online conveniences are discussed based on the author's experience.

Alden, D. (1999). Experience with scripted role-play in environmental economics. *Journal of Economic Education, 30*(2), 127-132.

This article explores the use of simulations and games in tertiary education. It examines the extent to which academics use different simulation-based teaching approaches and how they perceive the barriers to adopting such techniques. Following a review of the extant literature, a typology of simulations is constructed. A staff survey within a UK higher education institution is conducted to investigate the use of the different approaches identified within the typology. The findings show significant levels of use of both computer- and non-computer-based simulations and games.

Alexander, S. (2005). Role play simulations for teaching. In J. McKenzie., S. Alexander, C.

Harper, & S. Anderson (Eds.), *Dissemination, adoption & adaptation of project innovations in higher education.* Retrieved April 18, 2007, from http://ro.uow.edu.au/asdpapers/42

The paper examines three questions related to the dissemination of online innovations in higher education. The project has facilitated the participation of others, enabling them to share in the project's outcomes. Its relevance to this paper lies in the collaborative nature of information dissemination.

Beaudouin-Lafon, M. (Ed.). (1998). *Computer supported cooperative work (CSCW).* London: John Wiley & Sons.

The use and potential of online interaction and Web-based teaching and learning have been little used in the higher level and most critical functions of public administration, such as the development, monitoring, and evaluation of public policies and programmes; the decision making for difficult and complex social problems; or for granting licenses and permissions with high social impact. This paper explores the application of the methodologies and technologies of computer-supported collaborative work in these directions. Again, the focus is on collaborative dissemination within a pedagogic institution.

Bell, M. (2002). Online role play: Anonymity, engagement, and risk. *Education Media International, 38*(4), 251-260.

Australia seems to have produced a fair number of case studies in online collaborative learning, and this study tracks the uptake of online role play in Australia from 1990 to 2006, examining its reusability. The study treats reuse on two levels: reuse of an existing online role play and reuse of an online role play as the model for another online role play. Transferring the use of existing role plays is a theme that could well be developed from the chapter.

Bender, T. (2005). Role playing in online education: A teaching tool to enhance student engagement and sustained learning. *Innovate, 1*(4). Retrieved April 14, 2007, from http://innovateonline.info/index.php?view=article&id=57

Tisha Bender advocates online role-playing as an engaging educational tool that promotes sustained learning, and she has found that role-playing connects students to the course material and to each other more intimately and successfully than a traditional lecture can. She provides technical tips for establishing an online theatre, describes three role-playing assignment models, and evaluates those models according to Bloom's taxonomy. She also reports student reactions to role-playing exercises and suggests concrete criteria for grading individual performances. In so doing, she demonstrates direction that some of the ideas expressed in this paper could follow in future research.

Bender, T. (2005). *Discussion-based online teaching to enhance student learning.* Sterling, VA: Stylus Publishing LLC.

In this text, Bender further develops the theme that if online learning is to promote learning, which she believes is accomplished through meaningful dialogue, the online instructor has to move beyond thinking about the technology to providing opportunities for discussion. She proposes that because most online courses are primarily text based, the best way to engage learners is through frequent, active, and substantive discussions. This is therefore a general support of online discussion as a part of full-time course syllabi.

Black, G. (2001). *A comparison of traditional, online and hybrid methods.* Retrieved April 14, 2007, from http://www.ipfw.edu/as/tohe/2001/Papers/black1.htm

This paper examines student perceptions of traditional, online, and hybrid (mixed mode) methods of learning in higher education. Hybrid approaches may also extend to providing students with both real office hours and virtual office hours, working in both face-to-face teams and virtual teams. This mixture of approaches delivers some flexibility into the delivery patterns of blended learning approaches.

Boud, D., Cohen, R., & Sampson, J. (Eds.). (2001). *Peer learning in higher education: Learning from and with each other.* London: Kogan Page.

This paper offers four reasons as to why peer learning in tutorials may not be as useful as teachers might assume. Additionally, four possible solutions to these problems are proposed, which include changes to teaching methodologies and assessment structures in courses that employ peer learning strategies. It therefore challenges assumptions about peer learning that should be considered when establishing frameworks of collaborative learning, thereby facilitating careful and more productive construction of interactive learning.

Brown, D. G. (2002). *The role you play in online discussions.* Retrieved April 14, 2007, from http://campustechnology.com/articles/39303

In this paper, Brown briefly outlines his findings that provide some solid evidence for the fact that in classes that are entirely online, asynchronous discussions and chat sessions—especially ones in which the tutor is a participant-leader—often become central to the learning experience.

Crook, C. (1994). *Computers and the collaborative experience of learning.* London: Routledge.

Crook analyses the variety of different ways in which computers can be part of the collaborative experience of learning, which presents the scope and range of possible online collaborative learning activities and strategies, and the contribution that online element of this can confer, either by injecting a collaborative element or by embellishing existing social interaction.

Davies, P. (1994). Learning through computer simulations. *Economics and Business Education, 2*(1). 30-35.

This paper offers an analysis of selected first-year teaching-learning environments in economics. Evidence is derived from 41 semistructured interviews conducted as part of the Enhancing Teaching-Learning Environments in Undergraduate Courses (ETL) Project with staff and students in three introductory economics modules from three different UK economics departments.

Fetherston, T. (2001). Pedagogical challenges for the World Wide Web. *Educational Technology Review, 9*(1), 25-32.

This paper commences by analysing the influence of historical views of knowledge, considering how this informed views about the nature of university teaching. The paper then critiques the traditional lecture-tutorial-examination approach to teaching at university, considers research about learning, and then questions why university teaching and learning practices continue to be resistant to, and often inconsistent with, fundamental principles of learning developed through sustained scholarly enquiry.

Francis, P., & Byrne, A. (1999). *Use of role-play exercises in teaching undergraduate astronomy and physics.* Australia: Astronomical Society Australia.

This article explores the use of simulations and games in tertiary education. It examines the extent to which academics use different simulation-based teaching approaches and how they perceive the barriers to adopting such techniques. Following a review of the extant literature, a typology of simulations is constructed. The findings show significant levels of use of both computer- and non-computer-based simulations and games. The study concludes by recommending improved promotion of simulation-based teaching through enhanced information provision on the various techniques available and their application across subject areas.

Freeman, M. A., & Capper, J. M. (1999). Exploiting the Web for education: An anonymous asynchronous role simulation. *Australian Journal of Educational Technology, 15*(1), 95-116.

This paper describes the learning and other outcomes of an anonymous asynchronous Web-based role simulation. In response to changes in the tertiary environment (e.g., increasing competition, new technologies, busier student population), universities are increasingly pursuing flexible learning strategies. Technology-enhanced teaching and learning systems, in particular the World Wide Web, have become common in many tertiary courses. The question of anonymity and the advantages it may confer to stimulate greater interaction is a theme that is briefly explored in the chapter.

Galea, C. (2001). Experiential simulations: Using Web-enhanced role-plays to teach applied business management. *Information Technology and Management, 2*, 473-489.

This paper discusses the successful use of online role play, which is demonstrated as useful in helping students understand how governments, stakeholders, and business organisations interact, how new policy subsequently gets developed, and the impact this has on the management of business organisations. As such, the simulation can be used in a variety of business courses such as business-government relations, business ethics, business and society, environmental business management, and so forth, which are areas that touch on the author's subject areas.

Gilroy. K (2001). Collaborative e-learning: The right approach. *ArsDigita Systems Journal.*

This paper focuses on innovative activities that support a social mode of learning in a collaborative setting, which encourages independent learning and, by increasing awareness of learning processes, develops autonomy and responsibility for learning. This requires the development of technologies that support authoring and scripting, collaboration, reflection of learning activities, and integrated learning activities. The theme of developing independence in learning is an outcome that the chapter's author would expect from online collaborative activity.

Ip, A., & Linser, R. (2001). Evaluation of a role-play simulation in political science. *The Technology Source.* Retrieved April 11, 2007, from http://horizon.unc.edu/TS

Ip and Linser figure prominently in the main reference list as authors exploring areas of online role play, and the discipline of political science does offer itself as being a rich area for beneficial role adoption and simulation exercises as evidenced by this paper.

Ip, A., Linser, R., & Naidu, S. (2001). *Simulated worlds: Rapid generation of Web-based role-play.* Retrieved August 15, 2007, from http://ausweb.scu.edu.au/aw01/papers/refereed/ip/paper.html

Here the authors broaden the discussion beyond one academic discipline to the consideration of the use of Web-based role play within a range of academic disciplines.

McConnell, D. (2000). *Implementing computer supported cooperative learning* (2nd ed.). London: Kogan Page.

This qualitative cross-case study explores the experiences that learners describe within online collaborative groups. The study context was a fully online graduate course on adult learning whose findings suggest that the small online groups demonstrated dynamics and processes that are characteristic of individual growth and development akin to the experiences of face-to-face groups.

McLaughlan, R. G. (2005). *Online text-based role-play simulation: The challenges ahead.*

Retrieved March 24, 2007, from http://www.siaa. asn.au/get/2411856278.pdf

This paper undertakes a description and analysis of the way in which Australian higher education students perform roles through the use of online role-play systems at the University of Melbourne.

McLaughlan, R. G., & Kirkpatrick, D. (2004). Online roleplay: Design for active learning. *European Journal of Engineering Education, 29*(4), 477-490.

This paper outlines features and applications of the Mekong E-sim, which is an online role play designed to enable students from different disciplines to work collaboratively to investigate and resolve issues related to economic development in the Mekong region of South East Asia. The Mekong E-sim facilitates student engagement and encourages high levels of distributed student interaction.

Packham, G., Cramphorn, C., & Miller, C. (2001). Module development through peer assisted student support: An initial evaluation. *Mentoring and Tutoring, 9*(2), 113-124.

This paper examines tutor perceptions of effective e-moderation. The methodology involved semistructured interviews with 35 e-moderators from the university and partner colleges. Analysis of the results revealed that effective e-moderators required specific qualities, characteristics, and organisational skills. Effective communication and responsive feedback were judged to be the most critical activities.

Palloff, R. M., & Pratt, K. (1999). *Building learning communities in cyberspace.* San Francisco: Jossey-Bass.

In *this paper*, Palloff and Pratt explore benefits, problems, and concerns related to computer-mediated distance education. While identifying that online groups go through the same stages of development as face-to-face groups (forming, norming, performing, storming, adjourning), they challenge the belief that the online classroom is no different from the traditional one.

Salmon, G. (2000). *E-moderating: The key to teaching and learning online.* London: Kogan Page.

No reading list on this subject would be complete or even respectable without a reference to Gilly Salmon in the area of e-moderation and online learning in general.

Yardley-Matwiejczuk, K. M. (1997). *Role play: Theory and practice.* London: Sage.

This book reports on a case study of an asynchronous, anonymous, online role play conducted within a teaching course for academic staff. Findings suggest that online role play may offer an effective learning process and that anonymity may be a key factor for participant involvement and comfort.

# Chapter XVII
# Mastering the Online Summative Assessment Life Cycle

**Simon Wilkinson**
*Medical Education Unit, University of Nottingham, UK*

**Heather Rai**
*Medical Education Unit, University of Nottingham, UK*

## ABSTRACT

*This chapter focuses on the use of computers for online summative assessment, in particular for objectively marked items. The aim of this chapter is to try and address the concerns of individuals wishing to pilot the introduction of online summative assessments in their own institutions. A five-stage development life cycle of online summative assessment—item development, quality assurance, item selection, examination delivery, and results analysis—is presented and discussed.*

## INTRODUCTION

Many institutions are already using computers for online formative assessment, but in a review looking at medical education, Cantillon, Irish, and Sales (2004) found the application of computers to the summative-assessment arena much more limited. Limiting factors preventing wider adoption of online summative assessment included lack of space and perceived security risks. The publication of failures (Harwood, 2005; Heintz & Jemison, 2005; Smailes, 2002) also does little to reassure the unconverted.

Although the rationale for online assessment has been well rehearsed, it is nevertheless useful to recap some pertinent arguments that support the use of online assessment in the summative area. Students entering higher education today come from a broad background of technology in both their school and home lives. They expect interaction, a visual experience, and rapid feedback from their activities (Oblinger, 2006). Additionally, as more and more online assessment is used in secondary education before these students enter university and in the workplace after students leave, if universities do not keep up with this trend, their courses are in danger of appearing outdated to students (Sim, Holifield, & Brown, 2004). Additionally, online examination broadens the assessment arsenal and creates a more holistically challenging assessment environment: no longer is it possible to be just good at written examinations.

From the point of view of teaching and administration staff, the move to assessing students online also offers a number of advantages. As student numbers increase in the United Kingdom along with time pressures on staff to produce research alongside their teaching, a system that can reduce marking loads has huge advantages. Results can be available as soon as an examination is finished and can be immediately reviewed by an examination board and released to students. A number of quality checks can also be performed as the results come in, resulting in the early detection of problematic questions. These issues are covered in detail below.

The chapter concentrates on the specific topic of computer-based assessment using a client-server architecture such as the Internet. The field of computer-assisted assessment is very wide and conceptually encompasses any form of assessment activity assisted wholly or in part by a computer. This includes endeavours such as student submission of coursework into virtual learning environments (VLEs), the use of online plagiarism detection systems such as Turnitin (http://www.turnitin.com), and investigating methods for marking free-text prose automatically. What the current chapter will concentrate on is the use of computer-based assessment for objectively marked items. This should be of interest to curriculum managers, educationalists, and module coordinators who have possibly built up experience in using paper-based examinations that can be automatically marked through optical mark recognition (OMR) systems. OMR is a form of computer-assessed assessment. As the computer does the marking, there is growing interest in using computers to present the assessments to students as well. Table 1 contains a comparison of the two approaches to using computers in assessment.

This chapter covers the use of computer-based assessment and it is this that will be discussed

*Table 1. Pros and cons of computer-based vs. computer-assisted assessment*

| **Computer-Based Assessment: Pros**<br>• Fast marking, scales well with additional examinees<br>• Examinees can alter answers quickly and clearly<br>• Interactive, adaptive, and multimedia question types possible<br>• Saves paper<br>• External examiner can have instant access to a paper electronically | **Optical Mark Recognition: Pros**<br>• Large-scale performance, simultaneous starts possible<br>• Low cost, only a single computer with OMR scanner required<br>• Low chance of any failures (apart from power cut) |
|---|---|
| **Computer-Based Assessment: Cons**<br>• Multiple failure risks, power/hardware/software<br>• High cost, powerful servers required together with large numbers of clients<br>• Students must learn how to use the assessment system (should be during formative papers)<br>• Staff must be trained in how to enter questions and taught the full capabilities of the system | **Optical Mark Recognition: Cons**<br>• Interactive, adaptive, and multimedia question types not possible<br>• Answer sheet not correctly completed<br>• Time required to (a) print question booklets and (b) scan answer sheets increases linearly with examinee cohort sizes<br>• Storage of past examination scripts<br>• Examination scripts must be securely couriered to external examiners |

from this point on.

It can be tempting to dive into the deep end, metaphorically speaking, and concentrate on either the software or the assessment system or try to buy powerful hardware, but the chapter starts by stepping back and reviewing the risks involved in moving online. By carefully considering the risks involved, a robust defense can be planned against them. The United Kingdom Collaboration for a Digital Repository (UKCDR, http://www.ukcdr.manchester.ac.uk) has posited that it should be possible to defend a successful assessment from three main perspectives: intellectually, legally, and technically. A fourth and important real-world consideration in the form of defending work economically is suggested by Schuwirth and van der Vleuten (2006). Having established a sound defensible assessment, the rest of the chapter is split into a five-stage development life cycle. There are a number of very similar life cycles, and again we borrow on the work of UKCDR that incorporates the following steps.

1. Item Development
2. Quality Assurance
3. Item Selection
4. Examination Delivery
5. Results Analysis

This gives the structure for the rest of the chapter and hopefully a useful and practical structure that may be applied easily to different institutions.

## BACKGROUND

The importance of good assessment is highlighted in Boud's (1995, p. 35) slightly flippant statement, "Students can, with difficulty, escape from the effects of poor teaching, they cannot (by definition if they want to graduate) escape the effects of poor assessment." However, changing the form of assessment from a written or OMR approach to a purely computer-based approach is inherently risky. If change is inevitably risky, then the question "Why change?" must be asked. The answer is the pursuit of greater return on investment: academic, economic, or time. In Figure 1, Hardwood and Warburton (2004) present a theoretical model that can be used to plot the risk and return of computer-assisted assessment (CAA) applications. The current authors would like to suggest that it is equally applicable to non-online assessment forms too.

As Figure 1 shows, the ideal point on the model is the risk efficient frontier whereby return is maximised for a given level of risk. The white dots represent different CAA cases that may be plotted on this model. $C_1$ is less efficient than $C_6$ as it has higher risk and less return. The key to moving a given CAA solution toward the risk efficient frontier ($RI_2$) is to consider risk from a number of different perspectives. Utilising the work from UKCDR (http://www.ukcdr.manchester.ac.uk/) and Schuwirth and van der Vleuten (2006), four key risk categories emerge: intellectual, legal, technical, and economic. We will now review each one from the point of view of defense—what can be done to minimise the

*Figure 1. Theoretical risk efficiency framework for CAA (Hardwood & Warburton, 2004)*

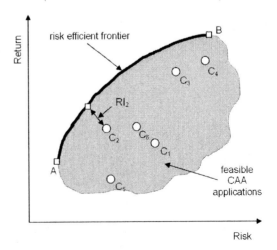

risks. Only after a department or institution has analysed its assessment practices from all these perspectives can online assessment be embraced for the correct reasons.

## Intellectual Defense

Being able to defend an assessment from an intellectual point of view is the most important of all the defense perspectives given the task is an inherently cognitive one. A detailed discussion of assessment design is outside the scope of this chapter, but key concepts are introduced here.

## Medium vs. Method

In 1964 McLuhan famously argued "the medium is the message" (p. 7), and this seems intuitively appealing with academics and technologists alike: with computer-based assessment, multimedia interactive questions can be used that are not possible with OMR. Dancy and Beichner (2000) found that examinees were less likely to misread physics questions when animations were used. It is therefore natural to conclude that it is the computer medium that is better than paper because it supports animation. However, this, as Clark (1994) asserts, is confusing medium with method. The gain in question clarity is a product of different instructional methods: animated vs. static. The same benefit could probably have been obtained, albeit less conveniently, by using a DVD and television in the assessment. When the method is kept the same between media, Clark argues that there is no difference in the learning outcomes. A five-stem multiple-choice question (MCQ) presented on paper will be equally intellectually challenging, valid, and reliable as the same question presented online. The true advantage of online assessment is not in the medium per se, but its increased spectrum of methods: animation, audio, interactivity, and so forth.

## Alignment

Assessment is only one component of the overall curriculum; to be effective, it must be aligned with these other endeavours. Brown (2001) presents a model in Figure 2 summarising the relationships between various parts of a course. Good assessment must relate back to course aims and clearly identified learning outcomes. An individual question is never inherently good, but only of high quality appropriately set within a well-planned curriculum.

## Reliability

The reliability of an assessment refers to its ability to reproduce the same results again and again. For example, would a student who got the highest score in one assessment get the highest score again in a very similar assessment? Would a student who passes in one assessment also pass in a different but very similar assessment? There is evidence that some of the unique properties of online assessment can influence question reliability. Dancy and Beichner (2000) found that a number of candidates misread a physics question

*Figure 2. Aligning assessment (Brown, 2001, p. 4)*

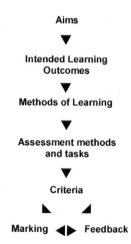

that used a static image and text. When presented as an animated image, such misreading did not occur, leading to a more reliable assessment.

## Validity

In general, validity is concerned with whether an assessment measures what it is designed to measure. Dent and Harden (2005, p. 305) use the following example to illustrate: "For example, a series of MCQs which test factual recall may be a valid measure of whether a student has read a textbook on diabetes but invalid as the indicator of whether that same student can actually manage a patient suffering from diabetes."

Moving assessments online can facilitate different forms of validity by using question types not possible using paper (Sim, Strong, & Holifield, 2005). Figure 3 shows five different states of an interactive question at the University of Nottingham testing students' procedural knowledge of how to correctly set up a Vacutainer™ for collecting blood samples. The question provides a simulated environment in which the user can drag and drop the various components as if they were real physical objects. The ability to visualise and interact with

such objects has greater assessment validity than a textual discussion of the same process. In addition to interactive simulations, high-quality images, animations, video, and sound (if headphones are used in the examination room) are all easy to incorporate in most online assessment systems. Hotspot questions can require students to place a mark anywhere on an image or diagram and these can be marked very accurately by the system. Students can also be required to label a diagram by dragging labels directly over an image. More complex simulations are also possible that allow a variety of interactions. One such system is the Tripartite Interactive Assessment Delivery System (TRIADS) created in a partnership between the University of Liverpool, University of Derby, and the Open University in the United Kingdom. Assessments are created in Authorware and are tailor made for each question. This can be a very labour-intensive approach but creates assessments that can test the students in a realistic scenario through a number of stages.

Although online assessment broadens the range of methods available to assessors and can improve validity, there is increased associated risk. A question using novel interaction techniques

*Figure 3. Interactive Flash™-based question testing examinees' procedural knowledge concerning blood-taking medical equipment*

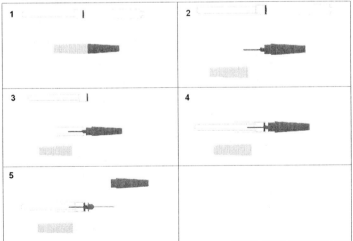

may not be understood by a student. Expressed in a different way, the correct answer would be selected by the examinee, but when confronted with an unknown interface, he or she may not know how to respond, thus affecting question reliability. Where possible, examinees should have exposure to online formative assessments even for well-understood question types such as MCQs. Olson and McDonald (2004) found students studying dentistry performed significantly higher on a summative examination after exposure to formative tests than those who had no exposure.

## Legal Defense

The legal implications for an examination system mainly cover copyright issues. If an online assessment uses graphics, video, or sound, the copyright for these materials must be obtained for them to be used in the system, especially if they are to be archived on the system for some time after the examination or possibly reused in further examinations. Related to this, there is also the possibility that academic staff may bring questions with them from other institutions that may still belong to those institutions rather than the individual, and conversely, take material away with them if they leave. A "take down" policy needs to be in place in case materials with such issues are discovered in use.

In addition to copyright law, online assessments should also comply with relevant health and safety legislation. Various medical conditions such as repetitive strain injury (RSI) have been linked to prolonged use of computers. While it is unlikely that a candidate will develop a serious medical condition from a single online examination, the international standard BS ISO/IEC 23988 (2007) does state that there should be a break for assessments longer than 1.5 hours. Adhering to such ratified guidelines limits the possibility that a candidate will claim any breaches in the standard as a reason for failing an examination

or, more seriously, as the basis for filing a civil law suit. Although most students will be familiar with computer use in higher education, it is still worthwhile to publish leaflets or write guidance online regarding basic computer health issues for online examinations: setting up contrast and brightness properly, having good posture, and taking breaks from looking at the screen.

Schuwirth and van der Vleuten (2006) argue that assessments must be acceptable. This is more an ethical consideration rather than a legal requirement, but it is nevertheless important to get key stakeholders to buy into the online assessment process. In an evaluation of multimedia online examinations, Liu, Papathanasiou, and Hao (2001) investigated students' and staffs' attitudes to multimedia in examinations and found very strong support for its use. They gave a number of reasons for this. First, it was felt that the assessment more closely matched the material that was being taught in a variety of courses, from arts to science. Second the presentation of more than one medium of information seemed to aid the students' recall, and this was also reflected in the students' feedback on the assessment. Third, the questions reflected real-world situations more accurately, and finally the students seemed to learn more in these assessments, which helped them as they continued their studies.

## Technical Defense

The technical components of an online assessment system are much wider than simply which software package is used. This chapter concentrates on discussing the issues surrounding one of the most popular types of assessment architectures: client-server. This is the classic Internet architecture whereby an end user sits at personal computer, the client, and requests pages to be sent from a Web site, the server. Importantly though, there are a lot of additional subsystems that lie between these two end points: routers, switches, network load balancers, and so on. Also, a range of operating systems and application software will run on the client and the server. What constitutes the assessment system is actually the entirety of all these constituent parts, not just what assessment software was licensed from company X. The key to the technical integrity of the overall system is to understand how the various subsystems are related to one another and what would happen to the end users (i.e., examinees) during an assessment if one or more subsystems failed. Each field of IT, such as desktop support, networking, and server configuration, is a complex discipline in its own right, so the reader is advised to seek guidance from a central IT department. The ability to recover from a technical failure if it happens is one of the key points of conducting successful online examinations. Disaster recovery must be planned up front so potentially erroneous decisions are not made in the heat of the moment. Although the literature surrounding high-profile summative failures is rather sparse, Harwood (2005) presents a frank account of the processes the University of Southampton followed after one of their assessment systems failed catastrophically.

## Economic Defense

It is a common fallacy to believe the economic return is higher for online assessment because it can mark questions over 10,000 times faster than OMR. While this is clearly a benefit, it is negated by potentially large server costs. The University of Nottingham Medical School utilises a powerful dedicated assessment server costing approximately £10,000. This represents a sizable investment over its anticipated 4-year life span. Also, because of its high reliance on online summative assessment and the resulting inconvenience a crash would cause, the university has chosen to invest a further £5,000 in a backup server. This substantially reduces the risk, but the additional financial outlay also reduces the return at the same time. Large computer rooms will also be required for large class sizes. Some institutions may already

have large computer suites for other purposes, in which case their economic return will be higher through greater utilisation; others will need to invest to bring their facilities up to scratch. Regardless of the actually required server, computer lab and infrastructure costs incurred, but as the cost per examination falls, more examinations can be scheduled for online delivery.

As well as hardware costs, the cost of the assessment software used is important. If a commercial system is chosen, then factors such as whether the license requires annual renewal or is for a lifetime is important. The predicted cost of future updates and any technical support costs over and above that which might be part of the basic license package must be considered. Alternatively, the cost of in-house programmers' salaries should be considered for any institutions developing their own assessment solutions. Regardless of whether a commercial or in-house solution is adopted, there will be the cost of departmental and institutional staff required to support the system: educationalists advising on the pedagogic approach and assessment strategies, trainers familiar in the assessment software, and IT support technicians. All these costs are relatively easy to quantify, but there are additional unseen and often difficult to measure costs: costs such as lost staff productivity because of poor usability in a particular assessment system, or lost time due to a system being off line because the decision to save money purchasing a cheaper server that is less fault tolerant was made.

## ITEM DEVELOPMENT

As already mentioned, a number of people who have yet to experience online assessment believe the most important aspect to consider is either the assessment software selected for the job or the hardware on which it will be installed. While hardware and software choices are important, a factor we will revisit a little later on, it is the questions themselves that ultimately dictate the success of an assessment. Staff interested in adopting online assessment should view the situation in the same way as traditional paper examinations; the quality of the examination is not affected by the colour, weight, or quality of the paper on which the questions are written. The same is true for online assessment. There are simply more ways in which the "paper" may go wrong; ways to prevent this from happening will be explored in more detail later.

The first step in item development is the actual question-writing process. In small departments that assess individual modules, identifying the individuals writing questions may not be problematic. However, for subjects such as medicine where there are a potentially large number of individuals who could be involved (lecturers, readers, subject experts, etc.) across multiple schools and departments, either a coordinator needs to take responsibility for the question item development process or some sort of assessment committee should be formed.

Having recruited subject-matter experts, in most cases, some form of training will be necessary. A second common fallacy in any assessment is that being a subject-matter expert in the field being assessed is the sole qualification for being a good question setter, and this is especially true for online assessment. Item developers should be familiar with three important aspects of question writing in addition to subject content. First, the capabilities of the assessment software chosen by the school or institution should be covered. Frequently, staff simply wish to write multiple-choice questions and use online assessment merely as the delivery vehicle. To do so is to ignore the specific additional capabilities afforded by IT: interactivity, adaptability, and multimedia aspects. However, it is the experience of the current authors that any training and examples demonstrated, where possible, should use as content the subject matter of the target audience rather than generic examples for maximum clarity.

Second, information about how to write high-quality questions that may be defended intellectually is important: this step is common between online and off-line question writing life cycles. Case and Swanson (2002) provide an excellent guide to writing high-quality items. Although it is aimed at the medical sciences, its concepts may be easily abstracted and applied to other fields. Case and Swanson cover recurrent issues such as writing questions that "test-wise" students will be able to use to work out the answer as well as issues relevant to item difficulty and technical item flaws such as double negatives and grammatical cues. In a similar vein, Holsgrove and Elzubeir (1998) report on a study they conducted that shows that assumptions regarding statements such as *rarely*, *commonly*, *never*, and *always* are commonly misunderstood. When asked to attach numeric values to such statements, subject-matter experts differ widely in their interpretation. Where possible, Holsgrove and Elzubeir suggest that such absolute terms be avoided in question writing. In addition to the guidelines provided by Case and Swanson regarding cognitive difficulty, Bloom (1956) presents a taxonomy of six levels of increasing cognitive engagement: knowledge, comprehension, application, analysis, synthesis, and evaluation, which may be used for the classification of questions according to the cognitive processes used by the student to answer them.

Educating staff about disabilities is a second factor relevant to item development. This could include an overview of the range of disabilities, how to prioritise needs against the prevalence of a particular disability, and what can be changed within the assessment system as a whole (hardware, software, location, and time) to accommodate and not disadvantage students in this category.

Third, it is important that staff, even though they are experts in a specialist field, know where and how their work fits into the overall curriculum of a module or course. The concept of curriculum alignment is important to ensure that the objectives of a module, the material delivered, and how it is assessed all aligns (Brown, 2001). Methods to help achieve alignment include the structured use of online VLEs or curriculum map systems whereby all the learning outcomes of a course, module, or session can be tied together in a hierarchical system. The form that this training takes will probably need to be flexible to suit busy teaching staff. Scheduled workshops, one-to-one tuition, and online help systems can all be sources of help. A range of staff will contribute to this help, including educationalists, people with broad experience of the curriculum, and IT experts familiar in the hardware and software systems employed.

The advantage of using server-based assessment systems is that it is very easy to collaborate when developing items without physically meeting the other question setters. Many systems provide mechanisms for working in groups. However, care is needed when there are multiple item writers. For example, when selecting the assessment software, one should look for systems that can provide some form of locking mechanism. If an author tries to edit a question that is already being amended by a different author, the assessment system should display a warning notice and only display a read-only version of the question to the second author. As well as locking mechanisms, automatic audit trails are useful so that in the event of problems with a question, it is easy to look back through a change log to see which author performed the last edit.

## QUALITY ASSURANCE

It is very easy for an individual question setter to be too close to his or her own work and to miss issues in a question that could lead to problems during an examination. One of the most frequently used quality assurance mechanisms is to organise a peer review amongst appropriate subject-matter experts. The first step toward doing this should be

the construction of a written policy that identifies the members of staff that will be responsible for quality assurance. Providing timescales is also critical when organising large numbers of assessments across different courses and cohorts. Most institutions will usually employ some form of internal quality review process whereby members of staff from the school or faculty will review the questions as drafted by the original author. If problems with a particular item are found, the quality assurance policy for a department needs to clearly articulate the resolution process. For example, is it the role of the reviewers to (a) amend the item themselves and inform the original author, or (b) communicate their comments to the author with a view to having only that author make changes to a question. Some assessment systems will assist in this process whereby a list of amendments may be called up for an item in the question bank together with times and dates and the authors who conducted the changes.

It is useful, from time to time, to test the rigor of a quality assurance process by artificially inserting known erroneous items that should be identified and corrected by the process. This should obviously be conducted without informing any reviewers, and someone should take overall leadership of the process to review if and when the test items are identified in the process.

Where possible, all quality reviews should be done not just online, but online using the same assessment software as will be used to deliver the final assessment to students. The most common problem to slip through review processes that the current authors have witnessed is formatting issues that have arisen when, for example, a member of staff copies and pastes an original question from a word processor into the target assessment system. Sometimes minor formatting such as superscript characters can be lost, but this can have a dramatic effect on the meaning of a question. For example, the numbers 205 and $20^5$ are quite different.

As has been discussed, the quality assurance of question items is of paramount importance to a successful assessment, but it is important not to forget the assessment software itself. Generally, software from large commercial organisations will have been used by enough institutions to have uncovered all the common bugs. However, there are no easy ways to ensure that software is free from all defects. Before running a summative examination online, it is useful to perform some set tests that will detect problems in the marking routines.

1.  Do not answer any items; the score should be zero.
2.  Answer all items correctly, and percentage score should be 100%
3.  Answer all items incorrectly, and score should be zero.

If any bugs are discovered, during examination delivery as well, there should be clear channels to report such problems with the software engineers responsible for the product. Ideally, any planned assessments should be put on hold until a resolution to the problem is found, or, depending on the nature of the problem, different question types can be used that do not have the bug. Testing should also be performed after a new version of the software is installed.

## ITEM SELECTION AND STORAGE

Item storage might have already been required since the item development stage. As discussed in the last section, the cutting and pasting of information from external systems, such as word processors, into the assessment system can introduce unwanted formatting errors. One way around this problem is to use assessment systems with a high degree of usability and to train subject-matter experts in how to enter questions directly into the target system.

Server-based assessment systems are popular for item storage because they provide a central repository for items. Security is easier to enforce with a single entry point (i.e., one authentication system) and backing up data onto another server or to tape is simplified.

The specification of the client-side computers that the students will use during the examination is not problematic today; modern desktop computers have a surplus of power for running Web-based examinations. However, the server that hosts and serves each assessment is a different issue. Unfortunately, it is difficult to provide specific server sizing within this chapter due to the different natures of software and the fast pace of change in hardware development. However, some basic heuristics can be suggested for a successful fault-tolerant server hardware platform.

1.  **Reliability**
    When an online assessment begins, all the client computers that the students are using will send their requests back to a single Web server that holds the examination paper. The main drawback of this client-server architecture is that it introduces a single point of failure: if the server stops, then none of the students can complete the examination. In practice there are a number of different things that can be done to minimise this risk. With primary storage (RAM), error-correcting code (ECC) modules can be specified on some servers to minimise errors that could crash software. In terms of secondary memory (hard disks), RAID 5 is a useful configuration. A RAID 5 arrangement requires a minimum of three separate hard disks to be installed within the server, and the reading and writing of data is spread across these disks with additional parity data being written in order to check for any errors in this process. This results in a system whereby if one disk failed entirely, the system would still be capable

of retrieving, through the additional parity data, all the information.[1] High-end servers will normally come supplied with two power supplies and two or more network connection ports. Where possible, the two network connections should go to different switches on different parts of the network so that Internet traffic to and from the server can be routed even if one switch fails. Finally, a large uninterruptible power supply (UPS) system should be installed that can power the server until either a backup generator starts or main power is restored.

2.  **Storage**
    As mentioned under reliability above, a server must have enough primary and secondary memory to support the maximum class size expected for an online assessment. The higher the number of simultaneous users, the more primary memory (RAM) will be required to run the assessment. Factors influencing secondary memory (hard disk) size include the amount of data that need to be stored: the amount of multimedia data used in questions, the total number of assessments planned for any given time period, and the number of students at each examination.

3.  **Performance**
    It is convenient to discuss the performance of a server here together with reliability and storage, but it is only really critical in the next phase, examination delivery. On the whole, the greater the number of students starting an examination simultaneously, the greater the hardware power required. Heintz and Jemison (2005) stress the importance of benchmarking and simulating examination delivery. Although there are software applications that can be used to simulate examination load, these should not replace real-world test sessions in noncritical (i.e., nonsummative) periods. A good way of doing this is to hold one or more invigilated and compulsory formative examinations with the same cohort that is scheduled to take the final summative examination. On the basis of these load tests, a couple of different strategies can be employed: (a) a staggered start of the examinees in blocks (Heintz & Jemison), or (b) starting the whole cohort simultaneously in a similar way to a paper examination if the system can respond fast enough.

4.  **Independence**
    Where financially possible, a dedicated assessment server should be used that is independent of other systems. Heintz and Jemison (2005) report on a situation where second-year students studying in a virtual learning environment created a load that resulted in 12 first-year examination students not being able to complete an online assessment on the same server. The failure reported by Harwood (2005) was also caused by an existing system operating at maximum load being used to host additional load, which pushed it over the edge.

In addition to appropriate hardware, the capabilities of the assessment software can play a key role in item storage. Each system is capable of storing pieces of data such as the question lead-in and options that form part of the question, but it is also important to be able to store associated metadata. These metadata will not be seen by the students during examination delivery but makes overall staff administration of large question banks easier. The amount of metadata stored will differ between assessment systems, but most will include the following types for each question

1.  Name of question author
2.  Time and date item was created
3.  Time and date item was last edited
4.  Keywords
5.  Difficulty level (i.e., Bloom's taxonomy)

When working in complex domains, it is likely that multiple authors will wish to author items for a single examination. In such cases, the assessment software should support some sort of group or team working and be able to stop editing conflicts. When using the stateless architecture of the Web it is very easy for one author to inadvertently overwrite the changes made by a different author who is working unbeknown to the first author at the same time. Some systems can prevent this situation from occurring by effectively placing a lock when the first author goes into an item for editing. Any subsequent authors are informed that the item is locked and that they will only be presented with a read-only version.

Establishing a deletion policy is good practice when dealing with mature question banks. Some assessment systems will produce errors if a member of staff wishes to run a report on a student cohort who took an examination some time ago that uses one or more questions that have been deleted from the bank. Many disciplines are periodically inspected by governing professional bodies and increasingly institutions are providing guest accounts for these institutions to log into VLEs and online assessment systems. In the past it has been relatively easy to find past data filed carefully by year within physical filing cabinets, but moving all this information into the electronic domain raises the dangers because it is so easy to delete electronic data. A reliable and regular backup of an assessment system (question items, papers, user accounts, and past examination results) should be made, ideally to a separate and secure location away from the primary assessment server. An archive of backups is also invaluable if past data that have been deleted also need to be retrieved. Just as the quality assurance process should be periodically tested, so too should the backup procedures.

Excluding adaptive assessment systems, there are two distinct methods of creating papers from items in a question bank. The first, as with a paper-based examination, is for the examination authors to specifically select which questions will be used and the order in which they will be listed. The second method utilises the power of the computer to randomly generate numbers and thereby pick out questions from the bank. Two subtypes of randomisation are possible: (a) all examinees receive the same questions within the examination, but the order of presentation is randomised, and (b) the questions used on an examination paper are randomised such that different examinees will answer slightly different question sets. This latter type of randomisation is often favoured for reducing plagiarism as neighbouring students will have different questions. However, their use in summative assessment raises issues of examination paper comparability. Can it be proven that the difficulty of a paper presented to student $x$ is the same as the paper presented to student $y$?

With a paper now formed, an appropriate pass mark needs to be set. One of the inherent problems with many of the question types used in objective examinations is that the correct answer is visible on screen. There is a chance that an examinee will select the correct answer not because they know the subject matter but merely through blind luck. There have been a few different approaches to try and counter this lucky guesswork. Historically UK medical schools employed large numbers of true-false-abstain questions. Each stem on an item was worth one mark if answered correctly. However, because the probability of getting it correct anyway was 50:50, one mark was deducted if the examinee was wrong. An *abstain* button is added to allow examinees who are unsure to refrain from answering, and thus the score is zero for that particular stem. However, this form of question writing has all but died out to be replaced with a broader spectrum of question types: extended matching, multiple choice, multiple response, ranking, and image hotspots to name a few. Using negative marking with each of these types can be quite complicated, for example, applying a negative marking scheme to a multiple-response question requiring an examinee to select three items from a list of eight. An alternative, as suggested by Harper (2003), is to incorporate some form of correction for guessing at the postexamination grading stage. It is possible to calculate the statistically expected mark for each type of objective question within a CAA system. A five-stem multiple-choice question marked out of one would have an expected mark based on a probability of 0.2. After calculating the expected mark of each question individually, it is then necessary to scale an examinee's marks to take account of this guessing factor. Harper describes using a spreadsheet for this purpose; however, some assessment systems (for example, TouchStone, http://www.nottingham.ac.uk/nle/about/touchstone) can perform such calculations automatically. This not only saves time but is more reliable. One potentially negative aspect of the overall process of generating these expected marks is that they do assume that examinees answer all questions.

A third technique, frequently used within medical fields, is the use of standards setting. The process uses teams of subject-matter experts to discuss each item on a paper separately and to make some form of collective decision regarding how many borderline candidates will get the item correct. There are a number of different techniques for doing this, with Ebel (1972) and Angoff (1971) being two of the more common. Although both techniques do not explicitly take into account the probability of selecting a correct answer by chance, the overall calculated pass marks are usually significantly above what could be achieved through guessing alone, so the probability can be dismissed. Where possible it is recommended that an assessment system with built-in support for the standards setting process is used when setting pass marks in this way. It is time consuming to set up spreadsheets to perform standards setting manually, and there is always the risk that the questions may be inadvertently changed when copying from the assessment system into the spreadsheet or vice versa.

## EXAMINATION DELIVERY

With an assessment paper created and the pass mark established, the next phase of the life cycle is the actual delivery to students under examination conditions. It is probably accurate to say that it is this stage of the life cycle that is most feared when considering online assessment. The main reason is that the window of opportunity in which problems can be solved is much shorter than any of the other phases. Rooms are booked and examinees have turned up; if a system does not respond as expected, some sort of contingency plan must be put into place if a resolution to a particular problem is not nearly instantaneous. Although disaster recovery will be covered later, there can be no substitute for rigorous and comprehensive planning of the examination delivery stage. Three main issues dominate: (a) security, (b) software usability, and (c) administration. There is an international standard produced by the British Standards Institute entitled Code of Practice for the Use of Information Technology (IT) in the Delivery of Assessments (BS ISO/IEC 23988, 2007), which covers many aspects of examination delivery in generic terms.

## Security

In the secondary education arena, there have been some high-profile breaches of security whereby examination papers have been read by unauthorised parties. Because computer-based assessment systems do not print examination papers, this risk is removed; however, a considerable range of new criteria must be considered. The avenues for potential security breaches can be broken down into two broad categories: external and internal.

External security risks are possible with any server attached to the Internet. Hackers anywhere worldwide are constantly using methods and software systems to root out vulnerable servers. When breached, a hacker might crash the server and thereby stop an examination, or use the assessment server to send out spam e-mail, which will affect its performance. Networking and security experts from the parent institution should be involved in the assessment process to ensure external loopholes are discovered and patched before the hackers can exploit them. This process is not simply an initial system setup activity, but an ongoing virtual battle in cyberspace. A firewall (either hardware or software) is a system that controls requests and protocols accepted and transmitted by a server. Most assessment systems will require HTTP (hypertext transfer protocol) or ideally HTTPS (encrypted; HTTP over secure socket layer) protocols, so a firewall can be used to deny access to other protocols such as FTP (file transfer protocol) and e-mail. All software subsystems should be patched and kept up to date; this includes operating system (Windows, Linux, etc.), Web servers (Apache, IIS, etc.), and applications software that would include scripting languages (PHP, .NET, etc.) and often a database (MySQL, Oracle, MS SQL, etc.). Patches and updates are publicised to the community through Web sites and boards; ideally, security patches should be installed soon after a vulnerability is published rather than at a set period of time. However, it may be prudent that if an online examination is going to run in 2 days time, then a patch could wait until after the assessment has been completed just in case there are some incompatibilities with the new patch that may take time to resolve.

Keeping external hackers from breaching a server is critical, but it is important to remember internal security issues, too. For example, from the point of view of examination delivery, a system should only deliver an online assessment to a relevant cohort of students studying a specific module at the prescribed time and only to the examination room used. Usually a Web server will deliver pages 24 hours a day to any computer worldwide, but good assessment systems are able to limit access using any combination of course, module, year of study, time and date, and room.

The room is important if two sittings of an examination are required through lack of computers. It is important that students in the second group cannot log into the examination paper while the first group is taking the assessment. Also, in marked contrast to many paper examinations, when using two or more sittings, it is advisable not to allow students to leave early and inform students not yet examined what the questions are. Restricting access to appropriate staff is another key security issue: who has access to system-wide privileges, who can add and alter questions, and who can only run reports. Some assessment systems, for instance, those built within VLEs, will utilise the authentication systems within the overall VLE architecture. Other systems will employ authentication such as lightweight directory access protocol (LDAP) to ensure that only registered users can access the assessment system. More proprietary or homegrown systems may even use their own maintained lists of authorised users. In the last case, it is vital that key personnel are identified who are responsible for maintaining these lists every year as new students are registered with the institution. Whatever method of authentication is used, two important conceptual issues have to be considered: (a) identification, meaning which individuals can access a system, and (2) authorisation, meaning which parts of the system these individuals are allowed to access. For example, in terms of identification, it could be all students and teaching staff connected with a particular course or module; however, in terms of authorisation, the students will only be allowed to view and answer certain assessments at controlled times whereas staff will be able to add questions, edit, delete, and run reports.

Even within a group of legitimate examinees who are allowed to access an online examination, security is still very important. The importance of summative examination leads some students to plagiarise and otherwise falsify their work. In a study of school and further education examination,

Underwood (2006, p. 1) states, "Although there remains some debate on whether the incidence of academic malpractice is increasing, it is widely acknowledged that it is a very significant problem." Referencing the work of Hinman (as cited in Underwood), she suggests a three-pronged approach to reducing academic malpractice, summed up as the three *E*s.

1. **Ethics** (the virtues approach)
   The establishment of a code of practice that can be circulated in a transparent process to both students and staff
2. **Engineering** (the prevention approach)
   There are several steps that can be taken using the engineering approach.
   - Reduce recycling of past examination papers
   - Introduce seating plans; students sitting next to strangers are less likely to cheat."
   - Introduce visual barriers (see Figure 4) where adjacent workstations are close (BS ISO/IEC 23988, 2007)
   - Limit the materials students may bring into the examination room
   - Secure browser (Heintz and Jemison, 2005) or desktop whereby students cannot use any other part of the computer's functionality other than the examination itself. Normal facilities such as e-mail, access to the wider Internet, and chat must all be disabled for the duration of the examination.
3. **Enforcement** (the police approach)
   One enforcement approach is to use statistical analysis after an examination to detect when the answer patterns of two or more candidates are unlikely to be that similar by chance. Such techniques are then used with IP (Internet protocol) address recording and seating plans to see if the suspected individuals were physically in close proximity.

## Usability

Usability is a second important aspect that should be one of the key factors used when deciding which assessment system to install. It also runs right through the online assessment life cycle from staff entering items, forming papers, and peer review through to actual examination delivery for students. It is vital that students receive an accurate grade for their level of subject-matter understanding not their IT capabilities. The assessment system employed must effectively become transparent to the students. Failure to ensure high levels of usability will result in examinees either taking too long per item trying to understand how to answer the question and thus running out of time, or simply giving up and being awarded zero for one or more questions. Nielsen (2005) lists 10 heuristics that can be applied to any interactive software system to measure usability in a more objective manner. In addition to using systems with high usability, it is important to ensure examinees are exposed to the software before any summative examinations so they have time to familiarise themselves. Obviously providing access to the final examination paper is not an

*Figure 4. An example of physical barriers used to prevent plagiarism in a multipurpose computer lab where adjacent workstations are close. These barriers may be taken down and stored when the lab is not required for assessments*

option so one or ideally more formative assessments should be written in the same software as the final summative examination.

## Administration

Following on from usability, one of the first administrative activities should be to identify any examinees with special needs. Most countries will have a form of legislation designed to protect the interests of users with special needs or disabilities. In the United Kingdom there is the Special Educational Needs and Disability Act (SENDA, 2001), which is now enshrined in law. Many institutions use accessibility units or other places with similar titles to provide centres for advice for students with particular requirements. Having clearly documented protocols and networks of support established is important so that these units can feed back to, in many instances, a school or faculty-based administrative unit that may then need to speak to an IT expert to establish what is and what is not possible to change for a student. Broadly speaking, there may be four factors that may need to be accommodated or adjusted in some way: (a) the time of the assessment, (b) the place and physical properties of the examination environment, (c) properties and configuration of the assessment software, and (d) properties of the client-side hardware that the examinee will be using. With approximately 10% of males suffering from some type of colour blindness, making sure that colours do not combine in ambiguous ways should be a key design factor when writing examination questions. Colour can also influence the text perception of students with Scotopic Sensitivity Syndrome, sometimes categorised as a form of dyslexia. Some people with this syndrome use coloured acetate sheets to place in front of books when reading. In an online examination taken at the computer it should be possible, ideally, to change the background and if necessary foreground colours.

The next step in the administration of an online examination is to book appropriate computer labs. Such rooms should ideally be large enough to examine the entire cohort simultaneously or through two sittings. Booking in good time is important due to pressure from other departments to reserve the same spaces. Once a booking is confirmed, students should be notified of the computer lab details, often through a posting on a virtual learning environment or portal. In situations where a cohort has to be split into two to be examined, certain additional steps must be covered. For example, a list of which students have been assigned to each group is necessary. Also, decisions have to be made regarding stopping the two groups from communicating with each other. Two solutions are possible here: (a) the two groups are examined back to back with no one allowed to leave the examination room for either sitting, or (b) different examination papers are used for each group: either two manually created papers or the use of papers that randomly select questions. The accommodation of individuals with extra time should also be planned. It can take a few minutes and be potentially quite noisy if not supervised properly to get large numbers of students out of a big computer lab. Ideally, candidates with additional time, such as dyslexic students, should be examined in a separate computer lab. Where this is not possible, then the complete additional period of time permitted for these students should only start after all students have left the room.

In parallel with room booking should be communication and agreement with the central institutional IT support unit. Keeping such a unit informed of timetabled summative assessments is vital so that planned maintenance of client computers, servers, and networking infrastructure can be accommodated around the examination dates. In the United Kingdom, the Joint Academic Network (JANET) that is used by all major universities has what is referred to as an "at risk" period of 7am to 9am on Tuesday mornings. Where possible, online summative examinations should not be scheduled during known at-risk times.

It is good practice to request that students report to the relevant computer lab 10 to 15 minutes ahead of the scheduled examination start time. This provides plenty of time to log into the system with their user names and passwords (authentication). Invigilators and IT support personnel should either have printed password lists or have access to a computer to look up the log-in details of any student who forgets their details. It is also prudent for the assessment system administrators to create two or three temporary guest accounts that can be given out to any unexpected student who wishes to sit in the examination.

Invigilators should also be in possession of any faculty or departmental disaster recovery protocol documents. Such documents should be drawn up before embarking on any programme of online assessment. The disaster recovery document should ideally cover points from guidance sources such as BS ISO/IEC 23988 (2007), but be grounded in the specific practicalities of the assessment system used. For example, one of the most common disaster recovery activities is likely to be dealing with the crash of a single student's computer. In such circumstances, the invigilators or IT support staff should be able to take steps to move the student to a spare computer and to restart the examination with as little loss of data as possible. Some systems require the user to explicitly save information; some save information automatically between screens, and others save automatically at periodic intervals. Knowing the precise mechanisms used by the assessment system in use will allow the disaster recovery protocol document to be fine-tuned. Another event that should be planned for is a fire evacuation in the middle of an examination. Systems such as TouchStone (http://www.nottingham.ac.uk/nle/about/touchstone/) contain "fire exit" icons that when pressed do two things: (a) saves all data back to the server, and (b) blanks the screen so

that evacuating examinees cannot see the answers of their peers when leaving the lab.

## RESULTS ANALYSIS

With an assessment successfully delivered, the results need to be analysed. As already mentioned, the goal of online assessment is usually to make decisions or for certification. Either purpose normally requires the identification of candidates who are below a particular threshold and those who are above. Most assessment systems will provide such data in the form of some sort of class listing report. However, although on the face of them such reports appear quite simple, caution must still be exercised. The current authors have witnessed assessments where key stakeholders in the assessment process were not made fully aware of the correct pass mark, which unfortunately led to candidates being given incorrect results. This sort of communication breakdown is more likely to happen when changes are made to grading systems, for example, moving from a fixed pass mark to a standard set pass mark. To avoid such problems, the exact pass mark should be entered into the assessment software, and the output reports should display a pass or fail descriptor next to each student's name. Most reports of this type will include broad statistical data such as maximum, minimum, mean, and median scores for the cohort expressed as marks and percentages. These should be checked by the module coordinator or academic member of staff responsible for the assessment. In the United Kingdom, this manual checking of the results is an important legal step as under the Data Protection Act (1998) there are clauses that give protection against decisions based solely on personal data. It is advisable to discuss in more detail relevant legislation with a data protection officer at your institution. Assuming the marks appear roughly in line with what is expected, the marks will normally need to be transferred to some kind of student management information system. Each system will differ in the format of the required data; however, the goal is to try and ensure an automatic transfer process. The situation where data entry clerks are hand-transcribing marks into a student management system from a print-out of a report from an online assessment system should be avoided as transcription errors may not be detected. Most assessment systems will provide a variety of data outputs, the common being MS Excel files, comma-separated value (CSV) files, or XML (extensible markup language) files.

Having considered how the examinees performed, attention can be turned to how well the question items performed. There are a number of different forms of investigations that come under the umbrella term *item analysis*. At this point the reader is directed to the summary provided by McAlpine (2002) covering the most common three: classical test theory, item response theory, and Rasch measurement. The range of available analyses will depend on the specific assessment system being used; however, many systems will support some sort of data export that may then be entered into a specific statistical package for further processing. Where an item is found to have performed poorly, there should be agreed departmental policies for investigation. The first step is probably to check that the correct answer has been accurately set within the assessment system. If it has been incorrectly set, then the question should be corrected and the students' answers remarked (this step might be automatic in some systems). Alternatively, if the answer is correctly set on a poorly performing question, then a number of things may be done: (a) it could be removed from the paper and the students' responses remarked, (b) the results of the analysis can be communicated back to the question author(s) so it may be amended in future, and/or (c) changes to the curriculum can be made to explain concepts that were misunderstood by the majority of the cohort.

The results analysis phase, although the last part of the summative-assessment life cycle, represents the first step of the coming academic year, feeding into both future teaching plans and question writing.

## FUTURE TRENDS

Reduced time spent marking is probably the most often cited advantage of moving toward computer-based assessment, but it will be interesting to see how long it takes the marketplace to move from online assessment as merely delivery to it being an inherent part of what it means to be online. Systems such as TRIADS (http://www.derby.ac.uk/ciad/) and Perception (http://www.question-mark.com) support many different question types that are not possible on paper, but there is limited literature about the validity and reliability of these new forms. Intuitively, the ability to drag and drop labels onto an image, for example, appears convincing, but this needs to be studied scientifically. Research in this area will also be useful in encouraging more interactive question-type use as it can be all too easy for the creation of online assessments to become a form-filling exercise for simple multiple-choice questions, rather than using these systems in ways that really set them apart from examinations on paper. In addition to validity and reliability, research into how long it takes examinees to complete different question types would also make a useful contribution that should help question writers determine how long an examination should be.

The cost of online assessment is a second area that is likely to change in the future. As already mentioned, some of the costs of online assessment are considerable: thousands of pounds spent on server hardware, potentially large computer labs, and the license cost of the assessment software itself. Of course, offset against some of these costs are issues such as the computer lab having roles other than summative assessment. Many systems also support questionnaire creation that makes the license more economic. Then there are less tangible aspects to costs such as members of IT support staff spending more time maintaining systems. On the other side, compared with OMR-based assessment, online systems can mark substantially faster and more accurately (no ambiguous rubbing out), and can save paper and printing costs. A complete and comprehensive auditing of all these costs would be useful in the justification of online assessment. Of course, final decisions regarding whether to use online or off-line assessment will include additional factors other than simple economics as the quality of the assessment also needs to be taken into account, but an awareness of the costs would certainly be useful to enable the preparedness of the stakeholders.

## CONCLUSION

Most universities have good systems in place for the summative assessment of their modules and programmes. A range of techniques are frequently employed in combination, methods such as group work, project work, essays, vivas, practical-skills demonstrations, and objectively marked questions via OMR. The surrounding framework that supports these diverse assessment methods is also well established with question writers, administrators, invigilators, markers, and external examiners, all knowing what is required of them and how their work fits into the larger assessment picture. The current authors have experienced that when computer-based assessment is introduced, the online nature of the process causes confusion in these well-developed frameworks. The tendency is for the traditional stakeholders to pull back from the process and the work and responsibility be directed toward technical IT staff because it is perceived to be an IT issue. IT is obviously important for an online examination, but the same core principles

that make a traditional examination good hold true for computer-based assessments.

It is the intention of this chapter to demonstrate how computer-based assessment can and should be integrated into the wider assessment process. As mentioned in the introduction, there have been a few documented failures of high-profile summative examinations (Harwood, 2005; Heintz & Jemison, 2005; Smailes, 2002), and it is tempting to suggest that the commonality between them is IT failure. While it appears that it was hardware and network speed issues that lay behind the failures, the current authors believe that it was a failure to fully engage in the communications process between all parties that ultimately resulted in the cause of the failures. One of the difficulties of the communication process that must be overcome is differences in the language used between stakeholders. Academic staff will use a certain vocabulary, such as *pedagogy*, *curricular alignment*, and *cognitive difficulty*; administrators will use their terms such as *cohort*, *session*, *entry year*, and so on; and IT staff will use terms such as *load*, *performance*, and *bandwidth*. While the reader may think they are familiar with the terms listed here, making sure that all are understood and that the same meaning is attributed to them by all parties is vital. The terms *reliability* and *performance* will be used by both academics and IT specialists when referring to assessment, but the context of such terms are completely different.

It is hoped that the reader at this stage who is interested in trying to pilot the introduction of online summative assessment into his or her institution feels suitably informed to be able to start the process going. As just mentioned, this is a process that at its core is a communications exercise between a wide variety of different stakeholders. Those stakeholders must come together to create assessments, as described in the background section, that should be defendable intellectually, legally, technically, and economically. Keeping these four perspectives in mind, the chapter outlined some of the more important issues to be considered during each of the five stages of the assessment development life cycle suggested by UKCDR (http://www.ukcdr.manchester.ac.uk). Adopting the principles set out here should create an accountable and robust online assessment process that can withstand scrutiny.

## REFERENCES

Angoff, W. H. (1971). Norms, scales, and equivalent scores. In R. L. Thorndike (Ed.), *Educational measurement* (2nd ed., pp. 508-600). Washington, DC: American Education on Education.

Boud, D. (1995). Assessment and learning: Contradictory or complementary? In P. Knight (Ed.), *Assessment for learning in higher education* (pp. 35-48). London: Kogan.

Brown, G. (2001). *Assessment: A guide for lecturers.* York, United Kingdom: Learning and Teaching Support Network (LTSN).

BS ISO/IEC 23988. (2007). *Code of practice for the use of information technology (IT) in the delivery of assessments.* London: British Standards.

Cantillon, P., Irish, B., & Sales, D. (2004). Using computers for assessment in medicine. *British Medical Journal, 329,* 606-609.

Case, S. M., & Swanson, D. B. (2002). *Constructing written test questions for the basic and clinical sciences* (3rd ed.). Philadelphia: National Board of Medical Examiners.

Clark, R. E. (1994). Media will never influence learning. *Educational Technology Research and Development, 42*(2), 21-29.

Dancy, M., & Beichner, R. (2000). *Does animation influence the validity of assessment? An example from physics.* Retrieved August 16, 2007, from http://www.ncsu.edu/PER/Articles/DancyDissSummary.pdf

Data Protection Act. (1998). *Data Protection Act 1998.* Retrieved June 5, 2007, from http://www.opsi.gov.uk/acts/acts1998/19980029.htm

Dent, J. A., & Harden, R. M. (2005). *A practical guide for medical teachers.* Oxford, United Kingdom: Elsevier Limited.

Ebel, R. L. (1972). *Essentials of educational measurement.* Englewood Cliffs, NJ: Prentice-Hall.

Harper, R. (2003). Correcting computer-based assessments for guessing. *Journal of Computer Assisted Learning, 19*(1), 2-8.

Harwood, I. (2005). When summative computer-aided assessments go wrong: Disaster recovery after a major failure. *British Journal of Educational Technology, 36*(4), 587-597.

Heintz, J., & Jemison, J. (2005). *Online exams: Embrace the opportunity, avoid the pitfalls.* Paper presented at the 2005 Educause Annual Conference. Retrieved June 3, 2007, from http://connect.educause.edu/blog/podcaster/e2005_podcast_online_exams/2027?time=1165945815

Holsgrove, G., & Elzubeir, M. (1998). Imprecise terms in UK medical multiple-choice questions: What examiners think they mean. *Medical Education, 32*(4), 343-350.

Liu, M., Papathanasiou, E., & Hao, Y. (2001). Exploring the use of multimedia examination formats in undergraduate teaching: Results from the fielding testing. *Computers in Human Behaviour, 17*(3), 225-248.

McAlpine, M. (2002). *A summary of methods of item analysis.* Luton, United Kingdom: CAA Centre.

McLuhan, M. (1964). *Understanding media: The extensions of man.* London: Routledge & Kegan Paul Ltd.

Nielsen, J. (2005). *Ten usability heuristics.* Retrieved May 20, 2007, from http://www.useit.com/papers/heuristic/heuristic_list.html

Oblinger, D. (2006, September 5-7). *Listening to what we're seeing.* Keynote speech at the 2006 ALT-C Conference, Edinburgh, United Kingdom.

Olson, B. L., & McDonald, J. L. (2004). Influence of online formative assessment upon student learning in biomedical science courses. *Journal of Dental Education, 68*(6), 656-659.

Schuwirth, L. W. T., & van der Vleuten, C. P. M. (2006). *How to design a useful test: The principles of assessment.* Edinburgh, United Kingdom: Association for the Study of Medical Education.

Sim, G., Holifield, P., & Brown, M. (2004). Implementation of computer assisted assessment: Lessons from the literature. *ALT-J, 12*(3), 215-230.

Sim, G., Strong, A., & Holifield, P. (2005, July 5-6). *The design of multimedia assessment objects.* Paper presented at the Ninth CAA Conference, Loughborough, United Kingdom. Retrieved May 20, 2007, from http://www.caaconference.com/pastConferences/2005/proceedings/SimG_StrongS_HolifieldP.pdf

Smailes, J. (2002). *Experiences of using computer aided assessment within a virtual learning environment.* Retrieved May 20, 2007, from http://www.business.ltsn.ac.uk/events/BEST2002/Papers/smailes.pdf

*Special Educational Needs and Disability Act 2001.* (2001). Retrieved May 20, 2007, from http://www.opsi.gov.uk/acts/acts2001/20010010.htm

Underwood, J. (2006). *Digital technologies and dishonesty in examinations and tests.* London: Qualifications and Curriculum Authority.

## ADDITIONAL READING

Benyon, D., Crerar, M. A., & Wilkinson, S. (2001). *Individual differences and inclusive design: User interfaces for all. Concepts, methods, and tools.* Mahwah, NJ: Lawrence Erlbaum Associates, Inc.

This book covers usability issues for the wide variety of people who may need to use a system, and the range of situations in which they may use it.

Case, S. M., & Swanson, D. B. (2002). *Constructing written test questions for the basic and clinical sciences* (3rd ed.). Philadelphia: National Board of Medical Examiners.

The work focuses on the question-writing level for undergraduate medical students. However, much of the advice will apply equally to other science subjects.

Konur, O. (2007). Computer-assisted teaching and assessment of disabled students in higher education: The interface between academic standards and disability rights. *Journal of Computer Assisted Learning, 23*(3), 207-219.

Konur covers the issues around making adjustments for students with disabilities in online assessment.

Hopkins, K. D. (1998). *Educational and psychological measurement and evaluation* (8th ed.). Needham Heights, MA: Allyn & Bacon.

Hopkins addresses test validity and reliability, and constructing objective tests and standard setting. It has been a standard textbook on educational measurement since 1941 and is now in its eighth edition.

Joint Information Systems Committee (JISC). (2007). *Effective practice with e-assessment: An overview of technologies, policies and practice in further and higher education.* HEFCE. Retrieved June 14, 2007, from http://www.jisc.ac.uk/media/documents/themes/elearning/effprac_eassess.pdf

The work includes a series of case studies on institutions offering e-assessment and measures its impact on teaching and learning.

*Proceedings for CAA Conference.* (2006). Retrieved from http://www.caaconference.com

This is the full proceedings for the annual computer-assisted learning conference held every year in Loughborough, United Kingdom.

Sclater, N., & Howie, K. (2003). User requirements of the "ultimate" online assessment engine. *Computers & Education, 40*(3), 285-306.

This paper presents a model showing key user roles in a theoretically ultimate CAA system. The user requirements of these 21 different roles are explored and mapped onto two leading online assessment systems to analyse how closely they come to achieving this model.

Scottish Qualifications Authority. (2003). *SQA guidelines on online assessment for further education.* Retrieved June 14, 2007, from http://www.sqa.org.uk/files_ccc/GuidelinesForOnlineAssessment(Web).pdf

Here the SQA focuses on guidelines for Scottish further education colleges, but they have wider relevance and the work offers a very practical guide.

## ENDNOTE

[1] RAID 6 is similar to RAID 5 but requires a minimum of four separate hard disks and will not lose data even in the event of two individual disk failures.

# Compilation of References

Abbott, C., Grosbois, M., & Klein, M. (2005). A beautiful house built on sand: What makes e-communication projects succeed—and why are they so rare? *Technology, Pedagogy and Education, 14*(2), 225-239.

Abrami, P., Bernard, R., Wade, A., & Schmid, R. (2006). A review of e-learning in Canada: A rough sketch of the evidence, gaps and promising directions. *Canadian Journal of Learning and Technology, 32*(3), 119-139. Retrieved April 18, 2006, from http://www.cjlt.ca/content/vol32.3/abrami.html

Abrandt, M. (1997). Learning physiotherapy: The impact of formal education and professional experience. *Linköping Studies in Education and Psychology Dissertations, 50.*

Adams, C. (2007). On the "informed use" of PowerPoint: Rejoining Vallance and Towndrow. *Journal of Curriculum Studies, 39*(2), 229-233.

Admiraal, W., Veen, W., Korthagen, F., Lockhorst, D., & Wubbels, T. (1999). Tele-guidance to develop reflective practice: Experiences in four teacher education programmes across Europe. *Journal of Information Technology for Teacher Education, 8,* 1-21.

Agagnostopoulo, K. (2002). *Designing to learn and learning to design: An overview of instructional design models.* LTSN Generic Centre. Retrieved March 2007 from http://www.ltsn.ac.uk/genericcentre/index.asp?id=17113

Agostinho, S., Lefoe, G., & Hedberg, J. (1997, July 5-9). *Online collaboration for learning.* Paper presented at the Third Australian World Wide Web Conference (AusWeb97), Australia.

Alanko-Turunen, M. (2005). *Negotiating interdiscursivity in a problem-based learning tutorial site.* Unpublished doctoral dissertation, University of Tampere, Finland.

Aldrich, R. (1996). *Education for the nation.* London: Cassell.

Alexander, G. (2000). *Netiquette.* Retrieved August 21, 2007, from http://sustainability.open.ac.uk/gary/papers/netique.htm

Alexander, R. J. (2000). *Culture and pedagogy: International comparisons in primary education.* Oxford, United Kingdom: Blackwell Publishers.

Alexander, S. (2001). E-learning developments and experiences. *Education and Training, 43*(4/5), 240-248.

Allen, I., & Seaman, J. (2006). *Making the grade: Online education in the United States.* Needham, MA: The Sloan Consortium (Sloan-C). Retrieved July 7, 2007, from http://www.sloan-c.org/publications/survey/pdf/making_the_grade.pdf

Altenbaugh, R. (2004, September 21-23). Education, disability and the march of dimes. Paper presented at the European Conference on Educational Research, Rethymno, Crete.

Ambrose, A., & Gillespie, B. (2003). Information-literacy programmes and programme curricula: The case for integration. *Level, 3,* 1. Retrieved February 18, 2006, from http://level3.dit.ie/html/issue1_ambrose1.html

American Productivity and Quality Centre. (2002). *International benchmarking cleaning house: Planning, implementing and evaluating e-learning initiatives.*

*Consortium learning forum: Best practice report.* TX: Author.

An Bord Altranais (2000). *Review of scope of practice for nursing and midwifery – Final report.* Dublin: An Bord Altranais.

Ananova, N. (2000, October 15). *Norway wants Internet access for all.* Retrieved June 1, 2007, from http://www.hi-europe.co.uk/files/2000/9980.htm

Anderson, C. A. (1974). Sweden re-examines higher education: A critique of the U68 report. *Comparative Education, 10*(3), 167-180.

Anderson, N., & Henderson, M. (2004). E-PD: Blended models of sustaining teacher professional development in digital literacies. *E-Learning, 1*(3), 383-394.

Anderson, T. (2004). Teaching in an online learning context. In T. Anderson & F. Elloumi (Eds.), *Theory and practice of online learning* (pp. 271-294). Athabasca: Athabasca University. Retrieved September 1, 2007, from http://www.cde.athabascau.ca/online_book.

Anderson, T. (2004). Toward a theory of online learning. In T. Anderson & F. Elloumi (Eds.), *Theory and practice of online learning* (pp. 33-60). Athabasca, Canada: Athabasca University.

Anderson, T., Rourke, L., Garrison, D., & Archer, W. (2001). Assessing teaching presence in a computer conferencing environment. *Journal of Asynchronous Learning Networks, 5*(2). Retrieved September 1, 2007, from http://www.aln.org/alnweb/journal/jaln-vol5issue2v2.htm.

Angelo, T. (2001). Doing faculty development as if we value learning most. In D. Lieberman & C. Wehlburg (Eds.), *To improve the academy* (Vol. 19, pp. 97-112). Boston: Anker Publishing Company, Inc.

Angoff, W. H. (1971). Norms, scales, and equivalent scores. In R. L. Thorndike (Ed.), *Educational measurement* (2nd ed., pp. 508-600). Washington, DC: American Education on Education.

Anonymous. (2007). E-learning and disability in higher education. *British Journal of Educational Technology, 38*(2), 382-383.

Appleton, B. A. (1997). Patterns and software: Essential concepts and terminology. *Object Magazine Online, 3*(5), 20-25.

Aqui, Y. (2005, June 27-30). *Characteristics of the online learner: Experiences, participation level, and achievement.* Paper presented at the Meeting of the National Educational Computing Conference (NECC) of the International Society for Technology in Education, Philadelphia. Retrieved January 9, 2007 from http://center.uoregon.edu/ISTE/uploads/NECC2005/KEY_7030859/Aqui_Aqui_OnlineLearnerCharacteristicsNECC2005_RP.txt

Aram, E., & Noble, D. (1990). Educating prospective managers in the complexity of organizational life. *Management Learning, 30*(3), 321-342.

Arbaugh, J. B. (2004). Learning to learn online: A study of perceptual changes between multiple online course experiences. *Internet and Higher Education, 7,* 169-182.

Archer, L., & Hutchings, M. (2000). "Bettering yourself"? Discourses of risk, cost and benefit in ethnically diverse, young working-class non-participants' constructions of higher education. *British Journal of Sociology of Education, 21*(4), 555-573.

Armatas, C., Holt, D., & Rice, M. (2003). Impacts of an online-supported resources-based learning environment: Does one size fit all? *Distance Education, 24*(2), 141-158.

Armitage, S., & O'Leary, R. (2003). *A good guide for learning technologists* (eLearning Series No. 4). York: Learning and Teaching Support Network Generic Centre.

Ascough, R. S. (2002). Designing for online distance education: Putting pedagogy before technology. *Teaching Theology and Religion, 5,* 1-17.

Ashford, M., & Thomas, J. (2005). Interprofessional education. In H. Burgess & I. Taylor (Eds.), *Effective learning and teaching in social policy and social work* (pp. 124-137). Oxford, United Kingdom: Routledge Falmer.

Atkins, S., & Murphy, K. (1993). Reflection: A review of the literature. *Journal of Advanced Nursing, 18*(8), 1188-1192.

Aviv, R., Erlich, Z., Ravid, G., & Geva, A. (2003). Network analysis of knowledge construction in asynchronous learning networks. *Journal of Asynchronous Learning Networks, 7*(3). Retrieved March 10, 2007, from http://www.sloan-c.org/publications/jaln/v7n3/index.asp

Babbie, C. (1990). *Survey research methods.* Belmont, CA: Wadsworth.

Baets, W., & Van der Linden, G. (2000). *The hybrid business school: Developing knowledge management through management learning.* Amsterdam: Prentice Hall.

Baets, W., & Van der Linden, G. (2003). *Virtual corporate universities: A matrix of knowledge and learning for the new digital dawn.* Boston: Kluwer Academic.

Baets, W., Browaeys, M., & Walker, R. (2001). *ADAGIO: A methodology for designing corporate virtual universities.* Breukelen, The Netherlands: Nyenrode University Press.

Ball, S. J., Davies, J., David, M., & Reay, D. (2002). "Classification" and "judgement": Social class and the "cognitive structures" of choice of higher education. *British Journal of Sociology of Education, 23*(1), 51-72.

Barefoot, B. (2004, February). Higher education's revolving door: Confronting the problem of student drop out in U.S. colleges and universities. *Open Learning, 19*(1), 9-18.

Barnes, A. (1998). Email as a non-directed means of developing independent reflection in beginning teachers of foreign languages. *Journal of Information Technology for Teacher Education, 7*, 189-206.

Barr, R., & Tagg, J. (1995). From teaching to learning: A new paradigm for undergraduate education. *Change, 27*(6), 13-25.

Barrett, E., & Lally, V. (2000). Meeting new challenges in educational research training: The signposts for educational research CD Rom. *British Educational Research Journal, 26*(2), 271-290.

Barrows, H. (2002). Is it truly possible to have such a thing as dPBL? *Distance Education, 23*(1), 199-122.

Bassey, M. (1999). *Case study research in educational settings.* Buckingham, United Kingdom: Open University Press.

Bath, D., & Smith, C. (2004). Academic developers: An academic tribe claiming their territory in higher education. *International Journal for Academic Development, 9*(1), 9-27.

Bautista, A. (1998). A study of the possibilities of teacher education with computer-based telecommunications systems. *Journal of Information Technology for Teacher Education, 7*, 207-230.

Beath, C. (1991). Supporting the information technology champions. *MIS Quarterly, 15*(3), 355-372.

Beetham, H. (2002). *Understanding e-learning, e-tutoring for effective e-learning resources.* Higher Education Academy. Retrieved April 3, 2007, from http://www.ics.heacademy.ac.uk/events/displayevent.php?id=22

Beetham, H. (2005). E-learning research: Emerging issues? *ALT-J, Research in Learning Technology, 13*(1), 81-89.

Belbin, M. (1993). *Team roles at work.* Oxford, United Kingdom: Butterworth Heinemann.

Ben-Ari, M. (2001). Constructivism in computer science education. *Journal of Computers in Mathematics and Science Teaching, 20*(1), 45-73.

Bennett, S., & Lockyer, L. (2004). Becoming an online teacher: Adapting to a changed environment for teaching and learning in higher education. *Educational Media International, 41*(3), 231-244.

Bennett, S., & Marsh, D. (2002, January). Are we expecting online tutors to run before they can walk? *Innovations in Education and Teaching International, 39*(1), 14-20.

Bennis, W. G., & Nanus, B. (1985). *Leaders: The strategies for taking charge.* New York: Harper & Row.

Berge, Z. (1995). Facilitating computer conferencing: Recommendations from the field. *Educational Technology, 35*(1), 22-30.

Bergin, J. (2000, July 5-9). *Fourteen pedagogical patterns.* Paper presented at the Fifth European Conference on Pattern Languages of Programs (EuroPLoP 2000), Irsee, Germany.

Berkenkotter, C., & Huckin, T. (1995). *Genre knowledge in disciplinary communication.* New York: Lawrence Erlbaum.

Bielaczyc, K. (2001). Designing social infrastructure: The challenge of building computer-supported learning communities. In P. Dillenbourg, A. Eurelings, & K. Hakkarainen (Eds.), *European Perspectives on computer-supported collaborative learning.* (pp. 106–114). Maastricht: Maastricht McLuhan Institute.

Bigge, M. L., & Shermis, S. S. (2004). *Learning theories for teachers* (6th ed.). Boston: Pearson.

Biggs, J. (2003). *Teaching for quality learning at university* (2nd ed.). Buckingham, United Kingdom: Open University Press.

Billett. (2001). Knowing in practice: Re-conceptualising vocational expertise. *Learning and Instruction, 11*(6), 431-452.

Birbili, M. (2002). *Teaching educational research methods.* Retrieved March 10, 2007, from http://escalate.ac.uk

Bishop, A. P., Bruce, B., Lunsford, K. J., Jones, M.C., Nazarova, M., Linderman, D., Won, M., Heidorn P. B, Ramprakash, R., & Brock, A. (2004). Supporting community inquiry with digital resources. *Journal of Digital Information, 5*(3). Article No. 308. Retrieved September 1, 2007, from http://jodi.tamu.edu/Articles/v05/i03/Bishop/.

Blair, J. (2002). E-learning: A virtual challenge for educators. *Nursing Times, 98*(31), 34-35.

Blair, T. (2000). *The knowledge economy: Access for all.* Retrieved January 2007 from http://www.dti.gov.uk/knowledge2000/blair.htm

Blass, E., & Davis, A. (2003). Building on solid foundations: Establishing criteria for e-learning development. *Journal of Further and Higher Education, 27*(3), 227-245.

Bloom, B. S., Englehart, M. B., Furst, E. J., Hill, W. H., & Krathwohl, D. R. (1956). *Taxonomy of educational objectives: The classification of educational goals. Handbook I: The cognitive domain.* New York: Longman.

Blumberg, P. (2000). Evaluating the evidence that problem-based learners are self-directed learners: A review of the literature. In D. H. Evensen & C. E. Hmelo (Eds.), *Problem-based learning: A research perspective on learning interactions* (pp. 199-226). Mahwah, NJ: Lawrence Erlbaum Associates.

Blumner, J., Eliason, J., & Fritz, F. (2001). Beyond the reactive: WAC programs and the steps ahead. *The WAC Journal, 12*, 21-36.

Blythman, M., & Orr, S. (2002). A joined-up approach to student support. In M. Peelo & T. Wareham (Eds.), *Failing students in higher education* (pp. 35-47). Buckingham, United Kingdom: The Society for Research into Higher Education & Open University Press.

Boardman, K. (2002). *How to use a discussion board.* UK Centre for Legal Education. Retrieved December 14, 2000, from http://www.ukcle.ac.uk/resources/trns/discussions/index.html

Bodzin, A., & Park, J. P. (2002).Using a nonrestrictive web-based forum to promote reflective discourse with preservice science teachers. *Contemporary Issues in Technology and Teacher Education, 2*, 267-289. Retrieved September 1, 2007, from http://www.citejournal.org/vol2/iss3/science/article1.cfm.

Boekaerts, M., & Simons, P. R. J. (1995). *Leren en instructie: Psychologie van de leerling en het leerproces* [Learning and instruction: The psychology of the learner and his learning process]. Assen, The Netherlands: Dekker & Van de Vegt.

Bollens, J. C., & Marshall, D. R. (1973). *A guide to participation: Fieldwork, role-playing cases and other forms.* Englewood Cliffs, NJ: Prentice-Hall.

Bollentin, R. (1995). Byting back: Is technophobia keeping you off the Internet? *On the Internet Magazine*. Retrieved April 2007 from http://www.csudh.edu/psych/OTI.htm

Bompani, L., Ciancarini, P., & Vitali, F. (2002). XML-based hypertext functionalities for software engineering. *Annals of Software Engineering, 13*(1-4), 231-247.

Bonk, C. J., Kim, K., & Zeng, T. (in press). Future directions of blended learning in higher education and workplace learning setting. In *Handbook of blended learning: Global perspectives*. San Francisco: Pfeiffer Publishing. Retrieved March 24, 2006, from http://www.publicationshare.com/c083_bonk_future.pdf

Bonk, C., Kim, K.-J., & Zeng, T. (2006). Future directions of blended learning in higher education and workplace settings. In C. Bonk & C. R. Graham (Eds.), *Handbook of blended learning: Global perspectives, local designs* (pp. 550-568). San Francisco: Pfeiffer Publishing.

Boud, D. (1995). Assessment and learning: Contradictory or complementary? In P. Knight (Ed.), *Assessment for learning in higher education* (pp. 35-48). London: Kogan.

Boud, D., & Feletti, G. (1997). Changing problem-based learning: Introduction to the second edition. In D. Boud & G. Feletti (Eds.), *The challenge of problem-based learning* (pp. 1-14). London: Kogan Page.

Bourdieu, P. (1990). *The logic of practice*. Cambridge: Polity Press.

Bourdieu, P. (1997). The forms of capital. In A. H. Halsey, H. Lauder, & A. Stuart-Wells (Eds.), *Education, culture, economy and society* (pp. 46-58). Oxford, United Kingdom: Oxford University Press.

Bourdieu, P., & Passeron, J. C. (1977). *Reproduction in education, society and culture*. London: SAGE.

Bovy, R. (1981). Successful instructional methods: A cognitive information processing approach. *ECTJ, 29*(4), 203-217.

Bowles, M. S. (2004). *Relearning to e-learn*. Melbourne, Australia: Melbourne University Press.

Bradley, C., Haynes, R., & Boyle, T. (2005, September 6-8). Design for multimedia m-learning: Lessons from two case studies. In J. Cook & D. Whitelock (Eds.), *Exploring the Frontiers of E-Learning: Borders, Outposts and Migration. Research Proceedings of the 12th Association for Learning Technology Conference (ALT-C 2005)*, Manchester, United Kingdom (pp. 98-108).

Brew, A. (2002). Research and the academic developer: A new agenda. *International Journal for Academic Development, 7*(2), 112-122.

Brew, A. (2003). Making sense of academic development: Editorial. *International Journal for Academic Development, 11*(2), 73-77.

Brew, A. (2006). *Research and teaching: Beyond the divide*. Basingstoke, United Kingdom: Palgrave Macmillan.

Bricheno, P., Higgison, C., & Weedon, E. (2004). *The impact of networked learning on education institutions*. Bradford, United Kingdom: UHI Millennium Institute & Bradford University, INLEI Project. Retrieved March 17, 2007, from http://www.sfeuprojects.org.uk/inlei/Final_Report.pdf

Bridges, E., & Hallinger, P. (1997). Using problem-based learning to prepare educational leaders. *Peabody Journal of Education, 72*(2), 131-146.

Bridges, L. (1995). *Creating your classroom community*. New York: Stenhouse.

British Educational Communications and Technology Agency. (1999). *Learning on-line: Electronic learning resources in further education*. Coventry, United Kingdom: Author.

British Educational Communications and Technology Agency. (2003). *Ferl practitioners' programme: Transforming teaching and learning with ILT*. Coventry, United Kingdom: Author.

British Educational Communications and Technology Agency. (2005). *ICT and e-learning in further education: The challenge of change*. Coventry, United Kingdom: Author.

British Educational Communications and Technology Agency. (2007a). *2007 annual review.* Coventry, United Kingdom: Author.

British Educational Communications and Technology Agency. (2007b). *E-portfolios: Technical processes, assumptions and implications.* Retrieved August 2007 from http://partners.becta.org.uk/index. php?section=pv&catcode=_pv_ep_02&rid=13637&pa genum=3&NextStart=1

Broberg, C., Aars, M., Beckmann, K., Emaus, N., Lehto, P., Lähteenmäki, M.-L., et al. (2003). A conceptual framework for curriculum design in physiotherapy education: An international perspective. *Advances in Physiotherapy, 5,* 161-168.

Brookfield, S. (1993). Through the lens of learning: How the visceral experience of learning reframes teaching. In D. Boud, R. Cohen, & D. Walker (Eds.), *Using experience for learning* (pp. 21-32). Milton Keynes, United Kingdom: The Open University Press.

Brookfield, S. D., & Preskill, S. (1999). *Discussion as a way of teaching: Tools and techniques for university teachers.* Buckingham, United Kingdom: The Society for Research into Higher Education & Open University Press.

Brown, A. L. (1997). Transforming schools into communities of thinking and learning about serious matters. *American Psychologist, 52*(4), 399-413.

Brown, G. (2001). *Assessment: A guide for lecturers.* York, United Kingdom: Learning and Teaching Support Network (LTSN).

Brown, J. S., Collins, A., & Duguid, P. (1989). Situated cognition and the culture of learning. *Educational Researcher, 18*(1), 32-42.

Browne, T., Jenkins, M., & Walker, R. (2006). A longitudinal perspective regarding the use of VLEs by higher education institutions in the United Kingdom. *Interactive Learning Environments, 14*(2), 177-192.

BS ISO/IEC 23988. (2007). *Code of practice for the use of information technology (IT) in the delivery of assessments.* London: British Standards.

Bulman, C., & Schutz, S. (2004). *Reflective practice in nursing* (3rd ed.). Oxford: Blackwell.

Burbules, N., & Callister, T. (2000). Universities in transition: The promise and challenge of new technologies. *Teachers College Record, 102*(2), 271-293.

Burgstahler, S. (2002). Distance learning: Universal design, universal access. *AACE Journal, 10*(1), 32-61.

Butler, D., & Sellbom, M. (2002). Barriers for adopting technology for teaching and learning. *Educause Quarterly, 25*(2), 22-28. Retrieved May 25, 2007, from http://www.educause.edu/ir/library/pdf/eqm0223.pdf

Byers, S. (2000). *The importance of the knowledge economy.* Retrieved January 2007 from http://www.dti. gov.uk/knowledge2000/byers.htm

Cairncross, S., & Mannion, M. (2001). Interactive multimedia and learning: Realizing the benefits. *Innovations in Education and Teaching International, 38*(2), 156-164.

Campbell, G. (2005). There's something in the air: Podcasting in education. *Educause Review, 40*(6), 32-47. Retrieved May 16, 2007, from http://www.educause. edu/apps/er/erm05/erm056.asp

Candy, P. (1996). Promoting lifelong learning: Academic developers and the university as a learning organisation. *International Journal for Academic Development, 1*(1), 7-19.

Cantillon, P., Irish, B., & Sales, D. (2004). Using computers for assessment in medicine. *British Medical Journal, 329,* 606-609.

Carr, S. (2000, February 11). As distance education comes of age, the challenge is keeping the students. *The Chronicle of Higher Education.*

Case, S. M., & Swanson, D. B. (2002). *Constructing written test questions for the basic and clinical sciences* (3rd ed.). Philadelphia: National Board of Medical Examiners.

ChanLin, L. J., & Chan, K. C. (2007). Integrating inter-disciplinary experts for supporting problem-based learning. *Innovations in Education and Teaching International, 44*(2), 211-224.

Charlesworth, P., & Vician, C. (2003). Leveraging technology for chemical sciences education: An early assessment of WebCT usage in first-year chemistry courses. *Journal of Chemical Education, 80*(11), 1333-1337.

Charlin, B., Mann, K., & Hansen, P. (1998). The many faces of problem-based learning: A framework for understanding and comparison. *Medical Teacher, 20,* 323-330.

Chee, Y. (2002). Refocusing learning on pedagogy in a connected world. *On The Horizon, 10*(4), 7-13.

Chen, Q., & Yao, J. (2005). A cognitive model of Web design for e-learning. *International Journal of Innovation and Learning, 2*(1), 26-35.

Cheng, R., & Vassileva, J. (2005). Adaptive reward mechanism for sustainable online learning community. Proceedings *of the International Conference on Artificial Intelligence in Education* (pp.152-159). Retrieved September 1, 2007, from http://julita.usask.ca/Texte/aied2005-final.pdf

Chickering, A., & Ehrmann, S. (1996, October). Implementing the seven principles: Technology as lever. *American Association for Higher Education Bulletin,* pp. 3-6. Retrieved February 24, 2006, from http://www.tltgroup.org/programs/seven.html

Choi, H., & Park, J. (2006). Difficulties that an online novice instructor faced. *The Quarterly Review of Distance Education, 7*(3), 317-322.

Clark, J. (2000). *Flash access: Unclear on the concept.* Retrieved June 12, 2007, from http://www.alistapart.com/articles/unclear/

Clark, J. (2004). *Reader's guide to Sydney Olympics accessibility complaint.* Retrieved June 12, 2007, from http://www.contenu.nu/socog.html

Clark, R. (1994). Media will never influence learning. *Educational Technology Research & Development, 42*(2), 1042-1069.

Clark, R. E. (1994). Media will never influence learning. *Educational Technology Research and Development, 42*(2), 21-29.

Clark, R., & Mayer, R. (2003). *E-learning and the science of instruction.* San Francisco: Pfeiffer.

Clark, R., Nguyen, F., & Sweller, J. (2006). *Efficiency in learning.* San Francisco: Pfeiffer.

Clarke, C. (2003). *Towards a unified e-learning strategy: Consultation document.* London: The Stationary Office.

Clouder, L., & Deepwell, F. (2004). Reflections on unexpected outcomes: Learning from student collaboration in an online discussion forum. *Networked Learning Conference.* Retrieved October 25, 2007, from http://www.networkedlearningconference.org.uk/past/nlc2004/proceedings/individual_papers/clouderanddeepwell.htm

Cohen, A. (1987). Using verbal protocols in research on language learning. In C. Faerch & G. Kasper (Eds.), *Introspection in second language research* (pp. 82-95). Clevedon, United Kingdom: Multilingual Matters.

Coleman, J. (1971). Learning through games. In E. Avedon & B. Sutton-Smith (Eds.), *The study of games* (pp. 322-329). New York: John Wiley.

Collis, B. (1996). *Telelearning in a digital world: The future of distance learning.* London: International Thomson Computer Press.

Collis, B. (1999). Designing for difference: Cultural issues in the design of WWW based course support sites. *British Journal of Educational Technology, 30*(3), 201-215.

Collis, B., & Moonen, J. (2001). *Flexible learning in a digital world.* London: Kogan Page.

Collis, B., Bruijstens, H., & van der Veen, J. K. (2003). Course redesign for blended learning: Modern optics for technical professionals. *International Journal of Continuing Engineering Education and Lifelong Learning, 13*(1/2), 22-38.

Colyer, H., Helme, M., & Jones, I. (Eds.). (2005). *The theory-practice relationship in interprofessional education.* Retrieved June 25, 2007, from http://www.health.heacademy.ac.uk/publications/occasionalpaper/occ7.pdf

Committee of Vice-Chancellors and Principals. (1998). *From elitism to inclusion* (executive summary). London: Author.

Concannon, F., Flynn, A., & Campbell, M. (2005). What campus-based students think about the quality and benefits of e-learning. *British Journal of Educational Technology, 36*(3), 501-512.

Connolly, M., Jones, C., & Jones, N. (2007). New approaches, new vision: Capturing teacher experiences in a brave new online world. *Open Learning, 22*(1), 43-56.

Connolly, T., Jessup, L. M., & Valacich, J. S. (1990). Effects of anonymity and evaluative tone on idea generation in computer-mediated groups. *Management Science, 36*(6), 689-703.

Conole, G., & Fill, K. (2005). A learning design toolkit to create pedagogically effective learning activities. *Journal of Interactive Media in Education, 8*, 1-16.

Conole, G., & Oliver, M. (Eds.). (2007). Introduction. In *Contemporary perspectives in elearning research: Themes, methods and impact on practice* (pp. 5-8). London: Routledge.

Conole, G., de Laat, M., Dillon, T., & Darby, J. (2006). *Student experiences of technologies (LXP): Final report and appendices.* Retrieved June 25, 2007, from http://www.jisc.ac.uk/elp_learneroutcomes

Conole, G., de Laat, M., Dillon, T., & Darby, J. (2006, December). *An in-depth case study of students' experiences of e-learning: How is learning changing?* Paper presented at the Australian Society for Computers in Learning and in Tertiary Education Conference, Sydney, Australia. Retrieved August 8, 2007, from http://www.ascilite.org.au/conferences/sydney06/proceeding/pdf_papers/p127.pdf

Conole, G., White, S., & Oliver, M. (2007). The impact of e-learning on organisational roles and structures. In G. Conole & M. Oliver (Eds.), *Contemporary perspectives in e-learning research: Themes, methods and impact on practice* (pp. 69-81). Abingdon: Routledge.

Conrad, D. (2004, April). University instructors' reflec-

tions on their first online teaching experiences. *Journal of Asynchronous Learning Networks, 8*(2), 31-44.

Cook, D., & Dupras, D. (2004). A practical guide to developing effective Web-based learning. *Journal of General Internal Medicine, 19*, 698-707.

Cooper, B., & Rixon, A. (2001). Integrating post-qualification study into the workplace: The candidates experience. *Social Work Education, 20*(6), 701-716.

Cooper, M. (2006). Making online learning accessible to disabled students: An institutional case study. *ALT-J Research in Learning Technology, 14*, 103-115.

Corgan, R., Hammer, V., Margolies, M., &Crossley, C. (2004). Making your online course successful. *Business Education Forum, 58*(3), 51–53.

Costello, M. L., Brunner, P. W., & Hasty, K. (2002). Preparing students for the empowered workplace. *Active Learning in Higher Education, 3*(2), 117-127.

Cotlar, M., & Shimabukuro, J. N. (1995). Stimulating learning with electronic guest lecturing. In Z. L. Berge & M. Collins (Eds.), *Computer mediated communication and the online classroom: Vol. 3. Distance learning* (pp. 105-128). Cresskill, NJ: Hampton Press.

Cottrell, S. (2001). *Teaching study skills and supporting learning.* Basingstoke, United Kingdom: Palgrave Macmillan.

Cowan, J. (1998). *On becoming an innovative university teacher.* Buckingham, United Kingdom: Open University Press.

Cowan, J. (2003). Learning from experience. In P. Kahn & D. Baume (Eds.), *A guide to staff and educational development* (pp. 192-211). London: Routledge.

Creanor, L. (2002). A tale of two courses: A comparative study of tutoring online. *Open Learning, 17*(1), 57-68.

Creanor, L., Trinder, K., Gowan, D., & Howells, C. (2006). *The learner experience of e-learning (LEX): Final report.* Retrieved June 25, 2007, from http://www.jisc.ac.uk/uploaded_documents/LEX%20Final%20Report_August06.pdf

Cronjé, J. (2006). Paradigms regained: Toward integrating objectivism and constructivism in instructional design and the learning sciences. *Journal of Educational Technology Research and Development, 54*(4), 387-416.

Curzon, L. B. (2003). *Teaching in further education: An outline of principals and practice* (6th ed.). London: Continuum.

D'Andrea, V., & Gosling, D. (2001). Joining the dots: Reconceptualizing academic development. *Active Learning in Higher Education, 2*(1), 64-80.

Dancy, M., & Beichner, R. (2000). *Does animation influence the validity of assessment? An example from physics.* Retrieved August 16, 2007, from http://www.ncsu.edu/PER/Articles/DancyDissSummary.pdf

Data Protection Act. (1998). *Data Protection Act 1998.* Retrieved June 5, 2007, from http://www.opsi.gov.uk/acts/acts1998/19980029.htm

Davies, P. (1994). Fourteen years on, what do we know about access students? Some reflections on national statistical data. *Journal of Access Studies, 9*(1), 45-60.

Davies, P. (Ed.). (1995). *Adults in higher education: International experiences in access and participation.* London: Jessica Kingsley.

Davis, M. (2003). Barriers to reflective practice: The changing nature of higher education. *Active Learning in Higher Education, 4*(3) 243-255.

Dawson, R., & Newsham, R. (1997). Introducing software engineers to the real world. *IEEE Software, 14*(6), 37-43.

Dearing, R. (1997). *Higher education in the learning society: Report of the National Committee of Inquiry into Higher Education.* London: HMSO.

Deem, R., & Lucas, L. (2006). Learning about research: Exploring the learning and teaching/research relationship amongst educational practitioners studying in higher education. *Teaching in Higher Education, 11*(1), 1-18.

Dehmel, A. (2006). Making a European area of lifelong learning a reality? Some critical reflections on the European Union's lifelong learning policies. *Comparative Education, 42*(1), 49-62.

DeLacey, B. J., & Leonard, D. A. (2002). Case study on technology and distance in education at the Harvard Business School. *Educational Technology and Society, 5*(2).

Denis, B., Watland, P., Pirotte, S., & Verday, N. (2004). Roles and competencies of the e-tutor. *Proceedings of Networked Learning Conference 2004.* Retrieved June 25, 2007, from http://www2.uca.es/orgobierno/ordenacion/formacion/docs/jifpev5-doc4.pdf

Dennis, J. K. (2003). Problem-based learning in online vs. face-to-face environments. *Education for Health, 16*(2), 198-209.

Dent, J. A., & Harden, R. M. (2005). *A practical guide for medical teachers.* Oxford, United Kingdom: Elsevier Limited.

Department for Children, Schools and Families. (2007). *Five year strategy for children and learners.* Retrieved August 2007 from http://www.dfes.gov.uk/publications/5yearstrategy/chap3.shtml

Department for Education and Skills. (2002). *Success for all: Reforming further education and training. Our vision for the future.* London: Author.

Department for Education and Skills. (2004). *Widening participation.* London: The Stationery Office.

Department for Education and Skills. (2005). *Harnessing technology: Transforming learning and children's services.* London: Author.

Deveaux, D., & La Traon, Y. (2001, May 15). *XML to manage source engineering in object-oriented development: An example.* Paper presented at the International Workshop on XML Technologies and Software Engineering (XSE 2001), Toronto, Canada.

Dewey, J. (1933). *How we think. A restatement of the relation of reflective thinking to the educative process.* Boston: D. C. Heath.

DeWolfe Waddill, D. (2006). Action e-learning: An exploratory case study of action learning applied online.

*Human Resource Development International, 9*(2), 157-171.

Dick, W., & Carey, L. (2004). *The systematic design of instruction* (6th ed.). Boston: Allyn and Bacon.

Diercks-O'Brien, G. (2002). Implementing a virtual learning environment: A holistic framework for institutionalizing online learning. In R. Macdonald & J. Wisdom (Eds.), *Academic and educational development: Research, evaluation and changing practice in higher education (staff and educational development series)* (pp. 140-151). London: Kogan Page.

Dillon, J. T. (1990). *The practice of questioning.* London: Routledge.

Dolmans, D., Gijselars, W., Moust, J., de Grave, W., Wolfhagen, I., & van der Vleuten, C. (2002). Trends in research on the tutor in problem-based learning: Conclusions and implications for educational practice and research. *Medical Teacher, 24*(2), 173-180.

Donnelly, R. (2004). The effectiveness of teaching "online learning" in a problem-based learning classroom environment. In M. Savin-Baden & K. Wilkie (Eds.), *Challenging research into problem-based learning.* Buckingham, United Kingdom: SRHE/Open University Press.

Donnelly, R. (2005). Using technology to support project and problem-based learning. In T. Barrett, I. Mac Labhrainn, & H. Fallon (Eds.), *Handbook of enquiry & problem-based learning* (pp. 157- 177). Galway, Ireland: CELT.

Donnelly, R. (2006). The academic developer as tutor in PBLonline in higher education. In M. Savin-Baden & K. Wilkie (Eds.), *Problem-based learning online* (pp. 79-97). Buckingham, United Kingdom: Open University Press.

Donnelly, R., & O'Brien, F. (2003). Towards the promotion of effective e-learning practice for academic staff development in DIT. *Level 3.* Retrieved May 20, 2007, from http://level3.dit.ie/pdf/issue1_donnelly_obrien.pdf

Donnelly, R., & O'Farrell, C. (2006). Constructivist e-learning for staff engaged in continuous professional de-velopment. In J. O'Donoghue (Ed.), *Technology supported learning and teaching: A staff perspective* (pp. 146-159). Hershey, PA: Information Science Publishing.

Donnelly, R., & O'Rourke, K. (2007). What now? Evaluating e-learning CPD practice in Irish third-level education. *Journal of Further and Higher Education, 31*(1), 31-40.

Donnelly, R., & O'Rourke, K. (2007). What now? Evaluating elearning CPD practice in Irish third-level education. *Journal of Further and Higher Education, 31*(1), 31-41.

Donnelly, R., & Portimojärvi, T. (in press). Online problem-based learning in higher education: Shifting perceptions. In C. Howard, P. Rogers, J. Boettcher, G. Berg, L. Justice, & K. Schenk (Eds.), *Encyclopedia of distance learning* (2nd ed.). Hershey, PA: Idea Group Inc.

Doolittle, P. (1999). *Constructivism and online education.* Retrieved August 16, 2007, from http://edpsychserver.ed.vt.edu/workshops/tohe1999/text/doo2s.doc

Downes, S. (2005). E-learning 2.0. *E-Learn Magazine.* Retrieved June 12, 2007, from http://www.elearnmag.org/subpage.cfm?section=articles&article=29-1

Drew, S. (2001). Student perceptions of what helps them learn and develop in higher education. *Teaching in Higher Education, 6*(3), 309-331.

Driscoll, M. (2000). *Psychology of learning for instruction* (2nd ed.). Boston: Allyn and Bacon.

Driscoll, M. (2002). Blended learning: Let's get beyond the hype. *Learning and Training Innovations Newsline.* Retrieved August 7, 2007, from http://elearningmag.com/ltimagazine/article/articleDetail.jsp?id=11755

Driscoll, M. (2002, March 1). Blended learning: Let's get beyond the hype. *LTI Newsline.* Retrieved March 20, 2007, from http://www.ltimagazine.com/ltimagazine/article/articleDetail.jsp?id=11755

Drummond, I., Nixon, I., & Wiltshire, J. (1998). Personal transferable skills in higher education. *Quality Assurance in Education, 6*(1), 19-27.

Drury, H. (2004). Teaching academic writing on screen: A search for best practice. In L. Ravelli & R. Ellis (Eds.), *Analysing academic writing* (pp. 233-253). London: Continuum.

Du Bois-Reymond, M. (1998). I don't want to commit myself yet: Young people's life concepts. *Journal of Youth Studies, 1*(1), 63-79.

Duffy, T. M., & Jonassen, D. H. (1992). *Constructivist and the technology of instruction: A conversation.* NJ: Lawrence Erlbaum Associates.

Durkin, K., & Main, A. (2002). Discipline-based study skills support for first-year undergraduate students. *Active Learning in Higher Education, 3*(1), 24-39.

Dziuban, C., Hartman, J., & Moskal, P. (2004, March 30). Blended learning. *Educause Center for Applied Research, Research Bulletin, 7.* Retrieved March 15, 2007, from http://www.educause.edu/LibraryDetailPage/666?ID=ERB0407

EADTU. (2004). *Report of the eLearning Programme of Education and Culture, European Commission.* Retrieved March 15, 2007, from http://www.eadtu.nl/files/EADTUstatementEC.final.doc

Earl, L., Watson, N., Levin, B., Leithwood, K., Fullan, M., & Torrence, N. (2003). *Watching and learning: Final report of the external evaluation of England's national literacy and numeracy strategies.* London: DfES Publications.

Ebel, R. L. (1972). *Essentials of educational measurement.* Englewood Cliffs, NJ: Prentice-Hall.

Eckstein, J. (2000, July 5-9). *Learning to teach and learning to learn: Pedagogical and social issues in education.* Paper presented at the Fifth European Conference on Pattern Languages of Programs (EuroPLoP 2000), Irsee, Germany.

Edmonds, C. D. (2004). Providing access to students with disabilities in online distance education: Legal and technical concerns for higher education. *The American Journal of Distance Education, 18*(1), 51-62.

Edward, N. (2003). First impressions last. *Active Learning in Higher Education, 4*(3), 226-242.

Eklund, J., Kay, M., & Lynch, H. (2003). *E-learning: Emerging issues and key trends.* Australia: Australian National Training Authority.

Ellis, R. (2004). Supporting genre-based literacy pedagogy with technology: The implications for the framing and classification of the pedagogy. In L. Ravelli & R. Ellis (Eds.), *Analysing academic writing* (pp. 210-232). London: Continuum.

Entwistle, N. J. (1997). Contrasting perspectives on learning. In F. Marton, D. Hounsell, & N. Entwistle (Eds.), *The experience of learning: Implications for teaching and studying in higher education* (pp. 3-22). Edinburgh, United Kingdom: Scottish Academic Press.

Eraut, M. (2004) The practice of reflection. *Learning in Health and Social Care, 3*(2), 47–52.

Ertmer, P. A., Richardson, J. C., Belland, B., Camin, D., Connolly, P., & Coulthard, G. (2007). Using peer feedback to enhance the quality of student online postings: An exploratory study. *Journal of Computer-Mediated Communication, 12*(2), 412-433.

European Commission. (2002). *Making lifelong learning a reality for all.* Luxembourg: Office for Official Publications of the European Communities.

eXe. (2007). *eLearning XHTML editor.* Retrieved July 2007 from http://exelearning.org

Eynon, R. (2005). The use of the Internet in higher education: Academics' experiences of using ICTs for teaching. Aslib Proceedings: *New Information Perspectives, 57*(2), 168-180.

Fasli, M., & Michalakopoulos, M. (2005, August 30-September1). *Learning through game-like simulations.* Paper presented at the Sixth Higher Education Academy Information and Computer Sciences Conference (HEA-ICS), York, United Kingdom. Retrieved June 12, 2007, from http://www.ics.heacademy.ac.uk/italics/vol5iss2/MFasli.htm

Fazey, D., & Fazey, J. (2001). The potential for autonomy in learning: Perceptions of competence, motivation and locus of control in first-year undergraduate students. *Studies in Higher Education, 26*(3), 345-361.

Feenberg, A. (2001). Whither educational technology? *International Journal of Technology and Design Education, 11*(1), 83-91.

Ferrier, F. (1992, July 12-15). *Not more of the same stuff: Student dissatisfaction with postgraduate courses.* Paper presented at the 15th Annual Higher Education Research & Development Society of Australasia Conference, Sydney, Australia.

Fetherston, T. (2001). Pedagogical challenges for the World Wide Web. *Educational Technology Review, 9*(1), 25-32.

Fitzgibbon, K., & Jones, N. (2004, March). Jumping the hurdles: Challenges of staff development delivered in a blended learning environment. *Journal of Educational Media, 29*(1), 25-35.

Flanders, V. (2007). *Web pages that suck 2.0.* Retrieved June 11, 2007, from http://www.webpagesthatsuck.com

Fogg, B. J. (2003). *Persuasive technology: Using computers to change what we think and do.* San Francisco: Morgan Kaufmann Publishers, Inc.

Forsyth, I. (1996). *Teaching and learning materials and the Internet.* London: Kogan Page.

Foucault, M. (1988). *Politics, philosophy, culture: Interviews and other writings 1977-1984* (L. D. Kritzman, Ed.). London: Routledge.

Fox, S., & MacKeogh, K. (2003). Can e-learning promote higher-order learning without tutor overload? *Open Learning, 18*(2), 121-134.

Frailey, D. J. (1998). Opportunities for software engineering education. *Annals of Software Engineering, 6*(1-4), 131-144.

Fraser, K. (2001). Australasian academic developers' conceptions of the profession. *International Journal for Academic Development, 6*(1), 54-64.

Freeman, M., & Capper, J. (1999). Exploiting the Web for education: An anonymous asynchronous role simulation. *Australian Journal of Educational Technology, 15*(1), 95-116. Retrieved August 14, 2007, from http://www.ascilite.org.au/ajet/ajet15/freeman.html

Gagné, R. M., Wager, W. W., Golas, K. C., & Keller, J. M. (2005). *Principles of instructional design* (5th ed.). Belmont, CA: Thomson Wadsworth.

Gagné, R.M. (1985). *The conditions of learning and theory of instruction* (Fourth Edition). Holt, Rinehart, and Winston.

Gagné, R.M., Wagner, W.W., Gloas, K., & Keller, J.M. (2005). *Principles of instructional design* (5th ed.) Wadsworth.

Galanouli, D., & Collins, J. (2000). Using unmediated computer conferencing to promote reflective practice and confidence-building in initial teacher education. *Journal of Information Technology for Teacher Education, 9*(2), 237-254.

Gamache, P. (2002). University students as creators of personal knowledge: An alternative epistemological view. *Teaching in Higher Education, 7*(3), 277-293.

Garet, M., Porter, A., Desimone, L., Birman, B., & Yoon, K. (2001). What makes professional development effective: Results from a national sample of teachers. *American Educational Research Association Journal, 38*(4), 915-945.

Garrett, B. (2003). *School of Health and Social Care e-learning strategy.* Retrieved November 9, 2004, from http://www.brookes.ac.uk/virtual/documents/files/Health_and_SocialCareDraftSchoolRBLStrategy2003.doc

Garrett, R., & Verbik, L. (2004). *Online learning in Commonwealth universities: Selected data from the 2004 observatory survey: Part 2* (Rep. No. 21). London: The Observatory on Borderless Higher Education.

Garris, R., Ahlers, R., & Driskell, J. (2002). Games, motivation, and learning: A research and practice model. *Simulation & Gaming: An International Journal, 33*, 441-467.

Garrison, D. R. (2002). *Cognitive presence for effective asynchronous online learning: The role of reflective inquiry, self-direction and metacognition.* Paper presented at the Fourth Annual Sloan ALN Workshop, Boltons Landing, NY. Retrieved September 1, 2007, from http://www.communitiesofinquiry.com/documents/ SLOAN%20CP%20CHAPTER% 202003.DOC

Garrison, D. R., & Anderson, T. (2003). *E-learning in the 21st century: A framework for research and practice.* London: RoutledgeFalmer.

Garrison, D. R., Anderson, T., & Archer, W. (2000). Critical inquiry in a text-based environment: Computer conferencing in higher education. *The Internet and Higher Education, 2*(2-3), 87-105.

Garrison, D. R., Cleveland-Innes, M., & Fung, T. (2004). Student role adjustment in online communities of inquiry: Model and instrument validation. *Journal of Asynchronous Learning Networks, 8*(2), 1-7.

Garrison, D. R., Cleveland-Innes, M., Koole, M., & Kappleman, J. (2006). Revisiting methodological issues in transcript analysis: Negotiated coding and reliability. *The Internet and Higher Education, 9*(1), 1-8.

Garrison, D., Anderson, T., & Archer, W. (2000). Critical inquiry in a text-based environment: Computer conferencing in higher education. *Internet and Higher Education, 11*(2), 1-14.

Gayeski, D. (1996). Multimedia packages in education. In T. Plomp & D. Ely (Eds.), *International encyclopaedia of educational technology* (pp. 440-445). New York: Elsevier.

Geibert, R. (2000). Integrating web-based instruction into a graduate nursing program taught via videoconferencing: *Challenges and solutions. Computers in Nursing 18*(1), 26-34.

Gerbic, P. (2006, December 3-6). To post or not to post: Undergraduate student perceptions about participating in online discussions. In *Proceedings of the 23rd Annual Ascilite Conference: Who's Learning? Whose Technology?* (pp. 271-281). Retrieved May 15, 2007,

from http://www.ascilite.org.au/conferences/sydney06/ proceeding/pdf_papers/p124.pdf

Ghezzi, C., Jazayeri, M., & Mandrioli, D. (2003). *Fundamentals of software engineering* (2nd ed.). Upper Saddle River, NJ: Prentice-Hall.

Gibbs, G. (1992). *Improving the quality of student learning.* Oxford, United Kingdom: Oxford Centre for Staff Development.

Gibbs, G. (1994). *Improving student learning: Through assessment and evaluation.* Oxford, United Kingdom: Oxford Centre for Staff Development.

Gibbs, G. (2004, February). Editorial. *Open Learning, 19*(1), 3-7.

Gibbs, G. (2004, June 21-23). *The nature of educational development in a changing context.* Keynote Presentation at the International Consortium for Educational Development Conference, Ottawa, Canada.

Gil, L., Blanco, E., & Auli, J. (2000). The virtual laboratory concept applied to strain measurements. *European Journal of Engineering Education, 25*(3), 243-251.

Gillis, A., Jackson, W., Braid, A., MacDonald, P., & MacQuarrie, M. (2000). The learning needs and experiences of women using print-based and CD-ROM technology in nursing distance education. *Journal of Distance Education 15*(1), 1–20.

Gilroy, K. (2001). Collaborative e-learning: The right approach. *ArsDigita Systems Journal.*

Goodyear, P. (2001). *Effective networked learning in higher education: Notes and guidelines.* Retrieved June 25, 2007, from http://csalt.lancs.ac.uk/jisc/Guidelines_final.doc

Goodyear, P. (2001). Teaching online. In N. Hativa & P. Goodyear (Eds.), *Teacher thinking, beliefs and knowledge in higher education* (pp. 79-101). The Netherlands: Kluwer.

Gorard, S., Rees, G., & Fevre, R. (1999). Patterns of participation in lifelong learning: Do families make a difference? *British Educational Research Journal, 25*(4), 517-532.

Gosling, D. (2001). Educational development units in the UK: What are they doing five years on? *International Journal for Academic Development, 6*(1), 74-90.

Government of Ireland. (2000). *Equal Status Act.* Dublin, Ireland: Stationery Office. Retrieved June 12, 2007, from http://www.irishstatutebook.ie/2000/en/act/pub/0008/index.html

Graham, C., Cagiltay, K., Lim, B., Craner, J., & Duffy, T. (2001, March/April). Seven principles of effective teaching: A practical lens for evaluating online courses. *The Technology Source.* Retrieved July 4, 2007, from http://www.technologysource.org/article/seven_principles_of_effective_teaching

Gray, R. (2007). Bite-sized generation. *Human Resources,* pp. 37-38. Retrieved May 2007 from www.hrmagazine.co.uk

Greek, D. (2006). UK households snub Internet access. *Computeract!ve.* Retrieved May 2007 from http://www.itweek.co.uk/computeractive/news/2167328/growing-number-people-uk

Green, A., & Lucas, N. (Eds.). (1999). *FE and lifelong learning: Realigning the sector for the 21ˢᵗ century.* London: Institute of Education.

Guest, T. (2007). *Second lives.* London: Hutchison.

Guion, L. (n.d.). *Conducting an in-depth interview.* Retrieved August 21, 2007, from http://edis.ifas.ufl.edu/pdffiles/FY/FY39300.pdf

Gunawardena, C. N. (1995). Social presence theory and implications for interaction and collaborative learning in computer conferences. International *Journal of Educational Telecommunications, 1*(2/3), 147-166.

Hadjerrouit, S. (2005). Constructivism as guiding philosophy for software engineering education. *ACM SIGCSE Bulletin, 37*(4), 45-49.

Halsey, A. H. (1992). An international comparison of access to higher education. *Oxford Studies in Comparative Education, 1*(1), 11-36.

Ham, V., & Davey, R. (2005). Our first time: Two higher education tutors reflect on becoming a "virtual teacher."

*Innovations in Education & Teaching International, 42,* 257-264.

Hannifin, M., Land, S., & Oliver, K. (1983). Open learning environments: Foundations, methods, and models. In C. M. Reigeluth (Ed.), *Instructional design theories and models.* (pp. 115-140). Hillsdale, NJ: Lawrence Erlbaum.

Hara, N., & Kling, R. (2000). Students' distress with a Web-based distance education course: An ethnographic study of participants' experiences. *Information, Communication and Society, 3*(4), 557-579.

Harasim, L. (1989). On-line education: A new domain. In R. Mason & A. Kaye (Eds.), *Mindweave: Communication, computers and distance education* (pp. 50-62). Oxford, United Kingdom: Pergamon Press.

Harasim, L. (1989). On-line education: A new domain. In R. Mason & A. Kaye (Eds.), *Mindweave: Communication, computers and distance education* (pp. 50-62). Oxford, United Kingdom: Pergamon Press.

Harasim, L. (1993). Collaborating in cyberspace: Using computer conferences as group learning environments. *Interactive Learning Environments, 3*(2), 119-130.

Harland, T., & Staniforth, D. (2003). Academic development as academic work. *International Journal for Academic Development, 8*(1/2), 25-35.

Harley, D. (2007). Why study users? An environmental scan of use and users of digital resources in humanities and social sciences undergraduate education. *First Monday, 12*(1). Retrieved April 1, 2007, from http://firstmonday.org/issues/issue12_1/harley/index.html

Harper, R. (2003). Correcting computer-based assessments for guessing. *Journal of Computer Assisted Learning, 19*(1), 2-8.

Harrington, H. L., & Hathaway, R. S. (1994). Computer conferencing, critical reflection, and teacher development. *Teaching and Teacher Education, 10*(5), 543-554.

Harwood, I. (2005). When summative computer-aided assessments go wrong: Disaster recovery after a major failure. *British Journal of Educational Technology, 36*(4), 587-597.

Hayes, D. (2001). Professional status and an emerging culture of conformity amongst teachers in England. *Education, 3*(13), 43-49.

Hayes, D., Hill, J., Mannette-Wright, A., & Wong, H. (2006, October 21-23). *Team project patterns for college students*. Paper presented at the 13ᵗʰ Conference on Pattern Languages of Programs (PLoP 2006), Portland, OR.

Healey, M. (2003). Promoting lifelong professional development in geography education: International perspectives on developing the scholarship of teaching in higher education in the twenty-first century. *The Professional Geographer, 55*(1), 1-17.

Healy, M., & Jenkins, A. (2003). Discipline-based educational development. In H. Higgins & R. Macdonald (Eds.), *The scholarship of academic development* (pp. 47-57). Buckingham, United Kingdom: Society for Research into Higher Education & Open University Press.

HEFCE. (2005). *HEFCE strategy for e-learning*. Retrieved October 25, 2007, from http://www.hefce. ac.uk/pubs/hefce/2005/05_12/

Heikkilä, K., & Heikkilä, J. (2001). *Innovatiivisuutta etsimässä: Irtiottoa keskinkertaisuudesta* [Searching for innovation: Letting go of the average]. Jyväskylä, Finland: Gummerus.

Heintz, J., & Jemison, J. (2005). *Online exams: Embrace the opportunity, avoid the pitfalls*. Paper presented at the 2005 Educause Annual Conference. Retrieved June 3, 2007, from http://connect.educause.edu/blog/podcaster/e2005_podcast_online_exams/2027?time=1165945815

Hendricks, M., & Quinn, L. (2000). Teaching referencing as an introduction to epistemological empowerment. *Teaching in Higher Education, 5*(4), 447-457.

Her Majesty's Stationery Office (HMSO). (1995). *UK Disability Discrimination Act*. Retrieved June 12, 2007, from http://www.legislation.hmso.gov.uk/acts/acts1995/Ukpga_19950050_en_1.htm

Her Majesty's Stationery Office (HMSO). (2001). *UK Special Educational Needs and Disability Act*. Retrieved June 12, 2007, from http://www.legislation.hmso.gov.uk/acts/acts2001/20010010.htm

Herrington, J., & Oliver, R. (1995, December 4-6). *Critical characteristics of situated learning: Implications for instructional design of multimedia*. Paper presented at the Annual Conference of the Australasian Society for Computers in Learning in Tertiary Education (ASCLITE), Melbourne, Australia. Retrieved July 4, 2007, from http://www.ascilite.org.au/conferences/melbourne95/smtu/papers/herrington.pdf

Herrington, J., & Oliver, R. (2000). An instructional design framework for authentic learning environments. *Educational Technology Research and Development, 48*(3), 23-48.

*Hi-Caption™ software*. (n.d.). Retrieved June 12, 2007, from http://www.hisoftware.com/hmccflash/index.html

Hicks, O. (1997). Career paths of directors of academic staff development units in Australian universities: The emergence of a species? *The International Journal for Academic Development, 2*(2), 56-63.

Higgins, K., & O'Keeffe, D. (2004). *An online digital engineering module companion using biomedical applications*. Paper presented at the Fourth Annual Irish Educational Technology Users Conference, Waterford, Ireland.

Higher Education Funding Council for England (HEFCE). (2004). *Effective practice with e-learning: A good practice guide in designing for learning*. Retrieved March 10, 2007, from http://www.jisc.ac.uk/uploaded_documents/ACF5D0.pdf

Higher Education Funding Council for England. (1997). *The influence of neighbourhood type on participation in higher education* (Interim Report). Bristol, United Kingdom: Author.

Higher Education Funding Council for England. (2005). *January 2005/03 research report: Young participation in higher education*. Bristol, United Kingdom: Author. Retrieved from http://www.hefce.ac.uk/pubs/hefce/2005/05_03/05_03c.pdf

Higher Education Statistics Agency (HESA). (1994-2007). *First year UK domiciled HE students by qualifica-*

*tion aim, mode of study, gender and disability.* Retrieved June 12, 2007, from http://www.hesa.ac.uk

Hildreth, P., Kimble, C., & Wright, P. (2000). Communities of practice in the distributed international environment. *Journal of Knowledge Management, 4*(1), 27-37.

Hiltz, S. (1993). Correlates of learning in a virtual classroom. *International Journal of Man-Machine Studies, 39*, 71-98.

Hiltz, S. (1994). *The virtual classroom.* Norwood, NJ: Ablex Publishing Corporation.

Hiltz, S. R., & Goldman, R. (2005). *Learning together online: Research on asynchronous learning networks.* London: Lawrence Erlbaum.

Hinson, J., & LaPrairie, K. (2005). Learning to teach online: Promoting success through professional development. *Community College Journal of Research and Practice, 29*, 483-493.

Hmelo, C., & Evensen, D. (2000). Problem-based learning: Gaining insights on learning interactions through multiple methods of inquiry. In C. Hmelo & D. Evensen (Eds.), *Problem-based learning: A research perspective on learning interactions* (pp. 1-16). Mahwah, NJ: Lawrence Erlbaum.

Hmelo, C., & Evensen, D. (Eds.). (2000). *Problem-based learning: A research perspective on learning interactions.* Mahwah, NJ: Lawrence Erlbaum.

Hoare, S. (2001, March 6). Whip-hand. *Guardian Education,* p. 50.

Hodgson, A., & Spours, K. (2000, February 21). *Going to college or getting a job: Factors affecting attitudes to HE.* Paper presented at the Progression to Higher Education Working Seminar Series, London.

Holmes, B., & Gardner, J. (2006). *E-learning concepts and practice.* London: Sage Publications.

Holsgrove, G., & Elzubeir, M. (1998). Imprecise terms in UK medical multiple-choice questions: What examiners think they mean. *Medical Education, 32*(4), 343-350.

Hounsell, D. (1994). Educational development. In J. Bocok & D. Watson (Eds.), *Managing the university curriculum: Making common cause* (pp. 89-102). Buckingham, United Kingdom: Society for Research into Higher Education & Open University Press.

Hsieh, H., & Shannon, S. (2005). Three approaches to qualitative content analysis. *Qualitative Health Research, 15*(9), 1277-1288.

Hughes, G. (2007). Using blended learning to increase learner support and improve retention. *Teaching in Higher Education, 12*(3), 349-363.

Hwang, W., & Wang, C. (2004). A study of learning time patterns in asynchronous learning environments. *Journal of Computer Assisted Learning, 20*, 292-304.

IMS Global Learning Consortium. (2002). *IMS guidelines for developing accessible learning applications V.1.* Retrieved June 12, 2007, from http://www.imsglobal.org/accessibility/accessiblevers/index.html

IMS Global Learning Consortium. (2003). *IMS learner information package accessibility for LIP best practice and implementation guide Version 1.0 final specification.* Retrieved June 12, 2007, from http://www.imsglobal.org/accessibility/acclipv1p0/imsacclip_bestv1p0.html

IMS Global Learning Consortium. (2004). *IMS access for all meta-data overview, version 1.0 final specification.* Retrieved June 12, 2007, from http://www.imsglobal.org/accessibility/accmdv1p0/imsaccmd_oviewv1p0.html

Inglis, A., Ling, P., & Joosten, V. (1999). *Delivered digitally: Managing the transition to the knowledge media.* London: Kogan Page.

Institute for Learning. (2007). *CPD portal.* Retrieved April 2007 from http://www.ifl.ac.uk/cpd_portal/cpd_index.html

Institute of Electrical and Electronics Engineers (IEEE). (2002). *Draft standard for learning object metadata.* Retrieved November 4, 2006, from http://ltsc.ieee.org/wg12

Intrallect. (2004). *Learning objects repositories in UK universities: A survey.* Author.

*Intute Virtual Training Suite.* (2006). Retrieved February 14, 2006, from http://www.vts.rdn.ac.uk

Issroff, K., & Scanlon, E. (2002). Using technology in higher education: An activity theory perspective. *Journal of Computer Assisted Learning, 18*(1), 77-83.

Issroff, K., & Scanlon, E. (2005). Activity theory and higher education: Evaluating learning technologies. *Journal of Computer Assisted Learning, 21*, 430-439.

IUPUI Jump Start program prepares faculty to teach online. (2006, September 15). *Academic Leader.*

Ivanic, R., & Lea, M. (2006). New contexts, new challenges: The teaching of writing in UK higher education. In L. Ganobcsik-Williams (Ed.), *Teaching academic writing in UK higher education* (pp. 6-15). Basingstoke, United Kingdom: Palgrave Macmillan.

Jackson, P. (1968). *Life in classrooms.* Eastbourne, United Kingdom: Holt, Rinehart and Winston.

Jackson, P. (1971). The student's world. In M. Silberman (Ed.), *The experience of schooling* (pp. 76-84). Eastbourne, United Kingdom: Holt, Rinehart and Winston.

Jafari, A. (2004). The "sticky" eportfolio system: Tackling challenges and identifying attributes. *Educause Review, 39*(4), 38-48. Retrieved May 16, 2007, from http://www.educause.edu/apps/er/erm05/erm056.asp

Jakobsen, L. (2006). *What is the level of IT social services workers and what impact could this have on the implementation of the new electronically focused government social care initiatives?* Unpublished manuscript.

Jakobsen, L. (2007). *Evaluating the effectiveness of online training as a staff development tool.* Unpublished manuscript.

Janes, D. P. (2000). *Teaching online in a postgraduate certificate in technology-based distributed learning.* Paper presented to the International Online Tutoring Skills (OTiS) E-Workshop. Retrieved May 12, 2000, from http://otis.scotcit.ac.uk/casestudy/janes.doc

Jarvela, S., & Hakkinen, P. (2002). Web-based cases in teaching and learning: The quality of discussion and stage of perspective taking in asynchronous communication. *Interactive Learning Environments, 10*, 1-22.

Jarvenpaa, S., Knoll, K., & Leidner, D. (1998). Is anybody out there? Antecedents of trust in global virtual teams. *Journal of MIS, 14*, 29-38.

Jenkins, A., Healy, A., & Zetter, R. (2007). *Linking teaching and research in disciplines and departments.* Retrieved November 27, 2007, from http://www.heacademy.ac.uk/ourwork/research/teaching

Jenkins, M., Browne, T., & Walker, R. (2005). *VLE surveys: A longitudinal perspective between March 2001, March 2003 and March 2005 for higher education in the United Kingdom.* UCISA. Retrieved March 20, 2007, from http://www.ucisa.ac.uk/groups/tlig/vle/index_html

Jenkins, S. (2007). *UK television commercials 1955-1985. Martini: 1971.* Retrieved April 2007 from http://www.headington.org.uk/adverts/drinks_alcoholic.htm

Jennings, M. (2006, March). *SD9 teacher training transformation projects at National Institute of Adult Continuing Education.* Paper presented at the E-Guides Lead by Example national event, Birmingham, United Kingdom.

John, P., & Sutherland, R. (2005). Affordance, opportunity and the pedagogical implications of ICT. *Educational Review, 57*(4), 405-413.

Johnson, D. (2004). *Wadda I need that I ain't got? Courage is a technology skill.* Retrieved February 2007 from http://www.doug-johnson.com/handouts/courage.pdf

Johnson, G., & Howell, A. (2005). Attitude toward instructional technology following required vs. optional WebCT usage. *Journal of Technology and Teacher Education, 13*, 643-654.

Johnson, H. (2003). Product, process or pre-requisite? Information literacy as infrastructure for information networking. In *The new review of information networking* (pp. 2-20).

Johnson, M., Benbow, S. M., & Baldwin, R. C. (1999). An electronic patient record system and geriatric psychiatry: Considerations and implications. *Aging and Mental Health, 3*(3), 257-263.

Joint Information Systems Committee (JISC). (2005). *Study of environments to support eLearning in UK further and higher education.* Retrieved March 18, 2006, from http://www.jisc.ac.uk/uploaded_documents/eLearning_survey_2005.pdf

Joint Information Systems Committee. (2004). *Starting point: Definition of elearning.* Retrieved July 2007 from http://www.elearning.ac.uk/effprac/html/start_defin.htm

Jonassen, D. (1995). Supporting communities of learners with technology: A vision for integrating technology with learning in schools. *Educational Technology*, pp. 60-63.

Jonassen, D. (1996). *Computers in the classrooms: Mindtools for critical thinking.* Columbus, OH: Prentice Hall.

Jonassen, D. H. (1991). Objectivist vs. constructivist: Do we need a new philosophical paradigm? *Educational Technology Research and Development, 39*(3), 5-14.

Jonassen, D. H. (1996). *Computers in the classroom: Mindtools for critical thinking.* Columbus, OH: Merrill/Prentice-Hall.

Jonassen, D. H., & Grabowski, B. L. (1993). *Handbook of individual differences: Learning and instruction.* NJ: Lawrence Erlbaum Associates.

Jonassen, D., Mayes, T., & McAleese, R. (1993). A manifesto for a constructivist approach to uses of technology in higher education. In T. M. Duffy, J. Lowyck, & D. H. Jonassen, Designing *environments for constructive learning* (pp. 231-247).Berlin: Springer.

Jones, C. (2004). Networks and learning: Communities, practices and the metaphor of networks. *ALT-J, Research in Learning Technology, 12*(1), 81-93.

Jones, C., Turner, J., & Street, B. (Eds.). (1999). *Student writing in the university: Cultural and epistemological issues.* Amsterdam: John Benjamins.

Joy, E., & Garcia, F. (2000, June). Measuring learning effectiveness: A new look at no-significant-difference findings. *Journal of Asynchronous Learning Networks, 4*(1). Retrieved July 5, 2007, from http://www.sloan-c.org/publications/jaln/v4n1/pdf/v4n1_joygarcia.pdf

Joyes, G. (2002, June 7). *On-line learning and research methods: An ESCalate funded project.* Paper presented at the ESCalate Research Methods for Research Students Conference, London. Retrieved November 27, 2007, from http://www.escalate.ac.uk/diary/reports/7Junindex.php3

Joyes, G. (2006, June 7). *Generic e-learning materials: Exploring localisation and personalisation issues.* Paper presented at the Universitas 21 Elearning Conference, Guadalajara, Mexico. Retrieved March 11, 2007, from http://www.universitas21.com/elearning.html

Joyes, G. (2007). E-learning design for localisation and personalisation. *Malaysian Journal of Distance Education, 8*(2), 69-82.

Jung, I. (2005). Cost effectiveness of online teacher training. *Open Learning, 20*(2), 131-146.

Kamthan, P. (1999, March 7). *Java applets in education: Internet related technologies (IRT.ORG).* Retrieved April 1, 2007, from http://www.irt.org/articles/js151/index.com

Kamthan, P. (2007). On the prospects and concerns of integrating open source software environment in software engineering education. *Journal of Information Technology Education, 6*, 45-64.

Kandlbinder, P. (2000, July 2-5). *Peeking under the covers: Understanding the foundations of online academic staff development.* Paper presented at the Australian Society of Educational Technology & Higher Education Research & Development Society of Australasia Conference, Toowoomba, Australia.

Kanste, O. (2005). *Moniulotteinen hoitotyön johtajuus ja hoitohenkilöstön työuupumus terveydenhuollossa* [Multidimensional nursing leadership and burn-out among nurses in health care]. Unpublished doctoral dissertation, University of Oulu, Finland.

Compilation of References

Kanuka, H., & Anderson, T. (1998). Online social interchange, discord, and knowledge construction. *Journal of Distance Education, 13*(1), 57-74.

Kanuka, H., & Garrison, D. R. (2004). Cognitive presence in online learning. *Journal of Computing in Higher Education, 15*(2), 30-48.

Kappel, G., Pröll, B., Reich, S., & Retschitzegger, W. (2006). *Web engineering.* NJ: John Wiley and Sons.

Kearsley, G. (2000). *Online education: Learning and teaching in cyberspace.* Belmont, CA: Wadsworth/ Thomson Learning.

Keenan, C. (2005). *Stepping stones 2HE: Students working to bridge the transition gap.* Unpublished manuscript.

Keirsey, D. (1998). *Please understand me II.* Del Mar, CA: Prometheus Nemesis Book Company.

Kelly, D. (2000, August 18). Adventures on the cyber shop floor. *Times Higher Education Supplement.* Retrieved January 9, 2007, from http://www.thes.co.uk/search/story.aspx?story_id=63580

Kelly, D. (2002, July 1-4). *Being an online learner before becoming an online teacher: Ten lessons from experience.* Paper presented at the Improving University Learning and Teaching (IUT) Conference, Vilnius, Lithuania.

Kelly, P. (2006). What is teacher learning? A socio-cultural perspective. *Oxford Review of Education, 32*(4), 505-519.

Kezar, A. (2001). *Understanding and facilitating organisational change in the 21st century: Recent research and conceptualisations* (ASHE-ERIC Higher Education Report, Vol. 28, No. 4). San Francisco: Jossey Bass.

Kidney, G. (2004, June). When the cows come home: A proven path of professional development for faculty pursuing e-learning. *T.H.E. Journal, 31*(11). Retrieved July 3, 2007, from http://thejournal.com/articles/16803

Kim, K., & Bonk, C. (2006). The future of online teaching and learning in higher education: The survey says. *Educause Quarterly, 4,* 22-30. Retrieved January 10, 2007, from http://www.educause.edu/ir/library/pdf/EQM0644.pdf

King, F. (2002). A virtual student: Not an ordinary Joe. *The Internet and Higher Education, 5*(2), 157-166.

Kitzinger J. (1996). Introducing focus groups. In N. Mays & C. Pope (Eds.), *Qualitative research in health care* (pp. 36-45). London: B. M. J. Publishing Group.

Klemm, W. R., & Snell, J. R. (1996). Enriching computer-mediated group learning by coupling constructivism with collaborative learning. *Journal of Instructional Science and Technology.* Retrieved August 14, 2007, from http://www.usq.edu.au/electpub/e-jist/docs/old/vol1no2/article1.htm

Knapper, C. (2004, June 21-23). *University teaching and educational development: What have we achieved?* Keynote Presentation at the International Consortium for Educational Development Conference, Ottawa, Canada.

Knight, P. T. (2002). A systemic approach to professional development: Learning as practice. *Teaching and Teacher Education, 18*(3), 229-241.

Knightley, W. (2006). Tackling social exclusion through online learning: A preliminary investigation. *Journal of Access Policy and Practice, 4*(1), 20-38.

Knoll, K., & Jarvenpaa, S. (1995, January 3-6). Learning to work in distributed global teams. In *Proceedings of the 28th Hawaii Conference on Systems Sciences* (Vol. 4, pp. 92-101).

Kolb, D. (1984). *Experiential learning: Experience as the source of learning and development.* Englewood Cliffs, NJ.

Kolb, D. A. (1984). *Experiential learning.* NJ: Prentice Hall.

Kreijns, K., Kirschner, P., & Jochems, W. (2003). Identifying the pitfalls for social interaction in computer-supported collaborative learning environments: A review of the research. *Computers in Human Behaviour, 19*(3), 335-353.

Krug, S. (2006). *Don't make me think! A common sense approach to Web usability* (2nd ed.). Berkeley, CA: New Riders.

Ladousse, G. P. (1987). *Role play.* Oxford, United Kingdom: Oxford University Press.

Laing, C., Robinson, A., & Johnston, V. (2005). Managing the transition into higher education. *Active Learning in Higher Education, 6*(3), 243-255.

Lally, V., Timmis, S., Jones, C., & Banks, S. (2004) *E-research: Using multimedia for research methods teaching and learning. ESCalate project report.* Retrieved November 13, 2006, from http://escalate.ac.uk/1132

Land, R. (2004). *Educational development: Discourse, identity and practice.* Maidenhead, United Kingdom: Society for Research into Higher Education & Open University Press.

Land, S., & Hannafin, M. (2000). Student-centred learning environments. In D. H. Jonassen & S. M. Land (Eds.), *Theoretical foundations of learning environments* (pp. 1-23). Mahwah, NJ: Lawrence Erlbaum.

Lankshear, C., & Knobel, M. (2003). *New literacies: Changing knowledge and classroom learning.* Maidenhead, United Kingdom: Open University Press.

Lapadat, J. (2002). Written interaction: A key component in online learning. *Journal of Computer-Mediated Communication, 7*(4). Retrieved September 1, 2007, from http://jcmc.indiana.edu/vol7/issue4/lapadat.html.

Laurillard, D. (1993). *Rethinking university teaching: A framework for the effective use of educational technology.* London: Routledge.

Laurillard, D. (1994). How can learning technologies improve learning? *Law Technology Journal, 3*(2). Retrieved March 10, 2007, from http://www.law.warwick.ac.uk/ltj/3-2j.html

Laurillard, D. (2001). *Rethinking university teaching: A framework for the effective use of educational technology.* London: Routledge.

Laurillard, D. (2002). *Rethinking university teaching: A conversational framework for the effective use of learning technologies* (2nd ed.). London: Routledge Falmer.

Laurillard, D. (2006). *Kaleidoscope: A scientific vision.* Retrieved March 11, 2007, from http://www.noe-kaleidoscope.org/public/pub/lastnews/images/kal_vision.pdf

Laurillard, D., Swift, B., & Darby, J. (1992). Probing the not invented here syndrome. *The CTISS File, 14.*

Lave, J., & Wenger, E. (1991). *Situated learning: Legitimate peripheral participation.* Cambridge, United Kingdom: Cambridge University Press.

Le@rning Federation. (2007). *The Le@rning Federation accessibility specification V2.1.* Retrieved June 12, 2007, from http://www.thelearningfederation.edu.au/tlf2/sitefiles/assets/docs/specifications/Accessibility_Specification_V2.1.pdf

Lea, M. (2004). Academic literacies: A pedagogy for course design. *Studies in Higher Education, 29*(6), 739-756.

Lea, M., & Street, B. (1998). Student writing in higher education: An academic literacies approach. *Studies in Higher Education, 11*(3), 182-199.

Learning and Skills Network. (2007). *A professional development framework for e-learning.* Gillingham, United Kingdom: Impress.

Learning and Skills Network. (2007). *Effective teaching transforming teacher training through elearning.* London: Author.

Leidner, D., & Jarvenpaa, S. (1995). The use of information technology to enhance management school education: A theoretical view. *MIS Quarterly, 19*(3), 265-292.

Lessig, L. (2004). *Free culture: How big media uses technology and the law to lock down culture and control creativity.* New York: The Penguin Press.

Lethbridge, T. C. (1998). The relevance of software education: A survey and some recommendations. *Annals of Software Engineering, 6*(1-4), 91-110.

Lethbridge, T. C. (2000a). Priorities for the education and training of software engineers. *Journal of Systems and Software, 53*(1), 53-71.

Lethbridge, T. C. (2000b). What knowledge is important to a software engineer? *Computer, 33*(5), 44-50.

Levin, J., Kim, H., & Riel, M. (1990). Analyzing instructional interactions on electronic message networks. In L. Harasim (Ed.), *Online education: Perspectives on a new environment* (pp. 185-214). New York: Praeger.

Levy, P. (2007). Exploring and developing excellence: Towards a community of praxis. In A. Skelton (Ed.), *International perspectives on teaching excellence in higher education*. Routledge.

Lewin, C., Mavers, D., & Somekh, B. (2003). Broadening access to the curriculum through using technology to link home and school: A critical analysis of reforms intended to improve students' educational attainment. *The Curriculum Journal, 14*(1), 23-53.

Lewis, C. (2002). Driving factors for e-learning: An organisational perspective. *Perspectives: Policy and Practice in Higher Education, 6*(2), 50-54.

Lifelong Learning Sector Skills Council. (2005). *E-learning standards*. Retrieved July 2007 from http://www.lifelonglearninguk.org/documents/standards/e_learning.pdf

Lillis, T. (2001). *Student writing*. London: Routledge.

Lillis, T. (2006). Moving towards an "academic literacies" pedagogy: Dialogues of participation. In L. Ganobcsik-Williams (Ed.), *Teaching academic writing in UK higher education* (pp. 30-45). Basingstoke, United Kingdom: Palgrave Macmillan.

Lim, B. (2004).Challenges and issues in designing inquiry on the Web. *British Journal of Educational Technology, 35*(5), 627–643.

Ling, L. H. (2007). Community of inquiry in an online undergraduate information technology course. *Journal of Information Technology Education, 6*, 153-168.

Linser, R., & Ip, A. (2002, October 15-19). *Beyond the current e-learning paradigm: Applications of role play simulations (RPS). Case studies.* Paper presented at E-Learn 2002, AACE Conference, Montreal, Canada. Retrieved July 17, 2007, from http://www.simplay.net/papers/E-Learning.html

Lipman, M. (1991). *Thinking in education*. Cambridge: Cambridge University Press.

Lipponen, L., & Lallimo, J. (2004). From collaborative technology to collaborative use of technology: Designing learning oriented infrastructures. *Educational Media International, 41*(2), 111-116.

Littlejohn, A. (2005). Key issues in the design and delivery of technology-enhanced learning. In P. Levy & S. Roberts (Eds.), *Developing the new learning environment: The changing role of the academic librarian* (pp. 70-90). London: Facet Publishing.

Littlejohn, A., & Pegler, C. (2007). *Preparing for blended learning*. New York: Routledge.

Liu, M., Papathanasiou, E., & Hao, Y. (2001). Exploring the use of multimedia examination formats in undergraduate teaching: Results from the fielding testing. *Computers in Human Behaviour, 17*(3), 225-248.

Ljoså, E. (1998). The role of university teachers in a digital era. *European Journal of Open, Distance and ELearning*. Retrieved May 5, 2007, from http://www.eurodl.org/materials/contrib/1998/eden98/Ljosa.html

Lokken, F., & Womer, L. (2007). *Trends in e-learning: Tracking the impact of e-learning in higher education*. Washington, DC: Instructional Technology Council. Retrieved July 7, 2007, from http://www.itcnetwork.org/Trends_in_Elearning_2006.pdf

Lorensen, M., Sinkkonen, S., Lichtenberg, A., Jensdotir, A. B., Hamran, G., Johansson, B., et al. (2001). *Knowledge and skill requirements for nurse leaders in the primary health care service6s in the Nordic countries*. Oslo, Norway: Det Medisinske Fakultet, Institutt for sykepleievitenskap, Universitetet i Oslo.

Lusty, S. (1969). Educational technology. *Peabody Journal of Education, 47*(1), 53-56.

Lynch, K. L., & O'Riordan, K. (1998). Inequality in higher education: A study of class barriers. *British Journal of Sociology, 19*(4), 445-478.

Mace, R. (1997). *The principles of universal design.* Retrieved June 12, 2007, from http://www.design.ncsu. edu/cud/about_ud/udprinciplestext.htm

MacKinnon, D., & Manathunga, C. (2003). Going global with assessment: What to do when the dominant culture's literacy drives assessment. *Higher Education Research & Development, 22*(2), 131-144.

Mainka, C. (2007). Putting staff first in staff development for the effective use of technology in teaching. *British Journal of Educational Technology, 38*(1), 158-160.

Manathunga, C. (2002). Designing online modules: An Australian example in teacher education. *International Journal of Instructional Media, 29*(2), 185-195.

Mann, S. (2001). Alternative perspectives on the student experience: Alienation and engagement. *Studies in Higher Education, 26*(1), 7-19.

Martin, A. J., Jones, E. S., & Callan, V. J. (2005). The role of the psychological climate in facilitating employee adjustment during organizational change. *European Journal of Work and Organizational Psychology, 14*(3), 263-289.

Mason, R. (1991). Moderating educational computer conferencing. *DEOSNEWS, 1*(19). Retrieved October 25, 2007, from http://www.emoderators.com/papers/mason.html

Mason, R. (1998). *Globalising education: Trends and applications.* London: Routledge.

Mason, R. (2001). The Open University experience. In J. Stephenson (Ed.), *Teaching and learning online: Pedagogies for new technologies* (pp. 67-75). London: Kogan Page.

Matheos, K., Daniel, K., & McCalla, G. I. (2005). Dimensions for blended learning technology: Learners' perspectives. *Journal of Learning Design, 1*(1), 56-76. Retrieved August 10, 2007, from https://olt.qut.edu.au/udf/jld/index.cfm?fa=displayPage&rNum=1780740

Matheson, D. (1992). *Post-compulsory education in Suisse Romande.* Unpublished doctoral dissertation, University of Glasgow, Glasgow, United Kingdom.

Maxwell, W. E., & Kazlauskas, E. J. (1992). Which faculty development methods really work in community colleges? A review of research. *Community/Junior College Quarterly, 16*, 351-360.

Mayer, R., & Moreno, R. (2003). Nine ways to reduce cognitive load in multimedia learning. *Educational Psychologist, 38*(1), 43-52.

Maykut, P., & Morehouse, R. (1994). *Beginning qualitative research: A philosophic and practical guide.* London: Falmer Press.

McAlpine, L., & Emrick, A. (2003, August 26-30). *Discipline-based curriculum development: An opportunity for sustainable collegial faculty development.* Paper Presented at the 10th Biennial Conference of European Association for Research on Learning and Instruction, Padova, Italy.

McAlpine, L., & Gandell, T. (2003). Teaching improvement grants: What they tell us about professors' instructional choices for the use of technology in higher education. *British Journal of Educational Technology, 34*(3), 281-293.

McAlpine, M. (2002). *A summary of methods of item analysis.* Luton, United Kingdom: CAA Centre.

McBride, A. B. (2005). Nursing and the informatics revolution. *Nursing Outlook, 53*, 183-191.

McConnell, D. (2000). *Implementing computer supported co-operative learning* (2nd ed.). London: Kogan Page.

McConnell, D. (2005). Examining the dynamics of networked e-learning groups and communities. *Studies in Higher Education, 30*(1), 25-42.

McCredie, J. W. (2000). Planning for IT in Higher Education: It's not an oxymoron. *Educause Quarterly, 23*(4), 14-21.

McFarlane, A., Sparrowhawk, A., & Heald, Y. (2002). *Report on the educational use of games.* Teachers Evaluating Educational Multimedia. Retrieved June 12, 2007, from http://www.teem.org.uk/publications/teem_games-ined_full.pdf

McFarlane, L., & McLean, J. (2003). Education and training for direct care workers. *Social Work Education, 22*(4), 385-399.

McInnis, C. (2001). Researching the first year experience: Where to from here? *Higher Education Research & Development, 20*(2), 105-114.

McKeachie, W. (1996). *The professional evaluation of teaching* (Paper No. 33). American Council of Learned Societies. Retrieved May 14, 2007, from http://www.acls.org/op33.htm#McKeachie

McKenna, P. (2004). *Change your life in 7 days.* London: Bantam Press.

McKlin, T., Harmon, S., Evans, W., & Jones, M. (2001). Cognitive presence in web-based learning: *A content analysis of student's online discussion.* IT Forum, 60, Retrieved May 10, 2006, from http://eric.ed.gov/ERICDocs/data/ericdocs2sql/content_storage_01/0000019b/80/1a/86/0b.pdf.

McLaughlan, R. G. (2004). Using online role-play/simulations for creating learning experiences. *CAL-laborate, 7.* Retrieved August 14, 2007, from http://science.uniserve.edu.au/pubs/callab/vol7/mclaugh.html

McLuhan, M. (1964). *Understanding media: The extensions of man.* London: Routledge & Kegan Paul Ltd.

McMahon, M. (1997, December). *Social constructivism and the World Wide Web: A paradigm for learning.* Paper presented at the Australian Society for Computers in Learning and in Tertiary Education Conference, Perth, Australia. Retrieved May 2, 2007, from http://www.ascilite.org.au/conferences/perth97/papers/Mcmahon/Mcmahon.html

McMullin, B. (2005). Putting the learning back into learning technology. In G. O'Neill, S. Moore, & B. McMullin (Eds.), *Emerging issues in the practice of university learning and teaching* (pp. 67-76). Dublin: AISHE.

McNaught, C. (2000). Technology: The challenge of change. In R. King, D. Hill, & B. Hemmings (Eds.), *University and diversity* (pp. 88-102). Wagga Wagga, Australia: Keon Publications.

McPherson, M., & Nunes, M. B. (2004). *Developing innovation in online learning: An action research framework.* London: Routledge Falmer.

McShane, K. (2004). Integrating face to face and online teaching: Academics' role concept and teaching choices. *Teaching in Higher Education, 9*(1), 3-16.

McWilliam, E. (2002). Against professional development. *Educational Philosophy and Theory, 34*(3), 289-299.

*Media Access Generator (MAGpie) software.* (n.d.). Retrieved June 12, 2007, from http://ncam.wgbh.org/webaccess/magpie

Mercer, N. (1995). *The guided construction of knowledge.* Clevedon, United Kingdom: Multilingual Matters Ltd.

Mering, J., & Robbie, D. (2005, July 4-7). *Education and electronic learning: Does online learning assist learners and how can it be continuously improved?* Paper presented at the HERDSA Conference, Miri, Malaysia.

Metcalf, H. (1997). *Class and higher education: The participation of young people from lower social classes.* London: Council for Industry and Higher Education.

Metcalf, H. (2003). Increasing inequality in higher education: The role of term-time working. *Oxford Review of Education, 29*(3), 315-329.

Meyer, K. (2003). Face-to-face versus threaded discussions: The role of time and higher-order thinking. *Journal of Asynchronous Learning Networks, 7.* Retrieved April 20, 2007, from http://www.sloan-c.org/publications/jaln/v7n3/index.asp

Meyer, K. A. (2003). Face-to-face versus threaded discussions: The role of time and higher-order thinking. *Journal of Asynchronous Learning Networks, 7*(3), 55-65.

Middlehurst, R. (2002). Variations on a theme: Complexity and choice in a world of borderless education. *Journal of Studies in International Education, 6*(2), 134-155.

Middlehurst, R., & Woodfield, S. (2007). *Responding to the internationalization agenda: implications for institutional policy and practice.* Retrieved June 10, 2007, from http://www.heacademy.ac.uk

Miers, M., Clarke, B., Lapthorn, C., Pollard, K., Thomas, J., & Turtle, A. (2005). *Learning together on-line: Student and staff experience of interprofessional on-line groups.* Centre for Learning and Workforce Research in Health and Social Care, University of West of England. Retrieved June 25, 2007, from http://hsc.uwe.ac.uk/hsc/pdf/research/learning_together_online.pdf

Milliken, J., & Barnes, L. (2002). Teaching and technology in higher education: Student perceptions and personal reflections. *Computers & Education, 39*(3), 223-235.

Mirabella, V., Kimani, S., Gabrielli, S., & Catarci, T. (2004). Accessible e-learning material: A no-frills avenue for didactical experts. *The New Review of Hypermedia and Multimedia, 10*(2), 1-16.

Moallem, M. (2001). Applying constructivist and objectivist learning theories in the design of a Web-based course: Implications for practice. *Journal of Educational Technology and Society, 4*(3), 113-125.

Molesworth, M. (2004). Collaboration, reflection and selective neglect: Campus-based marketing students' experiences of using a virtual learning environment. *Innovations in Education and Training International, 41*(1), 79-92.

Monteith, M., & Smith, J. (2001). Learning in a virtual campus: The pedagogic implications of students' experiences. *Innovations in Education and Teaching International, 38*(2), 302-311.

Montgomery, S. (1995, November 1-4). Addressing diverse learning styles through the use of multimedia. In *Engineering Education for the 21st Century: Proceedings of the 25th Annual Frontiers in Education Conference* (pp. 3a2.13-3a2.21). Atlanta, GA.

Moon, J. (1999). *Reflection in learning and professional development.* London: Kogan Page.

Moore, M. G., Shattuck, K., & Al-Harthi, A. (2005). Cultures meeting cultures in online distance education. *Journal of E-Learning and Knowledge Society, 1*(2), 187-208.

Morgan, D. L. (1996). Focus groups. *Annual Review of Sociology, 22,* 129-152.

Morris, L. (2007, August 30-31). *Pick and mix: Getting the blend right.* Paper presented at the Annual Variety in Chemistry Education Conference, Leicester, United Kingdom.

Moses, I. (1987). Educational development units: A cross-cultural perspective. *Higher Education, 16,* 449-479.

Moule, P. (2006). E-learning for healthcare students: *Developing the communities of practice framework. 54*(3), 370-380.

Moule, P. (2007). Challenging the five-stage model for e-learning: A new approach. *ALT-J, Research in Learning Technology, 15*(1), 37-50.

Moursund, D. (1997). *The future of information technology in education.* Washington, DC: The International Society for Technology in Education.

Mundle, D. (2001, May 15). *Using XML for software process documents.* Paper presented at the International Workshop on XML Technologies and Software Engineering (XSE 2001), Toronto, Canada.

Munro, M., & Walsh, E. (2005, May 26-27). *Online tutors as online students: Preparing tutors to teach online.* Paper presented at the Sixth Annual Irish Educational Technology Users' Conference, Dublin, Ireland. Retrieved March 2, 2006, from http://ilta.learnonline.ie/course/view.php?id=18

Naidu, S., Ip, A., & Linser, R. (2000). Dynamic goal-based role play simulation on the Web: A case study. *Educational Technology & Society, 3*(3), 190-202.

Nam, C. S., & Smith-Jackson, T. L. (2007). Web-based learning environment: A theory-based design process for development and evaluation. *Journal of Information Technology Education, 6,* 23-43.

National Audit Office. (2002). *Improving student achievement in English higher education: Report by the Comptroller and Auditor General, HC 486.* London: The Stationery Office.

National Institute for Adult Continuing Education. (2004). *E-guides: Lead by example.* Leicester, United Kingdom: Author.

National Statistics Online. (2006). *Internet access.* Retrieved May 2007 from http://www.ststistics.gov.uk/CCI/nugget.asp?ID=8&Pos=&ColRank=1&Rank=374

Nicholl, H., & Higgins, A. (2004).Reflection in pre-registration nursing curricula. *Journal of Advanced Nursing, 46*(6), 578-585.

Nielsen, J. (2005). *Ten usability heuristics.* Retrieved May 20, 2007, from http://www.useit.com/papers/heuristic/heuristic_list.html

Nisbet, J., & Shucksmith, J. (1986). *Learning strategies.* London: Routledge.

Nixon, T., & Salmon, G. (1995, December 12-14). *Spinning your Web: Interactive computer-mediated conferencing its potential for learning and teaching in higher education.* Paper presented at the Society for Research into Higher Education Annual Conference, Edinburgh, United Kingdom.

Noel-Levitz, Inc. (2006). *National online learners' priorities report.* Iowa City, IA: Author.

North Carolina State University. (n.d.). *Profile of Ron Mace.* Retrieved May 16, 2007, from http://ncsudesign.org/content/index.cfm/fuseaction/alum_profile/departmentID/1/startRow/4

Northedge, A. (2003). Enabling participation in academic discourse. *Teaching in Higher Education, 8*(2), 169-180.

Nunes, M. B., & McPherson, M. (2003, July 9-11). *Constructivism vs. objectivism: Where is difference for designers of e-learning environments?* Paper presented at the Third IEEE International Conference on Advanced Learning Technologies (ICALT 2003), Athens, Greece.

O'Banion, T. (1997). *A learning college for the 21^st century.* Washington, DC: American Association of Community Colleges.

O'Neill, K., Singh, G., & O'Donoghue, J. (2004). Implementing elearning programmes for higher education: A review of the literature. *Journal of Information Technology Education, 3,* 313-323.

O'Reilly, M., & Brown, J. (2001). *Staff development by immersion in interactive learning online.* Lismore, Australia: Southern Cross University. Retrieved July 7, 2007, from http://ausweb.scu.edu.au/aw01/papers/refereed/o_reilly/paper.html

O'Reilly, T. (2005). *What is Web 2.0: Design patterns and business models for the next generation of software.* O'Reilly Network, September 30, 2005.

Oblinger, D. (2006, September 5-7). *Listening to what we're seeing.* Keynote Presentation at ALT-C, Edinburgh, United Kingdom.

Oblinger, D. (2006, September 5-7). *Listening to what we're seeing.* Keynote speech at the 2006 ALT-C Conference, Edinburgh, United Kingdom.

Oblinger, D., & Oblinger, J. (2005). Is it age or IT: First steps towards understanding the Net generation. In D. Oblinger & J. Oblinger (Eds.), *Educating the Net generation.* Boulder, CO: Educause. Retrieved March 19, 2007, from http://www.educause.edu/content.asp?page_id=6058&bhcp=1

Oblinger, D., & Oblinger, J. (Eds.). (2005). *Educating the Net generation.* Educause.

Office for National Statistics. (2006). *Internet access.* London: Author. Retrieved May 18, 2007, from http://www.statistics.gov.uk/CCI/nugget.asp?ID=8

Office of Population and Census Survey. (1993). *1991 census household composition in Great Britain.* London: HMSO.

Olaniran, B. A., Savage, G. T., & Sorenson, R. L. (1996). Experimental and experiential approaches to teaching face-to-face and computer-mediated group discussion. *Communication Education, 45*(3), 244-259.

Oliver, M. (2000). An introduction to the evaluation of learning technology. *Educational Technology & Society, 3*(4), 20-30.

Oliver, M. (2002). What do learning technologists do? *Innovations in Education and Teaching International, 39*(4), 245-252.

Oliver, M., & Trigwell, K. (2005). Can "blended learning" be redeemed? *E-Learning, 2*(1), 17-26.

Oliver, R. (2001). Developing online learning environments that support knowledge construction. In S. Stoney & J. Burns (Eds.), *Working for excellence in the e-conomy* (pp. 407-416). Churchlands, Australia: We-B Centre. Retrieved April 10, 2007, from http://elrond.scam.ecu.edu.au/oliver/2001/webepaper.pdf

Olson, B. L., & McDonald, J. L. (2004). Influence of online formative assessment upon student learning in biomedical science courses. *Journal of Dental Education, 68*(6), 656-659.

Olson, D. R. (1995). Conceptualizing the written word: An intellectual autobiography. *Written Communication, 12*(3), 277–297.

Osborne, R. (1999, February 9). *The institutional distribution of young people from low income groups.* Address to a Joint Meeting of the Quantitative Studies and Access Network and SRHE, London.

Owen, S., & Besley, S. (2006). *Funding policy watch: FE funding. 2007/08.* Retrieved August 2007 from http://www.edexcel.org.uk/VirtualContent/93790/Funding_Policy_Watch_2006_2_FE_Funding___2007_081.pdf

Oxford Brookes University Centre for E-Learning (OBU C4eL). (2005). *E-learning strategy 2005-2008: Embedding e-learning.* Retrieved August 21, 2007, from http://mw.brookes.ac.uk/download/attachments/1900739/Appendix+2-5+e-L+Strategy+2005-08+post+consultation+vers51.pdf?version=1

Ozga, J., & Sukhnandan, L. (1998). Undergraduate non-completion: Developing an explanatory model. *Higher Education Quarterly, 52*(3), 316-333.

Paas, F., Renkl, A., & Sweller, J. (2003). Cognitive load theory and instructional design: Recent developments. *Educational Psychologist, 38*(1), 1-4.

Page, A., & Donovan, K. (2005). *Elearning: A workbook for adult community learning.* Leicester, United Kingdom: National Institute of Adult Continuing Education.

Paget T. (2001). Reflective practice and clinical outcomes: Practitioners' views on how reflective practice has influenced their clinical practice. *Journal of Clinical Nursing, 10*(2), 204-214.

Palloff, R. M., & Pratt, K. (2005). *Collaborating online: Learning together in community.* San Francisco: Jossey-Bass.

Palloff, R., & Pratt, K. (2000). *Making the transition: Helping teachers to teach online.* Paper presented at EDUCAUSE: Thinking it through. Nashville, TN. Retrieved September 1, 2007, from http://168.144.129.112/Articles/Helping%20Teachers%20to%20Teach%20Online.pdf.

Palmer, B., & Major, C. (2004). Learning leadership through collaboration: The intersection of leadership and group dynamics in problem-based learning. In M. Savin-Baden & K. Wilkie (Eds.), *Challenging research in problem-based learning* (pp. 120-132). Maidenhead, United Kingdom: Open University Press.

Palmer, S. (2002). Enquiry-based learning can maximise a student's potential. *Psychology, Learning and Teaching, 2*(2), 82-86. Retrieved April 18, 2007, from http://www.psychology.heacademy.ac.uk/docs/pdf/p20030617_22palmer.pdf

Panda, S., & Juwah, C. (2006). Professional development of online facilitators in enhancing interactions and engagement: A framework. In C. Juwah (Ed.), *Interactions in online education: Implications for theory and practice* (pp. 207-227). London: Routledge.

Paradales, M., & Girod, M. (2006). Community of inquiry: Its past and present future. *Educational Philosophy and Theory, 38*(3), 299-309.

Parnas, D. L. (1999). Software engineering programs are not computer science programs. *IEEE Software, 16*(6), 19-30.

Parry, G. (1997). Patterns of participation in higher education in England: A statistical summary and commentary. *Higher Education Quarterly, 51*(1), 6-28.

Parsons, J., & Fostert, K. D. (2000). Using the Internet to build realism in teaching requirements analysis. *Journal of Information Systems Education, 11*(3-4), 141-145.

Patterson, D. A. (2005). Restoring the popularity of computer science. *Communications of the ACM, 48*(9), 25-28.

Paukkala, M., Pelkonen, M., Olkkonen, A., Jaroma, A., & Tossavainen, K. (2001). Hoitotyön johtamiskoulutus: Haasteena muuttuva toimintaympäristö ja uudet osaamisvaatimukset [Innovative approaches in education to improve modern nursing leadership and management skills]. *Sairaanhoitaja, 74*(4), 26-29.

Pavey, J. (2003). *Collaborating with communities.* Retrieved July 14, 2007, from http://www.heacademy.ac.uk/resources/detail/id216_leap_casestudy14_pavey

Pawan, F., Paulus, T., Yalcin, S., & Chang, C. (2003). Online learning: Patterns of engagement and interaction among in-service teachers. *Language, Learning and Technology, 7*(3), 119-140.

Pennington, G., & O'Neill, M. (1994). Enhancing the quality of teaching and learning in higher education. *Quality Assurance in Education, 2*(3), 13-18.

Perkins, D. N. (1993). Person plus: A distributed view of thinking and learning. In G. Salomon (Ed.), *Distributed cognitions: Psychological and educational considerations* (pp. 88-110). Cambridge, United Kingdom: Cambridge University Press.

Perry, B., & Edwards, R. N. (2005). Exemplary online educators: Creating a community of inquiry. *Turkish Online Journal of Distance Education, 6* (2). Retrieved May 12, 2006, from http://tojde.anadolu.edu.tr/tojde18/articles/article6.htm.

Peterson, D. (1992). *Life in a crowded place: Making a learning community.* Portsmouth: Heinemann Educational Books.

Phillips, R. (1998, February 4-5). *Models of learning appropriate to educational applications of information technology.* Paper presented at the Seventh Annual Teaching Learning Forum, Perth, Australia.

Phipps, R. (2000). *What's the difference?* Washington, DC: The Institute for Higher Education Policy.

Poikela, E., & Nummenmaa, A. R. (2006). Introduction. In E. Poikela & A. R. Nummenmaa (Eds.), *Understanding problem-based learning* (pp. 9-10). Tampere, Finland: Tampere University Press.

Poikela, E., & Poikela, S. (2006a). Learning and knowing at work: Professional growth as a tutor. In E. Poikela & A. R. Nummenmaa (Eds.), *Understanding problem-based learning* (pp. 183-207). Tampere, Finland: Tampere University Press.

Poikela, E., & Poikela, S. (2006b). Problem-based curricula: Theory, development and design. In E. Poikela & A. R. Nummenmaa (Eds.), *Understanding problem-based learning* (pp. 71-90). Tampere, Finland: Tampere University Press.

Portimojärvi, T. (2006). Synchronous and asynchronous communication in online PBL. In E. Poikela & A. R. Nummenmaa (Eds.), *Understanding problem-based learning* (pp. 91-104). Tampere, Finland: Tampere University Press.

Portimojärvi, T. (Forthcoming). *Ongelmaperustainen oppiminen verkossa* [Problem-based learning networked]. Unpublished doctoral dissertation, Tampereen Yliopisto, Finland.

*Possajennikov, A. (2005). Using formative assessment and role-playing as means of enhancing learning.* Retrieved July 14, 2007, from http://www.nottingham.ac.uk/teaching/resources/methods/assessment/usingfor316

Powell, S., & Green, H. (Eds.). (2007). *The doctorate worldwide.* Maidenhead, United Kingdom: Oxford University Press & Society for Research into Higher Education.

Pratt, N. (2006). Interactive teaching in numeracy lessons: What do children have to say? *Cambridge Journal of Education, 36*(2), 221-235.

Pratt, N. (2008). Multi-point e-conferencing with initial teacher training students in England: Pitfalls and potential. *Teaching and Teacher Education, 24*(6), 1476-1486.

Preece, J. (2000). *Online communities: Designing usability, supporting sociability.* Chichester, United Kingdom: John Wiley & Sons.

Prensky, M. (2001). *Digital game-based learning.* New York: McGraw-Hill.

Prensky, M. (2001a). Digital natives, digital immigrants. *On the Horizon, 9*(5).

Prensky, M. (2001b). Digital natives, digital immigrants: Part II. Do they really think differently? *On the Horizon, 9*(6).

Price, S., & Oliver, M. (2007). A framework for conceptualising the impact of technology on learning and teaching. *Journal of Educational Technology and Society, 10*(1), 16-27.

Privateer, P. M. (1999). Academic technology and the future of higher education: *Strategic paths taken and not taken. The Journal of Higher Education, 70*(1), 60-79.

Quinney, A. (2005). "Placements online": Student experiences of a Website to support learning in practice settings. *Social Work Education, 24*(4), 439-450.

Ramsden, P. (1992). *Learning to teach in higher education.* London: Routledge.

Ramsden, P. (2003). *Learning to teach in higher education* (2nd ed.). London: Routledge Falmer.

Reay, D. (1998). "Always knowing" and "never being sure": Familial and institutional habituses and higher education choice. *Journal of Education Policy, 13*(4), 519-529.

Redmond, B. (2004). *Reflection in action: Developing reflective practice in health and social services.* Aldershot: Ashgate Publishing.

Regan, B. (2005). *Best practices for accessible Flash design.* Retrieved June 12, 2007, from http://www. adobe.com/resources/accessibility/best_practices/ bp_fp.html

Reilly, C. (2005). Teaching by example: A case for peer workshops about pedagogy and technology. *Innovate, 1*(3). Retrieved May 22, 2007, from http://www.innovateonline.info/index.php?view=article&id=15

Reload. (2006). *Reload project.* Retrieved June 2007 from http://www.reload.ac.uk

Renzi, S., & Klobas, J. (2000). First steps toward computer-supported collaborative learning in large classrooms. *Educational Technology & Society, 3*(3), 317-328.

Rezaei, S. (2005, May 5-6). *Software engineering education in Canada.* Paper presented at the Western Canadian Conference on Computing Education (WCCCE 2005), Prince George, Canada.

Richardson, W. (2006). The new face of learning: What happens to time-worn concepts of classrooms and teaching when we can now go online and learn anything, anywhere, anytime? *Edutopia*, pp. 34-37. Retrieved February 2007 from http://www.edutopia.org/1648

Riley, L., & Smith, G. (1997). Developing and implementing IS: A case study analysis in social services. *Journal of Information Technology, 12*, 305-321.

Robbins. (1963). *Higher education: Report of the Committee on Higher Education under the Chairmanship of Lord Robbins.* London: HMSO.

Roberts, L. (1995). *A template for converting classrooms to distributed, asynchronous courses.* Retrieved February 4, 2006, from http://ww.unc.edu/cit/iat-archive/publications/roberts/template.html

Robins, K., & Webster, F. (1989). *The technical fix: Education, computers, and industry.* Basingstoke: Macmillan.

Robson, C. (1993). *Real world research: A resource for social scientists and practitioner-researchers.* London: Blackwell.

Rodger, S., & Brown, T. (2000). Enhancing graduate supervision in occupational therapy education through alternative delivery. *Occupational Therapy International, 7*(3), 163-172.

Rogers, D. L. (2000). A paradigm shift: Technology integration for higher education in the new millennium. *Educational Technology Review, 1*(13), 19-33.

Rogoff, B., Matusov, E., & White, C. (1996). Models of teaching and learning: Participation in a community of learners. In D. R. Olson & N. Torrance (Eds.) *The handbook of education and human development* (pp. 388-413). Oxford: Blackwell.

Rooney, J. (2003). Blending learning opportunities to enhance educational programming and meetings. *Association Management, 55*(5), 26-32.

Rosenberg, M. J. (2001). *E-learning strategies for delivering knowledge in the digital age.* New York: McGraw-Hill.

Ross, B. (1997). Towards a framework for problem-based curricula. In D. Boud & G. Feletti (Eds.), *The challenge of problem based learning* (pp. 28-35). London: Kogan Page.

Rothery, A., Dorup, J., & Cadewener, B. (2006). *EUNIS ELearning snapshots.* Retrieved March 10, 2007, from http://www.au.dk/elearning/ikt/publikationer/eunise-learningsnapshots.pdf

Rourke, L., & Anderson, T. (2002). Using peer teams to lead online discussions. *Journal of Interactive Media in Education, 1.* Retrieved September 1, 2007, from http://www-jime.open.ac.uk/2002/1/rourke-anderson-02-1.pdf.

Rourke, L., Anderson, T., Garrison, D., & Archer, W. (2001). Assessing social presence in asynchronous, text-based computer conferencing. *Journal of Distance Education, 14*(2), 51-70.

Rovai, A. (2002). Sense of community, perceived cognitive learning, and persistence in asynchronous learning networks. *Internet and Higher Education, 5,* 319-332.

Rovai, A. P. (2000). Building and sustaining community in asynchronous learning networks. *The Internet and Higher Education, 3*(4), 285-297.

Rovai, A. P., & Jordan, H. M. (2004). Blended learning and sense of community: A comparative analysis with traditional and fully online graduate courses. *International Review of Research in Open and Distance Learning, 5*(2), 1-13.

Rowntree, D. (1995). *The tutor's role in teaching via computer conferencing.* Retrieved August 21, 2007, from http://www.iet.open.ac.uk/pp/D.G.F.Rowntree/Supporting%20online.htm

Roy, M. H., & Elfner, E. (2002). Analyzing student satisfaction with instructional technology techniques. *Industrial and Commercial Training, 34*(7), 272-277.

Russell, T. (1999). *The no significant difference phenomenon.* Chapel Hill, NC: Office of Instructional Telecommunications, North Carolina State University.

Rust, C. (2002). The impact of assessment on student learning: How can the research literature practically help to inform the development of departmental assessment strategies and learner-centred assessment practices? *Active Learning in Higher Education, 3*(2), 145-158.

Ruth, S. (1997). Getting real about technology-based learning: The medium is NOT the message. *Educom Review, 32*(5), 32-37.

Saliou, P., & Ribaud, V. (2006, November 9-10). *Learning by doing software engineering.* Paper presented at Informatics Education Europe, Montpellier, France.

Salmon, G. (1998). Developing learning through effective online moderation. *Active Learning, 9* (December), 3–8.

Salmon, G. (2000). *E-moderating: The key to teaching and learning online.* London: Kogan-Page.

Salmon, G. (2000a). Computer-mediated conferencing for management learning at the Open University. *Management Learning, 31*(4), 491-502.

Salmon, G. (2002) Mirror, mirror, on my screen: Exploring online reflections. *British Journal of Educational Technology, 33*(4), 379-391.

Salmon, G. (2002). *E-tivities: The key to active online learning.* London: Routledge Falmer.

Salmon, G. (2003). *E-moderating: The key to teaching and learning online* (2nd ed.). London: Routledge Falmer, Taylor & Francis Books Ltd.

Salmon, G. (2004). *E-moderating: The key to teaching and learning online* (2nd ed.). London: Routledge Farmer.

Salmon, G. (2005). Flying not flapping: A strategic framework for e-learning and pedagogical innovation in higher education institutions. *ALT-J, Research in Learning Technology, 13*(3), 201-218.

Salmon, G. (2006). *Scaffolding for e-moderator's development: The early years.* Beyond Distance Research Alliance, University of Leicester. Retrieved January 9, 2007, from http://www.atimod.com/docs/atim12d-ec12doc%20(2).pdf

Salmon, G., & Giles, K. (1997, October 29-31). Moderating online. In *Proceedings of the Online Educa Conference*, Berlin, Germany. Retrieved March 10, 2007, from http://www.atimod.com/research/presentations/Mod.doc

Salter, G. (2003). Comparing online and traditional teaching: A different approach. *Campus-Wide Information Systems, 20*(4), 137-145.

Savin-Baden, M. (2000). *Problem-based learning in higher education: Untold stories.* Buckingham, United Kingdom: SRHE & Open University Press.

Savin-Baden, M. (2006). The challenge of using problem-based learning online. In M. Savin-Baden & K. Wilkie (Eds.), *Problem-based learning online* (pp. 3-13). Berkshire, United Kingdom: Open University Press.

Savin-Baden, M., & Major, C. (2004). *Foundations of problem-based learning.* Berkshire, United Kingdom: Open University Press.

Schmolitzky, A. (2007, July 4-8). *Patterns for teaching software in classroom.* Paper presented at the 12th European Conference on Pattern Languages of Programs (EuroPLoP 2007), Irsee, Germany.

Schön, D. (1983). *The reflective practitioner: How professionals think in action.* New York: Basic Books.

Schön, D. (1987). *Educating the reflective practitioner: Toward a new design for teaching and learning in the professions.* San Francisco: Jossey-Bass.

Schön, D. (1988). *Educating the reflective practitioner.* San Francisco: Jossey-Bass Publishers.

Schraw, G. (2001). Promoting general metacognitive awareness. In H. J. Hartman (Ed.), *Metacognition in learning and instruction: Theory, research and practice* (pp. 3-16). Boston: Kluwer.

Schuwirth, L. W. T., & van der Vleuten, C. P. M. (2006). *How to design a useful test: The principles of assessment.* Edinburgh, United Kingdom: Association for the Study of Medical Education.

Schwartzman, R. (2007). Refining the question: How can online instruction maximize opportunities for all students? *Communication Education, 56*(1), 113-117.

Scott, P. (1995). *The meaning of mass higher education.* Milton Keynes, United Kingdom: Open University Press, Society for Research into Higher Education.

Scottish Executive. (2004). *Students in higher education in Scotland 2002/03.* Edinburgh, United Kingdom: Author.

Scottish Higher Education Funding Council. (2004). *Higher education in Scotland: A baseline report.* Edinburgh, United Kingdom: Author.

Seale, J. (2006). *Disability and e-learning in higher education: Accessibility theory and practice.* Oxford, United Kingdom: Routledge.

Seale, J. K., & Cann, A. J. (2000). Reflection on-line or off-line: The role of learning technologies in encouraging students to reflect. *Computers and Education, 34*(3-4), 309-320.

Seely Brown, J. (2000). Growing up digital. *Change, 32*(2), 10-11.

Seffah, A., & Grogono, P. (2002, February 25-27). *Learner-centered software engineering education: From resources to skills and pedagogical patterns.* Paper presented to the 15th International Conference on Software Engineering Education and Training (CSEE&T 2002), Covington, KY.

Selinger, M. (1998). Forming a critical community through telematics. *Computers and Education, 30*(1), 23-30.

Selwyn, N. (2007). The use of computer technology in university teaching and learning: A critical perspective. *Journal of Computer Assisted Learning, 23*(2), 83-94.

Sense, A. (2007). Learning within project practice: Cognitive styles exposed. *International Journal of Project Management, 25*(1), 33-40.

Shank, P. (2001). *Asynchronous online learning instructor competencies.* Retrieved August 21, 2007, from http://www.learningpeaks.com/instrcomp.pdf

Sharpe, R. (2004). *A typology of effective interventions that support e-learning practice.* JISC.

Sharpe, R., & Benfield, G. (2005). The student experience of e-learning in higher education: A review of the literature. *Brookes EJournal of Learning and Teaching, 1*(3). Retrieved August 15, 2007, from http://www.brookes.ac.uk/publications/bejlt/volume1issue3/academic/sharpe_benfield.html

Sharpe, R., Benfield, B., & Francis, R. (2006). Implementing a university e-learning strategy: Levers for change within academic schools. *ALT-J, Research in Learning Technology, 14*(2), 135-151.

Sharpe, R., Benfield, G., Roberts, G., & Francis, R. (2006). *The undergraduate experience of blended e-learning: A review of UK literature and practice.*

Sharples, M. (2007, May 23-25). *Big issues in mobile learning.* Paper presented at the Eighth Annual Irish Educational Technology Users' Conference, Dublin, Ireland.

Shea, P., Pickett, A., & Pelt, W. (2003). A follow-up investigation of teaching presence in the SUNY learning network. *Journal of the Asynchronous Learning Network, 7*(2). Retrieved May 1, 2007, from http://www.aln.org/publications/jaln/v7n2/v7n2_shea.asp.

Sheard, A. G., & Kakabadse, A. P. (2004). A process perspective on leadership and team development. *Journal of Management Development, 23*(1), 7-106.

Shephard, K. (2003). Questioning, promoting and evaluating the use of streaming video to support student learning. *British Journal of Educational Technology, 34*(3), 295-308.

Shephard, K. (2004). The role of educational developers in the expansion of educational technology. *International Journal for Academic Development, 9*(1), 67-83.

Shivkumar, S. (2006, September 15-17). *Strategies for improving elearning effectiveness.* Paper presented at the International Workshop on E-Learning for Adult Continuing Education.

Sim, G., Holifield, P., & Brown, M. (2004). Implementation of computer assisted assessment: Lessons from the literature. *ALT-J, 12*(3), 215-230.

Sim, G., Strong, A., & Holifield, P. (2005, July 5-6). *The design of multimedia assessment objects.* Paper presented at the Ninth CAA Conference, Loughborough, United Kingdom. Retrieved May 20, 2007, from http://www.caaconference.com/pastConferences/2005/proceedings/SimG_StrongS_HolifieldP.pdf

Simon, H. (1996). *The sciences of the artificial* (3rd ed.). Cambridge, MA: The MIT Press.

Sinkkonen, S., & Taskinen, H. (2002). Johtamisosaamisen vaatimukset ja taso perusterveydenhuollossa hoitotyön johtajilla [Leadership and management competencies of nurse leaders in primary health care settings]. *Hoitotiede, 14*(3), 129-141.

Skilbeck, M., & Connell, H. (2000). *Access and equity in higher education: An international perspective on issues and strategies.* Dublin, Ireland: HEA.

*Skills for Access Project.* (2007). Retrieved June 12, 2007, from http://www.skillsforaccess.org.uk

Sloan, D., & Stratford, J. (2004, January 29). *Producing high quality materials on accessible multimedia.* Paper presented at the ILTHE Disability Forum. Retrieved June 12, 2007, from http://www.heacademy.ac.uk/embedded_object.asp?id=21627&filename=Sloan_and_Stratford

Sloan, D., Stratford, J., & Gregor, P. (2006). Using multimedia to enhance the accessibility of the learning environment for disabled students: Reflections from the Skills for Access project. *Association for Learning Technology Journal (ALT-J), 14*(1), 39-54.

Sloan, M. (2001). Web accessibility and the DDA. *The Journal of Information, Law and Technology (JILT), 2.* Retrieved June 12, 2007, from http://www2.warwick.ac.uk/fac/soc/law/elj/jilt/2001_2/sloan

Sloman, J. (2002). *Case study: The use of lecture time for workshops.* Retrieved April 17, 2007, from http://www.economicsnetwork.ac.uk/showcase/sloman_workshop.htm

Smagorinsky, P. (1994). *Speaking about writing: Reflections on research methodology.* London: Sage.

Smailes, J. (2002). *Experiences of using computer aided assessment within a virtual learning environment.* Retrieved May 20, 2007, from http://www.business.ltsn.ac.uk/events/BEST 2002/Papers/smailes.pdf

Smith, B. (2001). *Teaching online: New or transferable skills?* Higher Education Academy. Retrieved March 21, 2006, from http://www.heacademy.ac.uk/resources.asp?process=full_record&section=generic&id=455

Smith, F., Hardman, F., & Higgins, S. (2006). The impact of interactive whiteboards on teacher-pupil interaction in the national literacy and numeracy strategies. *British Educational Research Journal, 32*(3), 443-457.

Smith, H., & Higgins, S. (2006). Opening classroom interaction: The importance of feedback. *Cambridge Journal of Education, 36*(4), 485-502.

Smith, J. (2004). *Creating accessible Macromedia Flash content.* Retrieved June 12, 2007, from http://www.webaim.org/techniques/flash/?templatetype=3

Smith, P., & Ragan, T.J. (1999). Instructional Design (2nd ed.). John Wiley and Sons.

Smith, T. (2005). Fifty one competencies for online instruction. *The Journal of Educators Online, 2*(2). Retrieved December 21, 2006, from http://its.fvtc.edu/langan/BB6/Online%20Instructor%20Competencies.pdf

Solomon, P. (2005). Problem-based learning: A review of current issues relevant to physiotherapy education. *Physiotherapy Theory and Practice, 21*(1), 37-49.

Somekh, B. (2004). Taking the sociological imagination to school: An analysis of the (lack of) impact of information and communication technologies on education systems. *Technology, Pedagogy and Education, 13*(2), 163-180.

Sormunen, E. (2006). *Web searching, information literacy and learning: Web-SeaL.* Retrieved February 15, 2006, from http://www.info.uta.fi/tutkimus/Web-Seal/Research_plan.pdf

Southern, A. (2002). Can information and communication technologies support regeneration? *Regional Studies, 36*(6), 697-702.

*Special Educational Needs and Disability Act 2001.* (2001). Retrieved May 20, 2007, from http://www.opsi.gov.uk/acts/acts2001/20010010.htm

Spector, J. M. (2001). An overview of progress and problems in educational technology. *Interactive Educational Multimedia, 3*, 27-37.

Spratt, M. (1999). How good are we at knowing what learners like? *System, 27*, 141-155.

Steele D, Johnson Palensky J, Lynch T, Lacy N, Duffy S (2002). Learning preferences, computer attitudes and student evaluation of computerized education. *Medical Education, 36*(3), 225–232.

Stiles, M. J. (2000, April). *Effective learning and the virtual learning environment.* Keynote paper presented at EUNIS 2000: Towards Virtual Universities, Pozan, Poland.

Stodel, E. J., Thompson, T. L, & MacDonald, C. J. (2006). Learners' perspectives on what is missing from online learning: Interpretations through the community of inquiry framework. *The International Review of Research in Open and Distance Learning, 7*(3). Retrieved September 1, 2007, from http://www.irrodl.org/index.php/irrodl/article/viewArticle/325/743

Stracke, E. (2007). A road to understanding: A qualitative study into why learners drop out of a blended language learning environment. *ReCALL, 19*, 57-78.

Strauss, A., & Corbin, J. (1990). *Basics of qualitative research: Grounded theory procedures and techniques.* London: Sage Publications.

Surakka, S. (2007). What subjects and skills are important for software developers? *Communications of the ACM, 50*(1), 73-78.

Surry, D. W., Ensminger, D. C., & Haab, M. (2005). A model for integrating instructional technology into higher education. *British Journal of Educational Technology, 36*(2), 327-329.

Surry, D., & Land, S. (2000). Strategies for motivating higher education faculty to use technology. *Innovation in Education and Training International, 37*(2), 145-153.

Sutcliffe, M. (2002). *Simulations, games and role-play.* Retrieved April 14, 2007, from http://www.economics-network.ac.uk/handbook/games

Swales, J. (1990). *Genre analysis: English in academic and research settings.* Cambridge, United Kingdom: Cambridge University Press.

Swan, K., & Shea, P. (2005). The development of virtual learning communities. In S. R. Hiltz & R. Goldman (Eds.), *Learning together online: Research on asynchronous learning networks* (pp. 239-260). London: Lawrence Erlbaum.

Sweeney, J., O'Donoghue, T., & Whitehead, C. (2004). Traditional face-to-face and Web-based tutorials: A study of university students' perspectives on the roles of tutorial participants. *Teaching in Higher Education, 9*(3), 311-323.

Sydänmaanlakka, P. (2004). *Älykäs johtajuus: Ihmisten johtaminen älykkäissä organisaatioissa* [Smart leader-ship: Human management in smart organizations]. Hämeenlinna, Finland: Karisto.

Tait, J. (2004, February). The tutor/facilitator role in student retention. *Open Learning, 19*(1), 97-109.

Tauer, J. M., & Harackiewicz, J. M. (1999). Winning isn't everything: Competition, achievement orientation, and intrinsic motivation. *Journal of Experimental Social Psychology, 35*, 209-238.

Taylor, J. (2003, May). Managing staff development for online education: A situated learning model. *Journal of Higher Education Policy and Management, 25*(1), 75-87.

Taylor, S., & Spencer, E. (1994). *Individual commitment to lifelong learning: Individuals' attitudes. Report on the qualitative* (Research Series No. 31). Sheffield, United Kingdom: Employment Department.

Teekman, B. (2000) Exploring reflective thinking in nursing practice. *Journal of Advanced Nursing, 31*(5), 1125-1135.

Tett, L. (1999). Widening provision in higher education: Some non-traditional participants' experiences. *Research Papers in Education, 14*(1), 107-119.

Thomas, J. (2000). *A review of research on project based learning.* Retrieved May 21, 2007, from http://www.bie.org/files/researchreviewPBL.pdf

Thomas, L. (2001). *Widening participation in post-compulsory education.* London: Continuum.

Thomas, L. (2002). Student retention in higher education: The role of institutional habitus. *Journal of Educational Policy, 17*(4), 423-432.

Thomas, M. J. W. (2002). Learning within incoherent structures: The space of online discussion forums. *Journal of Computer Assisted Learning, 18*(3), 351-366.

Thompson, J. F. (1978). *Using roleplay in the classroom.* Bloomington, IN: Phi Kappa Delta Educational Foundation.

Thompson, K. (2001). Constructivist curriculum design for professional development. *Australian Journal of Adult Learning, 41*(1), 94-109.

Timmis, S., O'Leary, R., Cai, C., Harrison, C., Weedon, E., Trapp, A., et al. (2004). *Student and tutor roles and relationships (SOLE thematic reports series)*. Retrieved June 25, 2007, from http://sole.ilrt.bris.ac.uk/roles.pdf

Tinto, V. (1993). *Leaving college: Rethinking the causes and cures of student attrition* (2ⁿᵈ ed.). Chicago: Chicago University Press.

Tolley, R. J. (2007). *I wonder when we will get some advice on the interoperability of eportfolios: BECTa Communities*. Retrieved August 2007 from http://communities.becta.org.uk/WebX?14@586.bT1FaghlZER.0@.3c40f8c7/0

Tomayko, J. E. (1998). Forging a discipline: An outline history of software engineering education. *Annals of Software Engineering, 6*(1-4), 3-18.

Tonks, D., & Farr, M. (2003). Widening access and participation in UK higher education. *The International Journal of Educational Management, 17*(1), 26-36.

Topping, K. (1998). Peer assessment between students in colleges and universities. *Review of Educational Research, 68*(3), 249-276.

*Towards an information society in Western Asia: A declaration of principles.* (2003). Beirut, Lebanon: Western Asia Preparatory Conference for the World Summit on the Information Society.

Training and Development Agency for Schools. (2007). *Professional standards for teachers.* London: Author.

Trentin, G. (2006). The Xanadu project: Training faculty in the use of information and communication technology for university teaching. *Journal of Computer Assisted Learning, 22*(3), 182-196.

Turoff, M. (1989). The anatomy of a computer application innovation: Computer mediated communications (CMC). *Technological Forecasting and Social Change, 36*, 107-122.

Tuthill, G., & Klemm, E. (2002). Virtual field trips: Alternatives to actual field trips. *International Journal of Instructional Media, 29*(4), 453-468.

U.S. Department of Justice. (1990). *Americans with Disabilities Act of 1990 (ADA).* Retrieved June 12, 2007, from http://www.ada.gov/pubs/ada.htm

U.S. Department of Labor. (1973). *Section 508, Rehabilitation Act of 1973.* Retrieved June 12, 2007, from http://www.dol.gov/oasam/regs/statutes/sec508.htm

UK GRAD Programme. (2007). *Report of proceedings UK GRAD Programme Roberts policy forum.* Retrieved November 27, 2007, from http://www.grad.ac.uk

Underwood, J. (2006). *Digital technologies and dishonesty in examinations and tests.* London: Qualifications and Curriculum Authority.

Vallance, M., & Towndrow, P. A. (2007). Towards the "informed use" of information and communication technology in education: A response to Adams' "PowerPoint, habits of mind, and classroom culture." *Journal of Curriculum Studies, 39*(2), 219-227.

Vanderheiden, G. (1996). *Universal design...What it is and what it isn't.* Retrieved June 12, 2007, from http://trace.wisc.edu/docs/whats_ud/whats_ud.htm

Vartiainen, M., Kokko, N., & Hakonen, M. (2003, July 25-27). Competences in virtual organizations. In *Proceedings of the Third International Conference on Researching Work and Learning* (Vol. 1, pp. 209-219). Tampere, Finland.

Vaughan, N., & Garrison, D. (2005). Creating cognitive presence in a blended faculty development community. *The Internet and Higher Education, 8*(1), 1-12.

Viitala, R. (2004a). *Henkilöstöjohtaminen* [Personnel leadership]. Helsinki, Finland: Edita.

Viitala, R. (2004b). *Osaamisen johtaminen esimiestyössä* [Knowledge leadership]. Unpublished doctoral dissertation, University of Vaasa, Finland.

Vincent, A., & Shepherd, J. (1998). Experiences in teaching Middle-East politics via Internet role-play simulations. *Journal of Interactive Media in Education, 11.* Retrieved April 18, 2007, from http://www-jime.open.ac.uk/98/11/vincent-98-11-paper.html

Voelter, M. (2006, July 5-9). *Software architecture: A pattern language for building sustainable software architectures.* Paper presented at the 11th European Conference on Pattern Languages of Programs (EuroPLoP 2006), Irsee, Germany.

Vygotsky, L. (1978). *Mind in society: The development of higher psychological processes.* Cambridge: Harvard University Press.

Walker, R. (2003). *An investigation into virtual learner-centred solutions for competency-based management education.* Groningen, The Netherlands: Gopher Publishers.

Walker, R. (2005). Virtual learner-centred solutions for management education and training. In W. Baets (Ed.), *Knowledge management and management learning* (pp. 143-164). New York: Springer.

Walker, R., & Baets, W. (2000). Designing a virtual course environment for management education: A learner-centred approach. *Indian Journal of Open Learning, 9*(3), 299-317.

Walker, R., & Baets, W. (2002, June 6-8). Introducing "conversational" eLearning to management education: A comparison of student experiences from two MIS courses. In *Proceedings of the 10th European Conference on Information Systems,* Gdansk, Poland (pp. 1400-1409). Retrieved March 18, 2006, from http://is2.lse.ac.uk/asp/aspecis/20020130.pdf

Wang, Q., & Woo, H. L. (2007). Comparing asynchronous online discussions and face-to-face discussions in a classroom setting. *British Journal of Educational Technology, 38*(2), 272-286.

Watson, D. (2001). Pedagogy before technology: Re-thinking the relationship between ICT and teaching. *Education and Information Technologies, 6*(4), 251-266.

Weaver, D., Chenicheri, S. N., & Spratt, C. (2005, November 30-December 1). *Evaluation: WebCT and the student experience.* Paper presented at Making a Difference: Evaluations and Assessment Conference, Sydney, Australia.

Webb, M., & Cox, M. (2004). A review of pedagogy related to information and communications technology. *Technology, Pedagogy and Education, 13*(3), 235-286.

Weber, M. (1978). *Economy and society: An outline of interpretive sociology.* New York: Bedminster.

Webster, J., & Hackley, P. (1997). Teaching effectiveness in technology-mediated distance learning. *Academy of Management Review, 40*(6), 1282-1309.

Weinberg, G. M. (1992). *Quality software management: Vol. 1. Systems thinking.* New York: Dorset House.

Welk, D. (2006). The trainer's application of Vygotsky's "zone of proximal development" to asynchronous online training of faculty facilitators. *Online Journal of Distance Learning, 9*(4). Carrollton, GA: University of West Georgia Distance Education Center.

Welker, J., & Berardino, L. (2005). Blended learning: Understanding the middle ground between traditional classroom and fully online instruction. *Journal of Educational Technology Systems, 34*(1), 33-55.

Wells, G. (1993). Re-evaluating the IRF sequence: A proposal for the articulation of theories of activity and discourse for the analysis of teaching and learning in the classroom. *Linguistics and Education, 5*(1), 1-37.

Wenger, E. (1998). *Communities of practice: Learning, meaning and identity.* Cambridge, United Kingdom: Cambridge University Press.

Wenger, E. (1998). *Communities of practice: Learning, meaning, and identity.* Cambridge: Cambridge University Press.

West, L. (1996). *Beyond fragments.* London: Taylor and Francis.

Wheeler, S. (2005). *Creating social presence in digital learning environments: A presence of mind?* Featured paper for the TAFE conference, Queensland, Australia. Retrieved September 1, 2007, from http://videolinq.tafe.net/learning2005/papers/wheeler.pdf

White, S. A. (2006, September 17-22). *Critical success factors for institutional change: Some organizational perspectives*. In H. C. Davis & S. Eales (Eds.), *Proceedings of Critical Success Factors for Institutional Change: A Workshop of the European Conference of Digital Libraries (ECDL'06)*, Alicante, Spain (pp. 75-89). Retrieved March 10, 2007, from http://eprints.ecs.soton.ac.uk/13225/01/Critical_Success_Factors_for_Institutional_Change_latest.pdf

Whitelock, D., & Jelfs, A. (2003). Editorial: *Educational Media* special issue on blended learning. *Journal of Educational Media, 28*(2-3), 99-100.

Whitelock, D., & Jelfs, A. (2003). Editorial: Journal of Educational Media special issue on blended learning. *Journal of Educational Media, 28*(2-3), 99-100.

Wiley, D. (2004). *The reusability paradox*. Retrieved November 11, 2006, from http://cnx.org/content/m11898/latest/

Williams, J. (Ed.). (1997). *Negotiating access to higher education: The discourse of selectivity and equity*. Buckingham, United Kingdom: Society for Research into Higher Education & Open University Press.

Williams, J. B., & Goldberg, M. (2005). *The evolution of elearning*. Retrieved July 2007 from http://www.ascilite.org.au/conferences/brisbane05/blogs/proceedings/84_Williams.pdf

Wilson, B. (1996). What is a constructivist learning environment? In B. G. Wilson (Ed.), *Constructivist learning environments: Case studies in instructional design* (p. 38). Englewood Cliffs, NJ: Educational Technology.

Wilson, D., Varnhagen, S., Krupa, E., Kasprzak, S., Hunting, V., & Taylor, A. (2003). Instructors' adaptation to online graduate education in health promotion: A qualitative study. *Journal of Distance Education, 18*(2), 1-15.

Wilson, T. (2001, May). *Information overload: Myth, reality and implications for health care*. Retrieved January 2007 from http://informationr.net/tdw/publ/ppt/overload/tsld001.htm

Winch, C., & Wells, P. (1995). The quality of student writing in higher education: A cause for concern? *British Journal of Educational Studies, 43*(1), 75-87.

Wingate, U. (2006). Doing away with study skills. *Teaching in Higher Education, 11*(4), 457-465.

Wingate, U. (in press). A framework for transition: Supporting "learning to learn" in higher education. *Higher Education Quarterly*.

Wink. (2005). *DebugMode Wink*. Retrieved April 2007 from http://www.debugmode.com/wink/

Winn, W. (1993). A constructivist critique of the assumptions of instructional design. In T. Duffy, J. Lowyck, & D. Jonassen (Eds.), *Designing environments for constructive learning*. New York: Springer.

Winter, C. (2004, April 5-7). *The e-research project: Developing an IMM resource for supporting communities of learners through CSCL*. In S. Banks, P. Goodyear, V. Hodgson, C. Jones, V. Lally, McConnell, & C. Steeples (Eds.), *Fourth International Networked Learning 2004 Conference Proceedings*. Retrieved November 27, 2007, from http://www.networkedlearningconference.org.uk/past/nlc2004/proceedings/individual_papers/winter/htm

Wisker, G. (2000, April 23-24). Cross-cultural research supervision and research at a distance: Issues for postgraduate students and supervisors. In M. Kiley & G. Mullins (Eds.), *Quality in Postgraduate Research: Making Ends Meet. Proceedings of the 2000 Quality in Postgraduate Research Conference*, Adelaide, Australia (pp.43-49). Adelaide, Australia: University of Adelaide, Centre for Learning and Professional Development (CLPD).

Woodrow, M. (2000). Putting a price on a priority: Funding an inclusive higher education. *Widening Participation and Lifelong Learning, 2*(3), 1-5.

Woods, R. (2003). "Communal architect" in online classroom: Integrating cognitive and affective learning for maximum effort in Web-based learning. *Online Journal of Distance Learning Administration, 6*(1). Retrieved May 2007 from http://www.westga.edu/%7Edistance/ojdla/spring61/woods61.htm

Woodward, D., & Denicolo, P. (2004). *Review of graduate schools in the UK*. Lichfield, United Kingdom: Council for Graduate Education.

World Wide Web Consortium (W3C). (1999). *Web content accessibility guidelines 1.0.* Retrieved June 12, 2007, from http://www.w3.org/TR/WCAG10

Wright, W. A., & Miller, J. E. (2000). The educational developer's portfolio. *The International Journal for Academic Development, 5*(1), 20-29.

Yee, G., Xu, Y., Korba, L., & El-Khatib, K. (2006). Privacy and security in e-learning. In T. Shih & J. Hung (Eds.), *Future directions in distance learning and communication technologies* (pp. 52-75). Hershey, PA: Idea Group, Inc.

Yin, R. (1993). *Applications of case study research: Design and methods.* Newbury Park, CA: Sage Publications.

Yorke, M. (2001). Formative assessment and its relevance in retention. *Higher Education Research and Development, 20*(2), 115-123.

Young, J. (2002). "Hybrid" teaching seeks to end the divide between traditional and online instruction. *Chronicle of Higher Education*, p. A33. Retrieved February 20, 2007, from http://chronicle.com/free/v48/i28/28a03301.htm

Yu, C., & Brandenburg, T. (2006). I would have had more success if…Trials and tribulations of a first-time online instructor. *The Journal of Technology Studies, 32*(1), 43-52. Retrieved July 5, 2007, from http://scholar.lib.vt.edu/ejournals/JOTS/v32/v32n1/pdf/yu.pdf

Zhao, Y., Lei, J., Yan, B., Lai, C., & Tan, H. (2005, August). What makes the difference? A practical analysis of research on the effectiveness of distance learning. *Teachers College Record, 107*(8), 1836-1884.

Ziguras, C. (2001). Educational technology in transnational higher education in South East Asia: The cultural politics of flexible learning. *Journal of Educational Technology and Society, 4*(4), 8-18.

Zirkle, C. (2004). *Access barriers experienced by adults in distance education courses and programs: A review of the research literature.* Retrieved May 16, 2007, from http://hdl.handle.net/1805/273

Zuber-Skerritt, O. (1992). *Professional development in higher education: A theoretical framework for action research.* London: Kogan Page.

Zwarenstein, M., Reeves, S., Barr, H., Hammick, M., Koppel, I., & Atkins, J. (2000). Interprofessional education: Effects on professional practice and health care outcomes. *The Cochrane Database of Systematic Reviews* (Issue 3, Art. No. CD002213.DOI:10.1002/14651858. CD002213). Retrieved August 21, 2007, from http://www.mrw.interscience.wiley.com/cochrane/clsysrev/articles/CD002213/frame.html

# About the Contributors

**Roisin Donnelly** has over 15 years of experience in higher education both as a lecturer and researcher. She has taught in universities in Northern Ireland and was a lecturer and visiting research fellow in the University of New South Wales, Sydney. She is currently programme coordinator for DIT's MSc in applied e-learning, and tutors and supervises in the PG certificate, diploma, and MA programmes in third-level learning and teaching. She has a range of chapter and journal publications to reflect her teaching and research interests, including academic development, designing e-learning, supporting virtual communities, tranformative pedagogies, and blended problem-based learning (PBL).

**Fiona McSweeney** lectures in developmental psychology and research methods in the Department of Social Sciences of the Dublin Institute of Technology, and in the psychology of learning and research methods with Waterford Institute of Technology. She has also worked as a learning development officer in the DIT. Her research interests focus on the student experience of higher education, assessment, the impact of professional education on identity, academic mentoring, and the use of VLEs as a support for student learning and engagement in education. She is currently undertaking an Ed.D with The Open University in student and professional identity and support.

\* \* \*

After 15 years in business in strategic planning and decision support, **Walter Baets**, PhD, HDR, decided to pursue an academic career. He has held academic positions in Belgium, The Netherlands, and Spain, and is now associate dean for research and MBA director at Euromed Marseille Ecole de Management, and professor of complexity, knowledge, and innovation. He has published 10 books and more than 50 academic papers in the area of complexity, knowledge, and learning. His latest book is entitled *Complexity, Learning and Organizations: A Quantum Interpretation of Business* (Routledge, 2006).

**Sheena Banks** is e-learning research associate in the School of Education at the University of Sheffield. She has been involved in e-learning research and development for over 12 years, working on a range of national and international collaborative research and implementation projects. She is currently coordinator of the V-ResORT Project (Virtual Resources for Online Research Training), an HEFCE-funded FDTL5 project (Higher Education Funding Council for England, Fund for the Development of Teaching and Learning), developing a new pedagogic framework for the teaching of research methodology and methods online at the master's and doctoral level. She also coordinates the development of a virtual graduate school at the University of Sheffield, and is a member of the eChina UK project team working on e-learning development in China. She has published widely and her research interests are in networked collaborative learning, e-tutoring, intercultural e-tutoring in globalized contexts, and e-learning pedagogies for postgraduate learning.

**Tony Cunningham** is an assistant lecturer in the School of Construction Economics and Management and Real Estate in the Dublin Institute of Technology (DIT). He is a chartered quantity surveyor with 20 years experience in the Irish and UK construction industries. He currently teaches quantity surveying studies, construction and safety legislation, and construction contract administration. He completed the postgraduate diploma programme in third-level learning and teaching at DIT in 2006. In 2005, he developed a virtual learning environment (VLE) for a module he teaches on using WebCT software with the aim of supporting students by providing electronic access to course notes and some supplementary material.

**Ann Donohoe** is a lecturer in the School of Nursing, Midwifery and Health Systems at the University College Dublin (UCD). She is currently undertaking a PhD at the Centre for Teaching and Learning, UCD, which involves the development of a Web-based tool to facilitate nurses to engage in reflective practice. Her other research interests include the implementation of innovative teaching practices, the design of effective learning environments, and the development of online communities in education.

**Louise Jakobsen** is passionate about the potential technology has to enhance learning and support teaching. Currently the e-learning curriculum manager at Park Lane College Leeds, she has the responsibility for moving forward the e-learning agenda within the large further education (FE) college, and the supporting staff working in and around Leeds through that process. Her enthusiasm is evident through the various training, sharing, and motivating strategies that are used. She has worked in FE, adult and community learning, and local government for several years delivering high-class training to teachers, managers, care staff, and small and medium businesses. Louise has also been involved in developing resources and delivering training for and on behalf of national organisations including NIACE and THinK FE. She is currently halfway though completing an MS in multimedia and e-learning with the University of Huddersfield.

**Gordon Joyes** is associate professor in e-learning at the University of Nottingham and holds the Dearing Award for Excellence in Teaching and Learning. He works within the School of Education in the Institute for Research for Learning and Teaching in Higher Education (IRLTHE), which has a research focus on the student experience. He is an accomplished director of international e-learning projects involving both research and innovation and he is also an experienced online course developer and tutor. His current work involves research into collaborative design and design for reusable e-learning, and he has published extensively in these areas.

**Pankaj Kamthan** has been teaching in academia and industry for several years. He has also been a technical editor, participated in standards development, served on programme committees of international conferences, and is on the editorial board of the *International Journal of Technology Enhanced Learning* and the *International Journal of Teaching and Case Studies*. His professional interests and experience include knowledge representation, requirements engineering, and software quality.

**Diana Kelly** has been involved in academic development since 1989. She first became involved in e-learning in 1999 as a student in the UCLA (University of California, Los Angeles) Online Teaching certificate programme. Upon completion of the programme, she developed two Web-based academic development workshops in Blackboard. As head of lifelong learning for the Dublin Institute of Technology (2000-2003), the learning technology team was part of her responsibility. In 2007 Dr. Kelly developed the new Web site for the City University, London, MA in academic practice programme. Diana is a faculty mentor in the online doctoral programme in education offered by Walden University. At present, she is the dean of the School of Liberal Arts at San Diego Miramar College. Dr. Kelly earned her doctorate in Higher Education at the Claremont Graduate University in California.

**Sabine Little** currently works for CILASS (The Centre for Inquiry-Based Learning in the Arts and Social Sciences), an HEFCE-funded CETL (Centre for Excellence in Teaching and Learning) based at the University of Sheffield. She holds the position of learning development and research associate, specialising in support for networked learning and working with staff to incorporate inquiry-based learning (IBL) into their teaching. Her research interests include the role of the learning developer as a facilitator of inquiry-based learning communities and staff-student collaborations in learning and teaching development, evaluation, and research.

**Catherine Manathunga** is a senior lecturer in higher education in the University of Queensland (UQ) Graduate School and the Teaching and Educational Development Institute (TEDI) at UQ. She has published a coauthored monograph on educational history, *A Class of its Own: A History of Queensland University of Technology*, and has published in Australian, Irish, American, and British journals in the fields of international relations, research training, and academic development. She is the leading chief investigator on an Australian Research Council Linkage grant to investigate the preparation of research and innovation leaders for industry and has received substantial research and development funding from industry partners and universities. She has received a number of UQ and Australian national teaching awards for her academic development contribution to the UQ Graduate School and for enhancing research students' learning. She has acted as an educational consultant to several Australian universities and two universities internationally.

**Catherine Matheson** is a researcher in the University of Nottingham, United Kingdom. Over many years, Catherine has published articles and chapters and presented conference papers on issues surrounding access to higher education, the history of education, and culture and identity in education, as well as education and development, the transition from university to professional practice, and the development of professional identity.

**David Matheson** is a lecturer in the University of Nottingham, United Kingdom. David's research interests lie mainly in lifelong learning, education and development, the transition from university to professional practice, culture and identity in education, and the use of simulation in health care education. He has produced articles, chapters, and conference papers across all of these areas. He is the editor of *An Introduction to the Study of Education* (London, David Fulton), the third edition of which appeared in 2008.

**Claire McDonnell** has been a lecturer in organic chemistry in the School of Chemical and Pharmaceutical Sciences at Dublin Institute of Technology since 2000. She completed the postgraduate diploma programme in third-level learning and teaching at DIT in 2006. In 2004, she and a colleague, Christine O'Connor, developed a WebCT VLE to support the learning of first-year undergraduate chemistry students. Online quizzes with instant and detailed feedback were incorporated to allow the students to study at their own pace. She has contributed oral presentations to several national and international chemistry education conferences on how this VLE, in conjunction with several other changes to teaching practice, has helped to support the learning of the students concerned. She is currently involved in several community learning projects on a pilot basis and has used asynchronous online communication to facilitate some of the group work involved.

**Barry McIntyre** is a lecturer in marketing in the School of Business and Humanities in the Dun Laoghaire Institute of Art, Design and Technology (IADT) teaching strategic marketing management and marketing communications. He is a graduate of University College Dublin with a BComm and MBA, and also has a postgraduate certificate and postgraduate diploma in third-level learning and teaching from DIT. He is the immediate past chairman of the Irish Learning Technology Association (ILTA) and has presented numerous papers at this organisation's EdTech Conferences as well as Irish Marketing Teachers' Association conferences. He has been an active user of VLEs including Blackboard, WebCT, and Moodle to support learning for the past 12 years and is currently completing a master's thesis at DIT on the issues that arise for lecturers and students in relation to the use of a VLE.

**Theresa McKenna** has been a lecturer at the National College of Art and Design (NCAD) in Dublin, Ireland, since 1980. She studied at NCAD at the undergraduate level and then at Edinburgh College of Art and Goldsmiths College, London, at the postgraduate MA level in the visual arts. She works as a lecturer and personal tutor in an interdisciplinary programme teaching first-year students. As a practicing artist, she has exhibited widely in Ireland and abroad. Her only experience of e-learning was as part of the postgraduate certificate programme and the Designing E-Learning module in the diploma programme in third-level learning and teaching at DIT, before which her use of learning technology was very limited. She plans to adapt the online activity-centred module designed as part of the Designing E-Learning module and to run it as a pilot for her tutorial group during the academic year 2008 to 2009.

**Tim McMahon** is a teaching development officer based in the Centre for Teaching and Learning at UCD and is director of the centre until 2008. He was previously principal lecturer in educational development in the School of Education at Anglia Polytechnic University (APU), Cambridge and Chelmsford, UK, and was an invited professor in higher education research at the Centre for Research & Development in Higher Education, Hokkaido University, Sapporo, Japan. He is a member of the court of the University of Kent, a fellow of the Higher Education Academy (UK), and a fellow of the Royal Academy of Medicine in Ireland. His research interests include peer observation and mentoring in higher education, assessment for learning, using action research to improve teaching and learning in higher education, and facilitating the transition from second- to third-level education.

**Barry McMullin** is an associate professor in the School of Electronic Engineering of Dublin City University (DCU). He is also director of the e-Access laboratory at the Research Institute for Networks and Communications Engineering (RINCE). He has participated in several national and international projects concerned with Web accessibility policy and practice, including the 2005 EU-wide study of accessible e-government, commissioned by the UK Cabinet Office and the European Public Administration Network. He has been an invited expert member of the W3C (World Wide Web Consortium) Web Accessibility Initiative (WAI) Education and Outreach Working Group.

**Steve Millard** On graduating from York University in 1973 where he read economics, Steve worked in the training department of a large multinational firm in Paris before joining the School of Business and Management at Buckinghamshire New University in 1982, where he lectures in economics-related subjects and has been economics field chair since 1992. He has run the Teaching and Learning Forum since 2002, was appointed as a university senior teaching and learning fellow in February 2004, and has presented several papers at the annual conferences of the Institute of Teaching and Learning in Higher Education on the theme of motivating students.

**Morag Munro** is a learning technologist in DCU responsible for supporting academic staff in the design, development, implementation, and evaluation of technology-based learning. She is also a tutor in DCU's MSc programme in education and training management. She has extensive expertise in instructional design, multimedia development, and e-learning project management, including time spent in both tertiary and commercial e-learning sectors. She is the editor of the Association for Learning Technology (ALT) newsletter (http://newsletter.alt.ac.uk).

**Geraldine O'Neill** works in the Centre for Teaching and Learning, School of Education and Lifelong Learning, University College Dublin. In her time in the Centre for Teaching and Learning, she has been both director of the centre (2001-2005) and the coordinator of the graduate diploma and certificate programme in university teaching and learning (2003-2007). She been involved in the strategic development of teaching and learning in UCD and has linked with international partners to support many national and local teaching and learning projects. Geraldine's educational research interests include curriculum design, reflective practice, and problem-based learning. In 2005, she was coeditor of *Emerging Issues in the Practice of University Learning and Teaching* (http://www.aishe.org/readings/2005-1/) and more recently she coedited a collection of case studies in the assessment of student learning (O'Neill, Huntley-Moore, & Race, 2007, *Case Studies of Good Practices in Assessment of Student Learning in Higher Education*, http://www.aishe.org/readings/2007-1).

**Jillian Palwyn** qualified as a learning disability nurse (RNLD) in 1994 and joined the School of Health and Social Care as a lecturer and practitioner in 2000. Jillian soon became an enthusiast promoting e-learning throughout the school. Jillian attained her PCTHE in 2003 when she had the fortunate opportunity to develop her skills in using ICT. In 2004 Jillian was awarded an Oxford Brookes University Associate Teaching Fellowship; the award provided the opportunity for Jillian to design a project to develop interprofessional learning within the School of Health and Social Care. Jillian is a member of the University eLearning Coordinators Forum, the School of Health and Social Care eLearning Sub Group, and the Information Management Task Group. Jillian is currently undertaking an MSc with a focus on e-learning in professional education.

**Timo Portimojärvi** has been working as a senior researcher, teacher, tutor, and developer at the University of Tampere in Finland. His work on media education, online learning, and problem-based learning has been connected to primary and secondary school teacher education and continuing education. He has recently finished a development and education project on combining PBL and ICT, in which he worked as a teacher, researcher, and project manager. The 40 participants of the project were higher education teachers from Finnish educational institutions. He has recently completed a doctorate in education researching problem-based learning online. The key aspects of his current research are synchronous and asynchronous collaboration, distributed communities of learning, and socio-epistemic networks.

**Nick Pratt** qualified with a degree in engineering science from the University of Oxford in 1988 before teaching in Exeter for 7 years. He then joined the University of Plymouth and worked in mathematics education. Currently, he teaches in the Integrated Masters Programme. His research interests are in online learning, mathematics education, and professional learning. In particular he is interested in how sociocultural perspectives on learning can illuminate educative situations in a new light and on how nonformal learning contexts can provide different kinds learning experiences for participants. Nick is married with three children and lives and works in the southwest of England.

**Heather Rai** has worked as an e-learning developer in the Medical Education Unit at the University of Nottingham since 2004, producing e-learning and e-assessment materials for undergraduate students studying in the medicine degree course. Part of this role had involved programming interfaces for the creation of image hotspots and drag-and-drop labeling question types for the TouchStone online assessment system, which has been created within the Medical Education Unit. Alongside this work, she produces teaching resources with subject specialists within the faculty, using tools such as Adobe Flash in conjunction with video and audio. She is also a member of the teaching team in the Masters in Clinical Education course offered by the faculty, covering informatics in medical education and teaching clinical staff from many backgrounds to use technology effectively in their teaching.

**Rhona Sharpe** is based within the Oxford Centre for Staff and Learning Development (OCSLD) at Oxford Brookes University, UK. She has worked with e-learning in a variety of roles, initially as a lecturer and subsequently as educational developer, consultant, and researcher. Rhona has devised and run online courses for OCSLD including the Online Tutoring course, which has been running since 2004. She has undertaken projects funded by the Higher Education Academy and the Joint Information Systems Committee, exploring how practitioners change their practice and the learner's experience of e-learning. Rhona is a fellow of the Staff and Educational Development Association and the Higher Education Academy. In 2007, she coedited *Rethinking Pedagogy for a Digital Age* with Helen Beetham and is currently coeditor of the Association for Learning Technology journal *Research in Learning Technology* (ALT-J).

**Pirjo Vuoskoski** has a work history as an entrepreneur and a physiotherapist. Now she is working as a senior lecturer, tutor, developer, and researcher in an undergraduate-level physiotherapy degree programme at Mikkeli University of Applied Sciences in Savonlinna, Finland. Her work in physiotherapy education has been connected to curriculum and online and blended PBL development and research. She also has an active role in a national PBL network. She has recently finished a development project on online problem-based and project-based learning with five other universities of applied sciences in eastern Finland. At the moment, she is preparing her doctoral thesis on assessment in the context of clinical learning and problem-based physiotherapist education.

**Richard Walker** is e-learning development team manager at the University of York and is responsible for the deployment of the University's VLE, Yorkshare. He is also deputy chair of UCISA's Teaching and Learning Working Group. Previously, he held research and teaching posts at Nyenrode Business University and at the Euro-Arab Management School in Granada, Spain. He has published on learner-centred frameworks for blended learning in a variety of journals.

**Simon Wilkinson** has been involved with the use of information technology in higher education since starting a PhD in hypertext and cognitive styles at Napier University, Edinburgh, in 1995. In 1999 he began working on the TLTP3-86 project, which was to build the University of Nottingham Medical School's first virtual learning environment. In addition to traditional forms of information, the VLE has had since the outset online marked question types with negative marking. As the pressure came for more sophisticated assessment techniques, in 2002 Simon initiated a new development programme to build a dedicated assessment and survey system, now called TouchStone, which supports the pedagogic strategy of the medical school. Simon continues to oversee strategic developments of the VLE and TouchStone, focusing on issues such as standards setting and curriculum mapping.

**Ursula Wingate** is a lecturer in language in education in the Department of Education and Professional Studies at King's College London. Before joining King's, she worked as a researcher in the Department of Educational Studies, University of Oxford, and as an assistant professor at Hong Kong Baptist University. Her main research interests are students' transition from school to university, the development of academic writing, and online teaching and learning.

# Index

## A

academic developers  8
academic development  35, 36, 85
academic development programmes  85
academic development units  87
academic knowledge  292
academic writing  178
access  132
accessibility  133
action research  220, 221
active learning  247
asynchronous  329
asynchronous discussion fora  87
asynchronous participant interaction and discussion
89
attrition  36

## B

behaviourism  203
Blackboard™  89
blended contexts  27
blended learning  57, 85, 328
Bloom's taxonomy  114
blurring of roles  3
Bobby  131

## C

cascade  111
cascading  111
cascading style sheets  144
case studies  230
Chickering  41
CILASS  2
cognitive perspective  289
cognitive presence  266
cognitive psychology  291
collaborative learning  329

## community  291
community-of-inquiry framework  265
community of inquiry  4, 264
community of practice  295
computer-mediated  242
computer-mediated learning  242
constructivist learning  184
Cowan  40
CPBL  61
curriculum design  85

## D

defense  349
desktop audio-conferencing  290
desktop conferencing  313
developing lecturers  115
differentiation  109
digital learners  85
disabilities  354
disability  130
discussion board  64
discussion forum  92
distributed teamwork  311
doctoral programmes  222
drip-feed  333
drop out  37
Dublin Institute of Technology (DIT)  85

## E

e-conferencing  290
e-learning  108, 220
e-moderating  41
e-portfolios  113
e-tutor  60
economic  131
educational developer  2
educational research  221, 223
educational technologist  2

educational technology 264
Educational Technology in Higher Education 263
evaluation 186
experiential 39
experiential learning 40
experiential or situated learning 40

**F**

facilitated 40, 41
faculty [academic] developers 39
feedback 114
Five steps 117
forums 86
further education (FE) 108

**G**

Gamson 41
gender 146
geography 137
Gibbs 37
group work 25

**H**

habitus 144
hardware 353
health care education 310
hidden curriculum 144
higher degree studies 86
higher education 220

**I**

ICT 312
identity 146
ILT 109
information-literacy 68
information and communication technology 317
information learning technologies (ILTs) 109
inquiry-based learning 4
instructional design 243
instructional methods 350
interactivity 350
international guest lecturers 87
international guests 85
Internet generation 85, 86
interprofessional education (IPE) 20
interprofessional learning 21
interrogation 338
item development 349
item difficulty 354

**J**

journals 113

**L**

leadership 311
learner support 63
learning 242
learning communities 225
learning management system 203
learning materials 225
learning outcomes 36, 37, 48
learning resources 223
learning support 178
learning technologist 7
legislation 352
legitimate peripheral participation 182

**M**

managed learning environment (MLE) 116
mentors 290
Mikkeli University of Applied Sciences 310
multimedia 352
multipoint audio-conferencing 289

**N**

natural evolution 119
Net Gen 85
Net Generation 242
Net Gen students 85
no significant difference 36

**O**

online 85
online academic development programmes 86
online communication 59
online environment 117
online learning environments 118
online participation 337
online preinduction courses (OPICs) 178
online role play 328
online supervision 86

**P**

pattern 206
PBL 90, 311
pedagogic 221
pedagogic choice 228
pedagogy 222

persistence 37
personalisation 109
personality type 207
pilot study 189
placement-based learning 290
plagiarism 348
postgraduate education 221
postgraduate supervision 86
practical inquiry 266
preinduction 178
presence 266
problem-based learning 310
problem-based learning (PBL) 87
professional (placement) knowledge 296
professional development 36, 84, 109, 226
professional expertise 290, 291
professional learning 291

**Q**

quality 38, 348

**R**

redundancy 143
reflect 40
reflection 40
reflection in action 291
reflection on action 291
reflective approach 39
reflective practice 40, 267, 291
Reflective Practice and Nurse Education 267
Relationships Between Staff and 24
reliability 350
remote 92
remote postgraduate supervision 85
remote supervision 91
research framework 222
research methodology 222
research methods 221
results analysis 349
reuse 205
risk 349

**S**

security 356
security risks 347
seven principles 42
Seven Principles of Effective Teaching 41
situated learning 182

situated staff development 40
Sloan Consortium 37
social class 131
socially active 241
social networking 117, 205
social perspective 289
social presence 266
sociocultural perspective 300
software process 202
staff development 21, 115
Stephen Brookfield 40
strategy for e-learning 19
student-centred learning 241
student learning outcomes 37
student perspective 57
Students 24
support 179
synchronous and asynchronous conferencing (bulletin boards 86
synchronous chat sessions 87

**T**

teachers' roles 19
teaching 266
The Multiprofessional Team 5
The No Significant Difference Phenomenon 37
Tom Angelo 39
transition 179
tutor training 39

**U**

universal design 130, 133
University of California at Los Angeles 42
University of Queensland (UQ) 85

**V**

validity 351
virtual learning environment (VLE) 4, 63, 109, 312
Vygotsky 41

**W**

Walden University 45
WebCT™ 4, 89
WebCT™ Vista 4
web engineering 214
widening participation 179
winged messenger 3